INDIANA
RAILROAD LINES

RAILROADS PAST AND PRESENT
GEORGE M. SMERK, EDITOR

INDIANA
RAILROAD LINES

GRAYDON M. MEINTS

INDIANA UNIVERSITY PRESS
Bloomington and Indianapolis

This book is a publication of

Indiana University Press
601 North Morton Street
Bloomington, Indiana 47404-3797 USA

iupress.indiana.edu

Telephone orders 800-842-6796
Fax orders 812-855-7931
Orders by e-mail iuporder@indiana.edu

© 2011 by Graydon M. Meints

Manufactured in the United States of America

Library of Congress Cataloging-in-Publication Data

Meints, Graydon M.
Indiana railroad lines / Graydon M. Meints.
p. cm. — (Railroads past and present)
Includes bibliographical references and index.
ISBN 978-0-253-22359-3 (pbk. : alk. paper) 1. Railroads—Indiana—
History. I. Title.
TF24.I6M45 2011
385.09772—dc23
2011025355

1 2 3 4 5 16 15 14 13 12 11

I am pleased to dedicate this work to

FRANCIS H. PARKER

and

RICHARD S. SIMONS

who introduced me to railroading in Indiana and whose work

helped me immeasurably.

Also, this is to the memory of

OVID W. LAMPORT,

the division superintendent of the Cincinnati, Wabash &

Michigan Railroad at Wabash, Indiana in the 1880s, who

railroaded with his Bible on his desk.

CONTENTS

INDIANA
RAILROAD LINES

INTRODUCTION

Indiana is its own unique scene in the panorama of American railroading. Every Eastern company that reached Chicago or St. Louis had to build across Indiana. The level terrain in the northern part of the state allowed tangents that made high-speed runs an everyday commonplace. The earliest railroads built into and out of Indianapolis, the state capital, like spokes on a wheel. By the Twentieth Century this was supplemented by the most extensive electric interurban service in the country, also was anchored in Indianapolis. The knobs and hollows in the south demanded deep cuts and high fills, tunnels, long bridges, and heavy grades. The 5.89% grade needed to climb out of the Ohio River valley at Madison remains a national record. By 1900 lines crossed east to west, another half dozen from north to south, and others on diagonals across the state. The railroad network reached into almost all of the state; of Indiana's 92 counties only two, Ohio and Switzerland, had no rails. The rail system climbed to a peak of nearly 7,300 miles in 1913, and then began a steady decline. Today, regrettably, substantial parts of this steel network have disappeared, so that by 1999 some 3,000 miles of line had been taken up.

The first railroad train ran in Indiana in 1838. But this compilation is not a history of Indiana's railroads. The growth of Indiana's railroads has been covered very capably by Richard S. Simons and Francis H. Parker in their invaluable study, Railroads of Indiana. This invaluable work should be in the library of every student of Indiana's railroad history.

The work you hold in your hands deals only with one specific facet of a railroad system: the physical plant. It has been compiled because, as each year passes, more details of the construction of the Indiana railroad network, particularly the work of the early years, may slip into obscurity. The names of companies have become unclear, as well as what they built and when they built it. Inaccuracies have crept in and now have been repeated as certainties. This book attempts to put a sound footing under the construction, abandonment, and ownership of Indiana's railroad network. Hopefully it will provide a solid framework for historians to use when dealing with the physical plant and ownership record of Indiana's railroads. At the least, historians now have the correct names of companies and dates of construction.

Chapter 4 details all the intercity common carrier "steam" railroad lines that operated in the state of Indiana. Each individual line of each company has three sets of data: an arrangement of stations that lists all named and some unnamed locations along the line, a record of construction and abandonment or other disposition of the line, and a record of the owners of the line. One important limitation must be mentioned: privately-owned industrial railroads, operated by a company for its own convenience and which handle only the owner's traffic, are reported only so far as they could be found and had information reasonably available. Railroads within the confines of one factory or plant are not included.

Readers may question the company names used in Chapter 4. The spate of mergers that took place on Indiana roads after the formation of Penn Central in 1968, would have forced too many lines of too many original owners into one listing. Many still recall the earlier names of the constituents that went into Penn Central. It seemed better, to the compiler at least, to assume that the user will have some familiarity with the ownership of lines in the 1940s, when most of the trackage was in place. This choice of time is purely a personal one, but it is not intended to make finding a specific line in Chapter 4 more difficult. The user should find Chapter 1 of value in tracking between companies, and Chapter 3 for locating companies in a specific county.

Chapter 5 details all of the intercity electric interurban lines. Despite the admirable efforts of the Central Electric Railfans' Association, the documentation about the construction and abandonment of city street railway lines is far from complete. For this reason intercity electric roads are included but city lines are not. The Southern Indiana is included with the "steam" roads since it stopped using electric power early in its life and continues today as a conventional railroad. The Winona also discontinued using electricity late in its life but has been kept with the electric roads.

Any work of this sort, dealing as it does with myriad data and numbers, requires some inferences and assumptions to make complete the record for some lines. Whenever possible the source providing data is identified. Entries without a cited source are inferred from the presence or absence of entries in timetables, on maps, and, if all else fails, the author's best estimates. Hopefully this book will encourage others to undertake research that will yield new and more complete documentation. In any such a compilation as this, despite the best of efforts, errors can and very likely have crept in, and the author is solely responsible for them.

1

INDEX OF ALL RAILROAD AND INTERURBAN COMPANIES

Chicago & West Michigan		PM-L
Chicago, Attica & Southern	CAS	117-119
Chicago, Cincinnati & Louisville		NKP-LM
Chicago, Hammond & Western RR		IHB-W
Chicago, Indiana & Eastern		PRR-CM
Chicago, Indiana & Southern		LS-WD, WK; MC-J
Chicago, Indianapolis & Louisville		MON all
Chicago Junction Ry		IHB-AW, -W
Chicago, Lake Shore & Eastern Ry		EJE-S
Chicago, Milwaukee, St. Paul & Pacific	MILW	120-126
Chicago, Milwaukee & St. Paul		all MILW
Chicago-New York Electric Air Line	CNAL	318
Chicago, St. Louis & Pittsburgh		PRR-CR, -I, -L, -LE
Chicago Short Line Ry	CSL	127
Chicago, South Bend & Northern Indiana		NOIN-A, -B, -C
Chicago South Shore & South Bend	CSS	318-321
Chicago, Terre Haute & Southeastern		MILW-T, -TA, -TL, -TO, -TS, -TW
Cincinnati & Bedford		B&O-SB
Cincinnati & Chicago Air-Line		PRR-CR, -L
Cincinnati & Chicago		PRR-CR, -L
Cincinnati & Indianapolis Junction		B&O-IH
Cincinnati & Martinsville		CCC-GM
Cincinnati & Southern Ohio River		CCC-GA
Cincinnati & Terre Haute		CEI-J
Cincinnati, Bluffton & Chicago	CBC	127
Cincinnati, Connersville & Muncie		NKP-LF
Cincinnati, Findlay & Fort Wayne		B&O-F
Cincinnati, Hamilton & Dayton		B&O-F, ID, -IH
Cincinnati, Hamilton & Indianapolis		B&O-IH
Cincinnati, Indianapolis & Western		B&O-ID, -IH
Cincinnati, Indianapolis, St. Louis & Chicago		CCC-G, -GA, -GM, -H, -HO
Cincinnati, Lawrenceburg & Aurora	CLA	321-322
Cincinnati, Logansport & Chicago		PRR-CR
Cincinnati, Peru & Chicago		NKP-LM
Cincinnati, Richmond & Fort Wayne		GR&I-R
Cincinnati, Rockport & Southwestern		SOU-UE, -UF, -UR
Cincinnati, Wabash & Michigan		CCC-M
City of Madison Port Authority		see Madison
Cleveland, Cincinnati, Chicago & St. Louis	CCC	128-150; see also P&E
Cleveland, Columbus, Cincinnati & Indianapolis		CCC-I
Cleveland, Indiana & St. Louis		CI-A
Columbus & Indiana Central		PRR-I, -L, -LE
Columbus & Shelby		PRR-IC
Columbus, Chicago & Indiana Central		PRR-CR, -I, -L, -LE
Columbus, Hope & Greensburg		CCC-GC
Connersville & New Castle Junction		NKP-LF
Conrail (Consolidated Rail Corp.)	CR	151-156 (CCC, IU, LS, MC, P&E, PRR)
Corman, R. J.	RJC	157
Crawfordsville & Wabash		MON-SA
CSX Corporation	CSX	157 (B&O, BOCT, C&O, CEI, L&N, MON, PM)
CSX Transportation	CSX	158-160 (B&O, BOCT, C&O, CEI, L&N, MON, PM)
Dayton & Muncie Traction		INDR-BU
Dayton & Western Traction	DAWE	322-323
Delphos, Bluffton & Frankfort		NKP-TB
Detroit, Butler & St. Louis		WAB-M
Detroit, Eel River & Illinois		PRR-IE; WAB-ME

Gary & Connecting		GARY
Gary & Hobart Traction		GARY
Gary & Interurban		GARY
Gary & Southern Traction		GARY
Gary & Valparaiso		GARY
Gary & Western RR		IHB-G
Gary Connecting Rys		GARY
Gary, Hobart & Eastern Traction		GARY
Gary Railways	GARY	329-330
Goshen, South Bend & Chicago		CNAL
Griffith & Northern		EJE-G
Grand Rapids & Indiana		PRR-GR, -GS
Grand Trunk Western	GTW	169-171
Hammond & Blue Island RR		IHB-W
Havana, Rantoul & Eastern		IC-SR; WAB-PR
Henderson Bridge & Railroad Co.		L&N-S
Henderson Bridge Co.		L&N-S
Heritage	HERG	171
Hillsdale County	HCRC	171
Honey Creek	HCR	172
Hoosier Southern	HOS	172-173
Huntington, Tell City & Cannelton		SOU-UC
Illinois Central Gulf		see Illinois Central
Illinois Central	IC	173-177
Indian Creek	INDC	177
Indiana & Illinois Central		B&O-ID
Indiana & Illinois Southern		IC-NE
Indiana & Lake Michigan		MC-J
Indiana & Michigan		PM-L
Indiana & Ohio	INOH	178
Indiana Block Coal		CEI-EZ
Indiana, Bloomington & Western		P&E-A
Indiana Central		PRR-I
Indiana, Columbus & Eastern		D&W
Indiana Eastern	IERT	178
Indiana Electric		NOIN-B
Indiana Harbor Belt	IHB	179-181
Indiana Harbor		LS-WD
Indiana Hi-Rail	IHRC	181-184
Indiana, Illinois & Iowa		LS-WK; MC-J
Indiana Interstate	INTS	184-185
Indiana Midland		IMID 185-186
Indiana North & South		CEI-IA; CAS-A
Indiana Northeastern	INNE	186
Indiana Northern Ry	INOR	187
Indiana Northern Traction		INDR-C
Indiana Railroad	INRD	187-188
Indiana Railroad	INDR	331-347; all THIE
Indiana Railway		NOIN-B
Indiana Railways & Light		INDR-E
Indiana Service Corp.		INDR-F, -KA, -KB
Indiana Southern	ISRR	188-189
Indiana Stone		MON-SB
Indiana, State of		PRR-IM
Indiana Union Traction		INDR-A, -BU
Indianapolis & Bellefontaine		CCC-I

Indianapolis & Cincinnati RR		CCC-G, -GA, -H, -HO
Indianapolis & Cincinnati Ry		ISER
Indianapolis & Cincinnati Traction		ISER
Indianapolis & Eastern Ry		THIE-R
Indianapolis & Evansville		CEI-J
Indianapolis & Louisville		MON-SL, -SL2, -SL3
Indianapolis & Louisville Electric		INDR-L
Indianapolis & Louisville Traction		INDR-L
Indianapolis & Madison		NKP-LM; PRR-IEC, -IL, -IM
Indianapolis & Martinsville Rapid Transit		THIE-M
Indianapolis & Northwestern Traction		THIE-L, LC
Indianapolis & Plainfield Electric		THIE-A
Indianapolis & St. Louis		CCC-L
Indianapolis & Southeastern	ISER	348-349
Indianapolis & Vincennes		PRR-IG, -IV, -IVO
Indianapolis & Western Ry		THIE-D
Indianapolis, Bloomington & Western		CCC-S; P&E-A
Indianapolis, Cincinnati & Lafayette		CCC-G, -GA, -GM, -H, -HO
Indianapolis Coal Traction		THIE-A
Indianapolis, Columbus & Southern Traction		INDR-L
Indianapolis, Crawfordsville & Danville		P&E-A
Indianapolis, Crawfordsville & Danville Electric		THIE-C
Indianapolis, Crawfordsville & Western Traction		THIE-C
Indianapolis, Decatur & Springfield		B&O-ID
Indianapolis, Decatur & Western		B&O-ID
Indianapolis, Delphi & Chicago		MON-A, -I
Indianapolis, Greenwood & Suburban		INDR-L
Indianapolis, New Castle & Eastern Traction		INDR-AP, -N, -NM
Indianapolis, New Castle & Northeastern Tr.		INDR-N
Indianapolis, New Castle & Toledo Electric		INDR-N
Indianapolis, Peru & Chicago		NKP-LM; WAB-IM
Indianapolis, Pittsburg & Cleveland		CCC-I
Indianapolis, Shelbyville & Southwestern		ISER
Indianapolis Southern		IC-NI
Indianapolis Union	IU	189-191
Interstate Public Service Co.		INDR-L, -LC, -LN
J. K. Line	JKL	191
Jeffersonville		PRR-IA, -IC, -IL
Jeffersonville City & Suburban		INDR-LN
Jeffersonville, Madison & Indianapolis		PRR-IA, -IC, -ICA, -IL, -IM
Joliet & Northern Indiana		MC-WJ
Kankakee, Beaverville & Southern	KBSR	192
Kentucky & Indiana Bridge & RR		KIT-A
Kentucky & Indiana Terminal RR	KIT	193
Knightstown & Shelbyville		PRR-SK
Kokomo Belt RR	KKBL	193
Kokomo, Frankfort & Western Traction		INDR-E
Kokomo, Marion & Western Traction		INDR-E
Kokomo Rail Co.	KOKO	194
Lafayette & Indianapolis		CCC-H, -HO
Lafayette, Bloomington & Muncie		NKP-LP, -LS
Lafayette, Muncie & Bloomington		NKP-LP, -LS; WAB-PB
Lafayette Union RR		WAB-YL
LaGrange, Toledo & Eastern		SJV
Lake Erie & Fort Wayne RR		WAB-YF
Lake Erie & Louisville		PRR-IC, -ICA

Lake Erie & Western		NKP-LF, -LM, -LP, -LR, -LS
Lake Erie, Evansville & Southwestern		SOU-UE
Lake Erie, Wabash & St. Louis		WAB-M, -MM, -P
Lake Shore & Michigan Southern	LS	194-205
LaPorte & Michigan City Traction		NOIN-A
Lawrenceburg & Upper Mississippi		CCC-G, -GA
Lebanon & Thorntown Traction	LETH	349
Lebanon & Western		IC-SR
Lima, Delphos, Van Wert & Fort Wayne		FWVL
Logansport & Eel River Short Line	LERS	205
Logansport & Toledo		PRR-IE
Logansport, Crawfordsville & South Western		PRR-IF, -VF
Logansport, Rochester & Northern Traction		INDR-F
Louisville & Indiana RR	LIRC	205-206
Louisville & Jeffersonville Bridge	LJB	206
Louisville & Nashville	L&N	207-209 (CEI, MON)
Louisville & Northern Ry & Lighting		INDR-L, -LC, -LN
Louisville & Southern Indiana Traction		INDR-L, -LC
Louisville Bridge Co.	LBR	209
Louisville, Evansville & St. Louis Consolidated		SOU-U, -UC, -UF, -UR
Louisville, Evansville & St. Louis		SOU-U, -UC, -UE, -UF, -UR
Louisville, New Albany & Chicago		MON-A, -I, -N, -SA, -SB, -SBO, -SS, -SV
Louisville, New Albany & Corydon	LNAC	210
Louisville, New Albany & St. Louis Air Line		SOU-U
Louisville, New Albany & St. Louis		SOU-U
Madison	CMPA	210
Madison & Indianapolis		CCC-GM
Madison & Indianapolis		NKP-LM
Madison & Indianapolis		PRR-IEC, -IL, -IM
Marion & Bluffton Traction		INDR-AB
Marion, Bluffton & Eastern Traction		INDR-AB
Marion Electric Street		INDR-C, -CG
Martinsville & Franklin		CCC-GM
Maumee & Western	MAWE	211
MG Rail	MGR	227
Michigan Air Line		MC-N
Michigan Central	MC	211-216
Michigan City & Indianapolis		NKP-LM
Michigan Southern & Northern Indiana		LS-A, -T, -W
Michigan Southern	MISO	216
Midland Ry		CI-A
Missouri Pacific	MP	217 (CEI)
Monon	MON	217-229
Muncie & Portland Traction		INDR-AP
Muncie & State Line		NKP-LP, -LS
Muncie & Union City Traction		INDR-BU
Muncie & Western RR	M&W	229
Muncie Belt	MUNB	230
Muncie, Hartford & Fort Wayne		INDR-A
National Rail Passenger Corp.		see Amtrak
New Albany & Eastern		B&O-SV
New Albany & Salem		MON-A, -N, -SA, -SB, -SBO
New Castle & Rushville		NKP-LR
New Jersey, Indiana & Illinois	NJI	230
New York Central	NYC	231 (all CCC, IHB, LS, MC, P&E, part NKP)
New York, Chicago & St. Louis	NKP	231-242

Norfolk & Western	N&W	243 (all NKP, WAB)
Norfolk Southern	NS	244-247 (all NKP, SOU, WAB)
Northern Indiana RR		LS-A, -T, -W
Northern Indiana Ry	NOIN	350-352
Northern Indiana Power		INDR-E
North Western Grand Trunk		GTW-C
Ohio & Indiana		PRR-F
Ohio & Mississippi		B&O-SC, -SI, -SJ, -SV, -SW
Ohio Electric		D&W; FWVL
Ohio, Indiana & Western		CCC-S
Ohio, Indiana & Western		P&E-A
Orleans, West Baden & French Lick Springs		MON-F
Owensville Terminal	OWEN	247
Peninsular		GTW-C, -CO2, -CO4
Penn Central	PC	247-253 (all CCC, IU, LS, MC, P&E, PRR)
Pennsylvania	PRR	253-291
Peoria & Eastern	P&E	292-293
Peoria, Decatur & Evansville		IC-NH, -NM
Pere Marquette of Indiana		PM-C
Pere Marquette	PM	293-295
Perry County Port Authority		see Hoosier Southern
Peru & Detroit		WAB-MX
Peru & Indianapolis		NKP-LM
Pigeon River	PGRV	295
Pittsburgh, Cincinnati & St. Louis		PRR-CR, -I, -IA, -IC, -ICA, -IL, -IM, -L, -LE
Pittsburgh, Cincinnati, Chicago & St. Louis		PRR-CM, -CR, -I, -IA, -IC, -ICA, -IE, -IF, -IG, -IK, -IL, -IM, -IV, -IVO, -L, -LE, -LS, -V, -VB, -VF, -VP
Pittsburgh, Fort Wayne & Chicago		PRR-F
Plymouth Short Line	PLSL	295
Poseyville & Owensville	PORR	296
Public Service Co. of Evansville		SIGE
Public Service Co. of Indiana		INDR-L,-LC, -LN
Rantoul		IC-SR
Richmond Street & Interurban Ry		THIE-R, -RN
Rossville & Eastern Illinois		CEI-CJ
Rushville & Shelbyville		PRR-IC
St. Joseph, South Bend & Southern		MC-J
St. Joseph Valley Ry	SJV	352-354
St. Joseph Valley Traction		SJV
St. Louis & South Eastern		L&N-S, SE
St. Louis & Southeastern		L&N-S, SE
St. Louis, Alton & Terre Haute		CCC-L
St. Louis, Indianapolis & Eastern		IC-NE
Seaboard System	SBD	296-297 (part CEI, MON)
Shelby & Rush		PRR-IC
Shelbyville Lateral Branch		PRR-SL
Soo Line	SOO	297 (all MILW)
South Bend & Southern Michigan		NOIN-C
South Bend, LaPorte & Michigan City Tr.		NOIN-A
South East & St. Louis		L&N-S, -SE
Southern	SOU	297-302
Southern Indiana		MILW-T, -TA, -TL, -TS
Southern Indiana Gas & Electric Co.	SIGE	354-355
Southern Indiana Ry	SOIN	302-303
Southern Michigan		NOIN-C
Southern Ry of Indiana		SOU-U, -UC, -UE, -UF, -UR

Southwind Shortline RR	SWND	303
Springfield, Effingham & Southeastern		IC-NE
Sturgis, Goshen & St. Louis		LS-TS
Syracuse & Milford	SYM	303
Terre Haute & Indianapolis		MC-J; PRR-V, -VB, -VP
Terre Haute & Logansport		PRR-IF, -LS, -VF
Terre Haute & Richmond		PRR-V
Terre Haute & Southeastern		CEI-J
Terre Haute, Brazil & Eastern	THBE	304
Terre Haute Electric Co.		THIE-A
Terre Haute, Indianapolis & Eastern Traction	THIE	355-365
Terre Haute Traction & Light Co.		THIE-A, -P, -S, -T
Tippecanoe	TIP	304-305
Toledo & Chicago Interurban		INDR-KA, -KB
Toledo & Illinois		WAB-MM
Toledo & Wabash		WAB-M, -MM, -P
Toledo, Cincinnati & St. Louis		NKP-TB, -TS
Toledo, Delphos & Burlington		NKP-TB
Toledo, Logansport & Burlington		PRR-L, -LE
Toledo, Peoria & Western	TPW	305
Toledo, St. Louis & Kansas City		NKP-TB, -TS
Toledo, St. Louis & Western		NKP-TB, -TS
Toledo, Wabash & Western		WAB-M, -MM, -P
Twin Branch	TWBR	306
Union Traction of Indiana		INDR-all
Valparaiso & Northern Ry	V&N	365-366
Vandalia		PRR-IE, -IF, -IG, -IV, -IVO, -LS, -V, -VB, -VF, -VP
Vernon, Greensburg & Rushville		CCC-M
Wabash	WAB	306-314
Wabash Central	WABC	314
Wabash River Traction		INDR-F
Wabash, St. Louis & Pacific		all WAB
Warsaw, Goshen & White Pigeon		CCC-M
Western Indiana RR		EJE-GS
White Water Valley		CCC-GW
White Water Valley	WWV	314-315
Winimac Southern	WSRY	315-316
Winona & Warsaw Ry		WIN
Winona Interurban Ry		WIN
Winona RR	WIN	366-367
Winona Service Co.		WIN
Yankeetown Dock	YANK	316

2 DIRECTORY OF NAMED PLACES ON RAILROADS

Place name	County	Railroad
# place not located		
Abbott	Sullivan	MILW-TS 10.9
Aboite	Allen	now Roanoke Siding
Academie	Allen	LS-TF 90.7
Ackerman	LaPorte	PM-W 31.9
Acton	Marion	CCC-G 96.6
AD	Starke	ERIE-C 193.0
Adams	Allen	PRR-GR 86.6--PRR-F 314.4
Adams	Decatur	CCC-G 67.8
Adams	Lake	GTW-C 43.3
Adams	Monroe	MON-SA 212.2
Adamsboro	Cass	PRR-LE 5.7
Ade	Newton	LS-WD 55.0
Advance	Boone	CI-A 70.1
Aetna	Lake	CSS-A 56.9; IHB-G 7.2; WAB-MC 239.2
Ainsworth	Lake	GTW-C 45.2
Airline Jct.	Lake	MON-A 25.4--PRR-L 285.4
Akron	Fulton	ERIE-C 157.9; WIN-A 46.1
Albany	Delaware	NKP-LS 162.5
Albion	Noble	B&O-C 143.3
Alco	Lake	IHB-G 8.2
Alda	Madison	CCC-M 155.0
Aldine	Starke	ERIE-C 193.9
Alert	Decatur	MILW-T 320.1
Alexandria	Madison	CCC-M 153.5; NKP-LS 189.9
Alice	Knox	CEI-E 236.4
Alida	LaPorte	B&O-C 220.9--MON-M 45.0
Alliance	Madison	CCC-M 171.0
Allison	Warren	LS-WD 99.3
Alma	Putnam	CCC-L 42.9
Almeda	Putnam	PRR-V 37.2
Alpine	Fayette	CCC-GW 61.8
Altamont	Tippecanoe	CCC-H 170.2--NKP-LF 254.7
Altona	DeKalb	B&O-C 129.2
Ambia	Benton	NKP-LP 293.9
Ambler	LaPorte	CSS-A 28.7
Amboy	Miami	C&O-C 146.8; PRR-L 171.4
Ambridge	Lake	CSS-A 60.7
Ames	Montgomery	MON-SA 148.4--P&E-A 43.0--PRR-VC 52.0
Amity	Johnson	PRR-IL 25.1
Amo	Hendricks	PRR-V 24.9
AN	Fredericks	CCC-L 12.5
AN	Fulton	ERIE-C 158.6--(WIN-A 46.6)
Anderson	Madison	CCC-I 247.4--CCC-M 165.5; CI-A 18.8; PRR-CR 123.0
Andrews	Huntington	WAB-M 176.2
Andrews Yard	Huntington	WAB-M 177.0
Andromeda	Clay	MON-SL 54.5
Andry	LaPorte	CSS-A 26.6
Angola	Steuben	LS-TF 56.2--SJV-A 59.7
Angola Jct.	Steuben	SJV-A 58.7--SJV-B 0
Anita	Johnson	IC-NI 24.7
Anoka	Cass	PRR-CR 177.4--PRR-L 192.6
Anthony	Delaware	PRR-CM 34.0
Anthonys	Pulaski	MON-M 20.6

Antioch	Gibson	CCC-LE 139.7
Arcadia	Hamilton	NKP-LM 31.6
Arcola	Allen	PRR-F 328.2
Ardmore	St.Joseph	CSS-A 3.4
Argos	Marshall	NKP-C 431.0--NKP-LM 110.1
Ari	Allen	PRR-LE 70.4
Arlington	Rush	B&O-IH 92.1
Armstrong	Lawrence	MON-SS 14.8
Armstrong	Vanderburgh	IC-NM 237.6
Arnold Street	St.Joseph	GTW-C 99.5--LS-W 437.3
Arnolds	Elkhart	WIN-A 9.6
#Arnolds	Whitley	NKP-C 393
Artic	Dekalb	WAB-M 109.3
Ashboro	Clay	PRR-VB 8.8
Ashby	Franklin	CCC-GA 33.8
Ashby	Pike	CCC-T 95.4
Asherville	Clay	PRR-VP 4.5
Ash Grove	Tippecanoe	MON-A 110.2
Ashland	Henry	PRR-CR 98.3
Ashley-Hudson	Steuben	WAB-MC 121.4
Asphaltum	Jasper	now Crescent
Athens	Fulton	ERIE-C 163.2
Atherton	Vigo	CEI-E 167.3
Atkins	Lake	GTW-C 42.0
Atkinson	Benton	CCC-H 196.7
Atlanta	Hamilton	NKP-LM 34.5
Atterbury	Johnson	PRR-IL 28.5
Attica	Fountain	CAS-A 82.9--WAB-P 276.8--WAB-PC 0
Attica Shops	Fountain	CAS-A 83.5
Atwoods	Kosciusko	PRR-F 365.5
Auburn	DeKalb	B&O-C 124.7; LS-TF 75.4; PRR-LE 82.4
Auburn Jct.	DeKalb	B&O-C 124.7--LS-TF 76.6--PRR-LE 81.4
Augusta	Marion	CCC-H 120.4
Aurora	Dearborn	B&O-SC 25.8
Austin	Scott	PRR-IL 74.5
Averitt	Greene	MILW-T 222.3
Averys	Clinton	NKP-TB 201.9
Avilla	Noble	B&O-C 133.1--PRR-GS 113.6
Avoca	Lawrence	MON-SS 6.5
Avon	Fredericks	CCC-L 11.9
Avondale	Delaware	CI-A 0.7
Aylesworth	Porter	PRR-L 257.7
Aylsworth	Fountain	CAS-A 89.3
Aynes	Porter	PRR-L 257.0
Ayrshire	Pike	SOU-U 182.1
Azalia	Bartholomew	MILW-T 309.0
B	Elkhart	LS-A 438.7--LS-T 421.5; now CP 421
Babcock	Porter	B&O-C 232.7
Bailey	Porter	CSS-A 46.8
Baileytown	Porter	LS-W 485.5--LS-WM 14
Bainbridge	Putnam	MON-SA 168.7
Baker	Vigo	CEI-E 179.9
Balbec	Jay	CBC-A 36
Barce	Benton	CAS-A 58.7
Bargersville	Johnson	IC-NI 17.6
Baring Avenue	Lake	BOCT-A 3.9

Barnard	Putnam	B&O-ID 154.2
Barrett	Posey	IC-NM 223.3
Bart	Lake	PRR-F 434.4--EJE-A 45.7
Bass Lake (new)	Starke	ERIE-C 190.3--ERIE-CB 0
Bass Lake (old)	Starke	ERIE-CB 1.8
Bass Lake Jct.	Starke	now Bass Lake
Batesville	Ripley	CCC-G 47.8; CCC-GO1 48.0
Bath	Franklin	C&O-C 39.0
Battle Ground	Tippecanoe	MON-A 112.9
BC	Elkhart	LS-W 424.3
Beamer	Owen	MON-SL 15.3
Bear	Kosciusko	WIN-A 42.7
Beardstown	Pulaski	C&O-C 202.7
Beatrice	Porter	C&O-C 240.0
Beaver City	Newton	CAS-B 9.6
Beaver Dam	Kosciusko	WIN-A 41.7
Becker	Grant	PRR-L 160.0
Bedford	Lawrence	B&O-SB 10.8
Bedford	Lawrence	MILW-T 262.4--MILW-TO 0--MON-SB 245.8
Bedford Jct.	Lawrence	MON-SB 245.1--MON-SS 0.7
Beech Grove	Marion	now CP 103
Beech Grove	Vigo	B&O-IB 19.3
Beech Ridge	Lake	MON-ND 27.1
Beehunter	Greene	MILW-T 218.3--PRR-IV 86.2
Beeson(s)	Wayne	CCC-GW 74.1--NKP-LF 103.7
Belfast	LaPorte	NKP-LM 149.5--PM-W 26.5
Belknap	Vanderburgh	L&N-S 328.6
Bell	Tippecanoe	CCC-H 159.4
Belleview	Elkhart	CCC-M 39.3
Belshaw	Lake	LS-WD 28.2
Belt	Miami	WIN-A 65.5
Belt Crossing	Marion	CCC-G 106.9--IU-B 3.8
Belt Jct.	Marion	CCC-I 279.1--IU-B 0
Belt Jct.	Marion	MON-I 180.4--(IU-C 2.0)--(NKP-LM 3.2)
Belt Jct.	Vigo	MILW-T 182.0
Belt Yard	Vanderburgh	CEI-E 284.6--CEI-EB 0
Benadum	Delaware	C&O-C 110.3
Bend	Cass	PRR-LS 116.1
Bendix	St.Joseph	CSS-A 2.2
Bennett	Pike	CCC-T 91.0
Bennetts	Miami	NKP-LM 61.0
Bennetts Crossing	Rush	CCC-M 209.6
Bennettsville	Clark	MON-SB 307.3
Benton	Elkhart	WAB-MC 158.0
Bentonville	Fayette	PRR-IC 57.3--PRR-ICA 0
#Benwood	Clay	PRR-VKN 2
Berlein	Steuben	SJV-B 6.8
Berne	Adams	PRR-GR 58.8
Bethany Park	Morgan	PRR-IV 22.1
Bethevan	Grant	PRR-L 154.7
Beverly Shores	Porter	CSS-A 39.4
Bickels	Elkhart	SJV-A 3.0
Bicknell	Knox	PRR-IV 102.9--PRR-IVC 0
Bide-a-Wee	Fayette	CCC-GW 61.0
Big Four	Kosciusko	WIN-A 24.0
Bippus	Huntington	ERIE-C 135.7

Birchim	LaPorte	CSS-A 18.6
Birdseye	Dubois	SOU-U 214.5
Black Oak	Daviess	B&O-SW 164.7
Blackfoot Mine	Pike	CCC-TC 5.8
Blackhawk	Vigo	MILW-T 191.3--MILW-TS 0
Blaine	Jay	NKP-LS 150.4
Blanford	Vermillion	MILW-T 155.4
Blankenship	Martin	MILW-T 239.8
Blocher	Scott	B&O-SV 20.1
Bloomer	Madison	CI-A 23.7
Bloomfield	Greene	IC-NI 83.1; MON-SS 34.3
Bloomingdale	Parke	B&O-ID 184.1
Bloomington	Monroe	IC-NI 55.9--(IC-NB 0); MON-SA 220.5
Blountsville	Henry	C&O-C 90.4
Bluffton	Wells	CBC-A 23--NKP-LF 25.4--NKP-TB 123.4
BO	Lake	LS-W 502.6--B&O-C 251.9
Boggstown	Shelby	CCC-GM 92.7
Bolivar	Wabash	CCC-M 101.6--ERIE-C 144.3--HERG-A 0
Bonnell	Dearborn	CCC-G 31.4
Bonneyville	Elkhart	SJV-A 12.0
Boone	Cass	PRR-L 11.9/206.8--PRR-LO 206.8
Boone Grove	Porter	ERIE-C 219.7
Boonville	Warrick	SOU-UE 16.9--YANK-A 12
Borden	Clark	MON-SB 299.5
Boston	Wayne	C&O-C 54.9
Boswell	Benton	NKP-LP 286.6
Bothwells	Lake	GTW-C 38.8
Boulevard	Marion	MON-I 178.5
Bourbon	Marshall	PRR-F 373.0
Bowers	Montgomery	PRR-VF 64.6
Boyd	Clark	B&O-SV 50.3--PRR-IL 104.9
Boyd	Rush	CCC-M 195.1
Boyleston	Clinton	NKP-LP 228.0
Bracey	Wells	CBC-A 25
Bradley	Spencer	SOU-UR 4.4
Bradshaw	Vigo	MILW-T 159.8--MILW-TB 0
Branch	Johnson	CCC-GM 106.7
Brant	Marion	CCC-H 113.1--P&E-A 3.6
Braxton	Orange	MON-F 8.6
Brazil	Clay	B&O-IB 25.1--CEI-JB 0; CEI-EZ 184.5; CI-A 127.0; PRR-V 57.0--PRR-VB 0--PRR-VO 57.0
Brazil Clay Co.	Clay	CEI-EZ 183.6
Brazil Shop	Vigo	B&O-IB 24.6
Bremen	Marshall	B&O-C 181.4
Brems	Starke	NKP-C 436.4
Bretzville	Dubois	SOU-U 203.9
Brevoorts	Knox	CCC-LV 116.4
Brewersville	Jennings	CCC-M 243.4
Briant	Randolph	PRR-GR 50.3
Brice	Jay	NKP-LS 141.4
Bridge Jct.	Vigo	MILW-T C 7.1
Bridgeport	Clark	MON-SB 303.8
Bridgeport	Marion	PRR-V 8.8
Bridgeton	Parke	CI-A 116.0--CI-FWTHS 0
Brightwood Yard	Marion	CCC-I 278.6
Brimfield	Noble	LS-T 386.4

Bringhurst	Carroll	PRR-IF 95.6
Bristol	Elkhart	LS-A 430.5; SJV-A 9.0
Broad	Henry	NKP-LF 83.6--PRR-CR 101.9
Broad Ripple	Marion	MON-I 175.3
Broadway	Allen	PRR-F 320.2
Broadway	Lake	PRR-F 440.4
Brook	Bartholomew	PRR-IL 37.9
Brook	Newton	CAS-B 5.9
Brookfield	Shelby	CCC-G 94.8
Brooklyn	Morgan	PRR-IV 21.5
Brookston	White	MON-A 106.2
Brookville	Franklin	CCC-GW 43.5
Brow	Ripley	CCC-G 40.6
Brownell	Miami	WAB-MX 7--WIN-A 60.8
Brown Hill	Clark	MON-SB 302.8
Brownsburg	Hendricks	P&E-A 14.0
Browns Crossing	Morgan	PRR-IV 35.5
Brownstown	Jackson	B&O-SW 97.8
Browns Valley	Montgomery	PRR-VF 40.4
Browns Valley Jct.	Montgomery	CI-A 91.7
Brownsville	Union	B&O-IH 59.2
Bruce Lake	Fulton	PRR-LS 138.4
Bruceville	Knox	PRR-IV 109.3
Buchanan Street	Lake	CSS-A 59.7
Buck Creek	Tippecanoe	WAB-P 247.4
Buckeye	Huntington	NKP-TB 133.3
Buckeye Mine	Greene	PRR-IG 5.5 + 0.7
Buckskin	Gibson	CCC-T 114.8
Buff	Lake	B&O-C 249.4
Buffaloville	Spencer	SOU-UC 2.9
#Buff Hill	Lawrence	MILW-TO 6
Buffington	Lake	EJE-S 9.7; LS-W 501.0; PRR-F 446.3
Bunker Hill	Miami	NKP-LM 66.2; PRR-L 182.2
Burdick	Porter	LS-W 476.8
Burkes	LaPorte	CAS-A 8.2
Burket	Kosciusko	NKP-C 415.9
Burnett	Vigo	CEI-EZ 175.0--CCC-I 63.9
Burnett Siding	Vigo	CEI-EZ 176.5
Burnettsville	White	PRR-LF 12.1
Burney	Decatur	CCC-GC 70.7
Burns	Elkhart	LS-TS 6.5
Burns City	Martin	now Crane
Burns Harbor	Porter	LS-W 485.7
Burr Oak	Marshall	NKP-C 440.4
Burrows	Carroll	WAB-P 227.8
Bushrod	Greene	PRR-IG 0--PRR-IV 84.9
Busseron	Knox	CEI-E 222.6
Butler	DeKalb	LS-T 359.1; PRR-LE 93.1; WAB-M 114.9
Butlerville	Jennings	B&O-SC 65.6
BX	Marion	CCC-L 1.6--IU-B 8.7
BY	Lake	LS-WK 73.1--(MON-N 52.6)
C. I. Crossing	Madison	CCC-M 165.8--CI-A 18.6
Caborn	Posey	L&N-S 336.0
Cale	Martin	MILW-T 245.1
Caledonia	Clay	CI-A 123.8
Caledonia	Sullivan	IC-NE 106.3

Calumet	Lake	CSS-AO 65.7
Calumet Avenue	Lake	BOCT-A 5.2; CSS-A 68.5; MC-W 264.2
Calumet Tower	Lake	BOCT-A 2.7--EJE-GW 0.7--IHB-A 2.0
Cambria	Clinton	MON-I 129.7
Cambridge City	Wayne	CCC-GW 81.0; NKP-LF 97.2; PRR-I 134.9--PRR-ICA 63.4
Camby	Marion	PRR-IV 11.3
Camden	Carroll	PRR-IF 101.3
Cammack	Delaware	NKP-LS 179.7
Campbells	Morgan	PRR-IV 27.3
Campbellsburg	Washington	MON-SB 271.8
Caney	Clark	PRR-IL 91.7
Cannelburg	Daviess	B&O-SW 160.0
Cannelton	Perry	SOU-UC 22.7
Cantaloupe	Knox	CEI-E 245.2
Capehart	Daviess	CCC-T 72.5
Carbon	Clay	CI-A 121.2--CCC-L 52.8
Carlisle	Sullivan	CEI-E 213.2
Carlos City	Randolph	CCC-S 74.5
Carmein	Elkhart	SJV-A 4.6
Carmel	Hamilton	MON-I 167.8
Carpentersville	Putnam	MON-SA 165.5
Carr	Lawrence	B&O-SB 4.8
Carrolls Crossing	Allen	LS-TF 88.4
Cartersburg	Hendricks	PRR-V 16.8
Carthage	Rush	CCC-M 193.1; PRR-SK 4.5
Carwood	Clark	now Bridgeport
Cary	Putnam	MON-SA 173.0
Cass	Cass	now Danes
Cass	Sullivan	IC-NE 103.0--MON-SL2 4.0
Cassville	Howard	NKP-LM 59.2
Castleton	Marion	NKP-LM 12.1
Cataract	Owen	MON-SL 6.4
Cates	Fountain	NKP-TC 258.5
Catlin	Parke	CEI-ER 17.8--PRR-VF 17.8
Cavanaugh	Lake	CSS-A 63.4--CSS-AO 63.4; EJE-G 6.7--EJE-GS 0
Cayuga	Vermillion	CEI-E 141.1--NKP-TC 266.5
Cayuga Mine	Vermillion	NKP-TC-1 1.2
Cedar	DeKalb	PRR-LE 76.3
Cedar Grove	Franklin	CCC-GW 36.7
Cedar Lake	Lake	MON-A 39.5
Cement	Putnam	MON-SA 180.6
Cementville	Clark	PRR-IL 102.7
Center	Howard	PRR-CR 153.9
Center Street	Kosciusko	WIN-A 24.6--WIN-B 0.2
Centerpoint	Clay	PRR-VP 8.3
Centerton	Morgan	PRR-IV 23.8
Centerville	Wayne	PRR-I 125.6
Chain Lakes	St.Joseph	CSS-A 5.9
Chalmers	White	MON-A 102.1
Chalottesville	Hancock	PRR-I 158.7
Chambers	LaPorte	PM-W 11.9
Chandler	Warrick	SOU-UE 11.6
Chappell	Daviess	B&O-SI 171.4--CCC-T 78.4
Charlestown	Clark	B&O-SV 40.3
Chase	Benton	NKP-LP 284.3
Chatterton	Warren	CAS-A 74.2

Cherry Grove	Montgomery	MON-SA 141.0
Chester	Wayne	PRR-GR 4.3
Chesterfield	Madison	CCC-I 242.3; CI-A 13.7
Chesterton	Porter	LS-W 481.1
Chili	Miami	PRR-LE 21.1--(WIN-A 57.8)--WAB-MX 10.5; WIN-A 58.1
Chrisney	Spencer	SOU-UR 7.9
Churubusco	Whitley	PRR-LE 66.1
Cicero	Hamilton	NKP-LM 28.6
City Limits	Elkhart	SJV-A 1.5
CK	St.Joseph	LS-W 444.2--(MC-J 5.9)
Clanricarde	LaPorte	ERIE-C 209.3
Clark Road	Lake	CSS-A 61.8
Clarke	Clark	B&O-SV 38.4
Clarke	Lake	PRR-F 443.8
Clarke Jct.	Lake	BOCT-A 0.5--PRR-F 445.7--WAB-MC 246.7
Clarks	Pulaski	MON-M 19.1
#Clarks Depot	Shelby	PRR-SL
Clarks Hill	Tippecanoe	CCC-H 158.9--NKP-TC 217.8; also now CP 158
Clarksville	Clark	PRR-IA 1.6
Clay City	Clay	CCC-T 26.1; MON-SL 27.7
Claypool	Kosciusko	CCC-M 87.5--NKP-C 410.9
Clayton	Hendricks	PRR-V 20.1
Clear Creek	Monroe	MON-SB 224.2--MON-SBO 224.2
Clemer	Kosciusko	NKP-C 420.8
Clermont	Marion	P&E-A 9.6--PRR-IF 12.6
Clifford	Bartholomew	PRR-IC 6.4
Clifty	Shelby	now CP 77
Clifty Switch	Bartholomew	PRR-IM 3.5
Climax	Clay	CCC-T 18.8
Cline	Gibson	CCC-T 105.6
Cline Avenue	Lake	PRR-F 447.4
Clinton	Vermillion	CEI-E 162.9--CEI-EU 0
Clinton Yard	Vermillion	MILW-T 153.8--MILW-TW 0
Cloverdale	Putnam	MON-SA 189.2
Cloverland	Clay	PRR-VO 63.1
Clymers	Cass	PRR-IF 109.2--WAB-P 224.3
Coal Bluff	Vigo	B&O-IB 16.9--CCC-L 58.6
Coal City	Owen	CCC-T 31.2
Coal Creek	Fountain	CEI-EC 24.0
Coalmont	Clay	MILW-T 200.3--MILW-TK 0
Coatesville	Hendricks	PRR-V 27.9
Cobb	Vigo	CCC-L 59.0
Coburg	Porter	B&O-C 223.4
Cochrane	Dearborn	B&O-SC 27.3
Cochrane Jct.	Dearborn	B&O-SC 30.3
Code	Dearborn	CCC-G 35.7
Coe	Pike	CCC-TC 5.8
Coesse	Whitley	PRR-F 333.9
Colburn	Tippecanoe	WAB-P 243.8
Cold Springs	Dearborn	B&O-SC 37.4
Cole	Grant	PRR-CM 8.7
Colehour Yard Office	Lake	PRR-F 453.1
Colfax	Clinton	CCC-H 153.2
Colfax Tower	Clinton	CCC-H 154.0--PRR-VC 68.6
College	Elkhart	WIN-A 1.5
College Avenue	Marion	CCC-G 108.9--IU-EA 0.7

College Avenue	Vigo	MILW-T 179.0
Collett	Jay	PRR-GR 38.9
Collins	Whitley	PRR-LE 62.1
Columbia	Miami	WIN-A 66.7
Columbia Avenue	Lake	BOCT-A 4.8; MC-W 263.7
Columbia City	Whitley	PRR-F 338.7; PRR-LE 56.0
#Columbia No. 5 Mine	Clay	PRR-VP 8.0 + 1.0
Columbus	Bartholomew	CCC-GC 88.6; PRR-IL 41.0--PRR-IC 0--PRR-IM 0--PRR-IEC 0
Commiskey	Jennings	B&O-SV 10.3
Commodore Mine	Clay	CCC-T 29.1
Concord	DeKalb	B&O-C 117.8
Conlog	Noble	PRR-GS 117.3
Conner	Randolph	CCC-I 218.8
Connersville	Fayette	B&O-IH 67.3--NKP-LF 109.0; CCC-GW 68.5
#Conovers	Shelby	PRR-SL
Conrad	Newton	LS-WD 38.5
Converse	Miami	C&O-C 143.7; PRR-CM 0--PRR-L 168.6
Cook	Kosciusko	WIN-A 29.7
Cook	Lake	LS-WD 19.8
Cook	LaPorte	CSS-A 31.0
Corinne	Owen	PRR-IV 46.4--PRR-IVG 0
Cortland	Jackson	MILW-T 294.6
Corunna	DeKalb	LS-T 373.4
Cory	Clay	CCC-T 15.6
Corydon	Harrison	LNAC-A 0
Corydon Jct.	Harrison	LNAC-A 7.7--SOU-U 251.2
Corymbo	LaPorte	MC-W 223.6
Cottage Grove	Union	B&O-IH 48.2--C&O-C 46.5
County Line	Vigo	CCC-T 12.6
Courter	Miami	NKP-LM 79.8
Covington	Fountain	P&E-A 72.1--WAB-PC 14.8; CEI-EC 15.4
Cowan	Delaware	NKP-LF 71.6
Coxton	Lawrence	MILW-T 256.6--MILW-TG 0
CP 11	Elkhart	LS-A 425.4
CP 22	Dearborn	CCC-G 22.3
CP 39	Dearborn	CCC-G 39.7
CP 60	Decatur	CCC-G 60.2
CP 61	Decatur	CCC-G 61.7
CP 63	Decatur	CCC-G 63.0
CP 64	Decatur	CCC-G 64.2
CP 66	Decatur	CCC-G 66.1
CP 72	Vigo	CCC-L 72.0--CCC-T 0--PRR-VT2 73.3
CP 76	Vigo	CCC-L 76.3
CP 77	Shelby	CCC-G 77.3
CP 79	Vigo	CCC-L 79.9
CP 82	Shelby	CCC-G 82.6--PRR-IC 23.8
CP 84	Shelby	CCC-G 84.7
CP 89	Shelby	CCC-G 89.3--CCC-GW 89.3
CP 103	Marion	CCC-G 103.7
CP 139	Boone	CCC-H 139.4--PRR-IF 30.6
CP 143	Boone	CCC-H 143.4
CP 155	Clinton	CCC-H 155.7
CP 158	Tippecanoe	CCC-H 158.2
CP 169	Tippecanoe	CCC-H 169.1
CP 21st Street	Elkhart	LS-W 422.5

CP 226	LaPorte	MC-W 226.2
CP 238	Porter	MC-W 238.9
CP 247	Madison	CCC-I 247.8--CCC-M 165.4
CP 247-A	Madison	CCC-M 166.6--CCC-IA 247.2
CP 358	DeKalb	LS-T 358.5--PRR-LE 93.7--WAB-M 114.9
CP 367	DeKalb	LS-T 367.1--LS-TF 70.4
CP 379	Noble	PRR-GS 120.2--LS-T 379.7
CP 395	Noble	LS-T 395.4
CP 397	Noble	LS-T 397.7
CP 412	Elkhart	LS-T 412.4
CP 415	Elkhart	LS-T 415.6
CP 482	Porter	see PO
CP Ringo	Vigo	see CP 72
CP WG	St.Joseph	LS-W 426.4
Craig	Decatur	CCC-GC 64.2--CCC-M 225.0
Craig	Miami	WIN-A 48.29
Craigville	Wells	NKP-TB 117.8
Crandall	Harrison	SOU-U 253.5
Crane	Martin	MILW-T 236.0
#Crawford Mine	Clay	PRR-VP 4.0 + 2.0
Crawford No. 8 Mine	Clay	PRR-VB 5.8 + 0.8
Crawfordsville	Montgomery	MON-SA 147.3; P&E-A 43.8; PRR-VF 52.5
Crawfordsville Jct	Montgomery	see Ames
Crescent	Jasper	MON-ND1 4
Creston	Lake	MON-A 41.5
Crete	Randolph	CCC-S 64.9
Crisman	Porter	MC-W 246.1
Crocker	Porter	EJE-A 53.5--WAB-MC 230.5
Cromwell	Noble	B&O-C 153.5
Crooked Creek	LaGrange	PRR-GS 145.5
Crooked Lake	Steuben	SJV-A 55.6
Crothersville	Jackson	PRR-IL 70.5
Crown Hill	Vermillion	MILW-TC 6.2
Crown Point	Lake	ERIE-C 232.9
Crums Point	St.Joseph	now Crumstown
Crumstown	St.Joseph	GTW-C 91.6
Crystal	Dubois	SOU-UF 66.2
Cudahy	Lake	CSS-AO 64.1; IHB-AC 1.3
Culver	Marshall	PRR-LS 148.8
Cumberland	Marion	PRR-I 176.8
Cumberland Lodge	Lake	LS-WD 30.9
Cummins	St.Joseph	CSS-A 0.9
Curryville	Wells	NKP-TB 116.6
Curtis	Lake	LS-W 498.3
Curtis Yard	Lake	B&O-C 246.4
Curtisville	Tipton	PRR-CR 142.1
Custer	LaGrange	SJV-A 44.7
Cutler	Carroll	PRR-IF 92.2
Cuzco	Dubois	SOU-UF 69.5
CW	Grant	C&O-C 162.7--WAB-P 204.4
CX	Elkhart	CCC-M 55.5--LS-T 411.1--LS-TS 0
Cyclone	Clinton	MON-I 142.2
Cynthiana	Posey	CCC-LE 143.1; CEI-EM 277.4
Cypress	Vanderburgh	now Vaughan
DA	Adams	ERIE-C 96.3--NKP-TB 108.5--PRR-GR 70.4
Dabney	Ripley	B&O-SC 55.1

Daggett	Owen	CCC-T 32.4
Dale	Boone	CCC-H 132.4
Dale	Marion	PRR-IL 1.7--IU-B 5.9
Dale	Spencer	SOU-UE 36.8
Daleville	Delaware	CCC-I 240.0; CI-A 11.6
Dana	Vermillion	B&O-ID 199.1
Danes	Cass	WAB-P 213.0
Danville	Fredericks	CCC-L 19.3
Dark Hollow	Lawrence	MON-SS 3.9
Darlington	Montgomery	PRR-VF 60.1
David	Hancock	CCC-I 262.3
Davis	LaPorte	CSS-A 30.3; PRR-F 404
Davis	Marion	PRR-IF 6.9--PRR-V 6.9
Davy	Vanderburgh	CCC-LE 151.3
Daylight	Vanderburgh	CCC-T 125.0
Dayton	Tippecanoe	NKP-LP 249.5
DE	St.Joseph	PRR-LS 182.2
De Gonia	Warrick	SOU-UE 21.8
De Pauw	Harrison	SOU-U 244.4
Dearborn	Dearborn	B&O-SC 21.9--CCC-GA 24.9
Deasy	Cass	PRR-L 8.9
Decatur	Adams	ERIE-C 96.0; PRR-GR 70.7; NKP-TB 108.2
Decker	Knox	CEI-E 246.3
Deeds	Miami	NKP-LM 85.4
Deerfield	Randolph	PRR-L 133.9
DeForest	Warrick	SOU-UE 13
Delaware	Ripley	B&O-SC 47.4; B&O-SO1 47.0
Delco	Madison	CCC-I 246.7--PRR-CR 122.2
Della	Jasper	MON-ND 3.3
DeLong	Fulton	ERIE-C 179.7--PRR-LS 143.1
Delphi	Carroll	MON-I 111.0--WAB-P 238.6
DeMotte	Jasper	LS-WK 65.6
Denham	PUlaski	PRR-L 231.4
Deniston	Clinton	NKP-LP 239.0
Denver	Miami	NKP-LM 81.9; PRR-LE 18.8
Deputy	Jefferson	B&O-SV 14.9
DeSoto	Delaware	NKP-LS 167.2
Dewey	Vigo	(CEI-E 174.7)--MILW-T 174.7--(PRR-VF 2.8)
Dewey (Jct.)	Vigo	CEI-E 173.8--(PRR-VF 3.7)--PRR-VT1 2.9
#Diamond	Monroe	MON-SB
Diamond Jct.	Vigo	B&O-IB 16.8
#Diamond Mine	Clay	B&O-IB 16.8/spur 3.5
#Dibliss	Huntington	CBC-A
Dickason	Vermillion	CEI-E 137.6
Dickason Pit	Vermillion	CEI-E 138.1
Dillon	LaPorte	NKP-LM 137.3--WAB-MC 200.5
Dillsboro	Dearborn	B&O-SC 33.9
Dinwiddie	Lake	MON-ND 32.2
Disko	Fulton	ERIE-C 152.8
Ditney	Warrick	CCC-T 121.4
Ditney Hill	Warrick	CCC-T 122.7
Dix	Miami	WIN-A 50.89
Dix	Shelby	CCC-G 95.6
Dixie Line Mine	Vigo	CEI-EZ 179.3
DK	Lake	LS-WD 14.6--(MON-N 33.5)
Dodd	Lawrence	B&O-SB 7.3

Donaldson	Marshall	PRR-F 391.7
Doran	Kosciusko	WIN-A 39.70
Doran	Porter	PM-C 131.5
Doubling Track	Benton	CAS-A 64.4
Douglas	Gibson	SOU-U 167.2
Dow	Madison	CCC-M 162.6--PRR-CR 124.8
Doyle	Miami	NKP-LM 77.7
Drawbridge	LaPorte	MC-W 228.5
Dresden	Greene	MON-SS 22.2
Drew	Delaware	C&O-C 103.5--PRR-CM 38.1
Duane	Vigo	CCC-L 69.2
Dublin	Wayne	PRR-I 137.3
Dublin Jct.	Wayne	PRR-I 138.4--PRR-IC 62.0
Dubois	Dubois	SOU-UF 62.8
Duff	Daviess	CCC-T 77.2--CCC-TW 0
Duff	Dubois	SOU-U 194.9
Dugger	Sullivan	IC-NE 101.1
Duncan	Floyd	SOU-U 262.4
Dundee	Madison	NKP-LS 194.1
Dune Acres	Porter	CSS-A 45.2; IHB-G 15.2
Dune Park	Porter	CSS-A 43.6; LS-W 486.7--IHB-G 16.2
Dunfee	Whitley	NKP-C 381.9
#Dunham	Jackson	B&O-SV 92
Dunkirk	Jay	PRR-L 128.4
Dunlap	Elkhart	LS-T 416.1
Dunlaps	Elkhart	CCC-M 50.2
Dunn	Benton	LS-WD 75.8
Dunns	Jasper	CAS-A 9.8
Dunreith	Henry	NKP-LR 94.1--PRR-I 148.9
Dupont	Jefferson	PRR-IM 32.0
Durbin	Hamilton	CI-A 31.5
Durham	LaPorte	LS-W 469.8
DX	Marion	CCC-I 280.1--CCC-S 136.4
DY	Benton	LS-WD 80.4--(NKP-LP 291.5)
Dyer	Lake	EJE-A 31.3--MON-A 29.1; MC-WJ 15.4
Eagles	Putnam	PRR-V 49.8
Eagletown	Hamilton	CI-A 46.8
Earl	Decatur	CCC-M 240.4
Earl Park	Benton	CCC-H 208.9
East Almeda	Putnam	PRR-V 35.9
East Avilla	Noble	B&O-C 132.1
East Bart	Lake	PRR-F 433.0
East Chicago	Lake	CSS-A 66.2; CSS-AO 67.0; EJE-GS 2.8
East Dublin	Wayne	PRR-I 137.0
East Gary	Lake	B&O-C 243.7; MC-WJ 0--MC-W 249.8
East Gibson	Hendricks	PRR-V 14.9
East Graw	Miami	PRR-L 174.8
East Haven	Wayne	PRR-I 121.7
East Kirk	Jay	PRR-L 126.8
East Marion	Hendricks	PRR-V 28.0
East North Judson	Starke	PRR-L 235.8
East Pinola	LaPorte	LS-W 466.6
East Rockville	Parke	CI-A 106.9
Eastside	Marion	CCC-S 135.8--IU-B 0.5
East Summit	Hendricks	PRR-V 20.3
East Upland	Grant	PRR-L 144.1

East Wanatah	LaPorte	PRR-F 413.2
East Wayne Yard	Allen	NKP-F 366.3
Eastwood	Marion	CCC-I 277.8
East Yard	Tippecanoe	WAB-P 253.5
East Yard	Vigo	PRR-V 70.9--PRR-VT1 0
Eaton	Delaware	NKP-LF 55.0
Eckerty	Crawford	SOU-U 219.4
Economy	Wayne	C&O-C 79.6
Eddy	LaGrange	WAB-MC 140.9
Edgerton	Allen	NKP-F 354.1
Edinburg	Johnson	PRR-IEC 10.5--PRR-IL 30.6--PRR-SK 0
Edwardsport	Knox	PRR-IV 98.5
Eel (River)	Clay	CCC-T 22.0
Eel River Mining Co.	Owen	CCC-T 34.1
Effner	Newton	PRR-LF 61.2
#Ehrlich	Clay	PRR-VB 4
8th Avenue	Vanderburgh	CCC-LE 160.0--L&N-SE 324.7--CEI-EB 287.4
Eighteenth Street	Cass	PRR-L 195.9
Elberfeld	Warrick	CCC-T 119.8
Elberfeld Mine	Warrick	CCC-T 120.4
Elizabethtown	Bartholomew	MILW-T 312.7; PRR-IM 8.0
Elk	Morgan	PRR-IV 29.5
Elkhart	Elkhart	CCC-M 44.8; LS-A 438.9--LS-T 421.6--LS-W 421.6; SJV-A 0
Ellettsville	Monroe	MON-SA 213.1
Elliott	Vanderburgh	CCC-T 122.8
Elliston	Greene	CCC-T 48.0--IC-NI 35.2--MON-SS 36.0
Elm	Cass	PRR-L 197.1--WAB-P 218.7
Elmer	Newton	CAS-B 18.8
Elmwood	Miami	WIN-A 66.8
Elnora	Daviess	CCC-T 61.2--MILW-T 224.1
Elvin	Johnson	PRR-IL 21.4
Elwood	Madison	NKP-LS 198.7; PRR-CR 137.8
Elwren	Monroe	IC-NI 65.0
Emison	Knox	CEI-E 224.7
Empire	Lake	CSS-AO 65.2
Emporia	Madison	CCC-M 172.7
English	Crawford	SOU-U 228.9
English Lake	Starke	C&O-C 217.5; PRR-L 241.5
Enos	Newton	LS-WD 44.8
Enosville	Pike	CCC-TC 3.7
Epileptic Village	Henry	CCC-S 93.6
Erie	Fulton	WIN-A 46.6--ERIE-C 158.6
Erwin	Posey	CEI-EM 298.4
Etna Green	Kosciusko	PRR-F 369.3
Evanston	Spencer	SOU-UC 11.9
Evansville	Vanderburgh	CEI-E 287.2--IC-NM 247.8--L&N-SE 325.0--(CCC-LE 160.3); CEI-EO 286.5--(CCC-T 134.4)--(SOU-UE 0)
Ewington	Decatur	CCC-GC 66.8
F	Benton	CCC-H 211.9--LS-WD 66.3
Fair Ground	Kosciusko	WIN-A 25.9
Fair Grounds	Marion	MON-I 178.1
Fair Oaks	Jasper	CAS-A 26.6--MON-A 62.2
Fairfield	Howard	NKP-LM 49.2
Fairland	Shelby	now CP 89
Fairlawn	Elkhart	WIN-A 2.81
Fairmount	Grant	CCC-M 142.8--PRR-CM 17.9

Falmouth	Fayette	PRR-IC 52.7
Fargo	Benton	NKP-LP 281.1
Farmer	Rush	CCC-M 196.4
Farmers	Owen	PRR-IV 65.8
Farmersburg	Sullivan	CEI-E 192.9
Farmland	Randolph	CCC-I 215.8
Farrabee	Washington	MON-SB 290.2
Fayette	Vigo	MILW-T 170.5
Fayne	Henry	PRR-CR 105.0
Felkner	Kosciusko	WIN-A 14.0
Fenns	Shelby	PRR-IC 19.2
Ferdinand	Dubois	FERD-A 7.4
Ferdinand	Dubois	now Johnsburg
Ferguson	Allen	NKP-LF 8.3
Fern	Cass	PRR-LE 2.5
Fern	Putnam	CCC-L 44.6
#Fiat	Jay	CBC-A 37
Fickle	Clinton	NKP-TC 215.0
Fillmore	Putnam	CCC-L 32.6; PRR-V 32.5
Finney	Warren	CEI-CJ 117.9
Fisher	St.Joseph	CSS-A 5.4
Fishers	Hamilton	NKP-LM 16.2
Flat Rock	Shelby	PRR-IC 12.4
#Flatwood	Lawrence	MON-SS 10
Fleming	Jackson	B&O-SW 81.7
Flint	Tippecanoe	WAB-P 268.8
Flora	Carroll	PRR-IF 97.0
Florida	Madison	PRR-CR 127.3
FN	Porter	LS-W 486.3
Fogg	Washington	MON-SB 284.0
Foley	Henry	NKP-LF 80.8--PRR-CR 104.1
Fontanet	Vigo	CCC-L 60.2
Foraker	Elkhart	WAB-MC 166.5
Foresman	Newton	CAS-A 41.5
Forest	Clinton	NKP-TB 194.6
Forest	Vigo	CCC-L 64.2
Forest City	Jasper	LS-WK 69.2
Forsythe	Porter	now State Park Siding
Fort	Cass	PRR-L 197.6
Fort	Clinton	PRR-VF 78.0
Fort Benjamin Harrison	Marion	CCC-I 273.4
Fort Branch	Gibson	CEI-E 266.6
Fort Ritner	Lawrence	B&O-SW 113.7
Fortner Mine	Clay	PRR-VO 59.5 + 0.7
Fortville	Hancock	CCC-I 263.1
Fort Wayne	Allen	LS-TF 96.2; WAB-M 146.5--(B&O-F 80.7); NKP-F 371.6--NKP-C 371.6--(NKP-LF 0); PRR-F 319.8--(PRR-GR 91.9--PRR-GS 91.9)
Fort Wayne Crossing	Porter	GTW-C 52.7--PRR-F 426.9
Foster	Warren	P&E-A 76.5
Fountain	Fountain	WAB-PC 7.2
#Fountain	Warren	C&EI-EC
Fountain City	Wayne	PRR-GR 8.9
Fountaintown	Shelby	B&O-IH 103.6
Four Mile Road	Allen	NKP-F 367.2
Fourteenth Street	Cass	PRR-L 196.6

Fowler	Benton	CCC-H 202.2
Fowlerton	Grant	C&O-C 121.0--PRR-CM 22.1
Fox	Grant	CCC-M 126.5
Frances	Johnson	IC-NI 11.6
Francesville	Pulaski	MON-M 8.6
Francisco	Gibson	SOU-U 170.0
Frank	Clinton	PRR-IF 48.1--PRR-VF 78.3--MON-I 136.0
Frankfort	Clinton	MON-I 136.0; NKP-LP 234.2; NKP-TB 206.2--
		NKP-TC 206.2; PRR-IF 78.6
Franklin	Johnson	CCC-GM 101.8--PRR-IL 20.3
Frankton	Madison	PRR-CR 132.8
Free	Benton	LS-WD 72.0
Freedom	Owen	PRR-IV 62.8
Freeland Park	Benton	CEI-CF 9.7
Freetown	Jackson	MILW-T 285.2
Fremont	Steuben	LS-TF 48.9
French Lick	Orange	MON-F 17.7--SOU-UF 79.0
Friendswood	Hendricks	PRR-IV 12.8
Fritchton	Knox	B&O-SI 183.3
Fruitdale	Brown	IC-NI 33.9
Fruitridge Avenue	Vigo	PRR-V 70.4
FS	LaPorte	LS-W 469.8
Fulton	Fulton	C&O-C 180.4
Fulton Road	Lake	CSS-A 52.7
Furnessville	Porter	CSS-A 42.0; MC-W 236.6
G&W Junction	Lake	IHB-G 8.6
G. T. Crossing	Lake	MON-A 25.8--(GTW-C 31.6)
Gadsden	Boone	CI-A 54.8
Galena	LaPorte	CSS-A 20.5
Gallaudet	Marion	CCC-G 100.2
Galveston	Cass	PRR-CR 165.9
Gar Creek	Allen	WAB-MM 83.3
Garden	Bartholomew	PRR-IL 42.5
Garden	Marshall	B&O-C 191.9
Garden City	Starke	LS-WK 22.6
Garfield	Montgomery	PRR-VF 56.8
Garrett	DeKalb	B&O-C 128.0
Gary	Lake	B&O-C 244.9--LS-W 496.0; CSS-A 58.9; EJE-S 14.2;
		MC-W 255.1; PRR-F 442.9; WAB-MC 241.1
Gart Mine	Clay	PRR-VHN 1.5
Gas City	Grant	PRR-L 152.2
Gaston	Delaware	C&O-C 113.6
Gem	Hancock	PRR-I 174.1
Geneva	Adams	PRR-GR 54.2
Gentryville	Spencer	SOU-UE 31.0
Georgetown	Floyd	SOU-U 259.4
Georgia	Lawrence	B&O-SW 131.9
Germantown	Wayne	PRR-I 133.1
Germnay	Fulton	now Pershing
Gessie	Vermillion	CEI-E 131.0
#Giberson	Lawrence	MILW-TG 3.2
Gibson	Gibson	CEI-E 257.9
Gibson	Lake	IHB-A 3.7--IHB-AS 0--IHB-G 0--LS-WD 4.2--MC-W 261.7
Gibson Transfer	Porter	MC-W 260.3
Gibson Yard	Lake	IHB-A 5.0
Gifford	Jasper	MON-ND 11.4--MON-ND1 0

Gilead	Miami	WIN-A 50.6
Gilman	Madison	NKP-LS 184.4
Ginger Hill	St.Joseph	LS-WK 9.5
Gings	Rush	PRR-IC 48.4
Gladstone	Pike	CCC-T 90.0
Glass Rock	Orange	MON-F 11
Glen	Wayne	PRR-CR 72.4--PRR-I 117.4
Glen Ayr Mine	Vigo	PRR-V 66.7 + 1.9
Glen Cliff	Warren	CAS-A 81.3
Glendora	Sullivan	MILW-TS 15.6-MILW-TSA 15.2
Glenn	Marion	CCC-H 122.9
Glenn Interlocking	Marion	CCC-H 123.6
Glen Park	Lake	now South Gary on NKP-C
Glenwood	Rush	B&O-IH 77.2
Glezen	Pike	CCC-T 100.4
GN	Decatur	CCC-G 62.1--CCC-M 223.6
Goldsmith	Tipton	NKP-LP 215.0
Goodland	Newton	CAS-A 48.5--PRR-LF 48.9
Goodman	Grant	PRR-L 161.0
Goshen	Elkhart	CCC-M 55.3; LS-T 411.5; WIN-A 0
Gosport	Owen	MON-SA 203.9; PRR-IV 45.0
Gosport Jct.	Owen	MON-SA 203.1--PRR-IV 44.1
GR	Fulton	ERIE-C 171.8
GR	Montgomery	PRR-VF 56.5
Grabill	Allen	WAB-M 130.6
Graham	Daviess	CCC-T 74.3
Graham	Fountain	NKP-TC 244.5
Graham	Jennings	now Grayford
Grammer	Bartholomew	MILW-T 317.6
Grand Trunk	Porter	PRR-F 426.9--(GTW-C 52.7)
Grandy	Kosciusko	CCC-M 78.3
Granger	St.Joseph	CCC-M 35.7--GTW-C 110.9
Grape Island	Lake	MON-ND 26.4
Grass Creek	Fulton	PRR-LS 129.8
Grasselli	Lake	EJE-GS 2.1--IHB-A 2.5--IHB-AC 0--IHB-AW 0--LS-WD 3.1
#Grassnere	Lake	MON-A 48
Gravel Hill	Benton	CCC-H 205.7
Gravel Pit	Fountain	CEI-EC 13.1
Gravel Pit	Warren	CAS-A 79.5
Gravel Pit	Vigo	CCC-L 72.8
Gravelton	Kosciusko	B&O-C 169.9
Gray Jct.	Gibson	CCC-T 107.2--CCC-TC 0
Grayford	Jennings	PRR-IM 26.3
Greencastle	Putnam	CCC-L 39.1; CCC-LO 39.0--MON-SA 177.8; PRR-V 38.9
Greenfield	Hancock	PRR-I 167.2
Greens Fork	Wayne	PRR-CR 83.6
Greensburg	Decatur	CCC-G 61.4; CCC-M 223.5
Greentown	Howard	NKP-TB 171.9
Greenwood	Johnson	PRR-IL 10.7
Greenwood	Vigo	CCC-T 2.2
Gregory	Elkhart	SJV-A 6.8
Grey	Grant	C&O-C 126.0
Gridley	Madison	CI-A 17.2--CCC-I 245.7--CCC-IA 245.7--PRR-CR 121.4
Griff	Vigo	CCC-L 72.2
Griffin	Posey	IC-NM 220.7
Griffith	Lake	C&O-C 254.0--EJE-A 36.2--ERIE-C 240.2--

		GTW-C 36.1--MC-WJ 10.3
Grismore	Noble	LS-T 399.7
Grover	Vigo	now Fayette
Groverton	Starke	PRR-F 394.3
GU	Parke	PRR-VF 32.7--(B&O-ID 176.4)
Gudgel	Gibson	CCC-T 108.8
Guernsey	White	MON-I 93.8
Guilford	Dearborn	CCC-G 27.9; CCC-GO2 28.1
Guion	Parke	B&O-ID 176.4--(PRR-VF 32.7); PRR-VF 32.3
Guthrie	Lawrence	MON-SB 235.4
Gwynneville	Shelby	B&O-IH 96.2
HA	Starke	LS-WK 27.5--PRR-F 397.9
Hadley	Allen	NKP-C 377.4
Hadley	Fredericks	CCC-L 23.8
Hagerstown	Wayne	CCC-GW 87.7--PRR-CR 90.3
Haley	Vigo	CEI-E 176.5--CCC-L 70.5
Hamilton	Steuben	WAB-MC 113.2
Hamlet	Starke	LS-WK 27.6; PRR-F 397.9
Hammond	Lake	CSS-A 68.9; IHB-A 6.9; EJE-GS 5.8--ERIE-C 248.5--
		MON-A 20.7--NKP-C 503.8--MC-W 264.9
Hamrick	Putnam	PRR-V 43.5
Hancock	Kosciusko	WIN-A 20.6
Handy	Benton	LS-WD 80.4--NKP-LP 291.5
Hanfield	Grant	NKP-TB 147.6
Hanna	LaPorte	PM-W 8.9--PRR-F 408.6
#Hanover	Shelby	PRR-SK
Hardenburg	Dearborn	CCC-GA 23.5
Harley	Carroll	MON-I 115.8
Harmony	Clay	PRR-V 53.2
Harper	Decatur	CCC-M 238.9
Harris	Marshall	PRR-LS 163.7
Harrisburg	Washington	now Norris
Harrison	Dearborn	CCC-GW 25.4
Harrisville	Randolph	CCC-I 202.7
Harrodsburg	Monroe	MON-SB 232.8--MON-SBO 230.9
Hart	Delaware	CCC-I 232.7
Hartford City	Blackford	NKP-LF 47.4--PRR-L 138.1
Hartman	Wabash	WAB-M 190.3
Hartsdale	Lake	EJE-A 33.8--MC-WJ 12.8--PRR-L 281.7; LS-D 10.3
Hartwell	Pike	SOU-UH 3.4
Hartwell Jct.	Pike	SOU-U 188.1--SOU-UH 0
Harwood	Vanderburgh	CCC-LE 157.7--IC-NM 245.5--(CEI-EB 285.1); CEI-EB 283.9
Haskells	LaPorte	GTW-C 63.9--MON-M 43.1
Haubstadt	Gibson	CEI-E 269.7
Haw	Bartholomew	PRR-IM 2.0
Hawkins Spur	Benton	LS-WD 70.0
Hawthorne Yards	Marion	PRR-IK 2.0
Hawton	Sullivan	MILW-TL 8.1--MILW-TS 13.0
Hayden	Jennings	B&O-SW 78.9--B&O-SO2 78.8
Hays	Lake	GTW-C 34.0--LS-WD 9.2
Hazelrigg	Boone	now CP 143
Hazelrigg Interl.	Boone	CCC-H 144.1
Hazleton	Gibson	CEI-E 248.7
HC	Lake	LS-W 503.2--IHB-A
Heath	Boone	CI-A 56.3
Hebron	Porter	PRR-L 262.5

Hedrick	Warren	IC-SR 6.4
Hege	Jennings	PRR-IM 11.8
Helmer	Steuben	WAB-MC 126.5--WAB-MS 0
Helmsburg	Brown	IC-NI 38.9
Heltonville	Lawrence	MILW-T 270.0
Henderson	Rush	CCC-M 198.6
Henry	Henry	C&O-C 92.6
Henryville	Clark	PRR-IL 89.3
Hepburn	Posey	CEI-EM 288.9
Herbst	Grant	NKP-TB 162.2
Herr	Boone	PRR-IF 24.6
HF	St.Joseph	LS-W 436.9--LS-WK 0.2
Hibbard	Marshall	NKP-C 438.9--PRR-LS 151.7
Hick	Lake	was BO on B&O-C
Hicks	LaPorte	CSS-A 16.8
High Street	St.Joseph	GTW-C 101.1--NYC-W 435.8
Highlands	Lake	ERIE-C 243.3; LS-WD 7.2
Hillisburg	Clinton	NKP-LP 225.1
Hills	Wayne	PRR-I 122.1
Hillsborough	Fountain	P&E-A 59.3
Hillsdale	Vermillion	B&O-ID 192.7--CEI-E 154.6
Hillside	LaPorte	CSS-A 19.4
#Hilltop	Spencer	SOU-UE 39
Hilt	LaPorte	PM-W 24.6
Hitchcock	Washington	MON-SB 277.2
HM	LaPorte	LS-W 473.4--(MON-M 51.1)
Hoagland	Allen	PRR-GR 79.6
Hobart	Lake	EJE-A 45.7; NKP-C 488.3; PRR-F 434.5
Hobbs	Tipton	NKP-LS 204.4
Hoffman	Noble	PRR-GS 121.5
#Hollowell	Vermillion	B&O-ID 195
Holton	Ripley	B&O-SC 58.1
Homer	Rush	PRR-IC 35.2
Honey Creek	Henry	PRR-CR 111.5
Hoosier	Greene	MILW-T 209.7
Hoover(s)	Cass	C&O-C 170.0--PRR-LE 10.1
Hope	Bartholomew	CCC-GC 77.4
Horace	Decatur	CCC-M 230.5
Horton	Hamilton	MON-I 159.9
Hosmer	Pike	CCC-T 100.7
Hovey	Posey	IC-NM 217.3
Howard	Knox	PRR-IV 100.0
Howe	LaGrange	PRR-GS 143.7
(Howell Yard	Vanderburgh	CCC-LE 161.6)
Howesville	Clay	MON-SL 35.8
Hubbard	St.Joseph	now Warren
Hubbell	Owen	CCC-T 35.0
Huber	Fayette	CCC-GW 71.6
Hudson Lake	LaPorte	CSS-A 15.2; LS-W 451.8
Hugo	Allen	NKP-LF 3.5--WAB-M 149.2
Hulman Street	Vigo	MILW-T 179.9--MILW-TA 0
Hunt	Marion	PRR-IF 9.5
Hunter	Marion	CCC-S 131.2
Hunters	Monroe	MON-SA 217.9
Huntertown	Allen	PRR-GS 104.1
Hunterville	Allen	LS-TF 86.4

Huntingburg	Dubois	SOU-U 199.6--SOU-UE 47.7--SOU-UF 47.7
Huntington	Huntington	CBC-A 0; ERIE-C 126.6; WAB-M 170.4
Hurlburt	Porter	ERIE-C 222.4
Huron	Lawrence	B&O-SW 138.0
#Hurricane	Rush	B&O-IH 75
HY	Lake	C&O-C 260.6--ERIE-C 246.8
Hyde	Ripley	CCC-G 46.9
Hymera	Sullivan	CEI-EN 201.3; MILW-TS 8.8
Hynds	Morgan	PRR-IV 34.2
I.I.& I.Jct.	St.Joseph	GTW-C 99.0--LS-N2 3.2--NJI-A 0
ID	Marion	PRR-I 186.8--(IU-E 0.9)
Idaville	White	PRR-LF 15.1
IJ	Marion	B&O-ID 125.5--CCC-L 1.0--IU-W 1.0--P&E-A 1.0
Ilene	Greene	MILW-T 219.7
Indian Springs	Martin	MILW-T 244.2
Indiana Bituminous Coal Mine		
	Vermillion	NKP-TC2 0.8
Ind. Girls School	Marion	P&E-A 7.4
Indiana Harbor	Lake	B&O-C 251.3; EJE-S 6.7; IHB-A 0--LS-W 502.8--LS-WD 0; PRR-F 448.1
Indiana Hbr. Canal	Lake	PRR-F 448.5
Indianapolis	Marion	IU-E 0--IU-S 0--IU-W 0--(B&O-IH 124.5--B&O-ID 124.5-- (CCC-G 109.6--CCC-H 110.0--CCC-I 283.8--CCC-S 140.1-- (IC-NI 0--MON-I 183.5--NKP-LM 0--P&E-A 0-- (PRR-I 187.7--PRR-IF 0--PRR-IL 0--PRR-IV 0--PRR-V 0)
#Indio	Fountain	NKP-TC 256
Indo	DeKalb	B&O-C 113.8
Ingalls	Madison	CCC-I 260.4
Ingle	Pike	CCC-T 101.8
Ingle	Vanderburgh	CEI-E 276.3
Inglehart	Vanderburgh	CCC-T 127.1
#Ingleton	Pike	SOU-U 179
Inverness	Steuben	SJV-A 52.6
Inwood	Marshall	PRR-F 377.7
Ironton	Martin	B&O-SW 146.1
#Irvington	Marion	B&O-IH 118; PRR-I 183.0
Island No. 20 Mine	Greene	PRR-IG 5.5 + 0.8
Ivanhoe	Lake	EJE-G 5.6--IHB-G 2.1--MC-W 259.6
#Jackson	Vermillion	CEI-E
#Jackson Hill	Vermillion	MILW-TD 3.0
Jamestown	Boone	P&E-A 27.7
Janney	Delaware	C&O-C 117.8
Jasonville	Greene	MILW-T 203.0
Jasper	Dubois	SOU-UF 54.2
Jax	Wayne	PRR-I 126.9
JD	Jackson	B&O-SW 87.3--PRR-IL 58.9
JD	LaPorte	LS-W 463.8--PM-W 23.12
Jeff	Jefferson	PRR-IM 36.9
Jefferson	Clinton	NKP-TC 210.4
Jeffersonville	Clark	B&O-SJ 53.0; PRR-IL 107.2--PRR-IA 0
Jeffries	Kosciusko	WIN-A 37.7
Jessups	Parke	CEI-ER 14.9--PRR-VF 14.9
JK	St.Joseph	LS-WK 2.7--MC-J 0--NJI-A 1.7
Johnsburg	Dubois	SOU-UE 41.0
Johnsfield	LaPorte	CSS-A 36.2
Johnson	Gibson	CCC-LE 136.3

Johnsonville	Warren	WAB-P 291.2
Jolietville	Hamilton	CI-A 48.7
Jonesboro	Grant	C&O-C 127.3; CCC-M 138.3
Jonesville	Bartholomew	PRR-IL 51.8
Jordan	Daviess	CCC-T 76.6
Jordan	Owen	MON-SL 12.9
Judson	Parke	PRR-VF 29.9
Judyville	Warren	CEI-CJ 120.4
Julian	Newton	CAS-A 39.5
Julietta	Marion	B&O-IH 113.5
Junction	Allen	PRR-GS 93.3--PRR-F 321.1
Junction	Miami	WAB-M 200.2--WAB-MX 2.3
Kaley	St.Joseph	now Bendix
Kankakee	LaPorte	NKP-LM 135.5
KD	Marion	B&O-ID 126.3--IU-B 9.1--P&E-A 1.8
KD	Parke	PRR-VF 22.7
Keiser	Porter	CSS-A 40.4
Keller	Elkhart	SJV-A 5.6
Keller	Vigo	MILW-T 187.6
Kempton	Tipton	NKP-LP 219.2
Kendallville	Noble	PRR-GS 120.2--NYC-T 379.7
Kennard	Henry	CCC-S 104.1
Kennedy	Spencer	SOU-UC 6.8
Kenneth	Cass	PRR-L 5.7--PRR-LF 5.7
Kent	Grant	CCC-M 133.4--PRR-L 156.9; NKP-TB 154.2
Kents	Newton	CAS-A 31.2
Kentland	Newton	LS-WD 61.7; PRR-LF 57.2
Kentucky Avenue	Marion	IU-W 0.3
#Kercheval	Spencer	SOU-UR 2
Kern	Rush	CCC-M 203.5
Kern	Warren	P&E-A 74.4
Kern Pit	Warren	P&E-A 73.9
Kersey	Jasper	LS-WK 63.5--MON-ND 22.0
Ketchams	Monroe	MON-SB 227.5
Kewanna	Fulton	C&O-C 189.8--PRR-LS 134.8
#Keystone	Clay	MILW-TK 5.1
Keystone	Wells	NKP-LF 36.3
Kickapoo	Warren	CAS-A 79.8
Kilverys Sand Pit	Porter	MC-W 245.6
Kimmell	Noble	B&O-C 150.1
King	Gibson	CEI-E 262.8
King	Miami	WIN-A 53.97
Kingman	Fountain	CAS-A 106.0
Kingsbury	LaPorte	B&O-C 207.1; GTW-C 74.8; NKP-LM 136.9; WAB-MC 205.6
Kingsbury Wye	LaPorte	WAB-MC 203.0
Kingsland	Wells	ERIE-C 109.3; NKP-LF 19.0
Kirby	Monroe	IC-NI 60.8
Kirk	Knox	PRR-IV 105.5
Kirk Yard	Lake	EJE-S 12.4
Kirk Yard Jct.	Lake	EJE-G 9.0--EJE-S 11.7
Kirklin	Clinton	MON-I 146.9
Kirkpatrick	Montgomery	NKP-TC 223.7
Kitchell	Union	C&O-C 50.9
Kitley Avenue	Marion	PRR-IK 1.9
Kizer	St.Joseph	NJI-A 4.1

Klondike Mine	Clay	PRR-VO 60.5 + 1.0
Klondyke Jct.	Parke	see West Melcher
KN	Newton	LS-WD 61.9--(PRR-LF 57.2)
KN	St.Joseph	B&O-C 199.1--LS-WK 19.5--NKP-LM 130.7
Kneipp Sanitarium	Noble	PRR-GS 127.9
Knightstown	Henry	CCC-M 187.5; PRR-I 153.9--PRR-SK 0
Knightsville	Clay	PRR-V 55.0--PRR-VP 0
Kniman	Jasper	CAS-A 18.8
Knowles	Gibson	CEI-EM 276.0
Knox	Henry	CCC-M 186.2
Knox	Starke	LS-WK 33.9--NKP-C 451.5
#Knox Consol. Mine	Knox	PRR-IVK 1.6
Kokomo	Howard	NKP-LM (old) 54.4; NKP-LM (new) 54.5--NKP-TB 181.1; PRR-CR 159.5
Kokomo Jct.	Howard	NKP-LM 54.8--PRR-CR 159.6
Koleen	Greene	MON-SS 26.3
Kolsem Jct.	Vermillion	MILW-T 158.4--MILW-TD 0
Kouts	Porter	ERIE-C 213.7--PRR-L 253.1
Kraft	Marion	PRR-V 3.0--PRR-IV 3.0--PRR-VK 1.4
Kurtz	Jackson	MILW-T 280.7
Kyana	Dubois	SOU-U 209.0
LaCrosse	LaPorte	CAS-A 0--MON-N 31.6--(PRR-L 246.6)--PRR-LV 0; C&O-C 220.5--(PM-W 0.3); PM-W 0--PRR-L 246.3
Ladoga	Montgomery	CI-A 81.3--MON-SA 157.8
Lafayette	Tippecanoe	MON-SA (old) 120.0; MON-SAN (new) 120.0 NKP-LP 258.7--(CCC-H 174.0); WAB-P 255.4
Lafayette Jct.	Tippecanoe	MON-SAN 121.2--MON-SA 121.5--NKP-LP 257.7--WAB-P 257.2
LaFontaine	Wabash	CCC-M 123.6
LaGrange	LaGrange	PRR-GS 138.4; SJV-A 32.7
Lagro	Wabash	WAB-M 183.2
Lake	Lake	now East Gary
Lake Bruce	Fulton	C&O-C 194.1
Lake Ciecott	Cass	PRR-LF 8.7
Lake Gage	Steuben	SJV-A 51.5
Lake Jct.	Lake	LS-WJ 0.4--PRR-F 451.4
Lake Park	LaPorte	CSS-A 15.8
Lake Shore	LaPorte	CSS-A 36.7
Lake Street	Kosciusko	WIN-A 24.8
Laketon	Wabash	ERIE-C 146.7; PRR-LE 33.2
Lake Village	Newton	LS-WD 36.4
Lake Wabee	Kosciusko	SYM-A 5
Lakeville	St.Joseph	PRR-LS 172.2--WAB-MC 184.8
LaLumiere	LaPorte	CSS-A 23.8
#Lambert	Bartholomew	CCC-GC 83
Lamott	Posey	L&N-S 337.4
Lancaster	Clay	CCC-T 28.1
Lancaster Jct.	Clay	CCC-T 27.6--CEI-JL 0
Land	Johnson	PRR-IL 15.5
Landess	Grant	NKP-TB 146.5
LaOtto	Noble	PRR-GS 108.7--PRR-LE 73.7
LaPaz	Marshall	B&O-C 189.8
LaPaz Jct.	Marshall	B&O-C 189.2--PRR-LS 167.4
Lapel	Madison	CI-A 28.0
Lapland	Montgomery	CI-A 86.9
LaPorte	LaPorte	LS-W 463.4; NKP-LM 147.5; PM-W 23.1

LaPorte Jct.	LaPorte	NKP-LM 146.3--(LS-W 462.4)
Larwill	Whitley	PRR-F 346.2
#Laster	Greene	CCC-T 53
Latta	Greene	MILW-T 204.1--MILW-TL 0
Latta	Kosciusko	WIN-A 31.8
Laura	Jasper	MON-ND 14.1
Laurel	Franklin	CCC-GW 57.7
Lawlers	Newton	CAS-A 28.6
Lawrence	Marion	CCC-I 274.6
Lawrenceburg	Dearborn	B&O-SC 22.1; CCC-GA 25.1
Lawrenceburg Jct.	Dearborn	CCC-G 22.3 (aka CP 22)
Lawrenceport	Lawrence	BEST-A 1.4
Lawton	Pulaski	C&O-C 198.0
Layton	Fountain	P&E-A 68.7
Lebanon	Boone	CI-A 61.4; CCC-H 138.3; PRR-IF 31.6
Lee	White	MON-A 83.1
#Leeland	Kosciusko	B&O-C 159
Leesburg	Kosciusko	CCC-M 73.0; WIN-A 18.1-
Leipsic	Orange	MON-SB 265.1
Leiters	Fulton	ERIE-C 177.8
Lena	Parke	CCC-L 48.7
Lena Park	Starke	C&O-C 210.0
Lennox	Carroll	now Yeoman
Leonard	Franklin	CCC-GW 52.7
Leroy	Lake	PRR-L 273.4
Letts	Decatur	CCC-M 232.4
Letts Corner	Decatur	now Letts
Lewis	Vigo	MILW-T 195.4
Lewis Creek	Shelby	PRR-IC 15.1
Lewiston	Jasper	MON-ND 7.7
Lewisville	Henry	PRR-I 144.6
Lexington	Scott	B&O-SV 25.1
Liberty	Union	B&O-IH 53.0
Liberty	Vigo	CCC-T 7.8
Liberty Centre	Wells	NKP-TB 129.4
Liberty Mills	Wabash	PRR-LE 40.5
#Liberty View	Porter	C&O-C 227
Libertyville	Vigo	now Bradshaw
Liggett	Vigo	PRR-V 77.4
Ligonier	Noble	LS-T 396.3
Limedale	Putnam	MON-SA 180.0--PRR-V 40.3
Lincoln	Cass	PRR-CR 168.8
Lincoln City	Spencer	SOU-UC 0--SOU-UE 33.5--(SOU-UR 0)
Linden	Montgomery	MON-SA 137.0--NKP-TC 228.5
Linker	Allen	PRR-F 316.3
Linnsburg	Montgomery	P&E-A 37.8
Linton	Greene	IC-NE 95.4--MILW-T 212.4; PRR-IG 5.3
Linton Summit	Greene	PRR-IG 13.4
Linwood	Madison	CCC-M 158.6
Lippe	Posey	L&N-S 331.2
Little	Pike	CCC-T 101.4
Liverpool	Lake	MC-WJ 2.9--PRR-F 437.4
Lizton	Hendricks	P&E-A 22.3
Lochiel	Benton	CAS-A 55.7
Log	Cass	PRR-LE 3.1
Logan	Lawrence	MON-SB 238.6

Logansport	Cass	PRR-L 197.3; WAB-P 218.5
Lomax	Starke	ERIE-C 204.7
London	Shelby	CCC-G 93.3
Lone Star Coal Co.	Vigo	CCC-L 61.2
Long Cliff	Cass	PRR-IF 113.3
Long Lake	Porter	CSS-A 52.3
Longnecker	Dearborn	CCC-GW 28.7
Longwood	Fayette	B&O-IH 73.0
Loogootee	Martin	B&O-SW 155.5
Losantville	Randolph	C&O-C 86.5; CCC-S 83.5
Lost River	Orange	MON-F 3.8
Lottaville	Lake	GTW-C 39.6
Love	Miami	WIN-A 55.93
Lovett	Jennings	B&O-SV 6.7
Lowell	Lake	MON-A 44.8
Lucerne	Cass	PRR-LS 124.3
Lydick	St.Joseph	LS-W 443.7--MC-J 5.9; CSS-A 6.8
Lyford	Vermillion	CEI-E 164.2
Lyle	Gibson	SOU-U 157.1
Lynn	Randolph	CCC-S 69.3--PRR-GR 15.3
Lyons	Fayette	now Lyonsville
Lyonsville	Fayette	B&O-IH 62.9
Lynnville Mine	Warrick	CCC-TK 5.5; YANK-A 0
Lyons	Greene	PRR-IV 83.2
Machler	LaPorte	PM-W 2.0
Mackey	Gibson	CCC-T 112.7
Mackie	Fountain	NKP-TC 253.1
Macksville	Vigo	PRR-V 75.3
Macy	Miami	NKP-LM 89.0
Madison	Jefferson	PRR-IM 45.2
Magee	LaPorte	PM-W 17.5--WAB-MC 209.6
Magley	Adams	ERIE-C 102.9
Magnesia Springs	Franklin	CCC-GW 41.4
Mahalasville	Morgan	CCC-GM 121.2
Mahoning	Lake	LS-W 503.5; PRR-F 448.9
Malden	Porter	C&O-C 230.9
Malott Park	Marion	NKP-LM 7.4
Manchester	Dearborn	CCC-GO2 32.0
Manchester	Montgomery	MON-SA 144.0
Mancourt	Owen	CCC-T 32.0
Manilla	Rush	PRR-IC 33.0
Manitou	Fulton	ERIE-C 165.0
Mansfield	Parke	CI-FWTHS 4.5
Manson	Clinton	PRR-VF 73.7
Maple Avenue	Vigo	MILW-T 172.2
Maples	Allen	PRR-F 309.9
Maplewood	Hendricks	B&O-ID 143.9
Marco	Greene	PRR-IV 88.0
Mardenis	Huntington	WAB-M 165.8
Marengo	Crawford	SOU-U 236.3
#Marietta	Shelby	PRR-SL 8
Marion	Grant	C&O-C 132.4; CCC-M 132.7; NKP-TB 153.5; PRR-L 157.3
Marion	Hendricks	PRR-V 29.0
Marion	Shelby	PRR-SK 19.5
Markle	Huntington	CBC-A 9; ERIE-C 118.0
Markles	Vigo	CCC-L 66.8

Markleville	Madison	CCC-M 174.8
Marlin	Martin	B&O-SW 147.7
Mars Hill	Marion	PRR-IVO 4.3--PRR-IV 6.2
Marshall	Marshall	PRR-LS 160.2
Marshall	Parke	B&O-ID 180.7
Marshfield	Warren	WAB-P 288.7
Marta	Sullivan	MILW-TS 4.7
Martin	Vanderburgh	IC-NM 235.8
Martinsville	Morgan	CCC-GM 127.3--PRR-IV 30.6
Mary No. 2 Mine	Vigo	B&O-IB 16.8
Marysville	Clark	B&O-SV 30.1
Massachusetts Ave.	Marion	CCC-I 281.9--MON-I 181.7--NKP-LM 1.9
Massey	Gibson	CCC-T 103.3
Mathews	Grant	PRR-CM 26.4
Mathews	Owen	CCC-T 32.5
Maumee No. 26	Greene	PRR-IG 8.8
Mauzy	Rush	B&O-IH 79.0
Max	Boone	CI-A 67.9
Maxwell	Hancock	CCC-S 117.7
Maynard	Lake	GTW-C 31.6--PRR-L 284.8; MON-A 25.5
Mays	Rush	NKP-LR 98.2
Maysville	Daviess	CCC-T 79.7--CCC-TW 5.6
Maywood	Marion	PRR-IV 5.7
McCally	LaGrange	SJV-A 38.4
McClelland	Vigo	B&O-IB 20.3
McCook Avenue	Lake	BOCT-A 3.2
McCool	Porter	B&O-C 234.8--EJE-A 52.1
McCordsville	Hancock	CCC-I 268.0
McCoy	Decatur	CCC-G 57.2
McCoysburg	Jasper	MON-A 80.0--MON-ND 0
McDoel	Monroe	MON-SA 221.5--MON-SB 221.5
McGlinn	Jasper	MON-ND 17.4
McGrawsville	Miami	PRR-L 176.8
McGray	Gibson	CEI-EM 268.1
McKee	Wells	CBC-A 21
MD	Benton	CCC-H 192.6--(NKP-LF 277.3)
Mead	Decatur	CCC-G 72.2
Meade	St.Joseph	CSS-A 1.9
Meadow	LaPorte	PM-W 0.3--(C&O-C 222.0)
Meadowbrook	Porter	CSS-A 47.5
Mecca	Parke	B&O-IB 4.5
Mecca Jct.	Parke	B&O-IB 2.9
Mecca Mine	Parke	B&O-IB 2.9/spur+1.5
Medaryville	Pulaski	MON-M 15.2
Medford	Delaware	C&O-C 96.7
Medora	Jackson	B&O-SW 105.4
Meer	LaPorte	CSS-A 29.8
Mellott	Fountain	NKP-TC 241.7
Memphis	Clark	PRR-IL 93.4
Mentone	Kosciusko	NKP-C 419.8--WIN-A 35.7
Mentor	Dubois	SOU-U 213.3
Merom	Sullivan	IC-NE 118.7
Merrick	LaPorte	PM-C 119.9
Merrillville	Lake	C&O-C 248.7
Messick	Henry	CCC-S 90.7
Metamora	Franklin	CCC-GW 51.9

Mexico	Miami	PRR-LE 14.3
Miami	Miami	NKP-LM 63.0
Michigan Avenue	Lake	LS-WD 1.6
Michigan City	LaPorte	CSS-A 34.0; LS-WM 0; PM-C 125.3; MC-W (old) 228.8; MC-W (new) 228.9--(NKP-LM 159.4); MON-M 59.8
Michigantown	Clinton	NKP-TB 199.0
Middlebury	Elkhart	LS-TS 9.3; SJV-A 16.4
Middlefork	Jefferson	PRR-IM 35.3
Middletons	Howard	NKP-TB 187.0
Middletown	Henry	PRR-CR 115.3
Midland	Clay	MON-SL 42.0--MILW-T 206.7
Midland	Greene	MILW-T 205.9
Midwest	Porter	CSS-A 49.8
Mier	Grant	C&O-C 141.0
Mike	Allen	WAB-M 146.0--(PRR-F 319.2)
Milan	Ripley	B&O-SC 42.6
Milford	Kosciusko	CCC-M 67.5; SYM 6.8; WIN-A 12.3
Milford Jct.	Kosciusko	B&O-C 165.7--CCC-M 166.3--WIN-A 11.0
Mill Creek	LaPorte	GTW-C 84.5
Mill Grove	Blackford	PRR-L 132.5
Millard	Vigo	CCC-L 72.4
Miller	Gibson	CEI-E 252.3
Miller	Lake	B&O-C 241.4; CSS-A 55.0
Millers	Lake	IHB-G 10.8; LS-W 491.0
Millersburg	Elkhart	LS-T 403.3
Millersburg	Elkhart	WAB-MC 154.0
Milligan	Parke	B&O-ID 172.3
Milltown	Crawford	SOU-U 240.6
Millville	Henry	PRR-CR 95.6
Milroy	Rush	CCC-M 212.1
Milton	Wayne	CCC-GW 78.8; NKP-LF 99.0
Mineral City	Greene	MON-SS 29.7
Mineral Springs	Porter	now Dune Acres
Minich	Greene	PRR-IV 72.2
#Minshall Mine	Pasrke	PRR-VG 15.1 + 3
Mishawaka	St.Joseph	GTW-C 104.0; LS-W 432.7; LS-WE 12.4
Mitchell	Elkhart	SJV-A 4.3
Mitchell	Lawrence	B&O-SW 126.4--MON-SB 255.3
Mitchellville	Marion	B&O-ID 132.6; PRR-IF 11.3
Modoc	Randolph	CCC-S 80.0
Moffitts	Jasper	CAS-A 24.2
Mohawk	Hancock	CCC-S 121.5
Mongo	LaGrange	SJV-A 41.1
Monon	White	MON-A 88.4--MON-I 88.4--MON-M 0
Monroe	Adams	PRR-GR 64.8
Monroeville	Allen	PRR-F 304.2
Montclair	Hendricks	B&O-ID 147.0
Monterey	Pulaski	ERIE-C 183.7
Montezuma	Parke	B&O-ID (old) 191.8; B&O-ID (new) 191.1
Montezuma	Vermillion	CEI-E 153.3
Montgomery	Daviess	B&O-SW 162.5
Monticello	White	MON-I 98.6; PRR-LF 21.6
Montmorenci	Tippecanoe	NKP-LP 267.6
Montpelier	Blackford	NKP-LF 39.3
Moody	Jasper	MON-ND 5.5
Moore	DeKalb	PRR-LE 88.5

Moorefield	Marion	B&O-ID 130.3; P&E-A 2.1
Mooreland	Henry	CCC-S 87.6
Moore's Hill	Dearborn	B&O-SC 40.1
Mooresville	Morgan	PRR-IV 18.7
Moran	Clinton	PRR-IF 85.8
Morehous	Elkhart	LS-A 434.6
Morgantown	Morgan	CCC-GM 115.8--IC-NI 30.1
Morocco	Newton	CAS-B 13.0; LS-WD 49.6
Morris	Ripley	CCC-G 45.3
Morristown	Shelby	B&O-IH 99.0; PRR-SK 12.5
Mott	Harrison	SOU-U 251.9
Moundhaven	Franklin	CCC-GW 39.3
Mt. Ayr	Newton	CAS-A 35.6
Mt. Comfort	Hancock	CCC-S 125.6
Mt. Jackson	Marion	CCC-L 2.6
Mt. Olive	Martin	MILW-T 248.4
Mt. Perry	Marion	IC-NI 7.4
Mounts	Gibson	CEI-EM 274.4
Mount Summit	Henry	NKP-LF 78.6
Mt. Vernon	Posey	CEI-EM 302.1; L&N-S 341.4
Mt. Vernon Jct.	Gibson	CEI-E 265.3--CEI-EM 265.3
MS	Lake	BOCT-W--LS-W 505.7--LS-WJ 0
Mudlavia	Warren	CAS-A 81.0
Mulberry	Clinton	NKP-LP 243.5
Muncie	Delaware	CI-A 41.1; C&O-C 103.1; CCC-I 229.6--NKP-LF 65.7--NKP-LS 173.7; PRR-CM 1.0
Munster	Lake	GTW-C 31.4
Murdock	Lawrence	MON-SB 241.4
Murray	Wells	CBC-A 18
MY	Fredericks	CCC-L 9.4--(PRR-IF 8.6 as South Hunt)
Nabb	Scott	B&O-SV 28.6
Nails	Allen	B&O-F 69.6
Nappanee	Elkhart	B&O-C 173.9
Nash	Fredericks	CCC-L 20.3
ND	Lake	C&O-C 256.9--ERIE-C 243.6--LS-WD 7.2
NE	Allen	NKP-F 365.4--WAB-M 140.5
NE	Lake	LS-W 500.1
Nebeker	Fountain	WAB-PC 11.1
Nebraska	Jennings	B&O-SC 62.0
Needham	Johnson	CCC-GM 96.3
#Needmore Quarry	Lawrence	MON-SB 241.4 + 2
Nelson	Greene	PRR-IV 72.9
Nevada	Tipton	PRR-CR 152.4
New Albany	Floyd	B&O-SV 54.0--KIT-A 0--MON-SB 317.5--PRR-IA 4.6--SOU-U 268.3
New Albany-State St.	Floyd	PRR-IA 4.6
New Britton	Hamilton	NKP-LM 17.7
New Carlisle	St.Joseph	CSS-A 13.6; LS-W 450.1
New Castle	Henry	CCC-S 95.8; NKP-LF 84.0--NKP-LR 84.0; PRR-CR 101.5
New Chicago	Lake	MC-WJ 1.8
New Era	DeKalb	LS-TF 81.6
New Goshen	Vigo	MILW-TB 3.9
New Harmony	Posey	IC-NH 6.3
New Haven	Allen	NKP-F 365.0; WAB-M 140.5--WAB-MM 88.5
New Lebanon	Sullivan	IC-NE 114.4
New Lisbon	Henry	NKP-LF 91.1

New Market	Montgomery	PRR-VF 45.6
New Palestine	Hancock	B&O-IH 109.7
New Paris	Elkhart	CCC-M 62.0; WIN-A 6.1
New Paris Jct.	Elkhart	CCC-M 61.3--(WAB-MC 161.4)
New Point	Decatur	CCC-G 54.0
New Richmond	Montgomery	NKP-TC 232.4
New Ross	Montgomery	CI-A 75.6--P&E-A 32.8
New Trenton	Franklin	CCC-GW 32.2
New Waverly	Cass	WAB-P 209.2
Newberry	Greene	CCC-T 55.9
Newland	Jasper	MON-ND 9.5
Newman	Wayne	PRR-I 119.8--PRR-CR 74.9--(PRR-GR 0.3)
Newport	Vermillion	CEI-E 146.9
Newton	Newton	PRR-LF 53.1
Newton	Wabash	ERIE-C 146.1--PRR-LE 33.9
Nickel	Porter	NKP-C 473.9
Niles	Delaware	NKP-LS 161.0
Nisbet	Vanderburgh	CCC-LE 147.0
Noblesville	Hamilton	CI-A 37.2; NKP-LM 22.2
#Nolands	Wayne	PRR-CR 87
Nora	Marion	MON-I 172.4
Norman	Jackson	MILW-T 276.5
Norris	Washington	MON-SB 286.9
#North Bedford	Owen	PRR-IVG 4.3
North Burr	Hendricks	PRR-IF 19.6
North Crane	Tippecanoe	CCC-H 165.9
North Delphi	Carroll	MON-I 110.4
North Fort Wayne	Allen	LS-TF 94.8
North Grove	Miami	PRR-L 174.0
North Hayden	Lake	LS-WD 25.8
North Howell	Vanderburgh	L&N-S 323.4--L&N-SE 323.4
North Indianapolis	Marion	CCC-HO 113.4
North Judson	Starke	C&O-C 213.3--ERIE-C 199.4--LS-WK 43.3--PRR-L 237.3
North Liberty	St.Joseph	LS-WK 13.6--WAB-MC 192.9
North Madison	Jefferson	PRR-IM 43.0
North Manchester	Wabash	CCC-M 99.0; PRR-LE 37.1
North Metz	Steuben	SJV-B 9.8
North Rushville	Rush	PRR-IC 44.1
North Salem	Hendricks	B&O-ID 151.3
North Street	Marion	CCC-HO 110.8
North Terre Haute	Vigo	CEI-E 173.3
North Vernon	Jennings	B&O-SC 72.2--B&O-SW 72.2--B&O-SV 0-- CCC-M 248.9--PRR-IM 21.5
North Y	Floyd	MON-SB 316.6--MON-SV 316.6
Norton	Dubois	SOU-UF 72.2
Nortonburg	Bartholomew	CCC-GC 81.4
#Norton Creek	Vermillion	CEI-E
Notre Dame	St.Joseph	MC-N 9.6
NS	Wayne	PRR-CR 85.1
Nulltown	Fayette	CCC-GW 63.9
Nutwood	St.Joseph	PRR-LS 175.7
#Nyesville	Parke	PRR-VF 28.5 + 2
NX	St.Joseph	LS-W 437.7--LS-N2 2.8
NX	Warren	LS-WD 94.6
Oak	LaGrange	LS-TS 12.7
Oakalla	Putnam	CCC-LO 42.8

Oakdale	Jennings	B&O-SC 68.4
Oakdale	Miami	WIN-A 66.1
Oak Hill	Porter	CSS-A 46.1
Oakland Avenue	Elkhart	LS-W 422.2
Oakland City	Gibson	CCC-T 106.2--SOU-U 175.6
Oakland City Jct.	Gibson	CCC-TC 2.8
Oaklandon	Marion	CCC-I 269.8
Oakley	Miami	C&O-C 155.2
Oak Ridge	Lake	CSS-A 60.3
Oaktown	Knox	CEI-E 220.0
Oakville	Delaware	NKP-LF 73.5
Oakwood	LaPorte	NKP-LM 152.4
Ober	Starke	NKP-C 445.6
Ockley	Carroll	MON-I 120.1
Odon	Daviess	MILW-T 230.3
Ogden Dunes	Porter	CSS-A 50.9; LS-W 488.3
Olin	Warren	P&E-A 74.0
Olive	St.Joseph	CSS-A 10.4
#Olive Hill	Wayne	PRR-CR 80
Oliver	Posey	CEI-EM 291.8
Olivers	St.Joseph	GTW-C 99.2; LS-N2 3.2--LS-WK 1.1
Onward	Cass	PRR-L 187.0
Oolitic	Lawrence	MILW-TO 4.8
Ora	Starke	ERIE-C 187.4
Orestes	Madison	NKP-LS 192.6
Orland	Steuben	SJV-A 47.7
Orleans	Orange	MON-SB 261.5--MON-F 0
Osborn	Lake	IHB-A 4.3--IHB-AS 0.9--LS-WD 4.9--NKP-C 500.3
Osceola	St.Joseph	LS-W 427.1
Osgood	Ripley	B&O-SC 51.5
Ossian	Wells	NKP-LF 15.6
Otes	Grant	CCC-M 128.7
Otis	LaPorte	LS-W 473.4--MON-N 51.1
Otisco	Clark	B&O-SV 33.4
#Otter Creek (Mine)	Clay	PRR-VKN 5
Otter Creek Jct.	Vigo	CEI-E 171.9--CEI-ER 5.6--CEI-EZ 171.9--PRR-VC 5.8
Otterbein	Benton	NKP-LP 271.2
Owasco	Carroll	MON-I 122.2
Owensburg	Greene	MON-SS 18.9
Owensville	Gibson	CEI-EM 271.5
Oxford	Benton	CAS-A 66.2--NKP-LP 279.4
Packertown	Kosciusko	NKP-C 406.3
Packy	Grant	PRR-L 150.5
Page	Randolph	CCC-S 68.9
#Paisley	Lake	MON-A 40
Palmer	Lake	ERIE-C 226.0
Palmerton	Fountain	P&E-A 70.2
Paoli	Orange	MON-F 7.6
Paragon	Morgan	PRR-IV 38.4
Paris	Jefferson	B&O-SV 12.5
#Parke No. 8 Mine	Parke	PRR-VF 12.2 + 1
Parker City	Randolph	CCC-I 219.9
#Parkwood	Floyd	SOU-U 266
Parr	Jasper	MON-A 65.8
#Parry	Wayne	PRR-GR
Pashan	LaGrange	LS-TS 14.3

Pass	Clark	SOIN-A 3.5
Patoka	Gibson	CEI-E 255.3
Patricksburg	Owen	MON-SL 19.1
Patton	White	MON-I 101.7
Paul	Porter	CSS-A 51.5
Pawnee	Montgomery	CI-A 85.6
Paxton	Sullivan	CEI-E 209.3
Peabody	Whitley	NKP-C 389.9
Peabody Jct.	Greene	MILW-T 205.2
Peacock	Fountain	WAB-PC 0.4
Pearl Street	Madison	CCC-M 165.7
Pecksburg	Hendricks	PRR-V 22.7
Peerless	Lawrence	MON-SB 240.2
Pekin	Washington	MON-SB 293.4
Pence	Warren	CEI-CJ 114.2
Pence Switch	Jasper	MON-ND 23.8
Pendleton	Madison	CCC-I 255.4 (new); CCC-IO 255.3 (old)
P.R.R. Crossing	Madison	CCC-M 166.3--(PRR-YA 0.9)
#Pennville	Jay	CBC-A 42
Penobscot	Montgomery	CI-A 88.9
Peoria	Franklin	C&O-C 33.1
Percy Jct.	Newton	CAS-A 46.0--CAS-B 0
Percy Siding	Newton	CAS-A 45.6
Perkins	Newton	PRR-LF 52.7
Perrysville	Vermillion	CEI-E 134.2
Pershing	Fulton	ERIE-C 173.9
Perth	Clay	CCC-L 55.6
Peru	Grant	C&O-C 160.4; NKP-LM 73.9; WAB-M/P 202.5-- (WAB-MX 0); WIN-A 67.8
Peru Yard	Miami	NKP-LM 74.3
Peters	Jackson	PRR-IL 54.5
Petersboro	Pike	CCC-T 94.3
Peterson	Adams	NKP-TB 113.1
#Petroleum	Wells	CBC-A 33
Pettysville	Miami	PRR-LE 23.6
Philadelphia	Hancock	PRR-I 170.9
Phoenix	Grant	C&O-C 134.0
Pierces	Lake	GTW-C 44.4
Pierceton	Kosciusko	PRR-F 350.5
Pierceville	Ripley	B&O-SC 45.2
Pigeon	Spencer	SOU-UE 29.1
Pike	Boone	PRR-IF 37.2
Pimento	Vigo	CEI-E 189.8
Pine	Lake	LS-W 499.3
Pine	Marion	PRR-I 185.3
Pine	St.Joseph	NJI-A 11.6--WAB-MC 187.4
Pine Jct.	Lake	B&O-C 248.8--BOCT-A 0
Pine Jct.	Marion	B&O-IH 121.9
Pine Village	Warren	CAS-A 71.2
Pinola	LaPorte	LS-W 467.5
Piqua Road	Allen	PRR-F 317.5
Pittsboro	Hendricks	P&E-A 17.9
Pittsburg	Carroll	MON-I 107.9
Plainfield	Hendricks	PRR-V 13.5
Plainview	St.Joseph	CSS-A 12.9
Plainville	Daviess	CCC-T 67.8

Pleasant Hill	LaGrange	SJV-A 35.3
Pleasant Lake	Steuben	LS-TF 60.5
Pleasant Mills	Adams	NKP-TB 102.7
Pleasant Ridge	Jasper	MON-A 77.0
Pleasant Valley	Elkhart	SJV-A 14.0
Plummer	Greene	CCC-T 51.1
Plymouth	Marshall	NKP-LM 118.3--PRR-C 383.9--PRR-LS 159.0
PO	Porter	LS-W 482.2--MC-W 240.7--PM-C 136.6-- EJE-A 56.7
Pogue	Newton	CAS-B 17.3
Polo	Fulton	WIN-A 44.68
Poneto	Wells	NKP-LF 31.5
Poplar Street	Vigo	CEI-E 178.3
Port Chester	Porter	CSS-A 44.2
Portage	St.Joseph	CSS-A 3.8
Porter	Porter	LS-W 482.2; MC-W 240.6
Portland	Jay	CBC-A 52--PRR-GR 43.2--NKP-LS 145.8
Poseyville	Posey	CEI-EM 281.8--IC-NM 229.2
Post	Marion	CCC-I 272.7
Potter Switch	Jasper	MON-ND 24.9
Powers	Jay	PRR-L 121.2
Prairie	Vigo	PRR-V 68.6
Prairie City	Clay	PRR-VB 5.5
Prairie Avenue	St.Joseph	MC-J 2.1
Prairie Switch	Allen	WAB-M 154.8
Preble	Adams	ERIE-C 100.9
Prescott	Shelby	CCC-G 77.4
Preston	Vigo	CCC-L 68.6--MILW-T 175.2--PRR-VT1 2.1
Princeton	Gibson	CEI-E 259.0; SOU-U 162.5
Princeton Jct.	Gibson	CEI-E 258.2--SOU-U 161.4
Prison Track	LaPorte	MC-W 229.8
Prosser Spur	Lawrence	B&O-SW 134
Purcell	Knox	CEI-E 241.0
Putnamville	Putnam	MON-SA 183.0
QN	St.Joseph	LS-WK 13.7--WAB-MC 192.9
Quaker	Vermillion	MILW-T 142.5
#Quarry	Martin	B&O-SW 151
#Quarry Spur	Huntington	CBC-A
Queensville	Jennings	PRR-IM 17.4
Quincy	Owen	MON-SA 195.3
R. B. Jct.	Vermillion	CEI-E 128.9
Raber	Whitley	NKP-C 386.9
Raccoon	Putnam	B&O-ID 164.7
Race	Cass	PRR-L 196.0
Radley	Grant	PRR-CM 12.8
Radnor	Carroll	MON-I 118.6
Railroad Avenue	Lake	CSS-AO 66.7--BOCT-spur
Raintown	Hendricks	P&E-A 20.6
Raleigh	Madison	CCC-I 257.3 (new); CCC-I 258.2 (old)
Ramsey	Harrison	SOU-U 248.0
Randle	Jasper	MON-ND 1.6
Range Line	Lake	MON-ND 30.1
Range Road	Fountain	P&E-A 58.1
Raub	Benton	CCC-H 213.9
Raubs	Tippecanoe	now South Raub
Ray	Miami	WIN-A 57.8--(PRR-LE 21.1)
Ray	Steuben	LS-TF 44.8

Raymond	Franklin	C&O-C 36.1
Rays Crossing	Shelby	PRR-IC 29.0
Reagan	Clinton	PRR-IF 41.8
Red Key	Jay	NKP-LS 156.7--PRR-L 124.9
Reddington	Jackson	MILW-T 304.4
Reed	Jackson	PRR-IL 53.9
Reed	Lawrence	MON-SS 5.5
Reeds	Kosciusko	CCC-M 83.2
Reedville	Hancock	B&O-IH 106.0
Reelsville	Putnam	PRR-V 47.7
Reiffsburg	Wells	CBC-A 30
Remington	Jasper	PRR-LF 41.5
Renner	Blackford	PRR-L 141.9
Reno	Fredericks	CCC-L 27.8
Rensselaer	Jasper	MON-A 73.0
Republic	Lake	BOCT-A 3.3
Rex	Tippecanoe	CCC-H 163.3
Reynolds	White	MON-A 95.8--PRR-LF 26.9
#Rhein	Henry	NKP-LF 80
Riceville	Crawford	SOU-U 216.5
Rich	Grant	PRR-CM 2.5
Rich Valley	Wabash	WAB-M 194.2
Richards	Gibson	CCC-TK 9.9
Richmond	Wayne	C&O-C 63.0; PRR-I 119.6--(PRR-GR 0)
Ridgeville	Randolph	PRR-GR 33.0--PRR-L 117.3
Riley	Hancock	PRR-I 164.8
Riley	Vigo	CCC-T 10.3
Rileysburg	Vermillion	now R. B. Jct.
Rincon	Greene	CCC-T 41.3
Rincon Jct.	Greene	CCC-T 41.2--PRR-IV 73.8
Riolado	Posey	L&N-S 349.1
#Ripley	Noble	B&O-C 138
Ripley	Pulaski	PRR-L 226.9
Risden	St.Joseph	CSS-A 10.8
Ritchies	Spencer	SOU-UR 11.3
Rivare	Adams	ERIE-C 91.5
Riverside	Fountain	WAB-P 272.2
Riverside	LaPorte	MON-M 27.6
Riverton	Sullivan	IC-NE 120.4
Rivervale	Lawrence	B&O-SW 121.0--B&O-SB 0--BEST-A 0
RN	Lake	LS-WD 5.1--(NKP-C 500.3)
RN	Randolph	CCC-S 83.8--C&O-C 88.0
Roachdale	Putnam	B&O-ID 159.8--MON-SA 162.2
Roann	Wabash	PRR-LE 27.2
Roanoke	Huntington	WAB-M 161.7
Roanoke Siding	Huntington	WAB-M 157.3
Rob Roy	Fountain	CAS-A 87.0
Robertsdale	Lake	LS-W 506.6--IHB-WR 4.0
Robinson	Greene	MON-SS 23.8
Roby	Lake	PRR-F 452.1
Rob Roy Mine	Clay	PRR-V 55.2 + 1.6
Rock Creek	Jennings	PRR-IM 10.5
Rockfield	Carroll	WAB-P 232.1
Rockford	Jackson	PRR-IL 56.9
Rock Hill	Spencer	SOU-UR 12.8
Rock Island	Marion	CCC-H 122.8

#Rock Ledge	Lawrence	MILW-T 280
Rockport	Spencer	SOU-UR 16.8
Rockport Jct.	Spencer	SOU-UE 32.5--SOU-UR 1.0
Rockville	Parke	CEI-ER 22.9--PRR-VF 22.9
Rockwood	Greene	MON-SS 28.0
#Roeske	LaPorte	NKP-LM 155
Rogers	Pike	CCC-T 88.9
Rogers	Posey	IC-NH 3.3
Rohm	Vanderburgh	L&N-S 315.3
Rolling Prairie	LaPorte	LS-W 456.4
Rome City	Noble	PRR-GS 127.3
Romney	Tippecanoe	MON-SA 132.9
Romona	Owen	PRR-IV 49.7
#Rose	DeKalb	WAB-M 118
Rose Hill	Wabash	CCC-M 94.2
Rose Lawn	Newton	MON-A 56.5
Rosebud	Warrick	CCC-T 117.1
Roseburgh	Grant	NKP-TB 159.2
Rosedale	Parke	B&O-IB 12.5--CEI-ER 12.2--PRR-VF 12.2
Ross	Dearborn	CCC-G 30.4
Ross	Lake	MC-WJ 7.8
Rosston	Boone	CI-A 51.8
Rossville	Clinton	MON-I 125.6
Roulos	Allen	B&O-F 74.7
Round House	LaPorte	MON-M 57.7
Royal Center	Cass	PRR-L 208.3
Royerton	Delaware	NKP-LF 60.4
RS	Fulton	ERIE-C 167.9--(NKP-LM 97.7)
Rudd	Owen	PRR-IV 57.5
Rugby	Bartholomew	CCC-GC 74.5
Rugby	St.Joseph	now Lydick
Runnion Avenue	Allen	NKP-C 372.7
Rupel	St.Joseph	LS-WK 5.4
Rushville	Rush	B&O-IH 85.1; CCC-M 204.5--NKP-LR 107.9; PRR-IC 42.2
Russellville	Putnam	B&O-ID 169.5
Russiaville	Howard	NKP-TB 190.4
Rutland	Marshall	NKP-C 437.3
RX	Wabash	ERIE-C 148.1
#Rynear	Fountain	P&E-A 62
SA	Newton	PRR-LF 60.2
Sagunay	LaPorte	CSS-A 17.5
St. Anthony	Dubois	SOU-U 206.9
St. Bernice	Vermillion	MILW-T 152.3
St. Joe	DeKalb	B&O-C 115.4; WAB-M 122.7
St. John	Lake	LS-WD 15.1; MON-A 33.5
St. John Yard	Lake	LS-WD 12.4
St. Johns	DeKalb	LS-TF 80.1
St. Joseph	Clark	MON-SB 309.4
St. Louis Crossing	Bartholomew	PRR-IC 9.2
St. Mary of the Woods	Vigo	CCC-L 75.7
St. Marys Sdg.	St.Joseph	MC-N 9.4
St. Paul	Decatur	CCC-G 72.7
St. Philips	Posey	now Lippe
Salem	Washington	MON-SB 282.1
Saline City	Clay	CCC-T 20.0--PRR-VB 11.5
Salters	Fayette	B&O-IH 68.8

Saltillo	Washington	MON-SB 270.1
Samaria	Johnson	CCC-GM 111.1
San Pierre	Starke	LS-WK 49.5--MON-M 23.3
Sand Creek	Parke	CI-A 105.3--PRR-VF 26.6
Sand Pit	Lake	EJE-G 4.7
Sand Pit	Lawrence	MON-SB 249.2
Sandborn	Knox	PRR-IV 91.7
Sanders	Monroe	MON-SBO 226.9
Sandford	Vigo	now CP 79
Sandusky	Decatur	CCC-M 217.6
Sandy Hook	Daviess	CCC-T 86.8
Sandy Hook	Porter	PRR-L 255.5
#San Pedro Mine	Clay	PRR-VO 66.0 + 1.5
Santa Fe	Miami	C&O-C 152.7
Saratoga	Randolph	PRR-L 110.2
Sardinia	Decatur	MILW-T 322.7; on CCC-M now Harper
Saxony	Lake	C&O-C 259.5
Schererville	Lake	PRR-L 280.1
Schneider	Lake	LS-WD 32.9; LS-WK 78.6
Scipio	Jennings	PRR-IM 14.5
Scircleville	Clinton	NKP-LP 222.9
Scottsburg	Scott	PRR-IL 79.3
Seafield	White	PRR-LF 32.8
Sedalia	Clinton	PRR-IF 87.9
Sedley	Porter	GTW-C 50.3
Seelyville	Vigo	PRR-V 64.5--PRR-VO 65.2
Sellersburg	Clark	PRR-IL 99.6; SOIN-A 4.2
Selma	Delaware	CCC-I 223.3
Servia	Wabash	ERIE-C 141.9
Seventh Street	Vigo	PRR-V 72.9
Sexton	Rush	NKP-LR 101.2
Seyberts	LaGrange	LS-TS 20.4
Seymour	Jackson	B&O-SW 87.2; MILW-T 299.8; PRR-IL 59.0
SG	Lake	LS-WD 32.9--LS-WK 78.5
Shadeland	Tippecanoe	WAB-P 260.2
Shady Grove	Vigo	MILW-TS 2.4--MILW-TSA 2.4
Shadyside	Porter	CSS-A 48.0
Sharps	Delaware	CI-A 5.4
Sharpsville	Tipton	NKP-LM 46.3
Shawswick	Lawrence	MILW-T 267.0
Shearson	Lake	CSS-AO 64.8; EJE-GS 1.9--EJE-GW 0
Sheff	Benton	CCC-H 211.2; LS-WD 66.1
Shelburn	Sullivan	CEI-E 198.6
Shelby	Fountain	WAB-PC 12.3
Shelby	Lake	LS-WK 73.4; MON-A 52.6
Shelbyville	Shelby	CCC-G 82.8; PRR-IC 24.0--PRR-SK 26-- PRR-SL 16
Sheridan	Hamilton	MON-I 155.4
Sheridan	LaPorte	CSS-A 35.7
Sherwood	Decatur	now Earl
Shideler	Delaware	NKP-LF 57.4
Shields	Jackson	B&O-SW 94.3
Shimps Siding	St.Joseph	MC-J 9.1
Shipshewana	LaGrange	LS-TS 16.4; SJV-A 23.1
Shipshewana Lake	LaGrange	SJV-A 21.8
Shirley	Hancock	CCC-M 181.0--CCC-S 107.3
Shoals	Martin	B&O-SW 147.1

Shop	Kosciusko	WIN-A 23.8
Shops	Daviess	B&O-SI 170.7
Shops	Miami	C&O-C 161.3
Shops	LaPorte	CSS-A 32.4
Shops	Tippecanoe	MON-A 117.9--MON-SA 117
Sidney	Kosciusko	NKP-C 403.3
Silex	Owen	PRR-IV 43.1
Silver Lake	Kosciusko	CCC-M 91.4
Silverwood	Fountain	NKP-TC 263.2
Simpson	Huntington	CBC-A 3--ERIE-C 122.4
Simpsons Spur	Clay	CCC-L 54.4
Sims	Grant	NKP-TB 165.9
Skelton	Gibson	CCC-LE 133.8
Sleeth	Carroll	MON-I 105.8
Sloan	Warren	IC-SR 5.7--LS-WD 94.1
Smalls	Porter	GTW-C 48.3
Smedley	Washington	MON-SB 275.3
Smith	Floyd	MON-SB 310.9
Smith	Knox	CEI-E 229.5
Smith	LaPorte	CSS-A 22.0
Smiths Mill	Allen	B&O-F 63.8
Smithson	White	MON-A 98.2
Smithville	Monroe	MON-SBO 227.7
Smythe	Vanderburgh	SOU-UE 4.1
Snow Hill	Randolph	PRR-GR 18.6
Soldiers Home	Grant	CCC-M 135.5
Solitude	Posey	CEI-EM 295.7
Solsberry	Greene	IC-NI 70.2
Somerville	Gibson	CCC-T 110.8--CCC-TS 0
Sommers	Porter	GTW-C 52.2
South Anderson Yard	Madison	CCC-IA 247.9--CCC-M 166.7
South Bend	St.Joseph	CSS-A 0; LS-W 436.7--(GTW-C (new) 100.2); GTW-CO2 (old) 100.5; MC-N 11.7; NJI-A 0; PRR-LS 182.3--MC-J -2.6
South Bend Airport	St.Joseph	CSS-B 2.8
South Burr	Hendricks	PRR-IF 17.9
South Gary	Lake	MC-WJ 5.4--NKP-C 493.2
South Hammond	Lake	MON-A 23.2
South Howell	Vanderburgh	L&N-S 321.8
South Hunt	Marion	PRR-IF 8.6--(CCC-L 9.4 as MY)
South Lebanon	Boone	PRR-IF 30.6
South Milford	LaGrange	WAB-MC 131.8
South Raub	Tippecanoe	MON-SA 129.5
South Richmond	Wayne	C&O-C 61.9
South Vincennes	Knox	CCC-LV 119.0
South Wanatah	LaPorte	MON-M 37.7--NKP-C 468.0
South Whitley	Whitley	NKP-C 397.2--PRR-LE 47.1
Southport	Marion	PRR-IL 7.1
Spades	Ripley	CCC-G 41.8
Sparksville	Jackson	B&O-SW 110.6
Sparr	Elkhart	SJV-A 3.5
Speed	Clark	PRR-IL 98.3; SOIN-A 5.5
Speedway	Marion	B&O-ID 129.1; P&E-A 4.6
Speicher	Wabash	CCC-M 109.1
Spencer	Owen	PRR-IV 53.8
Spencerville	Dekalb	WAB-M 125.3

Spiceland	Henry	NKP-LR 91.7
Sponsler	Greene	MILW-T 214.7--PRR-IG 3.6
Spriggsboro	Porter	NKP-C 480.7
Spring Cave	Owen	MON-SA 197.8
Spring Hill	Vigo	CCC-T 5.1
Spring Hill Tower	Vigo	CEI-E 181.7--(CCC-T 4.7 as X)--MILW-T 182.7
Springfield	Posey	CEI-EM 293.6
Springmans Cross.	Porter	GTW-C 48.9
Springport	Henry	NKP-LF 75.7
Springville	LaPorte	CSS-A 27.6
Springville	Lawrence	MON-SS 11.0
Spy Run	Allen	PRR-GS 94.6
SS&S Jct.	St.Joseph	see JK
SS&S Jct.	St.Joseph	MC-J 0.0--GTW-C 99.0--NJI-A 1.7
Stacer	Gibson	CEI-E 273.6
Standard	Lake	CSS-AO 68.0; PRR-F 450.6
Standard	Sullivan	CEI-E 196.8--CEI-EH 196.8
Standard Pit	Vermillion	CEI-E 159.8
Star City	Pulaski	PRR-L 216.5
State Line	Warren	WAB-P 294.2
State Line Jct.	Newton	CAS-B 21.0
State Park Siding	Porter	CSS-A 43.4
Staunton	Clay	PRR-VO 60.8
#Stave Track	Clay	PRR-VB 2
Stearleys	Clay	PRR-VP 6.5
Steenberg	St.Joseph	LS-WK 7.4
Steubenville	Steuben	LS-TF 63.5--WAB-MC 117.8
Stevenson	Warrick	SOU-UE 7.4
Stewart	Warren	CEI-CJ 116.0--LS-WD 90.1
Stewartsville	Posey	IC-NH 0--IC-NM 226.23
Stillwell	LaPorte	GTW-C 80.2--NKP-LM 139.6
Stinesville	Monroe	MON-SA 207.8
Stockport	Delaware	PRR-CM 31.6
Stockton	Lake	EJE-G 8.3--EJE-S 10.8
Stockwell	Tippecanoe	CCC-H 161.7
#Stoddart	Vigo	MILW-T 172
Stone	Randolph	PRR-GR 28.9
Stone Bluff	Fountain	CAS-A 91.6
Stoners	Allen	LS-TF 84.7
Stonington	Lawrence	BEST-A 3.0
Stony Creek	LaGrange	WAB-MC 151.4
Stoutsburg	Jasper	LS-WK 61.1
Straight Line Jct.	Vanderburgh	CEI-E 283.0--CEI-J 133.5--CCC-T 130.9
Straughn	Henry	PRR-I 141.3
Stroh	LaGrange	WAB-MS 4.6
Sullivan	Sullivan	CEI-E 203.7--IC-NE 110.0; MILW-TS 18.5
Sulphur Springs	Henry	PRR-CR 108.5
Suman	Porter	B&O-C 226.7
Summit	DeKalb	LS-TF 64.7
Summit	Hendricks	PRR-V 21.2
#Summit	Tippecanoe	NKP-LP 264
Summit Grove	Vermillion	CEI-E 158.4
Summitville	Madison	CCC-M 148.1
Sumner	Warren	CEI-EC 7.0
Sunman	Ripley	CCC-G 39.9
#Sunnyside	Marion	CCC-L 6

Superior	Parke	CI-A 118.6
Surprise	Jackson	MILW-T 289.5
Surrey	Jasper	MON-A 68.1
Swanington	Benton	CAS-A 61.3--(CCC-H 199.6); CCC-H 198.6
Swans	Noble	PRR-GS 110.4
Swayzee	Grant	NKP-TB 164.2--PRR-CM 5.9
Sweeneys	St.Joseph	NJI-A 8.6
Sweetser	Grant	C&O-C 138.0; PRR-L 163.2
Swifts	LaPorte	GTW-C 83.3
Switz City	Greene	IC-NE 89.4--IC-NI 89.4--MON-SS 40.5--PRR-IV 79.8
Sycamore	Howard	NKP-TB 169.0
Syracuse	Kosciusko	B&O-C 160.6--SYM-A 0
Tab	Warren	LS-WD 86.3
Taft	Madison	CCC-I 250.9--CCC-IA 250.1
Taggart	Morgan	CCC-GM 123.9
Talbot	Benton	NKP-LP 290.6
Tamarack	Porter	CSS-A 38.5
Tangier	Parke	CAS-A 110.0
Taswell	Crawford	SOU-U 222.8
Taylor	Tippecanoe	MON-SA 126.5
Taylor	Warren	CEI-EC 10.3
Taylorsville	Bartholomew	PRR-IL 34.5
Tecumseh	Gibson	CCC-TK 12.1
Tecumseh Jct.	Gibson	CCC-T 114.9--CCC-TK 0
Tee Lake	LaPorte	CSS-A 23.1
Teegarden	Marshall	B&O-C 193.5
Tefft	Jasper	LS-WK 53.5
Tell City	Perry	SOU-UC 20.0
Temple	Crawford	SOU-U 231.8
Templeton	Benton	CCC-H 193.3; NKP-KP 277.3
Tennyson	Warrick	SOU-UE 26.8
Tenth Street	LaPorte	CSS-A 35.1--MC-W 229.7--MON-M 59.0
Terhune	Boone	MON-I 151.5
Terre Coupee	St.Joseph	CSS-A 11.8; LS-W 448.5
Terre Haute	Vigo	CCC-L 71.6; MILW-TA 1.9; CEI-E 177.5--PRR-V 72.7--(PRR-VF 0)
Thatcher	Dearborn	CCC-G 23.0
Thayer	Lake	MON-A 54.1
3rd Street	Grant	CCC-M 133.0--NKP-TB 153.8
30th Street	Marion	CCC-H 115.2
Thomas	Daviess	CCC-T 82.5
Thomaston	LaPorte	NKP-C 463.0--PM-W 6.1
Thornburg	Wayne	C&O-C 82.3
Thorne	Marion	PRR-I 180.8--PRR-IK 0
Thornhope	Pulaski	PRR-L 212.8
Thornton	Lawrence	MON-SB 240.9
Thorntown	Boone	CCC-H 147.5
Thurman	Allen	WAB-M 137.0
Tilden	Hendricks	B&O-ID 139.9
Tile Siding	Montgomery	P&E-A 49.8
Tillmans	Allen	B&O-F 67.4
Tiosa	Fulton	NKP-LM 104.0
Tippecanoe	Marshall	NKP-C 424.4
Tipton	Tipton	NKP-LM 39.7--NKP-LP 209.3--NKP-LS 209.3
Tocsin	Wells	ERIE-C 105.9
Tod Avenue	Lake	BOCT-A 3.7

Tolleston	Lake	IHB-G 5.1--MC-W 256.3--PRR-F 441.8; WAB-MC 241.4
Tolleston Jct.	Lake	CSS-A 59.9
Topeka	LaGrange	WAB-MC 146.0
Toto	Starke	LS-WK 38.4
Towsley	Allen	B&O-F 65.1
Tracy	LaPorte	B&O-C 208.4
Trafalgar	Johnson	CCC-GM 109.0
Trail Creek	LaPorte	CSS-A 32.0
Treaty	Wabash	CCC-M 119.1
Tremont	Porter	CSS-A 43.1
Trevlac	Brown	IC-NI 41.3
Troy	Perry	SOU-UC 17.6
Tulip	Greene	IC-NI 77.5
Tunnelton	Lawrence	B&O-SW 117.7
Turkey Creek	Lake	GTW-C 41.2
Turner	Clay	PRR-VO 58.4
Twelve Mile	Cass	C&O-C 174.5
Twin Branch	St.Joseph	LS-WE 8.9
Twin Lake	LaGrange	LS-TS 23.2
Twin Lakes	Marshall	PRR-LS 154.8
Tyner	Marshall	NKP-LM 125.0
UK	Noble	now CP 379
Uncas	Parke	CI-A 113.3
Underwood	Clark	PRR-IL 84.8
Union	Huntington	now Mardenis
Union	Vigo	CEI-E 177.5--PRR-V 72.6
Union Center	LaPorte	B&O-C 207.2
Union City	Randolph	B&O-TU 47.3; CCC-I 198.8; PRR-L 103.8
Uniondale	Wells	CBC-A 15; ERIE-C 112.6
Union Mills	LaPorte	GTW-C 70.1
Union Track Jct.	Vanderburgh	CEI-E 285.8--CEI-EO 285.8--(SOU-UE 0.7)
Unionville	Monroe	IC-NI 49.7
Upland	Grant	PRR-L 145.1
Upton	Posey	L&N-S 345.5
Urbana	Wabash	CCC-M 106.1
Valentine	LaGrange	PRR-GS 134.4
Valley Mill(s)	Marion	PRR-IV 8.5
Valley View	Franklin	CCC-GW 54.1
Vallonia	Jackson	B&O-SW 101.0
Valparaiso	Porter	GTW-C 55.8; NKP-C 477.0; PRR-F 424.1; PRR-LV 10
Van	Cass	PRR-LE 1.2--PRR-IF 114.5--PRR-L 198.3--
		PRR-LO 198.3--(PRR-LS 114.5)
Van	Vigo	MILW-T 176.7
Van Buren	Grant	NKP-TB 143.9
Van Jct.	Marion	PRR-VK 0
Van Loon	Lake	EJE-G 3.5--NKP-C 497.9
Van Nuys	Henry	now Epileptic Village
Vance	Delaware	C&O-C 102.8--CCC-I 228.5--PRR-CM 41.8
Vandale	Whitley	PRR-F 339.2--PRR-LE 55.3
#Vandalia	Clay	PRR-VB 8
Vandalia Jct.	St.Joseph	GTW-C 97.5--MC-J 0.1--NJI-A 1.7
Vandalia No. 20 Mine	Greene	PRR-IG 8.6 + 0.7
Vaughan	Vanderburgh	L&N-S 318.6
Veedersburg	Fountain	CAS-A 95.7--NKP-TC 249.1--P&E-A 64.7
Velpen	Pike	SOU-U 190.1
Vermont	Howard	NKP-TB 175.7

Vernia	Floyd	MON-SB 315.6
Vernon	Jennings	PRR-IM 23.1
Verona	Cass	PRR-LS 120.5
VI	Floyd	MON-SV 317.7--KIT-A 0
Vicksburg	Greene	MON-SL 43.1--MON-SL2 0; MILW-T 208.0
#Victor	Monroe	IC-NB 9
Victoria	Greene	IC-NE 97.6--MON-SL 47.1
Vienna	Scott	PRR-IL 81.7
Vigo	Vigo	CCC-T 0.2--PRR-V 73.5
Vincennes-Main Street	Knox	CCC-LV 120.4--(CEI-E 235.6)
Vincennes-U. D.	Knox	B&O-SI 188.6--CEI-E 234.7--CCC-LV 121.2-- (PRR-IV 117.0); PRR-IV 117.8
Vine	Shelby	now CP 82
Virgie	Jasper	CAS-A 21.6
Virginia Street	Lake	CSS-A 58.5; PRR-F 439.9
Vistula	Elkhart	now CP 11
Vollmer	Knox	CEI-E 244.0
WA	Warren	CEI-CJ 116.0--LS-WD 90.1
Wabash	Allen	PRR-F 319.2--WAB-M 146.0; now Mike on WAB-M
Wabash	Wabash	CCC-M 113.4; WAB-M 188.8
Wabash Avenue	Vigo	CEI-E 178.0
Wabash Jct.	Allen	B&O-F 80.0--WAB-M 145.8
Wabash Jct.	Miami	WIN-A 64.1
Wabash River Ordnance	Vermillion	CEI-E 151.0
Wade	LaPorte	C&O-C 221.5--MON-N 32.5
Wadena	Benton	CAS-A 53.7
Wadesville	Posey	CEI-EM 286.5
Wagner	Lake	CSS-A 53.3
Wagoners	Fulton	NKP-LM 91.5
Wakarusa	Elkhart	WAB-MC 171.3
Waldron	Shelby	CCC-G 75.3
Walesboro	Bartholomew	PRR-IL 45.7
Walkerton	St.Joseph	B&O-C 199.1; LS-WK 19.6; NKP-LM 130.7
Wallace Jct.	Owen	MON-SA 194.0--MON-SL 0
Wallen	Allen	PRR-GS 99.6
Wallner	Lawrence	BEW-A 2.8
Walnut	Marshall	NKP-LM 105.6
#Walnut Corner	Jay	CBC-A
Walnut Grove	Vermillion	CEI-E 143.7
Walton	Cass	PRR-CR 172.2
Walton	Parke	CI-A 114.4
Walton Avenue	Allen	B&O-F 79.5
Wanatah	LaPorte	MON-M 39.4--PRR-F 414.9
Wansford	Vanderburgh	CEI-E 283.6
Warren	Huntington	NKP-TB 137.2
Warren	St.Joseph	CSS-A 8.7
Warsaw	Kosciusko	CCC-M 79.7--PRR-F 358.7; WIN-A 24.7--WIN-B 0
Warwick	St.Joseph	MC-J 10.9
Washington	Daviess	B&O-SI 170.4--B&O-SW 170.4; CCC-TW 2.7
Washington Street	Marion	CCC-I 283.1--IU-E 0.7--(MON-I 182.9)
Waterford	Elkhart	CCC-M 58.3
Waterloo	DeKalb	LS-T 367.0--LS-TF 70.4
Watson	Clark	B&O-SJ 46.6--B&O-SV 46.6
#Watson	Clay	PRR-VB 8
Waveland	Montgomery	CI-A 94.8; PRR-VF 37.2
Waveland Jct.	Montgomery	CI-A 95.9--PRR-VF 36.0

Wawaka	Noble	LS-T 390.9
Wawasee	Kosciusko	B&O-C (new) 157.8; (old) 158.4
Wayne	Wayne	C&O-C 67.5
Waynetown	Montgomery	P&E-A 54.0
WB	DeKalb	now CP 358
WD	Huntington	ERIE-C 134.0
Wea	Tippecanoe	WAB-P
#Webster	LaPorte	B&O-C 217.5
Webster	Wayne	C&O-C 69.0
Websters	St.Joseph	MC-N 6.7
Weisburg	Dearborn	CCC-G 36.8; CCC-GO2 37.7
Weishaars	Newton	CAS-B 2.4
Wellsboro	LaPorte	B&O-C 213.8--GTW-C 71.1--PM-W 15.1
Wendel	Posey	IC-NM 233.8
Wesley	Fountain	P&E-A 50.7
West Baden	Orange	MON-F 16.6--SOU-UF 80.0
West Clinton	Vermillion	MILW-T 153.8--MILW-TC 0
West Clinton	Vermillion	now Clinton Yard
West Dana	Vermillion	B&O-ID 200.8--MILW-T 146.1
West Davis	Marion	PRR-V 8.0
West Dublin	Henry	PRR-I 138.7
Westfield	Hamilton	CI-A 43.6--MON-I 163.4
#West Gary	Lake	IHB-G
West Gibson	Hendricks	PRR-V 16.0
West Good	Grant	PRR-L 162.9
West Graw	Miami	PRR-L 178.9
West Kirk	Jay	PRR-L 130.5
West Lebanon	Warren	IC-SR 0--WAB-P 284.9--(WAB-PR 0)
West Limedale	Putnam	PRR-V 41.4
West Marion	Putnam	PRR-V 30.0
West Melcher	Parke	B&O-IB 0--B&O-ID 190.1--CAS-A 119.6
West Monroeville	Allen	PRR-F 305.5
West Montezuma	Vermillion	now Montezuma
West Nappanee	Elkhart	B&O-C 175.4
Westphalia	Knox	PRR-IV 94.9
West Plymouth	Marshall	PRR-F 386.3
West Point	Tippecanoe	WAB-P 265.3
Westport	Decatur	CCC-M 236.5--MILW-T 325.9
West Ridgeville	Randolph	PRR-L 118.1
West Riley	Hancock	PRR-I 166.3
West Star City	Pulaski	PRR-L 217.4
West Street	Marion	B&O-ID 124.9--CCC-L 0.4--IU-W 0.4-PRR-V 0.4
West Summit	Hendricks	PRR-V 22.0
West Terre Haute	Vigo	PRR-V 75.1
West Union	Parke	CAS-A 116.1
West Union City	Randolph	PRR-L 105.2
West Vandale	Whitley	PRR-F 341.1
Westville	LaPorte	MON-M 47.1--WAB-MC 217.2
West Warsaw	Kosciusko	PRR-F 359.7
West Wayne	Allen	NKP-C 372.6--(LS-TF 97.4)
Whartons	St.Joseph	NJI-A 6.6
Wheatfield	Jasper	CAS-A 13.3--LS-YK 58.1
Wheatland	Knox	B&O-SI 176.7
Wheeler	Porter	NKP-C 484.6; PRR-F 430.7
Wheeling	Delaware	PRR-CM 28.6
Whistler	Miami	WIN-A 52.28

Whitaker	Morgan	PRR-IV 41.0
#Whitcomb	Jennings	B&O-SW 74
White Oak	Lake	CSS-AO 67.5
Whiteland	Johnson	PRR-IL 15.3
Whitestown	Boone	CCC-H 130.6
Whitesville	Montgomery	MON-SA 153.9
Whiting	Lake	B&O-C 254.9--BOCT-W 3.7; EJE-GW 3.6; IHB-W 4.1; LS-W 505.4; PRR-F 459.8
Whiting Jct.	Lake	BOCT-A 4.4--BOCT-W 0
Whiting-Lake Front	Lake	EJE-S 4.5
Wickliffe	Porter	now Ogden Dunes
#Wiggs	Bartholomew	PRR-IM 5
#Wilcox	Vanderburgh	IC-NM 240
Wilders	LaPorte	CAS-A 3.4--ERIE-C 206.1--MON-N 28.1
Wilhelm	LaPorte	CSS-A 25.1
Wilkinson	Hancock	CCC-S 109.0
Willard Avenue	LaPorte	CSS-A 34.7
Williams	Adams	PRR-GR 77.2
Williams	Elkhart	LS-TS 4.2
Williams	Lawrence	MILW-T 251.3
Williams Crossing	Morgan	CCC-GM 118.7
Williamsburg	Wayne	C&O-C 73.9
Williamsport	Warren	WAB-P 283.5
Williamstown	Decatur	CCC-M 215.2
Willow Branch	Hancock	CCC-S 113.1
Willow Creek	Porter	B&O-C 236.9--MC-W 246.6--WAB-MC 233.7
Willow Valley	Martin	B&O-SW 141.4
Wilson	Clark	MON-SB 305.3
Wilson	Porter	CSS-A 49.3
Wilson	Posey	CEI-EM 283.3
Winchester	Randolph	CCC-I 207.9--PRR-GR 24.5
Windfall	Tipton	PRR-CR 146.4
Windsor Jct.	Vigo	now Bradshaw
Winfield	Lake	ERIE-C 228.5
Wingate	Montgomery	NKP-TC 237.7
Winimac	Pulaski	PRR-L 222.4
Winkfield	Henry	CCC-M 183.5
Winona Lake	Kosciusko	PRR-F 357.1; WIN-B 2.0
Winslow	Pike	SOU-U 183.8
Winter Street	Allen	PRR-F 318.6
Winthrop	Warren	CAS-A 76.6
Winthrop Siding	Warren	CAS-A 76.2
Wirt	Jefferson	PRR-IM 38.9
Witts	Union	C&O-C 52.9
Wolcott	White	PRR-LF 35.8
Wolcottville	LaGrange	PRR-GS 129.4--WAB-MC 136.8
Wolf Lake	Lake	IHB-WR 3.0
Woodburn	Allen	WAB-MM 78.7
#Woodford	Wayne	PRR-GR
#Woods	Dubois	SOU-U 196
Woods	Marion	IU-B 8.6--PRR-V 1.6
Woods	Monroe	MON-SA 215.5
Woods	Randolph	PRR-GR 19.6
Woodside	Owen	CEI-JL 3.0
Woodville	Porter	B&O-C 229.6
Worthington	Greene	CCC-T 39.8; PRR-IV 72.3

Worthington Jct.	Greene	CCC-T 40.0--(PRR-IV 72.5)
Worthy	Vermillion	CEI-E 150.8
WR	LaPorte	LS-W 462.4--(NKP-LM 146.3 as LaPorte Jct.)
Wren	Jennings	PRR-IM 21.6
Wren	Kosciusko	WIN-A 18.4
Wright	Grant	PRR-CM 15.7
Wright	Kosciusko	WIN-A 12.0
WRO Jct.	Vermillion	CEI-E 149.7
WX	DeKalb	now CP 367
Wyatt	St.Joseph	WAB-MC 179.2
Wynkoop	Whitley	PRR-LE 51.5
X	Starke	LS-WK 33.9--(NKP-C 451.5)
X	Vigo	CCC-T 4.7--(CEI-E 181.7)--(MILW-T 182.7)
Yankeetown Dock	Warrick	YANK-A 22
Yeddo	Fountain	CAS-A 102.8
Yellow Bank	Franklin	CCC-GW 47.0
Yeoman	Carroll	MON-I 104.4
Yockey	Lawrence	MON-SB 251.7
Yoder	Allen	NKP-LF 12.1
Yoder	LaGrange	SJV-A 27.6
York Switch	Benton	LS-WD 66.1
Yorktown	Delaware	CCC-I 235.3
Yost	Elkhart	CCC-M 57.5
Young	Vigo	CEI-E 186.2
Youngs	LaPorte	PM-W 29.9
Zadoc	Jasper	CAS-A 17.0--MON-ND 18.5
#Zeller Mine	Clay	PRR-VB 5.8 + 1.7
Zelma	Lawrence	MILW-T 274.5
Zigler	St.Joseph	CSS-A 9.5
Zionsville	Boone	CCC-H 125.2

3 DIRECTORY OF RAILROADS AND INTERURBANS BY COUNTY

The names of companies given in this chapter are those that appear in chapters 4 and 5, and list the lines each road operated in the county, and also the subsequent owning companies. The names of preceding owning companies are given in the *OWNERSHIP* record for each individual line. If both railroads and interurban companies operated in a county, the railroads are listed above and the interurbans below a dashed line.

ADAMS
Chicago & Indiana
Erie
Erie Western
Indiana Hi-Rail: IHRC-[NKP-TB]
New York, Chicago & St. Louis: NKP-TB
Norfolk & Western: see New York, Chicago & St. Louis
Norfolk Southern: see New York, Chicago & St. Louis
Penn Central: see Pennsylvania
Pennsylvania: PRR-GR

Bluffton, Geneva & Celina
Fort Wayne & Decatur

ALLEN
Baltimore & Ohio: B&O-F
C&NC
Chesapeake & Ohio: see Baltimore & Ohio
Chessie System: see Baltimore & Ohio
Conrail: see Lake Shore & Michigan Southern; Pennsylvania
CSX Corporation: see Baltimore & Ohio
CSX Transportation: see Baltimore & Ohio
Fort Wayne Union
Indiana Hi-Rail: IHRC-[WAB-MM]
Lake Shore & Mich. Southern: LS-TF
Maumee & Western
New York Central: see Lake Shore & Mich. Southern
New York, Chicago & St. Louis: NKP-C, -F, -LF
Norfolk & Western: see New York, Chicago & St. Louis; Wabash
Norfolk Southern: see New York, Chicago & St. Louis; Wabash
Penn Central: see Lake Shore & Mich. Southern; Pennsylvania
Pennsylvania: PRR-F, -GR, -GS, -LE
Wabash: WAB-M, -ME, -MM, -YF

Fort Wayne & Decatur
Fort Wayne, Van Wert & Lima
Indiana Railroad: INDR-A, -F, -KA

BARTHOLOMEW
Cleveland, Cinci., Chi. & St. Louis: CCC-GC
Conrail: see Cleveland, Cincinnati, Chicago & St. Louis; Pennsylvania
Louisville & Indiana
New York Central: see Cleveland, Cincinnati, Chicago & St. Louis
Penn Central: see Cleveland, Cincinnati, Chicago & St. Louis
Pennsylvania: PRR-IC, -IEC, -IL, -IM

Indiana Railroad: INDR-L

BENTON
Bee Line
Benton Central
Chicago & Eastern Illinois, C&EI-CF, -IA
Chicago, Attica & Southern
Cleveland, Cincinnati, Chicago & St. Louis: CCC-H
Conrail: see Cleveland, Cincinnati, Chicago & St. Louis; Lake Shore & Mich. Southern
CSX Corporation: see Chicago & Eastern Illinois
CSX Transportation: see Chicago & Eastern Illinois
Kankakee, Beaverville & Southern
Lake Shore & Michigan Southern: LS-WD
Louisville & Nashville: see Chicago & Eastern Illinois
New York, Chicago & St. Louis: NKP-LP
Norfolk & Western: see New York, Chicago & St. Louis; Wabash
Norfolk Southern: see New York, Chicago & St. Louis; Wabash
Penn Central: see Cleveland, Cincinnati, Chicago & St. Louis
Seaboard System: see Chicago & Eastern Illinois
Wabash: WAB-PB

BLACKFORD
Conrail: see Pennsylvania
New York, Chicago & St. Louis: NKP-LF
Norfolk & Western: see New York, Chicago & St. Louis
Norfolk Southern: see New York, Chicago & St. Louis
Penn Central: see Pennsylvania
Pennsylvania: PRR-L

Indiana Railroad: INDR-A

BOONE
Central Indiana
Cleveland, Cincinnati, Chicago & St. Louis: CCC-H
Conrail: see Cleveland, Cincinnati, Chicago & St. Louis; Pennsylvania; Peoria & Eastern
CSX Corporation: see Monon
CSX Transportation: see Monon
Louisville & Nashville: see Monon
Monon: MON-I
New York Central: see Cleveland, Cincinnati, Chicago & St. Louis; Peoria & Eastern
Penn Central: see Cleveland, Cincinnati, Chicago & St. Louis; Pennsylvania; Peoria & Eastern
Pennsylvania: PRR-IF
Peoria & Eastern
Seaboard System: see Monon

Indiana Railroad: see Terre Haute, Indianapolis & Eastern
Lebanon & Thorntown
Terre Haute, Indianapolis & Eastern: THIE-C, -L, -LC

BROWN
Illinois Central, IC-NI
Indiana RR

CARROLL
Conrail: see Pennsylvania
CSX Corporation: see Monon
CSX Transportation: see Monon
Louisville & Nashville: see Monon

Monon: MON-I
Pennsylvania: PRR-IF
Seaboard System: see Monon
Wabash: WAB-P
Winimac Southern

Indiana Railroad: INDR-F

CASS
A & R Line
Chesapeake & Ohio
Chessie System: see Chesapeake & Ohio
Conrail: see Pennsylvania
CSX Corporation: see Chesapeake & Ohio
CSX Transportation: see Chesapeake & Ohio
Logansport & Eel River Short Line
Norfolk & Western: see Wabash
Norfolk Southern: see Wabash
Penn Central: see Pennsylvania
Pennsylvania: PRR-CR, -L, -LE, -LF, -LO, -LS
Toledo, Peoria & Western
Wabash: WAB-ME, -P
Winimac Southern

Indiana Railroad: INDR-DA, -F

CLARK
Baltimore & Ohio: B&O-SV, -SJ
Chesapeake & Ohio: see Baltimore & Ohio
Chessie System: see Baltimore & Ohio
Conrail: see Pennsylvania
CSX Corporation: see Baltimore & Ohio, Monon
CSX Transportation: see Baltimore & Ohio, Monon
Louisville & Indiana
Louisville & Jeffersonville Bridge
Louisville & Nashville: see Monon
Louisville Bridge
MG Rail
Monon: MON-SB
Penn Central: see Pennsylvania
Pennsylvania: PRR-IA, -IL, -IW
Seaboard System: see Monon
Southern Indiana

Indiana Railroad: INDR-L, -LC, -LN

CLAY
Baltimore & Ohio: B&O-IB
Central Indiana
Chesapeake & Ohio: see Baltimore & Ohio
Chessie System: see Baltimore & Ohio
Chicago & Eastern Illinois, C&EI-EZ, -IA, -J, -JA, -JL, -JL1
Chicago, Milwaukee, St. Paul & Pacific, MILW-T, -TK
Cleveland, Cincinnati, Chicago & St. Louis: CCC-L, -LC, -T
Conrail: see Cleveland, Cincinnati, Chicago & St. Louis; Pennsylvania
  (continued)

CLAY (continued)
CSX Corporation: see Baltimore & Ohio, Chicago & Eastern Illinois, Monon
CSX Transportation: see Baltimore & Ohio, Chicago & Eastern Illinois, Monon
Louisville & Nashville: see Chicago & Eastern Illinois, Monon
Monon: MON-SL
New York Central: see Cleveland, Cincinnati, Chicago & St. Louis
Penn Central: see Cleveland, Cincinnati, Chicago & St. Louis; Pennsylvania
Pennsylvania: PRR-V, -VB, -VB2, -VHN, -VKN, -VO, -VP
Seaboard System: see Chicago & Eastern Illinois, Monon
Terre Haute, Brazil & Eastern

Indiana Railroad: see Terre Haute, Indianapolis & Eastern
Terre Haute, Indianapolis & Eastern: THIE-A

CLINTON
Central RR of Indianapolis
Cleveland, Cincinnati, Chicago & St. Louis: CCC-H
Conrail: see Cleveland, Cincinnati, Chicago & St. Louis; Pennsylvania
CSX Corporation: see Monon
CSX Transportation: see Monon
Louisville & Nashville: see Monon
Monon: MON-I
New York Central: see Cleveland, Cincinnati, Chicago & St. Louis
New York, Chicago & St. Louis: NKP-LP, -TB, -TC
Norfolk & Western: see New York, Chicago & St. Louis
Norfolk Southern: see New York, Chicago & St. Louis
Penn Central: see Cleveland, Cincinnati, Chicago & St. Louis; Pennsylvania
Pennsylvania: PRR-IF, -VF
Seaboard System: see Monon

Indiana Railroad: INDR-E; see also Terre Haute, Indianapolis & Eastern
Terre Haute, Indianapolis & Eastern: THIE-L

CRAWFORD
Norfolk Southern: see Southern
Southern: SOU-U

DAVIESS
Baltimore & Ohio: B&O-SW, -SW1, -SI
Chesapeake & Ohio: see Baltimore & Ohio
Chessie System: see Baltimore & Ohio
Chicago & Eastern Illinois, C&EI-J
Chicago, Milwaukee, St. Paul & Pacific, MILW-T
Cleveland, Cincinnati, Chicago & St. Louis: CCC-T, -TW
Conrail: see Cleveland, Cincinnati, Chicago & St. Louis
CSX Corporation: see Baltimore & Ohio
CSX Transportation: see Baltimore & Ohio
Indiana Southern
Louisville & Nashville: see Chicago & Eastern Illinois
New York Central: see Cleveland, Cincinnati, Chicago & St. Louis
Penn Central: see Cleveland, Cincinnati, Chicago & St. Louis
Seaboard System: see Chicago & Eastern Illinois
Soo Line: see Chicago, Milwaukee, St. Paul & Pacific

DEARBORN
Baltimore & Ohio: B&O-SC
Central RR of Indiana
Chesapeake & Ohio: see Baltimore & Ohio
Chessie System: see Baltimore & Ohio
Cleveland, Cincinnati, Chicago & St. Louis: CCC-G, -GA, -GL, -GO2, -GW
Conrail: see Cleveland, Cincinnati, Chicago & St. Louis
CSX Corporation: see Baltimore & Ohio
CSX Transportation: see Baltimore & Ohio
Indiana & Ohio
New York Central: see Cleveland, Cincinnati, Chicago & St. Louis
Penn Central: see Cleveland, Cincinnati, Chicago & St. Louis

Cincinnati, Lawrenceburg & Aurora

DECATUR
Central RR of Indiana
Cleveland, Cincinnati, Chicago & St. Louis: CCC-G, -GC, -M
Conrail: see Cleveland, Cincinnati, Chicago & St. Louis
New York Central: see Cleveland, Cincinnati, Chicago & St. Louis
Penn Central: see Cleveland, Cincinnati, Chicago & St. Louis

Indianapolis & Southeastern

DEKALB
Auburn Port Authority
Baltimore & Ohio: B&O-C, -[LS-TF]
Chesapeake & Ohio: see Baltimore & Ohio
Chessie System: see Baltimore & Ohio, Chesapeake & Ohio
Conrail: see Lake Shore & Michigan Southern; Pennsylvania
CSX Corporation: see Baltimore & Ohio
CSX Transportation: see Baltimore & Ohio
Lake Shore & Michigan Southern: LS-T, -TF
New York Central: see Lake Shore & Mich. Southern
Norfolk & Western: see Wabash
Norfolk Southern: see Wabash
Penn Central: see Lake Shore & Mich. Southern; Pennsylvania
Pennsylvania: PRR-LE
Wabash: WAB-M, -ME

Indiana Railroad: INDR-KA, -KB

DELAWARE
Central Indiana
Chesapeake & Ohio
Chessie System: see Chesapeake & Ohio
Cleveland, Cincinnati, Chicago & St. Louis: CCC-I
Conrail: see Cleveland, Cincinnati, Chicago & St. Louis; Pennsylvania
CSX Corporation: see Chesapeake & Ohio
CSX Transportation: see Chesapeake & Ohio
Muncie & Western
Muncie Belt
New York Central: see Cleveland, Cincinnati, Chicago & St. Louis
New York, Chicago & St. Louis: NKP-LF, -LS
   (continued)

DELAWARE (continued)
Penn Central: see Cleveland, Cincinnati, Chicago & St. Louis; Pennsylvania
Pennsylvania: PRR-CM

Indiana Railroad: INDR-A, -AP, -B, -BU, -NM

DUBOIS
Dubois County
Ferdinand
French Lick, West Baden & Southern
Indiana Hi-Rail, IHRC-[SOU-UF]
Norfolk Southern: see Southern
Southern: SOU-U, -UE, -UF

ELKHART
Baltimore & Ohio: B&O-C
Chesapeake & Ohio: see Baltimore & Ohio
Chessie System: see Baltimore & Ohio
Cleveland, Cincinnati, Chicago & St. Louis: CCC-M
Conrail: see Cleveland, Cincinnati, Chicago & St. Louis; Lake Shore & Michigan Southern
CSX Corporation: see Baltimore & Ohio
CSX Transportation: see Baltimore & Ohio
Indiana Interstate
Lake Shore & Michigan Southern: LS-A, -T, -TS, -W, -WE
Michigan Southern
New York Central: see Cleveland, Cincinnati, Chicago & St. Louis; Lake Shore & Michigan Southern
Norfolk & Western: see Wabash
Norfolk Southern: see Wabash
Penn Central: see Cleveland, Cincinnati, Chicago & & St. Louis; Lake Shore & Michigan Southern
Wabash: WAB-MC

Northern Indiana
St Joseph Valley
Winona

FAYETTE
Baltimore & Ohio: B&O-IH
Chesapeake & Ohio: see Baltimore & Ohio
Chessie System: see Baltimore & Ohio
Cleveland, Cincinnati, Chicago & St. Louis: CCC-GW
Conrail: see Cleveland, Cincinnati, Chicago & St. Louis; Pennsylvania
CSX Corporation: see Baltimore & Ohio
CSX Transportation: see Baltimore & Ohio
Indiana Hi-Rail, IHRC-[CCC-GW]
New York Central: see Cleveland, Cincinnati, Chicago & St. Louis
New York, Chicago & St. Louis: NKP-LF
Norfolk & Western: see New York, Chicago & St. Louis
Norfolk Southern: see New York, Chicago & St. Louis
Penn Central: see Cleveland, Cincinnati, Chicago & St. Louis; Pennsylvania
Pennsylvania: PRR-IC, -ICA
Whitewater Valley

Indianapolis & Southeastern

FLOYD
Baltimore & Ohio: B&O-SV
Chesapeake & Ohio: see Baltimore & Ohio
Chessie System: see Baltimore & Ohio
Conrail: see Pennsylvania
CSX Corporation: see Baltimore & Ohio, Monon
CSX Transportation: see Baltimore & Ohio, Monon
Kentucky & Indiana Terminal
Louisville & Nashville: see Monon
Monon: MON-SB, -SV
Norfolk Southern: see Southern
Penn Central: see Pennsylvania
Pennsylvania: PRR-IA
Seaboard System: see Monon
Southern: SOU-U

Indiana Railroad: INDR-LN

FOUNTAIN
Chicago & Eastern Illinois, C&EI-IA
Chicago, Attica & Southern
Conrail: see Peoria & Eastern
CSX Corporation: see Chicago & Eastern Illinois
CSX Transportation: see Chicago & Eastern Illinois
Louisville & Nashville: see Chicago & Eastern Illinois
New York Central: see Peoria & Eastern
New York, Chicago & St. Louis: NKP-TC
Norfolk & Western: see New York, Chicago & St. Louis; Wabash
Norfolk Southern: see New York, Chicago & St. Louis; Wabash
Penn Central: see Peoria & Eastern
Peoria & Eastern
Seaboard System: see Chicago & Eastern Illinois
Wabash: WAB-P, -PC

FRANKLIN
Chesapeake & Ohio
Chessie System: see Chesapeake & Ohio
Cleveland, Cincinnati, Chicago & St. Louis: CCC-GW
Conrail: see Cleveland, Cincinnati, Chicago & & St. Louis
CSX Corporation: see Chesapeake & Ohio
CSX Transportation: see Chesapeake & Ohio
Indiana & Ohio
New York Central: see Cleveland, Cincinnati, Chicago & St. Louis
Penn Central: see Cleveland, Cincinnati, Chicago & & St. Louis
Whitewater Valley

FULTON
Central RR of Indianapolis
Chesapeake & Ohio
Chessie System: see Chesapeake & Ohio
Chicago & Indiana
Conrail: see Pennsylvania
CSX Corporation: see Chesapeake & Ohio
CSX Transportation: see Chesapeake & Ohio
Erie
   (continued)

FULTON (continued)
Erie Western
Fulton County
Indiana Hi-Rail, IHRC-[NKP-LM]
New York, Chicago & St. Louis: NKP-LM
Norfolk & Western: see New York, Chicago & St. Louis; Wabash
Norfolk Southern: see New York, Chicago & St. Louis; Wabash
Penn Central: see Pennsylvania
Pennsylvania: PRR-LS
Wabash: WAB-IM

Winona

GIBSON
Chicago & Eastern Illinois, C&EI-E, -EM, -J
Cleveland, Cincinnati, Chicago & St. Louis: CCC-LE, -T, -TC
Conrail: see Cleveland, Cincinnati, Chicago & St. Louis
CSX Corporation: see Chicago & Eastern Illinois
CSX Transportation: see Chicago & Eastern Illinois
Indiana Southern
Louisville & Nashville: see Chicago & Eastern Illinois
New York Central: see Cleveland, Cincinnati, Chicago & St. Louis
Norfolk Southern: see Southern
Owensville Terminal
Penn Central: see Cleveland, Cincinnati, Chicago & St. Louis
Poseyville & Owensville
Seaboard System: see Chicago & Eastern Illinois
Southern: SOU-U, -UA

Southern Indiana Gas & Electric

GRANT
Central RR of Indianapolis
Chesapeake & Ohio
Chessie System: see Chesapeake & Ohio
Cleveland, Cincinnati, Chicago & St. Louis: CCC-M
Conrail: see Cleveland, Cincinnati, Chicago & St. Louis; Pennsylvania
CSX Corporation: see Chesapeake & Ohio
CSX Transportation: see Chesapeake & Ohio
Indiana Hi-Rail, IHRC-[NKP-TB]
Kokomo Rail
New York Central: see Cleveland, Cincinnati, Chicago & St. Louis
New York, Chicago & St. Louis: NKP-TB
Norfolk & Western: see New York, Chicago & St. Louis
Norfolk Southern: see New York, Chicago & St. Louis
Penn Central: see Cleveland, Cincinnati, Chicago & St. Louis; Pennsylvania
Pennsylvania: PRR-CM, -L
Wabash Central

Indiana Railroad: INDR-AB, -C, -CG, -E

GREENE
Chicago & Eastern Illinois, C&EI-J
Chicago, Milwaukee, St. Paul & Pacific, MILW-T, -TL, -TLA
Cleveland, Cincinnati, Chicago & St. Louis: CCC-T
Conrail: see Cleveland, Cincinnati, Chicago & St. Louis; Pennsylvania

CSX Corporation: see Chicago & Eastern Illinois, Monon
CSX Transportation: see Chicago & Eastern Illinois, Monon
Illinois Central, IC-NE, -NE1, -NI
Indiana RR
Indiana Southern
Louisville & Nashville: see Chicago & Eastern Illinois, Monon
Monon: MON-SL, -SL2, -SL3, -SL4, -SS
New York Central: see Cleveland, Cincinnati, Chicago & St. Louis
Penn Central: see Cleveland, Cincinnati, Chicago & St. Louis; Pennsylvania
Pennsylvania: PRR-IG, -IV
Soo Line: see Chicago, Milwaukee, St. Paul & Pacific

HAMILTON
Central Indiana
CSX Corporation: see Monon
CSX Transportation: see Monon
Indiana Hi-Rail, IHRC-[MON-I]
Indiana RR
Louisville & Nashville: see Monon
Monon: MON-I
New York, Chicago & St. Louis: NKP-LM
Norfolk & Western: see New York, Chicago & St. Louis; Wabash
Norfolk Southern: see New York, Chicago & St. Louis; Wabash
Seaboard System: see Monon
Wabash: WAB-IM

Indiana Railroad: INDR-D

HANCOCK
Baltimore & Ohio: B&O-IH
Carthage, Knightstown & Shirley
Chesapeake & Ohio: see Baltimore & Ohio
Chessie System: see Baltimore & Ohio
Cleveland, Cincinnati, Chicago & St. Louis: CCC-I, -M, -S
Conrail: see Cleveland, Cincinnati, Chicago & St. Louis; Pennsylvania
CSX Corporation: see Baltimore & Ohio
CSX Transportation: see Baltimore & Ohio
Indiana Eastern
Indiana Midland
New York Central: see Cleveland, Cincinnati, Chicago & St. Louis
Penn Central: see Cleveland, Cincinnati, Chicago & St. Louis; Pennsylvania
Pennsylvania: PRR-I

Indianapolis & Southeastern
Indiana Railroad: INDR-B, -N; see also Terre Haute, Indianapolis & Eastern
Terre Haute, Indianapolis & Eastern: THIE-R

HARRISON
Louisville, New Albany & Corydon
Norfolk Southern: see Southern
Southern: SOU-U

HENDRICKS
Baltimore & Ohio: B&O-ID
Chesapeake & Ohio: see Baltimore & Ohio
    (continued)

HENDRICKS (continued)
Chessie System: see Baltimore & Ohio
Cleveland, Cincinnati, Chicago & St. Louis: CCC-L
Conrail: see Cleveland, Cincinnati, Chicago & St. Louis; Pennsylvania; Peoria & Eastern
CSX Corporation: see Baltimore & Ohio
CSX Transportation: see Baltimore & Ohio
Indiana Southern
New York Central: see Cleveland, Cincinnati, Chicago & St. Louis; Peoria & Eastern
Penn Central: see Cleveland, Cincinnati, Chicago & St. Louis; Pennsylvania; Peoria & Eastern
Pennsylvania: PRR-IF, -IV, -V
Peoria & Eastern

Indiana Railroad: see Terre Haute, Indianapolis & Eastern
Terre Haute, Indianapolis & Eastern: THIE-A, -C, -D

HENRY
Carthage, Knightstown & Shirley
Chesapeake & Ohio
Chessie System: see Chesapeake & Ohio
Cleveland, Cincinnati, Chicago & St. Louis: CCC-M, -S
Conrail: see Cleveland, Cincinnati, Chicago & St. Louis; Pennsylvania
CSX Corporation: see Chesapeake & Ohio
CSX Transportation: see Chesapeake & Ohio
Indiana Eastern
Indiana Hi-Rail, IHRC-[NKP-LF], IHRC-[NKP-LR]
Indiana Midland
New York Central: see Cleveland, Cincinnati, Chicago & St. Louis
New York, Chicago & St. Louis: NKP-LF, -LR
Norfolk & Western: see New York, Chicago & St. Louis
Norfolk Southern: see New York, Chicago & St. Louis
Penn Central: see Cleveland, Cincinnati, Chicago & St. Louis; Pennsylvania
Pennsylvania: PRR-CR, -I, -SK

Indiana Railroad: INDR-BM, -N, -NM; see also Terre Haute, Indianapolis & Eastern
Terre Haute, Indianapolis & Eastern: THIE-R, -RN

HOWARD
Central RR of Indianapolis
Conrail: see Pennsylvania
Kokomo Belt
New York, Chicago & St. Louis: NKP-LM, -TB
Norfolk & Western: see New York, Chicago & St. Louis; Wabash
Norfolk Southern: see New York, Chicago & St. Louis; Wabash
Penn Central: see Pennsylvania
Pennsylvania: PRR-CR
Wabash: WAB-IM
Winimac Southern

Indiana Railroad: INDR-D, -DA, -E

HUNTINGTON
Chicago & Indiana
Cincinnati, Bluffton & Chicago
Erie
Erie Western
Indiana Hi-Rail, IHRC-[NKP-TB]

New York, Chicago & St. Louis: NKP-LE, -TB
Norfolk & Western: see New York, Chicago & St. Louis; Wabash
Norfolk Southern: see New York, Chicago & St. Louis; Wabash
Wabash: WAB-M
Wabash Central

Indiana Railroad: INDR-AB, -F

JACKSON
Baltimore & Ohio: B&O-SW
Chesapeake & Ohio: see Baltimore & Ohio
Chessie System: see Baltimore & Ohio
Conrail: see Pennsylvania
CSX Corporation: see Baltimore & Ohio
CSX Transportation: see Baltimore & Ohio
Louisville & Indiana
Penn Central: see Pennsylvania
Pennsylvania: PRR-IL

Indiana Railroad: INDR-L

JASPER
Chicago & Eastern Illinois, C&EI-IA
Chicago, Attica & Southern
Conrail: see Lake Shore & Michigan Southern; Pennsylvania
CSX Corporation: see Monon
CSX Transportation: see Monon
Lake Shore & Michigan Southern: LS-WK
Louisville & Nashville: see Monon
Monon: MON-A, -ND, -ND1
New York Central: see Lake Shore & Michigan Southern
Penn Central: see Lake Shore & Michigan Southern; Pennsylvania
Pennsylvania: PRR-LF
Seaboard System: see Monon
Toledo, Peoria & Western

JAY
Cincinnati, Bluffton & Chicago
Conrail: see Pennsylvania
R. J. Corman
Erie Western
New York, Chicago & St. Louis: NKP-LS
Norfolk & Western: see New York, Chicago & St. Louis
Norfolk Southern: see New York, Chicago & St. Louis
Penn Central: see Pennsylvania
Pennsylvania: PRR-GR, -L

Indiana Railroad: INDR-AP

JEFFERSON
Baltimore & Ohio: B&O-SV
Chesapeake & Ohio: see Baltimore & Ohio
Chessie System: see Baltimore & Ohio
Conrail: see Pennsylvania
CSX Corporation: see Baltimore & Ohio
    (continued)

JEFFERSON (continued)
  CSX Transportation: see Baltimore & Ohio
  Madison
  Penn Central: see Pennsylvania
  Pennsylvania: PRR-IM

JENNINGS
  Baltimore & Ohio: B&O-SC, -SV, -SO2, -SW
  Chesapeake & Ohio: see Baltimore & Ohio
  Chessie System: see Baltimore & Ohio
  Cleveland, Cincinnati, Chicago & St. Louis: CCC-M
  Conrail: see Cleveland, Cincinnati, Chicago & St. Louis; Pennsylvania
  CSX Corporation: see Baltimore & Ohio
  CSX Transportation: see Baltimore & Ohio
  Madison
  New York Central: see Cleveland, Cincinnati, Chicago & St. Louis
  Penn Central: see Cleveland, Cincinnati, Chicago & St. Louis; Pennsylvania
  Pennsylvania: PRR-IM

JOHNSON
  Cleveland, Cincinnati, Chicago & St. Louis: CCC-GM-S
  Conrail: see Cleveland, Cincinnati, Chicago & St. Louis; Pennsylvania
  Illinois Central, IC-NI
  Indiana RR
  Louisville & Indiana
  New York Central: see Cleveland, Cincinnati, Chicago & St. Louis
  Penn Central: see Cleveland, Cincinnati, Chicago & St. Louis; Pennsylvania
  Pennsylvania: PRR-IEC, -IL, -SL

  Indiana Railroad: INDR-L

KNOX
  Baltimore & Ohio: B&O-SI
  Chesapeake & Ohio: see Baltimore & Ohio
  Chessie System: see Baltimore & Ohio
  Chicago & Eastern Illinois, C&EI-E
  Cleveland, Cincinnati, Chicago & St. Louis: CCC-LV
  Conrail: see Cleveland, Cincinnati, Chicago & St. Louis; Pennsylvania
  CSX Corporation: see Baltimore & Ohio, Chicago & Eastern Illinois
  CSX Transportation: see Baltimore & Ohio, Chicago & Eastern Illinois
  Indiana Interstate
  Louisville & Nashville: see Chicago & Eastern Illinois
  New York Central: see Cleveland, Cincinnati, Chicago & St. Louis
  Norfolk & Western: see Wabash
  Norfolk Southern: see Wabash
  Penn Central: see Cleveland, Cincinnati, Chicago & St. Louis; Pennsylvania
  Pennsylvania: PRR-IV, -IVC, -IVK
  Seaboard System: see Chicago & Eastern Illinois
  Wabash: WAB-CV

KOSCIUSKO
  Baltimore & Ohio: B&O-C
  Chesapeake & Ohio: see Baltimore & Ohio
  Chessie System: see Baltimore & Ohio
  Cleveland, Cincinnati, Chicago & St. Louis: CCC-M
    (continued)

KOSCIUSKO (continued)
Conrail: see Cleveland, Cincinnati, Chicago & St. Louis; Pennsylvania
CSX Corporation: see Baltimore & Ohio
CSX Transportation: see Baltimore & Ohio
New York Central: see Cleveland, Cincinnati, Chicago & St. Louis
New York, Chicago & St. Louis: NKP-C
Norfolk & Western: see New York, Chicago & St. Louis
Norfolk Southern: see New York, Chicago & St. Louis
Penn Central: see Cleveland, Cincinnati, Chicago & St. Louis; Pennsylvania
Pennsylvania: PRR-F
Syracuse & Milford

Winona

LAGRANGE
Conrail: see Lake Shore & Michigan Southern
Indiana Interstate
Indiana Northeastern
Lake Shore & Michigan Southern: LS-TS
New York Central: see Lake Shore & Michigan Southern
Norfolk & Western: see Wabash
Norfolk Southern: see Wabash
Penn Central: see Lake Shore & Michigan Southern
Pigeon River
Wabash: WAB-MC

St. Joseph Valley

LAKE
Amtrak
Baltimore & Ohio: B&O-C
Baltimore & Ohio Chicago Terminal
Chesapeake & Ohio; see also Baltimore & Ohio
Chessie System: see Baltimore & Ohio, Chesapeake & Ohio
Chicago & Indiana
Chicago Short Line
Conrail: see Lake Shore & Michigan Southern; Michigan Central; Pennsylvania
CSX Corporation: see Baltimore & Ohio, Chesapeake & Ohio, Monon
CSX Transportation: see Baltimore & Ohio, Chesapeake & Ohio, Monon
Elgin, Joliet & Eastern
Erie
Erie Western
Grand Trunk Western
Indiana Harbor Belt
Lake Shore & Michigan Southern: LS-W, -WD, -WJ, -WK
Louisville & Nashville: see Monon
Michigan Central: MC-W, -WJ
Monon: MON-A, -ND
New York Central: see Lake Shore & Michigan Southern; Michigan Central
New York, Chicago & St. Louis: NKP-C
Norfolk & Western: see New York, Chicago & St. Louis; Wabash
Norfolk Southern: see New York, Chicago & St. Louis; Wabash
Penn Central: see Lake Shore & Michigan Southern; Michigan Central; Pennsylvania
Pennsylvania: PRR-F, -L
    (continued)

LAKE (continued)
Seaboard System: see Monon
Wabash: WAB-MC

Chicago South Shore & South Bend
Gary & Interurban

LAPORTE
Amtrak
Baltimore & Ohio: B&O-C
Chesapeake & Ohio; see also Baltimore & Ohio, Pere Marquette
Chessie System: see Baltimore & Ohio, Chesapeake & Ohio, Pere Marquette
Chicago & Eastern Illinois, C&EI-IA
Chicago & Indiana
Chicago, Attica & Southern
Conrail: see Lake Shore & Michigan Southern; Michigan Central; Pennsylvania
CSX Corporation: see Baltimore & Ohio, Chesapeake & Ohio, Monon, Pere Marquette
CSX Transportation: see Baltimore & Ohio, Chesapeake & Ohio, Monon, Pere Marquette
Erie
Erie Western
Grand Trunk Western
Lake Shore & Michigan Southern: LS-W, -WM
Louisville & Nashville: see Monon
Michigan Central: MC-W
Monon: MON-M
New York Central: see Lake Shore & Michigan Southern; Michigan Central
New York, Chicago & St. Louis: NKP-C, -LM
Norfolk & Western: see New York, Chicago & St. Louis; Wabash
Norfolk Southern: see New York, Chicago & St. Louis; Wabash
Penn Central: see Lake Shore & Michigan Southern; Michigan Central; Pennsylvania
Pennsylvania: PRR-F, -L, -LV
Pere Marquette
Seaboard System: see Monon
Wabash: WAB-IM, -MC

Chicago-New York Electric Air Line
Chicago South Shore & South Bend
Northern Indiana

LAWRENCE
Baltimore & Ohio: B&O-SB, -SO3, -SW
Bedford & Wallner
Bedford Stone
Chesapeake & Ohio: see Baltimore & Ohio
Chessie System: see Baltimore & Ohio
Chicago, Milwaukee, St. Paul & Pacific, MILW-T, -TG, -TO
CSX Corporation: see Baltimore & Ohio, Monon
CSX Transportation: see Baltimore & Ohio, Monon
Monon: MON-SB, -SS
Seaboard System: see Monon
Soo Line: see Chicago, Milwaukee, St. Paul & Pacific

MADISON
Carthage, Knightstown & Shirley
Central Indiana
    (continued)

MADISON (continued)
Central Indiana & Western
Cleveland, Cinci., Chi. & St. Louis: CCC-I, -IA, -IO, -M
Conrail: see Cleveland, Cincinnati, Chicago & St. Louis; Pennsylvania
Indian Creek
Indiana Eastern
Indiana Midland
New York Central: see Cleveland, Cincinnati, Chicago & St. Louis
New York, Chicago & St. Louis: NKP-LS, -YE
Norfolk & Western: see New York, Chicago & St. Louis
Norfolk Southern: see New York, Chicago & St. Louis
Penn Central: see Cleveland, Cincinnati, Chicago & St. Louis; Pennsylvania
Pennsylvania: PRR-CR, -YA

Indiana Railroad: INDR-B, -BM, -C, -DC

MARION
Baltimore & Ohio: B&O-IH, -ID
Chesapeake & Ohio: see Baltimore & Ohio
Chessie System: see Baltimore & Ohio
Cleveland, Cincinnati, Chicago & St. Louis: CCC-G, -H, -HO, -I, -L, -S
Conrail: see Cleveland, Cincinnati, Chi. & St. Louis; Indianapolis Union; Pennsylvania; Peoria & Eastern
CSX Corporation: see Baltimore & Ohio, Monon
CSX Transportation: see Baltimore & Ohio, Monon
Illinois Central, IC-NI
Indiana Hi-Rail, IHRC-[MON-I]
Indiana RR
Indiana Southern
Indianapolis Union
Louisville & Indiana
Louisville & Nashville: see Monon
Monon: MON-I
New York Central: see Cleveland, Cincinnati, Chicago & St. Louis; Peoria & Eastern
New York, Chicago & St. Louis: NKP-LM
Norfolk & Western: see New York, Chicago & St. Louis; Wabash
Norfolk Southern: see New York, Chicago & St. Louis; Wabash
Penn Central: see Cleveland, Cincinnati, Chicago & St. Louis; Pennsylvania; Peoria & Eastern
Pennsylvania: PRR-I, -IF, -IK, -IL, -IV -IVO, -V, -VK
Peoria & Eastern
Seaboard System: see Monon
Wabash: WAB-IM

Beech Grove Traction
Indianapolis & Southeastern
Indiana Railroad: INDR-B, -D, -L, -N; see also Terre Haute, Indianapolis & East.
Terre Haute, Indianapolis & Eastern: THIE-A, -C, -D, -L, -M, -R

MARSHALL
Baltimore & Ohio: B&O-C
Central RR of Indianapolis
Chesapeake & Ohio: see Baltimore & Ohio
Chessie System: see Baltimore & Ohio
Conrail: see Pennsylvania
CSX Corporation: see Baltimore & Ohio
CSX Transportation: see Baltimore & Ohio
    (continued)

MARSHALL (continued)
Fulton County
Indiana Hi-Rail, IHRC-[NKP-LM]
New York, Chicago & St. Louis: NKP-C, -LM
Norfolk & Western: see New York, Chicago & St. Louis; Wabash
Norfolk Southern: see New York, Chicago & St. Louis; Wabash
Penn Central: see Pennsylvania
Pennsylvania: PRR-F, -LS
Plymouth Short Line
Wabash: WAB-IM

MARTIN
Baltimore & Ohio: B&O-SO4, -SO5, -SO6, -SW
Chesapeake & Ohio: see Baltimore & Ohio
Chessie System: see Baltimore & Ohio
Chicago, Milwaukee, St. Paul & Pacific, MILW-T
CSX Corporation: see Baltimore & Ohio
CSX Transportation: see Baltimore & Ohio
Soo Line: see Chicago, Milwaukee, St. Paul & Pacific

MIAMI
Central RR of Indianapolis
Chesapeake & Ohio
Chessie System: see Chesapeake & Ohio
Conrail: see Pennsylvania
CSX Corporation: see Chesapeake & Ohio
CSX Transportation: see Chesapeake & Ohio
Indiana Hi-Rail, IHRC-[NKP-LM]
Kokomo Rail
New York, Chicago & St. Louis: NKP-LM
Norfolk & Western: see New York, Chicago & St. Louis; Wabash
Norfolk Southern: see New York, Chicago & St. Louis; Wabash
Penn Central: see Pennsylvania
Pennsylvania: PRR-CM, -L, -LE
Wabash: WAB-IM, -M, -ME, -MX, -P

Indiana Railroad: INDR-D, -F
Winona

MONROE
CSX Corporation: see Monon
CSX Transportation: see Monon
Illinois Central, IC-NB, -NI
Indiana RR
Louisville & Nashville: see Monon
Monon: MON-SA, -SB, -SBO
Seaboard System: see Monon

MONTGOMERY
Central Indiana
Conrail: see Pennsylvania; Peoria & Eastern
CSX Corporation: see Monon
CSX Transportation: see Monon
Louisville & Nashville: see Monon
Monon: MON-SA
New York Central: see Peoria & Eastern

New York, Chicago & St. Louis: NKP-TC
Norfolk & Western: see New York, Chicago & St. Louis
Norfolk Southern: see New York, Chicago & St. Louis
Penn Central: see Pennsylvania; Peoria & Eastern
Pennsylvania: PRR-VF
Peoria & Eastern
Seaboard System: see Monon

Indiana Railroad: see Terre Haute, Indianapolis & Eastern
Terre Haute, Indianapolis & Eastern: THIE-C, -LC

MORGAN
Cleveland, Cincinnati, Chicago & St. Louis: CCC-GM
Conrail: see Cleveland, Cincinnati, Chicago & St. Louis; Peoria & Eastern
Indiana RR
Indiana Southern
New York Central: see Cleveland, Cincinnati, Chicago & St. Louis; Peoria & Eastern
Penn Central: see Cleveland, Cincinnati, Chicago & St. Louis; Pennsylvania; Peoria & Eastern
Pennsylvania: PRR-IV

Indiana Railroad: see Terre Haute, Indianapolis & Eastern
Terre Haute, Indianapolis & Eastern: THIE-M

NEWTON
Chicago & Eastern Illinois, C&EI-IA, -IB
Chicago, Attica & Southern
Conrail: see Lake Shore & Michigan Southern; Pennsylvania
CSX Corporation: see Chicago & Eastern Illinois, Monon
CSX Transportation: see Chicago & Eastern Illinois, Monon
Lake Shore & Michigan Southern: LS-WD
Louisville & Nashville: see Chicago & Eastern Illinois, Monon
Monon: MON-A
New York Central: see Lake Shore & Michigan Southern
Penn Central: see Lake Shore & Michigan Southern; Pennsylvania
Pennsylvania: PRR-LF
Seaboard System: see Chicago & Eastern Illinois, Monon
Toledo, Peoria & Western

NOBLE
Baltimore & Ohio: B&O-C
Chesapeake & Ohio: see Baltimore & Ohio
Chessie System: see Baltimore & Ohio
Conrail: see Lake Shore & Michigan Southern; Pennsylvania
CSX Corporation: see Baltimore & Ohio
CSX Transportation: see Baltimore & Ohio
Lake Shore & Michigan Southern: LS-T
Michigan Southern
New York Central: see Lake Shore & Michigan Southern
Penn Central: see Lake Shore & Michigan Southern; Pennsylvania
Pennsylvania: PRR-GS, -LE

Indiana Railroad: INDR-KA

OHIO
No railroads

ORANGE
CSX Corporation: see Monon
CSX Transportation: see Monon
French Lick, West Baden & Southern
Louisville & Nashville: see Monon
Monon: MON-F, -SB
Norfolk Southern: see Southern
Seaboard System: see Monon
Southern: SOU-UF

French Lick & West Baden

OWEN
Chicago & Eastern Illinois, C&EI-J, -JL
Cleveland, Cincinnati, Chicago & St. Louis: CCC-T
Conrail: see Cleveland, Cincinnati, Chicago & St. Louis; Pennsylvania
CSX Corporation: see Chicago & Eastern Illinois, Monon
CSX Transportation: see Chicago & Eastern Illinois, Monon
Indiana Southern
Louisville & Nashville: see Chicago & Eastern Illinois, Monon
Monon: MON-SA, -SL
New York Central: see Cleveland, Cincinnati, Chicago & St. Louis
Penn Central: see Cleveland, Cincinnati, Chicago & St. Louis; Pennsylvania
Pennsylvania: PRR-IV, -IVG
Seaboard System: see Chicago & Eastern Illinois, Monon

PARKE
Baltimore & Ohio: B&O-ID, -IB
Central Indiana
Chesapeake & Ohio: see Baltimore & Ohio
Chessie System: see Baltimore & Ohio
Chicago & Eastern Illinois, C&EI-ER, -IA
Chicago, Attica & Southern
Cleveland, Cincinnati, Chicago & St. Louis: CCC-L
Conrail: see Cleveland, Cincinnati, Chicago & St. Louis; Pennsylvania
CSX Corporation: see Baltimore & Ohio, Chicago & Eastern Illinois
CSX Transportation: see Baltimore & Ohio, Chicago & Eastern Illinois
Louisville & Nashville: see Chicago & Eastern Illinois
New York Central: see Cleveland, Cincinnati, Chicago & St. Louis
Penn Central: see Cleveland, Cincinnati, Chicago & St. Louis; Pennsylvania
Pennsylvania: PRR-VF
Seaboard System: see Chicago & Eastern Illinois

Indiana Railroad: see Terre Haute, Indianapolis & Eastern
Terre Haute, Indianapolis & Eastern: THIE-T

PERRY
Hoosier Southern
Indiana Hi-Rail, IHRC-[SOU-UC]
Norfolk Southern: see Southern
Southern: SOU-UC

PIKE
Algers, Winslow & Western
Chicago & Eastern Illinois, C&EI-J
Cleveland, Cincinnati, Chicago & St. Louis: CCC-T, -TC, -TK, -TS

Conrail: see Cleveland, Cincinnati, Chicago & St. Louis
CSX Corporation: see Chicago & Eastern Illinois
CSX Transportation: see Chicago & Eastern Illinois
Louisville & Nashville: see Chicago & Eastern Illinois
Indiana Southern
New York Central: see Cleveland, Cincinnati, Chicago & St. Louis
Norfolk Southern: see Southern
Penn Central: see Cleveland, Cincinnati, Chicago & St. Louis
Seaboard System: see Chicago & Eastern Illinois
Southern: SOU-U, -UH

PORTER
Amtrak
Baltimore & Ohio: B&O-C
Chesapeake & Ohio; see also Baltimore & Ohio, Pere Marquette
Chessie System: see Baltimore & Ohio, Chesapeake & Ohio, Pere Marquette
Chicago & Indiana
Conrail: see Lake Shore & Michigan Southern; Michigan Central; Pennsylvania
CSX Corporation: see Baltimore & Ohio, Chesapeake & Ohio, Pere Marquette
CSX Transportation: see Baltimore & Ohio, Chesapeake & Ohio, Pere Marquette
Elgin, Joliet & Eastern, EJE-G
Erie
Erie Western
Grand Trunk Western
Indiana Harbor Belt, IHB-G
Lake Shore & Michigan Southern: LS-W, -WM
Michigan Central: MC-W
New York Central: see Lake Shore & Michigan Southern; Michigan Central
New York, Chicago & St. Louis: NKP-C
Norfolk & Western: see New York, Chicago & St. Louis
Norfolk Southern: see New York, Chicago & St. Louis
Penn Central: see Lake Shore & Michigan Southern; Michigan Central; Pennsylvania
Pennsylvania: PRR-F, -FR, -L, -LV
Pere Marquette

Chicago-New York Electric Air Line
Chicago South Shore & South Bend
Gary & Interurban
Valparaiso & Northern

POSEY
Chicago & Eastern Illinois, C&EI-EM
Cleveland, Cincinnati, Chicago & St. Louis: CCC-LE
Conrail: see Cleveland, Cincinnati, Chicago & St. Louis
CSX Corporation: see Chicago & Eastern Illinois, Louisville & Nashville
CSX Transportation: see Chicago & Eastern Illinois, Louisville & Nashville
Evansville Terminal
Illinois Central, IC-NH, -NM
Indiana Hi-Rail, IHRC-[IC-NM]
Louisville & Nashville; see also Chicago & Eastern Illinois
New York Central: see Cleveland, Cincinnati, Chicago & St. Louis
Owensville Terminal
Penn Central: see Cleveland, Cincinnati, Chicago & St. Louis
Poseyville & Owensville
Seaboard System: see Chicago & Eastern Illinois, Louisville & Nashville
Southwind Shortline

PULASKI
A & R Line
Chesapeake & Ohio
Chessie System: see Chesapeake & Ohio
Chicago & Indiana
Conrail: see Pennsylvania
CSX Corporation: see Chesapeake & Ohio, Monon
CSX Transportation: see Chesapeake & Ohio, Monon
Erie
Erie Western
Fulton County
J. K. Line
Louisville & Nashville: see Monon
Monon: MON-M
Penn Central: see Pennsylvania
Pennsylvania: PRR-L
Seaboard System: see Monon
Tippecanoe

PUTNAM
Baltimore & Ohio: B&O-ID
Chesapeake & Ohio: see Baltimore & Ohio
Chessie System: see Baltimore & Ohio
Cleveland, Cincinnati, Chicago & St. Louis: CCC-L, -LO
Conrail: see Cleveland, Cincinnati, Chicago & St. Louis; Pennsylvania
CSX Corporation: see Baltimore & Ohio, Monon
CSX Transportation: see Baltimore & Ohio, Monon
Louisville & Nashville: see Monon
Monon: MON-SA
New York Central: see Cleveland, Cincinnati, Chicago & St. Louis
Penn Central: see Cleveland, Cincinnati, Chicago & St. Louis; Pennsylvania
Pennsylvania: PRR-V
Seaboard System: see Monon
Terre Haute, Brazil & Eastern

Indiana Railroad: see Terre Haute, Indianapolis & Eastern
Terre Haute, Indianapolis & Eastern: THIE-A

RANDOLPH
Baltimore & Ohio: B&O-TU
Chesapeake & Ohio; see also Baltimore & Ohio
Chessie System: see Baltimore & Ohio
Cleveland, Cincinnati, Chicago & St. Louis: CCC-I, -S
Conrail: see Cleveland, Cincinnati, Chicago & St. Louis; Pennsylvania
CSX Corporation: see Baltimore & Ohio
CSX Transportation: see Baltimore & Ohio
New York Central: see Cleveland, Cincinnati, Chicago & St. Louis
Penn Central: see Cleveland, Cincinnati, Chicago & St. Louis; Pennsylvania
Pennsylvania: PRR-GR, -L

Indiana Railroad: INDR-BU

RIPLEY
Baltimore & Ohio: B&O-SC, -SO1
Central RR of Indiana

Chesapeake & Ohio: see Baltimore & Ohio
Chessie System: see Baltimore & Ohio
Cleveland, Cincinnati, Chicago & St. Louis: CCC-G, -GO1
Conrail: see Cleveland, Cincinnati, Chicago & St. Louis
CSX Corporation: see Baltimore & Ohio
CSX Transportation: see Baltimore & Ohio
New York Central: see Cleveland, Cincinnati, Chicago & St. Louis
Penn Central: see Cleveland, Cincinnati, Chicago & St. Louis

RUSH
Baltimore & Ohio: B&O-IH
Carthage, Knightstown & Shirley
Chesapeake & Ohio: see Baltimore & Ohio
Chessie System: see Baltimore & Ohio
Cleveland, Cincinnati, Chicago & St. Louis: CCC-M
Conrail: see Cleveland, Cincinnati, Chicago & St. Louis; Pennsylvania
CSX Corporation: see Baltimore & Ohio
CSX Transportation: see Baltimore & Ohio
Honey Creek
Indiana Eastern
Indiana Hi-Rail, IHRC-[NKP-LR]
Indiana Midland
New York Central: see Cleveland, Cincinnati, Chicago & St. Louis
New York, Chicago & St. Louis: NKP-LR
Norfolk & Western: see New York, Chicago & St. Louis
Norfolk Southern: see New York, Chicago & St. Louis
Penn Central: see Cleveland, Cincinnati, Chicago & St. Louis; Pennsylvania
Pennsylvania: PRR-IC, -SK

Indianapolis & Southeastern

SAINT JOSEPH
Baltimore & Ohio: B&O-C
Chesapeake & Ohio: see Baltimore & Ohio
Chessie System: see Baltimore & Ohio
Chicago & South Bend
Cleveland, Cincinnati, Chicago & St. Louis: CCC-M
Conrail: see Cleveland, Cincinnati, Chicago & St. Louis; Lake Shore & Michigan Southern; Michigan
    Central; Pennsylvania
CSX Corporation: see Baltimore & Ohio
CSX Transportation: see Baltimore & Ohio
Indiana Northern
Lake Shore & Michigan Southern: LS-N2, -W, -WE, -WK
Michigan Central: MC-J, -N, -N2
Michigan Southern
New Jersey, Indiana & Illinois
New York Central: see Cleveland, Cincinnati, Chicago & St. Louis; Lake Shore & Michigan Southern;
    Michigan Central
New York, Chicago & St. Louis: NKP-LM
Norfolk & Western: see New Jersey, Indiana & Illinois; New York, Chicago & St. Louis; Wabash
Norfolk Southern: see New Jersey, Indiana & Illinois; New York, Chicago & St. Louis; Wabash
Penn Central: see Cleveland, Cincinnati, Chicago & St. Louis; Lake Shore & Michigan Southern; Michigan
    Central; Pennsylvania
Pennsylvania: PRR-LS
    (continued)

SAINT JOSEPH (continued)
Twin Branch
Wabash: WAB-IM, -MC

Chicago South Shore & South Bend
Northern Indiana

SCOTT
Baltimore & Ohio: B&O-SV
Chesapeake & Ohio: see Baltimore & Ohio
Chessie System: see Baltimore & Ohio
CSX Corporation: see Baltimore & Ohio
CSX Transportation: see Baltimore & Ohio
Conrail: see Pennsylvania
Louisville & Indiana
Penn Central: see Pennsylvania
Pennsylvania: PRR-IL

Indiana Railroad: INDR-L

SHELBY
Baltimore & Ohio: B&O-IH
Central RR of Indiana
Chesapeake & Ohio: see Baltimore & Ohio
Chessie System: see Baltimore & Ohio
Cleveland, Cincinnati, Chicago & St. Louis: CCC-G, -GM
Conrail: see Cleveland, Cincinnati, Chicago & St. Louis; Pennsylvania
CSX Corporation: see Baltimore & Ohio
CSX Transportation: see Baltimore & Ohio
New York Central: see Cleveland, Cincinnati, Chicago & St. Louis
Penn Central: see Cleveland, Cincinnati, Chicago & St. Louis; Pennsylvania
Pennsylvania: PRR-IC, -SK, -SL

Indianapolis & Southeastern

SPENCER
Hoosier Southern
Indiana Hi-Rail, IHRC-[SOU-UC], IHRC-[SOU]UR]
Norfolk Southern: see Southern
Southern: SOU-UC, -UE, -UR

Evansville & Ohio Valley

STARKE
Chesapeake & Ohio
Chessie System: see Chesapeake & Ohio
Chicago & Indiana
Conrail: see Lake Shore & Michigan Southern; Pennsylvania
CSX Corporation: see Chesapeake & Ohio, Monon
CSX Transportation: see Chesapeake & Ohio, Monon
Erie
Erie Western
J. K. Line
Lake Shore & Michigan Southern: LS-WK
Louisville & Nashville: see Monon
Monon: MON-M

New York Central: see Lake Shore & Michigan Southern
New York, Chicago & St. Louis: NKP-C
Norfolk & Western: see New York, Chicago & St. Louis
Norfolk Southern: see New York, Chicago & St. Louis
Penn Central: see Lake Shore & Michigan Southern; Pennsylvania
Pennsylvania: PRR-F, -L
Seaboard System: see Monon
Tippecanoe

STEUBEN
Conrail: see Lake Shore & Michigan Southern
Hillsdale County
Indiana Northeastern
Lake Shore & Michigan Southern: LS-TF
New York Central: see Lake Shore & Michigan Southern
Norfolk & Western: see Wabash
Norfolk Southern: see Wabash
Penn Central: see Lake Shore & Michigan Southern
Pigeon River
Wabash: WAB-MC

St. Joseph Valley

SULLIVAN
Chicago & Eastern Illinois, C&EI-E, -EN, -ENJ, -ENS, -ES, -ESP, -ESM, -EP
Chicago, Milwaukee, St. Paul & Pacific, MILW-TL, -TLA, -TS, -TSA, -TSB
CSX Corporation: see Chicago & Eastern Illinois, Monon
CSX Transportation: see Chicago & Eastern Illinois, Monon
Illinois Central, IC-NE, -NE2, -NE3
Indiana RR
Louisville & Nashville: see Chicago & Eastern Illinois, Monon
Monon: MON-SL, -SL2
Seaboard System: see Chicago & Eastern Illinois, Monon
Soo Line: see Chicago, Milwaukee, St. Paul & Pacific

Indiana Railroad: see Terre Haute, Indianapolis & Eastern
Terre Haute, Indianapolis & Eastern: THIE-S

SWITZERLAND
No railroads

TIPPECANOE
Cleveland, Cincinnati, Chicago & St. Louis: CCC-H
Conrail: see Cleveland, Cincinnati, Chicago & St. Louis
CSX Corporation: see Monon
CSX Transportation: see Monon
Kankakee, Beaverville & Southern
Louisville & Nashville: see Monon
Monon: MON-A, -SA, -SAN
New York Central: see Cleveland, Cincinnati, Chicago & St. Louis
New York, Chicago & St. Louis: NKP-LP, -TC
Norfolk & Western: see New York, Chicago & St. Louis; Wabash
Norfolk Southern: see New York, Chicago & St. Louis; Wabash
Penn Central: see Cleveland, Cincinnati, Chicago & St. Louis
    (continued)

TIPPECANOE (continued)
Seaboard System: see Monon
Wabash: WAB-P, -PB, -YL

Indiana Railroad: INDR-F; see Terre Haute, Indianapolis & Eastern
Terre Haute, Indianapolis & Eastern: THIE-L

TIPTON
Central RR of Indianapolis
Conrail: see Pennsylvania
Indiana RR
New York, Chicago & St. Louis: NKP-LM, -LP, -LS
Norfolk & Western: see New York, Chicago & St. Louis; Wabash
Norfolk Southern: see New York, Chicago & St. Louis; Wabash
Penn Central: see Pennsylvania
Pennsylvania: PRR-CR
Wabash: WAB-IM

Indiana Railroad: INDR-D, -DC

UNION
Baltimore & Ohio: B&O-IH
Chesapeake & Ohio; also see Baltimore & Ohio
Chessie System: see Baltimore & Ohio, Chesapeake & Ohio
CSX Corporation: see Baltimore & Ohio
CSX Transportation: see Baltimore & Ohio

VANDERBURGH
Chicago & Eastern Illinois, C&EI-E, -EB, -EO, -EJ, -J
Cleveland, Cincinnati, Chicago & St. Louis: CCC-LE, -T
Conrail: see Cleveland, Cincinnati, Chicago & St. Louis
CSX Corporation: see Chicago & Eastern Illinois, Louisville & Nashville
CSX Transportation: see Chicago & Eastern Illinois, Louisville & Nashville
Evansville Terminal
Illinois Central, IC-NM
Indiana Hi-Rail, IHRC-[IM]
Indiana Southern
Louisville & Nashville; see also Chicago & Eastern Illinois
New York Central: see Cleveland, Cincinnati, Chicago & St. Louis
Norfolk Southern: see Southern
Penn Central: see Cleveland, Cincinnati, Chicago & St. Louis
Seaboard System: see Chicago & Eastern Illinois, Louisville & Nashville
Southern: SOU-UE

Evansville & Ohio Valley
Evansville Suburban & Newburgh
Southern Indiana Gas & Electric

VERMILLION
Baltimore & Ohio: B&O-ID
Chesapeake & Ohio: see Baltimore & Ohio
Chessie System: see Baltimore & Ohio
Chicago & Eastern Illinois, C&EI-E, -CJ, -EU
Chicago, Milwaukee, St. Paul & Pacific, MILW-T, -TC, -TD
CSX Corporation: see Baltimore & Ohio
CSX Transportation: see Baltimore & Ohio

New York, Chicago & St. Louis: NKP-TC, -TC1, -TC2
Norfolk & Western: see New York, Chicago & St. Louis
Norfolk Southern: see New York, Chicago & St. Louis
Soo Line: see Chicago, Milwaukee, St. Paul & Pacific

Indiana Railroad: see Terre Haute, Indianapolis & Eastern
Terre Haute, Indianapolis & Eastern: THIE-T

VIGO
Baltimore & Ohio: B&O-IB
Chesapeake & Ohio: see Baltimore & Ohio
Chessie System: see Baltimore & Ohio
Chicago & Eastern Illinois, C&EI-E, -EP, -ER, -EZ, -J
Chicago, Milwaukee, St. Paul & Pacific, MILW-T, -TA, -TB, -TB2, -TS, -TSA
Cleveland, Cincinnati, Chicago & St. Louis: CCC-L, -LU, -T
Conrail: see Cleveland, Cincinnati, Chicago & St. Louis; Pennsylvania
CSX Corporation: see Baltimore & Ohio, Chicago & Eastern Illinois
CSX Transportation: see Baltimore & Ohio, Chicago & Eastern Illinois
Louisville & Nashville: see Chicago & Eastern Illinois
New York Central: see Cleveland, Cincinnati, Chicago & St. Louis
Penn Central: see Cleveland, Cincinnati, Chicago & St. Louis; Pennsylvania
Pennsylvania: PRR-V, -VF, -VM, -VT1, -VT2, -VT3
Seaboard System: see Chicago & Eastern Illinois
Soo Line: see Chicago, Milwaukee, St. Paul & Pacific
Terre Haute, Brazil & Eastern

Indiana Railroad: see Terre Haute, Indianapolis & Eastern
Terre Haute, Indianapolis & Eastern: THIE-A, -P, -S, -T

WABASH
Chicago & Indiana
Cleveland, Cincinnati, Chicago & St. Louis: CCC-M
Conrail: see Cleveland, Cincinnati, Chicago & St. Louis; Pennsylvania
Erie
Erie Western
Heritage
New York Central: see Cleveland, Cincinnati, Chicago & St. Louis
Norfolk & Western: see Wabash
Norfolk Southern: see Wabash
Penn Central: see Cleveland, Cincinnati, Chicago & St. Louis; Pennsylvania
Pennsylvania: PRR-LE
Wabash: WAB-M, -ME

Indiana Railroad: INDR-C, -F

WARREN
Bee Line
Chicago & Eastern Illinois, C&EI-EJ, -EC, -IA
Chicago, Attica & Southern
Conrail: see Lake Shore & Michigan Southern; Peoria & Eastern
Illinois Central, IC-SR
Lake Shore & Michigan Southern: LS-WD
Missouri Pacific: see part Chicago & Eastern Illinois
New York Central: see Lake Shore & Michigan Southern; Peoria & Eastern
    (continued)

WARREN (continued)
Norfolk & Western: see Wabash
Norfolk Southern: see Wabash
Penn Central: see Lake Shore & Michigan Southern; Peoria & Eastern
Peoria & Eastern
Wabash: WAB-P, -PR

WARRICK
Chicago & Eastern Illinois, C&EI-J
Cleveland, Cincinnati, Chicago & St. Louis: CCC-T
Conrail: see Cleveland, Cincinnati, Chicago & St. Louis
Indiana Southern
Louisville & Nashville: see Chicago & Eastern Illinois
New York Central: see Cleveland, Cincinnati, Chicago & St. Louis
Norfolk Southern: see Southern
Penn Central: see Cleveland, Cincinnati, Chicago & St. Louis
Southern: SOU-UE
Yankeetown Dock

Evansville & Ohio Valley
Evansville Suburban & Newburgh

WASHINGTON
CSX Corporation: see Monon
CSX Transportation: see Monon
Louisville & Nashville: see Monon
Monon: MON-SB
Seaboard System: see Monon

WAYNE
Chesapeake & Ohio
Chessie System: see Chesapeake & Ohio
Cleveland, Cincinnati, Chicago & St. Louis: CCC-GW
Conrail: see Cleveland, Cincinnati, Chicago & St. Louis; Pennsylvania
CSX Corporation: see Chesapeake & Ohio
CSX Transportation: see Chesapeake & Ohio
Indiana Hi-Rail, IHRC-[CCC-GW], IHRC-[NKP-LF]
New York Central: see Cleveland, Cincinnati, Chicago & St. Louis
New York, Chicago & St. Louis: NKP-LF
Norfolk & Western: see New York, Chicago & St. Louis
Norfolk Southern: see New York, Chicago & St. Louis
Penn Central: see Cleveland, Cincinnati, Chicago & St. Louis; Pennsylvania
Pennsylvania: PRR-CR, -GR, -I, -IC, -ICA

Dayton & Western
Indiana Railroad: see Terre Haute, Indianapolis & Eastern
Terre Haute, Indianapolis & Eastern: THIE-R, -RM

WELLS
Chicago & Indiana
Cincinnati, Bluffton & Chicago
Erie
Erie Western
Indiana Hi-Rail, IHRC-[NKP-TB]
New York, Chicago & St. Louis: NKP-LF, -TB
Norfolk & Western: see New York, Chicago & St. Louis; Wabash

Norfolk Southern: see New York, Chicago & St. Louis; Wabash
Wabash Central

Bluffton, Geneva & Celina
Indiana Railroad: INDR-A, -AB

WHITE
Conrail: see Pennsylvania
CSX Corporation: see Monon
CSX Transportation: see Monon
Louisville & Nashville: see Monon
Monon: MON-A, -I, -M
Penn Central: see Pennsylvania
Pennsylvania: PRR-LF
Seaboard System: see Monon
Toledo, Peoria & Western

WHITLEY
Conrail: see Pennsylvania
New York, Chicago & St. Louis: NKP-C
Norfolk & Western: see New York, Chicago & St. Louis; Wabash
Norfolk Southern: see New York, Chicago & St. Louis; Wabash
Penn Central: see Pennsylvania
Pennsylvania: PRR-F, -LE
Wabash: WAB-ME

4 COMPANY LISTING OF RAILROAD LINES OF TRACK

A & R LINE

LOGANSPORT-WINIMAC (ARLN-[PRR-L])
See Pennsylvania line PRR-L for arrangement of stations, prior construction/abandonment record, and prior ownership

CONSTRUCTION/ABANDONMENT

Date	Act	End points	MP	Change	Main	Source	Note
1995	P	Van-Winimac	198.9-225.2	+26.3	26.3	1	

OWNERSHIP

| 1995 | | A & R Line | | | | | |

ACQUISITION/DISPOSITION RECORD
See ownership record above for line ARLN-[PRR-L]

ACT COLUMN KEY
P Purchased from Winimac Southern

SOURCES
1 Simons and Parker, *Railroads of Indiana.*

ALGERS, WINSLOW & WESTERN

CATO MINE LINE (AWW-A)

	Mileage	County	Crossings, junctions, etc.
Oakland City Jct.	0	Pike	J/CCC-TC 2.8, J/AWW-B 0
(Bridge)	4.0	"	B/SOU-U 181.2
Cato Mine	10.1	"	

CONSTRUCTION/ABANDONMENT

Date	Act	End points	MP	Change	Main	Source	Note
1927	B	Oakland City Jct.-Cato M.	0-10.1	+10.1	10.1		

OWNERSHIP

| 1927 | | Algers, Winslow & Western | | | | | |

ENOS MINE LINE (AWW-B)

	Mileage	County	Crossings, junctions, etc.
Oakland City Jct.	0	Pike	J/CCC-TC 2.8, J/AWW-A 0
(Junction)	2.2	"	J/AWW-BB 0
Enos Mine	4.2	"	

CONSTRUCTION/ABANDONMENT

Date	Act	End points	MP	Change	Main	Source	Note
1950 ca.	P	Line	0-4.2	+4.2	4.2		

OWNERSHIP

| 1950 | | Algers, Winslow & Western | | | | | |

ENOS MINE LINE (AWW-BB)

	Mileage	County	Crossings, junctions, etc.
(Junction)	0	Pike	J/AWW-B 2.2
Blackfoot Mine	5.7	"	

CONSTRUCTION/ABANDONMENT

Date	Act	End points	MP	Change	Main	Source	Note
1950 ca.	B	Line	0-5.7	+5.7	5.7		

OWNERSHIP

| 1950 | | Algers, Winslow & Western | | | | | |

ALGERS, WINSLOW & WESTERN

ACQUISITION/DISPOSITION RECORD

Date	Act	AWW-	End points	Change	Main	Note
1927	B	A	Oakland City Jct.-Cato Mine	+10.1	10.1	
1950 ca.	P	B	Oakland City Jct.-Enos Mine	+4.2		
ca.	B	BB	(Junction)-Blackfoot Mine	+5.7	20.0	

ACT COLUMN KEY
B Built by Algers, Winslow & Western
P Purchased from Cleveland, Cincinnati, Chicago & St. Louis

SOURCES
1. Simons and Parker, *Railroads of Indiana*.

NOTES
General. In 1973 the Southern Ry bought a one-half interest in this company; this interest was transferred subsequently to Norfolk Southern.

AMTRAK (NATIONAL RAIL PASSENGER CORP.)

PORTER-KALAMAZOO LINE (AMK-[M-W])
See Michigan Central line MC-W for arrangement of stations, construction record, and prior ownership.

CONSTRUCTION/ABANDONMENT

Date	Act	End points	MP	Change	Main	Source	Note
1976/4/1	P	Niles MI-PO	222.7-240.7	+18.0	18.0		

OWNERSHIP

1976	Amtrak (National Rail Passenger Corp.)

ACQUISITION/DISPOSITION RECORD
See ownership record above for line AMK-[MC-W]

ACT COLUMN KEY
P Purchased from Penn Central

AUBURN PORT AUTHORITY

MAIN LINE (AUBN-[LS-TF])

	Mileage	County	Crossings, junctions, etc.
Auburn Jct.	0	DeKalb	J/B&O-C 124.7
Auburn	1.2	"	
(End of track)	1.7	"	

CONSTRUCTION/ABANDONMENT

Date	Act	End points	MP	Change	Main	Source	Note
1981	PL1	Line	0-1.7	<+1.7>	0	1	

OWNERSHIP

1981	Auburn Port Authority
1981	Baltimore & Ohio (controlled by Chesapeake & Ohio) lease line
1987/4/30	Chesapeake & Ohio, merge Baltimore & Ohio
1987/9/2	CSX Transportation, merge Chesapeake & Ohio

ACQUISITION/DISPOSITION RECORD
See ownership record above for line AUBN-[LS-TF]

ACT COLUMN KEY
PL1 Purchased from Baltimore & Ohio and leased back to Baltimore & Ohio

SOURCES
1 Simons and Parker, *Railroads of Indiana*.

BALTIMORE & OHIO

CHICAGO DIVISION (B&O-C)

	Mileage	County	Crossings, junctions, etc.
Willard OH	0		
Hicksville OH	107.9		
(OH/IN state line)	110.3		
Indo	113.8	DeKalb	
St. Joe	115.4	"	
(Crossing)	116.5	"	X/WAB-M 122.7
Concord	117.8	"	
Auburn	124.7	"	
Auburn Jct.	124.7	"	X/LS-TF 76.6, X/PRR-LE 81.4
Garrett	128.0	"	
Altona	129.2	"	
East Avilla	132.1	Noble	
Avilla	133.1	"	X/PRR-GS 113.6
Ripley	138	"	
Albion	143.3	"	
Kimmell	150.1	"	
Cromwell	153.5	"	
Wawasee	157.8	Kosciusko	old MP 158.4
Leeland	159	"	
Syracuse	160.6	"	J/SYM-A 0
Milford Jct.	165.7	"	X/CCC-M 166.3, X/WIN-A 11.0
Gravelton	169.9	"	
Nappanee	173.9	Elkhart	
West Nappanee	175.4	"	
Bremen	181.4	Marshall	
LaPaz Jct.	189.2	"	X/PRR-LS 54.0
LaPaz	189.8	"	
Garden	191.9	"	
Teegarden	193.5	"	
Walkerton	199.1	St. Joseph	X/LS-WK 19.5, X/NKP-LM 130.7
Kingsbury	207.1	LaPorte	
Union Center	207.2	"	
Tracy	208.4	"	
Wellsboro	213.8	"	X/GTW-C 71.1, X/PM-W 15.05
Webster	217.5	"	
Alida	220.9	"	X/MON-M 45.0
Coburg	223.4	Porter	
Suman	226.7	"	
Woodville	229.6	"	B/V&N-A 7.6
Babcock	232.7	"	
(continued)			

BALTIMORE & OHIO

CHICAGO DIVISION (B&O-C) (continued)

	Mileage [Willard OH]	County	Crossings, junctions, etc.
Babcock	232.7	Porter	
McCool	234.8	"	X/EJE-A 52.1
Willow Creek	236.9	"	X/MC-W 246.6, X/WAB-MC 233.7
(Bridge)	241.1	Lake	B/CSS-A 54.9
Miller	241.4	"	
East Gary	243.7	"	
Gary	244.9	"	
Curtis Yard	246.4	"	
(Bridge)	248.3	"	B/EJE-G 8.1
Pine Jct.	248.8	"	J/BOCT-A 0
Buff	249.4	"	
Indiana Harbor	251.3	"	
Hick	251.9	"	X/LS-W 502.6
Whiting	254.9	"	J/BOCT-W 3.7
(IN/IL state line)	256.6		
100th Street IL	257.3		
CR	258.1		
Rock Island Jct.	258.5		
Chicago IL			

CONSTRUCTION/ABANDONMENT

Date	Act	End points	MP	Change	Main	Source	Note
1874/11/23	B4	OH-IL state lines	110.3-256.6	+146.3	146.3	2	

OWNERSHIP

1874	Baltimore, Pittsburg & Ohio RR (B4), controlled by Baltimore & Ohiio
1876	Baltimore & Ohio RR, acquire Baltimore, Pittsburg & Ohio
1963	Chesapeake & Ohio Ry, control of Baltimore & Ohio
1973/6/15	Chessie System, control of Chesapeake & Ohio
1980/11/1	CSX Corp., merge Chessie System (with control of C&O)
1986/7/1	CSX Transportation, control of C&O (from CSX Corp.)
1987/4/30	Chesapeake & Ohio, merge Baltimore & Ohio
1987/9/2	CSX Transportation, merge Chesapeake & Ohio

FORT WAYNE LINE (B&O-F)

	Mileage	County	Crossings, junctions, etc.
Findlay OH	0		
Baldwin OH	62.6		
(OH/IN state line)	62.7		
Smiths Mill	63.8	Allen	
Towsley	65.1	"	
Tillmans	67.4	"	
Nails	69.6	"	
Roulos	74.7	"	
Gravel Pit	76.1	"	
Walton Avenue	79.5	"	
Wabash Jct.	80.0	"	J/WAB-M 145.8
--via WAB-M			
(Fort Wayne	80.7)	"	

CONSTRUCTION/ABANDONMENT

Date	Act	End points	MP	Change	Main	Source	Note
1895	B8	OH state line-Wabash Jct.	62.7-80.0	+17.3	17.3	2	
1919	X	OH state line-Wabash Jct.	62.7-80.0	-17.3	0	2	

OWNERSHIP

1895	Findlay, Fort Wayne & Western Ry (B8)
1901	Cincinnati, Hamilton & Dayton, leased Findlay, Ft. Wayne & W.
1903/7/6	Cincinnati, Findlay & Fort Wayne Ry, reorganized Findlay, Ft. Wayne & W., leased by CH&D

BALTIMORE & OHIO

OHIO DIVISION, DAYTON & UNION RR (B&O-TU)

	Mileage [Dayton]	County	Crossings, junctions, etc.
Miami City Jct. OH	0.6		
Hill Grove OH	44.3		
(OH/IN state line)	47.1		
Union City	47.3	Randolph	J/CCC-I 198.8

CONSTRUCTION/ABANDONMENT

Date	Act	End points	MP	Change	Main	Source	Note
1852	B10	OH state line-Union City	47.1-47.3	+0.2	0.2		
1991	X	OH state line-Union City	47.1-47.3	-0.2	0		

OWNERSHIP

1852	Greenville & Miami RR (B10)
1863	Dayton & Union RR (owned by CH&D and CCC&SL), reorganize Greenville & Miami
1936	Baltimore & Ohio RR, merge Dayton & Union
1963	Chesapeake & Ohio Ry, control of Baltimore & Ohio
1973/6/15	Chessie System, control of Chesapeake & Ohio
1980/11/1	CSX Corp., merge Chessie System (with control of C&O)
1986/7/1	CSX Transportation, control of C&O (from CSX Corp.)
1987/4/30	Chesapeake & Ohio, merge Baltimore & Ohio
1987/9/2	CSX Transportation, merge Chesapeake & Ohio

INDIANAPOLIS DIVISION, HAMILTON SUBDIVISION (B&O-IH)

	Mileage [Cincinnati]	County	Crossings, junctions, etc.
Hamilton OH	25.4		
Belt Jct.	26.9		
College Corner OH	44.9		
(OH/IN state line)	45.0	Union	
Cottage Grove	48.2	"	X/C&O-C 46.5
Liberty	53.0	"	
Brownsville	59.2	"	
Lyonsville	62.9	Fayette	f. Lyons
Connersville	67.3	"	J/NKP-LF 109.0
(Bridge)	67.7	"	B/CCC-GW 69.0
Salters	68.8	"	
Longwood	73.0	"	
Hurricane	75	Rush	
Glenwood	77.2	"	
Mauzy	79.0	"	
Rushville	85.1	"	
(Crossing)	85.2	"	X/PRR-IC 42.1
(Crossing)	85.4	"	X/CCC-M 204.5, J/NKP-LR 107.9
Arlington	92.1	"	
Gwynneville	96.2	Shelby	
Morristown	99.0	"	
Fountaintown	103.6	"	
Reedville	106.0	Hancock	
New Palestine	109.7	"	
Julietta	113.5	Marion	
Irvington	118	"	
(Bridge)	118.2	"	B/PRR-IK 1.4
(Crossing)	121.6	"	X/IU-B 2.6
Pine Jct.	121.9	"	
State Street	122.4	"	
(Junction)	123.6	"	J/IU-E 0.9
--via IU-E			
(Indianapolis	124.5)	"	

BALTIMORE & OHIO

INDIANAPOLIS DIVISION, HAMILTON SUBDIVISION (B&O-IH) (continued)

CONSTRUCTION/ABANDONMENT

Date	Act	End points	MP	Change	Main	Source	Note
1852	B1	OH state line-Rushville	45.0-85.1	+40.1	40.1	1	
1867	B:	Rushville-Indianapolis	85.1-123.6	+38.5	78.6	1	

OWNERSHIP

1852	Cincinnati & Indianapolis Junction RR (B1), of part
1872	Cincinnati, Hamilton & Indianapolis RR, bought Cinci. & Indpls. Jct.
1886	Cincinnati, Hamilton & Dayton RR, began operated Cinci., Ham. & Indpls.
1902	Cincinnati, Indianapolis & Western RR, merged Cinci., Ham. & Indpls.
1902	Cincinnati, Hamilton & Dayton RR, leased Cincinnati, Indianapolis & W.
1927	Baltimore & Ohio RR, bought Cincinnati, Hamilton & Dayton
1963	Chesapeake & Ohio Ry, control of Baltimore & Ohio
1973/6/15	Chessie System, control of Chesapeake & Ohio
1980/11/1	CSX Corp., merged Chessie System (with control of C&O)
1986/7/1	CSX Transportation, control of C&O (from CSX Corp.)
1987/4/30	Chesapeake & Ohio, merged Baltimore & Ohio
1987/9/2	CSX Transportation, merged Chesapeake & Ohio

INDIANAPOLIS DIVISION, DECATUR SUBDIVISION (B&O-ID)

	Mileage [Cincinnati]	County	Crossings, junctions, etc.
(Indianapolis	124.5)	Marion	
--via IU-W			
West Street	124.9	"	J/IU-W 0.4
IJ	125.5	"	X/CCC-L 1.0
KD	126.3	"	X/IU-B 9.4
Speedway	129.1	"	
Moorefield	130.3	"	
Mitchellville	132.6	"	B/PRR-IF 11.3
Tilden	139.9	Hendricks	
Maplewood	143.9	"	
Montclair	147.0	"	
North Salem	151.3	"	
Barnard	154.2	Putnam	
Roachdale	159.8	"	X/MON-SA 162.2
Raccoon	164.7	"	
Russellville	169.5	"	
Milligan	172.3	Parke	
Guion	176.4	"	X/PRR-VF 32.7
Marshall	180.7	"	
Bloomingdale	184.1	"	
West Melcher	190.1	"	J/B&O-IB 0, J/CAS-A 119.6 aka Klondyke Jct.
Montezuma	191.1	"	old MP 191.8
Hillsdale	192.7	Vermillion	X/CEI-E 154.6
Hollowell	195	"	
Dana	199.1	"	
West Dana	200.8	"	X/MILW-T 146.1
(IN/IL state line)	201.2		
Scotland IL	204.8		
Decatur	277.3		
(continued)			

BALTIMORE & OHIO

INDIANAPOLIS DIVISION, DECATUR SUBDIVISION (B&O-ID) (continued)
CONSTRUCTION/ABANDONMENT

Date	Act	End points	MP	Change	Main	Source	Note
1873	B3	Hillsdale-IL state line	192.9-201.2	+8.3	8.3	1	
1880	B5	Indianapolis-Hillsdale	124.9-192.9	+68.0	76.3	1	

1989	X	Russellville-Bloomingdale	169.5-184.1	-14.6		1	
1989	X	Mitchellville-Roachdale	132.5-159.2	-26.7	35.0	1,2	
1990	X	Roachdale-Russellville	159.2-169.5	-10.3	24.7	1,2	1
1992	X	Speedway-Mitchellville	129.2-132.5	-3.3	21.4	1	
1994	X	Bloomingdale-Montezuma	184.1-191.4	-7.3	14.1	1	

OWNERSHIP

1873	Indiana & Illinois Central Ry (B3), of part
1875	Indianapolis, Decatur & Springfield Ry (B5), bought Indiana & Ill. Cent.
1887/12	Indianapolis, Decatur & Western Ry, bought Indpls., Decatur & Spgfld.
1902	Cincinnati, Indianapolis & Western RR, acquired Indpls, Decatur & W.
1902	Cincinnati, Hamilton & Dayton RR, leased Cincinnati, Indianapolis & W.
1927	Baltimore & Ohio RR, bought Cincinnati, Hamilton & Dayton
1963	Chesapeake & Ohio Ry, control of Baltimore & Ohio
1973/6/15	Chessie System, control of Chesapeake & Ohio
1980/11/1	CSX Corp., merged Chessie System (with control of C&O)
1986/7/1	CSX Transportation, control of C&O (from CSX Corp.)
1987/4/30	Chesapeake & Ohio, merged Baltimore & Ohio
1987/9/2	CSX Transportation, merged Chesapeake & Ohio

INDIANAPOLIS DIVISION, BRAZIL SUBDIVISON (B&O-IB)

	Mileage	County	Crossings, junctions, etc.
West Melcher	0	Parke	J/B&O-ID 190.1, J/CAS-A 119.6
Mecca Jct.	2.9	"	J/spur to Mecca Mine, 1.5 miles
Mecca	4.5	"	
Oakville	10.6	"	
(Crossing)	12.1	"	X/PRR-VF 12.2
Rosedale	12.5	"	
Mary No. 2 Mine	15.6	Vigo	
Diamond Jct.	16.8	"	J/spur to Diamond Mine, 3.5 miles
Coal Bluff	16.9	"	X/CCC-L 59.0
Beech Grove	19.3	"	
McClelland	20.3	"	
Brazil	25.1	Clay	J/PRR-V 57.0

CONSTRUCTION/ABANDONMENT

Date	Act	End points	MP	Change	Main	Source	Note
1922	P1	West Melcher-Brazil	0-25.1	+25.1	25.1	2,3	
1965	X	West Melcher-Brazil	0-25.1	-25.1	0	2	3

OWNERSHIP

1922	Baltimore & Ohio RR, bought line from Chicago & Eastern Illinois
1963	Chesapeake & Ohio Ry, control of Baltimore & Ohio

ST. LOUIS DIVISION, CINCINNATI SUBDIVISION (B&O-SC)

	Mileage	County	Crossings, junctions, etc.
Cincinnati OH	0		
Columbia Park OH	19.1		
(OH/IN state line)	19.8		
Dearborn	21.9	Dearborn	X/CCC-GA 24.9
Lawrenceburg	22.1	"	
(continued)			

BALTIMORE & OHIO

ST. LOUIS DIVISION, CINCINNATI SUBDIVISION (B&O-SC) (continued)

Lawrenceburg	22.1	Dearborn	
Aurora	25.8	"	
Cochrane	27.3	"	
Cochrane Jct.	30.3	"	
Dillsboro	33.9	"	
Cold Springs	37.4	"	
Moore's Hill	40.1	"	
Milan	42.6	Ripley	
Pierceville	45.2	"	
(Junction)	45.5	"	J/B&O-SO1 45.5
Delaware	47.4	"	
Osgood	51.5	"	J/B&O-SO1 51.9
Dabney	55.1	"	
Holton	58.1	"	
Nebraska	62.0	Jennings	
Butlerville	65.6	"	
Oakdale	68.4	"	
North Vernon	72.2	"	J/B&O-SW 72.2, J/B&O-SV 0, X/CCC-M 248.9, J/PRR-IM 21.5

CONSTRUCTION/ABANDONMENT

Date	Act	End points	MP	Change	Main	Source	Note
1857	B2	Cincinnati OH-Pierceville	19.8-45.5	+25.7		1	1
1857	B2	Osgood-North Vernon	51.5-72.2	+20.7	46.4	1	1
1901	B9	Pierceville-Osgood	45.5-51.5	+6.0	52.4	2	

OWNERSHIP

1857	Ohio & Mississippi RR (B2)
1893	Baltimore & Ohio Southwestern RR, bought Ohio & Mississippi
1900/7	Baltimore & Ohio RR, bought Baltimore & Ohio Southwestern
1963	Chesapeake & Ohio Ry, control of Baltimore & Ohio
1973/6/15	Chessie System, control of Chesapeake & Ohio
1980/11/1	CSX Corp., merged Chessie System (with control of C&O)
1986/7/1	CSX Transportation, control of C&O (from CSX Corp.)
1987/4/30	Chesapeake & Ohio, merged Baltimore & Ohio
1987/9/2	CSX Transportation, merged Chesapeake & Ohio

ST. LOUIS DIVISION, LOUISVILLE SUBDIVISION (B&O-SV)

	Mileage	County	Crossings, junctions, etc.
North Vernon	0	Jennings	J/B&O-SC 72.7, J/B&O-SW 72.7, J/CCC-M 248.9, J/PRR-IM 21.5
Lovett	6.7	"	
Commiskey	10.3	"	
Paris	12.5	Jefferson	
Deputy	14.9	"	
Blocher	20.1	Scott	
Lexington	25.1	Scott	
Nabb	28.6	"	
Marysville	30.1	Clark	
Otisco	33.4	"	
Clarke	38.4	"	
Charlestown	40.3	"	
(Junction)	41.6	"	J/MGR-A 6.2
(Junction)	45.0	"	J/MGR-A 0
Watson	46.6	"	J/B&O-SJ 0
(Crossing)	47.1	"	X/SOIN-A 0.2
Boyd	50.3	"	X/PRR-IL 104.9
New Albany	54.0	Floyd	J/KIT-A 0
--via KIT-A			
(Louisville KY		57.6	

BALTIMORE & OHIO

ST. LOUIS DIVISION, LOUISVILLE SUBDIVISION (B&O-SV) (continued)

CONSTRUCTION/ABANDONMENT

Date	Act	End points	MP	Change	Main	Source	Note
1869	B2	North Vernon-Watson	0-46.6	+46.6	46.6	1	
1887	B6	Watson-New Albany	46.6-54.0	+7.4	54.0	1	

1980	Y	In North Vernon	0-0.4	(0.4)			
1980	X	North Vernon-Nabb	0.4-28.5	-28.1	25.5	1	
1985	X	Nabb-Charleston	28.5-40.3	-11.8	13.7	1	

OWNERSHIP

1869	Ohio & Mississippi RR (B2), of part
1887	New Albany & Eastern Ry (B6), of part
1888	Ohio & Mississippi, bought New Albany & Eastern
1893	Baltimore & Ohio Southwestern RR, bought Ohio & Mississippi
1900/7	Baltimore & Ohio RR, bought Baltimore & Ohio Southwestern
1963	Chesapeake & Ohio Ry, control of Baltimore & Ohio
1973/6/15	Chessie System, control of Chesapeake & Ohio
1980/11/1	CSX Corp., merged Chessie System (with control of C&O)
1986/7/1	CSX Transportation, control of C&O (from CSX Corp.)
1987/4/30	Chesapeake & Ohio, merged Baltimore & Ohio
1987/9/2	CSX Transportation, merged Chesapeake & Ohio

ST. LOUIS DIVISION, JEFFERSONVILLE SUBDIVISION (B&O-SJ)

	Mileage [North Vernon]	County	Crossings, junctions, etc.
Watson	46.6	Clark	J/B&O-SV 46.6
(Junction)	47.2	"	J/SOIN-A 0
(Junction)	52.8	"	J/LJB 0
Jeffersonville	53.0	"	
(Junction)	53.5	"	J/PRR-IL 108.0

CONSTRUCTION/ABANDONMENT

Date	Act	End points	MP	Change	Main	Source	Note
1869	B2	New Albany-Jeffersonville	46.6-52.8	+6.2	6.2	1	
1872	B2	In Jeffersonville	52.8-45.5	+0.7	6.9		

OWNERSHIP

1869	Ohio & Mississippi RR (B2)
1893	Baltimore & Ohio Southwestern RR, bought Ohio & Mississippi
1900/7	Baltimore & Ohio RR, bought Baltimore & Ohio Southwestern
1963	Chesapeake & Ohio Ry, control of Baltimore & Ohio
1973/6/15	Chessie System, control of Chesapeake & Ohio
1980/11/1	CSX Corp., merged Chessie System (with control of C&O)
1986/7/1	CSX Transportation, control of C&O (from CSX Corp.)
1987/4/30	Chesapeake & Ohio, merged Baltimore & Ohio
1987/9/2	CSX Transportation, merged Chesapeake & Ohio

ST. LOUIS DIVISION, BEDFORD BRANCH (B&O-SB)

	Mileage	County	Crossings, junctions, etc.
Rivervale	0	Lawrence	J/B&O-SW 121.0
Sheeks	3.8	"	
Carr	4.8	"	
Palestine	6.3	"	
Dodd	7.3	"	
Lehman	8.6	"	
Bedford	10.3	"	
(Junction)	10.8	"	X/MILW-T 262.3, J/MON-SB 245.8

BALTIMORE & OHIO

ST. LOUIS DIVISION, BEDFORD BRANCH (B&O-SB) (continued)

CONSTRUCTION/ABANDONMENT

Date	Act	End points	MP	Change	Main	Source	Note
1893	B7	Rivervale-Bedford	0-10.8	+10.8	10.8	1	
1924	X	Rivervale-Bedford	0-10.8	-10.8	0	2	

OWNERSHIP

1893	Cincinnati & Bedford Ry (B7)
1893/11/18	Baltimore & Ohio Southwestern RR, bought Cincinnati & Bedford
1900/7	Baltimore & Ohio RR, bought Baltimore & Ohio Southwestern
1963	Chesapeake & Ohio Ry, control of Baltimore & Ohio
1973/6/15	Chessie System, control of Chesapeake & Ohio
1980/11/1	CSX Corp., merged Chessie System (with control of C&O)
1986/7/1	CSX Transportation, control of C&O (from CSX Corp.)
1987/4/30	Chesapeake & Ohio, merged Baltimore & Ohio
1987/9/2	CSX Transportation, merged Chesapeake & Ohio

PIERCEVILLE-OSGOOD OLD MAIN (B&O-SO1)

	Mileage [Cincinnati]	County	Crossings, junctions, etc.
(Junction)	45.5	Ripley	J/B&O-SC 45.5
Delaware	47.0	"	
Osgood	51.9	"	J/B&O-SC 51.5

CONSTRUCTION/ABANDONMENT

Date	Act	End points	MP	Change	Main	Source	Note
1857	B2	Pierceville-Osgood	45.5-51.9	+6.4	6.4	1	
1901	X	Pierceville-Osgood	45.5-51.9	-6.4	0	2	

OWNERSHIP

1857	Ohio & Mississippi RR (B2)
1893	Baltimore & Ohio Southwestern RR, bought Ohio & Mississippi
1900/7	Baltimore & Ohio RR, bought Baltimore & Ohio Southwestern

NORTH VERNON-HAYDEN OLD MAIN LINE (B&O-SO2)

	Mileage [Cincinnati]	County	Crossings, junctions, etc.
(Junction)	74.0	Jennings	J/B&O-SW 74.0
Hayden	78.8	"	
(Junction)	79.2	"	J/B&O-SW 79.3

CONSTRUCTION/ABANDONMENT

Date	Act	End points	MP	Change	Main	Source	Note
1857	B2	Line	74.0-79.2	+5.2	5.2	1	
1901	X	Line	74.0-79.2	-5.2	0	2	

OWNERSHIP

1857	Ohio & Mississippi RR (B2)
1893	Baltimore & Ohio Southwestern RR, bought Ohio & Mississippi
1900/7	Baltimore & Ohio RR, bought Baltimore & Ohio Southwestern

OLD MAIN EAST OF HURON (B&O-SO3)

	Mileage [Cincinnati]	County	Crossings, junctions, etc.
(Junction)	134.3	Lawrence	J/B&O-SW 134.3
Moorestown	134.7	"	
(Junction)	137.2	"	J/B&O-SW 137.2
(Junction)	138.6	"	J/B&O-SW 137.9

BALTIMORE & OHIO

OLD MAIN EAST OF HURON (B&O-SO3) (continued)

CONSTRUCTION/ABANDONMENT

Date	Act	End points	MP	Change	Main	Source	Note
1857	B2	Line	134.2-138.6	+4.3	4.3	1	
1901	X	Line	134.2-138.6	-4.3	0	2	

OWNERSHIP

1857	Ohio & Mississippi RR (B2)
1893	Baltimore & Ohio Southwestern RR, bought Ohio & Mississippi
1900/7	Baltimore & Ohio RR, bought Baltimore & Ohio Southwestern

OLD MAIN WEST OF HURON (B&O-SO4)

	Mileage [Cincinnati]	County	Crossings, junctions, etc.
(Junction)	139.1	Martin	J/B&O-SW 139.1
(Junction)	140.2	"	J/B&O-SW 139.9
(continued)			

OLD MAIN WEST OF HURON (B&O-SO4) (continued)

CONSTRUCTION/ABANDONMENT

Date	Act	End points	MP	Change	Main	Source	Note
1857	B2	Line	139.1-140.2	+1.1	1.1	1	
1901	X	Line	139.1-140.2	-1.1	0	2	

OWNERSHIP

1857	Ohio & Mississippi RR (B2)
1893	Baltimore & Ohio Southwestern RR, bought Ohio & Mississippi
1900/7	Baltimore & Ohio RR, bought Baltimore & Ohio Southwestern

WILLOW VALLEY OLD MAIN (B&O-SO5)

	Mileage [Cincinnati]	County	Crossings, junctions, etc.
(Junction)	141.6	Martin	J/B&O-SW 141.6
(Junction)	143.9	"	J/B&O-SW 142.7

CONSTRUCTION/ABANDONMENT

Date	Act	End points	MP	Change	Main	Source	Note
1857	B2	Line	141.6-143.9	+2.3	2.3	1	
1901	X	Line	141.6-143.9	-2.3	0	2	

OWNERSHIP

1857	Ohio & Mississippi RR (B2)
1893	Baltimore & Ohio Southwestern RR, bought Ohio & Mississippi
1900/7	Baltimore & Ohio RR, bought Baltimore & Ohio Southwestern

LOOGOOTEE OLD MAIN (B&O-SO6)

	Mileage [Cincinnati]	County	Crossings, junctions, etc.
(Junction)	153.6	Martin	J/B&O-SW 153.6
(Junction)	155.7	"	J/B&O-SW 155.2

CONSTRUCTION/ABANDONMENT

Date	Act	End points	MP	Change	Main	Source	Note
1857	B2	Line	153.6-155.7	+2.1	2.1	1	
1901	X	Line	153.6-155.7	-2.1	0	2	

OWNERSHIP

1857	Ohio & Mississippi RR (B2)
1893	Baltimore & Ohio Southwestern RR, bought Ohio & Mississippi
1900/7	Baltimore & Ohio RR, bought Baltimore & Ohio Southwestern

BALTIMORE & OHIO
ST. LOUIS DIVISION, WASHINGTON SUBDIVISION (B&O-SW)

	Mileage [Cincinnati]	County	Crossings, junctions, etc.
North Vernon	72.2	Jennings	J/B&O-SC 72.2, J/B&O-SV 0, X/CCC-M 248.9, J/PRR-IM 21.5
Whitcomb	74	"	
(Junction)	74.0	"	J/B&O-SO2 74.0
Hayden	78.9	"	
(Junction)	79.3	"	J/B&O-SO2 79.2
Fleming	81.7	Jackson	
JD	87.3	"	X/PRR-IL 58.9
Dunham	92	"	
Shields	94.3	"	
Brownstown	97.8	"	
Vallonia	101.0	"	
Medora	105.4	"	
Sparksville	110.6	"	
Fort Ritner	113.7	Lawrence	
Tunnelton	117.7	"	
Rivervale	121.0	"	J/B&O-SB 0, J/BEST-A 0
Mitchell	126.4	"	X/MON-SB 255.3
Georgia	131.9	"	
Prosser Spur	134	"	
(Junction)	134.3	"	J/B&O-SO3 134.3
(Junction)	137.2	"	J/B&O-SO3 137.2
(Junction)	137.9	"	J/B&O-SO3 138.6
Huron	138.0	"	
(Junction)	139.1	Martin	J/B&O-SO4 139.1
(Junction)	139.9	"	J/B&O-SO4 140.2
Willow Valley	141.4	"	
(Junction)	141.6	"	J/B&O-SO5 141.6
(Junction)	142.7	"	J/B&O-SO5 143.9
Ironton	146.1	"	
Shoals	147.1	"	
Marlin	147.7	"	
Quarry	151	"	
(Junction)	153.6	"	J/B&O-SO6 153.6
(Junction)	155.2	"	J/B&O-SO6 155.7
Loogootee	155.5	"	
Cannelburg	160.0	Daviess	
Montgomery	162.5	"	
Black Oak	164.7	"	
(Junction)	169.6	"	J/B&O-SW1 0
Washington	170.4	"	J/B&O-SI 170.4, X/CCC-TW 2.7

CONSTRUCTION/ABANDONMENT

Date	Act	End points	MP	Change	Main	Source	Note
1857	B2	North Vernon-MP 74	72.2-74.0	+1.8		1	1
1857	B2	Hayden-MP 134.3	79.3-134.3	+55.0		1	
1857	B2	At Huron	137.9-139.1	+1.2		1	
1857	B2	MP 139.9-Willow Valley	139.9-141.6	+1.7		1	
1857	B2	Around Shoals	142.7-153.6	+10.9		1	
1857	B2	Loogootee-Washington	155.2-170.4	+15.2	85.8	1	
1901	B9	MP 74-Hayden	74.0-79.3	+5.3		2	
1901	B9	East of Huron	134.3-137.9	+3.6		2	
1901	B9	West of Huron	139.1-139.9	+0.8		2	
1901	B9	West of Willow Valley	141.6-142.7	+1.1		2	
1901	B9	East of Loogootee	153.6-155.2	+1.6	98.2	2	

(continued)

BALTIMORE & OHIO

ST. LOUIS DIVISION, WASHINGTON SUBDIVISION (B&O-SW) (continued)
OWNERSHIP

1857	Ohio & Mississippi RR (B2)
1893	Baltimore & Ohio Southwestern RR, bought Ohio & Mississippi
1900/7	Baltimore & Ohio RR, bought Baltimore & Ohio Southwestern
1963	Chesapeake & Ohio Ry, control of Baltimore & Ohio
1973/6/15	Chessie System, control of Chesapeake & Ohio
1980/11/1	CSX Corp., merged Chessie System (with control of C&O)
1986/7/1	CSX Transportation, control of C&O (from CSX Corp.)
1987/4/30	Chesapeake & Ohio, merged Baltimore & Ohio
1987/9/2	CSX Transportation, merged Chesapeake & Ohio

MINE SPUR (B&O-SW1)

	Mileage	County	Crossings, junctions, etc.
(Junction)	0	Daviess	J/B&O-SW 169.6
(Mines)	2.5	"	

CONSTRUCTION/ABANDONMENT

Date	Act	End points	MP	Change	Main	Source	Note
							4

ST. LOUIS DIVISION, ILLINOIS SUBDIVISION (B&O-SI)

	Mileage [Cincinnati]	County	Crossings, junctions, etc.
Washington	170.4	Daviess	old MP 169.8, J/B&O-SW 170.4, X/CCC-TW 2.7
Shops	170.7	"	
Chappell	171.4	"	X/CCC-T 78.4
Wheatland	176.7	Knox	
Fritchton	183.3	"	
Vincennes	188.6	"	X/CEI-E 234.7--J/PRR-IV 116.9-- J/CCC-LV 121.2
(IN/IL state line)	189.4		
Beman IL	193.5		
East St. Louis IL	335.5		

CONSTRUCTION/ABANDONMENT

Date	Act	End points	MP	Change	Main	Source	Note
1857	B2	Washington-IL state line	170.4-189.4	+19.0	19.0	1	1

OWNERSHIP

1857	Ohio & Mississippi RR (B2)
1893	Baltimore & Ohio Southwestern RR, bought Ohio & Mississippi
1900/7	Baltimore & Ohio RR, bought Baltimore & Ohio Southwestern
1963	Chesapeake & Ohio Ry, control of Baltimore & Ohio
1973/6/15	Chessie System, control of Chesapeake & Ohio
1980/11/1	CSX Corp., merged Chessie System (with control of C&O)
1986/7/1	CSX Transportation, control of C&O (from CSX Corp.)
1987/4/30	Chesapeake & Ohio, merged Baltimore & Ohio
1987/9/2	CSX Transportation, merged Chesapeake & Ohio

AUBURN SPUR (B&O-[LS-TF])

	Mileage	County	Crossings, junctions, etc.
Auburn Jct.	0	DeKalb	J/B&O-C 124.7
Auburn	1.2	"	
(End of track)	1.7	"	
(continued)			

BALTIMORE & OHIO

AUBURN SPUR (B&O-[LS-TF]) (continued)
CONSTRUCTION/ABANDONMENT

Date	Act	End points	MP	Change	Main	Source	Note
1976	P2	Line	0-1.7	+1.7	1.7	2	
1981	SL1	Line	0-1.7	-1.7			

OWNERSHIP

1976	Baltimore & Ohio RR, control by Chesapeake & Ohio
1981	Auburn Port Authority, buy line from Baltimore & Ohio
1981	Baltimore & Ohio RR, (control by Chessie System), lease Auburn Port Authority
1986/7/1	CSX Transportation, control of C&O (from CSX Corp.)
1987/4/30	Chesapeake & Ohio, merge Baltimore & Ohio
1987/9/2	CSX Transportation, merge Chesapeake & Ohio

ACQUISITION/DISPOSITION RECORD

Date	Act	B&O-	End points	Change	Main	Note
1852	B1	IH	OH state line-Rushville	+40.1		
	B10	TU	OH state line-Union City	+0.2	40.3	
1857	B2	SC,SO1	Cincinnati OH-North Vernon	+52.8		
	B2	SW,SO2-6	North Vernon-Washington	+100.8		
	B2	SI	Washington-IL state line	+19.0	212.9	1
1867	B1	IH	Rushville-Indianapolis	+38.5	251.4	
1869	B2	SV	North Vernon-Watson	+46.6		
	B2	SJ	New Albany-Jeffersonville	+6.2	304.2	
1872	B2	SJ	In Jeffersonville	+0.7	304.9	
1873	B3	ID	Hillsdale-IL state line	+8.3	313.2	
1874/11/23	B4	C	OH-IL state lines	+146.3	459.5	
1880	B5	ID	Indianapolis-Hillsdale	+68.0	527.5	
1887	B6	SV	Watson-New Albany	+7.4	534.9	
1893	B7	SB	Rivervale-Bedford	+10.8	545.7	
1895	B8	F	OH state line-Fort Wayne	+18.0	563.7	
1901	B9	SC	Main line segment	+6.0		
	X	SO1	Main line segment	-6.4		
	B9	SW	Main line segments	+12.4		
	X	SO2-SO6	Main line segments	-15.0	560.7	
1919	X	F	OH state line-Fort Wayne	-18.0	542.7	
1922	P1	IB	West Melcher-Brazil	+25.1	567.8	
1924	X	SB	Rivervale-Bedford	-10.8	557.0	

In 1963 this company became controlled by Chesapeake & Ohio. Its Acquisition/Disposition Record is continued in two places: under Baltimore & Ohio and under Chesapeake & Ohio.

1965	X	IB	West Melcher-Brazil	-25.1	531.9	3

On 1973/6/15 control of Chesapeake & Ohio (and its control of Baltimore & Ohio) was transferred to Chessie System. Its Acquisition/Disposition Record is continued in two places: under Baltimore & Ohio and under Chessie System.

1976	P2 [LS-TF]	In Auburn	+1.7	533.6	
1980	X,Y	SV	North Vernon-Nabb	-28.5	505.1

On 1980/11/1 CSX Corporation merged Chessie System (with control of Chesapeake & Ohio). The Acquisition/Disposition Record is continued in two places: under Baltimore & Ohio and under CSX Corporation.

1981	SL1 [LS-TF]	In Auburn	<1.7>	505.1	
1985	X	SV	Nabb-Charleston	-11.8	493.3

On 1986/7/1 CSX Transportation obtained control acquired control of Chesapeake & Ohio (and its control of Baltimore & Ohio) from CSX Corporation. On 1987/4/30 Chesapeake & Ohio merged Baltimore & Ohio and on 1987/9/2 CSX Transportation merged Chesapeake & Ohio. The Acquisition/Disposition Record is continued in two places: under Baltimore & Ohio and under CSX Transportation.

BALTIMORE & OHIO

ACQUISITION/DISPOSITION RECORD (continued)

Date	Act	B&O-	End points	Change	Main	Note
1989	X	ID	Russellville-Bloomingdale	-14.6		
	X	ID	Mitchellville-Roachdale	-26.7	452.0	
1990	X	ID	Roachdale-Russellville	-10.3	441.7	2
1991	X	TU	OH state line-Union City	-0.2	441.5	
1992	X	ID	Speedway-Mitchellville	-3.3	438.2	
1994	X	ID	Bloomingdale-Montezuma	-7.3	430.9	

ACT COLUMN KEY
B1 Built by Cincinnati & Indianapolis Junction RR
B2 Built by Ohio & Mississippi RR
B3 Built by Indiana & Illinois Central Ry
B4 Built by Baltimore, Pittsburg & Ohio RR
B5 Built by Indianapolis, Decatur & Springfield Ry
B6 Built by New Albany & Eastern Ry
B7 Built by Cincinnati & Bedford Ry
B8 Built by Findlay, Fort Wayne & Western Ry
B9 Built by Baltimore & Ohio RR
B10 Built by Greenville & Miami RR
P1 Purchased from Chicago & Eastern Illinois
P2 Purchased from Penn Central
S2 Sold to Conrail
SL1 Sold to Auburn Port Authority and leased back from that company
X   Abandoned
SOURCES
1 Indiana, *Indiana State Rail Plan.*
2 Simons and Parker, *Railroads of Indiana.*
3 Sulzer. *Ghost Railroads of Indiana.*

NOTES
1. This line was built to a 6 foot gauge and converted to standard gauge in July 1871.
2. It appears that 0.6 miles in Roachdale was retained as industrial track.
3. Source 3 states that 1.2 mile of line was conveyed to Pennsylvania RR as industrial track.
4. The construction or abandonment date could not be determined and this line is not included in the Acqusition/Disposition Record.

BALTIMORE & OHIO CHICAGO TERMINAL

MAIN LINE (BOCT-A)

	Mileage	County	Crossings, junctions, etc.
Pine Jct.	0	Lake	J/B&O-C 248.8
(Junction)	0.3	"	J/WAB-MC 246.7
Clarke Jct.	0.5	"	X/PRR-F 445.7
Calumet Tower	2.7	"	X/LS-WD 2.10, X/EJE-GW 0.7, X/IHB-A 2.0
McCook Avenue	3.2	"	
Republic	3.3	"	
Tod Avenue	3.7	"	
Baring Avenue	3.9	"	
Whiting Jct.	4.4	"	J/BOCT-W 0
(Bridge)	4.6	"	B/CSS-A 68.1
Columbia Avenue	4.8	"	
Calumet Avenue	5.2	"	X/PRR-FR 7.6
(IN/IL state line)	7.2		
Dolton	10.7		
Blue Island Jct. IL	14.9		
(continued)			

BALTIMORE & OHIO CHICAGO TERMINAL

MAIN LINE (BOCT-A) (continued)

CONSTRUCTION/ABANDONMENT

Date	Act	End points	MP	Change	Main	Source	Note
1895 ca.	B2	Line	0-6.0	+6.0	6.0		

OWNERSHIP

1895	Chicago Terminal Transfer RR (B2)
1910	Baltimore & Ohio Chicago Terminal RR, reorganize Chicago Terminal Transfer

WHITING BRANCH (BOCT-W)

	Mileage	County	Crossings, junctions, etc.
Whiting Jct.	0	Lake	J/BOCT-A 4.4
(Crossing)	2.0	"	X/IHB
(Junction)	3.4	"	J/IHB-W 4.1
(Crossing)	3.5	"	X/PRR-F 450.8
(MS)	3.7	"	X/LS-W 505.74
Whiting	3.7	"	J/B&O-C 254.5

CONSTRUCTION/ABANDONMENT

Date	Act	End points	MP	Change	Main	Source	Note
1890	B1	Line	0-3.7	+3.7	3.7		

OWNERSHIP

1890	Chicago & Calumet Terminal RR (B1)
1898	Chicago Terminal Transfer RR, acquire Chicago & Calumet Terminal
1910	Baltimore & Ohio Chicago Terminal RR, reorganize Chicago Terminal Transfer

ACQUISITION/DISPOSITION RECORD

Date	Act	BOCT	End points	Change	Main	Note
1890	B1	W	Line	+3.7	3.7	
1895 ca.	B2	A	Line	+6.0	9.7	

ACT COLUMN KEY
B1   Built by Chicago & Calumet Terminal RR
B2   Built by Chicago Terminal Transfer RR

NOTES
General. The company also had a number of other industrial spurs which are not detailed herein.

BEDFORD & WALLNER

MAIN LINE (BEW-A)

	Mileage	County	Crossings, junctions, etc.
(Bedford)	0	Lawrence	J/??
Wallner	2.8	"	

CONSTRUCTION/ABANDONMENT

Date	Act	End points	MP	Change	Main	Source	Note
1907	B	Bedford-Wallner	0-2.8	+2.8	2.8	1	
1927	X	Bedford-Wallner	0-2.8	-2.8	0	1	1

OWNERSHIP

1907	Bedford & Wallner RR

ACQUISITION/DISPOSITION RECORD
See ownership record above for line BEW-A

ACT COLUMN KEY
B   Built by Bedford & Wallner
X   Abandoned

BEDFORD & WALLNER

SOURCES
1 Simons and Parker, *Railroads of Indiana.*

NOTES
1 Source 1 states that the line was sold to Chicago, Indianapolis & Louisville in 1927 and operated as an industrial spur until 1935.

BEDFORD STONE RY

MAIN LINE (BEST-A)

	Mileage	County	Crossings, junctions, etc.
Rivervale	0	Lawrence	J/B&O-SW 121.0
Lawrenceport	1.4	"	
Stonington	3.0	"	

CONSTRUCTION/ABANDONMENT

Date	Act	End points	MP	Change	Main	Source	Note
1901/6	B	Rivervale-Stonington 0-	3.0	+3.0	3.0	1	
1917	X	Rivervale-Stonington 0-	3.0	-3.0	0	1	

OWNERSHIP
1901   Bedford Stone Ry

ACQUISITION/DISPOSITION RECORD
See ownership record above for line BEST-A

ACT COLUMN KEY
B Built by Bedford Stone Ry
X Abandoned

SOURCES
1 Simons and Parker, *Railroads of Indiana.*

BEE LINE

MAIN LINE (BLR-[LS-WD])
See Lake Shore & Michigan Southern line LS-WD for arrangement of stations, prior construction/abandonment record, and prior ownership

CONSTRUCTION/ABANDONMENT

Date	Act	End points	MP	Change	Main	Source	Note
1994/10	P	Handy-Stewart	80.4-91.2	+10.8	10.8	1	

OWNERSHIP
1994   Bee Line RR

ACQUISITION/DISPOSITION RECORD
See ownership record above for line BLR-[LS-WD]

ACT COLUMN KEY
P Purchased from Conrail

SOURCES
1 Simons and Parker, *Railroads of Indiana.*

BENTON CENTRAL

MAIN LINE (BENC-[CCC-H])
See Cleveland, Cincinnati, Chicago & St. Louis line CCC-H for arrangement of stations, prior construction/abandonment record, and prior ownership

CONSTRUCTION/ABANDONMENT

Date	Act	End points	MP	Change	Main	Source	Note
1988 ca.	P	Templeton-Swanington	192.6-198.6	+6.0	6.0	1	1
1989	S	Templeton-Swanington	192.6-198.6	[6.0]	0	1	

OWNERSHIP

1988	Benton Central RR

ACQUISITION/DISPOSITION RECORD
See ownership record above for line BENC-[CCC-H]

ACT COLUMN KEY
P Purchased from Conrail
S Sold to Kankakee, Beaverton & Southern

SOURCES
1 Simons and Parker, *Railroads of Indiana.*

NOTES
1. Source 1 states that the line was not operated by the owner before its sale in 1989.

C&NC RR

LIBERTY CENTER OH-WOODBURN (CNC-[NKP-LR])
See New York, Chicago & St. Louis line NKP-LR for arrangement of stations, prior construction/abandonment record, and prior ownership

CONSTRUCTION/ABANDONMENT

Date	Act	End points	MP	Change	Main	Source	Note
1998	L	Liberty Center OH-Woodburn	75.7-78.7	+3.0	3.0		

OWNERSHIP

1998	C&NC RR Corp

ACQUISITION/DISPOSITION RECORD
See ownership record above for line CNC-[NKP-LR]

ACT COLUMN KEY
L Leased from Norfolk Southern, transferred from Indiana Hi-Rail

CARTHAGE, KNIGHTSTOWN & SHIRLEY

MAIN LINE (CAKS-[CCC-M])
See Cleveland, Cincinnati, Chicago & St. Louis line CCC-M for arrangement of stations, prior construction/-abandonment record, and prior ownership. See also Indiana Eastern and Indiana Midland for prior operators.

CONSTRUCTION/ABANDONMENT

Date	Act	End points	MP	Change	Main	Source	Note
1987/4	P	Carthage-Emporia	193.2-172.7	+20.5	20.5	1	1
1988	X	Knightstown-Emporia	188.2-172.7	-15.5	5.0	1	

OWNERSHIP

1987/4	Carthage, Knightstown & Shirley RR

CARTHAGE, KNIGHTSTOWN & SHIRLEY

ACQUISITION/DISPOSITION RECORD
See ownership record above for line CAKS-[CCC-M]

ACT COLUMN KEY
P Purchased from Conrail
X Abandoned

SOURCES
1 Simons and Parker, *Railroads of Indiana*.

NOTES
1. The record is unclear, but it appears that the transfer of property was by purchase rather than by assignment of lease. The road now operates only as a tourist line.

CENTRAL INDIANA

MAIN LINE (CI-A)

	Mileage	County	Crossings, junctions, etc.
Muncie	0	Delaware	J/NKP-LF 66.7
Avondale	0.7	"	
Sharps	5.4	"	
Daleville	11.6	"	
Chesterfield	13.7	Madison	
Gridley	17.2	"	X/CCC-IA 245.7
East Yard	18.1	"	X/PRR-CR 122.2
(Crossing)	18.5	"	X/CCC-M 165.8
Anderson	18.8	"	
(Crossing)	19.2	"	X/CCC-I 248.3
(Junction)	20.5	"	J/PRR-YA 3.1
Bloomer	23.7	"	
Lapel	28.0	"	
Durbin	31.5	Hamilton	
Noblesville	37.2	"	X/NKP-LM 22.0
Westfield	43.6	"	X/MON-I 163.4
Eagletown	46.8	"	
Jolietville	48.7	"	
Rosston	51.8	Boone	
Gadsden	54.8	"	
Heath	56.3	"	
(Crossing)	61.2	"	X/CCC-H 138.0
Lebanon	61.4	"	
(Bridge)	61.8	"	B/PRR-IF 31.5
Max	67.9	"	
Advance	70.1	"	
New Ross	75.6	Montgomery	X/P&E-A 32.8
Ladoga	81.3	"	X/MON-SA 157.8
Pawnee	85.6	"	
Lapland	86.9	"	
Penobscot	88.9	"	
Browns Valley Jct.	91.7	"	
Waveland	94.8	"	
Waveland Jct.	95.9	"	J/PRR-VF 36.0
--via PRR-VF			
Sand Creek	105.3	Parke	J/PRR-VF 26.6
East Rockville	106.9	"	
Uncas	113.3	"	
(continued)			

CENTRAL INDIANA

MAIN LINE (CI-A) (continued)

	Mileage [Muncie]	County	Crossings, junctions, etc.
Uncas	113.3	Parke	
Walton	114.4	"	
Bridgeton	116.0	"	
Superior	118.6	"	
Carbon	121.2	Clay	X/CCC-L 52.8
Caledonia	123.8	"	
Brazil	127.0	"	J/PRR-V 57.0

CONSTRUCTION/ABANDONMENT

Date	Act	End points	MP	Change	Main	Source	Note
1876	B1	East Yard-Noblesville	18.1-37.5	+19.4	19.4	3	
1885	B2	Noblesville-Westfield	37.5-44.3	+6.8	26.2	3	
1886	B2	Westfield-Eagletown	44.3-47.4	+3.1	29.3	3	
1887	B2	Eagletown-Ladoga	47.4-81.3	+33.9	63.2	3	
1888	B2	Ladoga-Browns Valley Jct.	81.3-91.7	+10.4	73.6	3	
1890	B2	Browns Vall. Jct.-Waveland	91.7-94.8	+3.1		3	
1890	B2	Waveland-Waveland Jct.	94.8-95.9	+1.1	77.8	1	
1891	B4	Bridgeton-Carbon	116.0-121.2	+5.2	83.0	1	
1892	B3	Sand Creek-Bridgeton	105.3-116.0	+10.7	1	1	
1892	B3	Carbon-Brazil	121.2-127.0	+5.8	99.5	1	
1899	B3	Anderson-Muncie	18.1-0	+18.1	117.6	2	
1928	X	Muncie-East Yard	0-18.1	-18.1		2,3	
1928	X	Ladoga-Waveland Jct.	82.1-95.9	-13.8		2,3	
1928	X	Sand Creek-Brazil	105.3-127.0	-21.7	64.0	2,3	
1929	X	Advance-Ladoga	70.4-82.1	-11.7	52.3	2,3	
1943	X	Lebanon-Advance	62.1-70.4	-8.3	44.0	2,3	
1976	X	Westfield-Gadsden	40.8-54.6	-13.8	30.2	1,2	

1982	X	Gadsden-Lebanon	54.6-62.1	-7.5	22.7	1,2	
1986	X	Lapel-Westfield	28.0-42.7	-14.7		2	
1986	S1	Anderson-Lapel	18.7-28.0	[9.3]		2	
1986	Y	In Anderson	18.2-18.7	(0.5)	0		

OWNERSHIP

1876	Anderson, Lebanon & St. Louis RR (B1), of part
1881/12/23	Cleveland, Indiana & St. Louis Ry, reorganize AL&SL
1885/7/8	Midland Ry (B2), bought Cleveland, Indiana & St. Louis
1891	Chicago & South Eastern Ry (B3), bought Midland Ry
1891	Fort Wayne, Terre Haute & Southwestern (B4), of part
1892	Chicago & South Eastern Ry, leased FWTH&SW
1901	Chicago & South Eastern Ry, bought FWTH&SW
1903/3/16	Central Indiana Ry, reorganize Chicago & South Eastern, controlled by PRR and CCC&SL
1930/2/1	New York Central, leased Cleveland, Cincinnati, Chicago & St. Louis
1968/2/1	Penn Central, merge Pennsylvania and New York Central
1976/4/1	Conrail, purchase of Penn Central and Central Indiana

MANSFIELD BRANCH (CI-FWTHS)

	Mileage	County	Crossings, junctions, etc.
Bridgeton	0	Parke	J/CI-A 116.0
Mansfield	4.5	"	

CONSTRUCTION/ABANDONMENT

Date	Act	End points	MP	Change	Main	Source	Note
1891	B4	Bridgeton-Mansfield	0-4.5	+4.5	4.5	3	
1899	X	Bridgeton-Mansfield	0-4.5	-4.5	0	3	

OWNERSHIP

1891	Fort Wayne, Terre Haute & Southwestern (B4)

CENTRAL INDIANA

ACQUISITION/DISPOSITION RECORD
See ownership record above for line CI-A

ACT COLUMN KEY
B1 Built by Anderson, Lebanon & St. Louis Rr
B2 Built by Midland Ry
B3 Built by Chicago & South Eastern Ry
B4 Built by Fort Wayne, Terre Haute & Southwestern RR
S1 Sold to Central Indiana & Western as line CI&W-[CI-A]
X Abandoned

SOURCES
1 Indiana, *1995 Indiana State Rail Plan.*.
2 Simons and Parker, *Railroads of Indiana.*
3 Sulzer, *Ghost Railroads of Indiana.*

NOTES
1. The company used trackage rights between Waveland Jct. and Sand Creek over the Terre Haute & Logansport, see Pennsylvania line PRR-IF.

CENTRAL INDIANA & WESTERN RR

MAIN LINE (CEIW-[CI-A])
See Central Indiana line CI-A for arrangement of stations, prior construction/abandonment record, and prior ownership

CONSTRUCTION/ABANDONMENT

Date	Act	End points	MP	Change	Main	Source	Note
1986	P	Anderson-Lapel	19.7-29.0	+9.3	9.3	1	

OWNERSHIP

1986	Central Indiana & Western RR

ACQUISITION/DISPOSITION RECORD
See ownership record above for line CEIW-[CI-A]

ACT COLUMN KEY
P Purchased from Conrail

SOURCES
1 Simons and Parker, *Railroads of Indiana.*

CENTRAL RR OF INDIANA

MAIN LINE (CIND-[CCC-G])
See Cleveland, Cincinnati, Chicago & St. Louis line CCC-G for arrangement of stations, prior construction/abandonment record, and prior ownership.

CONSTRUCTION/ABANDONMENT

Date	Act	End points	MP	Change	Main	Source	Note
1991/12/31	P	OH state line-Shelbyville	21.5-82.6	+61.1	61.1	1	1

OWNERSHIP

1991	Central RR of Indiana

CENTRAL RR OF INDIANA

LAWRENCEBURG BRANCH (CIND-[CCC-GA])
See Cleveland, Cincinnati, Chicago & St. Louis line CCC-GA for arrangement of stations, prior construction/-abandonment record, and prior ownership.

CONSTRUCTION/ABANDONMENT

Date	Act	End points	MP	Change	Main	Source	Note
1991/12/31	P	(Junction)-Lawrenceburg	23.0-25.4	+2.4	2.4	1	
1994 ca.	X	(Junction)-MP 24.5	23.0-24.5	-1.5	0.9		2

OWNERSHIP
1991		Central RR of Indiana

IN LAWRENCEBURG (CIND-[CCC-GL])
See Cleveland, Cincinnati, Chicago & St. Louis line CCC-GL for arrangement of stations, prior construction/-abandonment record, and prior ownership.

CONSTRUCTION/ABANDONMENT

Date	Act	End points	MP	Change	Main	Source	Note
1991/12/31	P	In Lawrenceburg	25.5-27.6	(+2.1)	0	1	

OWNERSHIP
1991		Central RR of Indiana

BATESVILLE OLD MAIN (CIND-[CCC-GO1])

See Cleveland, Cincinnati, Chicago & St. Louis line CCC-GO1 for arrangement of stations, prior construction/-abandonment record, and prior ownership.

CONSTRUCTION/ABANDONMENT

Date	Act	End points	MP	Change	Main	Source	Note
1991/12/31	P	In Batesville	48.7-50.3	(+1.6)	0	1	

OWNERSHIP
1991		Central RR of Indiana

ACQUISITION/DISPOSITION RECORD

Date	Act	CIND-	End points	Change	Main	Note
1991/12/31	P	[CCC-G]	OH state line-Shelbyville	+61.1		
1991/12/31	P	[CCC-GA]	(Junction)-Lawrenceburg	+2.4		
1991/12/31	P	[CCC-GL]	In Lawrenceburg	(+2.1)		
1991/12/31	P	[CCC-GO1]	Batesville Old Main	(+1.6)	63.5	
1994 ca.	X	[CCC-GA]	(Junction)-MP 24.5	-1.5	62.0	

ACT COLUMN KEY
P Purchased from Conrail
X Abandoned

SOURCES
1. Simons and Parker, *Railroads of Indiana.*

NOTES
1. The company also has trackage rights over Conrail from Shelbyville to Indianapolis.
2. With this abandonment the company obtained trackage rights on CSX line B&O-SC to reach its own line.

CENTRAL RR OF INDIANAPOLIS

TIPTON-ARGOS LINE (CERA-[NKP-LM])
See New York, Chicago & St. Louis line NKP-LM for arrangement of stations, prior construction/abandonment record, and prior ownership.

CONSTRUCTION/ABANDONMENT

Date	Act	End points	MP	Change	Main	Source	Note
1989/8/14	L	Tipton-Argos	39.7-108.6	+68.9		1	
1989	LS	Peru-Argos	74.2-108.6	-34.4	34.5	1	
1996 ca.	XL	Kokomo-Peru	57.5-74.2	-16.7	17.8		

OWNERSHIP
1989   Central RR of Indianapolis, owned by Central Properties Co.

MARION-FRANKFORT LINE (CERA-[NKP-TB])
See New York, Chicago & St. Louis line NKP-TB for arrangement of stations, prior construction/abandonment record, and prior ownership.

CONSTRUCTION/ABANDONMENT

Date	Act	End points	MP	Change	Main	Source	Note
1989/8/14	L	Marion-Frankfort	153.8-206.2	+52.4	52.4	1	
1998	XL	Kokomo-Frankfort	183.5-206.2	-22.7	29.7		

OWNERSHIP
1989   Central RR of Indianapolis, owned by Central Properties Co

ACQUISITION/DISPOSITION RECORD

Date	Act	CIND-	End points	Change	Main	Note
1989/8/14	L	[NKP-LM]	Tipton-Argos	+68.9		
/8/14	L	[NKP-TB]	Marion-Frankfort	+52.4		
	LS	[NKP-LM]	Peru-Argos	-34.4	86.9	
1996 ca.	XL	[NKP-LM]	Kokomo-Peru	-16.7	70.2	
1998	XL	[NKP-TB]	Kokomo-Frankfort	-22.7	47.5	

ACT COLUMN KEY
L   Leased from Norfolk Southern
LS Subleased to Indiana Hi-Rail
XL Lease terminated

SOURCES
1. Simons and Parker, *Railroads of Indiana.*

NOTES
 General 1. From 1899 until the mid 1950s another company of the same name operated an industrial road in Indianapolis, which company was leased to Cleveland, Cincinnati, Chicago & St. Louis afer Feb. 7, 1917.
 General 2. This company also operates Central RR of Indiana, Kokomo Rail Corp., and Winimac Southern, which see.

CHESAPEAKE & OHIO

CHICAGO DIVISION (C&O-C)

	Mileage	County	Crossings, junctions, etc.
Cincinnati OH	0		
Newkirk OH	30.5		
(OH/IN state line)	33.0		
Peoria	33.1	Franklin	
Raymond	36.1	"	
Bath	39.0	"	
Cottage Grove	45.0	Union	X/B&O-IH 48.2
(continued)			

CHESAPEAKE & OHIO

CHICAGO DIVISION (C&O-C) (continued)

	Mileage [Cincinnati]	County	Crossings, junctions, etc.
Cottage Grove	45.0	Union	X/B&O-IH 48.2
Kitchell	50.9	"	
Witts	52.9	"	
Boston	54.9	Wayne	
South Richmond	61.9	"	
Richmond	63.0	"	
(Bridge)	63.5	"	B/PRR-I 119.7
(Bridge)	65.5	"	B/PRR-GR 2.2
Wayne	67.5	"	
Webster	69.0	"	
Williamsburg	73.9	"	
Economy	79.6	"	
Thornburg	82.3	"	
Losantville	86.5	Randolph	
(Crossing)	87.1	"	X/CCC-S 83.8
Blountsville	90.4	Henry	
Henry	92.6	"	
Medford	96.7	Delaware	
(Bridge)	102.5	"	B/CCC-I 228.5
(Bridge)	102.7	"	B/NKP-LS 172.7
Muncie	103.1	"	
(Crossing)	103.5	"	X/NKP-LF 62.2
Drew	103.5	"	X/PRR-CM 38.1
Benadum	110.3	"	
Gaston	113.6	"	
Janney	117.8	"	
Fowlerton	121.0	Grant	X/PRR-CM 22.1
Grey	126.0	"	
Jonesboro	127.3	"	
(Bridge)	131.3	"	B/CCC-M 134.1, B/NKP-TB 154.9
Marion	132.4	"	
Phoenix	134.0	"	
Sweetser	138.0	"	
Mier	141.0	"	
(Bridge)	142.9	Miami	B/PRR-L 168.0
Converse	143.7	"	
Amboy	146.8	"	
Santa Fe	152.7	"	
Oakley	155.2	"	
Peru	160.4	"	
Shops	161.3	"	
(Crossing)	162.0	"	X/NKP-LM 72.6
CW	162.7	"	X/WAB-P 204.4
Hoovers	170.0	Cass	X/PRR-LE 10.1
Twelve Mile	174.5	"	
Fulton	180.4	Fulton	
Kewanna	189.8	"	X/PRR-LS 21.7
Lake Bruce	194.1	"	
Lawton	198.0	Pulaski	
Beardstown	202.7	"	
Lena Park	210.0	Starke	
North Judson	213.3	"	X/ERIE-C 199.4, X/LS-WK 433.3
English Lake	217.5	"	
LaCrosse	220.5	LaPorte	X/PM-W 0.3
Wade	221.5	"	X/MON-N 32.5
(continued)			

CHESAPEAKE & OHIO

CHICAGO DIVISION (C&O-C) (continued)

	Mileage [Cincinnati]	County	Crossings, junctions, etc.
Wade	221.5	LaPorte	
Liberty View	227	Porter	
Malden	230.9	"	
Beatrice	240.0	"	
Merrillville	248.7	Lake	
Griffith	254.0	"	X/EJE-A 36.2, X/ERIE-C 240.2, X/GTW-C 36.1, X/MC-WJ 10.3
Highlands	256.9	"	X/LS-WD 7.2
Saxony	259.5	"	
HY	260.6	"	J/ERIE-C 246.8
(Hammond)	263.0)	"	

CONSTRUCTION/ABANDONMENT

Date	Act	End points	MP	Change	Main	Source	Note
1902	B1	Muncie-North Judson	103.1-213.3	+110.2		1	
1902	B1	North Judson-Beatrice	213.3-240.0	+26.7	195.0	1	
1904	B2	Peoria-Cottage Grove	33.0-45.0	+12.0		1	
1904	B2	Beatrice-Griffith	240.0-254.0	+14.0	221.0	1	
1907	B2	Griffith-HY	254.0-260.6	+6.6	227.6	1	

1982	X	Malden-HY	231.0-260.6	-29.6	198.0	1	
1987	X	Twelve Mile-Santa Fe	174.5-153.8	-20.7	177.3	1	1
1988	X	Twelve Mile-North Judson	174.5-212.5	-38.0	139.3	1,2	
1989	X	Richmond-Marion	62.9-134.2	-71.3	68.0	1,2	
1992	S1	Marion-Amboy	134.2-146.8	[12.6]	55.4	1	

OWNERSHIP

1901	Cincinnati, Richmond & Muncie RR (B1)
1902	Cincinnati, Richmond & Muncie, merged Chicago & Cincinnati
1903	Chicago, Cincinnati & Louisville RR (B2), merged Cinci., Rich. & Muncie and another road
1904	(Pere Marquette RR, control of Chicago, Cincinnati & Louisville)
1905	(Cincinnati, Hamilton & Dayton, leased Pere Marquette)
1910/7/2	Chesapeake & Ohio Ry of Indiana (controlled by Chesapeake & Ohio), reorganize Chi., Cinci., & Louisv. and cancel PM lease of CC&L
1934	Chesapeake & Ohio, merged C&O of Indiana
1973/6/15	Chessie System, control of Chesapeake & Ohio
1980/11/1	CSX Corp., merged Chessie System (with control of C&O)
1986/7/1	CSX Transportation, control of C&O (from CSX Corp.)
1987/9/2	CSX Transportation, merger of Chesapeake & Ohio

ACQUISITION/DISPOSITION RECORD

For period prior to 1947 see record above for line C&O-C.

On 1947/4/1 this company merged Pere Marquette. The Acquisition/Disposition Record is continued in two places: under the original company and under Chesapeake & Ohio. The property acquired was:

Line desig.	End points	MP	Main
[PM-C]	New Buffalo MI-Porter	117.9-136.6	18.7
[PM-W]	LaCrosse-New Buffalo MI	0-33.0	33.0
		TOTAL	51.7

1947 YEAR   C&O=227.6 PM=51.7 SYSTEM=279.3

In 1963 this company acquired control of Baltimore & Ohio. The B&O Acquisition/-Disposition Record is continued in two places: under the original constituent companies and under Chesapeake & Ohio. The property acquired was:

Line desig.	End points	MP	Main
[B&O-C]	Willard OH-Chicago IL	110.3-256.6	146.3
[B&O-IN]	Hamilton OH-Indianapolis	45.0-123.6	78.6
[B&O-IS]	Indianapolis-Springfield	124.9-201.2	76.3
(continued)			

CHESAPEAKE & OHIO

ACQUISITION/DISPOSITION RECORD (continued)

[B&O-IB]	Brazil-West Melcher	0-25.1	25.1
[B&O-SC]	Cincinnati OH-N. Vernon	19.8-72.2	52.4
[B&O-SW]	N. Vernon-Washington	72.2-170.4	98.2
[B&O-SI]	Washington-St. Louis MO	170.4-189.4	19.0
[B&O-SV]	N. Vernon-Louisville KY	0-54.0	54.0
[B&O-SJ]	Watson-Jeffersonville	46.6-53.5	6.9
[B&O-TU]	In Union City	47.1-47.3	0.2
	1963 YEAR	B&O=557.0 C&O=227.6 PM=51.7 SYSTEM=836.4	

Date	Act	C&O--	End points	Change	Main	Note
1965	X	[B&O-IB]	West Melcher-Brazil	-25.1		
		YEAR	B&O=531.9 C&O=227.6 PM=51.7 SYSTEM=		811.3	

On 1973/6/15 Chessie System acquired control of this company. The Acquisition/-Disposition Record is continued in two places: under the original constituent companies and under Chessie System.

On 1980/11/1 CSX Corporation merged Chessie System (and its control of Chesapeake & Ohio). The Acquisition/Disposition Record is continued in two places: under the original constituent companies and under CSX Corporation.

1982	X	C	Malden-HY	-29.6	198.0	

On 1986/7/1 CSX Transportation obtained control and on 1987/9/2 merged Chesapeake & Ohio. The Acquisition/Disposition Record is continued in two places: under Chesapeake & Ohio and under CSX Transportation.

1987	X	C	Twelve Mile-Santa Fe	-20.7	177.3	1
1988	X	C	Twelve Mile-North Judson	-38.0	139.3	
1989	X	C	Richmond-Muncie	-71.3	68.0	
1992	S1	C	Marion-Amboy	[12.6]	55.4	

ACT COLUMN KEY
B1 Built by Cincinnati, Richmond & Muncie RR
B2 Built by Chicago, Cincinnati & Louisville RR
S1 Sold to Kokomo Rail Corp.
X   Abandoned

SOURCES
1. Indiana, *1995 Indiana State Rail Plan.*
2. Simons and Parker, *Railroads of Indiana.*

NOTES
1. The segment between MP 162.2 and MP 162.7 apparently was conveyed to Norfolk Southern as industrial track.

CHESSIE SYSTEM

On 1973/6/15 Chessie System acquired control of Chesapeake & Ohio. Its Acquisition/-Disposition Record is continued in two places: under the original constituent companies and under Chessie System. The property acquired was:

CHS-Line desig.	End points	MP	Main
[B&O-C]	Willard OH-Chicago IL	110.3-256.6	146.3
[B&O-IN]	Hamilton OH-Indianapolis	45.0-123.6	78.6
[B&O-IS]	Indianapolis-Springfield	124.9-201.2	76.3
[B&O-SC]	Cincinnati OH-N. Vernon	19.8-72.2	52.4
[B&O-SW]	N. Vernon-Washington	72.2-170.4	98.2
[B&O-SI]	Washington-St. Louis MO	170.4-189.4	19.0
[B&O-SV]	N. Vernon-Louisville KY	0-54.0	54.0
[B&O-SJ]	Watson-Jeffersonville	46.6-53.5	6.9
[B&O-TU]	At Union City	47.1-47.3	0.2
(continued)			

CHESSIE SYSTEM

The property acquired was: (continued)

CHS- Line desig.		End points		MP	Main
[C&O-C]		Cincinnati OH-Hammond		33.0-260.6	227.6
[PM-C]		New Buffalo MI-Porter		117.9-136.6	18.7
[PM-W]		LaCrosse-New Buffalo MI		0-33.0	33.0
				TOTAL	811.2
1973	YEAR		B&O=531.9 C&O=227.6 PM=51.7 SYSTEM=811.2		

Date	Act	CHS-	End points		Change
1976	P2	[LS-TF]	In Auburn	+1.7	
YEAR			B&O=533.6 C&O=227.6 PM=51.7 SYSTEM=812.9		
1980	X	[B&O-SV]	North Vernon-Nabb	-28.5	
YEAR			B&O=505.1 C&O=227.6 PM=51.7 SYSTEM=784.4		

On 1980/11/1 this company was conveyed to CSX Corporation. Its Acquisition/Disposition Record is continued in two places: under the original constituent companies and under CSX Corporation.

ACT COLUMN KEY
P2   Purchased from Penn Central
X   Abandoned

CHICAGO & EASTERN ILLINOIS

EVANSVILLE DIVISION (CEI-E)

	Mileage	County	Crossings, junctions, etc.
Chicago IL	0		
Danville	123.1		
Brewer IL	126.5		
IL/IN state line	128.6		
R. B. Jct.	128.9	Vermillion	f. Rileysburg
Gessie	131.0	"	
Perrysville	134.2	"	
Dickason	137.6	"	
Dickason Pit	138.1	"	
Cayuga	141.1	"	X/NKP-TC 266.5
Walnut Grove	143.7	"	
Newport	146.9	"	
WRO Jct.	149.7	"	
Worthy	150.8	"	
Wabash River Ordnance	151.0	"	

(continued)

CHICAGO & EASTERN ILLINOIS

EVANSVILLE DIVISION (CEI-E) (continued)

	Mileage [Chicago]	County	Crossings, junctions, etc.
Montezuma	153.3	Vermillion	f. West Montezuma
Hillsdale	154.6	"	X/B&O-ID 192.7
Summit Grove	158.4	"	
Standard Pit	159.8	"	
(Junction)	162.2	"	J/CEI-EU 0
Clinton	162.9	"	
Lyford	164.2	"	
Atherton	167.3	Vigo	
Otter Creek Jct.	171.9	"	J/CEI-EZ 171.9, J/PRR-VC 5.8
North Terre Haute	173.3	"	
Dewey	173.8	"	J/PRR-VT1 2.9
(Crossing)	174.7	"	X/MILW-T 174.7, J/PRR-VT3 72.9
Haley	176.5	"	J/CCC-L 70.5
Terre Haute	177.5	"	X/PRR-V 72.6
(Junction)	177.8	"	J/conn to PRR-V 72.4, 0.4 mi.
Wabash Avenue	178.0	"	
Poplar Street	178.3	"	
Baker	179.9	"	
Spring Hill	181.7	"	X/CCC-T 4.7, X/MILW-T 182.7
Young	186.2	"	
Pimento	189.8	"	
(Junction)	192.1	"	J/CEI-EP 0
Farmersburg	192.9	Sullivan	
New Pittsburg Jct.	193.4	"	J/CEI-EN 0
(Junction)	196.4	"	J/industrial road
Standard	196.8	"	J/CEI-ES 196.8
Standard	196.8	Sullivan	J/CEI-ES 196.8
Shelburn	198.6	"	
Sullivan	203.7	"	X/IC-NE 110.0
Paxton	209.3	"	
Carlisle	213.2	"	
Oaktown	220.0	Knox	
Busseron	222.6	"	
Emison	224.7	"	
Smith	229.5	"	
Vincennes	234.7	"	X/B&O-SI 188.6, CCC-LV 121.4, J/PRR-IV 117.0
Alice	236.4	"	
Purcell	241.0	"	
Vollmer	244.0	"	
Cantaloupe	245.2	"	
Decker	246.3	"	
Hazleton	248.7	Gibson	
Miller	252.3	"	
Patoka	255.3	"	
Gibson	257.9	"	
Princeton Jct.	248.2	"	X/SOU-U 161.4
Princeton	259.0	"	
King	262.8	"	
Mt. Vernon Jct.	265.3	"	J/CEI-EM 265.3
Fort Branch	266.6	"	
Haubstadt	269.7	"	
Stacer	273.6	"	
Ingle	276.3	Vanderburgh	
(Junction)	279.5	"	J/CEI-EB 279.5
Straight Line Jct. (continued)	283.0	"	J/CEI-J 133.5, J/CCC-T 130.9

CHICAGO & EASTERN ILLINOIS

EVANSVILLE DIVISION (CEI-E) (continued)

	Mileage [Chicago]	County	Crossings, junctions, etc.
Straight Line Jct.	283.0	Vanderburgh	
Wansford	283.6	"	
Belt Yard	284.6	"	J/CEI-EJ 0
Union Track Jct.	285.8	"	J/CEI-EO 285.8, J/SOU-UE 0.7
Evansville (2nd)	287.2	"	J/L&N-SE 325.0

CONSTRUCTION/ABANDONMENT

Date	Act	End points	MP	Change	Main	Source	Note
1853	B1	Terre Haute-Union Trk.Jct.	177.5-285.8	+108.3	108.3	1	
1860	B1	Terre Haute-Otter Creek J.	177.5-171.9	+5.6	113.9		
1871/10/26	B2	Otter Cr.J.-Danville IL	171.9-128.6	+43.3	157.2	2	
1872	B1	Union Trk.Jct.-Evansville	285.8-287.2	+1.4	158.6		
1947	B15	Alice-Decker	236.4-246.3	-0.04	158.6	2	2
1976	Y	MP 279.5-Evansville	279.5-287.2	(7.7)	150.9		

OWNERSHIP

1853	Evansville & Crawfordsville (B1), of part
1871	Evansville, Terre Haute & Chicago (B2), of part
1877/3/5	Evansville & Terre Haute (B8), rename Evansville & Crawfordsville
1880	Chicago & Eastern Illinois, lease ETH&C
1899/12/27	Chicago & Eastern Illinois, buy ETH&C
1911/7/20	Chicago & Eastern Illinois, merge E&TH
1920/12/13	Chicago & Eastern Illinois Ry, reorganize C&EI RR
1940/6/27	Chicago & Eastern Illinois RR (B15), reorganize C&EI Ry
1967/5/12	Missouri Pacific RR, buy C&EI
1967	Louisville & Nashville RR, buy line Danville-Evansville
1983/1	Seaboard System, merge Louisville & Nashville
1986/7/1	CSX Transportation, merge Seaboard System

EVANSVILLE NEW LINE (CEI-EB)

	Mileage	County	Crossings, junctions, etc.
(Junction)	279.5	Vanderburgh	J/CEI-E 279.5
(Junction)	281.5	"	J/CCC-LV 154.1
Harwood	283.9	"	
(Crossing)	285.1	"	X/IC-NM 245.5
8th Avenue	287.4	"	J/L&N-SE 324.7

CONSTRUCTION/ABANDONMENT

Date	Act	End points	MP	Change	Main	Source	Note
1976	B16	MP 279.5-MP 281.5	279.5-281.5	+2.0			
1976	P1	MP 281.5-8th Avenue	281.5-287.4	+5.9	7.9		

OWNERSHIP

1976	Louisville & Nashville (B16)
1983/1	Seaboard System, merge Louisville & Nashville
1986/7/1	CSX Transportation, merge Seaboard System

EVANSVILLE ORIGINAL MAIN (CEI-EO)

	Mileage	County	Crossings, junctions, etc.
Union Track Jct.	285.8	Vanderburgh	J/CEI-E 285.8, J/SOU-UE 0.7
Evansville (1st)	286.5	"	

CONSTRUCTION/ABANDONMENT

Date	Act	End points	MP	Change	Main	Source	Note
1853	B1	In Evansville	285.8-286.5	+0.7	0.7	1	
1976	Y	In Evansville	285.8-286.5	(0.7)	0		

(continued)

CHICAGO & EASTERN ILLINOIS

EVANSVILLE ORIGINAL MAIN (CEI-EO) (continued)
OWNERSHIP

1853	Evansville & Crawfordsville (B1)
1877/3/5	Evansville & Terre Haute, rename Evansville & Crawfordsville
1911/7/20	Chicago & Eastern Illinois, merge E&TH
1920/12/13	Chicago & Eastern Illinois Ry, reorganize C&EI RR
1940/6/27	Chicago & Eastern Illinois RR, reorganize C&EI Ry
1967/5/12	Missouri Pacific RR, buy C&EI
1967	Louisville & Nashville RR, buy line Evansville Belt
1983/1	Seaboard System, merge Louisville & Nashville
1986/7/1	CSX Transportation, merge Seaboard System

EVANSVILLE BELT LINE (CEI-EJ)

	Mileage	County	Crossings, junctions, etc.
Belt Yard	0	Vanderburgh	J/CEI-E 284.6
(Crossing)	2.2	"	X/IC-NM 246.6
(Crossing)	2.8	"	X/CC-LE 159.2
(End)	4.0	"	

CONSTRUCTION/ABANDONMENT

Date	Act	End points	MP	Change	Main	Source	Note
1882	B7	In Evansville	0-4.0	+4.0	4.0	1	
1976	Y	In Evansville	0-4.0	(4.0)	0		

OWNERSHIP

1882	Evansville Belt Ry (B7)
1911/7/20	Chicago & Eastern Illinois, merged Evansville Belt
1920/12/13	Chicago & Eastern Illinois Ry, reorganize C&EI RR
1940/6/27	Chicago & Eastern Illinois RR, reorganize C&EI Ry
1967/5/12	Missouri Pacific RR, bought C&EI
1967	Louisville & Nashville RR, bought line Evansville Belt
1983/1	Seaboard System, merged Louisville & Nashville
1986/7/1	CSX Transportation, merged Seaboard System

JUDYVILLE BRANCH (CEI-CJ)

	Mileage [Chicago]	County	Crossings, junctions, etc.
Rossville Jct. IL	107.1	Vermillion IL	
Johannott IL	110.1	"	
(IL/IN state line)	113.5		
Pence	114.2	Warren	
Stewart	116.0	"	X/LS-WD 90.1
Finney	117.9	"	
Judyville	120.4	"	

CONSTRUCTION/ABANDONMENT

Date	Act	End points	MP	Change	Main	Source	Note
1903	B13	Rossville Jct IL-Judyville	113.5-120.4	+6.9	6.9	1	
1973 ca.	X	Rossville Jct IL-Judyville	113.5-120.4	-6.9	0	2	

OWNERSHIP

1903	Rossville & Eastern Illinois (B13)
1903	Chicago & Eastern Illinois RR, buy Rossville & Eastern Illinois
1920/12/13	Chicago & Eastern Illinois Ry, reorganize C&EI RR
1940/6/27	Chicago & Eastern Illinois RR, reorganize C&EI Ry
1967/5/12	Missouri Pacific RR, buy C&EI

CHICAGO & EASTERN ILLINOIS

FREELAND PARK BRANCH (CEI-CF)

	Mileage [Chicago]	County	Crossings, junctions, etc.
Milford IL	88.1		
Stockland	94.5		
Dawson Park IL	97.1		
(IL/IN state line)	97.9		
Freeland Park	99.7	Benton	

CONSTRUCTION/ABANDONMENT

Date	Act	End points	MP	Change	Main	Source	Note
1901/11/1	B14	Milford IL-Freeland Park	97.9-99.7	+1.8	1.8	3	
1950/3/7	X	Milford IL-Freeland Park	97.9-99.7	-1.8	0	3	4

OWNERSHIP

1901	Chicago & Eastern Illinois RR (B14)
1920/12/13	Chicago & Eastern Illinois Ry, reorganize C&EI RR
1940/6/27	Chicago & Eastern Illinois RR, reorganize C&EI Ry

UNIVERSAL MINE BRANCH (CEI-EU)

	Mileage	County	Crossings, junctions, etc.
(Junction)	0	Vermillion	J/CEI-EU 162.2
Universal Mine	8.5	"	

CONSTRUCTION/ABANDONMENT

Date	Act	End points	MP	Change	Main	Source	Note
1920 ca.	B15	Line	0-8.5	+8.5	8.5		
1994	X	Line	0-8.5	-8.5	0	1,2	

OWNERSHIP

1920/12/13	Chicago & Eastern Illinois Ry (B15)
1940/6/27	Chicago & Eastern Illinois RR, reorganize C&EI Ry
1967/5/12	Missouri Pacific RR, bought C&EI
1967	Louisville & Nashville RR, bought line Evansville Belt
1983/1	Seaboard System, merged Louisville & Nashville
1986/7/1	CSX Transportation, merged Seaboard System

COAL CREEK BRANCH (CEI-EC)

	Mileage	County	Crossings, junctions, etc.
Bismarck IL	0		
(IL/IN state line)	5.0		
Sumner	7.0	Warren	
Taylor	10.3	"	
Gravel Pit	13.1	"	
Fountain			
Covington	15.4	"	
Covington Jct.	15.6	"	X/P&E-A 72.1
Coal Creek	24.0	"	

CONSTRUCTION/ABANDONMENT

Date	Act	End points	MP	Change	Main	Source	Note
1872/8	B3A	Covington-Coal Creek	15.6-24.0	+8.4	8.4	3	
1873/7	B3A	Bismarck IL-Covington	5.0-15.6	+10.6	19.0	3	
1879/6/15	X	Bismarck IL-Covington	5.0-15.6	-10.6	8.4	3	5
1888	X	Covington-Coal Creek	15.6-24.0	-8.4	0	3	

OWNERSHIP

1872	Chicago, Danville & Vincennes RR (B3A)
1877/2	State Line & Covington RR, reorganize Chicago, Danville & Vincennes
1877/9/1	Chicago & Eastern Illinois RR, merge State Line & Covington

CHICAGO & EASTERN ILLINOIS

ROCKVILLE BRANCH (CEI-ER)

	Mileage [Terre Haute]	County	Crossings, junctions, etc.
Otter Creek Jct.	5.6	Vigo	J/CEI-E 171.9
Rosedale	12.2	Parke	
Jessups	14.9	"	
Catlin	17.8	"	
Rockville	22.9	"	

CONSTRUCTION/ABANDONMENT

Date	Act	End points	MP	Change	Main	Source	Note
1860	B1	Rockville-Otter Creek Jct.	5.6-22.9	+17.3	17.3	1	
1872	L1	Rockville-Otter Creek Jct.	5.6-22.9	<17.3>	0	2	
1924	S2	Rockville-Otter Creek Jct.	5.6-22.9	[<17.3.]		2	

OWNERSHIP

1860	Evansville & Crawfordsville (B1)
1872	Logansport, Crawfordsville & South Western, lease line from E&C
1877/3/5	Evansville & Terre Haute, rename Evansville & Crawfordsville
1911/7/20	Chicago & Eastern Illinois, merge E&TH
1920/12/13	Chicago & Eastern Illinois Ry, reorganize C&EI RR

BRAZIL BRANCH (CEI-EZ)

	Mileage [Chicago]	County	Crossings, junctions, etc.
Otter Creek Jct.	171.9	Vigo	J/CEI-E 171.9
Burnett	175.0	"	X/CCC-I 63.9
Burnett Siding	176.5	"	
Dixie Line Mine	179.3	"	
Brazil Clay Co.	183.6	Clay	
Brazil	184.4	"	
(Junction)	184.6	"	J/PRR-V 57.1

CONSTRUCTION/ABANDONMENT

Date	Act	End points	MP	Change	Main	Source	Note
1878	B5	Otter Creek Jct.-Brazil	171.9-184.6	+12.7	12.7	1	

1977	X	Otter Creek Jct.-Brazil	171.9-184.6	-12.7	0	1	

OWNERSHIP

1878	Indiana Block Coal RR (B5)
1880	Chicago & Eastern Illinois RR, lease Indiana Block Coal RR
1899	Chicago & Eastern Illinois RR, buy Indiana Block Coal RR
1920/12/13	Chicago & Eastern Illinois Ry, reorganize C&EI RR
1940/6/27	Chicago & Eastern Illinois RR, reorganize C&EI Ry
1967/5/12	Missouri Pacific RR, buy C&EI
1967	Louisville & Nashville RR, buy line

LACROSSE-BRAZIL LINE (CEI-IA)

For arrangement of stations, see Chicago, Attica & Southern line CAS-A and Baltimore & Ohio line B&O-IB

CONSTRUCTION/ABANDONMENT

Date	Act	End points	MP	Change	Main	Source	Note
1874	B4	Attica-Veedersburg	82.9-95.7	+12.8	12.8	2,3	
1882	B5	Veedersburg-Yeddo	95.7-102.8	+7.1	19.9	2,3	
1883	B9	Attica-Fair Oaks	82.9-26.6	+56.3	76.2	2,3	
1885	B9	Yeddo-Brazil	102.8-144.7	+41.9	118.1	2,3	
1887	B12	Fair Oaks-LaCrosse	26.6-0	+26.6	144.7	2,3	1
1922/12/2	S1	LaCrosse-West Melcher	0-119.6	-119.6		1,3	
1922	S5	West Melcher-Brazil	119.6-144.7	-25.1	0	1,3	

(continued)

CHICAGO & EASTERN ILLINOIS

LACROSSE-BRAZIL LINE (CEI-IA) (continued)
OWNERSHIP

1874	Indiana North & South RR (B4), of part
1879	Chicago & Block Coal RR (B5), buy Indiana North & South
1883	Chicago & Great Southern Ry (B9), merge Chicago & Block Coal
1886/4	Chicago & Indiana Coal Ry (B12), merge C&GS and Indiana Ry
1892/6/1	Chicago & Eastern Illinois, lease C&IC
1894/6/6	Chicago & Eastern Illinois, merge C&IC
1922/12/2	Chicago, Attica & Southern RR, buy LaCrosse-West Melcher
1922	Baltimore & Ohio buy line, West Melcher-Brazil

STATE LINE JCT. BRANCH (CEI-IB)
For arrangement of stations, see Chicago, Attica & Southern line CAS-B.

CONSTRUCTION/ABANDONMENT

Date	Act	End points	MP	Change	Main	Source	Note
1888	B12	Percy Jct.-State Line Jct.	0-21.0	+21.0	21.0	2,3	
1922/12/2	S1	Percy Jct.-State Line Jct.	0-21.0	-21.0	0	1,3	

OWNERSHIP

1888	Chicago & Indiana Coal Ry (B12)
1892/6/1	Chicago & Eastern Illinois, leased C&IC
1894/6/6	Chicago & Eastern Illinois, merged C&IC
1922/12/2	Chicago, Attica & Southern RR, bought C&EI line

EVANSVILLE & INDIANAPOLIS LINE (CEI-J)
For arrangement of stations and subsequent ownership see Cleveland, Cincinnati, Chicago & St. Louis line CCC-T.

CONSTRUCTION/ABANDONMENT

Date	Act	End points	MP	Change	Main	Source	Note
1876 ca.	B3	Terre Haute-Clay City	0-25.5	+25.5	25.5	1	
1882	B6	Clay City-Worthington	25.5-39.3	+13.8	39.3	1	
1884 ca.	B10	Str. Line Jct.-Maysville	133.5-82.3	+51.2	90.5	1	
1885 ca.	B11	Worthington-Maysville	39.3-82.3	+43.0	133.5	1	1
1920/6/3	S3	Line	0-133.5	-133.5	0	2	

OWNERSHIP

1876	Cincinnati & Terre Haute (B3), of part
1878	Terre Haute & Southeastern (B6), bought Cincinnati & Terre Haute
1884	Indianapolis & Evansville (B10), of part
1885	Evansville, Washington & Brazil (B11), of part
1886/1	Evansville & Indianapolis RR, merge TH&SE, I&E, and EW&B
1899 ca.	Chicago & Eastern Illinois, acquired E&I
1920/6/3	Evansville, Indianapolis & Terre Haute Ry, bought line

BRAZIL BRANCH (CEI-JB)
For arrangement of stations, see Pennsylvania line PRR-VB.

CONSTRUCTION/ABANDONMENT

Date	Act	End points	MP	Change	Main	Source	Note
1888 ca.	L1	Brazil-Saline City	0-11.5	+11.5	11.5	3	
1916	XL	Brazil-Saline City	0-11.5	-11.5	0		

OWNERSHIP

1888	Evansville & Indianapolis RR
1899 ca.	Chicago & Eastern Illinois, acquired E&I

(See Pennsylvania line PRR-VB for subsequent Ownership and Construction/Abandonment record)

CHICAGO & EASTERN ILLINOIS

LANCASTER BRANCH (CEI-JL)

	Mileage	County	Crossings, junctions, etc.
Lancaster Jct.	0	Clay	J/CCC-T 27.6
(Junction)	1.0	"	J/CEI-JL1 0
Woodside	3.0	Owen	

CONSTRUCTION/ABANDONMENT

Date	Act	End points	MP	Change	Main	Source	Note
1880	B6	Lancaster Jct.-Woodside	0-3.0	+3.0	3.0	3	
1910 ca.	X	MP 1.0-Woodside	1.0-3.0	-2.0	1.0	3	
1917	X	MP 0.4-MP 1.0	0.4-1.0	-0.6	0.4	3	
1919	X	Lancaster Jct.-MP 0.4	0-0.4	-0.4	0	3	

OWNERSHIP

1880	Terre Haute & Southeastern (B6)
1886/1	Evansville & Indianapolis RR, merge TH&SE
1899 ca.	Chicago & Eastern Illinois, acquire E&I

HARRISON MINE SPUR (CEI-JL1)

	Mileage	County	Crossings, junctions, etc.
(Junction)	0	Clay	J/CEI-JL 1.0
(Harrison Mines)	1.0	"	

CONSTRUCTION/ABANDONMENT

Date	Act	End points	MP	Change	Main	Source	Note
1885 ca.	B6	Line	0-1.0	+1.0	1.0	3	
1917	X	Line	0-1.0	-1.0	0	3	

OWNERSHIP

1885	Terre Haute & Southeastern (B6)
1886/1	Evansville & Indianapolis RR, merge TH&SE
1899 ca.	Chicago & Eastern Illinois, acquire E&I

NEW PITTSBURG BRANCH (CEI-EN)

	Mileage	County	Crossings, junctions, etc.
New Pittsburg Jct.	0	Sullivan	J/CEI-E 193.4
(Crossing)	2	"	X/MILW-TSA
Biddles Switch		"	
Lewis		"	
Jackson Hill Jct.		"	J/CEI-ENJ 0
New Pittsburg	8.1	"	

CONSTRUCTION/ABANDONMENT

Date	Act	End points	MP	Change	Main	Source	Note
1887	B8	Line	0-8.1	+8.1	8.1	3	
1900	X	Line	0-8.1	-8.1	0	3	

OWNERSHIP

1887	Evansville & Terre Haute (B8)

JACKSON HILL BRANCH (CEI-ENJ)

	Mileage	County	Crossings, junctions, etc.
Jackson Hill Jct.	0	Sullivan	J/CEI-EN
Hymera	1	"	J/CEI-ES 204.3
(Hymera Jct.)	2	"	
Star City Jct.	3	"	J/CEI-ENS 0, J/CEI-ES 202
Jackson Hill	6.7		

CHICAGO & EASTERN ILLINOIS

JACKSON HILL BRANCH (CEI-ENJ) (continued)
CONSTRUCTION/ABANDONMENT

Date	Act	End points	MP	Change	Main	Source	Note
1893	B8	Line	0-6.7	+6.7	6.7	3	
1900 ca.	X	Line	0-6.7	-6.7	0		

OWNERSHIP
| 1893 | | Evansville & Terre Haute (B8) | | | | | |

STAR CITY BRANCH (CEI-ENS)

	Mileage	County	Crossings, junctions, etc.
Star City Jct.	0	Sullivan	J/CEI-ENJ 3, J/CEI-ES 202
Star City	2.3	"	

CONSTRUCTION/ABANDONMENT

Date	Act	End points	MP	Change	Main	Source	Note
1893	B8	Star City Jct.-Star City	0-2.3	+2.3	2.3	3	
1900 ca.	X	Star City Jct.-Star City	0-2.3	-2.3	0		

OWNERSHIP
| 1893 | | Evansville & Terre Haute (B8) | | | | | |

SULLIVAN COUNTY COAL BRANCH (CEI-ES)

	Mileage [Chicago]	County	Crossings, junctions, etc.
Standard	196.8	Sullivan	J/CEI-E 196.8
(Crossing)	197.9	"	X/MILW-TSA
Kolsem Jct.	198.9	"	J/CEI-ESM 198.9
(Jackson Hole Mine	200.5)	"	
Abbott	201.9	"	X/MILW-TS 11.0
Star City Jct.	202	"	J/CEI-ENJ 3, J/CEI-ENS 0
Hymera Jct.	203.4	"	J/CEI-ESP 203.4
Hymera	204.3	"	J/CEI-ENJ 1

CONSTRUCTION/ABANDONMENT

Date	Act	End points	MP	Change	Main	Source	Note
1900	B14	Standard-Hymera	196.8-204.3	+7.5	7.5	3	7
1937	X	MP 201-Hymera	201.0-204.3	-3.3	4.2	3	
1942	X	MP 199.5-MP 201	199.5-201.0	-1.5	2.7	3	
1965 ca.	X	Standard-MP 199.5	196.8-199.5	-2.7	0		

OWNERSHIP
1900		Chicago & Eastern Illinois RR (B14)					
1920/12/13		Chicago & Eastern Illinois Ry, reorganize C&EI RR					
1940/6/27		Chicago & Eastern Illinois RR, reorganize C&EI Ry					

NEW PITTSBURG SPUR (CEI-ESP)

	Mileage	County	Crossings, junctions, etc.
Hymera Jct.	203.4	Sullivan	J/CEI-ES 203.4
New Pittsburg	208.2	"	

CONSTRUCTION/ABANDONMENT

Date	Act	End points	MP	Change	Main	Source	Note
1900	B14	Hymera Jct.-New Pittsburg	203.4-208.2	+4.8	4.8	3	
1921	X	MP 206.4-New Pittsburg	206.4-208.2	-1.8	3.0	3	
1930	X	MP 205.4-MP 206.4	205.4-206.4	-1.0	2.0	3	
1931 ca.	X	Hymera Jct.-MP 205.4	203.4-205.4	-2.0	0	3	

OWNERSHIP
| 1900 | | Chicago & Eastern Illinois RR (B14) | | | | | |
| 1920/12/13 | | Chicago & Eastern Illinois Ry, reorganize C&EI RR | | | | | |

CHICAGO & EASTERN ILLINOIS

MILDRED BRANCH (CEI-ESM)

	Mileage	County	Crossings, junctions, etc.
Kolsem Jct.	198.9	Sullivan	J/CEI-ES 198.9
Peerless	202.4	"	

CONSTRUCTION/ABANDONMENT

Date	Act	End points	MP	Change	Main	Source	Note
1900 ca.	B14	Kolsem Jct.-Peerless	198.9-202.4	+3.5	3.5		
1955	X	Kolsem Jct.-Peerless	198.9-202.4	-3.5	0	3	

OWNERSHIP

1900	Chicago & Eastern Illinois RR (B14)
1920/12/13	Chicago & Eastern Illinois Ry, reorganize C&EI RR

MT. VERNON SUBDIVISION (CEI-EM)

	Mileage [Chicago]	County	Crossings, junctions, etc.
Mt. Vernon Jct.	265.3	Gibson	J/CEI-E 265.3
McGray	268.1	"	
Owensville	271.5	"	
Mounts	274.4	"	
Knowles	276.0	"	
(Bridge)	277.2	Posey	B/CCC-LE 142.8
Cynthiana	277.4	"	
Poseyville	281.8	"	X/IC-NM 229.2
Wilson	283.3	"	
Wadesville	286.5	"	
Hepburn	288.9	"	
Oliver	291.8	"	
Springfield	293.6	"	
Solitude	295.7	"	
Erwin	298.4	"	
(Crossing)	301.2	"	X/L&N-S 342.0
Mt. Vernon (End of track)	302.1	"	

CONSTRUCTION/ABANDONMENT

Date	Act	End points	MP	Change	Main	Source	Note
1883	B8	Mt. Vernon Jct.-Mt. Vernon	265.3-302.1	+36.8	36.8	1	
1982	Y	In Mt. Vernon	300.5-302.1	(1.6)			
1982	X	Poseyville-Mt. Vernon	281.8-300.5	-18.7	16.5	1	
1987	X	Mt. Vernon Jct.-Owensville	265.3-270.8	-5.5		1	
1987	S4	Owensville-Poseyville	270.8-281.8	[11.0]	0	2	
1998 ca.	X	Owensville-Cynthiana	270.8-277.2	[-6.4]	0		

OWNERSHIP

1883	Evansville & Terre Haute (B8)
1911/7/20	Chicago & Eastern Illinois, merge E&TH
1920/12/13	Chicago & Eastern Illinois Ry, reorganize C&EI RR
1940/6/27	Chicago & Eastern Illinois RR, reorganize C&EI Ry
1967/5/12	Missouri Pacific RR, buy C&EI
1967	Louisville & Nashville RR, buy line Mt. Vernon Jct.-Mt. Vernon
1983/1	Seaboard System, merge Louisville & Nashville
1986/7/1	CSX Transportation, merge Seaboard System

CHICAGO & EASTERN ILLINOIS

NEW PITTSBURGH BRANCH (CEI-EP)

	Mileage	County	Crossings, junctions, etc.
(Junction)	0	Vigo	J/CEI-E 192.1
New Pittsburgh		Sullivan	
Old Pittsburgh		"	
Rose Hill	9.7	"	

CONSTRUCTION/ABANDONMENT

Date	Act	End points	MP	Change	Main	Source	Note
1910 ca.	B14	Line	0-9.7	+9.7	9.7		6
1920 ca.	X	Line	0-9.7	-9.7	0		6

OWNERSHIP

1910	Chicago & Eastern Illinois RR (B14)

ACQUISITION/DISPOSITION RECORD

Date	Act	CEI-	End points	Change	Main	Note
1853	B1	E,EO	Terre Haute-Evansville	+109.0	109.0	
1860	B1	E,ER	Rockville-Terre Haute	+22.9	131.9	
1871/10/26	B2	E	Otter Creek Jct.-Danville IL	+43.3	175.2	
1872	L1	ER	Rockville-Otter Creek Jct.	<17.3>		
	B1	E	In Evansville	+1.4		
/8	B3A	EC	Covington-Coal Creek	+8.4	167.7	
1873/7	B3A	EC	Bismarck IL-Covington	+10.6	178.3	
1874	B4	IA	Attica-Veedersburg	+12.8	191.1	
1876 ca.	B3	J	Terre Haute-Clay City	+25.5	216.6	
1878	B5	EZ	Otter Creek Jct.-Brazil	+12.7	229.3	
1879/6/15	X	EC	Bismarck IL-Covington	-10.6	218.7	5
1880	B6	JL	Lancaster Jct.-Woodside	+3.0	221.7	
1882	B5	IA	Veedersburg-Yeddo	+7.1		
	B6	J	Clay City-Worthington	+13.8		
	B7	EJ	Evansville Belt	+4.0	246.6	
1883	B8	EM	Mt. Vernon Jct.-Mt. Vernon	+36.8		
	B9	IA	Attica-Fair Oaks	+56.3	339.7	
1884 ca.	B10	J	Str't Line Jct.-Maysville	+51.2	390.9	
1885	B9	IA	Yeddo-Brazil	+41.9		
ca.	B11	J	Worthington-Maysville	+43.0		1
ca.	B6	JL1	Harrison Mine Spur	+1.0	476.8	
1887	B8	EN	New Pittsburg Jct.-New Pittsburg	+8.1		
	B12	IA	Fair Oaks-LaCrosse	+26.6	511.5	1
1888	B12	IB	Percy Jct.-State Line Jct.	+21.0		
ca.	L1	JB	Brazil-Saline City	+11.5		3
	X	EC	Covington-Coal Creek	-8.4	535.6	
1893	B8	ENJ	Jackson Hill Branch	+6.7		
	B8	ENS	Star City Jct.-Star City	+2.3	544.6	
1900	X	EN	New Pittsburg Jct.-New Pittsburg	-8.1		
ca.	X	ENJ	Jackson Hill Branch	-6.7		
ca.	X	ENS	Star City Jct.-Star City	-2.3		
	B14	ES	Standard-Hymera	+7.5		7
	B14	ESP	Hymera Jct.-New Pittsburg	+4.8		
ca.	B14	ESM	Kolsem Jct.-Peerless	+3.5	543.3	
1901/11/1	B14	CF	Milford IL-Freeland Park	+1.8	545.1	
1903	B13	CJ	Rossville Jct IL-Judyville	+6.9	552.0	
1910 ca.	X	JL	MP 1.0-Woodside	-2.0	550.0	
1916	XL	JB	Brazil-Saline City	-11.5	538.5	
1917	X	JL	MP 0.4-MP 1.0	-0.6		
	X	JL1	Harrison Mine Spur	-1.0	536.9	
1919	X	JL	Lancaster Jct.-MP 0.4	-0.4	536.5	

(continued)

CHICAGO & EASTERN ILLINOIS

ACQUISITION/DISPOSITION RECORD (continued)

Date	Act	C&EI-	End points	Change	Main	Note
1920 ca.	B15	EU	Clinton-Universal Mine	+8.5		
/6/3	S3	J	Str.Line Jct.-Terre Haute	[133.5]	411.5	
1921	X	ESP	MP 206.4-New Pittsburg	-1.8	409.7	
1922/12/2	S1	IA	LaCrosse-West Melcher	-119.6		
12	S5	IA	West Melcher-Brazil	-25.1		
12/2	S1	IB	Percy Jct.-State Line Jct.	-21.0	244.0	
1924	S2	ER	Rockville-Otter Creek Jct.	[<17.3>]	244.0	
1930	X	ESP	MP 205.4-MP 206.4	-1.0	243.0	
1931 ca.	X	ESP	Hymera Jct.-MP 205.4	-2.0	241.0	
1937	X	ES	MP 201-Hymera	-3.3	237.7	
1942	X	ES	MP 199.5-MP 201	-1.5	236.2	
1947	B12	E	Alice-Decker	-	236.2	2
1950/3/7	X	CF	Milford IL-Freeland Park	-1.8	234.4	4
1955	X	ESM	Kolsem Jct.-Peerless	-3.5	230.9	
1965 ca.	X	ES	Standard-MP 199.5	-2.7	228.2	

On 1967/5/12 Chicago & Eastern Illinois was conveyed to Missouri Pacific, which in turn conveyed all lines but one to Louisville & Nashville. The C&EI Acquisition/Disposition Record is continued in two places: under Chicago & Eastern Illinois and under the name of the new owning company. The lines conveyed were:

Line desig.	End points	MP	to L&N	to MP	Note
[CEI-E]	IL state line-Evansville	128.6-287.2	158.6		
[CEI-EO]	In Evansville	285.8-286.5	0.7		
[CEI-EJ]	In Evansville	0-4.0	4.0		
[CEI-EU]	Clinton-Universal Mine	0-8.5	8.5		
[CEI-EZ]	Otter Creek Jct.-Brazil	171.9-184.6	12.7		
[CEI-EM]	Mt. Vernon Jc.-Mt. Vernon	265.3-302.1	36.8		
[CEI-CJ]	IL state line-Judyville	113.5-120.4		6.9	
	TOTAL		221.3	6.9	
			CEI =228.2		

Date	Act	CEI-	End points	Change	Main	Note
1973 ca.	X	CJ	Rossville Jct IL-Judyville	-6.9	221.3	
1976	P1	EB	In Evansville	+5.9		
	B16	EB	In Evansville	+2.0		
	Y	E	MP 279.5-Evansville	(7.7)		
	Y	EO	In Evansville	(0.7)		
	Y	EJ	In Evansville	(4.0)	216.8	
1977	X	EZ	Otter Creek Jct.-Brazil	-12.7	204.1	
1982	X	EM	Poseyville-Mt. Vernon	-18.7		
	Y	EM	In Mt. Vernon	(1.6)	183.8	

Effective 1983/1/1 the Louisville & Nashville merged into the Seaboard System. The Acquisition/Disposition Record for Louisville & Nashville is continued in two places: under Louisville & Nashville and under Seaboard System. Louisville & Nashville acquired lines are continued under their original constituent companies and under Seaboard System.

On 1986/7/1 the Seaboard System was renamed CSX Transportation. The Acquisition/-Disposition Record foR Louisville & Nashville is continued in two places: under Louisville & Nashville and under CSX Transportation.

1987	X	EM	Mt. Vernon Jct.-Owensville	-5.5		
	S4	EM	Owensville-Poseyville	[11.0]	167.3	
1994	X	EU	Clinton-Universal	-8.5	158.8	
1998 ca.	X	EM	Owensville-Cynthiana	[-6.4]	158.8	

CHICAGO & EASTERN ILLINOIS

ACT COLUMN KEY
B1   Built by Evansville & Crawfordsville RR
B2   Built by Evansville, Terre Haute & Chicago Ry
B3   Built by Cincinnati & Terre Haute Ry
B3A Built by Chicago, Danville & Vincennes RR
B4   Built by Indiana North & South RR
B5   Built by Chicago & Block Coal RR
B6   Built by Terre Haute & Southeastern RR
B7   Built by Evansville Belt Ry
B8   Built by Evansville & Terre Haute RR
B9   Built by Chicago & Great Southern Ry
B10 Built by Indianapolis & Evansville RR
B11 Built by Evansville, Washington & Brazil RR
B12 Built by Chicago & Indiana Coal Ry
B13 Built by Rossville & Eastern Illinois RR
B14 Built by Chicago & Eastern Illinois RR
B15 Built by Chicago & Eastern Illinois Ry
B16 Built by Louisville & Nashville
L1   Leased from Terre Haute & Indianapolis
P1   Purchased from Penn Central
S1   Sold to Chicago, Attica & Southern
S2   Sold to Pennsylvania RR
S3   Sold to Evansville, Indianapolis & Terre Haute Ry
S4   Sold to Poseyville & Owensville RR
S5   Sold to Baltimore & Ohio
X   Abandoned
XL   Lease terminated
Y   Converted to yard/industrial track

SOURCES
1. Indiana, *1995 Indiana State Rail Plan.*
2. Simons and Parker, *Railroads of Indiana.*
3. Sulzer, *Ghost Railroads of Indiana.*

NOTES
General. Source 3 states the company owned a number of branches and spurs to coal mines in the vicinity of Clinton and Sullivan which have not been documented and are not included herein.
1. Source I states that this segment was built by the Evansville & Terre Haute on behalf of the owner.
2. The line reconstruction between Alice and Decker reduced line mileage by about 0.1 miles. No change in the Construction/Abandonment Record has been made for this change.
3. The means of transfer of the Brazil-Saline City segment from the Terre Haute & Indianapolis to the Evansville & Indianapolis is not certain but is assumed to be by lease inasmuch as the segment reverted to the Vandalia RR, the successor of the TH&I.
4. Date shown is date abandonment authorized by ICC.
5. With this abandonment trackage rights were obtained over Peoria & Eastern line P&E-A between Danville and Covington Jct.
6. The construction or abandonment dates could not be determined and this line is not included in the Acquisition/Disposition Record.
7. This construction apparently used the line of CEI-ENJ between Hymera and Star City Jct.

CHICAGO & INDIANA RR

MAIN LINE (CHIN-A)
See Erie line ERIE-C for arrangement of stations, prior construction/abandonment record, and prior ownership

CONSTRUCTION/ABANDONMENT
Date	Act	End points	MP	Change	Main	Source	Note
1979/6	T1	OH state line-Hammond	89.1-248.3	+159.2	159.2	1	1
1980/1	XT	OH state line-Hammond	89.1-248.3	-159.2	0	1	

OWNERSHIP
1979	Chicago & Indiana RR (T1)

ACQUISITION/DISPOSITION RECORD
See ownership record above for line CHIN-A

ACT COLUMN KEY
T1 Transfer to Chicago & Indiana from Erie
XT Transfer cancelled

SOURCES
1. Simons and Parker, *Railroads of Indiana.*

NOTES
1. The method of transfer to the Chicago & Indiana is unclear, but it is presumed to be by lease

CHICAGO & SOUTH BEND RR

MAIN LINE (CHSB-YA)
This road was an industrial road in South Bend and is not included in the Mileage table.

CONSTRUCTION/ABANDONMENT
Date	Act	End points	MP	Change	Main	Source	Note
1892	B	In South Bend		(+0.9)	(0.9)	1	
1918	X	In South Bend		(-0.9)	0	1	

OWNERSHIP
1892	Chicago & South Bend RR

ACQUISITION/DISPOSITION RECORD
See ownership record above for line CHSB-YA

ACT COLUMN KEY
B Built by Chicago & South Bend RR
X Abandoned

SOURCES
1. Simons and Parker, *Railroads of Indiana.*

CHICAGO, ATTICA & SOUTHERN

MAIN LINE (CAS-A)
	Mileage	County	Crossings, junctions, etc.
LaCrosse	0	LaPorte	J/MON-N 31.6, J/PM-W 0, J/PRR-L 249.2
Wilders	3.4	"	X/ERIE-C 206.1
Burkes	8.2	"	
Dunns	9.8	"	
Wheatfield	13.3	Jasper	X/LS-YK 58.1
Zadoc	17.0	"	X/MON-ND 18.5
(continued)			

CHICAGO, ATTICA & SOUTHERN

MAIN LINE (CAS-A) (continued)

	Mileage [LaCrosse]	County	Crossings, junctions, etc.
Zadoc	17.0	Jasper	
Kniman	18.8	"	
Virgie	21.6	"	
Moffitts	24.2	"	
Fair Oaks	26.6	"	X/MON-A 62.2
Lawlers	28.6	Newton	
Kents	31.2	"	
Mt. Ayr	35.6	"	
Julian	39.5	"	
Foresman	41.5	"	
Percy Siding	45.6	"	
Percy Jct.	46.0	"	J/CAS-B 0
Goodland	48.5	"	X/PRR-LF 48.9
Wadena	53.7	Benton	
Lochiel	55.7	"	
Barce	58.7	"	
Swanington	61.3	"	X/CCC-H 199.6
Doubling Track	64.4	"	
Oxford	66.2	"	X/NKP-LP 279.4
Pine Village	71.2	Warren	
Chatterton	74.2	"	
Winthrop Siding	76.4	"	
Winthrop	76.6	"	
Gravel Pit	79.5	"	
Kickapoo	79.8	"	
Mudlavia	81.0	"	
Glen Cliff	81.3	"	
Attica	82.9	Fountain	X/WAB-P 276.8
Attica Shops	83.5	"	
Rob Roy	87.0	"	
Aylsworth	89.3	"	
Stone Bluff	91.6	"	
Veedersburg	95.7	"	X/NKP-TC 249.1, X/P&E-A 64.7
Yeddo	102.8	"	
Kingman	106.0	"	
Tangier	110.0	Parke	
West Union	116.1	"	
Fluor	119.4	"	
West Melcher	119.6	"	J/B&O-ID 190.1, J/B&O-IB 0

CONSTRUCTION/ABANDONMENT

Date	Act	End points	MP	Change	Main	Source	Note
1874	B1	Attica-Veedersburg	82.9-95.7	+12.8	12.8	1,2	
1882	B2	Veedersburg-Yeddo	95.7-102.8	+7.1	19.9	1,2	
1883	B3	Attica-Fair Oaks	82.9-26.6	+56.3	76.2	1,2	
1885	B3	Yeddo-West Melcher	102.8-119.6	+16.8	93.0	1,2	
1887/1	B3	Fair Oaks-LaCrosse	26.6-0	+26.6	119.6	1,2	1
1943/6/30	X	LaCrosse-Percy Jct.	0-43.0	-43.0		1,2	2
1943/9/10	X	Veedersburg-West Melcher	95.7-119.6	-23.9	52.7	1,2	2,3
1946/4/12	X	Percy Jct.-Veedersburg	43.0-95.7	-52.7	0	1,2	2

OWNERSHIP

1874	Indiana North & South RR (B1), of part
1882	Chicago Block Coal RR (B2)
1883	Chicago & Great Southern Ry (B3)
1886/4	Chicago & Indiana Coal Ry (B4), merger of C&GS and Indiana Ry
1892/6/1	Chicago & Eastern Illinois, leased C&IC
1894/6/6	Chicago & Eastern Illinois, merged C&IC
1922/12/2	Chicago, Attica & Southern RR, bought C&EI line

CHICAGO, ATTICA & SOUTHERN

BRANCH (CAS-B)

	Mileage	County	Crossings, junctions, etc.
Percy Jct.	0	Newton	J/CAS-A 46.0
Weishaars	2.4	"	
Brook	5.9	"	
Beaver City	9.6	"	
(Crossing)	12.4	"	X/LS-WD 49.56
Morocco	13.0	"	
Pogue	17.3	"	
Elmer	18.8	"	
State Line Jct.	21.0	"	J/C&EI

CONSTRUCTION/ABANDONMENT

Date	Act	End points	MP	Change	Main	Source	Note
1888	B4	Percy Jct.-State Line Jct.	0-21.0	+21.0	21.0	1,2	
1943/6/30	X	Morocco-State Line Jct.	13.0-21.0	-8.0	13.0	1,2	2
1946/4/12	X	Percy Jct.-Morocco	0-13.0	-13.0	0	1,2	2

OWNERSHIP

1888	Chicago & Indiana Coal Ry (B4)
1892/6/1	Chicago & Eastern Illinois, leased C&IC
1894/6/6	Chicago & Eastern Illinois, merged C&IC
1922/12/2	Chicago, Attica & Southern RR, bought C&EI line

ACQUISITION/DISPOSITION RECORD

Date	Act	CAS-	End points	Change	Main	Note
1874	B1	A	Attica-Veedersburg	+12.8	12.8	
1882	B2	A	Veedersburg-Yeddo	+7.1	19.9	
1883	B3	A	Attica-Fair Oaks	+56.3	76.2	
1885	B3	A	Yeddo-West Melcher	+16.8	93.0	
1887	B3	A	Fair Oaks-LaCrosse	+26.6	119.6	1
1888/1	B4	B	Percy Jct.-State Line Jct.	+21.0	140.6	
1943/6/30	X	A	LaCrosse-Percy Jct.	-43.0		2
9/10	X	A	Veedersburg-West Melcher	-23.9		2,3
6/30	X	B	Morocco-State Line Jct.	-8.0	65.7	2
1946/4/12	X	A	Percy Jct.-Veedersburg	-52.7		2
4/12	X	B	Percy Jct.-Morocco	-13.0	0	2

ACT COLUMN KEY
B1 Built by Indiana North & South RR
B2 Built by Chicago Block Coal RR
B3 Built by Chicago & Great Southern Ry
B4 Built by Chicago & Indiana Coal Ry
X   Abandoned

SOURCES
1. Simons and Parker, *Railroads of Indiana*.
2. Sulzer, *Ghost Railroads of Indiana*.

NOTES
General. The dates and type of transfer of ownership between the Indiana North & South, the Chicago Block Coal, and the Chicago & Great Southern is not clear in Source R.
1. Source 1 states that the company held trackage rights over the Chicago & West Michigan RR between LaCrosse and New Buffalo, Mich. A company map in the January 1930 *Official Guide* shows trackage rights between LaCrosse and Wellsboro.
2. Date that abandonment authorized by ICC.
3. Source 2 states that at abandonment some trackage was conveyed to Wabash RR.

CHICAGO, MILWAUKEE, ST. PAUL & PACIFIC

MAIN LINE (MILW-T)

	Mileage	County	Crossings, junctions, etc.
(Chicago IL	0)		
Humrick IL	138.3		
(IL/IN state line)	142.1		
Quaker	142.5	Vermillion	
West Dana	146.1	"	X/B&O-ID 200.8
St. Bernice	152.3	"	
Clinton Yard	153.8	"	J/MILW-TC 0 f. West Clinton
Blanford	155.4	"	
Kolsem Jct.	158.4	"	J/MILW-TD 0
Bradshaw	159.8	Vigo	J/MILW-TB 0, J/MILW-TB2 0
			f. Windsor Jct., f. Libertyville
Pine Ridge Jct.	165.5	"	J/spur to Pine Ridge Mine, 1.2 mi.
Fayette	166.8	"	

Fayette	170.5	"	f. Grover
Bridge Jct.	171.2	"	J/MILW-TB 7.1
Stoddart	172	"	
Maple Avenue	172.2	"	
Dewey	174.7	"	X/CEI-E 173.8
Preston	175.2	"	X/CCC-L 68.6, X/PRR-VT1 2.1
Van	176.7	"	
(Bridge)	177.3	"	B/PRR-V 70.3
College Avenue	179.0	"	
Hulman Street	179.9	"	J/MILW-TA 0
Belt Jct.	182.0	"	J/
Spring Hill	182.7	"	X/CEI-E 181.7, X/CCC-T 4.7
Keller	187.6	"	
Blackhawk	191.3	"	J/MILW-TS 0
Lewis	195.4	"	
Coalmont	200.3	Clay	J/MILW-TK 0
Jasonville	203.0	Greene	
Latta	204.1	"	J/MILW-TL 0
(Junction)	204.6	"	J/spur to mine, 1.9 mi.
Peabody Jct.	205.2	"	J/spur to Midland Mine, 1.5 mi.
Midland	205.9	"	
(Crossing)	206.7	"	X/MON-SL 42.0
Vicksburg	208.0	"	
Hoosier	209.7	"	
Linton	212.4	"	X/IC-NE 95.36
Sponsler	214.7	"	X/PRR-IG 3.6
Beehunter	218.3	"	X/PRR-IV 86.2
Ilene	219.7	"	
Averitt	222.3	"	
Elnora	224.1	Daviess	X/CCC-T 61.2
Epsom Jct.	227.1	"	J/spur to Marian Mine, 3.8 mi.
Odon	230.3	"	
(continued)			

CHICAGO, MILWAUKEE, ST. PAUL & PACIFIC

MAIN LINE (MILW-T) (continued)

	Mileage [Chicago]	County	Crossings, junctions, etc.
Odon	230.3	Daviess	
Crane	236.0	Martin	f. Burns City
Blankenship	239.8	"	
Indian Springs	244.2	"	
Cale	245.1	"	
Mt. Olive	248.4	"	
Rock Ledge	250	Lawrence	
Williams	251.3	"	
Coxton	256.6	"	J/MILW-TG 0
(Crossing)	262.3	"	X/MON-SB 245.7, X/B&O-SB 10.8
Bedford	262.4	"	J/MILW-TO 0
Shawswick	267.0	"	
Heltonville	270.0	"	
Zelma	274.5	"	
Norman	276.5	Jackson	
Kurtz	280.7	"	
Freetown	285.2	"	
Surprise	289.5	"	
Cortland	294.6	"	
Seymour	299.8	"	X/PRR-IL 58.4
Reddington	304.4	"	
Azalia	309.0	Bartholomew	
Elizabethtown	312.7	"	X/PRR-IM 8.0
Grammer	317.6	"	
Alert	320.1	Decatur	
Sardinia	322.7	"	
Westport	325.9	"	J/CCC-M 236.5

CONSTRUCTION/ABANDONMENT

Date	Act	End points	MP	Change	Main	Source	Note
1890	B1	Elnora-Westport	224.1-325.9	+101.8	101.8	1,2	
1900	B3	Terre Haute-Linton	179.9-212.4	+32.5	134.3	1	
1903	B3	IL state line-Fayette	142.1-166.8	+24.7			
1903	B3	Fayette-Terre Haute	170.5-179.9	+9.4	168.4	2	3
1905	B3	Linton-Elnora	212.4-224.1	+11.7	180.1	1	
1961	X	Seymour-Westport	299.8-325.9	-26.1	154.0	2	
1978	X	Bedford-Seymour	262.4-299.8	-37.4	116.6	2	
1980	X	IL state line-Fayette	142.1-166.8	-24.7	91.9	2	
1990 ca.	X	Fayette-Dewey	170.5-174.7	-4.2	87.7		

OWNERSHIP

1890	Evansville & Richmond RR (B1), of part
1897	Southern Indiana Ry (B3), bought Evansville & Richmond
1910	Chicago, Terre Haute & Southeastern Ry, reorganize Southern Indiana
1921/7/1	Chicago, Milwaukee & St. Paul RR, lease Chicago, Terre Haute & Southeastern
1928/1/13	Chicago, Milwaukee, St. Paul & Pacific RR, reorganize CM&SP, lease assigned
1948	Chicago, Milwaukee, St. Paul & Pacific RR, buy CTH&SE
1986/1/1	Soo Line, merge Chicago, Milwaukee, St. Paul & Pacific

TERRE HAUTE SPUR (MILW-TA)

	Mileage	County	Crossings, junctions, etc.
Hulman Street	0	Vigo	J/MILW-T 179.9
Terre Haute	1.9	"	

CONSTRUCTION/ABANDONMENT

Date	Act	End points	MP	Change	Main	Source	Note
1900	B3	Line	0-1.9	+1.9	1.9	1	
1980 ca.	X	Line	0-1.9	-1.9	0		

(continued)

CHICAGO, MILWAUKEE, ST. PAUL & PACIFIC

TERRE HAUTE SPUR (MILW-TA) (continued)
OWNERSHIP

1900	Southern Indiana Ry (B3), bought Evansville & Richmond
1910	Chicago, Terre Haute & Southeastern Ry, reorganize Southern Indiana
1921/7/1	Chicago, Milwaukee & St. Paul RR, lease Chicago, Terre Haute & Southeastern
1928/1/13	Chicago, Milwaukee, St. Paul & Pacific RR, reorganize CM&SP, lease assigned
1948	Chicago, Milwaukee, St. Paul & Pacific RR, buy CTH&SE

COAL CREEK BRANCH (MILW-TB)

	Mileage	County	Crossings, junctions, etc.
Windsor Jct.	0	Vigo	J/MILW-T 159.8
New Goshen	4	"	
Maple Grove		"	
Tallydale	5.2	"	
Bridge Jct.	7.1	"	J/MILW-T 171.2

CONSTRUCTION/ABANDONMENT

Date	Act	End points	MP	Change	Main	Source	Note
1913 ca.	B4	Windsor Jct.-Bridge Jct.	0-7.1	+7.1	7.1	2	
1940	X	Windsor Jct.-Tallydale	0-5.2	-5.2	1.9	2	
1956 ca.	X	Tallydale-Bridge Jct.	5.2-7.1	-1.9	0		

OWNERSHIP

1913	Chicago, Terre Haute & Southeastern Ry (B4)
1921/7/1	Chicago, Milwaukee & St. Paul RR, lease Chicago, Terre Haute & Southeastern
1928/1/13	Chicago, Milwaukee, St. Paul & Pacific RR, reorganize CM&SP, lease assigned

NEW GOSHEN BRANCH (MILW-TB2)

	Mileage	County	Crossings, junctions, etc.
Bradshaw	0	Vigo	J/MILW-T 159.8
New Goshen	3.9	"	

CONSTRUCTION/ABANDONMENT

Date	Act	End points	MP	Change	Main	Source	Note
??							1,2

OWNERSHIP

WEST CLINTON-CROWN HILL (MILW-TC)

	Mileage	County	Crossings, junctions, etc.
West Clinton	0	Vermillion	J/MILW-T 153.8
Crown Hill	6.2	"	

CONSTRUCTION/ABANDONMENT

Date	Act	End points	MP	Change	Main	Source	Note
1913 ca.	B4	West Clinton-Crown Hill	0-6.2	+6.2	6.2	2	
1956	X	West Clinton-Crown Hill	0-6.2	-6.2	0	1	

OWNERSHIP

1913	Chicago, Terre Haute & Southeastern Ry (B4)
1921/7/1	Chicago, Milwaukee & St. Paul RR, lease Chicago, Terre Haute & Southeastern
1928/1/13	Chicago, Milwaukee, St. Paul & Pacific RR, reorganize CM&SP, lease assigned
1948	Chicago, Milwaukee, St. Paul & Pacific RR, buy CTH&SE

CHICAGO, MILWAUKEE, ST. PAUL & PACIFIC

KOLSEM JCT.-JACKSON HILL MINE (MILW-TD)

	Mileage	County	Crossings, junctions, etc.
Kolsem Jct.	0	Vermillion	J/MILW-T 158.4
Jackson Hill Mine	3.1	"	

CONSTRUCTION/ABANDONMENT

Date	Act	End points	MP	Change	Main	Source	Note
1916 ca.	B4	Kolsem Jct.-Jackson Hill	0-3.1	+3.1	3.1	2	
1942	X	Kolsem Jct.-Jackson Hill	0-3.1	-3.1	0	1	

OWNERSHIP

1916	Chicago, Terre Haute & Southeastern Ry (B4)
1921/7/1	Chicago, Milwaukee & St. Paul RR, lease Chicago, Terre Haute & Southeastern
1928/1/13	Chicago, Milwaukee, St. Paul & Pacific RR, reorganize CM&SP, lease assigned

KEYSTONE BRANCH (MILW-TK)

	Mileage	County	Crossings, junctions, etc.
Coalmont	0	Clay	J/MILW-T 200.3
Keystone	5.1	"	

CONSTRUCTION/ABANDONMENT

Date	Act	End points	MP	Change	Main	Source	Note
1905	B3	Coalmont-Keystone	0-5.1	+5.1	5.1	2	
1910	X	Coalmont-Keystone	0-5.1	-5.1	0	2	

OWNERSHIP

1905	Southern Indiana Ry (B3)

SULLIVAN BRANCH (MILW-TS)

	Mileage	County	Crossings, junctions, etc.
Blackhawk	0	Vigo	J/MILW-T 191.3
Shady Grove	2.4	"	J/MILW-TSA 2.4
Marta	4.7	Sullivan	
Hymera	8.8	"	
Abbott	11.0	"	X/CEI-ES 201.9
Hawton	12.8	"	J/MILW-TL 8.1, J/MILW-TL 8.1
Glendora	15.6	"	J/MILW-TSA 15.2, J/MILW-TSB 0
Sullivan	18.5	"	

CONSTRUCTION/ABANDONMENT

Date	Act	End points	MP	Change	Main	Source	Note
1905	B3	Blackhawk-Sullivan	0-18.5	+18.5	18.5	1	
1943	X	Shady Grove-Abbott	2.4-11.7	-9.3	9.2	2	
1952	X	Glendora-Sullivan	15.6-18.5	-2.9	6.3	1,2	
1953	X	Hawton-north	11.7-12.8	-1.1	5.2	2	
1956	X	Blackhawk-Shady Grove	0-2.4	-2.4	2.8	2	
1962	X	Hawton-Glendora	12.8-15.6	-2.8	0	2	

OWNERSHIP

1905	Southern Indiana Ry (B3)
1910	Chicago, Terre Haute & Southeastern Ry, reorganize Southern Indiana
1921/7/1	Chicago, Milwaukee & St. Paul RR, lease Chicago, Terre Haute & Southeastern
1928/1/13	Chicago, Milwaukee, St. Paul & Pacific RR, reorganize CM&SP, lease assigned
1948	Chicago, Milwaukee, St. Paul & Pacific RR, buy CTH&SE

CHICAGO, MILWAUKEE, ST. PAUL & PACIFIC

SHELBURNE BRANCH (MILW-TSA)

	Mileage	County	Crossings, junctions, etc.
Shady Grove	2.4	Vigo	J/MILW-TS 2.4
Rood	4.5	"	
Baldridge	7.7	Sullivan	
Hart	8.5	"	
(Crossing)	10.3	"	X/CEI-EN 197.9
Shelburne	11.2	"	
Glendora	15.2	"	J/MILW-TS 15.6, J/MILW-TSB 0

CONSTRUCTION/ABANDONMENT

Date	Act	End points	MP	Change	Main	Source	Note
1905	B3	Shady Grove-Glendora	2.4-15.2	+12.8	12.8	2	
1915 ca.	X	Rood-Hart	4.5-8.5	-4.0	8.8	2	
1916	X	Shady Grove-Rood	2.4-4.5	-2.1	6.7	2	
1942	X	Hart-Glendora	8.5-15.2	-6.7	0	2	

OWNERSHIP

1905	Southern Indiana Ry (B3)
1910	Chicago, Terre Haute & Southeastern Ry, reorganize Southern Indiana
1921/7/1	Chicago, Milwaukee & St. Paul RR, lease Chicago, Terre Haute & Southeastern
1928/1/13	Chicago, Milwaukee, St. Paul & Pacific RR, reorganize CM&SP, lease assigned

JONAY MINE BRANCH (MILW-TSB)

	Mileage	County	Crossings, junctions, etc.
Glendora	0	Sullivan	J/MILW-TS 15.6, J/MILW-TSA 15.2
Joney Mine	2.9	"	

CONSTRUCTION/ABANDONMENT

Date	Act	End points	MP	Change	Main	Source	Note
??	B?	Line	0-2.9	+2.9			1
1962	X	Line	0-2.9	-2.9	0	2	1

OWNERSHIP

LATTA COAL BRANCH (MILW-TL)

	Mileage	County	Crossings, junctions, etc.
Latta	0	Greene	J/MILW-T 204.1
Lattas Creek Jct.	1.9	"	J/MILW-TLA 1.9
(Junction)	6.8	Sullivan	J/spur to coal mine, 2.4 mi.
Hawton	8.1	"	J/MILW-TS 12.8

CONSTRUCTION/ABANDONMENT

Date	Act	End points	MP	Change	Main	Source	Note
1905	B3	Latta-Hawton	0-8.1	+8.1	8.1		

OWNERSHIP

1905	Southern Indiana Ry (B3), bought Evansville & Richmond
1910	Chicago, Terre Haute & Southeastern Ry, reorganize Southern Indiana
1921/7/1	Chicago, Milwaukee & St. Paul RR, lease Chicago, Terre Haute & Southeastern
1928/1/13	Chicago, Milwaukee, St. Paul & Pacific RR, reorganize CM&SP, lease assigned
1948	Chicago, Milwaukee, St. Paul & Pacific RR, buy CTH&SE
1986/1/1	Soo Line, merge Chicago, Milwaukee, St. Paul & Pacific

CHICAGO, MILWAUKEE, ST. PAUL & PACIFIC

LATTAS CREEK BRANCH (MILW-TLA)

	Mileage	County	Crossings, junctions, etc.
Lattas Creek Jct.	1.9	Greene	J/MILW-TL 1.9
Antioch Jct.	2.2	"	
Gilmour	3.2	Sullivan	
Vigo	5.9	"	
Minnehaha	6.8	"	

CONSTRUCTION/ABANDONMENT

Date	Act	End points	MP	Change	Main	Source	Note
							1

GIBERSON BRANCH (MILW-TG)

	Mileage	County	Crossings, junctions, etc.
Coxton	0	Lawrence	J/MILW-T 256.6
Giberson	3.2	"	

CONSTRUCTION/ABANDONMENT

Date	Act	End points	MP	Change	Main	Source	Note
1910	B4	Coxton-Giberson	0-3.2	+3.2	3.2	S	
1935	X	Coxton-Giberson	0-3.2	-3.2	0	S	

OWNERSHIP

1910	Chicago, Terre Haute & Southeastern Ry (B4)
1921/7/1	Chicago, Milwaukee & St. Paul RR, lease Chicago, Terre Haute & Southeastern
1928/1/13	Chicago, Milwaukee, St. Paul & Pacific RR, reorganize CM&SP, lease assigned

OOLITIC BRANCH (MILW-TO)

	Mileage	County	Crossings, junctions, etc.
Bedford	0	Lawrence	J/MILW-T 262.4
(Crossing)	1.3	"	X/MON-SB 294.5
Oolitic	4.8	"	
Buff Hill	6	"	

CONSTRUCTION/ABANDONMENT

Date	Act	End points	MP	Change	Main	Source	Note
1893/5/1	B2	Bedford-Oolitic	0-4.8	+4.8	4.8	I,R	
1984	X	Bedford-Oolitic	0-4.8	-4.8	0	I,R	

OWNERSHIP

1893	Bedford Belt Ry (B2)
1910	Chicago, Terre Haute & Southeastern Ry, bought Bedford Belt
1921/7/1	Chicago, Milwaukee & St. Paul RR, lease Chicago, Terre Haute & Southeastern
1928/1/13	Chicago, Milwaukee, St. Paul & Pacific RR, reorganize CM&SP, lease assigned
1948	Chicago, Milwaukee, St. Paul & Pacific RR, buy CTH&SE

ACQUISITION/DISPOSITION RECORD

Date	Act	MILW-	End points	Change	Main	Note
1890	B1	T	Elnora-Westport	+101.8	101.8	
1893	B2	TO	Bedford-Oolitic	+4.8	106.6	
1900	B3	T	Terre Haute-Linton	+32.5		
	B3	TA	Line	+1.9	141.0	
1903	B3	T	IL state line-Terre Haute	+34.1	175.1	3
1905	B3	T	Linton-Elnora	+11.7		
	B3	TK	Coalmont-Keystone	+5.1		
	B3	TL	Latta-Hawton	+8.1		
	B3	TS	Blackhawk-Sullivan	+18.5		
	B3	TSA	Shady Grove-Glendora	+12.8	231.3	

(continued)

CHICAGO, MILWAUKEE, ST. PAUL & PACIFIC

ACQUISITION/DISPOSITION RECORD (continued)

Date	Act	MILW-	End points	Change	Main	Note
1910	B4	TG	Coxton-Giberson	+3.2		
	X	TK	Coalmont-Keystone	-5.1	229.4	
1913 ca.	B4	TB	Windsor Jct.-Bridge Jct.	+7.1		
ca.	B4	TC	West Clinton-Crown Hill	+6.2	242.7	
1915 ca.	X	TSA	Rood-Hart	-4.0	238.7	
1916	X	TSA	Shady Grove-Rood	-2.1		
ca.	B4	TD	Kolsem Jct.-Jackson Hill	+3.1	239.7	
1935	X	TG	Coxton-Giberson	-3.2	236.5	
1940	X	TB	Windsor Jct.-Tallydale	-5.2	231.3	
1942	X	TD	Kolsem Jct.-Jackson Hill	-3.1		
	X	TSA	Hart-Glendora	-6.7	221.5	
1943	X	TS	Shady Grove-Abbott	-9.3	212.2	
1952	X	TS	Glendora-Sullivan	-2.9	209.3	
1953	X	TS	Hawton-north	-1.1	208.2	
1956	X	TS	Blackhawk-Shady Grove	-2.4		
	X	TC	West Clinton-Crown Hill	-6.2		
ca.	X	TB	Tallydale-Bridge Jct.	-1.9	197.7	
1961	X	T	Seymour-Westport	-26.1	171.6	
1962	X	TS	Hawton-Glendora	-2.8	168.8	
1978	X	T	Bedford-Seymour	-37.4	131.4	
1980	X	T	IL state line-Fayette	-24.7		
ca.	X	TA	In Terre Haute	-1.9	104.8	
1984	X	TO	Bedford-Oolitic	-4.8	100.0	

Effective 1986/1/1 this company was conveyed to Soo Line. Its Acquisition/Disposition Record is continued in two places: under the Chicago, Milwaukee and under Soo Line. The lines conveyed were:

Line desig. SOO-	End points	MP	Main
[MILW-T]	Fayette-Bedford	170.5-262.4	91.9
[MILW-TL]	Latta Coal Branch	0-8.1	8.1
		TOTAL	100.0

Date	Act	MILW--	End points	Change	Main	Note
1990 ca.	X	T	Fayette-Dewey	-4.2	95.8	

ACT COLUMN KEY
B1 Built by Evansville & Richmond RR
B2 Built by Bedford Belt Ry
B3 Built by Southern Indiana Ry
B4 Built by Chicago, Terre Haute & Southeastern Ry
B5 Built by Chicago, Milwaukee, St. Paul & Pacific
X Abandoned

SOURCES
1. Indiana, *1995 Indiana State Rail Plan*.
2. Simons and Parker, *Railroads of Indiana*.

NOTES
General. This company owned a number of branches and spurs to coal mines in Vermillion, Clay, Greene, and Sullivan Counties which have not been documented and are not included in the Acquisition/Disposition Record.
 1. The dates of construction and/or abandonment could not be determined and this line is not included in the Acquisition/Disposition Record.
 2. This line was rebuilt on the grade of the Coal Creek Branch (MILW-TE).
 3. An unexplained discrepancy of 3.7 miles appears in some timetable mileages for the main line north of Terre Haute. This mileage discrepancy is adjusted as shown in the arrangement of stations for line MILW-T at Fayette.

CHICAGO SHORT LINE

MAIN LINE (CSL-A)
This road is an industrial road in the Whiting area and is not included in the Mileage table.

CONSTRUCTION/ABANDONMENT

Date	Act	End points	MP	Change	Main	Source	Note
1903	B					1	

OWNERSHIP

1903	Chicago Short Line Ry

ACT COLUMN KEY
B Built by Chicago Short Line Ry

SOURCES
1. Simons and Parker, *Railroads of Indiana.*

CINCINATI, BLUFFTON & CHICAGO

MAIN LINE (CBC-A)

	Mileage	County	Crossings, junctions, etc.
Huntington	0	Huntington	J/ERIE-C 126.3, J/WAB-M 169.7
Simpson	5	"	
Dibbliss		"	
Quarry Spur		"	
Markle	9	"	
Uniondale	15	Wells	
Murray	18	"	
McKee	21	"	
Bluffton	23	"	X/NKP-LF 25.4, X/NKP-TB 123.4
Bracey	25	"	
Reiffsburg	30	"	
Petroleum	33	"	
Fiat	37	Jay	
Balbec	39	"	
Pennville	42	"	
Walnut Corners		"	
(Crossing)	51	"	X/NKP-LS
Portland	52	"	J/PRR-GR 43.2

CONSTRUCTION/ABANDONMENT

Date	Act	End points	MP	Change	Main	Source	Note
1903/12/23	B1	Bluffton-Pennville	23-42	+19.0	19.0	2	
1904/1/1	B1	Pennville-Portland	42-52	+10.0	29.0	2	
1908/1/15	B1	Huntington-Bluffton	0-23	+23.0	52.0	2	
1917	X	Huntington-Portland	0-52	-52.0	0	1,2	

OWNERSHIP

1903	Cincinnati, Bluffton & Chicago RR (B1)

ACQUISITION/DISPOSITION RECORD
See ownership record above for line CBC-A above

ACT COLUMN KEY
B1 Built by Cincinnati, Bluffton & Chicago RR (B1)
X Abandoned

SOURCES
1. Simons and Parker, *Railroads of Indiana.*
2. Sulzer, *Ghost Railroads of Indiana.*

CINCINNATI, BLUFFTON & CHICAGO

NOTES General. Source 1 reports a 1.5-mile branch built from near Pennville to Twin Hills gravel pit which is not documented.

CLEVELAND, CINCINNATI, CHICAGO & ST. LOUIS

CLEVELAND-INDIANAPOLIS LINE (CCC-I)

	Mileage	County	Crossings, junctions, etc.
Cleveland OH	0		
Bellefontaine OH	140.8		
Ansonia OH	189.7		
Elroy OH	193.4		
(OH/IN state line)	198.6		
(Crossing)	198.7	Randolph	X/PRR-L 103.8
Union City	198.8	"	J/B&O-TU 47.3
Harrisville	202.7	"	
Winchester	207.9	"	X/PRR-GR 24.5
Farmland	215.8	"	
Conner	218.8	"	
Parker City	219.9	"	
Selma	223.3	Delaware	
(Bridge)	228.3	"	B/C&O-C 102.5
(Junction)	228.4	"	J/MUNB-A 0
Vance	228.5	"	J/PRR-CM 41.8
Muncie	229.6	"	
(Crossing)	229.7	"	X/NKP-LF 65.8
Hart	232.7	"	
Yorktown	235.3	"	
Daleville	240.0	"	
Chesterfield	242.3	Madison	
Gridley	245.7	"	J/CCC-IA 245.7
Delco	246.7	"	X/PRR-CR 122.2
Anderson	247.4	"	
CP 247	247.8	"	J/CCC-M 165.4
(Crossing)	248.3	"	X/CI-A 19.7
(Crossing)	248.9	"	X/PRR-YA 2.4
Taft	250.9	"	J/CCC-IA 250.1
(continued)			

CLEVELAND, CINCINNATI, CHICAGO & ST. LOUIS

CLEVELAND-INDIANAPOLIS LINE (CCC-I) (continued)

	Mileage [Cleveland]	County	Crossings, junctions, etc.
Taft	250.9	Madison	J/CCC-IA 250.1
(Junction)	254.0	"	J/CCC-IO 254.0
Pendleton (new)	255.4	"	
Raleigh (new)	257.3	"	J/CCC-IO 257.0
Raleigh (old)	258.2	"	
Ingalls	260.4	"	
David	262.3	Hancock	
David	262.3	Hancock	
Fortville	263.1	"	
McCordsville	268.0	"	
Oaklandon	269.8	Marion	
Post	272.7	"	
Fort Benjamin Harrison	273.4	"	
Lawrence	274.6	"	
Eastwood	277.8	"	
Brightwood Yard	278.6	"	
Belt Jct.	279.1	"	J/IU-B 0
DX	280.1	"	J/CCC-S 136.4, X/IU-C 0.5
Massachusetts Avenue	281.9	"	X/MON-I 181.7, x/NKP-LM 1.9
Washington Street	283.1	"	J/IU-E 0.7
--via IU-E			
(Indianapolis	283.8)	"	

CONSTRUCTION/ABANDONMENT

Date	Act	End points	MP	Change	Main	Source	Note
1851	B1	OH state line-MP 254.0	198.6-254.0	+55.4		1	1
1851	B1	MP 257.3-Indianapolis	257.3-283.8	+26.5	81.9	1	
1853	S1	Wash. St.-Indianapolis	283.1-283.8	-0.7	81.2		
1905 ca.	B13	MP 254.0-MP 257.3	254.0-257.3	+3.3	84.5	2	

OWNERSHIP

1851	Indianapolis & Bellefontaine RR (B1)
1855/2	Indianapolis, Pittsburg & Cleveland RR, rename Indpls. & Bellef.
1864/12/20	Bellefontaine RR, merge IP&C and Bellefontaine & Indiana
1868/5/16	Cleveland, Columbus, Cincinnati & Indianapolis RR, merge Bellefontaine and Cleveland, Columbus & Cincinnati
1889/6	Cleveland, Cincinnati, Chicago & St. Louis Ry (B13), merge CCC&I and Indianapolis & St. Louis
1930/2/1	New York Central, lease Cleveland, Cincinnati, Chicago & St. Louis
1968/2/1	Penn Central, assigned lease of Cleveland, Cincinnati, Chicago & St. Louis
1976/4/1	Conrail, buy Penn Central
1999/6/1	CSX Transportation, buy Conrail line

PENDLETON OLD MAIN (CCC-IO)

	Mileage [Cleveland]	County	Crossings, junctions, etc.
(Junction)	254.0	Madison	J/CCC-I 254.0
Pendleton (old)	255.3	"	
Raleigh	257.0	"	J/CCC-I 257.3

CONSTRUCTION/ABANDONMENT

Date	Act	End points	MP	Change	Main	Source	Note
1851	B1	Line	254.0-257.0	+3.0	3.0	2	
1905 ca.	X	Part of line	254.0-257.0	-1.0			13
1905 ca.	Y	Part of line	255.0-257.0	(2.0)	0		

1976 ca.	X	Part of line	255.0-256.1	(-1.1)	0		
1984	X	Line	256.1-257.0	(-0.9)	0	1	
(continued)							

CLEVELAND, CINCINNATI, CHICAGO & ST. LOUIS

PENDLETON OLD MAIN (CCC-IO) (continued)
OWNERSHIP

1851	Indianapolis & Bellefontaine RR (B1)
1855/2	Indianapolis, Pittsburg & Cleveland RR, rename Indianapolis & Bellefontaine
1864/12/20	Bellefontaine RR, merge IP&C and Bellefontaine & Indiana
1868/5/16	Cleveland, Columbus, Cincinnati & Indianapolis RR, merge Bellefontaine and Cleve., Col's & Cinci.
1889/6	Cleveland, Cincinnati, Chicago & St. Louis Ry, merge CCC&I and Indianapolis & St. Louis
1930/2/1	New York Central, lease Cleveland, Cincinnati, Chicago & St. Louis
1968/2/1	Penn Central, assigned lease of Cleveland, Cincinnati, Chicago & St. Louis
1976/4/1	Conrail, buy Penn Central
1999/6/1	CSX Transportation, buy Conrail line

ANDERSON CUTOFF (CCC-IA)

	Mileage [Cleveland]	County	Crossings, junctions, etc.
Gridley	245.7	Madison	J/CCC-I 245.7, X/PRR-CR 121.4, X/CI-A 17.2
(Crossing)	247.2	"	X/CCC-M 166.6
South Anderson Yard	247.9	"	
Taft	250.1	"	J/CCC-I 250.9

CONSTRUCTION/ABANDONMENT

Date	Act	End points	MP	Change	Main	Source	Note
1892 ca.	B19	Gridley-Taft	245.7-250.1	+4.4	4.4		

OWNERSHIP

1892	Cleveland, Cincinnati, Chicago & St. Louis Ry (B19)
1930/2/1	New York Central, lease Cleveland, Cincinnati, Chicago & St. Louis
1968/2/1	Penn Central, assigned lease of Cleveland, Cincinnati, Chicago & St. Louis
1976/4/1	Conrail, buy Penn Central
1999/6/1	CSX Transportation, buy Conrail line

BATESVILLE OLD MAIN (CCC-GO1)

	Mileage [Cincinnati]	County	Crossings, junctions, etc.
Hyde	46.9	Ripley	J/CCC-G 46.9
Batesville	47.8	"	
(Junction)	50.3	"	J/CCC-G 50.2

CONSTRUCTION/ABANDONMENT

Date	Act	End points	MP	Change	Main	Source	Note
1853/11/1	B4	Hyde-MP 50.3	46.9-50.3	+3.4	3.4	2	
1905 ca.	Y	Hyde-MP 48.7	46.9-48.7	(1.8)			
1905 ca.	X	MP 48.7-MP 50.3	48.7-50.3	-1.6	0		

OWNERSHIP

1853	Lawrenceburg & Upper Mississippi RR (B4), of part
1853/12/1	Indianapolis & Cincinnati RR (B5), received Lawrenceburg & Upper Miss.
1867/2	Indianapolis, Cincinnati & Lafayette RR, reorganize Indianapolis. & Cincinnati
1880/3	Cincinnati, Indianapolis, St. Louis & Chicago RR, merge Indpls, Cin. & Laf.
1889/6	Cleveland, Cincinnati, Chicago & St. Louis Ry, merge CISL&C
1930/2/1	New York Central, lease Cleveland, Cincinnati, Chicago & St. Louis
1968/2/1	Penn Central, assigned lease of Cleveland, Cincinnati, Chicago & St. Louis
1976/4/1	Conrail, buy Penn Central
1991/12/31	Central RR of Indiana, buy part of Conrail line

CLEVELAND, CINCINNATI, CHICAGO & ST. LOUIS

SPRINGFIELD-INDIANAPOLIS (CCC-S)

	Mileage	County	Crossings, junctions, etc.
Springfield OH	0		
Glen Karn OH	60.4		
(OH/IN state line)	61.6		
Crete	64.9	Randolph	
Page	68.9	"	
Lynn	69.3	"	
(Crossing)	69.6	"	X/PRR-GR 15.3
Carlos City	74.5	"	
Modoc	80.0	"	
Losantville	83.5	"	
RN	83.8	"	X/C&O-C 88.0
Mooreland	87.6	Henry	
Messick	90.7	"	
Epileptic Village	93.6	"	f. Van Nuys
(Bridge)	95.1	"	B/PRR-CR 102.9
New Castle	95.8	"	
Kennard	104.1	"	
Shirley	107.3	Henry-Hancock	X/CCC-M 181.0
Wilkinson	109.0	Hancock	
Willow Branch	113.1	"	
Maxwell	117.7	"	
Mohawk	121.5	"	
Mt. Comfort	125.6	"	
Hunter	131.2	Marion	
Eastside	135.8	"	X/IU-B 0.5
DX	136.4	"	J/CCC-I 280.1, J/IU-C 0.5
--via CCC-I and IU-E			
(Indianapolis	140.1)	"	

CONSTRUCTION/ABANDONMENT

Date	Act	End points	MP	Change	Main	Source	Note
1882	B14	OH state line-Indianapolis	61.6-136.4	+74.8	74.8	1,2	

1976	Y	In New Castle	95.3-96.9	(1.6)			
1976	Y	Hunter-DX	128.8-136.4	(7.6)			
1976	X	OH state line-Lynn	61.6-69.4	-7.8	57.8	1,2	
1977	X	Lynn-New Castle	69.4-95.3	-25.9		1,2	
1977	X	New Castle-Shirley	96.9-107.3	-10.4		1,2	
1977	X	Wilkinson-Hunter	109.0-128.8	-19.8	1.7	1,2	
1979/6	L2	Shirley-Wilkinson	107.3-109.0	<1.7>	0		
1985/1	LA1	Shirley-Wilkinson	107.3-109.0	<1.7>	0		
1987/4	X	Shirley-Wilkinson	107.3-109.0	<-1.7>	0	2	

OWNERSHIP

1882	Indianapolis, Bloomington & Western Ry (B14)
1887/11	Ohio, Indiana & Western Ry, reorganize Indiana, Bloomington & Western
1890/2/22	Cleveland, Cincinnati, Chicago & St. Louis, merged OI&W
1930/2/1	New York Central, leased Cleveland, Cincinnati, Chicago & St. Louis
1968/2/1	Penn Central Co., assigned lease of Cleveland, Cincinnati, Chi. & St. Louis
1969/10/1	Penn Central Transp. Co., acquired Penn Central Co.
1976/4/1	Conrail, purchase of Penn Central Transp.

ORIGINAL MAIN VIA LAWRENCEBURG (CCC-GL)

	Mileage [Cincinnati]	County	Crossings, junctions, etc.
(Junction)	25.5	Dearborn	J/CCC-GL 25.5
(Crossing)	25.7	"	X/B&O-SC 22.4
(Junction)	28.6	"	J/CCC-G 23.8
(continued)			

CLEVELAND, CINCINNATI, CHICAGO & ST. LOUIS

ORIGINAL MAIN VIA LAWRENCEBURG (CCC-GL) (continued)

CONSTRUCTION/ABANDONMENT

Date	Act	End points	MP	Change	Main	Source	Note
1853/11/1	B4	Line	25.5-28.6	+2.9	2.9		
1875	Y	In Lawrecenburg	25.5-27.6	(1.9)			
1875	X	Line	27.6-28.6	-1.0	0		

OWNERSHIP

1853	Lawrenceburg & Upper Mississippi RR (B4), of part
1853/12/1	Indianapolis & Cincinnati RR, received Lawrenceburg & Upper Mississippi
1867/2	Indianapolis, Cincinnati & Lafayette RR, reorganize Indpls. & Cinci.

LAWRENCEBURG JCT.-SUNMAN OLD MAIN LINE (CCC-GO2)

	Mileage [Cincinnati]	County	Crossings, junctions, etc.
(Junction)	23.8	Dearborn	J/CCC-G 23.8
Guilford	28.1	"	
Manchester	32.2	"	
Weisburg	37.7	"	
(Junction)	40.3	"	J/CCC-G 39.2

CONSTRUCTION/ABANDONMENT

Date	Act	End points	MP	Change	Main	Source	Note
1853/11/1	B4	MP 23.8-MP 40.3	23.8-40.3	+16.5	16.5	2	
1905 ca.	X	MP 23.8-MP 40.3	23.8-40.3	-16.5	0	2	

OWNERSHIP

1853	Lawrenceburg & Upper Mississippi RR (B4), of part
1853/12/1	Indianapolis & Cincinnati RR (B5), received Lawrenceburg & Upper Miss.
1867/2	Indianapolis, Cincinnati & Lafayette RR, reorganize Indpls. & Cinci.
1880/3	Cincinnati, Indianapolis, St. Louis & Chicago RR, merge Indpls, Cin. & Laf.
1889/6	Cleveland, Cincinnati, Chicago & St. Louis Ry, merge CISL&C

CINCINNATI-INDIANAPOLIS LINE (CCC-G)

	Mileage	County	Crossings, junctions, etc.
Cincinnati OH	0		
Valley Jct.	17.7		
(Junction)	18.4		J/CCC-GW 18.4
Elizabethtown	19.5		
(OH/IN state line)	21.5		
Lawrenceburg Jct. (CP 22)	22.3	Dearborn	
(Junction)	23.0	"	J/CCC-GA 23.0
Thatcher	23.0	"	
(Junction)	23.8	"	J/CCC-GO2 23.8, J/CCC-GL 28.6
Guilford	27.9	"	
Ross	30.4	"	
Bonnell	31.4	"	
Code	35.7	"	
Weisburg	36.8	"	
(Junction)	39.2	"	J/CCC-GO2 40.3
CP 39	39.7	"	
Sunman	39.9	Ripley	
Brow	40.6	"	
Spades	41.8	"	
Morris	45.3	"	
Hyde	46.9	"	J/CCC-GO1 46.9
Batesville	47.8	"	
(Junction)	50.2	"	J/CCC-GO1 50.3
New Point	54.0	Decatur	
(continued)			

CLEVELAND, CINCINNATI, CHICAGO & ST. LOUIS

CINCINNATI-INDIANAPOLIS LINE (CCC-G) (continued)

		Mileage [Cincinnati]	County	Crossings, junctions, etc.
New Point		54.0	Decatur	
McCoy		57.2	"	
CP 60		60.2	"	
Greensburg		61.4	"	
CP 61		61.7	"	
GN		62.1	"	X/CCC-M 223.0
CP 63		63.0	"	
CP 64		64.2	"	
CP 66		66.1	"	
Adams		67.8	"	
Mead		72.2	"	
St. Paul		72.7	"	
Waldron		75.3	Shelby	
Clifty (CP 77)		77.3	"	
Prescott		77.4	"	
Vine (CP 82)		82.6	"	X/PRR-IC 23.8
Shelbyville		82.8	"	
CP 84		84.7	"	
Fairland (CP 89)		89.3	"	J/CCC-GM 89.3
London		93.3	"	
Brookfield		94.8	"	
Dix		95.6	"	
Acton		96.6	Marion	
Gallaudet		100.2	"	
Beech Grove	(CP 103)	103.7	"	
Belt Crossing		106.9	"	X/IU-B 3.8
College Avenue		108.9	"	J/IU-EA 0.7
--via IU-EA and IU-E				
(Indianapolis		109.6)	"	

CONSTRUCTION/ABANDONMENT

Date	Act	End points	MP	Change	Main	Source	Note
1853/11/1	B4	MP 39.2-Hyde	39.2-46.9	+7.7		2	
1853/11/1	B4	MP 50.2-Indianapolis	50.2-108.9	+58.7	66.4	2	
1865	B5	OH state line-MP 23.0	21.5-23.0	+1.5	67.9		1
1875	B5A	MP 23.0-MP 23.8	23.0-23.8	+0.8	68.7		
1905 ca.	B18	MP 23.8-MP 39.2	23.8-39.2	+15.4		2	
1905 ca.	B18	Hyde-MP 50.2	46.9-50.2	+3.3	87.4	2	

1991/12/31 S4		OH state line-Shelbyville	21.5-82.6	-61.1	26.3	2	

OWNERSHIP

1853	Lawrenceburg & Upper Mississippi RR (B4), of part
1853/12/1	Indianapolis & Cincinnati RR (B5), received Lawrenceburg & Upper Miss.
1867/2	Indianapolis, Cincinnati & Lafayette RR (B5A), reorganize Indpls. & Cinci.
1880/3	Cincinnati, Indianapolis, St. Louis & Chicago RR, merge Indpls, Cin. & Laf.
1889/6	Cleveland, Cincinnati, Chicago & St. Louis Ry (B18), merge CISL&C
1930/2/1	New York Central, lease Cleveland, Cincinnati, Chicago & St. Louis
1968/2/1	Penn Central, assigned lease of Cleveland, Cincinnati, Chicago & St. Louis
1976/4/1	Conrail, buy Penn Central
1991/12/31	Central RR of Indiana, buy part of Conrail line
1999/6/1	CSX Transportation, buy part of Conrail line

CLEVELAND, CINCINNATI, CHICAGO & ST. LOUIS

WHITEWATER BRANCH (CCC-GW)

	Mileage [Cincinnati]	County	Crossings, junctions, etc.
(Junction)	18.4		
White Water Park	19.8		
Shaper	21.2		
(OH/IN state line)	24.7		
Harrison	25.4	Dearborn	
Longnecker	28.7	"	
New Trenton	32.2	Franklin	
Ashby	33.8	"	
Cedar Grove	36.7	"	
Moundhaven	39.3	"	
Magnesia Springs	41.4	"	
Brookville	43.5	"	
Yellow Bank	47.0	"	
Metamora	51.9	"	
Leonard	52.7	"	
Valley View	54.1	"	
Laurel	57.7	"	
Bide-a-Wee	61.0	Fayette	
Alpine	61.8	"	
Nulltown	63.9	"	
Connersville	68.5	"	
(Bridge)	69.0	"	B/B&O-IH 67.7
Huber	71.6	"	
Beeson	74.1	Wayne	J/NKP-LF 103.7
(End)	74.4	"	
Milton	78.8	"	
(Crossing)	80.9	"	X/PRR-ICA 63.3
Cambridge City	81.0	"	X/PRR-I 135.0
Hagerstown	87.7	"	J/PRR-CR 90.3

CONSTRUCTION/ABANDONMENT

Date	Act	End points	MP	Change	Main	Source	Note
1868/7/21	B7	OH line-Hagerstown	24.7-87.7	+63.0	63.0	2	
1931	X	Beesons-Hagerstown	74.4-87.7	-13.3	49.7	2	

1974	L1	Brookville-Connersville	43.9-68.0	<24.1>	25.6		
1975	XL	Brookville-Metamora	43.9.50.1	<+6.3>			
1975	X	Brookville-Metamora	43.9-50.1	-6.3	25.6		
1979	S6	OH line-Brookville	24.7-43.9	[19.2]	6.4		
1981/12	S10	Connersville-Beeson	68.0-74.1	[6.1]			8
1981 ca.	X	In Beeson	74.1-74.4	-0.3	0		
1984/4	S5	Metamora-Connersville	50.1-68.0	[17.9]	0		
1990/2	S5	In Connersville	68.0-69.1	[1.1]	0		

OWNERSHIP

1868	White Water Valley RR (B7), leased to Indpls., Cinci. & Lafayette
1871/5/1	Lease of WWV by IC&L terminated
1890	Cleveland, Cincinnati, Chicago & St. Louis Ry, lease White Water Valley
1915/6/16	Cleveland, Cincinnati, Chicago & St. Louis Ry, buy White Water Valley
1930/2/1	New York Central, lease Cleveland, Cincinnati, Chicago & St. Louis
1968/2/1	Penn Central, assigned lease of Cleveland, Cincinnati, Chicago & St. Louis
1976/4/1	Conrail, purchase of Penn Central

CLEVELAND, CINCINNATI, CHICAGO & ST. LOUIS

AURORA BRANCH (CCC-GA)

	Mileage [Cincinnati]	County	Crossings, junctions, etc.
(Junction)	23.0	Dearborn	J/CCC-G 23.0
Hardenburg	23.5	"	
Dearborn	24.9	"	X/B&O-SC 21.9
Lawrenceburg	25.1	"	
(Junction)	25.5	"	J/CCC-GL 25.5
Aurora	29.0	"	
(End of track)	29.2	"	

CONSTRUCTION/ABANDONMENT

Date	Act	End points	MP	Change	Main	Source	Note
1853/11/1	B4	MP 23.0-Lawrenceburg	23.0-25.5	+2.5	2.5	2	
1887	B16	Lawrenceburg-Aurora	25.5-29.2	+3.7	6.2	1	

1979	X	Lawrenceburg-Aurora	26.0-29.2	-3.2	3.0	1	
1991/12/31	S4	MP 23.0-Lawrenceburg	23.0-26.0	-3.0	0	1	

OWNERSHIP

1853	Lawrenceburg & Upper Mississippi RR (B4), of part
1853/12/1	Indianapolis & Cincinnati RR, received Lawrenceburg & Upper Mississippi
1867/2	Indianapolis, Cincinnati & Lafayette RR, reorganize Indpls. & Cinci.
1880/3	Cincinnati, Indianapolis, St. Louis & Chicago RR, merged Indpls, Cin. & Laf.
1887	Cincinnati & Southern Ohio River RR (B16), lease by CISL&C
1889/6	Cleveland, Cincinnati, Chicago & St. Louis Ry, merge CISL&C
1915	Cleveland, Cincinnati, Chicago & St. Louis Ry, buy C&SOR
1930/2/1	New York Central, leased Cleveland, Cincinnati, Chicago & St. Louis
1968/2/1	Penn Central, assigned lease of Cleveland, Cincinnati, Chicago & St. Louis
1976/4/1	Conrail, purchase of Penn Central

COLUMBUS BRANCH (CCC-GC)

	Mileage [Cincinnati]	County	Crossings, junctions, etc.
Craig	64.2	Decatur	J/CCC-M 225.0
Ewington	66.8	"	
Burney	70.7	"	
Rugby	74.5	Bartholomew	
Hope	77.4	"	
Nortonburg	81.4	"	
Lambert	83	"	
Columbus	88.6	"	J/PRR-IL 41.0

CONSTRUCTION/ABANDONMENT

Date	Act	End points	MP	Change	Main	Source	Note
1884/5/5	B15	Craig-Columbus	64.2-88.6	+24.4	24.4	2	

1973	X	Craig-Columbus	64.2-86.1	-21.9		2	
1973	Y	In Columbus	86.1-88.6	(2.5)	(2.5)	2	
1976	X	In Columbus	86.1-88.6	(-2.5)	0		

OWNERSHIP

1884	Columbus, Hope & Greensburg RR (B15), controlled and leased by Cinci., Indpls., St.L. & Chicago
1930/2/1	New York Central, leased Cleveland, Cincinnati, Chicago & St. Louis
1968/2/1	Penn Central, assigned lease of Cleveland, Cincinnati, Chicago & St. Louis
1976/4/1	Conrail, purchase of Penn Central, merged Columbus, Hope & Greensburg

CLEVELAND, CINCINNATI, CHICAGO & ST. LOUIS

MARTINSVILLE BRANCH (CCC-GM)

	Mileage [Cincinnati]	County	Crossings, junctions, etc.
Fairland	89.3	Shelby	J/CCC-G 89.3
Boggstown	92.7	"	
Needham	96.3	Johnson	
Franklin	101.8	"	X/PRR-IL 20.3
Branch	106.7	"	
Trafalgar	109.0	"	
(End of track)	109.5	"	
Samaria	111.1	"	
Morgantown	115.8	Morgan	X/IC-NI 30.06
Williams Crossing	118.7	"	
Mahalasville	121.2	"	
Taggart	123.9	"	
Martinsville	127.3	"	J/PRR-IV 30.6

CONSTRUCTION/ABANDONMENT

Date	Act	End points	MP	Change	Main	Source	Note
1853/5/17	B3	Franklin-Martinsville	101.8-127.3	+25.5	25.5	1	2
1866/6/14	B6	Fairland-Franklin	89.3-101.8	+12.5	38.0	1	
1942	X	Martinsville-Trafalgar	127.3-109.5	-17.8	20.2	2	9
1961	X	Trafalgar-Franklin	109.5-101.8	-7.7	12.5	2	

1976	X	Fairland-Franklin	89.3-101.5	-12.5	0		

OWNERSHIP

1853	Martinsville & Franklin RR (B3), of part, leased to Madison & Indianapolis
1858/5/17	Madison & Indpls. lease of Martinsville & Franklin terminated
1865/9	Cincinnati & Martinsville RR (B6), of part, buy Martinsville & Franklin
1876/6	Indianapolis, Cincinnati & Lafayette RR, operate Cinci. & Martinsville
1877/1/27	Fairland, Franklin & Martinsville RR, reorganize Cinci. & Martinsville
1880/3	Cincinnati, Indianapolis, St. Louis & Chicago RR, merge FF&M
1889/6	Cleveland, Cincinnati, Chicago & St. Louis Ry, merge CISL&C
1930/2/1	New York Central, lease Cleveland, Cincinnati, Chicago & St. Louis
1968/2/1	Penn Central, assigned lease of Cleveland, Cincinnati, Chicago & St. Louis

INDIANAPOLIS-CHICAGO LINE (CCC-H)

	Mileage [Cincinnati	County	Crossings, junctions, etc.
(Indianapolis	110.0)	Marion	
--via IU-W and CCC-I			
(IJ	111.0)	"	
--via P&E-A			
Brant	113.1	"	J/P&E-A 3.5
30th Street	115.2	"	
(Junction)	116.7	"	J/CCC-HO 115.8
Augusta	120.4	"	
Rock Island	122.8	"	
Glenn	122.9	"	
Glenn Interlocking	123.6	"	
Zionsville	125.2	Boone	
Whitestown	130.6	"	
Dale	132.4	"	
(Crossing)	138.0	"	X/CI-A 61.2
Lebanon	138.3	"	
(Bridge)	138.7	"	B/PRR-IF 31.8
CP 139	139.4	"	
Hazelrigg (CP 143)	143.4	"	
(continued)			

CLEVELAND, CINCINNATI, CHICAGO & ST. LOUIS

INDIANAPOLIS-CHICAGO LINE (CCC-H) (continued)

	Mileage [Cincinnati]	County	Crossings, junctions, etc.
Hazelrigg (CP 143)	143.4	Boone	
Hazelrigg Interlocking	144.1	"	
Thorntown	147.5	"	
Colfax	153.2	Clinton	
Colfax Interlocking	154.0	"	X/PRR-VC 68.6
CP 155	155.7	"	
Clarks Hill (CP 158)	158.2	Tippecanoe	
Clarks Hill Interlocking	158.9	"	X/NKP-TC 217.8
Bell	159.4	"	
Stockwell	161.7	"	
Rex	163.3	"	
North Crane	165.9	"	
CP 169	169.1	"	
Altamont	170.2	"	J/NKP-LF 254.7
--via NKP-LF			
(Lafayette	174.0)	"	
--via NKP-LF			
MD	192.6	Benton	J/NKP-LF 277.3
Templeton	193.3	"	
Atkinson	196.7	"	
Swanington	198.6	"	
(Crossing)	199.6	"	X/CAS-A 61.3
Fowler	202.2	Benton	
Gravel Hill	205.7	"	
Earl Park	208.9	"	
Sheff	211.2	"	
F	211.9	"	X/LS-WD 66.26
Raub	213.9	"	
(IN/IL state line)	216.2		
Sheldon IL	219.0		
Kankakee IL	248.8		
Kankakee Jct. IL	249.4		

CONSTRUCTION/ABANDONMENT

Date	Act	End points	MP	Change	Main	Source	Note
1852/12/16	B2	Indianapolis-Altamont	116.7-170.2	+53.5	53.5	2	
1872/8/25	B11	Templeton-IL state line	192.6-216.2	+23.6	77.1	2	
1904	B18	Brant-MP 116.7	113.1-116.7	+3.6	80.7	2	

1976	X	Zionsville-Lebanon	125.4-137.0	-11.6	69.1	2	
1977/12/1	L3	Kankakee Jct IL-Sheldon IL	249.4-219.0	-			
1980	S2	Kankakee Jct IL-Sheldon IL	249.4-219.0	-		2	
1984	X	near Zionsville	123.4-125.4	-2.0	67.1	1,2	
1985	X	Lebanon-Altamont	137.0-170.2	-33.2	33.9	1,2	
1989	S2	Templeton-Swanington	192.6-198.6	[6.0]	27.9	2	
1994	S3	Swanington-Sheldon IL	198.6-216.2	[17.6]	10.3	2	

OWNERSHIP

1852	Lafayette & Indianapolis RR (B2)
1867/2/14	Indianapolis & Cincinnati RR, bought Lafayette & Indianapolis
1867/2/14	Indianapolis, Cincinnati & Lafayette RR (B11), reorganize Indpls. & Cinci
1880/3	Cincinnati, Indianapolis, St. Louis & Chicago RR, merged IC&L
1889/6	Cleveland, Cincinnati, Chicago & St. Louis Ry (B18), merged CISL&C
1930/2/1	New York Central, leased Cleveland, Cincinnati, Chicago & St. Louis
1968/2/1	Penn Central, assigned lease of Cleveland, Cincinnati, Chicago & St. Louis
1976/4/1	Conrail, purchase of Penn Central

CLEVELAND, CINCINNATI, CHICAGO & ST. LOUIS

OLD MAIN LINE IN INDIANAPOLIS (CCC-HO)

	Mileage [Cincinnati	County	Crossings, junctions, etc.
(Indianapolis)	109.6)	Marion	
--via IU-W			
(Junction)	109.8	"	J/IU-W 0.2
North Street	110.8	"	
(Junction)	113.2	"	J/IU-B 11.8
North Indianapolis	113.4	"	
(Junction)	115.8	"	J/CCC-H 116.7

CONSTRUCTION/ABANDONMENT

Date	Act	End points	MP	Change	Main	Source	Note
1852/12/16	B2	Line	109.6-115.8	+6.2	6.2	2	
1853	S1	Part of line	109.6-109.8	[0.2]	6.0		
1904	X	part of line	113.8-115.8	-2.0		2	
1904	Y	part of line	109.8-113.8	(4.0)	0	2	

OWNERSHIP

1852	Lafayette & Indianapolis RR (B2)
1867/2/14	Indianapolis & Cincinnati RR, bought Lafayette & Indianapolis
1867/2	Indianapolis, Cincinnati & Lafayette RR (B11), reorganize Indpls. & Cinci
1880/3	Cincinnati, Indianapolis, St. Louis & Chicago RR, merged IC&L
1889/6	Cleveland, Cincinnati, Chicago & St. Louis Ry, merged CISL&C
1930/2/1	New York Central, leased Cleveland, Cincinnati, Chicago & St. Louis
1968/2/1	Penn Central, assigned lease of Cleveland, Cincinnati, Chicago & St. Louis
1976/4/1	Conrail, purchase of Penn Central
1999/6/1	CSX Transportation, buy Conrail line

GREENCASTLE OLD MAIN (CCC-LO)

	Mileage [Indianapolis]	County	Crossings, junctions, etc.
(Junction)	36.4	Putnam	J/CCC-L 36.4
Greencastle	39.0	"	X/MON-SA 177.8
Oakalla	42.8	"	
(Junction)	47.9	"	J/CCC-L 47.3

CONSTRUCTION/ABANDONMENT

Date	Act	End points	MP	Change	Main	Source	Note
1870/7/4	B12	Line	36.4-47.9	+11.5	11.5	2	
1905 ca.	X	MP 36.4-Greencastle	36.4-39.0	-2.6		2	
1905 ca.	X	MP 40.6-MP 47.9	40.6-47.9	-7.3		2	
1905 ca.	Y	Greencastle-MP 40.6	39.0-40.6	(1.6)	0		

1984	X	Greencastle-MP 40.6	39.0-40.6	(-1.6)	0		1

OWNERSHIP

1870	Indianapolis & St. Louis RR (B12)
1889/6	Cleveland, Cincinnati, Chicago & St. Louis Ry, merged I&SL
1930/2/1	New York Central, leased Cleveland, Cincinnati, Chicago & St. Louis
1968/2/1	Penn Central, assigned lease of Cleveland, Cincinnati, Chicago & St. Louis
1976/4/1	Conrail, purchase of Penn Central

INDIANAPOLIS-ST. LOUIS LINE (CCC-L)

	Mileage	County	Crossings, junctions, etc.
(Indianapolis	0)	Marion	
--via IU-W			
West Street	0.4	"	J/IU-W 0.4
IJ	1.0	"	X/B&O-IS 125.5, J/P&E-A 1.0
BX	1.6	"	X/IU-B 9.1
(continued)			

CLEVELAND, CINCINNATI, CHICAGO & ST. LOUIS

INDIANAPOLIS-ST. LOUIS LINE (CCC-L) (continued)

	Mileage [Indianapolis]	County	Crossings, junctions, etc.
Mt. Jackson	2.6	Marion	
Sunnyside	6	"	
MY	9.4	Hendricks	X/PRR-IF 8.6
Avon	11.9	"	
AN	12.5	"	
Danville	19.3	"	
Nash	20.3	"	
Hadley	23.8	"	
Reno	27.8	"	
Fillmore	32.6	Putnam	
(Junction)	36.4	"	J/CCC-LO 36.4
(Crossing)	38.0	"	X/MON-SA 176.8
Greencastle	39.1	"	
Alma	42.9	"	
Fern	44.6	"	
(Junction)	47.3	"	J/CCC-LO 47.9
Lena	48.7	Parke	
Carbon	52.8	Clay	X/CI-A 121.2, J/CCC-LC 0
Simpsons Spur	54.4	"	
Perth	55.6	"	
Coal Bluff	58.6	Vigo	X/B&O-IB 16.9
Cobb	59.0	"	
Fontanet	60.2	"	J/CCC-LU 0
Lone Star Coal Co.	61.2	"	
Burnett	63.9	"	X/CEI-EZ 175.0
Forest	64.2	"	
Markles	66.8	"	
Preston	68.6	"	X/MILW-T 175.2, X/PRR-VT1 2.1
Duane	69.2	"	
Haley	70.5	"	X/CEI-E 176.5
Terre Haute	71.6	"	
CP 72	72.0	"	J/CCC-T 0, J/PRR-VT2 73.3 aka CP Ringo
Griff	72.2	"	
Millard	72.4	"	
Gravel Pit	72.8	"	
St. Mary of the Woods	75.7	"	
CP 76	76.3	"	
Sandford (CP 79)	79.9	"	
(IN/IL state line)	80.0		
Vermilion IL	84.0		
Mattoon IL	128.2		

CONSTRUCTION/ABANDONMENT

Date	Act	End points	MP	Change	Main	Source	Note
1856	B8	Terre Haute-IL state line	71.6-80.0	+8.4	8.4	2	
1870/7/4	B12	Indianapolis-MP 36.4	0.4-36.4	+36.0		2	
1870/7/4	B12	MP 47.3-Terre Haute	47.3-71.6	+24.3	68.7	2	
1905 ca.	B18	MP 36.4-MP 47.3	36.4-47.3	+10.9	79.6	2	

OWNERSHIP

1856	St. Louis, Alton & Terre Haute RR (B8), of part
1867	Indianapolis & St. Louis RR (B12), of part, leased SLA&TH
1889/6	Cleveland, Cincinnati, Chicago & St. Louis Ry (B18), merged SLA&TH and I&SL
1930/2/1	New York Central, leased Cleveland, Cincinnati, Chicago & St. Louis
1968/2/1	Penn Central, assigned lease of Cleveland, Cincinnati, Chicago & St. Louis
1976/4/1	Conrail, purchase of Penn Central

CLEVELAND, CINCINNATI, CHICAGO & ST. LOUIS

OTTER CREEK MINE SPUR (CCC-LC)

	Mileage	County	Crossings, junctions, etc.
Carbon	0	Clay	J/CCC-L 52.8
Otter Creek Mine	2	"	

CONSTRUCTION/ABANDONMENT

Date	Act	End points	MP	Change	Main	Source	Note
							3

OWNERSHIP

??	Indianapolis & St. Louis RR (B12)
1889/6	Cleveland, Cincinnati, Chicago & St. Louis Ry, merged I&SL

UNION MINE SPUR (CCC-LU)

	Mileage	County	Crossings, junctions, etc.
Fontanet	0	Vigo	J/CCC-L 60.2
Union Mine	1.5	"	

CONSTRUCTION/ABANDONMENT

Date	Act	End points	MP	Change	Main	Source	Note
??							3

OWNERSHIP

??	Indianapolis & St. Louis RR (B12)
1889/6	Cleveland, Cincinnati, Chicago & St. Louis Ry, merged I&SL

EI&TH (TERRE HAUTE-EVANSVILLE) (CCC-T)

	Mileage	County	Crossings, junctions, etc.
CP 72	0	Vigo	J/CCC-L 72.0
Vigo	0.2	"	X/PRR-V 73.5
Greenwood	2.2	"	
X	4.7	"	X/CEI-E 181.7, X/MILW-T 182.7
Spring Hill	5.1	"	
Liberty	7.8	"	
Riley	10.3	"	
County Line	12.6	"	
Cory	15.6	Clay	
Climax	18.8	"	
Saline City	20.0	"	J/PRR-VB 11.5
Eel (River)	22.0	"	
(Crossing)	25.6	"	X/MON-SL 27.7
Clay City	26.1	"	
Lancaster Jct.	27.6	"	J/CEI-JL 0
Lancaster	28.1	"	
Commodore Mine	29.1	"	
Coal City	31.2	Owen	
Mancourt	32.0	"	
Daggett	32.4	"	
Mathews	32.5	"	
Eel River Mining Co.	34.1	"	
Hubbell	35.0	"	
Worthington	39.8	Greene	
Worthington Jct.	40.0	"	(J/PRR-IV 72.5)
Rincon Jct.	41.2	"	X/PRR-IV 73.8
Rincon	41.3	"	
Elliston	48.0	"	X/MON-SS 36.0, B/IC-NI 85.2
Plummer	51.1	"	
Lester	53	"	
Newberry	55.9	"	
(continued)			

CLEVELAND, CINCINNATI, CHICAGO & ST. LOUIS

EI&TH (TERRE HAUTE-EVANSVILLE) (CCC-T) (continued)

	Mileage	County	Crossings, junctions, etc.
Newberry	55.9	"	
Elnora	61.2	Daviess	X/MILW-T 224.1
Plainville	67.8	"	
Capehart	72.5	"	
Graham	74.3	"	
Jordan	76.6	"	
Duff	77.2	"	J/CCC-TW 0
Chappell	78.4	"	X/B&O-SI 171.4
Maysville	79.7	"	J/CCC-TW 5.6
Thomas	82.5	"	
Sandy Hook	86.8	"	
Rogers	88.9	Pike	
Gladstone	90.0	"	
Bennett	91.0	"	
Petersboro	94.3	"	
Ashby	95.4	"	
Glezen	100.4	"	
Hosmer	100.7	"	
Little	101.4	"	
Ingle	101.8	"	
Massey	103.3	Gibson	
Cline	105.6	"	
Oakland City	106.2	"	X/SOU-U 175.6
Gray Jct.	107.2	"	J/CCC-TC 0
Gudgel	108.8	"	
Somerville	110.8	"	J/CCC-TS 0
Mackey	112.7	"	
Buckskin	114.8	"	
Tecumseh Jct.	114.9	"	J/CCC-TK 0
Rosebud	117.1	Warrick	
Elberfeld	119.8	"	
Elberfeld Mine	120.4	"	
Ditney	121.4	"	
Ditney Hill	122.7	"	
Elliott	122.8	Vanderburgh	
Daylight	125.0	"	
Inglehart	127.1	"	
Straight Line Jct.	130.9	"	J/CEI-E 283.0
--via CEI-E			
(Evansville	134.4)		

CONSTRUCTION/ABANDONMENT

Date	Act	End points	MP	Change	Main	Source	Note
1920/6/3	P1	Terre Haute-Str.Line Jct.	0-77.2	+77.2		2	3
1920/6/3	P1	Maysville-Str. Line Jct.	79.7-130.9	+51.2	128.4	2	3
1929	B19	Duff-Maysville	77.2-79.7	+2.5	130.9	2	3

1969 ca.	X,Y	Terre Haute-Spring Hill	0-5.5	-5.5			
1969	X	Worthington Jc.-Rincon Jc.	40.0-41.2	-1.2	124.2		
1981	X	Cory-Worthington Jct.	12.4-39.4	-27.0			6
1981	Y	At Worthington	39.4-40.0	(0.6)	96.6		
1984	X	At Worthington	39.4-40.0	(-0.6)			
1992	S9	Rincon Jct.-Str.Line Jct.	41.2-130.9	[89.7]	6.9		

OWNERSHIP

1920	Evansville, Indianapolis & Terre Haute Ry, purchased line
1930/2	Cleveland, Cincinnati, Chicago & St. Louis, leased EI&TH
1930/2/1	New York Central, leased Cleveland, Cincinnati, Chicago & St. Louis
1968/2/1	Penn Central, assigned lease of Cleveland, Cincinnati, Chicago & St. Louis
1976/4/1	Conrail, purchase of Penn Central

CLEVELAND, CINCINNATI, CHICAGO & ST. LOUIS

WASHINGTON BRANCH (CCC-TW)

	Mileage	County	Crossings, junctions, etc.
Duff	0	Daviess	J/CCC-T 77.2
Washington	2.7	"	X/B&O-SW/SW 170.4
Maysville	5.6	"	J/CCC-T 79.7

CONSTRUCTION/ABANDONMENT

Date	Act	End points	MP	Change	Main	Source	Note
1920/6/3	P1	Duff-Maysville	0-5.6	+5.6	5.6	R	3
1929	X	Washington-Maysville	2.3-5.6	-3.3	2.3	R	

1982	X,S	Duff-Washington	0-2.3	-2.3	0	I	5

OWNERSHIP

1920	Evansville, Indianapolis & Terre Haute Ry, purchased line
1930/2	Cleveland, Cincinnati, Chicago & St. Louis, leased EI&TH
1930/2/1	New York Central, leased Cleveland, Cincinnati, Chicago & St. Louis
1968/2/1	Penn Central, assigned lease of Cleveland, Cincinnati, Chicago & St. Louis
1976/4/1	Conrail, purchase of Penn Central

COE BRANCH (CCC-TC)

	Mileage	County	Crossings, junctions, etc.
Gray Jct.	0	Gibson	J/CCC-T 107.6
Oakland City Jct.	2.8	"	J/AWW-A 0, J/AWW-B 0
Enosville	3.7	Pike	
Coe	5.8	"	
Blackfoot Mine	5.8	"	

CONSTRUCTION/ABANDONMENT

Date	Act	End points	MP	Change	Main	Source	Note
1927 ca.	B19	Gray Jct.-Blackfoot Mine	0-5.8	+5.8	5.8		
1950 ca.	X	Oakland City Jct.-Bl. Mine	2.8-5.8	-3.0	2.8		

1992/4	S9	Gray Jct.-Oakland City Jct.	0-2.8	-2.8	0		

OWNERSHIP

1927	Evansville, Indianapolis & Terre Haute Ry (B19)
1930/2	Cleveland, Cincinnati, Chicago & St. Louis, leased EI&TH
1930/2/1	New York Central, leased Cleveland, Cincinnati, Chicago & St. Louis
1968/2/1	Penn Central, assigned lease of Cleveland, Cincinnati, Chicago & St. Louis
1976/4/1	Conrail, purchase of Penn Central

DICKEYVILLE BRANCH (CCC-TK)

	Mileage	County	Crossings, junctions, etc.
Tecumseh Jct.	0	Gibson	J/CCC-T 114.9
Lynnville Mine	5.5	"	J/YANK-A 0
Richards	9.9	"	
Tecumseh	12.1	"	

CONSTRUCTION/ABANDONMENT

Date	Act	End points	MP	Change	Main	Source	Note
1928 ca.	B19	Tecumseh-Jct.-Tecumseh	0-12.1	+12.1	12.1		
1954	X	Lynnville Mine-Tecumseh	7.8-12.1	-4.3	7.8		

1992/4	S9	Tecumseh Jct.-Lynnville M.	0-7.8	-7.8	0		

OWNERSHIP

1927	Evansville, Indianapolis & Terre Haute Ry (B19)
1930/2	Cleveland, Cincinnati, Chicago & St. Louis, leased EI&TH
1930/2/1	New York Central, leased Cleveland, Cincinnati, Chicago & St. Louis
1968/2/1	Penn Central, assigned lease of Cleveland, Cincinnati, Chicago & St. Louis
1976/4/1	Conrail, purchase of Penn Central

CLEVELAND, CINCINNATI, CHICAGO & ST. LOUIS

SOMERVILLE BRANCH (CCC-TS)

	Mileage	County	Crossings, junctions, etc.
Somerville	0	Gibson	J/CCC-T 110.8
(Junction)	6.7	"	J/SOU-U 168.5

CONSTRUCTION/ABANDONMENT

Date	Act	End points	MP	Change	Main	Source	Note
1924	B20	Line	0-6.7	+6.7	6.7	2	
1936	X	Line	0-6.7	-6.7	0	2	

OWNERSHIP

1924	Evansville, Indianapolis & Terre Haute Ry (B20)
1930/2	Cleveland, Cincinnati, Chicago & St. Louis, leased EI&TH
1930/2/1	New York Central, leased Cleveland, Cincinnati, Chicago & St. Louis

VINCENNES BRANCH (CCC-LV)

	Mileage [Danville]	County	Crossings, junctions, etc.
St. Francisville IL	111.4		J/CCC-LD 107.6
(IL/IN state line)	112.6		
Brevoorts	116.4	Knox	
South Vincennes	119.1	"	
Vincennes, Main Street	120.4	"	J/CEI-E 235.6
Vincennes, Union Depot	121.2	"	X/B&O-SI 188.6

CONSTRUCTION/ABANDONMENT

Date	Act	End points	MP	Change	Main	Source	Note
1885	P2	St. Francisville-Vincennes	112.6-121.2	+8.6	8.6	2	

1968	X	St. Francisville-Vincennes	112.6-121.2	-8.6	0		4

OWNERSHIP

1885	Cairo & Vincennes, lease to Wabash, St. Louis & Pacific canceled
1889	Cairo, Vincennes & Chicago RR, reorganize Cairo & Vincennes
1906	Cleveland, Cincinnati, Chicago & St. Louis, lease CV&C
1913	Cleveland, Cincinnati, Chicago & St. Louis, merge CV&C
1930/2/1	New York Central, lease Cleveland, Cincinnati, Chicago & St. Louis
1968/2/1	Penn Central, assigned lease of Cleveland, Cincinnati, Chicago & St. Louis
1976/4/1	Conrail, purchase Penn Central

EVANSVILLE BRANCH (CCC-LE)

	Mileage [Danville]	County	Crossings, junctions, etc.
YD	127.4		
(IL/IN state line)	131.8		
Skelton	133.8	Gibson	
Johnson	136.3	"	
Antioch	139.7	"	
(Bridge)	142.8	Posey	B/CEI-EM 277.2
Cynthiana	143.1	"	
Nisbet	147.0	Vanderburgh	
Davy	151.3	"	
Harwood	157.7	"	X/IC-NM 245.5
(Crossing)	159.2	"	X/CEI-EJ 2.8
8th Avenue	160.0	"	J/L&N-SE 324.7
--via L&N-SE			
(Evansville	160.3)	"	
(Howell Yard	161.6)	"	

CLEVELAND, CINCINNATI, CHICAGO & ST. LOUIS

EVANSVILLE BRANCH (CCC-LE) (continued)
CONSTRUCTION/ABANDONMENT

Date	Act	End points	MP	Change	Main	Source	Note
1911/7/1	B17	Evansville-Mt. Carmel	160.0-131.8	+28.2	28.2	R	

1976	X	Mt. Carmel-MP 154.1	131.8-154.1	-22.3		R	
1976	S8	In Evansville	154.1-160.0	-5.9		O	

OWNERSHIP

1911	Evansville, Mt. Carmel & Northern Ry (B17), controlled and leased by Clev., Cinci., Chgo & St. L.
1913 ??	Cleveland, Cincinnati, Chicago & St. Louis, merged EMC&N
1930/2/1	New York Central, leased Cleveland, Cincinnati, Chicago & St. Louis
1968/2/1	Penn Central, assigned lease of Cleveland, Cincinnati, Chicago & St. Louis
1976/4/1	Conrail, purchase of Penn Central

MICHIGAN DIVISION (CCC-M)

	Mileage	County	Crossings, junctions, etc.
Benton Harbor MI	0		
Beebe Siding			
(MI/IN state line)	33.4		

(MI/IN state line)	35.2		
Granger IN	35.7	St. Joseph	X/GTW-C 110.9
Belleview	39.3	Elkhart	
Elkhart	44.8	"	
(Crossing)	50.3	"	X/LS-A 438.3
Dunlaps	50.2	"	
Goshen	55.3	"	
CX	55.5	"	X/NYC-T 411.1, J/LS-TS 0
Yost	57.5	"	
Waterford	58.3	"	
New Paris Jct.	61.3	"	X/WAB-MC 161.4
New Paris	62.0	"	
Milford Jct.	66.3	Kosciusko	X/B&O-C 165.7
Milford	67.5	"	
(Junction)	68.2	"	J/SYM-A 6.8
Leesburg	73.0	"	
Grandy	78.3	"	
(Crossing)	79.6	"	X/WIN-B 0.2
Warsaw	79.7	"	X/PRR-F 358.7
Reeds	83.2	"	
Claypool	87.5	"	X/NKP-C 410.9
Silver Lake	91.4	"	
Rose Hill	94.2	Wabash	
North Manchester	99.0	"	X/PRR-LE 36.9
Bolivar	101.6	"	X/ERIE-C 144.4, J/HERG-A 0
Urbana	106.1	"	
Speicher	109.1	"	
(Bridge)	112.7	"	B/WAB-MC 187.6
Wabash	113.4	"	
Treaty	119.1	"	
LaFontaine	123.6	"	
Fox	126.5	Grant	
Otes	128.7	"	
Marion IN	132.7	"	
3rd Street	133.0	"	X/NKP-TB 153.8
Kent	133.4	"	X/PRR-L 156.9
(Bridge)	134.1	"	B/C&O-C 132.8
Soldiers Home	135.5	"	
Jonesboro	138.3	"	
(continued)			

CLEVELAND, CINCINNATI, CHICAGO & ST. LOUIS

MICHIGAN DIVISION (CCC-M) (continued)

	Mileage [Benton Harbor]	County	Crossings, junctions, etc.
Jonesboro	138.3	"	
Fairmount	142.8	"	X/PRR-CM 17.9
Summitville	148.1	Madison	
Alexandria	153.5	"	
(Crossing)	153.8	"	X/NKP-LS 189.9
Alda	155.0	"	
Linwood	158.6	"	
Dow	162.6	"	X/PRR-CR 124.8
CP 247	165.4	"	J/CCC-I 247.8
Anderson	165.5	"	
Pearl Street	165.7	"	
C. I. Crossing	165.8	"	X/CI-A 18.6
P. R. R. Crossing	166.3	"	X/PRR-YA 0.9
CP 247-A	166.6	"	X/CCC-IA 247.2
South Anderson Yard	166.7	"	
Alliance	171.0	"	
Emporia	172.7	"	
Markleville	174.8	"	
Shirley	181.0	Hancock	
(Crossing)	181.5	Henry	X/CCC-S 107.3
Winkfield	183.5	"	
Knox	186.2	"	
Knightstown	187.5	"	
(Crossing)	188.2	"	X/PRR-I 153.9
Carthage	193.1	Rush	
Boyd	195.1	"	
Farmer	196.4	"	
Henderson	198.6	"	
Kern	203.5	"	
(Junction)	203.8	"	J/NKP-LR 107.2
Rushville	204.5	"	X/B&O-IH 85.4
(Crossing)	204.7	"	X/PRR-IC 41.8
Bennetts Crossing	209.6	"	
Milroy	212.1	"	
Williamstown	215.2	Decatur	
Sandusky	217.6	"	
Greensburg	223.5	"	
GN	223.6	"	X/CC-G 62.8
Craig	225.0	"	X/CC-GC 64.2
Horace	230.5	"	
Letts	232.4	"	f. Letts Corner
Westport	236.5	"	J/MILW-T 325.9
Harper	238.9	"	f. Sardinia
Earl	240.4	"	f. Sherwood
Brewersville	243.4	Jennings	
North Vernon	248.9	"	J/B&O-SV 0, J/PRR-IM 21.5
--via B&O-SV			
(Louisville KY)			

CONSTRUCTION/ABANDONMENT

Date	Act	End points	MP	Change	Main	Source	Note
1870/8/15	B9	Warsaw-Goshen	79.7-55.3	+24.4	24.4		
1871	B10	North Manchester-Warsaw	99.0-79.7	+19.3	43.7		
1872	B10	Wabash-North Manchester	113.4-99.0	+14.4	58.1		
1873	B10	Marion-Wabash	132.7-113.4	+19.3	77.4		
(continued)							

CLEVELAND, CINCINNATI, CHICAGO & ST. LOUIS

MICHIGAN DIVISION (CCC-M)

CONSTRUCTION/ABANDONMENT (continued)

Date	Act	End points	MP	Change	Main	Source	Note
1875	B10	Fairmount-Marion	142.8-132.7	+10.1	87.5		
1876	B10	Anderson-Fairmount	165.5-142.8	+22.7	110.2		
1881	B13	Rushville-North Vernon	204.5-248.9	+44.4	154.6		
1882/7/3	B10	Goshen-Niles MI	23.8-55.3	+20.1		3	
1882/11/13	B10	Niles-Benton Harbor	23.8-0	-	174.7	3	
1891	B10	Rushville-Anderson	204.5-165.5	+39.0	213.7		
1942	X	Niles Jct. MI-CX	26.4-55.5	-20.3	193.4		

1973	X	Carthage-Greensburg	193.5-222.3	-28.8		2	
1973	Y	In Greensburg	222.3-223.5	(1.2)			
1973	X	Craig-North Vernon	225.0-248.9	-23.9	139.5	2	
1979/6	L2	Emporia-Carthage	173.5-193.5	<20.0>	119.5	2	
1982	X	Greensburg-Craig	223.5-225.0	-1.5			
1982	X	In Greensburg	222.3-223.5	(1.2)	118.0		
1985/1/8	LA1	Emporia-Carthage	173.5-193.5	<20.0>	118.0	2	
1987/4	S7	Emporia-Carthage	173.5-193.5	<20.0>		2	
1988	X	Emporia-Knightstown	173.5-188.2	[-14.7]	118.0	2	

OWNERSHIP

1870	Warsaw, Goshen & White Pigeon RR (B9), of part
1871	Cincinnati, Wabash & Michigan (B10), of part, merge WG&WP and other road
1881	Vernon, Greensburg & Rushville RR (B13), lease to Cin, Indpls, SL & Chi.
1889/6	Cleveland, Cincinnati, Chicago & St. Louis (B18), merge CISL&C and VG&R
1892/7/13	Cleveland, Cincinnati, Chicago & St. Louis, control of CW&M
1913/12/17	Cleveland, Cincinnati, Chicago & St. Louis, merge CW&M
1930/2/1	New York Central, lease Cleveland, Cincinnati, Chicago & St. Louis
1968/2/1	Penn Central, assigned lease of Cleveland, Cincinnati, Chicago & St. L.
1976/4/1	Conrail, purchase of Penn Central

ACQUISITION/DISPOSITION RECORD

Date	Act	CCC-	End points	Change	Main	Note
1851	B1	I,IO	OH state line-Indianapolis	+84.9	84.9	1
1852/12/16	B2	H,HO	Indianapolis-Lafayette	+59.7	144.6	
1853	S1	I	Wash. St.-Indianapolis	-0.7		
	S1	HO	In Indianapolis	-0.2		
/5/17	B3	GM	Franklin-Martinsville	+25.5		2
/11/1	B4	GA	MP 23.0-Lawrenceburg	+2.5		
/11/1	B4	GL	Lawrenceburg-MP 23.8	+2.9		
/11/1	B4	G,GO1&2	MP 23.8-Indianapolis	+86.3	260.9	
1856	B8	L	Terre Haute-IL state line	+8.4	269.3	
1865	B5	G	OH state line-MP 23.0	+1.5	270.8	
1866/6/14	B6	GM	Fairland-Franklin	+12.5	283.3	
1868/7/21	B7	GW	MP 18.4-Hagerstown	+63.0	346.3	
1870/7/4	B12	L,LO	Indianapolis-Terre Haute	+71.8		
/8/15	B9	M	Warsaw-Goshen	+24.4	442.5	
1871	B10	M	North Manchester-Warsaw	+19.3	461.8	
1872/8/25	B11	H	Templeton-IL state line	+23.6		
	B10	M	Wabash-North Manchester	+14.4	499.8	
1873	B10	M	Marion-Wabash	+19.3	519.1	
1875	B5A	G	MP 23.0-MP 23.8	+0.8		
	X	GL	Lawrenceburg-MP 23.8	-1.0		
	Y	GL	In Lawrenceburg	(1.9)		
	B10	M	Fairmount-Marion	+10.1	527.1	
1876	B10	M	Anderson-Fairmount	+22.7	549.8	
1881	B13	M	Rushville-North Vernon	+44.4	594.2	
1882/7/3	B10	M	Goshen-Niles MI	+20.1		
	B14	S	OH state line-Indianapolis	+74.8	689.1	
1884/5/5	B15	GC	Craig-Columbus	+24.4	713.5	

(continued)

CLEVELAND, CINCINNATI, CHICAGO & ST. LOUIS

ACQUISITION/DISPOSITION RECORD (continued)

Date	Act	CCC-	End points	Change	Main	Note
1887	B16	GA	Lawrenceburg-Aurora	+3.7	717.2	
1891	B10	M	Rushville-Anderson	+39.0	756.2	
1892 ca.	B19	IA	Gridley-Taft	+4.4	760.6	
1904	B18	H	At Indianapolis	+3.6		
	X,Y	HO	At Indianapolis	-6.0	758.2	
1905 ca.	X,Y	GO1	At Batesville	-3.4		
	B13	G	At Batesville	+3.3		
	X	GO2	Lawrenceburg Jct.-Sunman	-16.5		
	B13	G	Lawrenceburg Jct.-Sunman	+15.4		
	X,Y	IO	At Pendleton	-1.0		
	Y	IO	At Pendleton	(2.0)		
	B13	I	At Pendleton	+3.3		
	X,Y	LO	At Greencastle	-11.5		
	B13	L	At Greencastle	+10.9	756.7	
1906	P2	LV	St. Francisville-Vincennes	+8.6	765.3	
1911/7/1	B17	LE	Evansville-Mt. Carmel	+28.2	793.5	
1920/6/3	P1	T	Terre Haute-Str.Line Jct.	+134.0	927.5	
1924	B20	TS	Somerville Branch	+6.7	934.2	
1927 ca.	B19	TC	Coe Branch	+5.8	940.0	
1928 ca.	B29	TK	Tecumseh Branch	+12.1	952.1	
1929	B19	T	Duff-Maysville	+2.5		
	X	TW	Washington-Maysville	-3.3	951.3	
1931	X	GW	Beesons-Hagerstown	-13.3	938.0	
1936	X	TS	Somerville Branch	-6.7	931.3	
1942	X	M	Niles Jct. MI-CX	-20.3		
	X	GM	Martinsville-Trafalgar	-17.8	893.2	9
1950 ca.	X	TC	Part of Coe Branch	-3.0	890.2	
1954	X	TK	Part of Tecumseh Branch	-4.3	885.9	
1961	X	GM	Trafalgar-Franklin	-7.7	878.2	

On February 1, 1968, this company was conveyed to Penn Central. The Acquisition/-Disposition Record is continued to two places: under this company and under Penn Central.

Date	Act	CCC-	End points	Change	Main	Note
1968	X	LV	St. Francisville-Vincennes	-8.6	869.6	4
1969 ca.	X	T	Terre Haute-Spring Hill	-5.5		7
ca.	X	T	Worthington Jct.-Rincon Jct.	-1.2	862.9	
1973	X	M	Carthage-Rushville	-10.3		
	S11	M	In Rushville	[0.7]		
	X	M	Rushville-Greensburg	-17.8		
	Y	M	In Greensburg	(1.2)		
	X	M	Craig-North Vernon	-23.9		
	X	GC	Craig-Columbus	-21.9		
	Y	GC	In Columbus	(2.5)	784.6	
1974	L1	GW	Brookville-Connersville	<24.1>	760.5	
1975	XL	GW	Brookville-Metamora	<+6.2>		
	X	GW	Brookville-Metamora	-6.2	760.5	

On April 1, 1976, part of this company was conveyed to Conrail and part retained by the Penn Central trustees. The Acquisition/Disposition Record is continued to two places: under this company and under the name of the subsequent new owner. The property conveyed was:

Line desig.	End points	MP	to Conrail	to PennC	Note
[CCC-I]	OH state line-Wash. St.	198.6-283.1	84.5		
[CCC-IO]	Pendleton Old Main	245.0-247.0	(2.0)		
[CCC-IA]	Anderson Cutoff	245.7-250.1	4.4		
[CCC-G]	OH state line-College Av.	21.5-108.9	87.4		
[CCC-GO1]	Batesville Old Main	46.9-48.7	(1.8)		

(continued)

CLEVELAND, CINCINNATI, CHICAGO & ST. LOUIS

The property conveyed was: (continued)

Line desig.	End points	MP	to Conrail	to PennC	Note
[CCC-GA]	CP 23-Aurora	23.0-29.2	6.2		
[CCC-GC]	In Columbus	86.1-88.6		(2.5)	
[CCC-GW]	OH state line-Brookville	24.7-43.9		19.2	
[CCC-GW]	Connersville-Beeson	68.0-74.4	6.4		
[CCC-GM]	Fairland-Franklin	89.3-100.5		11.2	
[CCC-GM]	In Franklin	100.5-101.8	1.3		
[CCC-H]	Brant-Zionsville	113.1-125.4	12.3		
[CCC-H]	Zionsville-Lebanon	125.4-137.0		11.6	
[CCC-H]	Lebanon-Altamont	137.0-170.2	33.2		
[CCC-H]	Templeton-IL state line	192.6-216.2	23.6		
[CCC-L]	West St.-IL state line	0.4-80.0	79.6		
[CCC-LO]	Greencastle Old Main	39.0-40.6	(1.6)		
[CCC-T]	Spring Hill-Cory	5.5-12.4	6.9		
[CCC-T]	Cory-Worthington	12.4-39.4		27.0	
[CCC-T]	At Worthington	39.4-40.0	0.6		
[CCC-T]	Rincon Jct.-Str.Line Jct.	41.2-130.9	89.7		
[CCC-TW]	Duff-Washington	0-2.3	2.3		
[CCC-TC]	Gray Jc.-Oakland City Jc.	0-2.8	2.8		
[CCC-TK]	Tecumseh Jct.-Lynnville	0-7.8	7.8		
[CCC-LE]	IL state line-8th Ave.	131.8-160.0		28.2	
[CCC-S]	OH state line-New Castle	61.6-95.3		33.7	
[CCC-S]	In New Castle	95.3-96.9	1.6		
[CCC-S]	New Castle-Hunter	96.9-128.8		31.9	
[CCC-S]	Hunter-DX	128.8-136.4	7.6		
[CCC-M]	In Goshen	54.8-55.5	(0.7)		
[CCC-M]	CX-Emporia	55.5-173.5	118.0		
[CCC-M]	Emporia-Carthage	173.5-193.5		20.0	
[CCC-M]	In Greensburg	222.3-223.5	(1.2)		
[CCC-M]	Greensburg-Craig	223.5-225.0	1.5		

TOTAL SYSTEM 760.5   CR = 577.7   PC = 182.8

Date	Act	CCC-	End points	Change Conrail	PennC	Total	
1976	X	GM	Fairland-Franklin		-11.2		
	Y	GM	In Franklin	(1.3)			
	X	GC	In Columbus		(-2.5)		
	X	H	Zionsville-Lebanon		-11.6		
ca.	X	IO	In Pendleton	(-1.1)			
	X	LE	IL state line-Evansville		-22.3		
	S8	LE	In Evansville		[5.9]		
	X	S	OH state line-Lynn		-7.8		
	Y	S	In New Castle	(1.6)			
	Y	S	Hunter-DX	(7.6)			
YEAR				567.2	124.0	691.2	
1977	X	S	Lynn-New Castle		-25.9		
	X	S	New Castle-Shirley		-10.4		
	X	S	Wilkinson-Hunter		-19.8		
YEAR				567.2	67.9	635.1	
1979	X	GA	Lawrenceburg-Aurora	-3.2			
	S6	GW	OH state line-Brookville		[19.2]		
/6	L2	M	Emporia-Carthage	<20.0>			
/6	L2	S	Shirley-Wilkinson	<1.7>			
YEAR				564.0	27.0	591.0	
1981	X	T	Cory-Worthington	-27.0			6
	Y	T	At Worthington	(0.6)			
/12	S10	GW	Connersville-Beeson	[6.1]			
	X	GW	At Beeson	-0.3			
YEAR				557.0	0	557.0	
(continued)							

CLEVELAND, CINCINNATI, CHICAGO & ST. LOUIS

Date	Act	CCC-	End points	Change Conrail	PennC	Total	
1982	X	TW	Duff-Washington	-2.3			5
	X	M	Greensburg-Craig	-1.5			
	X	M	In Greensburg	(-1.2)			
YEAR				553.2	0	553.2	
1984	X	H	Near Zionsville	-2.0			
	X	IO	In Pendleton	(-0.9)			
	X	LO	Greencastle Old Main	(-1.6)			
	X	M	In Goshen	(-0.7)			
	X	T	At Worthington	(-0.6)			
/4	S5	GW	Metamora-Connersville			[[17.9]]	
YEAR				551.2	0	551.2	
1985	X	H	Lebanon-Altamont	-33.2			
	LA1	M	Emporia-Carthage	<<20.0>>			
YEAR				518.0	0	518.0	
1987/4	S7	M	Emporia-Carthage	[<20.0>]			
/4	X	S	Shirley-Wilkinson	<-1.7>			
YEAR				518.0	0	518.0	
1988	X	M	Emporia-Knightstown		[-14.7]		
YEAR				518.0	0	518.0	
1989	S2	H	Templeton-Swanington	[6.0]			
YEAR				512.0	0	512.0	
1990/2	S5	GW	In Connersville	[[0.7]]			
YEAR				512.0	0	512.0	
1991/12/31	S4	G	OH line-Shelbyville	[61.1]			
/12/31	S4	GA	CP 23-Lawrenceburg	[3.0]			
/12/31	S4	GL	In Lawrenceburg	[(1.9)]			
/12/31	S4	GO1	Batesville Old Main	[(1.8)]			
YEAR				447.9	0	447.9	
1992/4/11	S9	T	Rincon Jct.-Str.L.Jct.	[89.7]			
/4/11	S9	TK	Tecumseh Jct.-Lynnville	[7.8]			
/4/11	S9	TC	Gray Jct.-Oakland Cy. Jc.	[2.8]			
YEAR				347.6	0	347.6	
1994	S3	H	Swanington-IL state line	[17.6]			
	X	T	Rincon Jct.-Elnora	[-20.0]			
YEAR				330.0	0	330.0	

On 1999/6/1 Conrail was conveyed to CSX Transportation and Norfolk Southern. The lines conveyed were:

CSX/NS Line Desig		MP	to CSX	to NS
[CCC-I]	OH state line-Wash. St.	198.6-283.1	84.5	
[CCC-IA]	Anderson Cutoff	245.7-250.1	4.4	
[CCC-G]	Shelbyville-College Ave.	82.6-108.9	26.3	
[CCC-H]	Brant-Zionsville	113.1-123.4	10.3	
[CCC-L]	West St.-IL state line	0.4-80.0	79.6	
[CCC-T]	Spring Hill-Cory	5.5-12.4	6.9	
[CCC-S]	In New Castle	95.3-96.9	(1.6)	
[CCC-S]	Hunter-DX	128.8-136.4	(7.6)	
[CCC-M]	CX-Anderson	55.5-165.4		109.9
[CCC-M]	Anderson-Emporia	165.4-173.5	8.1	
		TOTAL	220.1	109.9 =330.0

ACT COLUMN KEY
B1   Built by Indianapolis & Bellefontaine RR
B2   Built by Lafayette & Indianapolis RR
B3   Built by Martinsville & Franklin RR
B4   Built by Lawrenceburg & Upper Mississippi RR
B5   Built by Indianapolis & Cincinnati RR
(continued)

CLEVELAND, CINCINNATI, CHICAGO & ST. LOUIS

ACT COLUMN KEY (continued)
B6   Built by Cincinnati & Martinsville RR
B7   Built by White Water Valley RR
B8   Built by St. Louis, Alton & Terre Haute RR
B9   Built by Warsaw, Goshen & White Pigeon RR
B10 Built by Cincinnati, Wabash & Michigan Ry
B11 Built by Cincinnati, Lafayette & Chicago RR
B12 Built by Indianapolis & St. Louis RR
B13 Built by Vernon, Greensburg & Rushville RR
B14 Built by Indianapolis, Bloomington & Western Ry
B15 Built by Columbus, Hope & Greensburg RR
B16 Built by Cincinnati & Southern Ohio River RR
B17 Built by Evansville, Mt. Carmel & Northern Ry
B18 Built by Cleveland, Cincinnati, Chicago & St. Louis Ry
B19 Built by Evansville, Indianapolis & Terre Haute Ry
L1   Leased to Whitewater Valley RR
L2   Leased to Indiana Eastern RR
L3   Leased to Kankakee, Beaverville & Southern RR
LA1 Lease assigned to Indiana Midland
P1   Purchased from Chicago & Eastern Illinois
P2   Purchased from Cairo, Vincennes & Chicago
S1   Sold to Indianapolis Union
S2   Sold to Benton Central
S3   Sold to Kankakee, Beaverville & Southern RR
S4   Sold to Central RR of Indiana
S5   Sold to Whitewater Valley
S6   Sold to Indiana & Ohio
S7   Sold to Carthage, Knightstown & Shirley
S8   Sold to Louisville & Nashville
S9   Sold to Indiana Southern
X   Abandoned
Y   Converted to yard/industrial track

SOURCES
1. Indiana, , *1995 Indiana State Rail Plan.*
2. Simons and Parker, *Railroads of Indiana.*
3. Michigan, *Aids, Gifts, Grants.*

NOTES
1. Source 2 gives Indianapolis-Pendleton segment service beginning on Dec. 11, 1850, and on Indianapolis-Union City segment beginning on Jan. 24, 1853.
2. The Martinsville-Franklin segment was not operated between May 1858 and June 1866.
3. The date of construction and/or abandonment could not be determined and is not included in the Acquisition/-Disposition Record.
4. The disposition of this segment could not be determined, but it may have been sold, in part, to another carrier.
5. That part east of MP 1.4 apparently was sold to CSX as industrial track.
6. Penn Central apparently did not use the section between Spring Hill and Riley between 1968 and 1976. Service was reinstated by Conrail in 1976 when the Cory-Worthington Jct. segment was abandoned. The section was reached by trackage rights.
7. Approximately three miles of this segment from Spring Hill toward Terre Haute apparently was retained as industrial track. Ownership of the segment could not be determined.
8. Until its sale this segment was operated by Conrail and reached via trackage rights over Norfolk & Western line N&W-[NKP-LF].
9. Some trackage in Martinsville and Morgantown was sold to Pennsylvania and Illinois Central respectively for use as industrial track.
10. Line CCC-IO served as the main line between 1851 and ca. 1906 and was 0.3 miles shorter than line CCC-I. When line CCC-I was built between MP 254.0 and MP 257.3 in ca. 1906 line CCC-IO was converted to industrial track and part of the line abandoned. The final segment from Raleigh eastward was removed in 1984.

CONRAIL

On April 1, 1976, some lines of Penn Central were conveyed to Conrail and some retained by Penn Central. The Acquisition/Disposition Record is continued in two places: under the name of the original pre-Penn Central company and under Conrail. The lines to Conrail were:

Line desig. CR-	End points	MP	Main
[CCC-I]	OH state line-Wash. St.	198.6-283.1	84.5
[CCC-IA]	Anderson Cutoff	245.7-250.1	4.4
[CCC-IO]	Pendleton Old Main	255.0-257.0	(2.0)
[CCC-G]	OH state line-College Av.	21.5-108.9	87.4
[CCC-GO1]	Batesville Old Main	46.9-	(1.8)
[CCC-GA]	CP 23-Aurora	23.0-29.2	6.2
[CCC-GM]	In Franklin	100.5-101.8	1.3
[CCC-GW]	Connersville-Beeson	68.0-74.4	6.4
[CCC-H]	Brant-Zionsville	113.1-125.4	12.3
[CCC-H]	Lebanon-Altamont	137.0-170.2	33.2
[CCC-H]	Templeton-IL state line	192.6-216.2	23.6
[CCC-L]	West St.-IL state line	0.4-80.0	79.6
[CCC-LO]	Greencastle Old Main	39.0-40.6	(1.6)
[CCC-T]	Spring Hill-Cory	5.5-12.4	6.9
[CCC-T]	At Worthington	39.4-40.0	0.6
[CCC-T]	Rincon Jct.-Str.Line Jct.	41.2-130.9	89.7
[CCC-TW]	Duff-Washington	0-2.3	2.3
[CCC-TC]	Gray Jc.-Oakland City Jc.	0-2.8	2.8
[CCC-TK]	Tecumseh Jct.-Lynnville	0-7.8	7.8
[CCC-S]	In New Castle	95.3-96.9	1.6
[CCC-S]	Hunter-DX	128.8-136.4	7.6
[CCC-M]	In Goshen	54.8-55.5	(0.7)
[CCC-M]	CX-Emporia	55.5-173.5	118.0
[CCC-M]	In Greensburg	222.3-223.5	(1.2)
[CCC-M]	Greensburg-Craig	223.5-225.0	1.5
[LS-T]	IN state line-B	355.4-421.5	66.1
[LS-A]	MI state line-Elkhart	420.1-438.8	14.7
[LS-TS]	Goshen-Shipshewana	0-16.9	16.9
[LS-TF]	In Waterloo	70.4-71.2	0.8
[LS-TF]	Waterloo-Auburn Jct.	71.2-76.7	5.5
[LS-TF]	In Fort Wayne	92.8-100.0	(7.2)
[LS-W]	Elkhart-MS	421.6-505.7	84.1
[LS-WE]	Elkhart & Western Branch	0-12.9	12.9
[LS-N2]	MC Connecting Branch	1.3-3.2	1.9
[LS-WK]	South Bend-IL state line	0.2-82.2	82.0
[LS-WD]	Osborn-IL state line	4.9-100.8	95.9
[LS-WJ]	MS-Lake Jct.	0-0.4	0.4
[MC-W]	PO-Ivanhoe	240.7-259.6	18.9
[MC-WJ]	Hartsdale-IL state line	12.8-15.7	2.9
[MC-N]	MI state line-South Bend	5.8-9.6	3.8
[MC-N2]	In South Bend	0-1.3	1.3
[P&E-A]	IJ-Speedway	1.0-6.2	5.2
[P&E-A]	Clermont-IL state line	9.0-79.9	70.9
[PRR-F]	OH line-IL line	300.4-453.3	152.9
[PRR-GR]	In Richmond	0.7-2.3	1.6
[PRR-GR]	In Ridgeville	33.0-34.2	1.2
[PRR-GR]	Decatur-Adams	70.4-86.6	16.2
[PRR-GS]	Junction-Kendallville	93.3-121.0	27.7
[PRR-L]	OH line-Van	103.6-198.3	94.7
[PRR-L]	Van-Boone	1.2-11.9	10.7
[PRR-L]	Boone-IL line	206.8-286.1	79.3

(continued)

CONRAIL

The lines to Conrail were: (continued)

Line desig. CR-	End points	MP	Main
[PRR-LS]	In Plymouth	159.1-160.9	1.8
[PRR-LS]	In South Bend	179.0-182.3	3.3
[PRR-LE]	Van-MP 3.4	1.2-3.4	2.2
[PRR-LE]	In North Manchester	36.9-38.0	1.1
[PRR-LE]	In Columbia City	55.3-56.6	1.3
[PRR-CM]	In Muncie	41.8-42.9	(1.1)
[PRR-YA]	Anderson Belt	0-3.1	(3.1)
[PRR-CR]	OH state line-Glen	68.5-72.4	3.9
[PRR-CR]	In Richmond	74.9-76.6	1.7
[PRR-CR]	New Castle-Anderson	100.5-127.0	26.5
[PRR-CR]	Anderson-Kokomo	127.0-155.7	28.7
[PRR-CR]	Kokomo-Anoka	155.7-177.4	21.7
[PRR-I]	OH line-Indianapolis	115.4-186.8	71.4
[PRR-IK]	Thorne-Hawthorne Yard	0-2.0	2.0
[PRR-IK]	In Hawthorne Yard	2.0-5.0	(3.0)
[PRR-IL]	Indianapolis-KY line	0.5-108.8	108.3
[PRR-IA]	Jeffersonville-Clarksville	0-1.6	1.6
[PRR-IW]	Boyd-Watson	0-4.0	4.0
[PRR-IM]	In Columbus	0-2.8	2.8
[PRR-IC]	In Columbus	0-3.8	3.8
[PRR-IC]	In Shelbyville	23.8-27.3	3.5
[PRR-IV]	Kraft-Vincennes	3.0-102.9	99.9
[PRR-IVO]	In Indianapolis	0.9-4.3	(3.4)
[PRR-IF]	Davis-Frank	6.9-48.1	41.2
[PRR-IF]	Frank-Van	78.3-114.5	36.2
[PRR-V]	Indianapolis-Seelyville	0.4-64.5	64.1
[PRR-V]	Seelyville-Prairie	65.3-69.9	4.6
[PRR-V]	Prairie-Union	69.9-72.4	(2.5)
[PRR-V]	Terre Haute-IL line	73.5-79.9	6.4
[PRR-VB2]	Brazil-Chinook Mine	0-6.0	(6.0)
[PRR-VO]	Brazil-Staunton	57.3-60.8	3.5
[PRR-VT1]	At East Yard	0-1.7	(1.7)
[PRR-VT2]	In Terre Haute	73.3-73.5	0.2
[PRR-VT3]	Prairie-Preston	69.9-72.4	2.5
[PRR-VK]	Van Jct.-Kraft	0-1.4	1.4

On April 1, 1976, Conrail acquired Indianapolis Union. The IU Acquisition/-Disposition Record is continued in two places: under Indianapolis Union and under Conrail. The lines conveyed were:

[IU-E]	Indpls.-E of Wash. St.	0-0.9	0.9
[IU-EA]	to College Ave.	0.3-0.7	0.4
[IU-S]	Indianapolis-south	0-0.5	0.5
[IU-W]	Indianapolis-IJ	0-1.0	1.0
[IU-B]	Belt Line	0-11.8	11.8
[IU-C]	Belt Line	0.5-2.0	1.5

1976/4/1 TOTALS   CCC=577.7 IU=16.1 LS=381.2 MC=26.9 PRR=933.9 P&E=76.1 CR System=2011.9

ACQUISITION/DISPOSITION RECORD

Date	Act	CR-	End points	Change	Main	Note
1976	Y	[CCC-GM]	In Franklin	(1.3)		
ca.	X	[CCC-IO]	In Pendleton	(-1.1)		
	Y	[CCC-S]	Hunter-DX	(7.6)		
	Y	[CCC-S]	In New Castle	(1.6)		
	Y	[LS-TF]	In Waterloo	(0.8)		
	S1	[LS-TF]	Auburn Jct.-Auburn	[1.7]		
	X	[LS-TF]	Waterloo-Auburn	-3.8		

(continued)

CONRAIL

ACQUISITION/DISPOSITION RECORD

Date	Act	CR-	End points	Change	Main	Note
	Y	[PRR-GR]	In Richmond	(1.6)		
	X	[PRR-CR]	Delco-Dow	(-2.7)		
	Y	[PRR-GR]	In Ridgeville	(1.2)		
	Y	[PRR-GS]	In Kendallville	(0.9)		
	Y	[PRR-IC]	In Shelbyville	(3.5)		
	Y	[PRR-IM]	In Columbus	(2.8)		
	Y	[PRR-LE]	In Columbia City	(1.3)		
	Y	[PRR-LE]	In North Manchester	(1.1)		
	Y	[PRR-LS]	In Plymouth	(1.8)		
	Y	[PRR-LS]	In South Bend	(3.3)		
1976 YEAR TOTALS		CCC=567.2 IU=16.1 LS=374.9 MC=26.9 PRR=916.4 P&E=76.1 CR System=1977.6				
1977	Y	[PRR-IC]	In Columbus	(3.8)		
YEAR TOTALS		CCC=567.2 IU=16.1 LS=374.9 MC=26.9 PRR=906.3 P&E=76.1 CR System =1973.8				
1979	X	[CCC-GA]	Lawrenceburg-Aurora	-3.2		
	L1	[LS-TG]	Goshen-Shipshewana	<16.9>		
	T	[PRR-GR]	In Decatur	(=1.5)		
YEAR TOTALS		CCC=564.0 IU=16.1 LS=358.0 MC=26.9 PRR=912.6 P&E=76.1 CR=1953.7				
1980	XL	[LS-TG]	Goshen-Shipshewana	<+16.9>		
	X	[LS-TG]	Goshen-Shipshewana	-16.2		
	Y	[LS-TG]	In Goshen	(0.7)		
/7	S2	[PRR-L]	Marion-Sweetser	[4.6]		
YEAR TOTALS		CCC=564.0 IU=16.1 LS=358.0 MC=26.9 PRR=908.0 P&E=76.1 CR System =1949.1				
1981	X	[PRR-I]	Cambridge City-Charlottesv.	-21.3		
/12	S3	[CCC-GW]	Connersville-Beeson	[6.1]		
ca.	X	[CCC-GW]	In Beeson	-0.3		
	Y	[CCC-T]	At Worthington	(0.6)		
YEAR TOTALS		CCC=557.0 IU=16.1 LS=358.0 MC=26.9 PRR=886.7 P&E=76.1 CR System =1920.8				
1982	X	[CCC-M]	Greensburg-Craig	-1.5		
	X	[CCC-M]	In Greensburg	(-1.2)		
	X	[CCC-TW]	Duff-Washington	-2.3		
	Y	[LS-WK]	High Street-JK	(2.8)		
	X	[LS-WK]	JK-wheatfield	-55.0		
	X	[P&E-A]	Crawfordsville-Olin	-28.0		
	S5	[PRR-CR]	OH state line-Glen	[3.9]		
	S5	[PRR-CR]	In Richmond	[1.7]		
	Y	[PRR-CR]	In Anderson	(7.7)		
	X	[PRR-CR]	Anderson-Kokomo	-28.7		
	S5	[PRR-GR]	In Richmond	[(1.6)]		
	X	[PRR-GS]	MP 97.8-Kendallville	-21.2		
	Y	[PRR-GS]	In Kendallville	(1.1)		
	Y	[PRR-GS]	Junction-MP 97.8	(4.5)		
	X	[PRR-I]	Centerville-Cambridge City	-10.1		
	X	[PRR-I]	Charlottesville-Thorne	-22.9		
	X	[PRR-I]	OH state line-Glen	-2.0		
	S5	[PRR-I]	Glen-Newman	[2.4]		
	Y	[PRR-I]	Thorne-MP 186.8	(6.0)		
	Y	[PRR-IK]	Line	(2.0)		
	X	[PRR-L]	Winimac-Crown Point	-48.8		
	X	[PRR-LE]	In Columbia City	(-1.3)		
	X	[PRR-V]	Davis-Greencastle	-28.1		
YEAR TOTALS		CCC=553.2 IU=16.1 LS=300.2 MC=26.9 PRR=695.6 P&E=48.1 CR System =1640.1				
1984	X	[CCC-IO]	In Pendleton	(-0.9)		
	X	[CCC-H]	Near Zionsville	-2.0		
	X	[CCC-LO]	Greencastle Old Main	(-1.6)		
	X	[CCC-M]	In Goshen	(-0.7)		
	X	[CCC-T]	In Worthington	(-0.6)		
	X	[LS-TF]	In Waterloo	(-0.8)		
	X	[LS-TG]	In Goshen	(-0.7)		

(continued)

CONRAIL

ACQUISITION/DISPOSITION RECORD (continued)

Date	Act	CR-	-End points	Change	Main	Note
	X	[LS-WE]	In Mishawaka	-0.7		
	X	[P&E-A]	At Speedway	-2.2		
	X	[PRR-CM]	In Muncie	(-1.1)		
1984	X	[PRR-GR]	In Ridgeville	(-1.2)		
	X	[PRR-GR]	In Decatur	(-1.5)		
	X	[PRR-GS]	In Kendallville	(-0.9)		
	X	[PRR-IA]	Jeffersonville-Clarksville	-1.6		
	X	[PRR-IC]	In Columbus	(-2.7)		
	X	[PRR-IC]	In Shelbyville	(-1.8)		
	X	[PRR-IV]	Sandborn-Bicknell	-10.5		
	X	[PRR-L]	Crown Point-IL state line	-11.9		
	X	[PRR-L]	In Winimac	-1.2		
	X	[PRR-L]	Sweetser-Anoka	-29.4		
	X	[PRR-LE]	In North Manchester	(-1.1)		
	X	[PRR-LE]	In South Bend	(-1.0)		
	X	[PRR-V]	Greencastle-Limedale	-5.3		
	X	[PRR-VO]	Brazil-Staunton	-3.5		
	X	[PRR-VB2]	Line	(-6.0)		
	X	[PRR-VT1]	At East Yard	(-1.7)		
YEAR TOTALS		CCC=551.2 IU=16.1 LS=299.5 MC=26.9 PRR=632.2 P&E=45.9 CR System =1571.8				
1985	X	[CCC-H]	Lebanon-Altamont	-33.2		
	X	[PRR-L]	In Winimac	-0.3		
/5	L2	[PRR-LS]	In Plymouth	<(1.8)>		
YEAR TOTALS		CCC=518.0 IU=16.1 LS=299.5 MC=26.9 PRR=631.9 P&E=45.9 CR System =1538.3				
1986	X	[LS-WE]	In Mishawaka	-2.4		
	X	[LS-TF]	In Fort Wayne	(-2.4)		
	X	[PRR-CR]	In Kokomo	-0.8		
	X	[PRR-IC]	In Shelbyville	(-1.7)		
YEAR TOTALS		CCC=518.0 IU=16.1 LS=297.1 MC=26.9 PRR=631.1 P&E=45.9 CR System =1535.1				
1987	X	[PRR-IC]	In Columbus	(-1.1)		
/5/1	S6	[PRR-V]	Limedale-Seelyville	[24.2]		
/5/1	S6	[PRR-V]	Prairie-Union	[(3.8)]		
/5/1	S6	[PRR-V]	Seelyville-Prairie	[4.6]		
/5/1	S6	[PRR-VT3]	Prairie-Preston	[2.5]		
	X	[PRR-V]	MP 69.9-Union	(-2.5)		
YEAR TOTALS		CCC=518.0 IU=16.1 LS=297.1 MC=26.9 PRR=599.8 P&E=45.9 CR System =1503.8				
1989	S2	[CCC-H]	Templeton-Swanington	[6.0]		
	S6	[PRR-LE]	Van-MP 3.4	[2.2]		
YEAR TOTALS		CCC=512.0 IU=16.1 LS=297.1 MC=26.9 PRR=597.6 P&E=45.9 CR System =1495.6				
1990	X	[PRR-LS]	In Plymouth	<(-1.8)>		
/2	S5	[CCC-GW]	In Connersville	[(0.7)]		
YEAR TOTALS		CCC=512.0 IU=16.1 LS=297.1 MC=26.9 PRR=597.6 P&E=45.9 CR System =1495.6				
1991/12/31	S4	[CCC-G]	OH line-Shelbyville	[61.1]		
/12/31	S4	[CCC-GO1]	Batesville Old Main	[(1.8)]		
/12/31	S4	[CCC-GA]	CP 23-Lawrenceburg	[3.0]		
/12/31	S4	[CCC-GL]	In Lawrenceburg	[(1.9)]		
YEAR TOTALS		CCC=447.9 IU=16.1 LS=297.1 MC=26.9 PRR=597.6 P&E=45.9 CR System =1431.5				
1992/4/11	S7	[CCC-T]	Rincon Jct.-Str.L.Jct.	[89.7]		
/4/11	S7	[CCC-TC]	Gray Jct.-Oakland Cy. Jc.	[2.8]		
/4/11	S7	[CCC-TK]	Tecumseh Jct.-Lynnville	[7.8]		
	X	[PRR-I]	East Haven-Centerville	-5.2		
	S5	[PRR-I]	Newman-East Haven	[1.5]		
/4/11	S7	[PRR-IV]	Kraft-Bicknell	[89.4]		
	X	[PRR-IVO]	In Indianapolis	(-3.4)		
YEAR TOTALS		CCC=347.6 IU=16.1 LS=297.1 MC=26.9 PRR=501.5 P&E=45.9 CR System =1235.1				
1993 ca.	X	[MC-N]	Niles MI-St Marys	-3.6		
	S5	[PRR-CR]	In Kokomo	[3.1]		
	S5	[PRR-CR]	New Castle-Foley	[3.6]		

(continued)

CONRAIL

ACQUISITION/DISPOSITION RECORD (continued)

Date	Act	CR--	End points	Change	Main	Note
	X	[PRR-CR]	Sulphur Springs-Anderson	-8.6		
/10/1	S8	[PRR-CR]	Foley-Sulphur Springs	[6.6]		
/3/20	S9	[PRR-CR]	Kokomo-Anoka	[17.8]		
	Y	[PRR-L]	In Union City	(1.8)		
	X	[PRR-L]	Union city-Red Key	-19.5		
/3/20	S9	[PRR-L]	Anoka-Van	[5.7]		
/3/20	S9	[PRR-L]	Boone-Winimac	[17.1]		
/3/20	S5	[PRR-L]	Van-Boone	[10.7]		
1993	X	[PRR-IF]	Frankfort-Bringhurst	-13.8		
	Y	[PRR-IF]	In Frankfort	(1.6)		
/3/20	S9	[PRR-IF]	Bringhurst-Van	[20.5]		
YEAR TOTALS		CCC=347.6 IU=16.1 LS=297.1 MC=23.3 PRR=371.1 P&E=45.9 CR System =1101.1				
1994	S3	[CCC-H]	Swanington-IL state line	[17.6]		
	X	[CCC-T]	Rincon Jct.-Elnora	[-20.0]		
/10	S10	[LS-WD]	Handy-Stewart	[10.8]		
/3/12	S11	[PRR-IL]	Southport-KY state line	[102.5]		
/3/12	S11	[PRR-IW]	Boyd-Watson	[4.0]		
/3/12	S11	[PRR-IM]	In Columbus	[(2.8)]		
YEAR TOTALS		CCC=330.0 IU=16.1 LS=286.3 MC=23.3 PRR=264.6 P&E=45.9 CR System =966.2				
1996	S12	[PRR-F]	Wabash-Clarke Jct.	[126.5]		
	X	[LS-WD]	Schneider-Sheff	-33.2		
	S4	[LS-WD]	Sheff-Free	[5.9]		
	X	[LS-WD]	Free-Handy	-8.4		
	X	[LS-WD]	Stewart-IL state line	-9.6		
/11	L3	[LS-WE]	Elkhart-Mishawaka	<9.8>		
	L3	[PRR-GS]	In Kendallville	<(1.1)>		
YEAR TOTALS		CCC=330.0 IU=16.1 LS=219.4 MC=23.3 PRR=138.1 P&E=45.9 CR System =772.8				

On 1999/6/1 Conrail was conveyed to CSX Transportation and Norfolk Southern. Its Acquisition/Disposition Record is continued in two places: under the name of the original constituent company and under the name of the new company. The lines conveyed were:

Line desig. CR-	End points	MP	to CSX	to NS	Note
[CCC-I]	OH state line-Wash. St.	198.6-283.1	84.5		
[CCC-IA]	Anderson Cutoff	245.7-250.1	4.4		
[CCC-G]	Shelbyville-College Ave.	82.6-108.9	26.3		
[CCC-H]	Brant-Zionsville	113.1-123.4	10.3		
[CCC-L]	West St.-IL state line	0.4-80.0	79.6		
[CCC-T]	Spring Hill-Cory	5.5-12.4	6.9		
[CCC-S]	In New Castle	95.3-96.9	(1.6)		
[CCC-S]	Hunter-DX	128.8-136.4	(7.6)		
[CCC-M]	CX-Anderson	55.5-165.4		109.9	
[CCC-M]	Anderson-Emporia	165.4-173.5	8.1		
[IU-E]	Indpls.-E of Wash. St.	0-0.9	0.9		
[IU-EA]	to College Ave.	0.3-0.7	0.4		
[IU-S]	Indianapolis-south	0-0.5	0.5		
[IU-W]	Indianapolis-IJ	0-1.0	1.0		
[IU-B]	Belt Line	0-11.8	11.8		
[IU-C]	Belt Line	0.5-2.0	1.5		
[LS-T]	IN state line-B	355.4-421.5		66.1	
[LS-A]	MI state line-Elkhart	420.1-438.8		14.7	
[LS-TF]	In Fort Wayne	95.2-100.0		(4.8)	
[LS-W]	Elkhart-IL state line	421.6-505.7		84.1	
[LS-N2]	MC Connecting Branch	1.3-3.2		1.9	
[LS-WK]	In South Bend	0.2-3.0		(2.8)	
[LS-WK]	Wheatfield-IL state line	58.0-82.2		24.2	
[LS-WD]	Osborn-Schneider	4.9-32.9			28.0

(continued)

CONRAIL

ACQUISITION/DISPOSITION RECORD (continued)

. The lines conveyed were:

Line desig. CR-	End points	MP	to CSX	to NS	Note
[LS-WJ]	MS-Lake Jct.	0-0.4		0.4	
[MC-WJ]	PO-Ivanhoe	240.7-259.6		18.9	
[MC-WJ]	Hartsdale-IL state line	12.8-15.7	2.9		
[MC-N]	St. Marys-South Bend	5.8-6.0		0.2	
[MC-N2]	In South Bend	0-1.3		1.3	
[P&E-A]	IJ-Brant	1.0-4.0	3.0		
[P&E-A]	Clermont-Crawfordsville	9.0-46.0	37.0		
[P&E-A]	Olin-IL state line	74.0-79.9	5.9		
[PRR-F]	OH state line-Wabash	300.4-319.2	18.8		
[PRR-F]	Clarke Jct.-IL state line	445.7-453.3	7.6		
[PRR-GR]	Decatur-Adams	70.4-86.6	16.2		
[PRR-GS]	In Fort Wayne	93.3-97.8		(4.5)	
[PRR-L]	Red Key-Marion	124.9-158.6		33.7	
[PRR-LS]	In South Bend	179.0-181.3		(2.3)	
[PRR-CR]	In Anderson	119.3-122.1	(2.8)		
[PRR-CR]	In Anderson	124.8-127.0	(2.2)		
[PRR-YA]	Anderson Belt	0-3.1	(3.1)		
[PRR-I]	Thorne-ID	180.8-186.8	(6.0)		
[PRR-IL]	Indianapolis-Southport	0.5-6.3	5.8		
[PRR-IK]	Thorne-Hawthorne Yard	0-5.0	(5.0)		
[PRR-IF]	Davis-Frank	6.9-48.1	41.2		
[PRR-IF]	Frank-Frankfort	78.3-78.6	0.3		
[PRR-IF]	In Frankfort	78.6-80.2	(1.6)		
[PRR-V]	Indianapolis-Davis	0.4-6.9	6.5		
[PRR-V]	Terre Haute-IL line	73.5-79.9	6.4		
[PRR-VT2]	In Terre Haute	73.3-73.5	0.2		
[PRR-VK]	Van Jct.-Kraft	0-1.4	1.4		

	Original Ownership	to CSX	to NS	CR System		
CCC		220.1	109.9	330.0		
IU		16.1		16.1		
LS			219.4	219.4		
MC		2.9	20.4	23.3		
PRR		104.4	33.7	138.1		
P&E		45.9		45.9		
TOTAL		389.4	383.4	772.8		

ACT COLUMN KEY

L1 Leased to Indiana Interstate
L2 Leased to Plymouth Shore Line
L3 Leased to Michigan Southern RR
S1 Sold to Baltimore & Ohio
S2 Sold to Honey Creek
S3 Sold to Indiana Hi-Rail
S4 Sold to Kankakee, Beaverville & Southern
S5 Sold to Norfolk Southern
S6 Sold to Terre Haute, Brazil & Eastern
S7 Sold to Indiana Southern
S8 Sold to Honey Creek
S9 Sold to Winimac Southern
S10 Sold to Bee Line
S11 Sold to Louisville & Indiana
S12 Sold to CSX Transportation
T   Transferred, apparently, from Penn Central
X   Abandoned
XL Lease cancelled

R. J. CORMAN

MAIN LINE (RJC-[NKP-LS])

See New York, Chicago & St. Louis line NKP-LS for arrangement of stations, prior construction/abandonment record, and prior ownership

CONSTRUCTION/ABANDONMENT

Date	Act	End points	MP	Change	Main	Source	Note
1993/8/21	L	Lima OH-Portland	136.3-145.8	+9.5	9.5	1	1

OWNERSHIP
1993   R. J. Corman RR Co.

ACQUISITION/DISPOSITION RECORD
See ownership record above for line

ACT COLUMN KEY
 L Leased from Norfolk Southern

SOURCES
1. Simons and Parker, *Railroads of Indiana.*

NOTES
1. Apparently the Indiana part of the line was not operated for the first year or two after the lease date.

CSX CORPORATION

On 1980/11/1 this company acquired Chessie System. Its Acquisition/Disposition Record is continued in two places: under the original constituent companies and under CSX Corporation. The property acquired was:

Line desig.	End points	MP	Main	Note
[B&O-C]	Willard OH-Chicago IL	110.3-256.6	146.3	
[B&O-IN]	Hamilton OH-Indianapolis	45.0-123.6	78.6	
[B&O-IS]	Indianapolis-Decatur IL	124.9-201.2	76.3	
[B&O-[LS-TF]	In Auburn	0-1.7	1.7	
[B&O-SC]	Cincinnati OH-N. Vernon	19.8-72.2	52.4	
[B&O-SW]	N. Vernon-Washington	72.2-170.4	98.2	
[B&O-SI]	Washington-St. Louis MO	170.4-189.4	19.0	
[B&O-SV]	Nabb-Louisville KY	28.5-54.0	25.5	
[B&O-SJ]	Watson-Jeffersonville	46.6-53.5	6.9	
[B&O-TU]	In Union City	47.1-47.3	0.2	
[C&O-C]	Cincinnati OH-Hammond	33.0-260.6	227.6	
[PM-C]	New Buffalo MI-Porter	117.9-136.6	18.7	
[PM-W]	LaCrosse-New Buffalo MI	0-33.0	33.0	
1980 YEAR TOTAL	B&O=505.1 C&O=227.6 PM=51.7 CSX System=784.4			

ACQUISITION/DISPOSITION RECORD

Date	Act	CSX--	End points	Change	Main	Note
1982	X	[C&O-C]	Malden-HY	-29.6		
YEAR TOTALS		B&O=505.1 C&O=198.0 PM=51.7 CSX System =754.8				
1985	X	[B&O-SV]	Nabb-Charleston	-11.8		
YEAR TOTALS		B&O=493.3 C&O=198.0 PM=51.7 CSX System =743.0				

On 1986/7/1 this company was conveyed to CSX Transportation. Its Acquisition/-Disposition Record is continued in two places: under the name of the original constituent companies and under CSX Corporation.

ACT COLUMN KEY
X Abandoned

CSX TRANSPORTATION CO.

On 1986/7/1 CSX Transportation acquired CSX Corporation and merged Seaboard System. Its Acquisition/Disposition Record is continued in two places: under the name of the original constituent companY and under CSX Transp. The property acquired was:

Line desig.	End points	MP	Main	Note
CSX-				
[B&O-C]	Willard OH-Chicago IL	110.3-256.6	146.3	
[B&O-IN]	Hamilton OH-Indianapolis	45.0-123.6	78.6	
[B&O-IS]	Indianapolis-Decatur IL	124.9-201.2	76.3	
[B&O-[LS-TF]	In Auburn	0-1.7	1.7	
[B&O-SC]	Cincinnati OH-N. Vernon	19.8-72.2	52.4	
[B&O-SW]	N. Vernon-Washington	72.2-170.4	98.2	
[B&O-SI]	Washington-St. Louis MO	170.4-189.4	19.0	
[B&O-SV]	Charleston-Louisville KY	40.3-54.0	13.7	
[B&O-SJ]	Watson-Jeffersonville	46.6-53.5	6.9	
[B&O-TU]	In Union City	47.1-47.3	0.2	
[C&O-C]	Cincinnati OH-Malden	33.0-231.0	198.0	
[CEI-E]	Danville IL-Evansville	128.6-279.5	150.9	
[CEI-E]	In Evansville	279.5-287.2	(7.7)	
[CEI-EB]	In Evansville	279.5-287.4	7.9	
[CEI-EO]	In Evansville	285.8-286.5	(0.7)	
[CEI-EJ]	Evansville Belt	0-4.0	(4.0)	
[CEI-EM]	Mt. Vernon Jct.-Poseyv.	265.3-281.8	16.5	
[CEI-EM]	In Mt. Vernon	300.5-302.1	(1.6)	
[CEI-EU]	Clinton-Universal	0-8.5	8.5	
[L&N-S]	Henderson KY-St. Louis MO	313.5-350.4	36.9	
[L&N-SE]	North Howell-Evansville	323.4-325.0	1.6	
[MON-A]	Chicago-Lafayette	19.2-117.9	98.7	
[MON-I]	Monon-Frankfort	88.4-137.5	49.1	
[MON-N]	Monon-Medaryville	0-15.2	15.2	
[MON-SA]	Lafayette-Bloomington	117.9-221.5	103.6	
[MON-SB]	Bloomington-New Albany	221.5-317.5	96.0	
[MON-SV]	In New Albany	316.6-317.7	1.1	
[MON-SBO]	Clear Creek-Sanders	224.2-226.9	2.7	
[MON-F]	In Orleans	0-0.6	0.6	
[PM-C]	New Buffalo MI-Porter	117.9-136.6	18.7	
[PM-W]	LaCrosse-New Buffalo MI	0-33.0	33.0	

1986/7/1 TOTALS   B&O=493.3 C&O=198.0 CEI=183.8 L&N=38.5 MON=367.0 PM=51.7 CSX System =1332.3

ACQUISITION/DISPOSITION RECORD

Date	Act	CSX--	End points	Change	Main	Note
1987	X	[C&O-C]	Twelve Mile-Santa Fe	-20.7		1
	X	[CEI-EM]	Mt. Vernon Jct.-Owensville	-5.5		
	S1	[CEI-EM]	Owensville-Poseyville	[11.0]		
YEAR TOTALS			B&O=493.3 C&O=177.3 CEI=167.3 L&N=38.5 MON=367.0 PM=51.7 CSX System =1295.1			
1988	X	[C&O-C]	Twelve Mile-North Judson	-38.0		
	X	[PM-W]	Wellsboro-New Buffalo MI	-17.4		
YEAR TOTALS			B&O=493.3 C&O=139.3 CEI=167.3 L&N=38.5 MON=367.0 PM=34.3 CSX System =1239.7			
1989	X	[C&O-C]	Richmond-Marion	-71.3		
	X	[B&O-ID]	Russellville-Bloomingdale	-14.6		
	X	[B&O-ID]	Mitchellville-Roachdale	-26.7		
YEAR TOTALS			B&O=452.0 C&O=68.0 CEI=167.3 L&N=38.5 MON=367.0 PM=34.3 CSX System =1127.1			
1990	X	[B&O-ID]	Roachdale-Russellville	-10.3		2
	X	[MON-A]	Airline Jct.-Hammond	-4.3		3
	X	[MON-F]	In Orleans	-0.6		
YEAR TOTALS			B&O=441.7 C&O=68.0 CEI=167.3 L&N=38.5 MON=362.1 PM=34.3 CSX System =1111.9			
1991	X	[B&O-TU]	In Union City	-0.2		
YEAR TOTALS			B&O=441.5 C&O=68.0 CEI=167.3 L&N=38.5 MON=362.1 PM=34.3 CSX System =1111.7			
1992	X	[B&O-ID]	Speedway-Mitchellville	-3.3		
	S2	[C&O-C]	Marion-Amboy	[12.6]		
	X	[MON-I]	Delphi-Frankfort	-25.3		

CSX TRANSPORTATION CO.
YEAR TOTALS B&O=438.2 C&O=55.4 CEI=167.3 L&N=38.5 MON=336.8 PM=34.3 CSX System =1070.5

Date	Act	CSX--	End points	Change	Main	Note
1993	X	[MON-A]	Airline Jct.-Maynard	-0.1		
	X	[MON-SB]	Bloomington-Bedford Jct.	-22.5		
	X	[MON-SBO]	Clear Creek-Sanders	-2.7		
	X	[MON-I]	Monticello-Delphi	-14.2		

YEAR TOTALS B&O=438.2 C&O=55.4 CEI=167.3 L&N=38.5 MON=297.3 PM=34.3 CSX System =1031.0

1994	X	[B&O-ID]	Bloomingdale-Montezuma	-7.3		
	X	[CEI-EU]	Clinton-Universal	-8.5		
	X	[MON-M]	In Medaryville	-0.4		
	B1	[MON-SAN]	In Lafayette	+1.9		
	X	[MON-SA]	In Lafayette	-2.2		
	X	[MON-SA]	Cloverdale-Gosport Jct.	-13.1		

YEAR TOTALS B&O=430.9 C&O=55.4 CEI=158.8 L&N=38.5 MON=283.5 PM=34.3 CSX System =1001.4

1995	X	[MON-SA]	Gosport Jct.-Ellettsville	-10.3		

YEAR TOTALS B&O=430.9 C&O=55.4 CEI=158.8 L&N=38.5 MON=273.2 PM=34.3 CSX System =991.1

1997	X	[MON-SA]	Ellettsville-Hunters	-4.3		

YEAR TOTALS B&O=430.9 C&O=55.4 CEI=158.8 L&N=38.5 MON=268.9 PM=34.3 CSX System =986.8

1998 ca.	X	[CEI-EM]	Owensville-Cynthiana	[-6.4]		

YEAR TOTALS B&O=430.9 C&O=55.4 CEI=158.8 L&N=38.5 MON=268.9 PM=34.3 CSX System =986.8

On 1999/6/1 CSC Transportation purchased part of Norfolk Southern:

Line desig.	End points	MP	Main	Note
[PRR-F]	Wabash-Clarke Jct.	319.2-445.7	126.5	

On 1999/6/1 CSX Transportation acquired part of Conrail. The lines acquired were:

[CCC-I]	OH state line-Wash. St.	198.6-283.1	84.5	
[CCC-IA]	Anderson Cutoff	245.7-250.1	4.4	
[CCC-G]	Shelbyville-College Ave.	82.6-108.9	26.3	
[CCC-H]	Brant-Zionsville	113.1-123.4	10.3	
[CCC-L]	West St.-IL state line	0.4-80.0	79.6	
[CCC-T]	Spring Hill-Cory	5.5-12.4	6.9	
[CCC-S]	In New Castle	95.3-96.9	(1.6)	
[CCC-S]	Hunter-DX	128.8-136.4	(7.6)	
[IU-E]	Indianapolis-E of Wash. St.	0-0.9	0.9	
[IU-EA]	to College Ave.	0.3-0.7	0.4	
[IU-S]	Indianapolis-south	0-0.5	0.5	
[IU-W]	Indianapolis-IJ	0-1.0	1.0	
[IU-B]	Belt Line	0-11.8	11.8	
[IU-C]	Belt Line	0.5-2.0	1.5	
[MC-WJ]	Hartsdale-IL state line	12.8-15.7	2.9	
[P&E-A]	IJ-Brant	1.0-4.0	3.0	
[P&E-A]	Clermont-Crawfordsville	9.0-46.0	37.0	
[P&E-A]	Olin-IL state line	74.0-79.9	5.9	
[PRR-F]	OH state line-Wabash	300.4-319.2	18.8	
[PRR-F]	Clarke Jct.-IL state line	445.7-453.3	7.6	
[PRR-GR]	Decatur-Adams	70.4-86.6	16.2	
[PRR-CR]	In Anderson	119.3-122.1	(2.8)	
[PRR-CR]	In Anderson	124.8-127.0	(2.2)	
[PRR-YA]	Anderson Belt	0-3.1	(3.1)	
[PRR-I]	Thorne-ID	180.8-186.8	(6.0)	
[PRR-IK]	Thorne-Hawthorne Yard	0-5.0	(5.0)	
[PRR-IL]	Indianapolis-Southport	0.5-6.3	5.8	
[PRR-IF]	Davis-Frank	6.9-48.1	41.2	
[PRR-IF]	Frank-Frankfort	78.3-78.6	0.3	
[PRR-IF]	In Frankfort	78.6-80.2	(1.6)	
[PRR-V]	Indianapolis-Davis	0.4-6.9	6.5	
[PRR-V]	Terre Haute-IL state line	73.5-79.9	6.4	
[PRR-VT2]	In Terre Haute	73.3-73.5	0.2	
[PRR-VK]	Van Jct.-Kraft	0-1.4	1.4	

CSX TRANSPORTATION CO.

YEAR B&O=430.9 C&O=55.4 CEI=158.8 CCC=220.1 IU=16.1 L&N=38.5 MC=2.9 MON=268.9
P&E=45.9 PRR=230.9 PM=34.3 CSX System=1502.7

On the lines acquired from Conrail and on lines previously owned, CSX Transportation granted trackage rights to Norfolk Southern on:

Line desig.	End points	MP	Main	Note
[CCC-I]	Muncie-Indianapolis	229.7-283.1	53.4	
[IU-]	Various in Indianapolis			
[P&E-A]	Clermont-Ames	9.6-43.0	33.4	
[PRR-F]	OH state line-Hobart	300.4-487.5	187.1	
[PRR-IL]	Indianapolis-Southport	0.5-6.3	5.8	
[PRR-V]	Indianapolis-Davis	0.4-6.9	6.5	
[PRR-IF]	Davis-Clermont	6.9-12.6	5.7	

CSX Transportation obtained trackage rights on lines owned by Norfolk Southern, on:

Line desig.	End points	MP	Main	Note
[LS-T]	OH state line-Elkhart	355.4-421.6	66.2	
[LS-W]	Elkhart-IL state line	421.6-508.2	86.6	
[LS-WD]	Osborn-Schneider	4.9-32.9	28.0	
[LS-WK]	Schneider-IL state line	78.5-82.2	4.7	
[MON-SA]	Lafayette Jct.-Ames	121.5-148.4	26.9	
[NKP-LF]	Muncie-New Castle	65.8-84.0	18.2	
[WAB-M]	Butler-St. Joe	114.3-122.7	8.4	
[WAB-P]	Lafayette Jct.-IL state line	257.2-294.3	37.1	

ACT COLUMN KEY
B1 Built by CSX Transportation
P1 Purchased from Norfolk Southern
S1 Sold to Poseyville & Owensville RR
S2 Sold to Kokomo Rail Corp.
X   Abandoned

SOURCES
1. Simons and Parker, *Railroads of Indiana.*

NOTES
1. The segment between MP 162.2 and MP 162.7 apparently was conveyed to Norfolk Southern as industrial track.
2. It appears that 0.6 miles in Roachdale was retained as industrial track.
3. This abandonment was replaced with trackage rights over Grand Trunk Western line GTW-C from Maynard to Thornton Jct. IL.

DUBOIS COUNTY

MAIN LINE (DCRR-[SOU-UF])
See Southern line SOU-UF for arrangement of stations, prior construction/abandonment record, and prior ownership

CONSTRUCTION/ABANDONMENT

Date	Act	End points	MP	Change	Main	Source	Note
1993/7/15	L	Huntingburg-Dubois	47.7-63.7	+16.0	16.0	1	

OWNERSHIP

1993		Dubois County RR					

ACQUISITION/DISPOSITION RECORD

See ownership record above for line DCRR-[SOU-UF]

ACT COLUMN KEY
L Leased from Norfolk Southern, upon termination of lease to Indiana Hi-Rail

SOURCES
1. Simons and Parker, *Railroads of Indiana.*

ELGIN, JOLIET & EASTERN

MAIN LINE (EJE-A)

	Mileage	County	Crossings, junctions, etc.
East Joliet IL	0		
Matteson	21.61		
Chicago Heights IL	24.91		
(IL/IN state line)	30.8		
Dyer	31.30	Lake	X/MON-A 29.1
Hartsdale	33.82	"	X/PRR-L 281.7
(Bridge)	34.1	"	B/LS-WD 10.6
Griffith	36.21	"	X/C&O-C 254.0, X/ERIE-C 240.2, X/GTW-C 36.1
(Junction)	36.4	"	J/EJE-G 0.1
(Crossing)	45.3	"	X/NKP-C 488.3
Hobart	45.72	"	X/PRR-F 434.4
McCool	52.11	Porter	X/B&O-C 234.8
Crocker	53.48	"	X/WAB-MC 230.5
Porter	56.71	"	J/LS-W 482.18, J/MC-W 240.70, J/PM-C 136.6

CONSTRUCTION/ABANDONMENT

Date	Act	End points	MP	Change	Main	Source	Note
1888	B1	Joliet IL-McCool	30.8-52.1	+21.3	21.3		
1893	B1	McCool-Porter	52.1-56.7	+4.6	25.9	2	
1984	X	Griffith-Porter	36.4-56.7	-20.3	5.6	1	

OWNERSHIP

| 1888 | Elgin, Joliet & Eastern Ry (B1) |

WHITING BRANCH (EJE-GW)

	Mileage	County	Crossings, junctions, etc.
Shearson	0	Lake	J/EJE-GS 1.9
(Crossing)	0.6	"	X/IHB-A 2.2, X/LS-WD 2.2
(Crossing)	0.7	"	X/CSS-AO 66.4
(Crossing)	0.8	"	X/BOCT-A 2.7
Whiting	3.6	"	

CONSTRUCTION/ABANDONMENT

Date	Act	End points	MP	Change	Main	Source	Note
1898 ca.	B1	Shearson-Whiting	0-3.6	+3.6	3.6	1	

OWNERSHIP

| 1898 | Elgin, Joliet & Eastern Ry |

GRIFFITH-GARY LINE (EJE-G)

	Mileage	County	Crossings, junctions, etc.
(Junction)	0.1	Lake	J/EJE-A 36.4
Van Loon	3.5	"	X/NKP-C 497.9
Sand Pit	4.7	"	
Ivanhoe	5.6	"	X/MC-W 259.58, X/IHB-G 2.1
(Bridge)	6.3	"	B/CSS-A 63.2
Cavanaugh	6.7	"	J/EJE-GS 0
(Bridge)	7.8	"	B/PRR-F 445.3
(Bridge)	8.0	"	B/WAB-MC 246.4
(Bridge)	8.1	"	B/B&O-C 248.3
(Junction)	8.2	"	J/conn. to EJE-S 10.8, 0.2 mi.
Kirk Yard Jct.	9.0	"	J/EJE-S 11.7

ELGIN, JOLIET & EASTERN

WHITING BRANCH (EJE-G) (continued)
CONSTRUCTION/ABANDONMENT

Date	Act	End points	MP	Change	Main	Source	Note
1898 ca.	B3	Line	0.1-9.0	+8.9	8.9		

OWNERSHIP

1898 ca.	Griffith & Northern (B3), controlled by Elgin, Joliet & Eastern
no date	Elgin, Joliet & Eastern Ry, merge Griffith & Northern

CAVANAUGH-SOUTH CHICAGO (EJE-GS)

	Mileage	County	Crossings, junctions, etc.
Cavanaugh	0	Lake	J/EJE-G 6.7
(Crossing)	1.7	"	X/CSS-AO 64.4
Shearson	1.9	"	J/EJE-GW 0
(Crossing)	2.1	"	X/IHB-A 2.6, X/LS-WD 3.1
(Crossing)	2.2	"	X/IHB-AW 0.1
East Chicago	2.8	"	
(Bridge)	3.7	"	B/CSS-A 67.2
Hammond	4.9	"	
(Crossing)	5.8	"	X/ERIE-C 248.5, X/MON-A 20.7, X/NKP-C 203.8
(IN/IL state line)	6.1		
State Line IL	6.1		
South Chicago IL	12.4		

CONSTRUCTION/ABANDONMENT

Date	Act	End points	MP	Change	Main	Source	Note
1897	P1	In Hammond	4.8-5.8	+1.0	1.0	2	
1898 ca.	B1	Shearson-Hammond	1.9-4.8	+2.9			
1898 ca.	B1	Hammond-State Line	5.8-6.1	+0.3	4.2		
1898 ca.	B1	Cavanaugh-Shearson	0-1.9	+1.9	6.1		
1933 ca.	X	Shearson-State Line	1.9-6.1	-4.2	1.9	1	

OWNERSHIP

1897	Elgin, Joliet & Eastern Ry

SOUTH CHICAGO-GARY (EJE-S)

	Mileage	County	Crossings, junctions, etc.
South Chicago IL	0		
(IL/IN state line)	2.9		
Whiting-Lake Front	4.5	Lake	
Indiana Harbor	6.7	"	
(Draw bridge)	7.8	"	
Buffington	9.7	"	
(Junction)	10.8	"	J/conn. to EJE-G 8.2, 0.2 mi.
Kirk Yard Jct.	11.7	"	J/EJE-G 9.0
Kirk Yard	12.4	"	
Gary	14.2	"	

CONSTRUCTION/ABANDONMENT

Date	Act	End points	MP	Change	Main	Source	Note
1896/4/1	B2	South Chicago IL-MP 10.8	2.9-10.8	+7.9	7.9		
ca.1906	B2	MP 10.8-Gary	10.8-14.2	+3.4	11.3		

OWNERSHIP

1896	Chicago, Lake Shore & Eastern Ry (B2)
1901	Elgin, Joliet & Eastern Ry, control of Chicago, Lake Shore & Eastern
1938/12/30	Elgin, Joliet & Eastern Ry, merge Chicago, Lake Shore & Eastern

ELGIN, JOLIET & EASTERN

ACQUISITION/DISPOSITION RECORD

Date	Act	EJE--	End points	Change	Main	Note
1888	B1	A	Joliet IL-McCool	+21.3	21.3	
1893	B1	A	McCool-Porter	+4.6	25.9	
1896/4/1	B2	S	South Chicago IL-MP 10.8	+7.9	33.8	
1897	P1	GS	In Hammond	+1.0	34.8	
1898 ca.	B3	G	Griffith-MP 8.2	+8.1		
ca.	B1	GW	Shearson-Whiting	+3.6		
ca.	B1	GS	Shearson-Hammond	+2.9		
ca.	B1	GS	Hammond-State Line	+0.3		
ca.	B1	GS	Cavanaugh-Shearson	+1.9	51.6	
1906 ca.	B2	S	MP 10.8-Gary	+3.4		
ca.	B1	G	MP 8.2-Kirk Yard Jct.	+0.8	55.8	
1933 ca.	X	GS	Shearson-State Line	-4.2	51.6	1
1984	X	A	Griffith-Porter	-20.3	31.3	

ACT COLUMN KEY
B1 Built by Elgin, Joliet & Eastern RR
B2 Built by Chicago, Lake Shore & Eastern Ry
B3 Built by Griffith & Northern
P1 Purchased Western Indiana RR
X   Abandoned

SOURCES
1 Indiana, *1995 Indiana State Rail Plan.*
R Simons and Parker, *Railroads of Indiana.*

NOTES
General 1. The EJ&E was owned by United States Steel Co. from 1901 to 1988.
General 2. In several areas this road was an industrial facility and many spurs and short branches have not been documented nor included in this work.
1. This abandonment was replaced with trackage rights over Indiana Harbor Belt line IHB-AW.

ERIE

MARION DIVISION (ERIE-C)

	Mileage	County	Crossings, junctions, etc.
Marion OH	0		
Wren OH	87.7		
(OH/IN state line)	89.1		
Rivare	91.5	Adams	
Decatur	96.0	"	
DA	96.3	"	X/PRR-GR 70.4
Preble	100.9	"	
Magley	102.9	"	
Tocsin	105.9	Wells	
Kingsland	109.3	"	X/NKP-LF 19.0
Uniondale	112.6	"	
Markle	118.0	Huntington	
Simpson	122.4	"	
(Crossing)	126.3	"	X/WAB-M 169.7
Huntington	126.6	"	J/CBC-A 0
WD	134.0	"	
Bippus	135.7	"	
Servia	141.9	Wabash	
Bolivar	144.3	"	X/CCC-M 101.6

(continued)

ERIE

MARION DIVISION (ERIE-C) (continued)

	Mileage [Marion OH]	County	Crossings, junctions, etc.
Bolivar	144.3	Wabash	X/CCC-M 101.6
Newton	146.1	"	X/PRR-LE 33.9
Laketon	146.7	"	
RX	148.1	"	
Disko	152.8	Fulton	
Akron	157.9	"	
AN	158.6	"	X/WIN-A 46.6
Athens	163.2	"	
Manitou	165.0	"	
RS	167.9	"	X/NKP-LM 98.2
Rochester	168.3	"	
GR	171.8	"	
Pershing	173.9	"	f. Germany
Leiters	177.8	"	
DeLong	179.7	"	X/PRR-LS 29.7
Monterey	183.7	Pulaski	
Ora	187.4	Starke	
Bass Lake	190.3	"	J/ERIE-CB 0 f. Bass Lake Jct.
AD	193.0	"	
Aldine	193.9	"	
North Judson	199.4	"	X/C&O-C 214.8 X/LS-WK 43.3 X/PRR-L 237.3
Lomax	204.7	"	
Wilders	206.1	LaPorte	X/CAS-A 3.4, X/MON-N 28.1
Clanricarde	209.3	Porter	
Kouts	213.7	"	X/PRR-L 253.1
Boone Grove	219.7	"	
Hurlburt	222.4	"	
Palmer	226.0	Lake	
Winfield	228.5	"	
Crown Point	232.9	"	
Griffith	240.2	"	X/EJE-A 36.2, X/MC-WJ 10.3, X/C&O-C 254.0, X/GTW-C 36.1
Highlands	243.3	"	
HD	243.6	"	x/LS-WD 7.15
HY	246.8	"	J/C&O-C 260.6
Hammond	248.3	"	
(Crossing, junction)	248.5	"	J/NKP-C 503.8, X/EJE-GS 5.8, X/IHB-A 6.9, X/MC-W 264.9

CONSTRUCTION/ABANDONMENT

Date	Act	End points	MP	Change	Main	Source	Note
1882	B1	OH state line-Hammond	89.1-248.3	+159.2	159.2	1	1
1977/9/25	T1	OH state line-Hammond	89.1-248.3	<159.2>	0	1	2
1979/6	XT	OH state line-Hammond	89.1-248.3	<+159.2>		1	
1979/6	T2	OH state line-Hammond	89.1-248.3	<159.2>	0	1	
1980/1	XT	OH state line-Hammond	89.1-248.3	<+159.2>		1	
1980/1	T3	Rochester-Monterey	168.3-183.7	<15.4>		1	
1980/1	S1	Monterey-North Judson	183.7-199.7	[16.0]		1	3
1980	X	OH state line-Monterey	89-1-168.3	79.2		1	
1980	X	North Judson-Hammond	199.7-248.3	48.6	0	1	
1983 ca.	XT	Rochester-Monterey	168.3-183.7	<+15.4>			
1983 ca.	X	Rochester-Monterey	168.3-183.7	15.4	0		

OWNERSHIP

1882	Chicago & Atlantic Ry (B1)
1890	Chicago & Erie RR (controlled by Erie RR), reorganize Chicago & Atlantic
1941	Erie RR, merge Chicago & Erie
1960	Erie-Lackawanna RR, merge Erie and Delaware, Lackawanna & Western
1968	Erie-Lackawanna Ry, reorganize Erie-Lackawanna

ERIE

BASS LAKE BRANCH (ERIE-CB)

	Mileage	County	Crossings, junctions, etc.
Bass Lake Jct.	0	Starke	J/ERIE-C 190.3
Lake Park	1.8	"	

CONSTRUCTION/ABANDONMENT

Date	Act	End points	MP	Change	Main	Source	Note
1898/6	B1	Bass Lake Jct.-Lake Park	0-1.8	+1.8	1.8	2	
1928/8	X	Bass Lake Jct.-Lake Park	0-1.8	-1.8	0	2	

OWNERSHIP

1898	Chicago & Erie RR (controlled by Erie RR)

ACQUISITION/DISPOSITION RECORD

Date	Act	ERIE-	End points	Change	Main	Note
1882	B1	C	OH state line-Hammond	+159.2	159.2	1
1898/6	B1	CB	Bass Lake Jct.-Lake Park	+1.8	161.0	S
1928/8	X	CB	Bass Lake Jct.-Lake Park	-1.8	159.2	
1977/9/25	T1	C	OH state line-Hammond	<159.2>	0	2
1979/6	XT	C	OH state line-Hammond	<+159.2>		
6	T2	C	OH state line-Hammond	<159.2>	0	
1980/1	XT	C	OH state line-Hammond	<+159.2>		
1	T3	C	Rochester-Monterey	<15.4>		
1	S1	C	Monterey-North Judson	[16.0]		3
	X	C	OH state line-Monterey	79.2		
	X	C	North Judson-Hammond	48.6	0	
1983 ca.	XT	C	Rochester-Monterey	<+15.4>		
ca.	X	C	Rochester-Monterey	15.4	0	

ACT COLUMN KEY
B1 Built by Chicago & Atlantic
S1 Sold to Tippecanoe RR
T1 Transferred to Erie Western
T2 Transferred to Chicago & Indiana
T3 Transferred to Fulton County
X Abandoned
XT Transfer cancelled

SOURCES
1. Simons and Parker, *Railroads of Indiana.*
2. Sulzer, *Ghost Railroads of Indiana.*

NOTES
1. Source 1 states that at the time the Chicago & Atlantic was constructed, it acquired a completed narrow gauge line extending from Huntington to Markle. No record of this company has been found.
2. The entire line in Indiana was operated by the Erie Western Ry. from Sept. 25, 1977, until June 1979, and by the Chicago & Indiana RR from June 1979 until January 1980. The method of transfer to Erie Western and to Chicago & Indiana is unclear, but it is presumed to be by lease.
3. The Monterey-North Judson segment was sold to the Tippecanoe RR which subsequently sold it to Daniel R. Frick who operates it under the name J. K. Line.

ERIE WESTERN

MAIN LINE (ERW-[ERIE-C])
See Erie line ERIE-C for arrangement of stations, prior construction/abandonment record, and prior ownership

CONSTRUCTION/ABANDONMENT

Date	Act	End points	MP	Change	Main	Source	Note
1977/9/25	T1	OH line-Hammond	89.1-248.3	+159.2	159.2	1	1
1979/6	XT	OH line-Hammond	89.1-248.3	-159.2	0	R	

OWNERSHIP
1977   Erie Western Ry

DECATUR-PORTLAND (ERW-[PRR-GR])
See Grand Rapids & Indiana line PRR-GR for arrangement of stations, prior construction/-abandonment record, and prior ownership

CONSTRUCTION/ABANDONMENT

Date	Act	End points	MP	Change	Main	Source	Note
1977/9/25	T2	Decatur-Portland	70.4-42.0	+28.4	28.4	1	1
1979/6	XT	Decatur-Portland	70.4-42.0	-28.4	0	1	

OWNERSHIP
1977   Erie Western Ry

ACQUISITION/DISPOSITION RECORD

Date	Act	ERW--	End points	Change	Main	Note
1977/9/25	T1	[ERIE-C]	OH state line-Hammond	+159.2		1
1977/9/25	T2	[PRR-GR]	Decatur-Portland	+28.4	187.6	1
1979/6	XT	[ERIE-C]	OH state line-Hammond	-159.2		
1979/6	XT	[PRR-GR]	Decatur-Portland	-28.4	0	

ACT COLUMN KEY
T1   Transfer to Erie Western from Erie
T2   Transfer to Erie Western from Penn Central
XT   Transfer cancelled

SOURCES
1. Simons and Parker, *Railroads of Indiana.*

NOTES
1. The method of transfer from the Erie and Penn Central to the Erie Western is unclear, but it is presumed to be by lease.

EVANSVILLE TERMINAL CO.

MAIN LINE (ETCI-[IC-NM])
See Illinois Central line IC-NM for arrangement of stations, prior construction/abandonment record, and prior ownership

CONSTRUCTION/ABANDONMENT

Date	Act	End points	MP	Change	Main	Source	Note
1996/7	P	IL state line-Evansville	216.7-246.2	+29.5	29.5	1	
1997	X	IL state line-Poseyville	216.7-227.5	-10.8	18.7	1	

OWNERSHIP
1996   Evansville Terminal Co.

ACQUISITION/DISPOSITION RECORD
See ownership record above for line ETCI-[IC-NM]

ACT COLUMN KEY
P Purchased from Indiana Hi-Rail

SOURCES
1. Simons and Parker, *Railroads of Indiana.*

FERDINAND

MAIN LINE (FERD-A)

	Mileage	County	Crossings, junctions, etc.
(Huntingburg)	0)	Dubois	
(Junction)	1.0	"	J/SOU-UE 46.7
Ferdinand	7.38	"	

CONSTRUCTION/ABANDONMENT

Date	Act	End points	MP	Change	Main	Source	Note
1909	B	Huntingburg-Ferdinand	0-6.4	+6.4	6.4	1	
1991/3/3	X	Huntingburg-Ferdinand	0-6.4	-6.4	0	2	

OWNERSHIP

1909	Ferdinand Ry
1911/10/13	Ferdinand RR, reorganize Ferdinand Ry

ACQUISITION/DISPOSITION RECORD
See ownership record above for line FERD-A

ACT COLUMN KEY
B Built by Ferdinand Ry
X Abandoned

SOURCES
1. Indiana, *1995 Indiana State Rail Plan.*
2. Simons and Parker, *Railroads of Indiana.*

FORT WAYNE UNION RY

MAIN LINE (FWU-A)
This was an industrial road in Fort Wayne, and is not included in the Mileage table.

CONSTRUCTION/ABANDONMENT

Date	Act	End points	MP	Change	Main	Source	Note
1925/6/1	B	In Fort Wayne		(+2.1)	0	1	

OWNERSHIP

1925	Fort Wayne Union Ry (see Note, General)
1989/5	Norfolk & Western, buy Fort Wayne Union

ACQUISITION/DISPOSITION RECORD
See ownership record above for line FWU-A

ACT COLUMN KEY
B Built by Fort Wayne Union Ry

SOURCES
1. Simons and Parker, *Railroads of Indiana.*

NOTES
 General. Initially this company was owned jointly by New York Central, Wabash, Pennsylvania, and New York, Chicago & St. Louis, and ownership passed to the successor owners as mergers occurred.

FRENCH LICK, WEST BADEN & SOUTHERN

MAIN LINE (FWS-[SOU-UF])
See Southern Ry line SOU-UF for arrangement of stations, prior construction/abandonment record, and prior ownership

CONSTRUCTION/ABANDONMENT

Date	Act	End points	MP	Change	Main	Source	Note
1978	P	Dubois-French Lick	63.7-79.0	+15.3	15.3	1	1

OWNERSHIP

1978	French Lick, West Baden & Southern Ry

ACQUISITION/DISPOSITION RECORD
See ownership record above for line WFS-[SOU-UF]

ACT COLUMN KEY
 P Purchased from Southern Ry

SOURCES
1. Simons and Parker, *Railroads of Indiana.*

NOTES
 1. This road is operated primarily as a tourist railroad.

FULTON COUNTY

ROCHESTER-MONTEREY (FULT-[ERIE-C])
See Erie line ERIE-C for arrangement of stations, prior construction/abandonment record, and prior ownership

CONSTRUCTION/ABANDONMENT

Date	Act	End points	MP	Change	Main	Source	Note
1980/1	T1	Rochester-Monterey	168.3-183.7	+15.4	15.4	1	
1983 ca.	XT	Rochester-Monterey	168.3-183.7	-15.4	0	1	

OWNERSHIP

1980	Fulton County RR

ROCHESTER-ARGOS (FULT-[NKP-LM])
See New York, Chicago & St. Louis line NKP-LM for arrangement of stations, prior construction/abandonment record, and prior ownership

CONSTRUCTION/ABANDONMENT

Date	Act	End points	MP	Change	Main	Source	Note
1998 ca.	P	Rochester-Argos	95.6-108.6	+13.0	13.0		

OWNERSHIP

1998	Fulton County RR

ACQUISITION/DISPOSITION RECORD
See ownership record above

ACT COLUMN KEY
P   Purchase from Norfolk Southern
T1   Transfer to Fulton County from Erie
XT   Transfer cancelled

SOURCES
1. Simons and Parker, *Railroads of Indiana.*

NOTES
 1. The method of transfer from the Erie to the Fulton County is unclear, but it is presumed to be by lease.

GRAND TRUNK WESTERN

CHICAGO DIV. (GTW-C)

	Mileage	County	Crossings, junctions, etc.
Chicago	0.0		
Oak Glen IL	28.63		
(Line IL/IN)	30.6		
(Crossing) IN	31.3	Lake	X/MON-N 25.8
Munster	31.4	"	
Maynard	31.56	"	X/PRR-L 284.8
Hays	33.97	"	X/LS-WD 9.2
Griffith	36.08	"	X/EJ&E-A 36.2, X/C&O-C 254.0,
			X/ERIE-C 240.6, X/MC-WJ 10.3
Bothwells	38.76	"	
Lottaville	39.62	"	
Turkey Creek	41.24	"	
Atkins	41.97	"	
Adams	43.29	"	
Pierces	44.35	"	
Ainsworth	45.20	"	
Smalls	48.29	Porter	
Springmans Cross.	48.93	"	
Sedley	50.34	"	
Sommers	52.24	"	
(Crossing)	52.6	"	X/NKP-C 481.4
Fort Wayne Crossing	52.69	"	X/PRR-F 426.9
Valparaiso	55.80	"	J/GTW-CO4 0
Haskells	63.89	LaPorte	X/MON-M 43.1
Union Mills	70.14	"	
Wellsboro	71.08	"	X/B&O-C 213.8, X/PM-W 15.05
Kingsbury	74.82	"	B/WAB-MC 205.6 (old 75.05)
Stillwell	80.17	"	X/NKP-LM 139.6
Swifts	83.31	"	
Mill Creek	84.51	"	
Crumstown	91.57	St.Joseph	f.Crums Point
Vandalia Jct.	97.5	"	X/MC-J 0.1, J/NJI-A 1.7
I.I.& I.Jct.	99.0	"	X/LS-N2 3.2, J/NJI-A 0
Olivers	99.16	"	
Arnold Street	99.52	"	J&X/LS-W 437.3, J/GTW-CO2 99.5
--via LS-W			
(South Bend	100.19)	"	
--via LS-W			
High Street	101.09	"	J/NYC-W 435.8
(Greenlawn Avenue)	102.4	"	J/GTW-CO2 102.1
------------------ (Mileage east is via GTW-CO2)			
(Greenlawn Avenue)	102.1	"	
Mishawaka	104.03	"	
(Junction)	104.1	"	J/LS-WE 12.9
Granger	110.88	"	X/CCC-M 35.7
(Line IN/MI)	111.1		
Edwardsburg MI	113.97		
Battle Creek MI	176.64		

CONSTRUCTION/ABANDONMENT

Date	Act	End points	MP	Change	Main	Source	Note
1872/Aut.	B1	Cassopolis-MP 102.1	111.1-102.1	+9.0	9.0	3	
1873/10/13	B1	MP 99.5-Valparaiso	99.5-55.8	+43.7	52.7	1	
1879/12	B2	Thornton Jct.-Valparaiso	30.6-55.8	+25.2	77.9	2	
1929	B3	High St-MP 102	101.1-102.4	+1.3	79.2		2
(continued)							

GRAND TRUNK WESTERN

CHICAGO DIV. (GTW-C) (continued)

OWNERSHIP

1872	Peninsular (B1) of part
1876	Chicago & Southern (B2) of part
1878/7/30	Chicago & Lake Huron, merge Port Huron & Lake Michigan and Peninsular
1878/8/5	Chicago & State Line, bought Chicago & Southern
1879	North Western Grand Trunk
1880/4/6	Chicago & Grand Trunk, merger of Chicago & Huron, Chicago & State Line, and Chicago & Northeastern, and North Western Grand Trunk; control by G T Ry Of Canada
1881	Grand Trunk Junction
1900/11/20	Grand Trunk Western Ry, reorganization of Chicago & Grand Trunk
1928/11/1	Grand Trunk Western RR (B3), merger of Grand Trunk Western Ry
1930/11/30	Grand Trunk Western RR, merger of Grand Trunk Junction

OLD MAIN LINE IN SOUTH BEND (GTW-CO2)

	Mileage [Chicago]	County	Crossings, junctions, etc.
Arnold Street	99.52	St.Joseph	J/GTW-C 99.5
South Bend (original depot)	100.46	"	
(Greenlawn Avenue)	102.1	"	J/GTW-C 102.4

CONSTRUCTION/ABANDONMENT

Date	Act	End points	MP	Change	Main	Source	Note
1872/Fall	B1	Greenlawn Ave.-South Bend	102.1-100.5	+1.6	1.6	3	1
1873/10/13	B1	South Bend-Arnold Street	100.5-99.5	+1.0	2.6	1	1
1929	X	Line	99.5-102.1	-2.6	0		3

OWNERSHIP

1872	Peninsular (B1)
1878/7/30	Chicago & Lake Huron, merger of Peninsular
1880/4/6	Chicago & Grand Trunk, merger of Chicago & Lake Huron
1900/11/20	Grand Trunk Western Ry, reorganization of Chicago & Grand Trunk
1928/11/1	Grand Trunk Western RR, merger of Grand Trunk Western Ry

OLD MAIN LINE IN VALPARAISO (GTW-CO4)

	Mileage	County	Crossings, junctions, etc.
Valparaiso	0	Porter	J/GTW-C 55.8
(Junction)	1.1	"	J/PRR-F----junction point not located

CONSTRUCTION/ABANDONMENT

Date	Act	End points	MP	Change	Main	Source	Note
1873/10/13	B1	Line	0-1.1	+1.1	1.1		
1879	X	Line	0-1.1	-1.1	0		

OWNERSHIP

1873	Peninsular (B1)
1878/7/30	Chicago & Lake Huron, merger of Peninsular

ACQUISITION/DISPOSITION RECORD

Date	Act	GTW--	End points	Change	Main	Note
1872/Aut.	B1	C,CO2	Battle Creek MI-South Bend	+10.6	10.6	1
1873/10/13	B1	C,CO2,CO4	So Bend-W of Valparaiso	+45.8	56.4	
1879/12	B2	C	Elsden Jct. IL-Valparaiso	+25.2		
	X	CO4	Valparaiso-W of Valparaiso	-1.1	80.5	
1929	B3	C	High St.-MP 102.1	+1.3		2
	X	CO2	High St.-MP 102.1	-2.6	79.2	3

GRAND TRUNK WESTERN

ACT COLUMN KEY
B1   Built by Peninsular
B2   Built by North Western Grand Trunk
B3   Built by Grand Trunk Western
X   Abandoned

SOURCES
1. Hopper, *Canadian National Railways: Syntopical History*.
2. Interstate Commerce Commission *Valuation Docket 445*
3. Michigan, *Aids, Gifts, Grants and Donations*.

NOTES
1. The original South Bend station was at MP 100.5 at Division (now Western Ave.) and Michigan Ave. The track was in the center of Western Ave
2. This construction also included obtaining trackage rights on 1.6 miles of the New York Central between Arnold Street and High Street and the use of the NYC South Bend station.
3. This segment was replaced by present main line GTW-C 99.5 to 102.4.

HERITAGE RR

MAIN LINE (HERG-A)

	Mileage	County	Crossings, junctions, etc.
Boliver	0	Wabash	J/CCC-M 101.6
(Laketon Refining Co.)	3.1	"	

CONSTRUCTION/ABANDONMENT

Date	Act	End points	MP	Change	Main	Source	Note
1991	B	Line	0-3.1	+3.1	3.1	1	1

OWNERSHIP

1991		Heritage RR (B)

ACQUISITION/DISPOSITION RECORD

Date	Act	HERG-	End points	Change	Main	Note

See ownership record above for line HERG-A

ACT COLUMN KEY
B Built by Heritage RR

SOURCES
1. Simons and Parker, *Railroads of Indiana*.

NOTES
1. The Heritage RR is a privately-owned industrial road and not a common carrier.

HILLSDALE COUNTY

HILLSDALE-STEUBENVILLE (HCRC-[LS-TF])
See Lake Shore & Michigan Southern line LS-TF for arrangement of stations, prior construction/abandonment record, and prior ownership

CONSTRUCTION/ABANDONMENT

Date	Act	End points	MP	Change	Main	Source	Note
1976/4/1	L	Hillsdale MI-Pleasant Lake	44.7-60.5	+15.8	15.8	R	
1986/4	L	Pleasant Lake-Steubenville	60.5-63.5	+3.0	18.8	R	
1992	TL	MI state line-Steubenville	44.7-63.5	-18.8	0	R	

OWNERSHIP

1976		Hillsdale County Ry

HILLSDALE COUNTY

ACQUISITION/DISPOSITION RECORD
See ownership record above for line HCRC-[LS-TF]

ACT COLUMN KEY
 L Leased from Penn Central, later Conrail
 TL Lease transferred to Indiana Northeastern

SOURCES
1. Simons and Parker, *Railroads of Indiana.*

HONEY CREEK

NEW CASTLE-SULPHUR SPRINS (HCR-[PRR-CR])
See Pennsylvania line PRR-CR for arrangement of stations, prior construction/abandonment record, and prior ownership

CONSTRUCTION/ABANDONMENT

Date	Act	End points	MP	Change	Main	Source	Note
1993/10/1	P	Foley-Sulphur Springs	104.1-110.7	+6.6	6.6	1	1

OWNERSHIP

1993		Honey Creek RR

MAIN LINE (HCR-[NKP-LR])
See New York, Chicago & St. Louis line NKP-LR for arrangement of stations, prior construction/abandonment record, and prior ownership

CONSTRUCTION/ABANDONMENT

Date	Act	End points	MP	Change	Main	Source	Note
1993/10/1	T	Rushville-Sexton	107.9-101.0	+6.9	6.9	1	1

OWNERSHIP

1993		Honey Creek RR

ACQUISITION/DISPOSITION RECORD

Date	Act	HCR-	-End points	Change	Main	Note
1993/10/1	P	[PRR-CR]	Foley-Sulphur Springs	+6.6		
1993/10/1	T	[NKP-LR]	Rushville-Sexton	+6.9	13.5	1

ACT COLUMN KEY
P Purchased from Conrail
T Leased or acquired from Indiana Hi-Rail

SOURCES
1. Simons and Parker, *Railroads of Indiana.*
NOTES
 1. This railroad company is owned by the Morristown Grain Co. and is not a common carrier.

HOOSIER SOUTHERN

LINCOLN CITY-CANNELTON (HOS-[SOU-UC])
See Southern line SOU-UC for arrangement of stations, prior construction/abandonment record, and prior ownership

CONSTRUCTION/ABANDONMENT

Date	Act	End points	MP	Change	Main	Source	Note
1994	L	Lincoln City-Tell City	0-19.8	+19.8	19.8	1	

OWNERSHIP

1994		Hoosier Southern RR

HOOSIER SOUTHERN

ROCKPORT JCT.-ROCKPORT (HOS-[SOU-UR])
See Southern line SOU-UR for arrangement of stations, prior construction/abandonment record, and prior ownership

CONSTRUCTION/ABANDONMENT

Date	Act	End points	MP	Change	Main	Source	Note
1996	L	Rockport Jct.-Rockport	1.0-16.8	+15.8	15.8	1	

OWNERSHIP
1996   Hoosier Southern RR

ACQUISITION/DISPOSITION RECORD

Date	Act	HCR--	End points	Change	Main	Note
1994	L	[SOU-UC]	Lincoln City-Tell City	+19.8	19.8	
1996	L	[SOU-UR]	Rockport Jct.-Rockport	+15.8	35.6	

ACT COLUMN KEY
L Leased from Norfolk Southern

SOURCES
1. Simons and Parker, *Railroads of Indiana.*

ILLINOIS CENTRAL

INDIANAPOLIS DISTRICT (IC-NI)

	Mileage	County	Crossings, junctions, etc.
(Indianapolis	0)	Marion	
--via IU-W			
(Junction)	0.2	"	J/IU-W 0.2
(Bridge)	1.7	"	B/IU-B 6.7
Mt. Perry	7.40	"	
Frances	11.63	Johnson	
Bargersville	17.6	"	
Anita	24.79	"	
Morgantown	30.06	"	X/CCC-GW 115.8
Fruitdale	33.9	Brown	
Helmsburg	38.86	"	
Trevlac	41.31	"	
Unionville	49.75	Monroe	
Bloomington	55.94	"	
(Bridge)	56.4	"	B/MON-SA 219.9
(Junction)	57.0	"	J/IC-NB 0.8
Kirby	60.79	"	
Elwren	65.02	"	
Solsberry	70.19	Greene	
Tulip	77.51	"	
Bloomfield	83.05	"	
(Bridge)	83.9	"	B/MON-SS 36.0
(Bridge)	85.2	"	B/CCC-T 48.2
Switz City	89.44	"	J/IC-NE 89.44, X/PRR-IV 79.8, J/MON-SS 40.5
(continued)			

ILLINOIS CENTRAL

INDIANAPOLIS DISTRICT (IC-NI) (continued)

CONSTRUCTION/ABANDONMENT

Date	Act	End points	MP	Change	Main	Source	Note
1905	B5	Indianapolis-Switz City	0.4-89.4	+89.2	89.0	1,2	
1986/3/18	S1	Indianapolis-Switz City	0.4-89.7	-89.2	0	2	

OWNERSHIP

1905	Indianapolis Southern Ry (B5), controlled by Illinois Central
1911	Illinois Central RR, merge Indianapolis Southern
1972/8	Illinois Central Gulf RR, merge Gulf, Mobile & Ohio

BLOOMINGTON SOUTHERN RR (IC-NB)

	Mileage	County	Crossings, junctions, etc.
(Bloomington	0)	Monroe	
(Junction)	1.1	"	J/IC-NI 57.0
Clear Creek	5.2	"	
Victor	9.3	"	

CONSTRUCTION/ABANDONMENT

Date	Act	End points	MP	Change	Main	Source	Note
1914	B6	Bloomington-Victor	1.1-9.3	+8.2	8.2	2	
1988	X	Bloomington-Victor	1.1-9.3	-8.2	0	2	3

OWNERSHIP

1914	Bloomington Southern RR (B6), controlled by Illinois Central
1972/8	Illinois Central Gulf RR, merge Gulf, Mobile & Ohio

EFFINGHAM DISTRICT (IC-NE)

	Mileage [Indianapolis]	County	Crossings, junctions, etc.
Switz City	89.44	Greene	J/IC-NI 89.44, X/PRR-IV 79.8, X/MON-SS 40.5
Linton	95.36	"	X/MILW-T 212.4
(Junction)	95.5	"	J/IC-NE1 0
Victoria	97.62	"	X/MON-SL 47.1
Dugger	101.08	Sullivan	J/IC-NE2 0
Cass	103.01	"	X/MON-SL2 4.0
(Junction)	104.4	"	J/IC-NE3 0
Caledonia	106.33	"	
Sullivan	110.01	"	X/CEI-E 203.7
New Lebanon	114.45	"	
Merom	118.70	"	
Riverton	120.38	"	
(IN/IL state line)	120.4		
Palestine IL	123.26		
Effingham IL	177.00		

CONSTRUCTION/ABANDONMENT

Date	Act	End points	MP	Change	Main	Source	Note
1880	B2	Switz City-IL state line	89.4-120.4	+31.0	31.0	1	1
1986/3/18	S1	Switz City-Sullivan	89.4-110.0	-20.6	10.4	2	
1989 ca.	S1	Sullivan-IL state line	110.0-120.4	-10.4	0	2	

OWNERSHIP

1880	Bloomfield RR (B2), controlled by Springfield, Effingham & SE (See also Monon line MON-SS)
1881/12/28	Springfield, Effington & Southeastern Ry ended control of Bloomfield
1883/4/9	Indiana & Illinois Southern Ry, buy Bloomfield
1886/5/12	Indiana & Illinois Southern RR, reorganize I&IS Ry
1890/2/6	St. Louis, Indianapolis & Eastern RR, reorganize I&IS RR
1899/11	Illinois & Indiana RR, reorganize SLI&E
1905	Illinois Central RR, acquired Illinois & Indiana
1972/8	Illinois Central Gulf RR, merge Gulf, Mobile & Ohio
1988/3	Illinois Central RR, rename Illinois Central Gulf

ILLINOIS CENTRAL

TEMPLETON MINE SPUR (IC-NE1)

	Mileage	County	Crossings, junctions, etc.
(Junction)	0	Greene	J/IC-NE 95.5
Templeton Mine	0.8	"	

CONSTRUCTION/ABANDONMENT

Date	Act	End points		MP	Change	Main	Source	Note
								4

SUNFLOWER MINE SPUR (IC-NE2)

	Mileage	County	Crossings, junctions, etc.
(Junction)	0	Sullivan	J/IC-NE 101.1
Sunflower Mine	1.0	"	

CONSTRUCTION/ABANDONMENT

Date	Act	End points		MP	Change	Main	Source	Note
								4

REBENT MINE SPUR (IC-NE3)

	Mileage	County	Crossings, junctions, etc.
(Junction)	0	Sullivan	J/IC-NE 104.4
Rebent Mine	1.5	"	

CONSTRUCTION/ABANDONMENT

Date	Act	End points		MP	Change	Main	Source	Note
								4

MATTOON DISTRICT (IC-NM)

	Mileage [Peoria]	County	Crossings, junctions, etc.
Mattoon IL	119.74		
Grayville IL	214.23		
(IL/IN state line)	216.7		
Hovey	217.28	Posey	
Griffin	220.74	"	
Barrett	223.34	"	
Stewartsville	226.23	"	J/IC-NH 0
Poseyville	229.23	"	X/CEI-EM 281.8
Wendel	233.85	"	
Martin	235.77	Vanderburgh	
Armstrong	237.59	"	
Wilcox	240	"	
Harwood	245.5	"	X/CCC-LE 157.7, (X/CEI-EB 285.1)
(Crossing)	246.6	"	X/CEI-EJ 2.2
Evansville	247.81	"	J/L&N-SE 325.0

CONSTRUCTION/ABANDONMENT

Date	Act	End points	MP	Change	Main	Source	Note
1881	B3	Mattoon IL-Evansville	216.7-247.8	+31.1	31.1	2	
1984	X,Y	In Evansville	246.6-247.8	-1.2	29.9	1	
1986	X	In Evansville	246.2-246.6	-0.4		1	
1986	S2	IL state line-Evansville	216.7-246.2	[29.5]	0	2	
1996/7	S3	IL state line-Evansville	216.7-246.2	[[29.5]]	0	2	
1997	X	IL state line-Poseyville	216.7-227.5	[-10.8]	0	2	

OWNERSHIP

1881	Peoria, Decatur & Evansville Ry (B3)
1900	Illinois Central RR, bought Peoria, Decatur & Evansville
1972/8	Illinois Central Gulf RR, merge Gulf, Mobile & Ohio
1988/3	Illinois Central RR, rename Illinois Central Gulf

ILLINOIS CENTRAL

NEW HARMONY BRANCH (IC-NH)

	Mileage	County	Crossings, junctions, etc.
Stewartsville	0	Posey	J/IC-NM 226.23
Rogers	3.31	"	
New Harmony	6.30	"	

CONSTRUCTION/ABANDONMENT

Date	Act	End points	MP	Change	Main	Source	Note
1881	B4	Stewartsville-New Harmony	0-6.3	+6.3	6.3	2	
1976	X	Stewartsville-New Harmony	0-6.3	-6.3	0	2	

OWNERSHIP

1881	Evansville & New Harmony Ry (B4)
1881	Peoria, Decatur & Evansville, ?acquired Evansville & New Harmony
1900	Illinois Central RR, bought Peoria, Decatur & Evansville
1972/8	Illinois Central Gulf RR, merge Gulf, Mobile & Ohio

RANTOUL DISTRICT (IC-SR)

	Mileage	County	Crossings, junctions, etc.
West Lebanon	0	Warren	J/WAB-P 284.9
Sloan	5.7	"	X/LS-WD 94.1
Hedrick	6.4	"	
(IN/IL state line)	8.4		
Alvin IL	12.36		
LeRoy IL	75.40		

CONSTRUCTION/ABANDONMENT

Date	Act	End points	MP	Change	Main	Source	Note
1878/12/1	B1	West Lebanon-LeRoy IL	0-8.4	+8.4	8.4	3	
1887/10/27	L1	West Lebanon-LeRoy IL	0-8.4		8.4	3	2
1937/4/7	X	West Lebanon-Hedrick	0-6.0	-6.0	2.4	3	
1943/2/14	X	Hedrick-IL state line	6.0-8.4	-2.4	0	S	

OWNERSHIP

1878	Havana, Rantoul & Eastern RR (B1)
1881	Wabash, St. Louis & Pacific, leased line
1884	Wabash, St. Louis & Pacific, terminated lease of line
1887	Lebanon & Western RR, reorganize Havana, Rantoul & Eastern
1887	Rantoul RR, (controlled and leased by Illinois Central) acquired L&W

ACQUISITION/DISPOSITION RECORD

Date	Act	IC-	End points	Change	Main	Note
1880	B2	NE	Switz City-IL state line	+31.0	31.0	1
1881	B3	NM	Mattoon IL-Evansville	+31.1		
1881	B4	NH	Stewartsville-New Harmony	+6.3	68.4	
1887/10/27	L1	SR	West Lebanon-LeRoy IL	+8.4	76.8	2
1905	B5	NI	Indianapolis-Switz City	+89.2	166.0	
1914	B6	NB	Bloomington-Victor	+8.2	174.2	
1937/4/7	X	SR	West Lebanon-Hedrick	-6.0	168.2	
1943/2/14	X	SR	Hedrick-IL state line	-2.4	165.8	
1976	X	NH	Stewartsville-New Harmony	-6.3	159.5	
1984	X,Y	NM	In Evansville	-1.2	158.3	
1986/3/18	S1	NI	Indianapolis-Switz City	[89.2]		
3/18	S1	NE	Switz City-Sullivan	[20.6]		
	X	NM	In Evansville	-0.4		
	S2	NM	IL state line-Evansville	[29.5]	18.6	
1988	X	NB	Bloomington-Victor	-8.2	10.4	3
1989 ca.	S1	NE	Sullivan-IL state line	[10.4]	0	
1996/7	S3	NM	IL state line-Evansville	[[29.5]]	0	
1997	X	NM	IL state line-Poseyville	[-10.8]	0	

ILLINOIS CENTRAL

ACT COLUMN KEY
B1 Built by Havana, Rantoul & Eastern RR
B2 Built by Bloomfield RR
B3 Built by Peoria, Decatur & Evansville Ry
B4 Built by Evansville & New Harmony Ry
B5 Built by Indianapolis Southern Ry
B6 Built by Bloomington Southern RR
L1 Lease of Rantoul RR
S1 Sold to Indiana RR
S2 Sold to Indiana Hi-Rail
S3 Sold to Evansville Terminal
X Abandoned

SOURCES
1. Indiana, *1995 Indiana State Rail Plan.*
2. Simons and Parker, *Railroads of Indiana.*
3. Sulzer, *Ghost Railroads of Indiana.*

NOTES
1. The line was built as narrow gauge and in 1887 converted to standard gauge.
2. The line was built as narrow gauge, and converted to standard gauge shortly after the Illinois Central acquired it.
3. Source 2 states that a section remains in use as an industrial facility.
4. The date of construction or abandonment could not be determined and this line is not included in the Acquisition/-Disposition Record.

INDIAN CREEK

ELWOOD-FRANKTON (INDC-[PRR-CR])
See Pennsylvania line PRR-CR for arrangement of stations, prior construction/-abandonment record, and prior ownership

CONSTRUCTION/ABANDONMENT

Date	Act	End points	MP	Change	Main	Source	Note
1980/7/20	P	Frankton-Elwood	132.8-137.4	+4.6	4.6	1	1

OWNERSHIP
1980   Indian Creek RR

ACQUISITION/DISPOSITION RECORD
See ownership record above for line INDC-[PRR-CR]

ACT COLUMN KEY
P Purchased from Conrail

SOURCES
1. Simons and Parker, *Railroads of Indiana.*

NOTES
1. This company is owned by Rydman & Fox, Inc., and is not a common carrier.

INDIANA & OHIO

MAIN LINE (INOH-[CCC-GW])
See Cleveland, Cincinnati, Chicago & St. Louis line CCC-GW for arrangement of stations, prior construction/-abandonment record, and prior ownership

CONSTRUCTION/ABANDONMENT

Date	Act	End points	MP	Change	Main	Source	Note
1979/6	P	Valley Jct.-Brookville	24.7-45.4	+20.7	20.7	1	

OWNERSHIP
1979   Indiana & Ohio RR

ACQUISITION/DISPOSITION RECORD
See ownership record above for line INOH-[CCC-GW]

ACT COLUMN KEY
 P Purchased from Penn Central

SOURCES
1. Simons and Parker, *Railroads of Indiana.*

INDIANA EASTERN

CARTHAGE-EMPORIA (IERT-[CCC-M])
See Cleveland, Cincinnati, Chicago & St. Louis line CCC-M for arrangement of stations, prior construction/abandonment record, and prior ownership

CONSTRUCTION/ABANDONMENT

Date	Act	End points	MP	Change	Main	Source	Note
1979/6	L	Carthage-Emporia	194.0-172.7	+21.3	21.3	1	
1985/1/8	LT	Carthage-Emporia	194.0-172.7	-21.3	0	1	

OWNERSHIP
1979   Indiana Eastern RR and Transportation Co

SHIRLEY-WILKINSON (IERT-[CCC-S])
See Cleveland, Cincinnati, Chicago & St. Louis line CCC-S for arrangement of stations, prior construction/abandonment record, and prior ownership and also and Indiana Eastern

CONSTRUCTION/ABANDONMENT

Date	Act	End points	MP	Change	Main	Source	Note
1979/6	T	Shirley-Wilkinson	107.3-109.0	+1.7	1.7		
1985/1/8	LT	Shirley-Wilkinson	107.3-109.0	-1.7	0		

OWNERSHIP
1979   Indiana Eastern RR and Transportation Co

ACQUISITION/DISPOSITION RECORD

Date	Act	IERT-	End points	Change	Main	Note
1979/6	L	[CCC-M]	Carthage-Emporia	+21.3		
/6	L	[CCC-S]	Shirley-Wilkinson	+1.7	23.0	
1985/1/8	LT	[CCC-M]	Carthage-Emporia	-21.3		
/6	LT	[CCC-S]	Shirley-Wilkinson	-1.7	0	

ACT COLUMN KEY
L   Leased from Penn Central
LT   Lease assigned to Indiana Midland

SOURCES
1. Simons and Parker, *Railroads of Indiana.*

NOTES
 General. The road operated under the service name "Hoosier Connection."

INDIANA HARBOR BELT

INDIANA HARBOR-MANNHEIM (IHB-A)

	Mileage	County	Crossings, junctions, etc.
Indiana Harbor	0	Lake	J/LS-W 503.19
(Crossing)	0.2	"	X/PRR-F 448.1
Whiting			
(Crossing)	2.0	"	X/BOCT-A 2.7
(Crossing)	2.1	"	X/CSS-AO 66.4
(Crossing)	2.2	"	X/EJE-GW 0.6
Grasselli	2.5	"	J/EJE-GS 2.1, J/IHB-AC 0, J/IHB-AW 0
(Bridge)	3.3	"	B/CSS-A 65.2
Gibson	3.7	"	X/MC-W 261.73, J/IHB-G 0, J/IHB-GS 0
Gibson Yard	5.0	"	
Hammond	6.9	"	X/ERIE-C 248.5, X/MON-A 20.7, X/NKP-C 203.8
(IN/IL state line)	7.2		
Dolton IL	11.8		
Mannheim IL			

CONSTRUCTION/ABANDONMENT

Date	Act	End points	MP	Change	Main	Source	Note
1907 ca.	T	Indiana Harbor-Gibson	0-3.7				1
1907 ca.	B	Gibson-IL state line	3.7-7.2	+3.5	3.5		
1958	P	Indiana Harbor-Gibson	0-3.7	+3.7	7.2		1

OWNERSHIP

1907	Indiana Harbor Belt RR

GIBSON-DUNE PARK (IHB-G)

	Mileage	County	Crossings, junctions, etc.
Gibson	0	Lake	J/IHB-A 3.7
Ivanhoe	2.1	"	X/EJE-G 5.6
Tolleston	5.2	"	X/PRR-F 441.8
(Bridge)	7.4	"	B/WAB-MC 239.2
(Bridge)	7.8	"	B/CSS-A 57.6
(Bridge)	8.0	"	B/B&O-C
(Bridge)	8.2	"	B/LS-W 494.5
Alco	8.2	"	
G&W Jct.	8.6	"	
Millers	10.8	"	
Dune Acres	15.2	Porter	
Dune Park	16.2	"	J/LS-W 486.7

CONSTRUCTION/ABANDONMENT

Date	Act	End points	MP	Change	Main	Source	Note
1910 ca.	B	Gibson-Dune Park	0-16.2	+16.2	16.2		2
1958	X	Gibson-Ivanhoe	0-2.1	-2.1			
1958	P	Gibson-Ivanhoe	0-2.1	+2.1	16.2		

OWNERSHIP

1910	Indiana Harbor Belt RR

GRASSELLI-CUDAHY (IHB-AC)

	Mileage	County	Crossings, junctions, etc.
Grasselli	0	Lake	J/IHB-A 2.5
Cudahy	1.6	"	

CONSTRUCTION/ABANDONMENT

Date	Act	End points	MP	Change	Main	Source	Note
1907 ca.	B	Grasselli-Cudahy	0-1.6	+1.6	1.6		

OWNERSHIP

1907	Indiana Harbor Belt RR

INDIANA HARBOR BELT

GIBSON-OSBORN LINE (IHB-AS)

	Mileage	County	Crossings, junctions, etc.
Gibson	0	Lake	J/IHB-A 3.7
Osborn	0.9	"	J/LS-WD 4.9, J/NKP-C 500.3

CONSTRUCTION/ABANDONMENT

Date	Act	End points	MP	Change	Main	Source	Note
1907 ca.	T	Gibson-Osborn	0-0.9	-			1
1958	P	Gibson-Osborn	0-0.9	+0.9	0.9		

OWNERSHIP

1958	Indiana Harbor Belt RR

GRASSELLI-STATE LINE (IHB-AW)

	Mileage	County	Crossings, junctions, etc.
Grasselli	0	Lake	J/IHB-A 2.5
(Crossing)	0.1	"	X/EJE-GS 2.2
(Bridge)	1.6	"	B/CSS-A 67.2
(IN/IL state line)	3.5		
State Line IL	3.6		J/IHB-W 0

CONSTRUCTION/ABANDONMENT

Date	Act	End points	MP	Change	Main	Source	Note
1896	B2	Graselli-IL state line	0-3.5	+3.5	3.5	2	

OWNERSHIP

1896	East Chicago Belt RR
1898	Chicago Junction, control of East Chicago Belt
1907	Indiana Harbor Belt RR, buy East Chicago Belt

STATE LINE-WHITING (IHB-W)

	Mileage	County	Crossings, junctions, etc.
State Line IL	0	Cook IL	J/IHB-AW 3.6
IL/IN state line	1.0		
(Crossing)	1.2	Lake	X/PRR-spur
(Junction)	1.3	"	J/IHB-WR 0
Whiting	4.1	"	J/BOCT-W 3.4

CONSTRUCTION/ABANDONMENT

Date	Act	End points	MP	Change	Main	Source	Note
1896	B1	Whiting-IL state line	4.1-1.0	+3.1	3.1	2	

OWNERSHIP

1896	Hammond & Blue Island RR
1897	Chicago, Hammond & Western RR, buy Hammond & Blue Island
1898	Chicago Junction, control of Chicago, Hammond & Western
1907	Indiana Harbor Belt RR, buy Chicago, Hammond & Western

ROBY BRANCH (IHB-WR)

	Mileage	County	Crossings, junctions, etc.
(Junction)	0	Lake	J/IHB-W 1.3
(IN/IL state line)	0.0		
(IL/IN state line)	2.5		
(Bridge)	3.9	"	B/PRR-F 452.6
(Junction)	4.0	"	J/LS-W 506.6

CONSTRUCTION/ABANDONMENT

Date	Act	End points	MP	Change	Main	Source	Note
1907 ca.	B1	IL state line-Roby	2.5-4.0	+1.5	1.5		

OWNERSHIP

1907	Indiana Harbor Belt RR

INDIANA HARBOR BELT

ACQUISITION/DISPOSITION RECORD

Date	Act	IHB-	End points	Change	Main	Note
1896	B1	W	Whiting-IL state line	+3.1		
	B2	AW	Grasselli-IL state line	+3.5	6.6	
1907 ca.	T	A	Indiana Harbor-Gibson	-		1
ca.	B	A	Gibson-IL state line	+3.5		
ca.	T	AS	Gibson-Osborn	-		1
ca.	B	AC	Grasselli-Cudahy	+1.6		
ca.	B1	WR	IL state line-Roby	+1.5	13.2	
1910 ca.	B	G	Gibson-Dune Park	+16.2	29.4	2
1958	P	A	Indiana Harbor-Gibson	+3.7		
	X	G	Gibson-Ivanhoe	-2.1		
	P	G	Gibson-Ivanhoe	+2.1		
	P	AS	Gibson-Osborn	+0.9	34.0	

ACT COLUMN KEY

B1 Built by Hammond & Blue Island RR
B2 Built by East Chicago Belt RR
B3 Built by Indiana Harbor Belt RR
P   Purchased from New York Central
T   Trackage rights obtained on New York Central/LS&MS/MC
X   Abandoned

SOURCES

1. Indiana, *1995 Indiana State Rail Plan.*
2. Simons and Parker, *Railroads of Indiana.*

NOTES

1. The original use of this segment was by trackage rights granted by the New York Central or one of its subsidiaries, and this segment is not included in the Mileage table until its subsequent acquisition by Indiana Harbor Belt.
2. This line was apparently built by the Lake Shore & Michigan Southern and the Gary & Western. It appears to have been used only by the Indiana Harbor Belt and therefore included in the Mileage table.

INDIANA HI-RAIL

CONNERSVILLE-BEESON (IHRC-[CCC-GW])
See Cleveland, Cincinnati, Chicago & St. Louis line CCC-GW for arrangement of stations, prior construction/abandonment record, and prior ownership

CONSTRUCTION/ABANDONMENT

Date	Act	End points	MP	Change	Main	Source	Note
1981/12	P1	Connersville-Beeson	68.0-74.1	+6.1	6.1	1	
1990/2	S1	In Connersville	68.0-69.1	-1.1	5.0		
1998	L11	Connersville-Beeson	69.1-74.1	<5.0>	0		

OWNERSHIP
1981   Indiana Hi-Rail Corp.

NEW CASTLE-CONNERSVILLE (IHRC-[NKP-LF)
See New York, Chicago & St. Louis line NKP-LF for arrangement of stations, prior construction/abandonment record, and prior ownership

CONSTRUCTION/ABANDONMENT

Date	Act	End points	MP	Change	Main	Source	Note
1989	L4	New Castle-Beesons	84.0-103.7	+19.7	19.7	1	
1998	XL	New Castle-Beesons	84.0-103.7	-19.7	0		1

OWNERSHIP
1989   Indiana Hi-Rail Corp.

INDIANA HI-RAIL

NEW CASTLE-RUSHVILLE (IHRC-[NKP-LR])
See New York, Chicago & St. Louis line NKP-LR for arrangement of stations, prior construction/abandonment record, and prior ownership

CONSTRUCTION/ABANDONMENT

Date	Act	End points	MP	Change	Main	Source	Note
1984 ca.	P2	New Castle-Rushville	84.0-107.9	+23.9	23.9	1	
1989	X	Mew Castle-Mays	84.0-96.2	-12.2	11.7		
1990	X	Mays-Sexton	96.2-101.2	-4.8	6.9		
1993/10	T	Sexton-Rushville	101.0-107.9	-6.9	0		

OWNERSHIP

1984		Indiana Hi-Rail Corp.

SHERIDAN-INDIANAPOLIS (IHRC-[MON-I])
See Monon line MON-I for arrangement of stations, prior construction/abandonment record, and prior ownership

CONSTRUCTION/ABANDONMENT

Date	Act	End points	MP	Change	Main	Source	Note
1985	L3	Sheridan-Indianapolis	155.4-181.7	+26.3	26.3	1	
1986 ca.	XL	Sheridan-Indianapolis	155.4-181.7	-26.3	0		

OWNERSHIP

1985		Indiana Hi-Rail Corp.

EVANSVILLE-NEWTON IL (IHRC-[IC-NM])
See Illinois Central line IC-NM for arrangement of stations, prior construction/-abandonment record, and prior ownership

CONSTRUCTION/ABANDONMENT

Date	Act	End points	MP	Change	Main	Source	Note
1986 ca.	P3	Newton IL-Evansville	216.7-246.2	+29.5	29.5	1	
1996/7	S2	Newton IL-Evansville	216.7-246.2	-29.5	0	1	

OWNERSHIP

1986		Indiana Hi-Rail Corp.

HUNTINGBURG-DUBOIS (IHRC-[SOU-UF])
See Southern Ry line SOU-UF for arrangement of stations, prior construction/-abandonment record, and prior ownership

CONSTRUCTION/ABANDONMENT

Date	Act	End points	MP	Change	Main	Source	Note
1989	L2	Huntingburg-Dubois	47.7-63.7	+16.0	16.0	1	
1993	LA1	Huntingburg-Dubois	47.7-63.7	-16.0	0	1	

OWNERSHIP

1989		Indiana Hi-Rail Corp.

LINCOLN CITY-CANNELTON (IHRC-[SOU-UC])
See Southern Ry line SOU-UC for arrangement of stations, prior construction/-abandonment record, and prior ownership

CONSTRUCTION/ABANDONMENT

Date	Act	End points	MP	Change	Main	Source	Note
1989	L2	Lincoln City-Cannelton	0-22.7	+22.7	22.7	1	
1994	XL	Lincoln City-Cannelton	0-22.7	-22.7	0		

OWNERSHIP

1989		Indiana Hi-Rail Corp.

INDIANA HI-RAIL

ROCKPORT JCT.-ROCKPORT (IHRC-[SOU-UR])
See Southern Ry line SOU-UR for arrangement of stations, prior construction/-abandonment record, and prior ownership

CONSTRUCTION/ABANDONMENT

Date	Act	End points	MP	Change	Main	Source	Note
1989	L2	Rockport Jct.-Rockport	1.0-16.8	+15.8	15.8	1	
1994	LA1	Rockport Jct.-Rockport	1.0-16.8	-15.8	0	1	

OWNERSHIP
| 1989 | | Indiana Hi-Rail Corp. |

LIBERTY CENTER OH-WOODBURN (IHRC-[WAB-MM])
See Wabash line WAB-MM for arrangement of stations, prior construction/abandonment record, and prior ownership

CONSTRUCTION/ABANDONMENT

Date	Act	End points	MP	Change	Main	Source	Note
1989	L2	Liberty Center OH-Woodburn	75.7-78.7	+3.0	3.0	1	
1998	XL	Liberty Center OH-Woodburn	75.7-78.7	-3.0	0		1

OWNERSHIP
| 1989 | | Indiana Hi-Rail Corp. |

DOUGLAS OH-MARION (IHRC-[NKP-TB])
See New York, Chicago & St. Louis line NKP-TB for arrangement of stations, prior construction/abandonment record, and prior ownership

CONSTRUCTION/ABANDONMENT

Date	Act	End points	MP	Change	Main	Source	Note
1989	L2	Douglas OH-Marion	99.9-153.8	+53.9	53.9	1	
1997	X	OH state line-Craigville	99.9-117.8	-17.9	36.0		
1998	XL	Craigville-Van Buren	117.8-144.2	-26.4			2
1998	XL	Van Buren-Marion	144.2-153.8	-9.6	0		

OWNERSHIP
| 1989 | | Indiana Hi-Rail Corp. |

PERU-ARGOS (IHRC-[NKP-LM])
See New York, Chicago & St. Louis line NKP-LM for arrangement of stations, prior construction/abandonment record, and prior ownership

CONSTRUCTION/ABANDONMENT

Date	Act	End points	MP	Change	Main	Source	Note
1989	LS2	Peru-Argos	74.2-108.6	+34.4	34.4	1	
1996 ca.	XL	Peru-Argos	74.2-108.6	-34.4	0		

OWNERSHIP
| 1989 | | Indiana Hi-Rail Corp. |

POSEYVILLE & OWENSVILLE LINE
Indiana Hi-Rail operated the Poseyville-Owensville line for its owners from 1987 to 1996. This mileage is reported under Poseyville & Owensville.

INDIANA HI-RAIL

ACQUISITION/DISPOSITION RECORD

Date	Act	IHRC--	End points	Change	Main	Note
1981/12	P1	[CCC-GW]	Connersville-Beeson	+6.1	6.1	
1984 ca.	P2	[NKP-LR]	New Castle-Rushville	+23.9	30.0	
1985	L3	[MON-I]	Sheridan-Indianapolis	+26.3	56.3	
1986 ca.	XL	[MON-I]	Sheridan-Indianapolis	-26.3		
	P3	[IC-NM]	IL state line-Evansville	+29.5	59.5	
1990/2	XL	[CCC-GW]	In Connersville	-1.1		
	X	[NKP-LR]	Mays-Sexton	-4.8	206.9	
1993/10	T	[NKP-LR]	Sexton-Rushville	-6.9		
	LA1	[SOU-UF]	Huntingburg-Dubois	-16.0	184.0	
1994	XL	[SOU-UC]	Lincoln City-Cannelton	-22.7		
	LA1	[SOU-UR]	Rockport Jct.-Rockport	-15.8	145.5	
1996/7	S2	[IC-NM]	IL state line-Evansville	[29.5]		
ca.	XL	[NKP-LM]	Peru-Argos	-34.4	81.6	
1997	X	[NKP-TB]	OH state line-Craigville	-17.9	63.7	
1998	L11	[CCC-GW]	Connersville-Beesons	<5.0>		
	XL	[NKP-LF]	New Castle-Beesons	-19.7		3
	XL	[NKP-TB]	Craigville-Van Buren	-26.4		2
	XL	[NKP-TB]	Van Buren-Marion	-9.6		
	XL	[WAB-MM]	Liberty Center OH-Woodburn	-3.0	0	1

ACT COLUMN KEY
L2   Leased from Southern Ry
L3   Leased from Seaboard System
L4   Leased from Norfolk Southern
L11 Leased to C&NC RR
LA1 Lease assigned from Indiana Hi-Rail to Hoosier Southern
LS2 Subleased from Central RR of Indianapolis
P1   Purchased from Conrail
P2   Purchased from Norfolk Southern
P3   Purchased form Illinois Central
S1   Sold to Whitewater Valley
S2   Sold to Evansville Terminal
T   Transferred to Honey Creek
X   Abandoned
XL   Lease terminated

SOURCES
1. Simons and Parker, *Railroads of Indiana.*

NOTES
1. Maumee & Western became the operator of this line.
2. Wabash Central became the operator of this line.
3. C&NCRR became the operator of this line.

INDIANA INTERSTATE

AT BICKNELL (INTS-[PRR-IV])
See Pennsylvania line PRR-IV for arrangement of stations, prior construction/abandonment record, and prior ownership

CONSTRUCTION/ABANDONMENT

Date	Act	End points	MP	Change	Main	Source	Note
1978	L	At Bicknell	??	+1.0	1.0	1	
1980	XL	At Bicknell	??	-1.0	0	1	

OWNERSHIP
1978   Indiana Interstate Ry

INDIANA INTERSTATE

AT BICKNELL (INTS-[PRR-IV])
See Pennsylvania line PRR-IV for arrangement of stations, prior construction/abandonment record, and prior ownership

CONSTRUCTION/ABANDONMENT

Date	Act	End points	MP	Change	Main	Source	Note
1978	L	At Bicknell	??	+1.0	1.0	1	
1980	XL	At Bicknell	??	-1.0	0	1	

OWNERSHIP

1978		Indiana Interstate Ry

GOSHEN-SHIPSHEWANA (INTS-[LS-TS])
See Lake Shore & Michigan Southern line LS-TS for arrangement of stations, prior construction/abandonment record, and prior ownership

CONSTRUCTION/ABANDONMENT

Date	Act	End points	MP	Change	Main	Source	Note
1979	L	Goshen-Shipshewana	0.7-16.9	+16.2	16.2	1	
1980/12	XL	Goshen-Shipshewana	0.7-16.9	-16.2	0	1	

OWNERSHIP

1979		Indiana Interstate Ry

ACQUISITION/DISPOSITION RECORD

Date	Act	INTS--	End points	Change	Main	Note
1978	L	[PRR-IV]	At Bicknell	+1.0	1.0	
1979	L	[LS-TS]	Goshen-Shipshewana	+16.2	17.2	
1980	XL	[PRR-IV]	At Bicknell	-1.0		
1980/12	XL	[LS-TS]	Goshen-Shipshewana	-16.2	0	

ACT COLUMN KEY
L   Leased from Conrail
X   Abandoned

SOURCES
1. Simons and Parker, *Railroads of Indiana.*

INDIANA MIDLAND

MAIN LINE (IMID-[CCC-M])
See Cleveland, Cincinnati, Chicago & St. Louis line CCC-M for arrangement of stations, prior construction/abandonment record, and prior ownership and also and Indiana Eastern

CONSTRUCTION/ABANDONMENT

Date	Act	End points	MP	Change	Main	Source	Note
1985/1/8	L	Carthage-Emporia	194.0-172.7	+21.3	21.3	R	
1987/4	LT	Carthage-Emporia	194.0-172.7	-21.3		R	
1987/4	X	At Carthage	194.0-193.2	<-0.8>	0		

OWNERSHIP

1985		Indiana Midland Ry

SHIRLEY-WILKINSON (IMID-[CCC-S])
See Cleveland, Cincinnati, Chicago & St. Louis line CCC-S for arrangement of stations, prior construction/abandonment record, and prior ownership and also and Indiana Eastern

CONSTRUCTION/ABANDONMENT

Date	Act	End points	MP	Change	Main	Source	Note
1985	L	Shirley-Wilkinson	107.3-109.0	+1.7	1.7	R	
1987/4	X	Shirley-Wilkinson	107.3-109.0	-1.7	0	R	

OWNERSHIP

1985		Indiana Midland Ry

INDIANA MIDLAND

ACQUISITION/DISPOSITION RECORD

Date	Act	IMID--	End points	Change	Main	Note
1985/1/8	L	[CCC-M]	Carthage-Emporia	+21.3		
1985	L	[CCC-S]	Shirley-Wilkinson	+1.7	23.0	
1987/4	LT	[CCC-M]	Carthage-Emporia	-21.3		
1987/4	X	[CCC-S]	Shirley-Wilkinson	-1.7	0	

ACT COLUMN KEY
L   Lease from Conrail assigned by Indiana Eastern
LT Lease from Conrail assigned to Carthage, Knightstown & Shirley
X   Abandoned

SOURCES
1. Simons and Parker, *Railroads of Indiana.*

INDIANA NORTHEASTERN

MONTPELIER-SOUTH MILFORD (INNE-[WAB-MC])
See Wabash line WAB-MC for arrangement of stations, prior construction/abandonment record, and prior ownership

CONSTRUCTION/ABANDONMENT

Date	Act	End points	MP	Change	Main	Source	Note
1992/12	L	Ashley-Hudson - S. Milford	121.4-131.8	+10.4	10.4	1	1
1993	L	Montpelier - Ashley-Hudson	107.2-121.4	+14.2	24.6	1	

OWNERSHIP
1992   Indiana Northeastern RR

HILLSDALE MI-STEUBENVILLE (INNE-[LS-TF])
See Lake Shore & Michigan Southern line LS-TF for arrangement of stations, prior construction/abandonment record, and prior ownership

CONSTRUCTION/ABANDONMENT

Date	Act	End points	MP	Change	Main	Source	Note
1992/12	P	MI state line-Steubenville	44.7-63.5	+18.8	18.8	1	2

OWNERSHIP
1992   Indiana Northeastern RR

ACQUISITION/DISPOSITION RECORD

Date	Act	INNE-	End points	Change	Main	Note
1992/12	L	[WAB-MC]	Ashley-Hudson - S. Milford	+10.4		1
1992/12	P	[LS-TF]	MI state line-Steubenville	+18.8	29.2	2
1993	L	[WAB-MC]	Montpelier - Ashley-Hudson	+14.2	43.4	

ACT COLUMN KEY
L   Leased from Norfolk Southern
P   Purchased Hillsdale County

SOURCES
1. Simons and Parker, *Railroads of Indiana.*

NOTES
1. This was an assignment of lease by Pigeon River RR
2. It appears that the Hillsdale County purchased the MI state line-Steubenville segment at about the time of its transfer to Indiana Northeastern. Its Michigan lines were operated under Designated Operator contract with the State of Michigan. The Michigan lines were owned by Penn Central until 1984 when the State of Michigan purchased them.

INDIANA NORTHERN

MAIN LINE (INOR-A)
This was an industrial road in South Bend, and is not included in the Mileage table.

CONSTRUCTION/ABANDONMENT

Date	Act	End points	MP	Change	Main	Source	Note
1893	B	In South Bend		(+2.0)	0	1	1

OWNERSHIP
1893   Indiana Northern Ry.

ACT COLUMN KEY
B Built by Indiana Northern Ry

SOURCES
1. Simons and Parker, *Railroads of Indiana.*

NOTES
1. This company was conveyed at an uncertain date to New Jersey, Indiana & Illinois.

INDIANA RAILROAD

MAIN LINE (INRD-[IC-NI])
See Illinois Central line IC-NI for arrangement of stations, prior construction/abandonment record, and prior ownership

CONSTRUCTION/ABANDONMENT

Date	Act	End points	MP	Change	Main	Source	Note
1986/3/18	P	Indianapolis-Switz Cit	0.4-89.4	+89.0	89.0	1	

OWNERSHIP
1986   Indiana RR, owned by Indianapolis Terminal Corp.
1995   CSX Transportation, control of Indiana RR, operated as separate entity

MAIN LINE (INRD-[IC-NE])
See Illinois Central line IC-NE for arrangement of stations, prior construction/abandonment record, and prior ownership

CONSTRUCTION/ABANDONMENT

Date	Act	End points	MP	Change	Main	Source	Note
1986/3/18	P	Switz City-Sullivan	89.4-110.0	+20.6	20.6	1	
1989 ca.	P	Sullivan-Newton IL	110.0-120.4	+10.4	31.0	1	

OWNERSHIP
1986   Indiana RR, owned by Indianapolis Terminal Corp.
     1995   CSX Transportation, control of Indiana RR, operated as separate entity

INDIANAPOLIS-TIPTON (INRD-[NKP-LM])
See New York, Chicago & St. Louis line NKP-LM for arrangement of stations, prior construction/abandonment record, and prior ownership

CONSTRUCTION/ABANDONMENT

Date	Act	End points	MP	Change	Main	Source	Note
1990	L	Indianapolis-Tipton	2.1-39.7	+37.6	37.6	1	
1996 ca.	XL	Indianapolis-Tipton	2.1-39.7	-37.6	0		

OWNERSHIP
1990   Indiana RR, owned by Indianapolis Terminal Corp.

INDIANA RAILROAD

ACQUISITION/DISPOSITION RECORD

Date	Act	INRD-	End points	Change	Main	Note
1986/3/18	P	[IC-NI]	Indianapolis-Switz City	+89.0		
1986/3/18	P	[IC-NE]	Switz City-Sullivan	+20.6	109.6	
1989 ca.	P	[IC-NE]	Sullivan-Newton IL	+10.4	120.0	
1990	L	[NKP-LM}	Indianapolis-Tipton	+37.6	157.6	
1996 ca.	XL	[NKP-LM]	Indianapolis-Tipton	-37.6	120.0	

ACT COLUMN KEY
L Leased from Norfolk Southern
P Purchased from Illinois Central Gulf
XL Lease terminated

SOURCES
1. Simons and Parker, *Railroads of Indiana.*

INDIANA SOUTHERN

MAIN LINE (ISRR-[PRR-IV])
See Pennsylvania line PRR-IV for arrangement of stations, prior construction/abandonment record, and prior ownership

CONSTRUCTION/ABANDONMENT

Date	Act	End points	MP	Change	Main	Source	Note
1992/4/11	P	Kraft-Sandborn	3.0-92.4	+89.4	89.4	1	

OWNERSHIP
1992   Indiana Southern RR, owned by RailTex

MAIN LINE (ISRR-[CCC-T])
See Cleveland, Cincinnati, Chicago & St. Louis line CCC-T for arrangement of stations, prior construction/abandonment record, and prior ownership

CONSTRUCTION/ABANDONMENT

Date	Act	End points	MP	Change	Main	Source	Note
1992/4/11	P	Rincon Jct.-Str. Line Jct.	41.2-130.9	+89.7	89.7	1	
1994	X	Rincon Jct.-Elnora	41.2-59.4	-18.2	71.5	1	1

OWNERSHIP
1992   Indiana Southern RR, owned by RailTex

AW&W CONNECTING LINE (ISRR-[CCC-TC])
See Cleveland, Cincinnati, Chicago & St. Louis line CCC-TC for arrangement of stations, prior construction/abandonment record, and prior ownership

CONSTRUCTION/ABANDONMENT

Date	Act	End points	MP	Change	Main	Source	Note
1992/4/11	P	Gray Jct.-Oakland City Jc.	0-2.8	+2.8	2.8	1	

OWNERSHIP
1992   Indiana Southern RR, owned by RailTex

LYNNVILLE MINE BRANCH (ISRR-[CCC-TK])
See Cleveland, Cincinnati, Chicago & St. Louis line CCC-TK for arrangement of stations, prior construction/abandonment record, and prior ownership

CONSTRUCTION/ABANDONMENT

Date	Act	End points	MP	Change	Main	Source	Note
1992/4/11	P	Tecumseh Jct.-Lynnville Mine	0-7.8	+7.8	7.8	1	

OWNERSHIP
1992   Indiana Southern RR, owned by RailTex

INDIANA SOUTHERN

ACQUISITION/DISPOSITION RECORD

Date	Act	ISRR-	-End points	Change	Main	Note
1992/4/11	P	[PRR-IV]	Kraft-Sandborn	+89.4		
/4/11	P	[CCC-T}	Rincon Jct.-Straight Line Jct.	+89.7		
/4/11	P	[CCC-TC]	Gray Jct.-Oakland City Jct.	+2.8		
/4/11	P	[CCC-TK]	Tecumseh Jct.-Lynnville Mine	+7.8	189.7	
1994	X	[CCC-T]	Rincon Jct.-Elnora	-18.2	171.5	1

ACT COLUMN KEY
P Purchased from Conrail
X Abandoned

SOURCES
1. Simons and Parker, *Railroads of Indiana.*

NOTES
1. Rights over Soo Line line MILW-T between Beehunter and Elnora were substituted for the abandoned segment.

INDIANAPOLIS UNION

MAIN LINE EAST (IU-E)

	Mileage	County	Crossings, junctions, etc.
Indianapolis	0	Marion	J/IU-S 0, J/IU-W 0
(Junction)	0.3	"	J/IU-EA 0.3
Washington Street	0.7	"	J/CCC-I 283.1
(Junction)	0.9	"	J/B&O-IH 123.6, J/PRR-I 186.8

CONSTRUCTION/ABANDONMENT

Date	Act	End points	MP	Change	Main	Source	Note
1851	B2	Indianapolis-Washington St.	0-0.7	+0.7	0.7		1
1853	B4	Washington St.-MP 0.9	0.7-0.9	+0.2	0.9		

OWNERSHIP
1851   Indianapolis & Bellefontaine RR (B2)
1853   Indianapolis Union RR (B4), buy line from Indianapolis. & Bellefontaine
1976/4/1   Conrail, buy Indianapolis Union

MAIN LINE EAST (IU-EA)

	Mileage	County	Crossings, junctions, etc.
(Junction)	0.3	Marion	J/IU-E 0.3
College Avenue	0.7	"	J/CCC-G 108.9

CONSTRUCTION/ABANDONMENT

Date	Act	End points	MP	Change	Main	Source	Note
1865	B4	Line	0.3-0.7	+0.4	0.4	1	

OWNERSHIP
1865   Indianapolis Union RR (B1)
1976/4/1   Conrail, buy Indianapolis Union

MAIN LINE SOUTH (IU-S)

	Mileage	County	Crossings, junctions, etc.
Indianapolis	0	Marion	J/IU-E 0, J/IU-W 0
(Junction)	0.5	"	J/PRR-IL 0.5

CONSTRUCTION/ABANDONMENT

Date	Act	End points	MP	Change	Main	Source	Note
1853	B4	Line	0-0.5	+0.5	0.5		1

OWNERSHIP
1853   Indianapolis Union RR (B4)
1976/4/1   Conrail, buy Indianapolis Union

INDIANAPOLIS UNION

MAIN LINE WEST (IU-W)

	Mileage	County	Crossings, junctions, etc.
Indianapolis	0	Marion	J/IU-E 0, J/IU-S 0
(Junction)	0.2	"	J/CCC-HO 109.8, J/IC-NI 0.2
Kentucky Avenue	0.3	"	J/PRR-IVO 0
West Street	0.4	"	J/CCC-L 0.4, J/PRR-V 0.4
IJ	1.0	"	J/B&O-IS 125.5, J/P&E-A 1.0

CONSTRUCTION/ABANDONMENT

Date	Act	End points	MP	Change	Main	Source	Note
1852	B3	Indianapolis-West St.	0-0.4	+0.4	0.4		1
1869	B4	West St.-IJ	0.4-1.0	+0.6	1.0		

OWNERSHIP

1852	Terre Haute & Richmond RR (B3)
1853	Indianapolis Union RR (B4), buy line from Terre Haute & Richmond
1976/4/1	Conrail, buy Indianapolis Union

BELT LINE (IU-B)

	Mileage	County	Crossings, junctions, etc.
(Junction)	0	Marion	J/CCC-I 279.1 (Belt Jct. on CCC-I)
(Crossing)	0.5	"	X/CCC-S 135.8, J/IU-C 0
(Crossing)	2.6	"	X/PRR-I 184.8
(Crossing)	2.6	"	X/B&O-IH 121.6
(Junction)	3.0	"	J/PRR-IK 5.0
(Crossing)	3.8	"	X/CCC-G 106.9 (Belt Crossing on CCC-G)
(Crossing)	6.1	"	X/PRR-IL 1.7(Dale on PRR-IL)
(Bridge)	6.7	"	B/IC-NI 1.7
(Crossing)	7.9	"	X/PRR-IVO 1.3
(Crossing)	8.9	"	X/PRR-V 1.6(Woods on PRR-V)
BX	9.1	"	X/CCC-L 1.6
KD	9.4	"	X/B&O-IS 126.3, X/P&E-A 1.8
(Junction)	11.8	"	J/CCC-HO 113.2

CONSTRUCTION/ABANDONMENT

Date	Act	End points	MP	Change	Main	Source	Note
1876	B4	Line	0-11.8	+11.8	11.8	R	

OWNERSHIP

1876	Indianapolis Union RR (B1)
1976/4/1	Conrail, buy Indianapolis Union

BELT LINE (IU-C)

	Mileage	County	Crossings, junctions, etc.
(Junction)	0	Marion	J/IU-B 0.5, J/CCC-S 135.8 (aka Eastside)
--via CCC-S			
DX	0.5	"	X/CCC-I 280.1
(Belt Jct.)	2.0	"	J/MON-I 180.4, J/NKP-LM 3.2

CONSTRUCTION/ABANDONMENT

Date	Act	End points	MP	Change	Main	Source	Note
1882 ca.	B4	Line	0.5-2.0	+1.5	1.5		

OWNERSHIP

1882	Indianapolis Union RR (B4)
1976/4/1	Conrail, buy Indianapolis Union

INDIANAPOLIS UNION

ACQUISITION/DISPOSITION RECORD

Date	Act	IU--	End points	Change	Main	Note
1851	B2	E	Indianapolis-Wash. St.	+0.7	0.7	1
1852	B3	W	Indianapolis-West St.	+0.4	1.1	1
1853	B4	S	Line	+0.5		
	B4	E	Washington St.-MP 0.9	+0.2	1.8	
1865	B4	EA	Line	+0.4	2.2	
1869	B4	W	West St.-IJ	+0.6	2.8	
1876	B1	B	Line	+11.8	14.6	
1882 ca.	B4	C	Line	+1.5	16.1	

On April 1, 1976, Indianapolis Union was conveyed to Conrail. The IU Acquisition/-Disposition Record is continued in two places: under Indianapolis Union and under Conrail. The lines conveyed were:

Line desig.	End points	MP	Main	Note
[IU-E]	Indianapolis-E of Wash. St.	0-0.9	0.9	
[IU-EA]	to College Ave.	0.3-0.7	0.4	
[IU-S]	Indianapolis-south	0-0.5	0.5	
[IU-W]	Indianapolis-IJ	0-1.0	1.0	
[IU-B]	Belt Line	0-11.4	11.8	
[IU-C]	Belt Line	0.5-2.0	1.5	
		TOTAL	16.1	

ACQUISITION/DISPOSITION RECORD
On 1999/6/1 Conrail's former Indianapolis Union lines were conveyed to CSX Transportation. The IU Acquisition/-Disposition Record is continued in two places: under IU and under CSX Transportation.

ACT COLUMN KEY
B1 Built by Madison & Indianapolis
B2 Built by Indianapolis & Bellefontaine RR
B3 Built by Terre Haute & Richmond RR
B4 Built by Indianapolis Union RR

SOURCES
1. Simons and Parker, *Railroads of Indiana.*

NOTES
 General. This company also owned industrial spurs and branches which are not documented herein and are not included in the Acquisition/Disposition Record.
 1. This segment was built by an owner of the Indianapolis Union prior to the IU's formation and was conveyed to IU at its organization.

J. K. LINE

MAIN LINE (JKL-[ERIE-C])
See Erie line ERIE-C for arrangement of stations, prior construction/abandonment record, and prior ownership

CONSTRUCTION/ABANDONMENT

Date	Act	End points	MP	Change	Main	Source	Note
1990/4	P	Monterey-North Judson	183.7-199.7	+16.0	16.0	1	

OWNERSHIP
| 1990 | | J. K. Line RR |

ACQUISITION/DISPOSITION RECORD
See ownership record above for line JKL-A

ACT COLUMN KEY
P Purchased from Tippecanoe RR

SOURCES
1. Simons and Parker, *Railroads of Indiana.*

KANKAKEE, BEAVERVILLE & SOUTHERN

KANKAKEE-TEMPLETON (KBSR-[CCC-H])
See Cleveland, Cincinnati, Chicago & St. Louis line CCC-H for arrangement of stations, prior construction/abandonment record, and prior ownership

CONSTRUCTION/ABANDONMENT

Date	Act	End points	MP	Change	Main	Source	Note
1977/12/1	L1	Kankakee Jct IL-Sheldon IL			0	1	
1980	P1	Kankakee Jct IL-Sheldon IL			0	1	
1989	P2	Templeton-Swanington	192.6-198.6	+6.0	6.0	1	
1994	P4	Swanington-Sheldon	198.6-216.2	+17.6	23.6	1	

OWNERSHIP

1977		Kankakee, Beaverville & Southern RR

LAFAYETTE-CHENEYVILLE (KBSR-[NKP-LP])
See New York Chicago & St. Louis line NKP-LP for arrangement of stations, prior construction/abandonment record, and prior ownership

CONSTRUCTION/ABANDONMENT

Date	Act	End points	MP	Change	Main	Source	Note
1989	P3	Lafayette-Cheneyville IL	262.2-294.4	+32.2	32.2	1	

OWNERSHIP

1989		Kankakee, Beaverville & Southern RR

SHEFF-FREE (KBSR-[LS-WD])
See Lake Shore & Mich. Southern line LS-WD for arrangement of stations, prior construction/abandonment record, and prior ownership

SHEFF-FREE (KBSR-[LS-WD]) (continued)
CONSTRUCTION/ABANDONMENT

Date	Act	End points	MP	Change	Main	Source	Note
1996	P4	Sheff-Free	66.1-72.0	+5.9	5.9	1	

OWNERSHIP

1996		Kankakee, Beaverville & Southern RR

ACQUISITION/DISPOSITION RECORD

Date	Act	KBSR--	End points	Change	Main	Note
1989	P2	[CCC-H]	Templeton-Swanington	+6.0		
	P3	[NKP-LP]	Lafayette-Cheneyville IL	+32.2	39.2	
1994	P4	[CCC-H]	Swanington-Sheldon	+17.6	56.8	
1996	P4	[LS-WD]	Sheff-Free	+5.9	62.7	

ACT COLUMN KEY
L1   Leased from Penn Central
P1   Purchased from Penn Central
P2   Purchased from Benton Central
P3   Purchased from Norfolk Southern
P4   Purchased from Conrail

SOURCES
1. Simons and Parker, *Railroads of Indiana.*

KENTUCKY & INDIANA TERMINAL

MAIN LINE (KIT-A)

	Mileage	County	Crossings, junctions, etc.
VI	0	Floyd	J/B&O-SV 54.0; J/MON-SV 317.7
(Bridge apron)			
(IN/KY state line)	0.4		
DI KY	1.5		
Louisville KY	6.4		

CONSTRUCTION/ABANDONMENT

Date	Act	End points	MP	Change	Main	Source	Note
1886	B	VI-KY state line	0-0.4	+0.4	0.4	1	

OWNERSHIP

1886	Kentucky & Indiana Terminal RR
1900	Kentucky & Indiana Bridge & RR Co., rename K&IT
1910	Kentucky & Indiana Terminal RR, rename K&IB&R

ACQUISITION/DISPOSITION RECORD
See ownership record above for line KIT-A

ACT COLUMN KEY
B Built by Kentucky & Indiana Terminal

SOURCES
1. Simons and Parker, *Railroads of Indiana.*

NOTES
General. This company was owned one-third each by Baltimore & Ohio, Monon, and Southern. It also was used by trains of the Cleveland, Cincinnati, Chicago & St. Louis which used the B&O tracks.

KOKOMO BELT

MAIN LINE (KKBL-A)
This was an industrial road in Kokomo, and is not included in the Mileage table.

CONSTRUCTION/ABANDONMENT

Date	Act	End points	MP	Change	Main	Source	Note
1889	B	In Kokomo				1	
	S	In Kokomo				1	

OWNERSHIP

1889	Kokomo Belt RR
1890	Kokomo Belt, control by Chicago, St. Louis & Pittsburgh, controlled by Pennsylvania (see Pennsylvania line PRR-CR for successors)
1902/7/18	Kokomo Belt, one-half ownership bought by Lake Erie & Western from Chicago, St. Louis & Pittsburgh
n. d.	Kokomo Belt, all ownership bought by Norfolk Southern

ACQUISITION/DISPOSITION RECORD
See ownership record above for line KKBL-A

ACT COLUMN KEY
B Built by Kokomo Belt RR
S Sold to Central RR of Indianapolis

SOURCES
1. Simons and Parker, *Railroads of Indiana.*

KOKOMO RAIL

MARION-AMBOY (KOKO-[C&O-C])
See Chesapeake & Ohio line C&O-C for arrangement of stations, prior construction/abandonment record, and prior ownership

CONSTRUCTION/ABANDONMENT

Date	Act	End points	MP	Change	Main	Source	Note
1992	P	Marion-Amboy	134.2-146.8	+12.6	12.6	1	

OWNERSHIP
1992   Kokomo Rail Co.

ACQUISITION/DISPOSITION RECORD
See ownership record above for line KOKO-[C&O-C]

ACT COLUMN KEY
P Purchased from CSX Transportation

SOURCES
1. Simons and Parker, *Railroads of Indiana.*

NOTES
General. Source 1 states this company is affiliated with and operated by Central RR of Indianapolis.

LAKE SHORE & MICHIGAN SOUTHERN

See also Cleveland, Cincinnati, Chicago & St. Louis; Michigan Central; and Peoria & Eastern for other New York Central properties.

OLD ROAD (LS-A)

	Mileage [Buffalo]	County	Crossings, junctions, etc.
Toledo OH	296.43		
Hillsdale MI	362.11		
CP 10 MI	422.55		f. Vistula East MI
(MI/IN state line)	424.09		
CP 11	425.4	Elkhart	f. Vistula
(Crossing)	430.1	"	X/SJV-A 9.3
Bristol	430.49	"	
Morehous	434.64	"	
(Crossing)	438.3	"	X/CCC-M 45.3
(Junction)	438.33	"	J/LS-WE 0
B (now CP 421)	438.71	"	J/LS-T 421.5
Elkhart	438.86	"	
(continued)			

LAKE SHORE & MICHIGAN SOUTHERN

OLD ROAD (LS-A) (continued)
CONSTRUCTION/ABANDONMENT

Date	Act	End points	MP	Change	Main	Source	Note
1851/10/4	B1	White Pigeon MI-Elkhart	420.1-438.8	14.7	14.7	2	6

OWNERSHIP

1851	Northern Indiana RR (B1), of part
1855/4/25	Michigan Southern & Northern Indiana, merge Michigan Southern
1869/4/6	Lake Shore & Michigan Southern, merge MS&NI and other roads
1915/1/1	New York Central, merge Lake Shore & Mich. Southern
1968/2/1	Penn Central, merge New York Central
1976/4/1	Conrail, buy Penn Central line
1999/6/1	Norfolk Southern, buy Conrail line

TOLEDO DIVISION (LS-T)

	Mileage [Buffalo]	County	Crossings, junctions, etc.
Toledo OH	288.34		
CP 352 OH	352.6		
MN	353.51		
(OH/IN state line)	355.35		
CP 358	358.46	DeKalb	J/PRR-LE 93.7, X/WAB-M 114.3 f. WB
Butler	359.09	"	
Waterloo	367.01	"	
CP 367	367.05	"	J/LS-TF 70.38,f. WX
Corunna	373.35	"	
Kendallville	379.72	Noble	
CP 379	379.74	"	X/PRR-GS 120.2, f. UK
Brimfield	386.44	"	
Wawaka	390.88	"	
CP 395	395.4	"	
Ligonier	396.27	"	
CP 397	397.7	"	
Grismore	399.67	"	
(Bridge)	403.0	Elkhart	B/WAB-MC 154.1
Millersburg	403.32	"	
CX	411.12	"	X/CCC-M 55.5, J/LS-TS 0
Goshen	411.50	"	
CP 412	412.4	"	
CP 415	415.6	"	
Dunlap	416.1	"	
B	421.45	"	J/LS-A 438.7now CP 421
Elkhart	421.61	"	J/LS-W 421.6

CONSTRUCTION/ABANDONMENT

Date	Act	End points	MP	Change	Main	Source	Note
1852	B1	Goshen-B	411.5-421.5	+10.0	10.0	1	
1858	B3	Toledo OH-Goshen	355.4-411.5	+56.1	66.1	3	

OWNERSHIP

1852	Northern Indiana RR (B1), of part
1855/4/25	Michigan Southern & Northern Indiana RR (B3), merge Northern Indiana and Michigan Southern
1869/4/6	Lake Shore & Michigan Southern, merge MS&NI and other roads
1915/1/1	New York Central, merge Lake Shore & Mich. Southern
1968/2/1	Penn Central, merge New York Central
1976/4/1	Conrail, buy Penn Central line
1999/6/1	Norfolk Southern, buy Conrail line

LAKE SHORE & MICHIGAN SOUTHERN

ELKHART & WESTERN BRANCH (LS-WE)

	Mileage	County	Crossings, junctions, etc.
(Junction)	0	Elkhart	J/LS-A 438.33
Twin Branch	8.92	St. Joseph	
(Junction)	12.1	"	J/TWBR-A 0
Mishawaka	12.41	"	
(Junction)	12.85	"	J/GTW-C 104.1

CONSTRUCTION/ABANDONMENT

Date	Act	End points	MP	Change	Main	Source	Note
1893	B9	Line		0-12.9	+12.9	12.9	

1986	X	At Mishawaka		9.8-12.9	-3.1	9.8	1
1996/11	L4	Elkhart-Mishawaka	0-9.8	<9.8>	0	R	

OWNERSHIP

1893	Elkhart & Western RR (B9)
1898	Lake Shore & Michigan Southern, lease Elkhart & Western
1915/1/1	New York Central, bought Elkhart & Western
1968/2/1	Penn Central Co., merge New York Central
1976/4/1	Conrail, buy Penn Central line
1996/11	Michigan Southern, lease line

G & M BRANCH (LS-TS)

	Mileage	County	Crossings, junctions, etc.
CX	0	Elkhart	J/LS-T 411.1
Williams	4.18	"	
Burns	6.48	"	
Middlebury	9.26	"	
(Crossing)	9.9	"	X/SJV-A 16.4
Oak	12.73	LaGrange	
Pashan	14.25	"	
Shipshewana	16.43	"	
Seyberts	20.42	"	
Twin Lake	23.24	"	
(Line IN/MI)	25.60		
Sturgis	29.0		

CONSTRUCTION/ABANDONMENT

Date	Act	End points	MP	Change	Main	Source	Note
1888 ca.	B6	Sturgis MI-Goshen	0-29.0	+25.6	25.6	2	
1960	X	Sturgis MI-Shipshewana	16.9-27.4	-8.7	16.9	3	

1979	L2	Goshen-Shipshewana	0-16.9	<16.9>	0	3	
1980	XL	Goshen-Shipshewana	0-16.9	<+16.9>			
1980	X	Goshen-Shipshewana	0.7-16.9	-16.2		1	
1980	Y	In Goshen	0-0.7	(0.7)	0		
1984	X	In Goshen	0-0.7	(-0.7)	0	1	

OWNERSHIP

1888	Canada & St. Louis (B6)
1889/10/29	Sturgis, Goshen & St. Louis, reorganization of Canada & St. Louis
1889/12/1	Sturgis, Goshen & St. Louis, leased by Lake Shore & Mich. Southern
1890	Lake Shore & Michigan Southern, lease part of Battle Creek & Sturgis
1915/6/11	New York Central, merge Sturgis, Goshen & St. Louis and LS&MS
1968/2/1	Penn Central, merge New York Central
1976/4/1	Conrail, buy Penn Central
1979	Indiana Interstate Ry, leased line
1980	Lease by Indiana Interstate terminated

LAKE SHORE & MICHIGAN SOUTHERN

FORT WAYNE BRANCH (LS-TF)

	Mileage	County	Crossings, junctions, etc.
Jackson MI	0		
Montgomery MI	41.16		
(Line MI/IN)	44.68		
Ray	44.79	Steuben	
Fremont	48.86	"	
(Bridge)	55.5	"	B/SJV-A 58.7
Angola	56.21	"	
Pleasant Lake	60.46	"	
Steubenville	63.45	"	X/WAB-MC 117.8
Summit	64.67	DeKalb	
WX	70.38	"	X/LS-T 367.0
Waterloo	70.43	"	
Auburn	75.44	"	
Auburn Jct.	76.58	"	X/B&O-C 124.7, X/PRR-LE 81.3
St. Johns	80.11	"	
New Era	81.63	"	
Stoners	84.68	Allen	
Hunterville	86.39	"	
Carrolls Crossing	88.39	"	
Academie	90.74	"	
North Fort Wayne	94.81	"	
Fort Wayne	96.24	"	
(Crossing)	97.4	"	X/NKP-C 372.6
(Crossing)	97.7	"	X/PRR-GS 93.6
(Crossing)	97.9	"	X/PRR-F 321.2
(End)	97.99	"	J/NKP-LF 1.6

CONSTRUCTION/ABANDONMENT

Date	Act	End points	MP	Change	Main	Source	Note
1870/1/17	B4	Reading MI-Angola	35.8-56.2	+11.5	11.5	2	
1870/12/5	B4	Angola-Fort Wayne	56.2-100.0	+43.8	55.3	2	

1973/1	X	Steubenville-Waterloo	63.5-70.4	-6.9			
1973	Y	In Ft. Wayne	92.8-100.0	(7.2)			
1973	X	Auburn Jct.-Fort Wayne	76.7-92.8	-16.1	25.1		
1976	S2	Auburn-Auburn Jct.	75.0-76.7	[1.7]			1
1976	X	Waterloo-Auburn	71.2-75.0	-3.8			
1976	Y	In Waterloo	70.4-71.2	(0.8)	18.8		
1976/4	L3	MI line-Pleasant Lake	44.7-60.5	<15.8>	3.0		
1984	X	In Waterloo	70.4-71.2	(-0.8)	3.0		
1986	X	In Fort Wayne	92.8-95.2	(-2.4)			
1986	L3	Pleasant Lake-Steubenville	60.5-63.5	<3.0>	0		
1992	S3	MI line-Steubenville	44.7-63.5	[-18.8]	0		

OWNERSHIP

1869	Fort Wayne, Jackson & Saginaw (B4)
1879/12/31	Fort Wayne & Jackson, reorganization of Ft. Wayne, Jackson & Saginaw
1882/8/24	Leased to Lake Shore & Michigan Southern
1915/1/1	Lease assigned to New York Central
1968/2/1	Lease assigned to Penn Central
1976/4/1	Conrail, bought part of line of Penn Central

LAKE SHORE & MICHIGAN SOUTHERN

WESTERN DIVISION (LS-W)

	Mileage [Buffalo]	County	Crossings, junctions, etc.
Elkhart	421.61	Elkhart	J/LS-A 438.9, J/LS-T 421.6
Oakland Avenue	422.2	"	
CP 21st Street	422.5	"	
BC	424.3	"	
CP WG	426.43	St.Joseph	
Osceola	427.12	"	
Mishawaka	432.72	"	
High Street	435.84	"	J/GTW-C 101.09
South Bend	436.70	"	
HF	436.89	"	J/LS-WK 0.19
Arnold Street	437.29	"	J/GTW-C 99.52
NX	437.72	"	X/LS-N2 2.84
Lydick	443.67	"	
CK	444.20	"	X/MC-J 5.89
Terre Coupee	448.48	"	
New Carlisle	450.09	"	
Hudson Lake	451.77	LaPorte	
Rolling Prairie	456.39	"	
WR	462.39	"	X/NKP-LM 146.3
LaPorte	463.41	"	
JD	463.76	"	X/PM-W 23.12
East Pinola	466.6	"	
Pinola	467.49	"	
FS	469.82	"	
Durham	469.82	"	
HM	473.35	"	X/MON-M 51.1
Otis	473.36	"	
Burdick	476.81	Porter	
Chesterton	481.08	"	
Porter	481.99	"	
PO	482.18	"	X/MC-W 240.70, J/PM-C 136.6, J/EJE-A 56.71
(Bridge)	484.9	"	B/CSS-A 47.2
Baileytown	485.5	"	J/LS-WM 14
Burns Harbor	485.7	"	
FN	486.27	"	
Dune Park	486.73	"	J/IHB-G 15.8
Ogden Dunes	488.30	"	
Millers	491.0	Lake	
(Bridge)	494.5	"	B/IHB-G 7.6
Gary	496.03	"	
Curtis	498.26	"	
Pine	499.26	"	
NE	500.09	"	
Buffington	501.01	"	
BO	502.64	"	X/B&O-C 251.9, X/IHB
Indiana Harbor	502.82	"	J/LS-WD 0
HC	503.19	"	J/IHB-A
Mahoning	503.54	"	
Whiting	505.38	"	
MS	505.74	"	J/LS-WJ 0, X/BOCT-W 3.7
Robertsdale	506.64	"	J/IHB-WR 4.0
(IN/IL state line)	508.17		
East Side IL	508.98		
Chicago IL	522.17		
(continued)			

LAKE SHORE & MICHIGAN SOUTHERN

WESTERN DIVISION (LS-W) (continued)

CONSTRUCTION/ABANDONMENT

Date	Act	End points	MP	Change	Main	Source	Note
1851/10/4	B1	Elkhart-South Bend	421.6-436.7	+15.1	15.1	1	
1852	B1	South Bend-IL state line	436.7-508.2	+71.5	86.6	1	

1976	X	MS-IL state line	505.7-508.2	-2.5	84.1	1	

OWNERSHIP

1852	Northern Indiana RR (B1), of part
1855/4/25	Michigan Southern & Northern Indiana RR, merge Northern Indiana and Michigan Southern
1869/4/6	Lake Shore & Michigan Southern, merge MS&NI and other roads
1915/1/1	New York Central, merge Lake Shore & Mich. Southern
1968/2/1	Penn Central, merge New York Central
1976/4/1	Conrail, buy Penn Central line
1999/6/1	Norfolk Southern, buy Conrail line

LAKE BRANCH (LS-WJ)

	Mileage	County	Crossings, junctions, etc.
MS	0	Lake	J/LS-W 505.7
Lake Jct.	0.4	"	J/PRR-F 451.4

CONSTRUCTION/ABANDONMENT

Date	Act	End points	MP	Change	Main	Source	Note
1968	B9	Line	0-0.4	+0.4	0.4		

OWNERSHIP

1968	Penn Central (B9)
1976/4/1	Conrail, buy Penn Central line

M. C. CONNECTING BRANCH (LS-N2)

	Mileage	County	Crossings, junctions, etc.
(Prop line MC/II&I)	1.31	St.Joseph	J/MC-N2 1.3
(Bridge, Portage Ave.)	1.32	"	
(Crossing)	2.3	"	X/CSS-A 1.3
(Switch, NYC wye)	2.66	"	
NX	2.84	"	X/LS-W 437.7
Olivers	3.23	"	X/GTW-C 99.0, J/LS-WK 1.1

CONSTRUCTION/ABANDONMENT

Date	Act	End points	MP	Change	Main	Source	Note
1905 ca.	B7	MP 1.3-MP 3.2	1.3-3.2	+1.9	1.9		

OWNERSHIP

1905	Indiana, Illinois & Iowa Ry (B7) (controlled by Lake Shore & Mich. So.)
1906/4/6	Chicago, Indiana & Southern (controlled by Lake Shore & Mich. Southern), merged Indiana, Illinois & Iowa
1915/1/1	New York Central, merger of Chicago, Indiana & Southern
1968/2/1	Penn Central, merger of New York Central
1976/4/1	Conrail, purchase of Penn Central
1999/6/1	Norfolk Southern, purchase of Conrail

NOTE. For ownership record of Michigan Central part, see Mich. Cent. line MC-N2.

LAKE SHORE & MICHIGAN SOUTHERN

KANKAKEE BRANCH (LS-WK)

	Mileage [South Bend]	County	Crossings, junctions, etc.
HF	0.19	St. Joseph	J/LS-W 436.9
Olivers	1.06	"	J/LS-N2 3.23
JK	2.67	"	X/MC-J 0, X/NJI-A 1.7 aka SS&S Jct.
Rupel	5.38	"	
Steenberg	7.35	"	
Ginger Hill	9.45	"	
North Liberty	13.57	"	
QN	13.70	"	X/WAB-MC 192.9
KN	19.50	"	X/B&O-C 199.1, X/NKP-LM 130.7
Walkerton	19.64	"	
Garden City	22.64	Starke	
HA	27.50	"	X/PRR-F 397.9
Hamlet	27.64	"	
Knox	33.89	"	
X	33.93	"	X/NKP-C 451.5
Toto	38.41	"	
North Judson	43.33	"	X/C&O-C 214.8, X/ERIE-C 199.7, X/PRR-L 237.3
San Pierre	49.48	"	X/MON-M 23.3
Tefft	53.54	Jasper	
Wheatfield	58.06	"	X/CAS-A 13.3
Stoutsburg	61.14	"	
Kersey	63.45	"	X/MON-ND 22.0
DeMotte	65.62	"	
Forest City	69.18	"	
BY	73.10	Lake	X/MON-N 52.6
Shelby	73.43	"	
SG	78.50	"	X/LS-WD 32.86
Schneider	78.58	"	
(IN/IL state line)	82.16		
Illinoi IL	82.72		
Kankakee IL	101.42		
Zearing IL	200.38		

CONSTRUCTION/ABANDONMENT

Date	Act	End points	MP	Change	Main	Source	Note
1883	B5	IL state line-North Judson	82.2-43.3	+38.9	38.9	1	
1886/12	B5	North Judson-Knox	43.3-33.9	+9.4	48.3	3	
1894/11	B7	Knox-South Bend	33.9-0.2	+33.7	82.0	3	

1982	Y	HF-JK	0.2-3.0	(2.8)			
1982	X	JK-Wheatfield	3.0-58.0	-55.0	24.2	1	

OWNERSHIP

1883	Indiana, Illinois & Iowa RR (B5), of part
1893	Indiana, Illinois & Iowa Ry (B7), of part, acquired II&I RR
1898/9/15	Indiana, Illinois & Iowa RR, reorganize II&I Ry
1898/9/15	Lake Shore & Michigan Southern, control of II&I RR
1906/4/6	Chicago, Indiana & Southern RR, acquire II&I RR, controlled by LS&MS
1915/1/1	New York Central, merge II&I RR and LS&MS and other roads
1968/2/1	Penn Central, merge New York Central
1976/4/1	Conrail, buy Penn Central line
1999/6/1	Norfolk Southern, buy Conrail line

LAKE SHORE & MICHIGAN SOUTHERN

DANVILLE LINE (LS-WD)

	Mileage	County	Crossings, junctions, etc.
Indiana Harbor	0	Lake	J/LS-W 502.82
Michigan Avenue	1.62	"	
Calumet	2.10	"	X/BOCT-A 2.7
(Crossing)	2.7	"	X/CSS-AO 66.4
(Crossing)	2.8	"	X/EJE-GW 0.6
Grasselli	3.10	"	X/EJE-GS 2.1
(Bridge)	3.9	"	B/CSS-A 65.2
Gibson	4.23	"	X/MC-W 261.7, X/IHB-A 3.7
Osborn	4.93	"	J/IHB-AS 0.9
RN	5.05	"	X/NKP-C 500.3
ND	7.15	"	X/C&O-C 256.9, X/ERIE-c 243.3
Highlands	7.40	"	
Hays	9.18	"	X/GTW-C 34.0
Hartsdale	10.28	"	
(Bridge)	10.6	"	B/MC-WJ 12.8, B/EJE-A 34.1
(Bridge)	10.9	"	B/PRR-L 281.5
St. John Yard	12.41	"	
DK	14.64	"	X/MON-N 33.5
St. John	15.09	"	
Cook	19.77	"	
North Hayden	25.84	"	
Belshaw	28.16	"	
Cumberland Lodge	30.86	"	
Schneider	32.85	"	
SG	32.86	"	X/LS-WK 78.5
Lake Village	36.36	Newton	
Conrad	38.51	"	
Enos	44.84	"	
Morocco	49.56	"	X/CAS-B 12.4
Ade	54.98	"	
Kentland	61.69	"	
KN	61.87	"	X/PRR-LF 57.2
Sheff	66.07	Benton	
F	66.26	"	X/CCC-H 211.9
York Switch	66.10	"	
Hawkins Spur	70.01		
Free	72.00	"	
Dunn	75.82	"	
Handy	80.35	"	
DY	80.37	"	X/NKP-LP 291.5
Tab	86.28	Warren	
WA	90.08	"	X/CEI-CJ 116.0
Stewart	90.10	"	
Sloan	94.05	"	X/IC-SR 5.7
NX	94.57	"	
Allison	99.33	"	
(IN/IL state line)	100.75		
Campbell IL	104.06		
Danville IL	109.29		

CONSTRUCTION/ABANDONMENT

Date	Act	End points	MP	Change	Main	Source	Note
1903	B8	Indiana Harbor-Osborn	0-4.9	+4.9	4.9	1	
1906	B10	Osborn-IL state line	4.9-100.8	+95.9	100.8	1	
1958	S4	Indiana Harbor-Osborn	0-4.9	[4.9]	95.9		3

1994/10	S1	Handy-Stewart	80.4-91.2	[10.8]	85.1		3
(continued)							

LAKE SHORE & MICHIGAN SOUTHERN

DANVILLE LINE (LS-WD) (continued)
CONSTRUCTION/ABANDONMENT

1996	X	Schneider-Sheff	32.9-66.1	-33.2		1
1996	S5	Sheff-Free	66.1-72.0	[5.9]		3
1996	X	Free-Handy	72.0-80.4	-8.4		1
1996	X	Stewart-Danville	91.2-100.8	-9.6	28.0	1

OWNERSHIP

1903	Indiana Harbor RR (B8), of part
1905	Chicago, Indiana & Southern RR (B10), merged Indiana Harbor RR
1915/1/1	New York Central, merged CI&S and LS&MS and other roads
1968/2/1	Penn Central, merge New York Central
1976/4/1	Conrail, buy Penn Central line
1999/6/1	Norfolk Southern, buy Conrail line

MICHIGAN CITY-BAILEYTOWN LINE (LS-WM)

	Mileage	County	Crossings, junctions, etc.
Michigan City	0	LaPorte	
Baileytown	14	Porter	J/LS-W 485.5

CONSTRUCTION/ABANDONMENT

Date	Act	End points	MP	Change	Main	Source	Note
1851	B2	Michigan City-Baileytown	0-14	+14.0	14.0		
1856	X	Michigan City-Baileytown	0-14	-14.0	0		

OWNERSHIP

1851	Buffalo & Mississippi RR (B2), controlled by Northern Indiana

ACQUISITION/DISPOSITION RECORD

Date	Act	LS-	End points	Change	Main	Note
1851/10/4	B1	A	White Pigeon MI-Elkhart	+14.7		6
/10/4	B1	W	Elkhart-South Bend	+15.1		
	B2	WM	Michigan City-Baileytown	+14.0	43.8	
1852	B1	T	Goshen-B	+10.0		
	B1	T	South Bend-IL state line	+71.5	125.3	
1856	X	WM	Michigan City-Baileytown	-14.0	111.3	
1858	B3	T	Toledo OH-Goshen	+56.1	167.4	
1870/1/17	B4	TF	Reading MI-Angola	+11.5		
/12/5	B4	TF	Angola-Fort Wayne	+43.8	222.7	
1883	B5	WK	IL state line-North Judson	+38.9	261.6	
1886/12	B5	WK	North Judson-Knox	+9.4	271.0	
1888 ca.	B6	TG	Sturgis MI-Goshen	+25.6	296.6	
1893	B9	WE	Elkhart & Western	+12.9	307.5	
1894/11	B7	WK	Knox-South Bend	+33.7	343.2	
1903	B8	WD	Indiana Harbor-Osborn	+4.9	348.1	
1905 ca.	B7	N2	MP 1.3-MP 3.2	+1.9	350.0	
1906	B10	WD	Osborn-IL state line	+95.9	445.9	
1958	S2	WD	Indiana Harbor-Osborn	[4.9]	441.0	3
1960	X	TG	Sturgis MI-Shipshewana	-8.7	432.3	

On 1968/2/1 this company was conveyed to Penn Central. Its Acquisition/Disposition Record is continued in two places: under the name of the former company and under the name of the new company. The lines conveyed were:

Line desig.	End points	MP	Main	Note
[LS-T]	IN state line-B	355.4-421.5	66.1	
[LS-A]	MI state line-Elkhart	420.1-438.8	14.7	
[LS-TS]	Goshen-Shipshewana	0-16.9	16.9	
[LS-TF]	MI state line-Ft. Wayne	44.7-100.0	55.3	
[LS-W]	Elkhart-IL state line	421.6-508.2	86.6	
[LS-WE]	Elkhart & Western Branch	0-12.9	12.9	
[LS-N2]	MC Connecting Branch	1.3-3.2	1.9	

(continued)

LAKE SHORE & MICHIGAN SOUTHERN

ACQUISITION/DISPOSITION RECORD (continued)
The lines conveyed were:

Line desig.	End points	MP	Main	Note
[LS-WK]	South Bend-IL state line	0.2-82.2	82.0	
[LS-WD]	Osborn-IL state line	4.9-100.8	95.9	
		TOTAL	432.3	

Date	Act	LS--	End points	Change	Main	Note
1968	B9	WJ	MS-Lake Jct.	+0.4	432.7	
1973/1	X	TF	Waterloo-Steubenville	-6.9		
	X	TF	Fort Wayne-Auburn Jct.	-16.1		
	Y	TF	In Fort Wayne	(7.2)	402.5	

On April 1, 1976, part of this company was conveyed to Conrail and part retained by the Penn Central trustees. The Acquisition/Disposition Record is continued to two places: under this company and under the name of the subsequent new owner. The property conveyed was:

Line desig.	End points	MP	to Conrail	to PennC	Note
[LS-T]	IN state line-B	355.4-421.5	66.1		
[LS-A]	MI state line-Elkhart	420.1-438.8	14.7		
[LS-TS]	Goshen-Shipshewana	0-16.9	16.9		
[LS-TF]	MI state line-Steubenvil.	44.7-63.5		18.8	
[LS-TF]	In Waterloo	70.4-71.2	0.8		
[LS-TF]	Waterloo-Auburn Jct.	71.2-76.7	5.5		
[LS-TF]	In Fort Wayne	92.8-100.0	(7.2)		
[LS-W]	Elkhart-MS	421.6-505.7	84.1		
[LS-W]	MS-IL state line	505.7-208.2		2.5	
[LS-WE]	Elkhart & Western Branch	0-12.9	12.9		
[LS-N2]	MC Connecting Branch	1.3-3.2	1.9		
[LS-WK]	South Bend-IL state line	0.2-82.2	82.0		
[LS-WD]	Osborn-IL state line	4.9-100.8	95.9		
[LS-WJ]	MS-Lake Jct.	0-0.4	0.4		
		TOTAL	381.2	21.3	System = 402.5

Date	Act	Line desig.	End points	Conrail change	PennC change	Note
1976	S2	TF	Auburn Jct.-Auburn	[1.7]		
	X	TF	Waterloo-Auburn	-3.8		
	Y	TF	In Waterloo	(0.8)		
	L3	TF	MI line-Pleasant Lake		<15.8>	
	X	W	MS-IL state line		-2.5	
YEAR TOTALS				374.9	3.0	System=377.9
1979	L2	TG	Goshen-Shipshewana	<16.9>		
YEAR TOTALS				358.0	3.0	System =361.0
1980	XL	TG	Goshen-Shipshewana	<+16.9>		
	X	TG	Goshen-Shipshewana	-16.2		
	Y	TG	In Goshen	(0.7)		
YEAR TOTALS				358.0	3.0	System =361.0
1982	X	WK	JK-wheatfield	-55.0		
	Y	WK	High Street-JK	(2.8)		
YEAR TOTALS				300.2	3.0	System =303.2
1984	X	TF	In Waterloo	(-0.8)		
	X	TG	In Goshen	(-0.7)		
	X	WE	In Mishawaka	-0.7		
YEAR TOTALS				299.5	3.0	System =302.5
1986	L3	TF	Pleasant Lake-Steubenville		<3.0>	
	X	TF	In Fort Wayne	(-2.4)		
	X	WE	In Mishawaka	-2.4		
YEAR TOTALS				297.1	0	System =297.1

(continued)

LAKE SHORE & MICHIGAN SOUTHERN

ACQUISITION/DISPOSITION RECORD (continued)

1992	S3	TF	MI line-Steubenville		[<18.8>]		
	YEAR TOTALS			297.1	0	System =297.1	
1994/10	S1	WD	Handy-Stewart	[10.8]			
	YEAR TOTALS			286.3	0	System =286.3	
1996	X	WD	Schneider-Sheff	-33.2			
	S5	WD	Sheff-Free	[5.9]			
	S	WD	Free-Handy	-8.4			
	X	WD	Stewart-IL state line	-9.6			
/11	L4	WE	Elkhart-Mishawaka	<9.8>			
	YEAR TOTALS			219.4	0	System =219.4	

On 1999/6/1 Conrail was conveyed to CSX Transportation and Norfolk Southern. Its Acquisition/Disposition Record is continued in two places: under the name of the original company and under the name of the new company. The lines conveyed were:

Line desig.	End points	MP	to CSX	to NS
[LS-T]	IN state line-B	355.4-421.5		66.1
[LS-A]	MI state line-Elkhart	420.1-438.8		14.7
[LS-TF]	In Fort Wayne	95.2-100.0		(4.8)
[LS-W]	Elkhart-MS	421.6-505.7		84.1
[LS-N2]	MC Connecting Branch	1.3-3.2		1.9
[LS-WK]	In South Bend	0.2-3.0		(2.8)
[LS-WK]	Wheatfield-IL state line	58.0-82.2		24.2
[LS-WD]	Osborn-Schneider	4.9-32.9		28.0
[LS-WJ]	MS-Lake Jct.	0-0.4		0.4
		TOTAL	0	219.4

ACT COLUMN KEY

B1 Built by Northern Indiana RR
B2 Built by Buffalo & Mississippi RR
B3 Built by Michigan Southern & Northern Indiana RR
B4 Built by Fort Wayne, Jackson & Saginaw
B5 Built by Indiana, Illinois & Iowa RR
B6 Built by Canada & St. Louis
B7 Built by Indiana, Illinois & Iowa Ry
B8 Built by Indiana Harbor RR
B9 Built by Elkhart & Western
B10 Built by Chicago, Indiana & Southern RR
B11 Built by Penn Central Co.
L1 Leased to Hillsdale County RR
L2 Leased to Indiana Interstate
L3 Leased to Hillsdale County
L4 Leased to Michigan Southern
LA1 Lease assigned to Indiana Northeastern
S1 Sold to Bee Line
S2 Sold to Baltimore & Ohio
S3 Sold to Indiana Northeastern
S4 Sold to Indiana Harbor Belt
S5 Sold to Kankakee, Beaverville & Southern
X   Abandoned

SOURCES

1. Indiana, *1995 Indiana State Rail Plan*.
2. Michigan, *Aids, Gifts, Grants*.
3. Simons and Parker, *Railroads of Indiana*.

LAKE SHORE & MICHIGAN SOUTHERN

NOTES
1. After 1976 the Baltimore & Ohio provided switching service from Auburn Jct. over the segment to serve several industries in Auburn. In 1981 the city-owned Auburn Port Authority purchased the line.
2. The abandonment authorized extended from Waterloo to Pleasant Lake but apparently the Steubenville-Pleasant Lake segment was not abandoned since it was subsequently conveyed to Hillsdale County RR in 1986.
3. The New York Central and succeeding owners retained trackage rights over this segment until 1986.

LOGANSPORT & EEL RIVER SHORT LINE CO.

MAIN LINE (LERS-[PRR-LE])
See Pennsylvania line PRR-LE for arrangement of stations, prior construction/-abandonment record, and prior ownership

CONSTRUCTION/ABANDONMENT

Date	Act	End points	MP	Change	Main	Source	Note
1989/7/1	P	Van-MP 3.4	1.2-3.4	+2.2	2.2	1	1

OWNERSHIP
1989   Logansport & Eel River Short Line

ACQUISITION/DISPOSITION RECORD
See ownership record above for line LERS-[PRR-LE]

ACT COLUMN KEY
P   Purchased from Conrail

SOURCES
1. Simons and Parker, *Railroads of Indiana.*

NOTES
1. Apparently this property was operated as a tourist railroad for a period of time before freight operations began on July 1, 1989.

LOUISVILLE & INDIANA

MAIN LINE (LIRC-[PRR-IL])
See Pennsylvania line PRR-IL for arrangement of stations, prior construction/-abandonment record, and prior ownership.

CONSTRUCTION/ABANDONMENT

Date	Act	End points	MP	Change	Main	Source	Note
1994/3/12	P	Southport-KY state line	6.3-108.8	+102.5	102.5	1	

OWNERSHIP
1994   Louisville & Indiana RR

WATSON BRANCH (LIRC-[PRR-IW])
See Pennsylvania line PRR-IW for arrangement of stations, prior construction/-abandonment record, and prior ownership.

CONSTRUCTION/ABANDONMENT

Date	Act	End points	MP	Change	Main	Source	Note
1994/3/12	P	Boyd-Watson	0-4.0	+4.0	4.0		

OWNERSHIP
1994   Louisville & Indiana RR

LOUISVILLE & INDIANA

IN COLUMBUS (LIRC-[PRR-IM])
See Pennsylvania line PRR-IM for arrangement of stations, prior construction/-abandonment record, and prior ownership.

CONSTRUCTION/ABANDONMENT

Date	Act	End points	MP	Change	Main	Source	Note
1994/3/12	P	In Columbus	0-2.8	(+2.8)	(2.8)		

OWNERSHIP

1994		Louisville & Indiana RR

ACQUISITION/DISPOSITION RECORD

Date	Act	LIRC-	End points	Change	Main	Note
1994/3/12	P	[PRR-IL]	Indianapolis-KY state line	+102.5		
/3/12	P	[PRR-IW]	Boyd-Watson	+4.0		
/3/12	P	[PRR-IM]	In Columbus	(2.8)	106.5	

ACT COLUMN KEY
P   Purchased from Conrail

SOURCES
1. Simons and Parker, *Railroads of Indiana.*

LOUISVILLE & JEFFERSONVILLE BRIDGE CO.

MAIN LINE (LJB-A)

	Mileage	County	Crossings, junctions, etc.
(Junction)	0	Clark	J/B&O-SV 52.8
Jeffersonville	0.2	"	
(IN/KY state line)	0.7		
Louisville KY-7th St.	3.3	Jefferson KY	

CONSTRUCTION/ABANDONMENT

Date	Act	End points	MP	Change	Main	Source	Note
1893	B	Line	0-0.7	+0.7	0.7	1	
1996	XS	Line	0-0.7	-0.7	0	1	1

OWNERSHIP

1893	Louisville & Jeffersonville Bridge Co., owned 2/3 by Cleveland, Cincinnati, Chicago & St. Louis, 1/3 by Chesapeake & Ohio
1917	Louisville & Jeffersonville Bridge & RR Co., ownership as above
1927	Louisville & Jeffersonville Bridge & RR Co., CCC&SL buy 100% ownership
1930/2/1	New York Central, leased Cleveland, Cincinnati, Chicago & St. Louis
1960 ca.	CCC&SL, apparently buy L&JB&R
1968/2/1	Penn Central, assigned lease of Cleveland, Cincinnati, Chicago & St. L.

ACQUISITION/DISPOSITION RECORD
See ownership record above for line LJB-A

ACT COLUMN KEY
B   Built by Louisville & Jeffersonville Bridge Co.
XS   Operations ended; approach tracks removed; bridge remains in place

SOURCES
1. Simons and Parker, *Railroads of Indiana.*

LOUISVILLE & NASHVILLE

ST. LOUIS DIVISION (L&N-S)

	Mileage [Nashville]	County	Crossings, junctions, etc.
Henderson KY	312.8		
(KY/IN state line)	313.5		
Rohm	315.3	Vanderburgh	
Vaughan	318.6	"	f. Cypress
South Howell	321.8	"	J/conn. to L&N-SE 323.6, 0.3 mi.
North Howell	323.4	"	J/L&N-SE 323.4
Belknap	328.6	"	
Lippe	331.2	Posey	f. St. Philips
Caborn	336.0	"	
Lamott	337.4	"	
(Junction)	340.2	"	J/SWND-A 0
Mt. Vernon	341.4	"	
(Crossing)	342.0	"	X/CEI-EM 301.2
Upton	345.5	"	
Riolado	349.1	"	
(IN/IL state line)	350.4		
Maunie IL			
McLeansboro	382.7		
Mt. Vernon	408.1		
East St. Louis IL	483.6		

CONSTRUCTION/ABANDONMENT

Date	Act	End points	MP	Change	Main	Source	Note
1872	B1	IL state line-North Howell	350.4-323.4	+27.0	27.0	1	
1885	B2	KY state line-North Howell	313.5-323.4	+9.9	36.9	1	

OWNERSHIP

1872	St. Louis & Southeastern (B1) Ry, of part
1872	St. Louis & South Eastern Ry, merge SL&SE and other roads
1880	South East & St. Louis Ry, acquire St. Louis & South Eastern
1881	Louisville & Nashville RR, lease & controll of South East & St. Louis
1885	Henderson Bridge Co. (B2), of part
1906	Henderson Bridge and Railroad, rename Henderson Bridge Co.
1906	Louisville & Nashville RR, buy Henderson Bridge and RR
1936	Louisville & Nashville, merge South East & St. Louis
1982/12/29	Seaboard System, merge Louisville & Nashville and others
1986/7/1	CSX Transportation, rename Seaboard System

IN EVANSVILLE (L&N-SE)

	Mileage	County	Crossings, junctions, etc.
North Howell	323.4	Vanderburgh	J/L&N-S 323.4 f. Howell Yard
(Junction)	323.6	"	J/connection to South Howell, 0.3 mi.
8th Avenue	324.7	"	J/CCC-LE 160.0
Evansville	325.0	"	J/CEI-E 287.2, J/IC-NM 247.8

CONSTRUCTION/ABANDONMENT

Date	Act	End points	MP	Change	Main	Source	Note
1872	B1	North Howell-Evansville	323.4-325.0	+1.6	1.6	1	

OWNERSHIP

1872	St. Louis & Southeastern (B1) Ry, of part
1872	St. Louis & South Eastern Ry, merge SL&SE and other roads
1880	South East & St. Louis Ry, acquire St. Louis & South Eastern
1881	Louisville & Nashville RR, lease and control South East & St. Louis
1936	Louisville & Nashville, merge South East & St. Louis
1982/12/24	Seaboard System, merge Louisville & Nashville and others
1986/7/1	CSX Transportation, rename Seaboard System

LOUISVILLE & NASHVILLE

ACQUISITION/DISPOSITION RECORD

Date	Act	L&N-	End points	Change	Main	Note
1872	B1	S	IL state line-North Howell	+27.0		
1872	B1	SE	North Howell-Evansville	+1.6	28.6	
1885	B2	S	KY state line-North Howell	+9.9	38.5	

In 1967 Louisville & Nashville acquired Chicago & Eastern Illinois. The constituent parts of the new company are reported under lines Louisville & Nashville (L&N) and Chicago & Eastern Illinois (CEI). Their Acquisition/Disposition Records are continued under the name of the former company and under Louisville & Nashville. The property acquired by L&N was:

Line desig. L&N-	End points	MP	Main	Note
[CEI-E]	IL state line-Evansville	128.6-287.2	158.6	
[CEI-EO]	In Evansville	285.8-286.5	0.7	
[CEI-EJ]	In Evansville	0-4.0	4.0	
[CEI-EU]	Clinton-Universal Mine	0-8.5	8.5	
[CEI-EZ]	Otter Creek Jct.-Brazil	171.9-184.6	12.7	
[CEI-EM]	Mt. Vernon Jc.-Mt. Vernon	265.3-302.1	36.8	
1967 YEAR TOTALS		L&N=38.5 CEI=221.3 SYSTEM=259.8		

On 1971/7/31 Louisville & Nashville acquired Monon RR. The constituent parts of the new company are reported under lines Louisville & Nashville (L&N) and Monon (MON). Their Acquisition/Disposition Records are continued under the name of the former company and also under the name of the new company. The property acquired was:

Line desig. L&N-	End points	MP	Main	Note
[MON-A]	Chicago-Lafayette	19.2-117.9	98.7	
[MON-I]	Monon-Indianapolis	88.4-181.7	93.3	
[MON-N]	Monon-Michigan City	0-60.0	60.0	
[MON-SA]	Lafayette-Bloomington	117.9-221.5	103.6	
[MON-SB]	Bloomington-New Albany	221.5-317.5	96.0	
[MON-SV]	In New Albany	316.6-317.7	1.1	
[MON-SBO]	Clear Creek-Snyders	224.2-226.9	2.7	
[MON-SS]	Bedford Jct.-Dark Hollow	0.7-2.5	1.8	
[MON-SL]	Wallace Jct.-Midland	0-42.0	42.0	
[MON-F]	Orleans-French Lick	0-17.7	17.7	
1971/7/31 TOTALS		L&N=38.5 CEI=221.3 MON=516.9 SYSTEM=776.7		

Date	Act	L&N-	End points	Change	Note
1976	P1	[CEI-EB]	In Evansville	+5.9	
	B3	CEI-EB	In Evansville	+2.0	
	Y	[CEI-E]	In Evansville	(7.7)	
	Y	[CEI-EO]	In Evansville	(0.7)	
	Y	[CEI-EJ]	Evansville Belt	(4.0)	
	X	[MON-F]	Paoli-Frenck Lick	-10.0	
	X	[MON-I]	Belt Jct.-Mass. Ave.	-1.3	
YEAR TOTALS			L&N=38.5 CEI=216.8 MON=505.6 SYSTEM=760.9		
1977	X	[CEI-EZ]	Otter Creek Jct.-Brazil	-12.7	
YEAR TOTALS			L&N=38.5 CEI=204.1 MON=505.6 SYSTEM=748.2		
1980	X	[MON-N]	Medaryville-Michigan City	-44.8	
YEAR TOTALS			L&N=38.5 CEI=204.1 MON=460.8 SYSTEM=703.4		
1981	X	[MON-SS]	Bedford Jct.-Dark Hollow	-1.8	
	X	[MON-F]	Orleans-Paoli	-7.1	
YEAR TOTALS			L&N=38.5 CEI=204.1 MON=451.9 SYSTEM=694.5		
1982	Y	[CEI-EM]	In Mt. Vernon	(1.6)	
	X	[CEI-EM]	Poseyville-Mt. Vernon	-18.7	
YEAR TOTALS			L&N=38.5 CEI=183.8 MON=451.9 SYSTEM=674.2		

(continued)

LOUISVILLE & NASHVILLE

ACQUISITION/DISPOSITION RECORD (continued)

Effective 1983/1/1 the Louisville & Nashville merged into the Seaboard System. The Acquisition/Disposition Record for Louisville & Nashville is continued in two places: under Louisville & Nashville and under Seaboard System. Louisville & Nashville acquired lines are continued under their original constituent companies and under Seaboard System.

On 1986/7/1 the Seaboard System was renamed CSX Transportation. The Acquisition/-Disposition Record foR Louisville & Nashville is continued in two places: under Louisville & Nashville and under CSX Transportation.

ACT COLUMN KEY

B1   Built by St. Louis & Southeastern Ry
B2   Built by Henderson Bridge Co.
B3   Built by Louisville & Nashville
P1   Purchased from Penn Central
S4   Sold to Poseyville & Owensville
X   Abandoned
Y   Converted to yard trackage

SOURCES

1. Indiana, *1995 Indiana State Rail Plan.*

LOUISVILLE BRIDGE CO.

MAIN LINE (LBR-A)

CONSTRUCTION/ABANDONMENT

Date	Act	End points	MP	Change	Main	Source	Note
1870/2/24	B						

OWNERSHIP

1870	Louisville Bridge Co., control by Jeffersonville, Madison & Indianapolis.
1871	Pittsburgh, Cincinnati & St. Louis Ry (control by Pennsylvania RR), lease JM&I
1890	Pittsburgh, Cincinnati & St. Louis, merge JM&I and other road
1890	Pittsburgh, Cincinnati, Chicago & St. Louis Ry (control by Pennsylvaniaa RR), merge PC&SL and others
1921/1/1	Pennsylvania RR, lease PCC&SL
1957 ca.	Ownership of PCC&SL transferred to Philadelphia, Baltimore & Washington
1968/2/1	Penn Central Co., merge PRR and New York Central
1969/10/1	Penn Central Transp. Co., acquire Penn Central Co.
1976/4/1	Conrail, buy Penn Central Transp.

ACQUISITION/DISPOSITION RECORD

See ownership record above for line LBR-A

ACT COLUMN KEY

B   Built by Louisville Bridge Co.

SOURCES

1. Indiana, *1995 Indiana State Rail Plan.*

NOTES

General. This company's bridge was used by the Jeffersonville, Madison & Indianapolis and its successors. In 1872 the Ohio & Mississippi (see Baltimore & Ohio) began using the bridge, and continued to until 1887. The Louisville, New Albany & Chicago (see Monon) also used the bridge from 1892 until 1900.

LOUISVILLE, NEW ALBANY & CORYDON RR

MAIN LINE (LNAC-A)

	Mileage	County	Crossings, junctions, etc.
Corydon	0	Harrison	
Corydon Jct.	7.7	"	J/SOU-U 251.2

CONSTRUCTION/ABANDONMENT

Date	Act	End points	MP	Change	Main	Source	Note
1883/12/1	B1	Corydon-Corydon Jct.	0-7.7	+7.7	7.7	1	1

OWNERSHIP

1883	Louisville, New Albany & Corydon Ry (B1)
1890/5/1	Louisville, New Albany & Corydon RR, reorganize LNA&C Rt

ACQUISITION/DISPOSITION RECORD
See ownership record above for line LNAC-A

ACT COLUMN KEY
B1   Built by Louisville, New Albany & Corydon Ry

SOURCES
1. Indiana, *1995 Indiana State Rail Plan.*
2. Sulzer, *Ghost Railroads of Indiana.*

NOTES
1. Source 2 reports a 3-mile extension from Corydon to Kings Cave was built sometime in 1889, and that 2 miles of this extension were abandoned in 1905. This work is not included in the Acquisition/Disposition record.

MADISON

MAIN LINE (CMPA-[PRR-IM])
See Pennsylvania line PRR-IM for arrangement of stations, prior construction/abandonment record, and prior ownership

CONSTRUCTION/ABANDONMENT

Date	Act	End points	MP	Change	Main	Source	Note
1977	P	Madison-North Vernon	45.2-19.4	+25.8	25.8	1	1

OWNERSHIP

1977	Madison RR

ACQUISITION/DISPOSITION RECORD
See ownership record above for line CMPA-[PRR-IM]

ACT COLUMN KEY
P   Purchased from Penn Central

SOURCES
1. Simons and Parker, *Railroads of Indiana.*

NOTES
1. Beginning Apr. 1, 1976, the line was operated under contract with the State of Indiana. In 1977-78 the City of Madison Port Authority purchased the line from Penn Central and retained Madison RR to operate the line.

MAUMEE & WESTERN

LIBERTY CENTER OH-WOODBURN (MAWE-[WAB-MM])
See Wabash line WAB-MM for arrangement of stations, prior constructionabandonment record, and prior ownership

CONSTRUCTION/ABANDONMENT

Date	Act	End points	MP	Change	Main	Source	Note
1998	P	Liberty Center OH-Woodburn	75.7-78.7	+3.0	3.0		

OWNERSHIP

1998	Maumee & Western

ACQUISITION/DISPOSITION RECORD
See ownership record above for line MAWE-[WAB-MM]

ACT COLUMN KEY
P Purchased from Norfolk Southern

MG RAIL

MAIN LINE (MGR-A)

	Mileage	County	Crossings, junctions, etc.
(Junction)	0	Clark	J/B&O-SV 45.0
(Junction)	6.2	"	J/B&O-SV 41.6

CONSTRUCTION/ABANDONMENT

Date	Act	End points	MP	Change	Main	Source	Note
1985	L	Line	0-6.2	(+6.2)	0	1	1

OWNERSHIP

1985	MG Rail, leased from State of Indiana

ACQUISITION/DISPOSITION RECORD
See ownership record above for line MGR-A

ACT COLUMN KEY
L Leased from State of Indiana

SOURCES
1. Simons and Parker, *Railroads of Indiana.*

NOTES

1. This line is an industrial road and is not included in the mileage table

MICHIGAN CENTRAL

WEST DIVISION (MC-W)

	Mileage	County	Crossings, junctions, etc.
	(Detroit, Third St.)		
Niles MI	191.90		
Grand Beach	222.09		
Vetterlys Crossing MI	222.44		
(MI/IN state line)	222.72		
Corymbo	223.58	LaPorte	
CP 226	226.2	"	
(Yard office)	227.30	"	
(Junction)	228.38	"	J/NKP-LM 159.0
Drawbridge	228.47	"	
(continued)			

MICHIGAN CENTRAL

WEST DIVISION (MC-W) (continued)

Drawbridge	228.47	LaPorte	
(Junction)	228.57	"	J/MON-N 60.0
Michigan City (old)	228.82	"	
Michigan City (new)	228.88	"	
Tenth Street	229.67	"	X/CSS-A 35.1
Prison Track	229.78	"	
Furnessville	236.60	Porter	
CP 238	238.9	"	
Porter	240.62	"	
PO	240.70	"	X/NYC-W 482.2, now CP 482
Kilverys Sand Pit	245.63	"	
Crisman	246.05	"	
Willow Creek	246.59	"	
(Crossing)	246.61	"	X/B&O-C 236.9
(Crossing)	246.64	"	X/WAB-MC 233.7
East Gary	249.78	Lake	J/MC-WJ 0 f. Lake
Gary	255.09	"	
(Crossing)	256.26	"	X/PRR-F 441.8
Tolleston	256.28	"	
Ivanhoe	259.58	"	
(Crossing)	259.58	"	X/EJ&E-G 5.6
Gibson Transfer	260.28	"	
Gibson	261.73	"	
(Crossing)	261.73	"	X/IHB-A 3.7, X/LS-WD 4.23
Columbia Ave.	263.71	"	
Calumet Ave.	264.23	"	
(Switch, E Chicago Belt)	264.49	"	
Hammond IN	264.68	"	
(Crossing)	264.87	"	X/NKP-C 503.8
(Crossing)	264.89	"	X/ERIE-C 248.5
(Crossing)	264.90	"	X/MON-A 20.7
Hammond (old sta.) IN	265.02	"	
(IN/IL state line)	265.17		
Calumet City IL	265.26		
--via IC			
(Chicago-12th St.	284.74)		
(End of track) IL	286.22		

CONSTRUCTION/ABANDONMENT

Date	Act	End points	MP	Change	Main	Source	Note
1849/4/23	B1	Niles-New Buffalo	191.9-218.9	+23.7		2	
1850/10/29	B1	New Buffalo-Mich. City	218.9-228.9	+10.0	6.2	2	2
1852/5/1	B1	Mich. City-Kensington	228.9-272.0	+43.1	42.5		3
1958	S1	Ivanhoe-Kensington	259.6-265.2	[5.6]	36.9		

1976/4/1	S2	Niles-Porter	227.2-240.7	[13.5]	24.5		

OWNERSHIP

1849	Michigan Central (B2)
1930/2/1	New York Central, leased Michigan Central
1968/2/1	Penn Central, merge New York Central, with lease of Michigan Central
1976/4/1	Amtrak, bought line, Niles-Porter, from Michigan Central
1976/4/1	Conrail, bought line, Porter west, from Michigan Central
1999/6/1	Norfolk Southern, bought Conraii

MICHIGAN CENTRAL

JOLIET BRANCH (MC-WJ)

	Mileage	County	Crossings, junctions, etc.	
East Gary	0.0	Lake	J/MC-W 249.78	
New Chicago	1.82	"		
Liverpool	2.93	"	X/PRR-F 437.4	
South Gary	5.38	"	X/NKP-C 493.2	f. Glen Park
Ross	7.78	"		
(Crossing)	10.21	"	X/EJ&E-G 0.1	
(Crossing)	10.33	"	X/ERIE-C 240.6	
(Crossing)	10.34	"	X/GTW-C 36.08	
Griffith	10.34	"		
(Bridge)	12.0	"	B/LS-WD 10.28	
Hartsdale	12.75	"	X/PRR-L 281.7	
(Crossing)	15.25	"	X/MON-N 29.0	
Dyer IN	15.44	"		
(IN/IL state line)	15.66			
(Bridge) IL	20.85			
Chicago Heights IL	21.36			
Joliet IL	44.46			
(End of track) IL	44.81			

CONSTRUCTION/ABANDONMENT

Date	Act	End points	MP	Change	Main	Source	Note
1854/9/7	B2	Line	0-44.8	+44.8	15.7		

1976	X	East Gary-Hartsdale	0-12.8	-12.8	2.9	2	

OWNERSHIP

1854	Joliet & Northern Indiana (B3), leased by Michigan Central
1930/2/1	New York Central, lease Michigan Central
1968/2/1	Penn Central, merge New York Central, with lease of Michigan Central
1976/4/1	Conrail, purchase Penn Central and Joliet & Northern Indiana
1999/6/1	CSX Transportation, purchase Conrail

SOUTH BEND BRANCH (MC-N)

	Mileage	County	Crossings, junctions, etc.
Lake Street MI	0.0		
Bertrand MI	4.80		
(MI/IN state line)	5.75		
Websters	6.86	St.Joseph	
St. Marys Sdg.	9.40	"	
Notre Dame	9.56	"	
(Junction)	9.61	"	J/MC-N2 0
South Bend	11.66	"	
(End of track)	11.72	"	

CONSTRUCTION/ABANDONMENT

Date	Act	End points	MP	Change	Main	Source	Note
1872	B3	MP 0.3-South Bend	5.8-11.7	+5.9	5.9	1	

1975 ca.	X	In South Bend	9.6-11.7	-2.1	3.8		
1984	X	Niles-St Marys IN	0.3-9.4	-3.6	0.2	2	

OWNERSHIP

1872	Michigan Air Line RR (B8), leased by Michigan Central
1916/9/27	Michigan Central (B2), merger of Michigan Air Line RR
1930/2/1	New York Central, lease of Michigan Central
1968/2/1	Penn Central, merge New York Central, with lease of Michigan Central
1976/4/1	Conrail, purchase Penn Central and Michigan Cental
1999/6/1	Norfolk Southern, purchase of Conrail

MICHIGAN CENTRAL

ST. JOSEPH BRANCH (MC-J)

	Mileage	County	Crossings, junctions, etc.
(Junction)	2.57	St.Joseph	J/PRR-LS 182.3
Prairie Avenue	1.95	"	
SS&S Jct.	0.0	"	
(Crossing)	0.08	"	X/GTW-C 99.0, X/NJI-A 1.7
Lydick	5.89	"	X/NYC-W 443.7, Rugby
(Crossing)	5.9	"	X/CSS-A 7.4
(Crossing)	5.9	"	X/NOIN-A
Shimps Siding	9.06	"	
Warwick	10.92	"	
(IN/MI state line)	11.70		
(Bridge)	14.87	Berrien MI	B/MC-W 205.32
Galien (old) MI	15.46		
St. Joseph MI	36.86		
(Junction)	36.97		J/PM-C 87.7
(St. Joseph, via PM)	37.14)		

CONSTRUCTION/ABANDONMENT

Date	Act	End points	MP	Change	Main	Source	Note
1890/8/4	B4	St. Joseph-Junction/PRR	11.7-2.6	+14.3	14.3	1	
1942/12/23	X	SS&S Jct.-Baroda MI	0-11.7	-11.7		2	1
1942	Y	In South Bend	-2.6-0	(2.6)	0		

1972	X	In South Bend	-2.6-0	(-2.6)	0	2	

OWNERSHIP

1890	Indiana & Lake Michigan (B19)
1890/8/4	Terre Haute & Indianapolis, lease Indiana & Lake Michigan
1899/1/20	St. Joseph, South Bend & Southern, reorganize Indiana & Lake Michigan
1900/2/23	SJSB&S leased to Indiana, Illinois & Iowa (controlled by Lake Shore & Mich. Southern)
1905/3/15	Bend & Southern, reorganize Indiana & Lake Michigan
1900/2/23	SJSB&S leased to Indiana, Illinois & Iowa lease of SJSB&S assigned to Michigan Central
1906/4/6	Chicago, Indiana & Southern (controlled by Lake Shore & Mich. Southern), merge Indiana, III. & Iowa
1915/1/1	New York Central, merge Chicago, Indiana & Southern
1930/2/1	New York Central, lease Michigan Central
1949 ca.	Michigan Central, buy SJSB&S
1968/2/1	Penn Central, merge New York Central, with lease of Michigan Central
1976/4/1	Conrail, purchase Penn Central and Joliet & Northern Indiana

M. C. CONNECTING BRANCH (MC-N2)

	Mileage	County	Crossings, junctions, etc.
(Junction)	0	St.Joseph	J/MC-N 9.61
(Bridge, St.Joseph River)	1.03	"	
(Prop line MC/NYC)	1.31	"	J/LS-N2 1.31
(Bridge, Portage Ave.)	1.32	"	
Olivers	3.23	"	

NOTE. For record of New York Central part between MP 1.3 and MP 3.2, see Lake Shore line LS-N2.

CONSTRUCTION/ABANDONMENT

Date	Act	End points	MP	Change	Main	Source	Note
1905 ca.	B3	MP 0-MP 1.3	0-1.3	+1.3	1.3		

OWNERSHIP

1905	Michigan Air Line RR (B8), leased to Michigan Central
1916/9/27	Michigan Central, merger of Michigan Air Line RR
1930/2/1	New York Central leased Michigan Central
1968/2/1	Penn Central, merger of New York Central (with lease of Michigan Central)
1976/4/1	Conrail, purchase of Penn Central
1999/6/1	Norfolk Southern, purchase of Conrail

MICHIGAN CENTRAL

ACQUISITION/DISPOSITION RECORD

Date	Act	MC-	End points	Change	Main	Note
1850/10/29	B1	W	New Buffalo MI-Mich. City	+6.2	6.2	
1852/5/1	B1	W	Mich. City-Kensington IL	+36.3	42.5	
1854/9/7	B2	WJ	Lake-Joliet IL	+15.7	58.2	
1872	B3	N	Niles MI-South Bend	+5.9	64.1	
1890/8/4	B4	J	St. Joseph MI-Junction/PRR	+14.3	78.4	
1905 ca.	B3	N2	In South Bend (MP 0-MP 1.3)	+1.3	79.7	
1942/12/23	X	J	SS&S Jct.-Baroda	-11.7		1
	Y	J	In South Bend	(2.6)	65.4	
1958	S1	W	Ivanhoe-Kensington	[5.6]	59.8	

On 1968/2/1 this company was conveyed to Penn Central. Its Acquisition/Disposition Record is continued in two places: under Michigan Central and under Penn Central. The lines conveyed were:

Line desig.	End points	MP	Main	Note
[MC-W]	MI state line-Ivanhoe	222.7-259.6	36.9	
[MC-WJ]	East Gary-IL state line	0-15.7	15.7	
[MC-N]	MI state line-South Bend	5.8-11.7	5.9	
[MC-N2]	In South Bend	0-1.3	1.3	
[MC-J]	In South Bend	0-2.6	(2.6)	
	TOTAL	59.8		

Date	Act	MC-	End points	Change	Main	Note
1972	X	J	In South Bend	(-2.6)	59.8	
1975 ca.	X	N	In South Bend	-2.1	57.7	

On April 1, 1976, part of this company was conveyed to Conrail, part to Amtrak, and part retained by the Penn Central trustees. The Acquisition/Disposition Record is continued to two places: under Michigan Central and under the name of the subsequent new owner. The property conveyed was:

Line desig.	End points	MP	to Conrail	to PennC	tp Amtrak
[MC-W]	MI state line-PO	222.7-240.7			18.0
[MC-W]	PO-Ivanhoe	240.7-259.6	18.9		
[MC-WJ]	East Gary-Hartsdale	0-12.8		12.8	
[MC-WJ]	Hartsdale-IL state line	12.8-15.7	2.9		
[MC-N]	MI state line-South Bend	5.8-9.6	3.8		
[MC-N2]	In South Bend	0-1.3	1.3		
		TOTALS	26.9	12.8	18.0
		SYSTEM	57.7		

Date	Act	Line desig.	End points	Conrail	PennC	Amtrak
1976/4/1	X	WJ	East Gary-Hartsdale		-12.8	
	YEAR TOTALS		CR=26.9 PC=0 AMK=18.0 MC=44.9			
1993 ca.	X	N	Niles MI-St Marys		-3.6	
	YEAR TOTALS		CR=23.3 PC=0 AMK=18.0 MC=41.3			

On 1999/6/1 Conrail was conveyed to CSX Transportation and Norfolk Southern. Its Acquisition/Disposition Record is continued in two places: under Michigan Central and under the name of the new owner. The lines conveyed were:

Line desig.	End points	MP	to CSX	to NS	
[MC-W]	PO-Ivanhoe	240.7-259.6	18.9		
[MC-WJ]	Hartsdale-IL state line	12.8-15.7	2.9		
[MC-N]	St Marys-MP 6	5.8-6.0		0.2	
[MC-N2]	In South Bend	0-1.3		1.3	
	TOTALS		20.4	2.9	SYSTEM =23.3

MICHIGAN CENTRAL

ACT COLUMN KEY
B1 Built by Michigan Central
B2 Built by Joliet & Northern Indiana
B3 Built by Michigan Air Line
B4 Built by Indiana & Lake Michigan
S1 Sold to Indiana Harbor Belt
S2 Sold to Amtrak
X   Abandoned

SOURCES
1. Michigan, *Aids, Gifts, Grants.*
2. Simons and Parker, *Railroads of Indiana.*

NOTES
1. The 2.57 miles of this line south of SS&S Jct. was part of the main line while the line was the property the Terre Haute & Indianapolis until 1899. After that time it was, apparently, used as a yard track, and remained in service after the abandonment of the part north of SS&S Jct.
2. This segment was built under an agreement with the Buffalo & Mississippi.
3. This segment was built under an agreement with Louisville, New Albany & Chicago.

MICHIGAN SOUTHERN

ELKHART & WESTERN (MISO-[LS-WE])
See Lake Shore & Michigan Southern line LS-WD for arrangement of stations, prior construction/abandonment record, and prior ownership

CONSTRUCTION/ABANDONMENT

Date	Act	End points	MP	Change	Main	Source	Note
1996/11	L	Elkhart-Mishawaka	0-9.8	+9.8	9.8	1	

OWNERSHIP

1996	Michigan Southern RR

IN KENDALLVILLE (MISO-[PRR-GS])
See Grand Rapids & Indiana line PRR-GS for arrangement of stations, prior construction/abandonment record, and prior ownership

CONSTRUCTION/ABANDONMENT

Date	Act	End points	MP	Change	Main	Source	Note
1996/11	L	In Kendallville	119.0-120.1	[Y]+1.1	0	1	

OWNERSHIP

1996	Michigan Southern RR

ACQUISITION/DISPOSITION RECORD

Date	Act	MISO-	End points	Change	Main	Note
1996/11	L	[LS-EW]	Elkhart-Mishawaka	+9.8		
1996/11	L	[PRR-GS]	In Kendallville	[Y]+1.1	9.8	

ACT COLUMN KEY
L Leased from Conrail

SOURCES
1. Simons and Parker, *Railroads of Indiana.*

MISSOURI PACIFIC

On 1967/5/12 this company acquired Chicago & Eastern Illinois. Shortly thereafter all lines purchased were sold to Louisville & Nashville except one line as detailed below. Its Acquisition/Disposition Record is continued in two places: under the name of the original company and under the name of the new company. The property acquired was:

Line desig. MP-	End points	MP	Main	Note
[CEI-CJ]	IL state line-Judyville	113.5-120.4	6.9	

ACQUISITION/DISPOSITION RECORD

Date	Act	MP	End points	Change	Main	Note
1973 ca.	X	[CEI-CJ]	IL state line-Judyville	-6.9	0	

ACT COLUMN KEY
X Abandoned

SOURCES
1. Simons and Parker, *Railroads of Indiana.*

MONON

NORTHERN DIVISION, 1st SUBDIVISION (MON-A)

	Mileage	County	Crossings, junctions, etc.
Chicago IL	0		
State Line IL	19.2		
(IL/IN state line)	19.2		
Hammond	20.7	Lake	X/EJE-GS 5.8, X/IHB-A 6.9, X/MC-W 264.9, J/NKP-C 503.8
South Hammond	23.2	"	
Airline Jct.	25.4	"	X/PRR-L 285.4
Maynard	25.5	"	
G. T. Crossing	25.8	"	X/GTW-C 31.6
Dyer	29.0	"	X/MC-WJ 15.3
(Crossing)	29.1	"	X/EJE-A 31.5
St. John	33.5	"	X/LS-WD 14.6
Cedar Lake	39.5	"	
Paisley	40	"	
Creston	41.5	"	
Lowell	44.8	"	
Grassmere	48	"	
Shelby	52.6	"	X/LS-WK 73.1
Thayer	54.1	"	
Rose Lawn	56.5	Newton	
Fair Oaks	62.2	Jasper	X/CAS-A 26.6
Parr	65.8	"	
(continued)			

MONON

NORTHERN DIVISION, 1st SUBDIVISION (MON-A) (continued)

	Mileage [Chicago]	County	Crossings, junctions, etc.
Surrey	68.1	"	
Rensselaer	73.0	"	
Pleasant Ridge	77.0	"	
McCoysburg	80.0	"	J/MON-ND 0
Lee	83.1	White	
Monon	88.4	"	J/MON-I 88.4, J/MON-M 0
Reynolds	95.8	"	X/PRR-LF 26.9
Smithson	98.2	"	
Chalmers	102.1	"	
Brookston	106.2	"	
Ash Grove	110.2	Tippecanoe	
Battle Ground	112.9	"	
Shops	117.9	"	J/MON-SA 117.9

CONSTRUCTION/ABANDONMENT

Date	Act	End points	MP	Change	Main	Source	Note
1853	B1	Shops-Monon	117.9-88.4	+29.5	29.5	1	
1878	B5	Monon-Rensselaer	88.4-73.0	+15.4	44.9	1	
1881	B6	Rensselaer-Dyer	73.0-29.0	+44.0	88.9	1	
1882	B6	Dyer-IL/IN state line	29.0-19.2	+9.8	98.7	1	
1948	B11	At Cedar Lake			98.7	2	1

1990	X	Hammond-Airline Jct.	21.1-25.4	-4.3	94.4	1,2	4
1993	X	Airline Jct.-Maynard	25.4-25.5	-0.1	94.3	1	

OWNERSHIP

1853	New Albany & Salem RR (B1) of part
1859/10/24	Louisville, New Albany & Chicago RR, rename NA&S
1869/6/24	Louisville, New Albany & Chicago Ry, reorganize LNA&C
1878	Indianapolis, Delphi & Chicago RR (B5) of part
1881	Louisville, New Albany & Chicago Ry (B6) of part
1881	Chicago & Indianapolis Air Line Ry, reorganized Ind, Delphi & Chi.
1881/12/15	LNA&C, bought Chi & Ipls Air Line
1897	Chicago, Indianapolis & Louisville Ry, reorganized LNA&C
1956/1/10	Monon RR, rename CI&L
1971/7/31	Louisville & Nashville RR, bought Monon RR
1982/12/29	Seaboard System RR, merge Louisville & Nashville
1986/7/1	CSX Transportation, rename Seaboard System

NORTHERN DIVISION, DINWIDDIE BRANCH (MON-ND)

	Mileage	County	Crossings, junctions, etc.
McCoysburg	0	Jasper	J/MON-N 80.0
Randle	1.6	"	
Della	3.3	"	
Moody	5.5	"	
Lewiston	7.7	"	
Newland	9.5	"	
Gifford	11.4	"	J/MON-ND1 0
Laura	14.1	"	
McGlinn	17.4	"	
Zadoc	18.5	"	J/CAS-A 17.0
Kersey	22.0	"	X/LS-WK 63.5
Pence Switch	23.8	"	
(continued)			

MONON

NORTHERN DIVISION, DINWIDDIE BRANCH (MON-ND) (continued)

	Mileage [McCoysburg]	County	Crossings, junctions, etc.
Pence Switch	23.8	Jasper	
Potter Switch	24.9	"	
Grape Island	26.4	Lake	
Beech Ridge	27.1	"	
Range Line	30.1	"	
Dinwiddie	32.2	"	
(End of track)	36.0	"	

CONSTRUCTION/ABANDONMENT

Date	Act	End points	MP	Change	Main	Source	Note
1900	B10	Randle-Kersey	1.6-22.0	+20.4	20.4	3	
1901	B10	McCoysburg-Randle	0-1.6	+1.6	22.0	3	
1903	B10	Kersey-Grape Island	22.0-26.4	+4.4	26.4	3	
1906	B10	Grape Island-Dinwiddie	26.4-31.2	+4.8	31.2	3	
1912 ca.	B10	Dinwiddie-MP 36.0	31.2-36.0	+4.8	36.0	3	
1935/12/5	X	Line	0-36.0	-36.0	0	3	5

OWNERSHIP

1900	Chicago & Wabash Valley RR (B10)
1900	Chicago & Wabash Valley Ry, rename of C&WV
1914	Chicago, Indianapolis & Louisville Ry, control of C&WV
1916	Chicago, Indianapolis & Louisville Ry, bought C&WV

NORTHERN DIVISION, CRESCENT BRANCH (MON-ND1)

	Mileage	County	Crossings, junctions, etc.
Gifford	0	Jasper	J/MON-ND 11.4
--line not located			
Crescent	4	"	f. Asphaltum

CONSTRUCTION/ABANDONMENT

Date	Act	End points	MP	Change	Main	Source	Note
1902	B10	Line	0-4	+4.0	4.0	3	
1910	X	Line	0-4	-4.0	0	3	

OWNERSHIP

1902	Chicago & Wabash Valley Ry (B10)

NORTHERN DIVISION, 2nd SUBDIVISION (MON-I)

	Mileage (Chicago)	County	Crossings, junctions, etc.
Monon	88.4	White	J/MON-N 88.4, J/MON-M 0
Guernsey	93.8	"	
Monticello	98.6	"	X/PRR-LF 21.5
Patton	101.7	"	
Yeoman	104.4	Carroll	f. Lennox
Sleeth	105.8	"	
Pittsburg	107.9	"	
North Delphi	110.4	"	
Delphi	111.0	"	X/WAB-P 238.6
Harley	115.8	"	
Radnor	118.6	"	
Ockley	120.1	"	
Owasco	122.2	"	
Rossville	125.6	Clinton	
(continued)			

MONON

NORTHERN DIVISION, 2nd SUBDIVISION (MON-I) (continued)

	Mileage (Chicago)	County	Crossings, junctions, etc.
Rossville	125.6	Clinton	
Cambria	129.7	"	
Frankfort	136.0	"	X/NKP-LP 234.7, X/NKP-C 206.7
(Crossing)	136.3	"	X/PRR-IF 78.3
Cyclone	142.2	"	
Kirklin	146.9	"	
Terhune	151.5	Boone	
Sheridan	155.4	Hamilton	
Horton	159.9	"	
Westfield	163.4	"	X/CI-A 43.6
Carmel	167.8	"	
Nora	172.4	Marion	
Broad Ripple	175.3	"	
Fair Grounds	178.1	"	
Boulevard	178.5	"	
Belt Jct.	180.4	"	J/IU-C 2.0
Massachusetts Avenue	181.7	"	J/CCC-I 281.9
--via CCC-I			
(Washington Street	182.9)	"	
--via IU)			
(Indianapolis	183.5)	"	

CONSTRUCTION/ABANDONMENT

Date	Act	End points	MP	Change	Main	Source	Note
1878	B5	Delphi-Monon	111.0-88.4	+22.6	22.6	1	
1882	B6	Mass. Ave.-Delphi	181.7-111.0	+70.7	93.3	1	

1976	X	Belt Jct.-Mass. Ave.	180.4-181.7	-1.3	92.0	1	
1985	X	Frankfort-Sheridan	137.5-155.4	-17.9			
	L1	Sheridan-Belt Jct.	155.4-180.4	<25.0>	49.1	1	
1986 ca.	XL	Sheridan-Belt Jct.	155.4-180.4	<+25.0>			
ca.	X	Sheridan-Belt Jct.	155.4-180.4	-25.0	49.1		
1992	X	Delphi-Frankfort	112.2-137.5	-25.3	23.8	1	
1993	X	Monticello-Delphi	98.0-112.2	-14.2	9.6	1	

OWNERSHIP

1878	Indianapolis, Delphi & Chicago RR (B5) of part
1881	Chicago & Indianapolis Air Line Ry, reorganize ID&C
1881/12/15	Louisville, New Albany & Chicago (B6), bought C&IAL
1897	Chicago, Indianapolis & Louisville Ry, reorganize LNA&C
1956/1/10	Monon RR, renamed CI&L
1971/7/31	Louisville & Nashville RR, bought Monon RR
1982/12/29	Seaboard System RR, merge Louisville & Nashville
1986/7/1	CSX Transportation, rename Seaboard System

NORTHERN DIVISION, 3rd SUBDIVISION (MON-M)

	Mileage	County	Crossings, junctions, etc.
Monon	0	White	J/MON-N 88.4, J/MON-I 88.4
Francesville	8.6	Pulaski	
Medaryville	15.2	"	
Clarks	19.1	"	
Anthonys	20.6	"	
San Pierre	23.3	Starke	X/LS-WK 49.48
Riverside	27.6	LaPorte	
Wilders	28.1	"	X/ERIE-C 206.4
LaCrosse	31.6	"	X/PRR-L 246.6, J/CAS-A 0
(continued)			

MONON

NORTHERN DIVISION, 3rd SUBDIVISION (MON-M)

	Mileage [Monon]	County	Crossings, junctions, etc.
LaCrosse	31.6	LaPorte	X/PRR-L 246.6, J/CAS-A 0
Wade	32.5	"	X/C&O-C 223.0
South Wanatah	37.7	"	X/NKP-C 468.0
Wanatah	39.4	"	X/PRR-F 414.9
Haskells	43.1	"	X/GTW-C 63.89
Alida	45.0	"	X/B&O-C 220.9
Westville	47.1	"	B/WAB-MC 217.2
Otis	51.1	"	X/LS-W 473.35
Round House	57.7	"	
(Crossing)	58.1	"	X/PM-C 126.7
(Crossing)	59.0	"	X/CSS-A 35.1
Michigan City	59.8	"	J/MC-W 228.57
(End of track)	60.0	"	

CONSTRUCTION/ABANDONMENT

Date	Act	End points	MP	Change	Main	Source	Note
1853	B1	Monon-Michigan City	0-59.8	+60.0	60.0	I	

1980	X	Medaryville-Michigan City	15.2-60.0	-44.8	15.2	I	
1994	X	In Medaryville	14.8-15.2	-0.4	14.8	I	

OWNERSHIP

1853	New Albany & Salem RR (B1)
1859/10/24	Louisville, New Albany & Chicago RR, rename NA&S
1869/6/24	Louisville, New Albany & Chicago Ry, reorganize LNA&C
1897	Chicago, Indianapolis & Louisville Ry, reorganize LNA&C
1956/1/10	Monon RR, renamed CI&L
1971/7/31	Louisville & Nashville RR, bought Monon RR
1982/12/29	Seaboard System RR, merge Louisville & Nashville
1986/7/1	CSX Transportation, rename Seaboard System

SOUTHERN DIVISION, 4th SUBDIVISION (MON-SA)

	Mileage (Chicago)	County	Crossings, junctions, etc.
Shops	117.9	Tippecanoe	J/MON-N 117.9
(Junction)	119.3	"	J/MON-SAN 119.3
Lafayette	120.0	"	
Lafayette Jct.	121.5	"	X/NKP-LP 257.7, J/MON-SA 121.2
(Bridge)	122.9	"	B/WAB-P 258.4
Taylor	126.5	"	
South Raub	129.5	"	f. Raubs
Romney	132.9	"	
Linden	137.0	Montgomery	X/NKP-TC 228.5
Cherry Grove	141.0	"	
Manchester	144.0	"	
Crawfordsville	147.3	"	
Ames	148.4	"	X/P&E-A 43.0, X/PRR-VC 52.0 aka. Crawfordsville Jct.
Whitesville	153.9	"	
Ladoga	157.8	"	X/CI-A 81.3
Roachdale	162.2	Putnam	X/B&O-ID 159.8
Carpentersville	165.5	"	
Bainbridge	168.7	"	
Cary	173.0	"	
(Crossing)	176.8	"	X/CCC-L 38.0
Greencastle	177.8	"	X/CCC-LO 39.0
(continued)			

MONON

SOUTHERN DIVISION, 4th SUBDIVISION (MON-SA) (continued)

	Mileage (Chicago)	County	Crossings, junctions, etc.
Greencastle	177.8	Putnam	
Whitesville	153.9	Montgomery	
Limedale	180.0	"	X/PRR-V 40.3
Cement	180.6	"	
Putnamville	183.0	"	
Cloverdale	189.2	"	
Wallace Jct.	194.0	Owen	J/MON-SL 0
Quincy	195.3	"	
Spring Cave	197.8	"	
Gosport Jct.	203.1	"	X/PRR-IV 44.1
Gosport	203.9	"	
Stinesville	207.8	Monroe	
Adams	212.2	"	
Ellettsville	213.1	"	
Woods	215.5	"	
Hunters	217.9	"	
(Bridge)	219.9	"	X/IC-NI 56.4
Bloomington	220.5	"	
McDoel	221.5	"	J/MON-SB 221.5

CONSTRUCTION/ABANDONMENT

Date	Act	End points	MP	Change	Main	Source	Note
1852	B2	Crawfordsille-Lafayette	147.3-120.0	+27.3	27.3	1	
1853	B1	McDoel-Gosport	221.5-203.9	+17.6		1	
1853	B1	Lafayette-Shops	120.0-117.9	+2.1	47.0	1	
1854	B1	Gosport-Crawfordsville	203.9-147.3	+56.6	103.6	1	

1994	X	In Lafayette	119.3-121.5	-2.2			
1994	X	Cloverdale-Gosport Jct.	190.0-203.1	-13.1	88.3	1	
1995	X	Gosport Jct.-Ellettsville	203.1-213.4	-10.3	78.0	1	
1997	X	Ellettsville-Hunters	213.4-217.7	-4.3	73.7	1	

OWNERSHIP

1852	Crawfordsville & Wabash RR (B2) of part
1852/6/17	New Albany & Salem RR (B1), bought C&W
1859/10/24	Louisville, New Albany & Chicago RR, rename NA&S
1869/6/24	Louisville, New Albany & Chicago Ry, reorganize LNA&C
1897	Chicago, Indianapolis & Louisville Ry, reorganize LNA&C
1956/1/10	Monon RR, renamed CI&L
1971/7/31	Louisville & Nashville RR, bought Monon RR
1982/12/29	Seaboard System RR, merge Louisville & Nashville
1986/7/1	CSX Transportation, rename Seaboard System

LAFAYETTE RIVERFRONT LINE (MON-SAN)

	Mileage [Chicago]	County	Crossings, junctions, etc.
(Junction)	119.3	Tippecanoe	J/MON-SA 119.3
Lafayette (2nd station)	120.0	"	
(Bridge)	120.2	"	B/NKP-LP 258.8
Lafayette Jct.	121.2	"	J/MON-SA 121.5
(continued)			

CONSTRUCTION/ABANDONMENT

Date	Act	End points	MP	Change	Main	Source	Note
1994	B12	In Lafayette	119.3-121.2	+1.9	1.9	R	

OWNERSHIP

1994	CSX Transportation (B12)

MONON

SOUTHERN DIVISION, 5th SUBDIVISION (MON-SB)

	Mileage (Chicago)	County	Crossings, junctions, etc.
McDoel	221.5	Monroe	J/MON-SA 221.5
Clear Creek	224.2	"	J/MON-SBO 224.2
Diamond		"	
Ketchams	227.5	"	
Harrodsburg	232.8	"	J/MON-SBO 230.9
Guthrie	235.4	Lawrence	
Logan	238.6	"	
Peerless	240.2	"	
Thornton	240.9	"	
Murdock	241.4	"	J/spur to Needmore Quarry, 2 mi.
(Crossing)	244.5	"	X/MILW-TO 1.3
Bedford Jct.	245.1	"	
(Junction)	245.3	"	J/MON-SS 0.7
(Crossing, Junction)	245.7	"	X/MILW-T 262.3, J/B&O-SB 10.8
Bedford	245.8	"	
Sand Pit	249.2	"	
Yockey	251.7	"	
Mitchell	255.3	"	X/B&O-SW 126.4
Orleans	261.5	Orange	J/MON-F 0
Leipsic	265.1	"	
Saltillo	270.1	Washington	
Campbellsburg	271.8	"	
Smedley	275.3	"	
Hitchcock	277.2	"	
Salem	282.1	"	
Fogg	284.0	"	
Norris	286.9	"	f. Harrisburg
Farrabee	290.2	"	
Pekin	293.4	"	
Borden	299.5	Clark	
Brown Hill	302.8		
Bridgeport	303.8	"	f. Carwood
Wilson	305.3	"	
Bennettsville	307.3	"	
St. Joseph	309.4	"	
Smith	310.9	Floyd	
Vernia	315.6	"	
North Y	316.6	"	J/MON-SV 316.6
New Albany	317.5	"	

CONSTRUCTION/ABANDONMENT

Date	Act	End points	MP	Change	Main	Source	Note
1851	B1	New Albany-Orleans	317.5-261.5	+56.0	56.0	1	
1853	B1	Orleans-Harrodsburg	261.5-232.8	+28.7		1	
1853	B1	Clear Creek-McDoel	224.2-221.5	+2.7	87.4	1	
1899/9/1	B8	Harrodsburg-Clear Creek	232.8-224.2	+8.6	96.0	3	

1993	X	Bloomington-Bedford Jct.	222.6-245.1	-22.5	73.5	1	

(continued)

MONON

SOUTHERN DIVISION, 5th SUBDIVISION (MON-SB) (continued)
OWNERSHIP

1851	New Albany & Salem RR (B1)
1859/10/24	Louisville, New Albany & Chicago RR, rename NA&S
1869/6/24	Louisville, New Albany & Chicago Ry, reorganize LNA&C
1897	Chicago, Indianapolis & Louisville Ry, reorganize LNA&C
1899	Indiana Stone RR (B8), control and lease by Chicago, Indianapolis & Louisv.
1916	Chicago, Indianapolis & Louisville Ry, buy Indiana Stone
1956/1/10	Monon RR, renamed CI&L
1971/7/31	Louisville & Nashville RR, bought Monon RR
1982/12/29	Seaboard System RR, merge Louisville & Nashville
1986/7/1	CSX Transportation, rename Seaboard System

LOUISVILLE LINE (MON-SV)

	Mileage [Chicago]	County	Crossings, junctions, etc.
North Y	316.6	Floyd	J/MON-SB 316.6
VI	317.7	"	J/KIT-A 0
--via KIT-A			
(IN/KY state line)	317.8		
DI	319.2		
Youngtown	319.4		
(Louisville KY)	324.1		

CONSTRUCTION/ABANDONMENT

Date	Act	End points	MP	Change	Main	Source	Note
1882	B6	North Y-VI	316.6-317.7	+1.1	1.1	H	3

OWNERSHIP

1882	Louisville, New Albany & Chicago Ry (B6)
1897	Chicago, Indianapolis & Louisville Ry, reorganize LNA&C
1956/1/10	Monon RR, renamed CI&L
1971/7/31	Louisville & Nashville RR, buy Monon RR
1982/12/29	Seaboard System RR, merge Louisville & Nashville
1986/7/1	CSX Transportation, rename Seaboard System

SOUTHERN DIVISION, ORIGINAL MAIN LINE (MON-SBO)

	Mileage [Chicago]	County	Crossings, junctions, etc.
Clear Creek	224.2	Monroe	J/MON-SB 224.2
Sanders	226.9	"	
Smithville	227.7	"	
Harrodsburg	230.9	"	J/MON-SB 232.8

CONSTRUCTION/ABANDONMENT

Date	Act	End points	MP	Change	Main	Source	Note
1853	B1	Clear Creek-Harrodsburg	224.2-230.9	+6.7	6.7	1	
1945	X	Sanders-Harrodsburg	226.9-230.9	-4.0	2.7	3	

1993	X	Clear Creek-Sanders	224.2-226.9	-2.7	0		

OWNERSHIP

1853	New Albany & Salem RR (B1)
1859/10/24	Louisville, New Albany & Chicago RR, rename NA&S
1869/6/24	Louisville, New Albany & Chicago Ry, reorganize LNA&C
1897	Chicago, Indianapolis & Louisville Ry, reorganize LNA&C
1956/1/10	Monon RR, renamed CI&L
1956/1/10	Monon RR, renamed CI&L
1971/7/31	Louisville & Nashville RR, bought Monon RR
1982/12/29	Seaboard System RR, merge Louisville & Nashville

MONON

SOUTHERN DIVISION, B. & B. BRANCH (MON-SS)

	Mileage (Bedford)	County	Crossings, junctions, etc.
Bedford Jct.	0.7	Lawrence	J/MON-SB 245.1
Dark Hollow	3.9	"	
Reed	5.5	"	
Avoca	6.5	"	
Flatwood	10	"	
Springville	11.0	"	
Armstrong	14.8	"	
Owensburg	18.9	Greene	
Dresden	22.2	"	
Robinson	23.8	"	
Koleen	26.3	"	
Rockwood	28.0	"	
Mineral City	29.7	"	
Bloomfield	34.3	"	
Elliston	36.0	"	X/CCC-T 48.0, B/IC-NI 85.2
Switz City	40.5	"	J/PRR-IV 79.8, J/IC-NI 89.4
(continued)			

CONSTRUCTION/ABANDONMENT

Date	Act	End points	MP	Change	Main	Source	Note
1877	B3	Bedford Jct.-Bloomfield	0.7-34.3	+33.6	33.6	1	
1878	B4	Bloomfield-Switz City	34.3-40.5	+6.2	39.8	1	
1935	X	Avoca-Switz City	6.7-40.5	-33.8	6.0	2	
1943	X	Dark Hollow-Avoca	2.5-6.7	-4.2	1.8	2	

1981	X	Bedford Jct.-Dark Hollow	0.7-2.5	-1.8	0	1	

OWNERSHIP

1877	Bedford, Springville, Owensburg & Bloomfield RR (B3) in part
1878	Bloomfield RR (B4) in part. (See also Illinois Central line IC-NE for additional line owned by this company.)
1883/4/24	Bedford & Bloomfield RR, buy BSO&B
1884/3/29	Bedford & Bloomfield RR, buy Bloomfield
1886/4/1	Louisville, New Albany & Chicago Ry, buy B&B
1897	Chicago, Indianapolis & Louisville Ry, reorganize LNA&C
1956/1/10	Monon RR, renamed CI&L
1971/7/31	Louisville & Nashville RR, buy Monon RR

SOUTHERN DIVISION, I & L BRANCH (MON-SL)

	Mileage	County	Crossings, junctions, etc.
Wallace Jct.	0	Owen	
Cataract	6.4	"	
Jordan	12.9	"	
Beamer	15.3	"	
Patricksburg	19.1	"	
Clay City	27.7	Clay	X/CCC-T 25.6
Howesville	35.8	"	
Midland	42.0	Greene	X/MILW-T 206.7, J/MON-SL3 0
Vicksburg	43.1	"	J/MON-SL2 0
Victoria	47.1	"	X/IC-NE 97.6, J/MON-SL4 0
(Crossing)	48.0	"	X/PRR-IG 8.0
Andromeda	54.5	Sullivan	
(continued)			

MONON

SOUTHERN DIVISION, I & L BRANCH (MON-SL) (continued)
CONSTRUCTION/ABANDONMENT

Date	Act	End points	MP	Change	Main	Source	Note
1907	B9	Wallace Jct.-Andromeda	0-54.5	+54.5	54.5	1	
1942	X	At Andromeda	50.2-54.5	-4.3	50.2	3	
1955 ca.	X	Midland-Andromeda	42.0-50.2	-8.2	42.0		

1984	X	Wallace Jct.-Midland	0-42.0	-42.0	0	1	

OWNERSHIP

1907	Indianapolis & Louisville RR (B9), leased to Chicago, Indpls. & Louisv.
1916/12	Chicago, Indianapolis & Louisville Ry, bought Indianapolis & Louisville
1956/1/10	Monon RR, rename of CI&L
1971/7/31	Louisville & Nashville RR, bought Monon RR
1982/12/29	Seaboard System RR, merge Louisville & Nashville
1986/7/1	CSX Transportation, rename Seaboard System

SOUTHERN DIVISION, CASS BRANCH (MON-SL2)

	Mileage	County	Crossings, junctions, etc.
Vicksburg	0	Greene	J/MON-SL 43.1
Cass	5.0	Sullivan	J/IC-NE 103.4

CONSTRUCTION/ABANDONMENT

Date	Act	End points	MP	Change	Main	Source	Note
1907/12/1	B9	Vicksburg-Cass	0-5.0	+5.0	5.0	3	
1945	X	MP 3.0-Cass	3.0-5.0	-2.0	3.0	3	
1947	X	MP 2.4-MP 3.0	2.4-3.0	-0.6	2.4	3	
1955 ca.	X	Vicksburg-MP 2.4	0-2.4	-2.4	0		

OWNERSHIP

1907	Indianapolis & Louisville RR (B9), leased to Chicago, Indpls. & Louisv.
1916/12	Chicago, Indianapolis & Louisville Ry, bought Indianapolis & Louisville

SOUTHERN DIVISION, LATTAS CREEK BRANCH (MON-SL3)

	Mileage	County	Crossings, junctions, etc.
Midland	0	Greene	J/MON-SL 42.0
Lattas Creek	4.0	"	

CONSTRUCTION/ABANDONMENT

Date	Act	End points	MP	Change	Main	Source	Note
1912/6	B9	Midland-Lattas Creek	0-4.0	+4.0	4.0	3	
1942	X	Midland-MP 2.6	0-2.6	-2.6	1.4	3	
1950 ca.	X	MP 2.6-Lattas Creek	2.6-4.0	-1.4	0	3	

OWNERSHIP

1912	Indianapolis & Louisville RR (B9), leased to Chicago, Indpls. & Louisv.
1916/12	Chicago, Indianapolis & Louisville Ry, bought Indianapolis & Louisville

SHIRLEY HILL MINE BRANCH (MON-SL4)

	Mileage	County	Crossings, junctions, etc.
Victoria	0	Greene	J/MON-SL 47.1
Shirley Hill Mine	7.5	"	

CONSTRUCTION/ABANDONMENT

Date	Act	End points	MP	Change	Main	Source	Note
1904/10	B9	Line		0-7.5	+7.5	7.5	S
1950 ca.	X	Line		0-7.5	-7.5	0	

OWNERSHIP

1904	Indianapolis & Louisville RR (B9), leased to Chicago, Indpls. & Louisv.
1916/12	Chicago, Indianapolis & Louisville Ry, bought Indianapolis & Louisville

MONON

SOUTHERN DIVISION, FRENCH LICK BRANCH (MON-F)

	Mileage	County	Crossings, junctions, etc.
Orleans	0	Orange	J/MON-SA 261.5
Lost River	3.8	"	
Paoli	7.6	"	
Braxton	8.6	"	
Glass Rock	11	"	
West Baden	16.6	"	
French Lick	17.7	"	J/SOU-UF 79.0

CONSTRUCTION/ABANDONMENT

Date	Act	End points	MP	Change	Main	Source	Note
1887	B7	Orleans-French Lick	0-17.7	+17.7	17.7	1	

1976	X	Paoli-Frenck Lick	7.7-17.7	-10.0	7.7	1	
1981	X	Orleans-Paoli	0.6-7.7	-7.1	0.6	1	
1990	X	In Orleans	0-0.6	-0.6	0	1	

OWNERSHIP

1887	Orleans, West Baden & French Lick Springs Ry (B7), controlled at inc. by Louisville, New Albany & Chicago
1897/3/31	Chicago, Indianapolis & Louisville Ry, reorganize LNA&C, merged OWB&FLS
1956/1/10	Monon RR, renamed CI&L
1971/7/31	Louisville & Nashville RR, bought Monon RR
1982/12/29	Seaboard System RR, merge Louisville & Nashville
1986/7/1	CSX Transportation, rename Seaboard System

ACQUISITION/DISPOSITION RECORD

Date	Act	MON-	End points	Change	Main	Note
1851	B1	SB	New Albany-Orleans	+56.0	56.0	
1852	B2	SA	Crawfordsille-Lafayette	+27.3	83.3	
1853	B1	SB	Orleans-Harrodsburg	+28.7		
	B1	SBO	Clear Creek-Harrodsburg	+6.7		
	B1	SB	Clear Creek-McDoel	+2.7		
	B1	SA	McDoel-Gosport	+17.6		
	B1	SA	Lafayette-Shops	+2.1		
	B1	N	Shops-Monon	+29.5		
	B1	M	Monon-Michigan City	+60.0	230.6	
1854	B1	SA	Gosport-Crawfordsville	+56.6	287.2	
1877	B3	SS	Bedford Jct.-Bloomfield	+33.6	320.8	
1878	B4	SS	Bloomfield-Switz City	+6.2		
	B5	I	Delphi-Monon	+22.6		
	B5	N	Monon-Rensselaer	+15.4	365.0	
1881	B6	N	Rensselaer-Dyer	+44.0	409.0	
1882	B6	N	Dyer-IL/IN state line	+9.8		
	B6	I	Mass. Ave.-Delphi	+70.7		
	B6	SV	North Y-VI	+1.1	490.6	3
1887	B7	F	Orleans-French Lick	+17.7	508.3	
1899/9/1	B8	SB	Harrodsburg-Clear Creek	+8.6	516.9	
1900	B10	ND	Randle-Kersey	+20.4	537.3	
1901	B10	ND	McCoysburg-Randle	+1.6	538.9	
1902	B10	ND1	Gifford-Crescent	+4.0	542.9	
1903	B10	ND	Kersey-Grape Island	+4.4	547.3	
1904/10	B9	SL4	Victoria-Shirley Hill Mine	+7.5	554.8	
1906	B10	ND	Grape Island-Dinwiddie	+4.8	559.6	
1907	B9	SL	Wallace Jct.-Andromeda	+54.5		
	B9	SL2	Vicksburg-Cass	+5.0	619.1	
1910	X	ND1	Gifford-Crescent	-4.0	615.1	

(continued)

MONON

ACQUISITION/DISPOSITION RECORD (continued)

Date	Act	MON-	End points	Change	Main	Note
1912 ca.	B10	ND	Dinwiddie-MP 36	+4.8		
/6	B9	SL3	Midland-Lattas Creek	+4.0	623.9	
1935/12/5	X	ND	McCoysburg-Dinwiddie	-36.0		5
	X	SS	Avoca-Switz City	-33.8	554.1	
1942	X	SL3	part Lattas Creek Branch	-2.6	551.5	
1943	X	SS	Dark Hollow-Avoca	-4.2	547.3	
1945	X	SBO	Sanders-Harrodsburg	-4.0		
	X	SL2	part Cass Branch	-2.0	541.3	
1947	X	SL2	part Cass Branch	-0.6	540.7	
1948	B11	A	At Cedar Lake	-	540.7	1
1950 ca.	X	SL3	part Lattas Creek Branch	-1.4		
ca.	X	SL4	Victoria-Shirley Hill Mine	-7.5	531.8	
1955 ca.	X	SL	Andromeda-MP 50.2	-12.5		
ca.	X	SL2	part Cass Branch	-2.4	516.9	

On 1971/7/31 the Monon was conveyed to Louisville & Nashville. The Acquisition/-Disposition Record is continued in two places: under Monon and under Louisville & Nashville.

1976	X	F	Paoli-Frenck Lick	-10.0		
	X	I	Belt Jct.-Mass. Ave.	-1.3	505.6	
1980	X	N	Medaryville-Michigan City	-44.8	460.8	
1981	X	SS	Bedford Jct.-Dark Hollow	-1.8		
	X	F	Orleans-Paoli	-7.1	451.9	

Effective 1983/1/1 the Louisville & Nashville merged into the Seaboard System. The Acquisition/Disposition Record for Monon is continued in two places: under Monon and under Seaboard System.

1984	X	SL	Wallace Jct.-Midland	-42.0	409.9	
1985	X	I	Frankfort-Sheridan	-17.9		
	L1	I	Sheridan-Belt Jct.	<25.0>	367.0	
1986 ca.	XL	I	Sheridan-Belt Jct.	<+25.0>		
	X	I	Sheridan-Belt Jct.	-25.0	367.0	

On 1986/7/1 the Seaboard System was renamed CSX Transportation. The Acquisition/-Disposition Record for Monon is continued in two places: under Monon and under CSX Transportation.

1990	X	F	In Orleans	-0.6		
	X	A	Hammond-Airline Jct.	-4.3	362.1	4
1992	X	I	Delphi-Frankfort	-25.3	336.8	
1993	X	A	Airline Jct.-Maynard	-0.1		
	X	SB	Bloomington-Bedford Jct.	-22.5		
	X	SBO	Clear Creek-Sanders	-2.7		
	X	I	Monticello-Delphi	-14.2	297.3	
1994	X	M	In Medaryville	-0.4		
	B12	SAN	In Lafayette	+1.9		
	x	SA	In Lafayette	-2.2		
	X	SA	Cloverdale-Gosport Jct.	-13.1	283.5	
1995	X	SA	Gosport Jct.-Ellettsville	-10.3	273.2	
1997	X	SA	Ellettsville-Hunters	-4.3	268.9	

ACT COLUMN KEY
B1   Built by New Albany & Salem RR
B2   Built by Crawfordsville & Wabash RR
B3   Built by Bedford, Springville, Owensburg & Bloomfield RR
B4   Built by Bloomfield RR
B5   Built by Indianapolis, Delphi & Chicago RR
(continued)

MONON

ACT COLUMN KEY (continued)
B6   Built by Louisville, New Albany & Chicago Ry
B7   Built by Orleans, West Baden & French Lick Springs Ry
B8   Built by Indiana Stone RR
B9   Built by Indianapolis & Louisville Ry B10   Built by Chicago & Wabash Valley RR/Ry
B11   Built by Chicago, Indianapolis & Louisville Ry
B12   Built by CSX Transportation
L1   Leased to Indiana Hi-Rail
X   Abandoned
XL   Lease terminated

SOURCES
1. Indiana, *1995 Indiana State Rail Plan*,
2. Simons, and Parker, *Railroads of Indiana*.
3. Sulzer, *Ghost Railroads of Indiana*.

NOTES
1. Four miles of line in the vicinity of Cedar Lake was relocated in 1948 without a change in overall mileage.
2. The date of construction and/or abandonment could not be determined and this line is not included in the Acquisition/Disposition record.
3. From 1882 to 1900 the Monon used trackage rights over Pennsylvania line PRR-IA between New Albany and Jeffersonville to reach the Louisville Bridge and Louisville Union Depot. After 1900 it began using the Kentucky & Indiana Terminal bridge from VI. Monon line MON-SV was built to connect the main line with both of these facilities.
4. This abandonment was replaced with trackage rights over Grand Trunk Western line GTW-C from Maynard to Thornton Jct. IL.
5. The date shown is the authorization for abandonment by the ICC.

MUNCIE & WESTERN

MAIN LINE (M&W-A)

(Junction)	Mileage 0	County Delaware	Crossings, junctions, etc. J/NKP-LF 67.2			

CONSTRUCTION/ABANDONMENT

Date	Act	End points	MP	Change	Main	Source	Note
1902	B	In Muncie	0-4.9	(+4.9)	(4.9)	1	1
1994	X	In Muncie	0-4.9	(-4.9)	0	1	

OWNERSHIP

1902	Muncie & Western RR

ACQUISITION/DISPOSITION RECORD
See ownership record above for line M&W-A

ACT COLUMN KEY
B   Built by Muncie & Western
X   Abandoned

SOURCES
1. Simons, and Parker, *Railroads of Indiana*.

NOTES
1. This was an industrial road in Muncie, and is not included in the Mileage table.

MUNCIE BELT

MAIN LINE (MUNB-A)

	Mileage	County	Crossings, junctions, etc.
(Junction)	0	Delaware	J/CCC-I 228.4

CONSTRUCTION/ABANDONMENT

Date	Act	End points	MP	Change	Main	Source	Note
no data							

OWNERSHIP

no date	Muncie Belt

ACQUISITION/DISPOSITION RECORD
See ownership record above for line MUNB-A

ACT COLUMN KEY
B Built by Muncie Belt
X Abandoned

SOURCES
1. Simons, and Parker, *Railroads of Indiana.*

NOTES
General. This was an industrial road in Muncie, and is not included in the Mileage table.

NEW JERSEY, INDIANA & ILLINOIS

MAIN LINE (NJI-A)

	Mileage	County	Crossings, junctions, etc.
South Bend	0	St. Joseph	J/GTW-C 99.0
(Crossing)	1.7	"	X/GTW-C 97.5, X/LS-WK 2.67, X/MC-J 0.1
Kizer	4.1	"	
Whartons	6.6	"	
Sweeneys	8.6	"	
Pine	11.6	"	J/WAB-MC 187.4

CONSTRUCTION/ABANDONMENT

Date	Act	End points	MP	Change	Main	Source	Note
1905	B	South Bend-Pine	0-11.6	+11.6	11.6	R	
1981	X	In South Bend	0-2.1	-2.1	9.5	I	

1998	X	South Bend-Pine	2.1-11.6	-9.5	0		

OWNERSHIP

1905	New Jersey, Indiana & Illinois RR (B1)
1926	Wabash RR, purchased NJI&I, operated as separate company
1982	Norfolk Southern, merged NJI&I

ACQUISITION/DISPOSITION RECORD
See ownership record above for line NJI-A

ACT COLUMN KEY
B Built by New Jersey, Indiana & Illinois RR
X Abandoned

SOURCES
1. Indiana, *1995 Indiana State Rail Plan,*
2. Simons, and Parker, *Railroads of Indiana.*

NEW YORK CENTRAL

On 1915/1/1 the New York Central was formed by the merger of a number of companies including Lake Shore & Michigan Southern. From 1915 through 1929 all Indiana all NYC mileage is reported by Lake Shore & Michigan Southern, which see.

On 1930/2/1 the New York Central leased Cleveland, Cincinnati, Chicago & St. Louis (CCC) and Michigan Central (MC). The Acquisition/Disposition Record is continued under each original constituent company. See each such company for detail of changes.

	CCC	LS	MC	P&E	=NYC
1930/2/1	951.3	445.9	79.7	78.9	1556.1
1931 YEAR	938.0	445.9	79.7	78.9	1542.8
1936 YEAR	931.3	445.9	79.7	78.9	1535.8
1942 YEAR	893.2	445.9	65.4	78.9	1483.4
1950 YEAR	890.2	445.9	65.4	78.9	1480.4
1954 YEAR	885.9	445.9	65.4	78.9	1476.1
1958 YEAR	885.9	441.0	59.8	78.9	1465.6
1960 YEAR	885.9	432.3	59.8	78.9	1456.9
1961 YEAR	878.2	432.3	59.8	78.9	1449.2
1968/2/1	878.2	432.3	59.8	78.9	1449.2

On 1968/2/1 New York Central was conveyed to Penn Central. The Acquisition/Disposition Record is continued under each original constituent company and under Penn Central.

NEW YORK, CHICAGO & ST. LOUIS

FORT WAYNE DIVISION (NKP-F)

	Mileage [Buffalo]	County	Crossings, junctions, etc.
Bellevue OH	248.5		
Payne OH	349.8		
(OH/IN state line)	354.0		
Edgerton	354.1	Allen	
New Haven	365.0	"	
NE	365.4	"	X/WAB-M 140.5
East Wayne Yard	366.3	"	
Four Mile Road	367.2	"	
Fort Wayne	371.6	"	J/NKP-C 371.6--(J/NKP-LF 0)

CONSTRUCTION/ABANDONMENT

Date	Act	End points	MP	Change	Main	Source	Note
1881/11/3	B15	OH state line-Ft. Wayne	354.0-371.6	+17.6	17.6	1,2	

OWNERSHIP
1881	New York, Chicago & St. Louis Ry (B15),
1882/10/26 to 1922/7	NYC&SL controlled by New York Central
1922/7	New York, Chicago & St. Louis RR, bought NYC&SL Ry
1964/10/16	Norfolk & Western Ry, bought New York, Chicago & St. Louis
1982/6/1	Norfolk Southern Corp., acquired Norfolk & Western

NEW YORK, CHICAGO & ST. LOUIS

CHICAGO DIVISION (NKP-C)

	Mileage [Buffalo]	County	Crossings, junctions, etc.
Fort Wayne	371.6	Allen	J/NKP-F 371.6
West Wayne	372.6	"	X/LS-TF 97.4
Runnion Avenue	372.7	"	
(Crossing)	373.0	"	X/PRR-GS 94.1
(Bridge)	375.2	"	B/PRR-F 324.6
Hadley	377.4	"	
Dunfee	381.9	Whitley	
Raber	386.9	"	
Peabody	389.9	"	
Arnolds	393	"	
South Whitley	397.2	"	X/PRR-LE 47.1
Sidney	403.3	Kosciusko	
Packertown	406.3	"	
Claypool	410.9	"	X/CCC-M 87.5
Burket	415.9	"	
Mentone	419.8	"	X/WIN-A 35.7
Clemer	420.8	"	
Tippecanoe	424.4	Marshall	
Argos	431.0	"	X/NKP-LM 110.1
Rutland	437.3	"	
Hibbard	438.9	"	X/PRR-LS 151.7
Burr Oak	440.4	"	
Ober	445.6	Starke	
Knox	451.5	"	X/LS-WK 33.93
Brems	436.4	"	
Thomaston	463.0	LaPorte	X/PM-W 6.1
South Wanatah	468.0	"	X/MON-M 37.7
Nickel	473.9	Porter	
Valparaiso	477.0	"	
Spriggsboro	480.7	"	
(Crossing)	481.4	"	X/GTW-C 52.6
Wheeler	484.6	"	
(Junction)	487.5	"	J/PRR-F 433.8
Hobart	488.3	Lake	X/EJE-A 45.3
South Gary	493.2	"	X/MC-WJ 5.4
Van Loon	497.9	"	X/EJE-G 3.5
Osborn	500.3	"	X/LS-WD 5.05, J/IHB-AS 0.9
Hammond	503.8	"	X/MC-W 264.9, X/IHB-A 6.9, J/ERIE-C 248.5, J/MON-A 20.8, X/EJE-GS 5.8
(IN/IL state line)	504.7		
State Line IL	504.7		

CONSTRUCTION/ABANDONMENT

Date	Act	End points	MP	Change	Main	Source	Note
1882/10/23	B15	Ft. Wayne- IL state line	371.6-504.7	+133.1	133.1	1	

OWNERSHIP

1882	New York, Chicago & St. Louis Ry (B15),
1882/10/26 to 1922/7	controlled by New York Central owners
1922/7	New York, Chicago & St. Louis RR, bought NYC&SL Ry
1964/10/16	Norfolk & Western Ry, bought New York, Chicago & St. Louis
1982/6/1	Norfolk Southern Corp., acquired Norfolk & Western

NEW YORK, CHICAGO & ST. LOUIS

CLOVER LEAF, DISTRICT 2 (NKP-TB)

	Mileage	County	Crossings, junctions, etc.
Toledo OH	0		
Wilshire OH	99.5		
(OH/IN state line)	99.9		
Pleasant Mills	102.7	Adams	
Decatur	108.2	"	
DA	108.5	"	X/PRR-GR 70.4
Peterson	113.1	"	
Curryville	116.6	Wells	
Craigville	117.8	"	
Bluffton	123.4	"	X/NKP-LF 25.4, X/CBC-A 23
Liberty Centre	129.4	"	
Buckeye	133.3	Huntington	
Warren	137.2	"	
Van Buren	143.9	Grant	
Landess	146.5	"	
Hanfield	147.6	"	
Marion	153.5	"	
(Crossing)	153.8	"	X/CCC-M 133.0
Kent	154.2	"	X/PRR-L 157.2
(Bridge)	154.9	"	B/C&O-C 132.8
Roseburgh	159.2	"	
Herbst	162.2	"	X/PRR-CM 5.9
Swayzee	164.2	"	
Sims	165.9	"	
Sycamore	169.0	Howard	
Greentown	171.9	"	
Vermont	175.7	"	
(Crossing)	180.9	"	X/PRR-CR 159.3
Kokomo	181.1	"	X/NKP-LM 54.4
Middletons	187.0	"	
Russiaville	190.4	"	
Forest	194.6	Clinton	
Michigantown	199.0	"	
Averys	201.9	"	
(Junction)	206.0	"	J/NKP-LP 234.0
Frankfort	206.2	"	J/NKP-TC 206.2

CONSTRUCTION/ABANDONMENT

Date	Act	End points	MP	Change	Main	Source	Note
1874/8/10	B11	Kokomo-Frankfort	181.1-206.2	+25.1	25.1	1,4	2,3,6
1878/10/11	B12	Bluffton-Warren	123.4-137.2	+13.8	38.9	4	3
1879	B13	OH state line-Bluffton	99.9-123.4	+23.5	62.4	2	3,4
1880/12/2	B13	Warren-Marion	137.2-153.5	+16.3	88.7	4	3,4
1881/7/24	B13	Marion-Kokomo	153.5-181.1	+27.6	106.3	4	3,4

1989/8/14	L5	Marion-Frankfort	153.8-206.2	<52.4>		4	
1989	L3	Douglas OH-Marion	99.9-153.8	<53.9>	0	4	
1997	X	OH state line-Craigville	99.9-117.8	<-17.9>	0	4	
1998	S3	Craigville-Van Buren	117.8-144.2	<[26.4]>			
1998	XL	Kokomo-Frankfort	183.5-206.2	<+22.7>	22.7		

OWNERSHIP

1874	Frankfort & Kokomo RR (B11)
1878	Delphos, Bluffton & Frankfort RR (B12)
1879/4/21	Toledo, Delphos & Burlington RR (B13), merge Delphos, Bluffton & Frankfort
1881/5/20	Toledo, Cincinnati & St. Louis RR, buy Frankfort & Kokomo.

(continued)

NEW YORK, CHICAGO & ST. LOUIS

CLOVER LEAF, DISTRICT 2 (NKP-TB) (continued)
OWNERSHIP

1882/1/23	Toledo, Cincinnati & St. Louis RR, buy Toledo, Delphos & Burlington RR
1886/6/12	Toledo, St. Louis & Kansas City RR, reorganize Toledo, Cinci. & St. L.
1900/7/9	Toledo, St. Louis & Western RR, reorganize Toledo, St. Louis & K. C.
1923/6/18	New York, Chicago & St. Louis RR, buy Toledo, St. Louis & Western
1964/10/16	Norfolk & Western Ry, buy New York, Chicago & St. Louis
1982/6/1	Norfolk Southern Corp., acquire Norfolk & Western

CLOVER LEAF, DISTRICT 3 (NKP-TC)

	Mileage [Toledo]	County	Crossings, junctions, etc.
Frankfort	206.2	Clinton	J/NKP-TB 206.2
(Crossing)	206.6	"	X/PRR-IF 78.1
(Crossing)	206.7	"	X/MON-I 136.0
(Junction)	207.9	"	J/NKP-LP 235.9
Jefferson	210.4	"	
Fickle	215.0	"	
Clark's Hill	217.8	Tippecanoe	X/CCC-H 158.9
Kirkpatrick	223.7	Montgomery	
Linden	228.5	"	X/MON-SA 137.0
New Richmond	232.4	"	
Wingate	237.7	"	
Mellott	241.7	Fountain	
Graham	244.5	"	
Veedersburg	249.1	"	X/CAS-A 95.7, X/P&E-A 64.7
Mackie	253.1	"	
Indio	256	"	
Cates	258.5	"	
Silverwood	263.2	"	
(Junction)	264.8	Vermillion	J/NKP-TC1 0, J/NKP-TC2 0
Cayuga	266.5	"	X/CEI-E 141.1
(IN/IL state line)	270.9		
Humrick IL	271.9		
Charleston IL	319.0		
(St. Louis MO	453.6)		

CONSTRUCTION/ABANDONMENT

Date	Act	End points	MP	Change	Main	Source	Note
1879	B14	Frankfort-Clark's Hill	206.2-217.8	+11.6	11.6	2,4	
1881	B14	Clark's Hill-IL state line	217.8-270.9	+53.1	64.7	4	

1987	X	Linden-IL state line	231.2-270.9	-39.7	25.0	2,4	
1988	X	Frankfort-Linden	209.3-231.2	-21.9		2	
1988	Y	In Frankfort	206.2-209.3	(3.1)	0		

OWNERSHIP

1879	Frankfort & State Line RR (B14)
1881/7	Toledo, Cincinnati & St. Louis RR, bought Frankfort & State Line
1886/6/12	Toledo, St. Louis & Kansas City RR, reorganized Toledo, Cinci. & St. L.
1900/7/9	Toledo, St. Louis & Western RR, reorganized Toledo, St. Louis & K. C.
1923/6/18	New York, Chicago & St. Louis RR, bought Toledo, St. Louis & Western
1964/10/16	Norfolk & Western Ry, bought New York, Chicago & St. Louis
1982/6/1	Norfolk Southern Corp., acquired Norfolk & Western

NEW YORK, CHICAGO & ST. LOUIS

CAYUGA MINE SPUR (NKP-TC1)

	Mileage	County	Crossings, junctions, etc.
(Junction)	0	Vermillion	J/NKP-TC 264.8
Cayuga Mine	1.2	"	

CONSTRUCTION/ABANDONMENT

Date	Act	End points	MP	Change	Main	Source	Note
							11

INDIANA BITUMINOUS COAL MINE SPUR (NKP-TC12)

	Mileage	County	Crossings, junctions, etc.
(Junction)	0	Vermillion	J/NKP-TC 264.8
Indiana Bituminous Coal Mine	0.8	"	

CONSTRUCTION/ABANDONMENT

Date	Act	End points	MP	Change	Main	Source	Note
							11

FORT WAYNE-CONNERSVILLE (NKP-LF)

	Mileage	County	Crossings, junctions, etc.
(Fort Wayne)	0)	Allen	
--via NKP-C and LS-TF			
(Junction)	1.6	"	J/LS-TF 98.0
Hugo	3.5	"	X/WAB-M 149.2
Ferguson	8.3	"	
Yoder	12.1	"	
Ossian	15.6	Wells	
Kingsland	19.0	"	X/ERIE-C 109.4
Bluffton	25.4	"	X/NKP-TB 123.4, X/CBC-A 23
Poneto	31.5	"	
Keystone	36.3	"	
Montpelier	39.3	Blackford	
Hartford City	47.4	"	X/PRR-L 138.1
Eaton	55.0	Delaware	
Shideler	57.4	"	
Royerton	60.4	"	
(Crossing)	62.3	"	X/C&O-C 105.0
(Crossing)	62.4	"	X/PRR-CM 40.9
Muncie	65.7	"	
(Crossing)	65.8	"	X/CCC-I 229.7, X/NKP-LS 173.8
(Junction)	66.7	"	J/CI-A 0
(Junction)	67.2	"	J/M&W-A 0
Cowan	71.6	"	
Oakville	73.5	"	
Springport	75.7	Henry	
Mount Summit	78.6	"	
Rhein	80	"	
Foley	80.8	"	J/PRR-CR 104.1
--via PRR-CR			
Broad	83.0	"	J/PRR-CR 101.9
New Castle	84.0	"	J/NKP-LR 84.0
New Lisbon	91.1	"	
Cambridge City	97.2	Wayne	X/PRR-I 135.1
(Crossing)	97.3	"	X/PRR-ICA 63.3
Milton	99.0	"	
Beesons	103.7	"	J/CCC-GW 74.1
Connersville	109.0	Fayette	J/B&O-IH 67.3
(continued)			

NEW YORK, CHICAGO & ST. LOUIS

FORT WAYNE-CONNERSVILLE (NKP-LF) (continued)
CONSTRUCTION/ABANDONMENT

Date	Act	End points	MP	Change	Main	Source	Note
1865	B5	Connersville-New Castle	109.0-84.0	+25.0	25.0	I	
1868	B6	New Castle-Broad	84.0-83.0	+1.0		I	9
1868	B6	Foley-Muncie	80.8-65.7	+15.1	41.1	I	9
1870	B7	Muncie-Fort Wayne	65.7-1.6	+64.1	105.2	I	
1953	X	In Muncie	62.3-65.8	-3.5	101.7	R	

1989	L3	New Castle-Beesons	84.0-103.7	[19.7]		R	
1989 ca.	X	Beesons-Connersville	103.7-109.0	-5.3	76.7		

OWNERSHIP

1865	Connersville & New Castle Junction RR (B5), of part
1868/1/2	Cincinnati, Connersville & Muncie RR (B6), merged C&NCJ
1869/6/8	Fort Wayne, Muncie & Cincinnati RR (B7), merged CC&M
1881/12/6	Fort Wayne, Cincinnati & Louisville RR, reorganized FWM&C
1890/5/28	Lake Erie & Western Ry, acquired Fort Wayne, Cincinnati & Louisville
1900/2/20	LE&W operated by Lake Shore & Michigan Southern
1922/7	New York, Chicago & St. Louis RR, bought Lake Erie & Western
1964/10/16	Norfolk & Western Ry, bought New York, Chicago & St. Louis
1982/6/1	Norfolk Southern Corp., acquired Norfolk & Western

RUSHVILLE BRANCH (NKP-LR)

	Mileage [Fort Wayne]	County	Crossings, junctions, etc.
New Castle	84.0	Henry	J/NKP-LF 84.0
Spiceland	91.7	"	
Dunreith	94.1	"	X/PRR-I 148.9
Mays	98.2	Rush	
Sexton	101.2	"	
(Junction)	107.2	"	J/CCC-M 203.8
Rushville	107.9	"	J/B&O-IH 85.4

CONSTRUCTION/ABANDONMENT

Date	Act	End points	MP	Change	Main	Source	Note
1881	B8	New Castle-Rushville	84.0-107.2	+23.2	23.2	2	

1973	P1	In Rushville	107.2-107.9	+0.7	23.9		
1984 ca.	S2	New Castle-Rushville	84.0-107.9	[23.9]	0		
1989	X	New Castle-Mays	84.0-96.2	[-12.2]	0	4	9
1990	X	Mays-Sexton	96.2-101.0	[-4.8]	0	4	
1993/10/1	T	Sexton-Rushville	101.0-107.9	[6.9]	0	4	

OWNERSHIP

1881	New Castle & Rushville RR (B8), controlled by Ft. Wayne, Cinci. & Louisv.
1886/11/11	Fort Wayne, Cincinnati & Louisville RR, merged New Castle & Rushville
1890/5/28	Lake Erie & Western Ry, acquired Fort Wayne, Cincinnati & Louisville
1922/7	New York, Chicago & St. Louis RR, bought Lake Erie & Western
1964/10/16	Norfolk & Western Ry, bought New York, Chicago & St. Louis
1973	Norfolk & Western, bought part from Penn Central
1982/6/1	Norfolk Southern Corp., acquired Norfolk & Western

ELWOOD, ANDERSON & LAPEL (NKP-YE)

	Mileage	County	Crossings, junctions, etc.
(Junction)	0	Madison	J/NKP-LS
(End)	1.1	"	
(continued)			

NEW YORK, CHICAGO & ST. LOUIS

ELWOOD, ANDERSON & LAPEL (NKP-YE) (continued)
CONSTRUCTION/ABANDONMENT

Date	Act	End points	MP	Change	Main	Source	Note
1892	B15	In Elwood	0-1.1	(+1.1)	0	4	
1930 ca.	X	In Elwood	0-1.1	(-1.1)	0		

OWNERSHIP

1892	Elwood, Anderson & Lapel (B15)
1929	New York, Chicago & St. Louis, buy Elwood, Anderson & Lapel

I & MC DIVISION (NKP-LM)

	Mileage	County	Crossings, junctions, etc.
(Indianapolis)	0)	Marion	
--via IU-E			
(Junction)	0.8)	"	
--via CCC-I			
Massachusetts Avenue	1.9	"	J/CCC-I 281.9
(Junction)	3.2	"	J/IU-C 2.0
Malott Park	7.4	"	
Castleton	12.1	"	
Fishers	16.2	Hamilton	
New Britton	17.2	"	
(Crossing)	22.0	"	X/CI-A 37.2
Noblesville	22.2	"	
Cicero	28.6	"	
Arcadia	31.6	"	
Atlanta	34.5	"	
Tipton	39.7	Tipton	X/NKP-LP/LS 209.3
Sharpsville	46.3	"	
Fairfield	49.2	Howard	
Kokomo (old)	54.4	"	
Kokomo (new)	54.5	"	X/NKP-TB 181.1
Kokomo Jct.	54.8	"	X/PRR-CR 159.6
Cassville	59.2	"	
Bennetts	61.0	Miami	
Miami	63.0	"	
Bunker Hill	66.2	"	X/PRR-L 182.2
(Crossing)	72.6	"	X/C&O-C 163.5
Peru	73.9	"	adj. WAB-M 202.5
(Crossing)	74.2	"	X/WAB-M 202.2
Peru Yard	74.3	"	
Doyle	77.7	"	
Courter	79.8	"	
Denver	81.9	"	x/PRR-LE 18.2
Deeds	85.4	"	
Macy	89.0	"	
Wagoners	91.5	Fulton	
Rochester	97.7	"	
RS	98.2	"	X/ERIE-C 167.9
Tiosa	104.0	"	
Walnut	105.6	Marshall	
Argos	110.1	"	X/NKP-C 431.0
Plymouth	118.3	"	X/PRR-C 383.9, X/PRR-LS 159.0
Tyner	125.0	"	
Walkerton	130.7	St.Joseph	
KN	130.9	"	X/B&O-C 199.1, X/LS-WK 19.5
Kankakee	135.5	LaPorte	
Kingsbury	136.9	"	
(continued)			

NEW YORK, CHICAGO & ST. LOUIS

I & MC DIVISION (NKP-LM) (continued)

	Mileage [Indianapolis]	County	Crossings, junctions, etc.
Kingsbury	136.9	LaPorte	
Walnut	105.6	Marshall	
Dillon	137.3	"	X/WAB-MC 200.5
Stillwell	139.6	"	X/GTW-C 80.17
LaPorte Jct.	146.3	"	X/LS-W 462.39
LaPorte	147.5	"	
Belfast	149.5	"	X/PM-W 26.50
Oakwood	152.4	"	
Roeske	155	"	
(Bridge)	156.6	"	B/PM-C 122.9
(Crossing)	157.3	"	X/CSS-A 32.5
(Junction)	159.0	"	J/MC-W 228.4
--via MC-W			
(Michigan City)	159.4)	"	

CONSTRUCTION/ABANDONMENT

Date	Act	End points	MP	Change	Main	Source	Note
1851/3/10	B1	Noblesville-Indianapolis	22.2-1.9	+20.3	20.3	1	
1853	B1	Peru-Noblesville	73.9-22.2	+51.7	72.0	1	
1855	B2	LaPorte-Plymouth	147.5-118.3	+29.2	101.2	2	
1869/9/4	B3	Plymouth-Peru	118.3-73.9	+44.4	145.6	1,2	
1871/4/9	B4	Michigan City-LaPorte	159.0-147.5	+11.5	157.1	1	

1974	X	In Indianapolis	1.9-2.1	-0.2	156.9	2	
1989	L5	Tipton-Argos	39.7-108.6	<68.9>			
1989	SL	Peru-Argos	73.9-108.6	<<34.7>>88.0			
1990	L6	Indianapolis-Tipton	2.1-39.7	<37.6>	50.4		
1996 ca.	LA1	Indianapolis-Tipton	2.1-39.7	<<37.6>>			
1996 ca.	XL	Kokomo-Argos	57.5-108.6	<+51.1>			
1996 ca.	X	Kokomo-Rochester	57.5-95.6	-38.1	63.4		
1997 ca.	L7	Kingsbury-Michigan City	135.5-159.0	<23.5>	39.9		
1998 ca.	S4	Rochester-Argos	95.6-108.6	[13.0]	26.9		

OWNERSHIP

1851	Peru & Indianapolis RR (B1), of part
1854	Madison & Indianapolis, lease Peru & Indianapolis
1855	Cincinnati, Peru & Chicago Ry (B2), of part
1862/3/28	Indianapolis & Madison, reorganize Madison & Indianapolis (with lease of Peru & Indpls.)
1864/3/11	Indianapolis, Peru & Chicago Ry, reorganize Peru & Indianapolis
1867/9/6	Chicago, Cincinnati & Louisville RR (B3), reorganize Cinci., Peru & Chicago and terminate lease of Madison & Indianapolis
1871	Michigan City & Indianapolis RR (B4), of part
1871/5/12	Indianapolis, Peru & Chicago Ry, buy Chicago, Cincinnati & Louisville
1871	Indianapolis, Peru & Chicago Ry, operate Michigan City & Indianapolis
1881/9	Wabash, St. Louis & Pacific, leased Indpls., Peru & Chicago
1886/11/13	lease by Wabash, St. Louis & Pacific terminated
1886/11/13	Lake Erie & Western Ry, buy Michigan City & Indianapolis
1887/3/30	Lake Erie & Western Ry, buy Chicago, Cincinnati & Louisville
1887/4/8	Lake Erie & Western Ry, buy Indianapolis, Peru & Chicago
1922/7	New York, Chicago & St. Louis RR, buy Lake Erie & Western
1964/10/16	Norfolk & Western Ry, bouy New York, Chicago & St. Louis
1982/6/1	Norfolk Southern Corp., acquire Norfolk & Western

NEW YORK, CHICAGO & ST. LOUIS

SANDUSKY DIVISION (NKP-LS)

	Mileage	County	Crossings, junctions, etc.
Sandusky OH	0		
Fort Recovery OH	134.8		
(OH/IN state line)	136.3		
Brice	141.1	Jay	
(Crossing)	145.7	"	X/PRR-GR 42.9
Portland	145.8	"	
(Crossing)	146	"	X/CBC-A 51
Blaine	150.4	"	
Red Key	156.7	"	X/PRR-L 124.9
Niles	161.0	Delaware	
Albany	162.5	"	
DeSoto	167.2	"	
(Bridge)	172.4	"	B/C&O-C 102.7
(Junction)	172.7	"	J/PRR-CM 0
Muncie	173.7	"	
(Crossing)	173.8	"	X/NKP-LF 65.8
Cammack	179.7	"	
Gilman	184.4	Madison	
Alexandria	189.9	"	X/CCC-M 153.8
Orestes	192.6	"	
Dundee	194.1	"	
Elwood	198.7	"	X/PRR-CR 137.5
Hobbs	204.4	Tipton	
Tipton	209.3	"	J/NKP-LP 209.3, X/NKP-LM 39.7

CONSTRUCTION/ABANDONMENT

Date	Act	End points	MP	Change	Main	Source	Note
1876/2/11	B9	Muncie-Tipton	173.7-209.3	+35.6	35.6	4	
1879	B10	OH state line-Muncie	136.3-173.7	+37.4	73.0	2	

1993/8/21	L4	Lima OH-Portland	136.3-145.8	<9.5>	63.5	4	

OWNERSHIP

1876	Lafayette, Muncie & Bloomington RR (B9), of part
1879/4/3	Muncie & State Line RR, reorganize LM&B
1879/4/30	Lafayette, Bloomington & Muncie, merge Muncie & State Line and other companies
1879/12/11	Lake Erie & Western Ry (B10), merge LB&M
1922/7	New York, Chicago & St. Louis RR, buy Lake Erie & Western
1964/10/16	Norfolk & Western Ry, buy New York, Chicago & St. Louis
1982/6/1	Norfolk Southern Corp., acquire Norfolk & Western

PEORIA DIVISION (NKP-LP)

	Mileage [Sandusky OH]	County	Crossings, junctions, etc.
Tipton	209.3	Tipton	J/NKP-LS 209.3, X/NKP-LM 39.7
Goldsmith	215.0	"	
Kempton	219.2	"	
Scircleville	222.9	Clinton	
Hillisburg	225.1	"	
Boyleston	228.0	"	
(Junction)	234.0	"	J/NKP-TB 206.0
Frankfort	234.2	"	
(Crossing)	234.6	"	X/PRR-IF 78.6
(Crossing)	234.7	"	X/MON-I 131.0
(Junction)	235.9	"	J/NKP-TC 207.9
Deniston	239.2	"	
(continued)			

NEW YORK, CHICAGO & ST. LOUIS

PEORIA DIVISION (NKP-LP) (continued)

	Mileage [Sandusky OH]	County	Crossings, junctions, etc.
Deniston	139.2	Clinton	
Mulberry	243.5	"	
Dayton	249.5	Tippecanoe	
Altamont	254.7	"	J/CCC-H 170.2
Lafayette Jct.	257.7	"	X/MON-SA 121.5, X/WAB-P 257.2
Lafayette	258.7	"	
(Bridge)	258.8	"	B/MON-SAN 120.2
Montmorenci	267.6	"	
Otterbein	271.2	Benton	
Templeton	277.3	"	J/CCC-H 192.6
Oxford	279.4	"	X/CAS-A 66.2
Fargo	281.1	"	
Chase	284.3	"	
Boswell	286.6	"	
Talbot	290.6	"	
Handy	291.5	"	X/LS-WD 80.37
Ambia	293.9	"	
(IN/IL state line)	294.4		
Cheneyville IL	298.0		
Peoria IL	415.5		

CONSTRUCTION/ABANDONMENT

Date	Act	End points	MP	Change	Main	Source	Note
1871/11	B9	Lafayette-Templeton	258.7-277.3	+18.6	18.6	R	
1872	B9	Templeton-IL state line	277.3-294.4	+17.1		I	1
1872	L1	Lafayette-IL state line	258.7-294.4	<35.7>	0		
1876	XL	Lafayette-IL state line	258.7-294.4	<+35.7>	35.7		
1876/2/11	B9	Tipton-Lafayette	209.3-258.7	+49.4	85.1	R	

1989	S1	Lafayette-Cheneyville IL	262.2-294.4	-32.2	52.9	R	

OWNERSHIP

1871	Lafayette, Muncie & Bloomington RR (B9), of part
1879/4/3	Muncie & State Line RR, reorganize LM&B
1879/4/30	Lafayette, Bloomington & Muncie, merged Muncie & State Line and other co.
1879/12/11	Lake Erie & Western Ry (B10), merged LB&M
1922/7	New York, Chicago & St. Louis RR, bought Lake Erie & Western
1964/10/16	Norfolk & Western Ry, bought New York, Chicago & St. Louis
1982/6/1	Norfolk Southern Corp., acquired Norfolk & Western

ACQUISITION/DISPOSITION RECORD

Date	Act	NKP-	End points	Change	Main	Note
--Lake Erie & Western trackage						
1851/3/10	B1	LM	Noblesville-Indianapolis	+20.3	20.3	
1853	B1	LM	Peru-Noblesville	+51.7	72.0	
1855	B2	LM	LaPorte-Plymouth	+29.2	101.2	
1865	B5	LF	Connersville-New Castle	+25.0	126.2	
1868	B6	LF	New Castle-Broad	+1.0		9
	B6	LF	Foley-Muncie	+15.1	142.3	
1869/9/14	B3	LM	Plymouth-Peru	+44.4	186.7	
1870	B7	LF	Muncie-Fort Wayne	+64.1	250.8	
1871/4/9	B4	LM	Michigan City-LaPorte	+11.5		
/11	B9	LP	Lafayette-Templeton	+18.6	280.9	
1872	B9	LP	Templeton-IL state line	+17.1		
	L1	LP	Lafayette-IL state line	<35.7>	262.3	1

(continued)

NEW YORK, CHICAGO & ST. LOUIS

ACQUISITION/DISPOSITION RECORD (continued)

Date	Act	NKP-	End points	Change	Main	Note
--Lake Erie & Western trackage						
1876	XL	LP	Lafayette-IL state line	<+35.7>		
/2/11	B9	LP	Lafayette-Tipton	+49.4		
/2/11	B9	LS	Muncie-Tipton	+35.6	383.0	
1879	B10	LS	OH state line-Muncie	+37.4	420.4	
1881	B8	LR	New Castle-Rushville	+23.2		
/9	L2	LM	Indianapolis-Michigan City	<157.1>	286.5	5
1886/11	XL	LM	Indianapolis-Michigan City	<+157.1>	443.6	8
--Toledo, St. Louis & Western trackage						
1874/8/10	B11	TB	Kokomo-Frankfort	+25.1	25.1	2,3,6
1878/10/14	B12	TB	Bluffton-Warren	+13.8	38.9	3
1879	B13	TB	OH state line-Bluffton	+23.5		3
	B14	TC	Frankfort-Clark's Hill	+11.6	74.0	
1880/12/12	B13	TB	Warren-Marion	+16.3	90.3	3,4
1881/7/24	B13	TB	Marion-Kokomo	+27.6		4
1881	B14	TC	Clark's Hill-IL state line	+53.1	171.0	
--New York, Chicago & St. Louis trackage						
1881/11/3	B15	F	OH state line-Ft. Wayne	+17.6	17.6	
1882/10/23	B15	C	Ft. Wayne- IL state line	+133.1	150.7	7
			TOTAL LE&W =443.6 TL&W =171.0 NYC&SL =150.7 NKP =765.3			
--merged lines						
1953	X	LF	In Muncie	-3.5	761.8	

On 1964/10/16 this company was conveyed to Norfolk & Western. Its Acquisition/-Disposition Record is continued in two places: under New York, Chicago & St. Louis and under Norfolk & Western.

1973	P1	LR	In Rushville	+0.7	762.5	
1974	X	LM	In Indianapolis	-0.2	762.3	

On 1982/6/1 Norfolk & Western was conveyed to Norfolk Southern. Its Acquisition/-Disposition Record is continued in two places: under New York, Chicago & St. Louis and under Norfolk Southern.

1984 ca.	L3	LR	New Castle-Rushville	<23.9>	738.4	
1987	X	TC	Linden-IL state line	-39.7	698.7	
1988	X	TC	Frankfort-Linden	-21.9		
	Y	TC	In Frankfort	(3.1)	673.7	
1989	X	LR	New Castle-Mays	<-12.2>		9,10
	S1	LP	Lafayette-Cheneyville IL	[32.2]		
	L3	LF	New Castle-Beesons	[19.7]		
	X	LF	Beesons-Connersville	-5.3		
	L5	LM	Tipton-Argos	<68.9>		
	SL	LM	Peru-Argos	<<34.7>>		
	L6	TB	Marion-Frankfort	<52.4>		
	L3	TB	Douglas OH-Marion	<53.9>	441.3	
1990	L6	LM	Indianapolis-Tipton	<37.6>		
	X	LR	Mays-Sexton	<-4.8>	403.7	
1993/8/21	L4	LS	OH state line-Portland	<9.5>		
/10/1	T	LR	Sexton-Rushville	[7.9]	386.3	
1996 ca.	L4.1	LM	Indianapolis-Tipton	<<37.6>>		
ca.	XL	LM	Kokomo-Argos	<+51.1>		
ca.	X	LM	Kokomo-Rochester	-38.1	399.3	
1997	L7	LM	Kingsbury-Michigan City	<23.5>		
	X	TB	OH state line-Craigville	<-17.9>	375.8	
1998	S4	LM	Rochester-Argos	[13.0]		
	S3	TB	Craigville-Van Buren	<[26.4]>		
	XL	TB	Kokomo-Frankfort	<+22.7>	385.5	

NEW YORK, CHICAGO & ST. LOUIS

ACT COLUMN KEY
B1   Built by Peru & Indianapolis RR
B2   Built by Cincinnati, Peru & Chicago Ry
B3   Built by Chicago, Cincinnati & Louisville RR
B4   Built by Michigan City & Indianapolis RR
B5   Built by Connersville & New Castle Junction RR
B6   Built by Cincinnati, Connersville & Muncie RR
B7   Built by Fort Wayne, Muncie & Cincinnati RR
B8   Built by New Castle & Rushville RR
B9   Built by Lafayette, Muncie & Bloomington RR
B10   Built by Lake Erie & Western Ry
B11   Built by Frankfort & Kokomo RR
B12   Built by Delphos, Bluffton & Frankfort RR
B13   Built by Toledo, Delphos & Burlington RR
B14   Built by Frankfort & State Line RR
B15   Built by Elwood, Anderson & Lapel RR
L1   Leased to Toledo, Wabash & Western
L2   Leased to Wabash, St. Louis & Pacific
L3   Leased to Indiana Hi-Rail
L4   Leased to R. J. Corman
L5   Leased to Central RR of Indianapolis
L6   Leased to Indiana RR
L7   Leased to Chicago South Shore & South Bend
LA1   Lease assigned to Indiana Transportation Museum
P1   Purchased from Penn Central
S1   Sold to Kankakee, Beaverville & Southern RR
S2   Sold to Indiana Hi-Rail
S3   Sold to Wabash Central
S4   Sold to Fulton County
SL   Subleased to Indiana Hi-Rail
T   Transferred to Honey Creek
X   Abandoned
XL   Lease terminated

SOURCES
1. Hampton, *The Nickel Plate Road.*
2. Indiana, *1995 Indiana State Rail Plan.*
3. Rehor, *The Nickel Plate Story.*
4. Simons and Parker, *Railroads of Indiana.*

NOTES
   1. The segment between Lafayette and the IL state line was leased to the Toledo, Wabash & Western from 1872 until 1876.
   2. The Frankfort-Kokomo segment was built to standard gauge and converted to narrow gauge in 1881.
   3. This line was built to narrow gauge and converted to standard gauge in 1887.
   4. Source 4 states Toledo-Kokomo through service began July 24, 1881.
   5. The entire line was leased to the Wabash, St. Louis & Pacific from Sept. 1881 until Nov. 1886.
   6. Source 1 states this line was opened to regular service July 4, 1875.
   7. In Oct. 1882 control of the entire New York, Chicago & St. Louis property was obtained by the Vanderbilt family and ownership assigned to the Lake Shore & Michigan Southern. This control ended with the July 1922 Interstate Commerce Commission order requiring the LS&MS to divest itself of the NYC&SL.
   8. In Feb. 1900 control of the entire Lake Erie & Western property was obtained by the New York Central & Hudson River and ownership assigned 50% to itself and 50% to the Lake Shore & Michigan Southern. This control ended with the July 1922 Interstate Commerce Commission order for the LS&MS to divest itself of the NYC&SL.
   9. This construction included trackage rights on Pennsylvania line PRR-CR.
   10. Approximately 1.2 miles in New Castle was retained as yard track.
   11. The dates of construction or abandonment could not be determined and this line is not included in the Acquisition/Disposition Record.

NORFOLK & WESTERN

ACQUISITION/DISPOSITION RECORD

On 1964/10/16 Norfolk & Western acquired New York, Chicago & St. Louis. The Acquisition/Disposition Record is continued in two places: under New York, Chicago & St. Louis and under Norfolk & Western. The property acquired was:

Line desig. N&W-	End points	MP	Main	Note
[NKP-C]	Fort Wayne-Chicago IL	371.6-504.7	133.1	
[NKP-F]	Bellevue OH-Fort Wayne	354.0-371.6	17.6	
[NKP-LF]	Fort Wayne-Muncie	1.6-62.3	60.7	
[NKP-LF]	Muncie-Foley	65.8-80.8	15.0	
[NKP-LF]	Broad-Connersville	83.0-109.0	26.0	
[NKP-LR]	New Castle-Rushville	84.0-107.2	23.2	
[NKP-LM]	Indianapolis-Michigan City	1.9-159.0	157.1	
[NKP-LS]	Sandusky OH-Tipton	136.3-209.3	73.0	
[NKP-LP]	Tipton-Peoria IL	209.3-294.4	85.1	
[NKP-TB]	Wilshire OH-Frankfort	99.8-206.2	106.3	
[NKP-TC]	Frankfort-St. Louis MO	206.2-270.9	64.7	

On 1964/10/16 Norfolk & Western leased Wabash. On 1970/3/1 Norfolk & Western purchased Wabash. The Acquisition/Disposition Record is continued in two places: under Wabash and under Norfolk & Western. The property acquired was:

Line desig. N&W-	End points	MP	Main	Note
[WAB-M]	Montpelier OH-Peru	109.3-202.5	93.2	
[WAB-MC]	Montpelier OH-Clarke Jct.	107.2-246.7	139.5	
[WAB-MM]	Toledo OH-New Haven	75.7-88.5	12.8	
[WAB-YF]	Lake Erie & Fort Wayne	0-2.0	(2.0)	
[WAB-P]	Peru-Tilton IL	202.5-294.3	91.8	
[WAB-YL]	Lafayette Union	0-2.2	(2.2)	
1964 TOTAL		NKP=761.8 WAB=337.3 SYSTEM=1099.1		

Date	Act	N&W-	-End points	Change	Main	Note
1973	P	[NKP-LR]	In Rushville	+0.7		
YEAR TOTALS			NKP=762.5 WAB=337.3 SYSTEM=1099.8			
1974	X	[NKP-LM] In Indianapolis		-0.2		
YEAR TOTALS			NKP=762.3 WAB=337.3 SYSTEM=1099.6			
1976	P	[PR-CR] Richmond-New Castle		+23.9	1	
YEAR TOTALS			NKP=762.3 PRR=23.9 WAB=337.3 SYSTEM=1123.5			

On 1982/6/1 Norfolk & Western was conveyed to Norfolk Southern. The Acquisition/Disposition Record is continued in two places: under the name of the original constituent companies and under Norfolk Southern.

ACT COLUMN KEY
P   Purchased from Penn Central
X   Abandoned

SOURCES
1. Indiana, *1995 Indiana State Rail Plan.*
2. Simons and Parker, *Railroads of Indiana.*

NOTES
1. Trackage rights were obtained on Penn Central lines PC-[PRR-CR] and PC-[PRR-I] between Richmond and Ohio state line.

NORFOLK SOUTHERN

ACQUISITION/DISPOSITION RECORD

On 1982/6/1 Norfolk Southern was formed to rename Southern Ry and to acquire Norfolk & Western and New Jersey, Indiana & Illinois. The Acquisition/Disposition Record is continued in two places: under the name of the original constituent companies and under Norfolk Southern. The property acquired was:

Line desig.	End points	MP	Main	Note
NS-				
[NJI-A]	South Bend-Pine	2.1-11.6	9.5	
[NKP-C]	Fort Wayne-Chicago IL	371.6-504.7	133.1	
[NKP-F]	Bellevue OH-Fort Wayne	354.0-371.6	17.6	
[NKP-LF]	Fort Wayne-Muncie	1.6-62.3	60.7	
[NKP-LF]	Muncie-Foley	65.8-80.8	15.0	
[NKP-LF]	Broad-Connersville	83.0-109.0	26.0	
[NKP-LR]	New Castle-Rushville	84.0-107.9	23.9	
[NKP-LM]	Indianapolis-Michigan City	2.1-159.0	156.9	
[NKP-LS]	Sandusky OH-Tipton	136.3-209.3	73.0	
[NKP-LP]	Tipton-Peoria IL	209.3-294.4	85.1	
[NKP-TB]	Wilshire OH-Frankfort	99.8-206.2	106.3	
[NKP-TC]	Frankfort-St. Louis MO	206.2-270.9	64.7	
[PRR-CR]	Richmond-New Castle	76.6-100.5	23.9	
[SOU-U]	Mt Carmel IL-New Albany	151.8-161.4	9.6	
[SOU-U]	In Princeton	163.0-165.3	(2.3)	
[SOU-U]	Princeton-New Albany	165.3-268.3	103.0	
[SOU-UA]	Princeton Bypass	0-2.4	2.4	
[SOU-UE]	Evansville-Huntingburg	0.7-47.7	47.0	
[SOU-UC]	Lincoln City-Cannelton	0-22.7	22.7	
[SOU-UR]	Rockport Jct.-Rockport	1.0-16.8	15.8	
[SOU-UF]	Huntingburg-Dubois	47.7-63.7	16.0	
[WAB-M]	Montpelier OH-Peru	109.3-202.5	93.2	
[WAB-MC]	Montpelier OH-Clarke Jct.	107.2-246.7	139.5	
[WAB-MM]	Toledo OH-New Haven	75.7-88.5	12.8	
[WAB-YF]	Lake Erie & Fort Wayne	0-2.0	(2.0)	
[WAB-P]	Peru-Tilton IL	202.5-294.3	91.8	
[WAB-YL]	Lafayette Union	0-2.2	(2.2)	
1982/6/1	NJI=9.5 NKP=762.3 PRR=23.9 SOU=216.5 WAB=337.3 NS SYSTEM=1349.5			

Date	Act	NS-	End points	Change	Main	Note
1982	P1	[PRR-CR]	OH state line-Glen	+3.9		
	P1	[PRR-CR]	In Richmond	+1.7		
	P1	[PRR-I]	Glen-Newman	+2.4		
	X	[WAB-MC]	Kingsbury-Clarke Jct.	-41.1		
	X	[WAB-YF]	Lake Erie & Fort Wayne	(-2.0)		
YEAR TOTALS			NJI=9.5 NKP=762.3 PRR=31.9 SOU=216.5 WAB=296.2 SYSTEM=1316.4			
1984	L2	[WAB-MC]	Ashley-Hudson - Wolcottv.	<15.4>		
	X	[WAB-MC]	Wakarusa IN-Wolcottville	-34.2		
ca.	L3	[NKP-LR]	New Castle-Rushville	<23.9>		
YEAR TOTALS			NJI=9.5 NKP=738.4 PRR=31.9 SOU=216.5 WAB=246.6 SYSTEM=1242.9			
1987	X	[NKP-TC]	Linden-IL state line	-39.7		
YEAR TOTALS			NJI=9.5 NKP=698.7 PRR=31.9 SOU=216.5 WAB=246.6 sYSTEM=1203.2			
1988	X	[NKP-TC]	Frankfort-Linden	-21.9		
	Y	[NKP-TC]	In Frankfort	(3.1)		
	X	[WAB-MC]	Pine-Wakarusa	-16.4		
YEAR TOTALS			NJI=9.5 NKP=673.7 PRR=31.9 SOU=216.5 WAB=230.2 SYSTEM=1161.8			
1989	X	[NKP-LR]	New Castle-Mays	<-12.2>	9,10	
	S7	[NKP-LP]	Lafayette-Cheneyville IL	[32.2]		
	L3	[NKP-LF]	New Castle-Beesons	<19.7>		
	X	[NKP-LF]	Beesons-Connersville	-5.3		

NORFOLK SOUTHERN

ACQUISITION/DISPOSITION RECORD (continued)

Date	Act	NS-	End points	Change	Main	Note
	L5	[NKP-LM]	Tipton-Argos	<68.9>		
	SL	[NKP-LM]	Peru-Argos	<<34.7>>		
	L6	[NKP-TB]	Marion-Frankfort	<52.4>		
	L3	[NKP-TB]	Douglas OH-Marion	<53.9>		
	L1	[SOU-UF]	Huntingburg-Dubois	<16.0>		
	L1	[SOU-UC]	Lincoln City-Cannelton	<22.7>		
	L1	[SOU-UR]	Rockport Jct.-Rockport	<15.8>		
	L3	[WAB-MM]	Liberty Center OH-Woodburn	<3.0>		
YEAR TOTALS			NJI=9.5 NKP=441.3 PRR=31.9 SOU=162.0 WAB=227.2 SYSTEM=871.9			
1990	L6	[NKP-LM]	Indianapolis-Tipton	<37.6>		
	X	[NKP-LR]	Mays-Sexton	<-4.8>	9	
YEAR TOTALS			NJI=9.5 NKP=403.7 PRR=31.9 SOU=162.0 WAB=227.2 SYSTEM=834.3			
1991	XL	[SOU-UC]	Lincoln City-Cannelton	<+22.7>		
YEAR TOTALS			NJI=9.5 NKP=403.7 PRR=31.9 SOU=184.7 WAB=227.2 SYSTEM=857.0			
1992/12	LA1	[WAB-MC]	Ashley-Hudson - S. Milford	<16.4>		
	XL	[WAB-MC]	S. Milford-Wolcottville	<+5.0>		
	X	[WAB-MC]	S. Milford-Wolcottville	-5.0		
	P1	[PRR-I]	Newman-East Haven	(+1.5)		
YEAR TOTALS			NJI=9.5 NKP=403.7 PRR=31.9 SOU=184.7 WAB=227.2 SYSTEM=857.0			
1993/9/21	L8	[NKP-LS]	OH state line-Portland	<9.5>		
/10/21	T	[NKP-LR]	Sexton-Rushville	[7.9]		
	P1	[PRR-CR]	New Castle-Foley	+3.6		
	P1	[PRR-CR]	In Kokomo	+3.1		
	LA1	[SOU-UF]	Hungtingburg-Dubois	<+-16.0>		
	L4	[WAB-MC]	Montpelier OH- Ashley-Hudson	<14.2>		
YEAR TOTALS			NJI=9.5 NKP=386.3 PRR=38.6 SOU=184.7 WAB=213.0 SYSTEM=832.1			
1994	S3	[SOU-UC]	Lincoln City-Tell City	[19.8]		
	X	[SOU-UC]	Tell City-Cannelton	-2.9		
	XL	[SOU-UR]	Rockport Jct.-Rockport	<+15.8>		
YEAR TOTALS			NJI=9.5 NKP=386.3 PRR=38.6 SOU=177.8 WAB=213.0 SYSTEM=825.2			
1996 ca.	LA2	[NKP-LM]	Indianapolis-Tipton	<<37.6>>		
ca.	XL	[NKP-LM]	Kokomo-Argos	<+51.1>		
ca,	X	[NKP-LM]	Kokomo-Rochester	-38.1		
	P1	[PRR-F]	Wabash-Clarke Jct.	+126.5		
	L2	[SOU-UR]	Rockport Jct.-Rockport	<15.8>		
YEAR TOTALS			NJI=9.5 NKP=399.3 PRR=165.1 SOU=162.0 WAB=213.0 SYSTEM=948.9			
1997	L7	[NKP-LM]	Kingsbury-Michigan City	<23.5>		
	X	[NKP-TB]	OH state line-Craigville	<-17.9>		
YEAR TOTALS			NJI=9.5 NKP=375.8 PRR=165.1 SOU=162.0 WAB=213.0 SYSTEM=925.4			
1998	X	[NJI- A]	South Bend-Pine	-9.5		
	S6	[NKP-LM]	Rochester-Argos	[13.0]		
	S5	[NKP-TB]	Craigville-Van Buren	<[26.4]>		
	XL	[NKP-TB]	Kokomo-Frankfort	<+22.7>		
	X	[WAB-MC]	Pine-Dillon	-13.1		
	S4	[WAB-MM]	Liberty Center OH-Woodburn	<[3.0]>		
YEAR TOTALS			NJI=0 NKP=385.5 PRR=165.1 SOU=162.0 WAB=199.9 SYSTEM=912.5			
1999/6/1	S1	[PRR-F]	Wabash-Clarke Jct.	[126.5]		
TOTALS			NJI=0 NKP=385.5 PRR=38.6 SOU=162.0 WAB=199.9 SYSTEM=786.0			

On 1999/6/1 Norfolk Southern acquired part of Conrail. The Acquisition/Disposition Record is continued in two places, under the original constituent company and under Norfolk Southern. The lines acquired were:

Line desig.	End points	MP	Main	Note
[CCC-M]	Goshen-Anderson	55.5-165.4	109.9	
[LS-T]	OH state line-Elkhart	355.4-421.5	66.1	
[LS-A]	MI state line-B	420.1-438.8	14.7	
[LS-TF]	In Fort Wayne	95.2-100.0	(4.8)	
(continued)				

NORFOLK SOUTHERN

ACQUISITION/DISPOSITION RECORD (continued)
The lines acquired were:

Line desig.	End points	MP	Main	Note
[LS-W]	Elkhart-IL state line	421.6-505.7	84.1	
[LS-N2]	MC Connecting Branch	1.3-3.2	1.9	
[LS-WK]	In South Bend	0.2-3.0	(2.8)	
[LS-WK]	Wheatfield-IL state line	58.0-82.2	24.2	
[LS-WD]	Osborn-Schneider	4.9-32.9	28.0	
[LS-WJ]	MS-Lake Jct.	0-0.4	0.4	
[MC-W]	Porter-Ivanhoe	240.7-259.6	18.9	
[MC-N]	St. Marys-South Bend	5.8-6.0	0.2	
[MC-N2]	In South Bend	0-1.3	1.3	
[PRR-GS]	In Fort Wayne	93.3-97.8	(4.5)	
[PRR-L]	Red Key-Marion	124.9-158.6	33.7	
[PRR-LS]	In South Bend	179.0-181.3	(2.3)	

1999/6/1 TOTALS   CCC=109.9 LS=219.4 MC=20.4 NJI=0 NKP=385.5 PRR=72.3 SOU=162.0 WAB=199.9
NS SYSTEM   =1169.4

On the lines acquired from Conrail and on lines previously owned, Norfolk Southern granted trackage rights to CSX Transportation on:

Line desig. NS-	End points	MP	Main	Note
[LS-T]	IN state line-Elkhart	355.4-421.6	66.2	
[LS-W]	Elkhart-IL state line	421.6-508.2	86.6	
[LS-WK]	Schneider-IL state line	78.5-82.2	4.7	
[LS-WD]	Osborn-Schneider	4.9-32.9	28.0	
[LS-WJ]	MS-Lake Jct.	0-0.4	0.4	
[NKP-LF]	Muncie-New Castle	65.8-84.0	18.2	
[WAB-M]	Butler-St. Joe	114.3-122.7	8.4	
[WAB-P]	Lafayette-IL state line	257.2-294.3	37.1	

Norfolk Southern obtained trackage rights on lines owned by CSX Transportation, on:

Line desig. CSX-	End points	MP	Main	Note
[CCC-I]	Muncie-Indianapolis	229.7-283.1	53.4	
[IU all lines]	Various in Indianapolis			
[MON-SA]	Lafayette-Ames	121.5-148.4	26.9	
[P&E-A]	Clermont-Ames	9.6-43.0	33.4	
[PRR-F]	OH state line-Hobart	300.4-487.5	187.1	
[PRR-IL]	Indianapolis-Southport	0.5-6.3	5.8	
[PRR-V]	Indianapolis-Davis	0.4-6.9	6.5	
[PRR-IF]	Davis-Clermont	6.9-12.6	5.7	

ACT COLUMN KEY
L2   Leased to Pigeon River
L3   Leased to Indiana Hi-Rail
L4   Leased to Indiana Northeastern
L5   Leased to Central RR of Indianapolis
L6   Leased to Indiana RR
L7   Leased to Chicago South Shore & South Bend
L8   Leased to R. J. Corman
LA1 Lease assigned from Pigeon River to Indiana Northeastern
LA2 Lease assigned to Indiana Transportation Museum
P1   Purchased from Conrail
S1   Sold to CSX Transportation
S2   Sold to Indiana Hi-Rail
S3   Sold to Perry County Port Authority and leased to Hoosier Southern
(continued)

NORFOLK SOUTHERN

ACT COLUMN KEY (continued)
S4   Sold to Maumee & Western
S5   Sold to Wabash Central
S6   Sold to Fulton County
S7   Sold to Kankakee, Beaverville & Southern
SL   Sbleased to Indiana Hi-Rail
T   Transferred to Honey Creek
X   Abandoned
XL   Lease terminated

OWENSVILLE TERMINAL

MAIN LINE (OWEN-[CEI-EM])
See Chicago & Eastern Illinois line CEI-EM for arrangement of stations, prior construction/abandonment record, and prior ownership, and also Poseyville & Owensville

CONSTRUCTION/ABANDONMENT

Date	Act	End points	MP	Change	Main	Source	Note
1996/7/22	P	Owensville-Poseyville	270.8-281.8	+11.0	11.0	1	
1998 ca.	X	Owensville-Cynthiana	270.8-277.2	-6.4	4.6		

OWNERSHIP
1996   Owensville Terminal Co., owned by RailAmerica

ACQUISITION/DISPOSITION RECORD
See ownership record above for line OWEN-[CEI-EM]

ACT COLUMN KEY
P Purchased from Poseyville & Owensville

SOURCES
1. Simons and Parker, *Railroads of Indiana.*

PENN CENTRAL

ACQUISITION/DISPOSITION RECORD

On Feb. 1, 1968, Penn Central was formed by acquiring Cleveland, Cincinnati, Chicago & St. Louis (CC); Lake Shore & Michigan Southern (LS); Michigan Central (MC); Pennsylvania (PRR); and Peoria & Eastern (P&E). The Acquisition/Disposition Records are continued in two places: under the name of the original constituent company and under the name of Penn Central. The property acquired was:

Line desig. PC-	End points	MP	Main	Note
[CCC-I]	OH line-Indianapolis	198.6-283.1	84.5	
[CCC-IA]	In Anderson	245.7-250.1	4.4	
[CCC-IO]	Pendleton Old Main	245.0-247.0	(2.0)	
[CCC-G]	Cincinnati-Indianapolis	21.5-108.9	87.4	
[CCC-GO1]	Batesville Old Main	46.9-48.7	(1.8)	
[CCC-GA]	Aurora Branch	23.0-29.2	6.2	
[CCC-GW]	OH line-Beesons	24.7-74.4	49.7	
[CCC-GC]	Craig-Columbus	64.2-88.6	24.4	
[CCC-GM]	Fairland-Trafalgar	89.3-101.8	12.5	
[CCC-H]	Brant-Altamont	113.1-170.2	57.1	
[CCC-H]	Templeton-IL line	192.6-216.2	23.6	
[CCC-L]	Indianapolis-IL line	0.4-80.0	79.6	
(continued)				

PENN CENTRAL

ACQUISITION/DISPOSITION RECORD (continued)

Line desig. PC-	End points	MP	Main	Note
[CCC-LO]	Greencastle Old Main	39.0-40.6		(1.6)
[CCC-T]	Terre Haute-Evansville	0-130.9	130.9	
[CCC-TW]	Washington Branch	0-2.3	2.3	
[CCC-TC]	Gray Jct.-Oakland City Jct.	0-2.8	2.8	
[CCC-TK]	Lynnville Mine Branch	0-7.8	7.8	
[CCC-LE]	Mt. Carmel-Evansville	131.8-160.0	28.2	
[CCC-LV]	St. Francisv.-Vincennes	112.6-121.2	8.6	
[CCC-S]	OH line-Indianapolis	61.6-136.4	74.8	
[CCC-M]	In Goshen	54.8-55.5		(0.7)
[CCC-M]	Goshen-North Vernon	55.5-248.9	193.4	
[LS-T]	OH line-Elkhart	355.4-421.5	66.1	
[LS-A]	MI line-Elkhart	424.1-438.8	14.7	
[LS-TS]	Goshen-Shipshewanna	0-16.9	16.9	
[LS-TF]	MI line-Fort Wayne	44.7-100.0	55.3	
[LS-W]	Elkhart-Chicago	421.6-508.2	86.6	
[LS-WE]	Elkhart & Western	0-12.9	12.9	
[LS-N2]	In South Bend	1.3-3.2	1.9	
[LS-WK]	South Bend-Kankakee	0.2-82.2	82.0	
[LS-WD]	Osborn-Danville	4.9-100.8	95.9	
[MC-W]	MI line-Ivanhoe	222.7-259.6	36.9	
[MC-N]	MI line-South Bend	5.9-11.7	5.9	
[MC-N2]	In South Bend	0-1.3	1.3	
[MC-J]	In South Bend	0-2.6		(2.6)
[MC-WJ]	East Gary-Joliet	0-15.7	15.7	
[P&E-A]	Indianapolis-Peoria	1.0-79.9	78.9	
[PRR-F]	OH line-Chicago	300.4-453.3	152.9	
[PRR-FE]	In East Chicago			
[PRR-GR]	Richmond-Fort Wayne	0.7-86.6	85.9	
[PRR-GS]	Fort Wayne-MI line	93.3-146.4	53.1	
[PRR-L]	Union City-Chicago	103.6-286.1	184.7	
[PRR-LE]	Logansport-Columbia City	1.2-57.2	56.0	
[PRR-LE]	Churubusco-Auburn	65.0-82.4	17.4	
[PRR-LF]	Logansport-Effner	5.7-61.3	55.6	
[PRR-LS]	Logansport-South Bend	115.9-182.3	66.4	
[PRR-CR]	OH line-Glen	68.5-72.4	3.9	
[PRR-CR]	Newman-Anoka	74.9-177.4	102.5	
[PRR-CM]	Mathews-Muncie	26.0-41.1	15.1	
[PRR-CM]	In Muncie	41.1-42.9		(1.8)
[PRR-I]	Columbus-Indianapolis	115.4-186.8	71.4	
[PRR-IK]	Thorne-Hawthorne Yard	0-2.0	2.0	
[PRR-IK]	In Hawthorne Yard	2.0-5.0		(3.0)
[PRR-IL]	Indianapolis-Louisville	0.5-108.8	108.3	
[PRR-IA]	Jeffersonv.-New Albany	0-4.6	4.6	
[PRR-IW]	Boyd-Watson	0-4.0	4.0	
[PRR-IM]	Columbus-Madison	0-45.2	45.2	
[PRR-IC]	Columbus-N. Rushville	0-44.3	44.3	
[PRR-IV]	Indianapolis-Vincennes	3.0-117.8	114.8	
[PRR-IG]	Bushrod-Linton	0-13.4	13.4	
[PRR-IF]	Indianapolis-Logansport	6.9-114.5	77.4	
[PRR-VK]	Van Jct.-Kraft	0-1.4	1.4	
[PRR-V]	Indianapolis-Seelyville	0.4-64.5	64.1	
[PRR-V]	Seelyville-IL state line	65.3-79.9	14.6	
[PRR-VO]	Brazil-Staunton	57.3-60.8	3.5	
[PRR-VM]	Macksville-south	0-5.6	5.6	
[PRR-VF]	Terre Haute-Frankfort	5.8-78.3	72.5	
[PRR-VT1]	East Yard-Dewey	0-2.9	2.9	

1968/2/1   CCC=878.2   LS=432.3   MC=59.8   P&E=78.9   PRR=1443.5   PC SYSTEM=2892.7
(continued)

PENN CENTRAL

ACQUISITION/DISPOSITION RECORD (continued)

Date	Act	PC-	End points	Change	Main	Note
1968	X	[CCC-LV]	St. Francisville-Vincennes	-8.6	4	
	B	[LS-WJ]	MS-Lake Jct.	+0.4		
	X	[PRR-LE]	Logansport-Mexico	-10.8		
YEAR TOTALS			CCC=869.6 LS=432.7 MC=59.8 P&E=78.9 PRR=1432.7 SYSTEM=2873.7			
1969 ca.	X	[CCC-T]	Terre Haute-Spring Hill	-5.5		7
ca.	X	[CCC-T]	Worthington Jct.-Rincon Jct.	-1.2		
	X	[PRR-V]	In Terre Haute	-1.1		
ca.	Y	[PRR-V]	East Yard-Union	(1.5)		
	B	[PRR-VT2]	In Terre Haute	+0.2		
	X	[PRR-VF]	Guion-Waveland	-4.3		
YEAR TOTALS			CCC=862.9 LS=432.7 MC=59.8 P&E=78.9 PRR=1426.0 SYSTEM=2860.9			
1972	X	[MC-J]	In South Bend	(-2.6)		
	X	[PRR-IC]	Flat Rock-Fenns	-6.2		
	X	[PRR-VF]	Rockville-Guion	-9.4		
	X	[PRR-VM]	MP 3.0-MP 5.6	-2.6		
YEAR TOTALS			CCC=862.9 LS=432.7 MC=59.8 P&E=78.9 PRR=1407.8 SYSTEM=2842.1			
1973	X	[CCC-M]	Carthage-Rushville	-10.3		
	S4	[CCC-M]	In Rushville	[0.7]		
	X	[CCC-M]	Rushville-Greensburg	-17.8		
	Y	[CCC-M]	In Greensburg	(1.2)		
	X	[CCC-M]	Craig-North Vernon	-23.9		
	X	[CCC-GC]	Craig-Columbus	-21.9		
	Y	[CCC-GC]	In Columbus	(2.5)		
/1	X	[LS-TF]	Waterloo-Steubenville	-6.9		
	X	[LS-TF]	Fort Wayne-Auburn Jct.	-16.1		
	Y	[LS-TF]	In Fort Wayne	(7.2)		
	X	[P&E-A]	Speedway-Clermont	-2.8		
	X	[PRR-IG]	Bushrod-Linton	-13.4		
	X	[PRR-LE]	Churubusco-Auburn	-17.4		
	X	[PRR-LS]	Plymouth-Nutwood	-15.1		
	X	[PRR-LS]	Culver-Plymouth	-10.5		
	Y	[PRR-V]	At East Yard	(1.0)		
	X	[PRR-VT1]	East Yard-Dewey	-1.2		
	Y	[PRR-VT1]	At East Yard	(1.7)		
	B	[PRR-VT3]	Prairie-Preston	+2.5		
	X	[PRR-VF]	Otter Creek Jct.-Rockville	-17.5		
	X	[PRR-VF]	Colfax-Frank	-7.1		
YEAR TOTALS			CCC=784.6 LS=402.5 MC=59.8 P&E=76.1 PRR=1325.4 SYSTEM=2648.4			
1974	L1	[CCC-GW]	Brookville-Connersville	<24.1>		
YEAR TOTALS			CCC=760.5 LS=402.5 MC=59.8 P&E=76.1 PRR=1325.4 SYSTEM=2624.3			
1975	XL	[CCC-GW]	Brookville-Metamora	<+6.2>		
	X	[CCC-GW]	Brookville-Metamora	-6.2		
ca.	X	[MC-N]	In South Bend	-2.1		
	X	[PRR-LE]	North Manchester-Columbia City	-17.3		
YEAR TOTALS			CCC=760.5 LS=402.5 MC=57.7 P&E=76.1 PRR=1308.1 SYSTEM=2604.9			

On April 1, 1976, some lines of Penn Central were conveyed to Conrail and to Amtrak, and some retained by Penn Central. The Acquisition/Disposition Record is continued in two places: under the name of the former pre-Penn Central company and under Conrail. The lines conveyed to Conrail and those retained by Penn Central were:

Line desig. PC-	End points	MP	to Conrail	with PennC	to Amtrak
[CCC-I]	OH state line-Wash. St.	198.6-283.1	84.5		
[CCC-IA]	Anderson Cutoff	245.7-250.1	4.4		
[CCC-IO]	Pendleton Old Main	255.0-257.0	(2.0)		
[CCC-G]	OH state line-College Av.	21.5-108.9	87.4		
(continued)					

PENN CENTRAL

ACQUISITION/DISPOSITION RECORD (continued)
The lines conveyed to Conrail and those retained by Penn Central were:

Line desig. PC-	End points	MP	to Conrail	with PennC	to Amtrak
[CCC-GO1]	Batesville Old Main	46.9-48.7	(1.8)		
[CCC-GA]	CP 23-Aurora	23.0-29.2	6.2		
[CCC-GC]	In Columbus	86.1-88.6		(2.5)	
[CCC-GW]	OH state line-Brookville	24.7-43.9		19.2	
[CCC-GW]	Connersville-Beeson	68.0-74.4	6.4		
[CCC-GM]	Fairland-Franklin	89.3-100.5		11.2	
[CCC-GM]	In Franklin	100.5-101.8	1.3		
[CCC-H]	Brant-Zionsville	113.1-125.4	12.3		
[CCC-H]	Zionsville-Lebanon	125.4-137.0		11.6	
[CCC-H]	Lebanon-Altamont	137.0-170.2	33.2		
[CCC-H]	Templeton-IL state line	192.6-216.2	23.6		
[CCC-L]	West St.-IL state line	0.4-80.0	79.6		
[CCC-LO]	Greencastle Old Main	39.0-40.6	(1.6)		
[CCC-T]	Spring Hill-Cory	5.5-12.4	6.9		
[CCC-T]	Cory-Worthington	12.4-39.4		27.0	
[CCC-T]	In Worthington	39.4-40.0	0.6		
[CCC-T]	Rincon Jct.-Str.Line Jct.	41.2-130.9	89.7		
[CCC-TW]	Duff-Washington	0-2.3	2.3		
[CCC-TC]	Gray Jc.-Oakland City Jc.	0-2.8	2.8		
[CCC-TK]	Tecumseh Jct.-Lynnville	0-7.8	7.8		
[CCC-LE]	IL state line-8th Ave.	131.8-160.0		28.2	
[CCC-S]	OH state line-New Castle	61.6-95.3		33.7	
[CCC-S]	In New Castle	95.3-96.9	1.6		
[CCC-S]	New Castle-Hunter	96.9-128.8		31.9	
[CCC-S]	Hunter-DX	128.8-136.4	7.6		
[CCC-M]	In Goshen	54.8-55.5	(0.7)		
[CCC-M]	CX-Emporia	55.5-173.5	118.0		
[CCC-M]	Emporia-Carthage	173.5-193.5		20.0	
[CCC-M]	In Greensburg	222.3-223.5	(1.2)		
[CCC-M]	Greensburg-Craig	223.5-225.0	1.5		
[LS-T]	IN state line-B	355.4-421.5	66.1		
[LS-A]	MI state line-Elkhart	420.1-438.8	14.7		
[LS-TS]	Goshen-Shipshewana	0-16.9	16.9		
[LS-TF]	MI state line-Steubenville	44.7-63.5		18.8	
[LS-TF]	In Waterloo	70.4-71.2	0.8		
[LS-TF]	Waterloo-Auburn Jct.	71.2-76.7	5.5		
[LS-TF]	In Fort Wayne	92.8-100.0	(7.2)		
[LS-W]	Elkhart-MS	421.6-505.7	84.1		
[LS-W]	MS-IL state line	505.7-508.2		0.5	
[LS-WE]	Elkhart & Western Branch	0-12.9	12.9		
[LS-N2]	MC Connecting Branch	1.3-3.2	1.9		
[LS-WK]	South Bend-IL state line	0.2-82.2	82.0		
[LS-WD]	Osborn-IL state line	4.9-100.8	95.9		
[LS-WJ]	MS-Lake Jct.	0-0.4	0.4		
[MC-W]	MI state line-PO	222.7-240.7			18.0
[MC-W]	PO-Ivanhoe	240.7-259.6	18.9		
[MC-WJ]	East Gary-Hartsdale	0-12.8		12.8	
[MC-WJ]	Hartsdale-IL state line	12.8-15.7	2.9		
[MC-N]	MI state line-South Bend	5.8-9.6	3.8		
[MC-N2]	In South Bend	0-1.3	1.3		
[P&E-A]	IJ-Speedway	1.0-6.2	5.2		
[P&E-A]	Clermont-IL state line	9.0-79.9	70.9		
[PRR-F]	OH line-IL line	300.4-453.3	152.9		

(continued)

PENN CENTRAL

ACQUISITION/DISPOSITION RECORD (continued)

Line desig. PC-	End points	MP	to Conrail	with PennC	to Amtrak
[PRR-GR]	In Richmond	0.7-2.3	1.6		
[PRR-GR]	Richmond-Decatur	2.3-33.0		30.7	
[PRR-GR]	In Ridgeville	33.0-34.2	1.2		
[PRR-GR]	Ridgeville-Decatur	34.2-70.4		36.2	
[PRR-GR]	Decatur-Adams	70.4-86.6	16.2		
[PRR-GS]	Junction-Kendallville	93.3-121.0	27.7		
[PRR-GS]	Kendallville-MI line	121.0-146.4		25.4	
[PRR-L]	OH line-Van	103.6-198.3	94.7		
[PRR-L]	Van-Boone	1.2-11.9	10.7		
[PRR-L]	Boone-IL line	206.8-286.1	79.3		
[PRR-LF]	Kenneth-Effner	5.7-61.3		55.6	
[PRR-LS]	MP 115.9-Culver	115.9-148.6		32.7	
[PRR-LS]	In Plymouth	159.1-160.9	1.8		
[PRR-LS]	Nutwood-South Bend	176.0-179.0		3.0	
[PRR-LS]	In South Bend	179.0-182.3	3.3		
[PRR-LE]	Van-MP 3.4	1.2-3.4	2.2		
[PRR-LE]	Mexico-North Manchester	14.2-36.9		22.7	
[PRR-LE]	In North Manchester	36.9-38.0	1.1		
[PRR-LE]	In Columbia City	55.3-56.6	1.3		
[PRR-LE]	In Columbia City	56.6-57.2		0.6	
[PRR-CR]	OH line-Glen	68.5-72.4	3.9		
[PRR-CR]	In Richmond	74.9-76.6	1.7		
[PRR-CR]	Newman-New Castle	76.6-100.5		23.9	
[PRR-CR]	New Castle-Anderson	100.5-127.0	26.5		
[PRR-CR]	Anderson-Kokomo	127.0-155.7	28.7		
[PRR-CR]	Kokomo-Anoka	155.7-177.4	21.7		
[PRR-CM]	Muncie-Mathews	26.0-41.1		15.1	
[PRR-CM]	In Muncie	41.1-41.8		(0.7)	
[PRR-CM]	In Muncie	41.8-42.9	(1.1)		
[PRR-I]	OH line-Indianapolis	115.4-186.8	71.4		
[PRR-IK]	Thorne-Hawthorne Yard	0-2.0	2.0		
[PRR-IL]	Indianapolis-KY line	0.5-108.8	108.3		
[PRR-IA]	Jeffersonville-Clarksville	0-1.6	1.6		
[PRR-IA]	Clarksville-New Albany	1.6-4.6		3.0	
[PRR-IW]	Boyd-Watson	0-4.0	4.0		
[PRR-IM]	In Columbus	0-2.8	2.8		
[PRR-IM]	Columbus-Madison	2.8-45.2		42.4	
[PRR-IC]	In Columbus	0-3.8	3.8		
[PRR-IC]	Columbus-Flat Rock	3.8-12.6		8.8	
[PRR-IC]	Fenns-Shelbyville	18.8-23.8		5.0	
[PRR-IC]	In Shelbyville	23.8-27.3	3.5		
[PRR-IC]	Shelbyville-N. Rushville	27.3-44.3		17.0	
[PRR-IV]	Kraft-Vincennes	3.0-102.9	99.9		
[PRR-IV]	Bicknell-Vincennes	102.9-117.8		14.9	
[PRR-IF]	Davis-Frank	6.9-48.1	41.2		
[PRR-IF]	Frank-Van	78.3-114.5	36.2		
[PRR-V]	Indianapolis-Seelyville	0.4-64.5	64.1		
[PRR-V]	Seelyville-Prairie	65.3-69.9	4.6		
[PRR-V]	Prairie-Union	69.9-72.4	(2.5)		
[PRR-V]	Terre Haute-IL line	73.5-79.9	6.4		
[PRR-VO]	Brazil-Staunton	57.3-60.8	3.5		
[PRR-VB2]	Brazil-Chinook Mine	0-6.0	(6.0)		
[PRR-VT1]	At East Yard	0-1.7	(1.7)		
[PRR-VT2]	In Terre Haute	73.3-73.5	0.2		
(continued)					

PENN CENTRAL

ACQUISITION/DISPOSITION RECORD (continued)

Line desig. PC-	End points	MP	to Conrail	with PennC	to Amtrak
[PRR-VT3]	Prairie-Preston	69.9-72.4	2.5		
[PRR-VM]	Macksville-south	0-3.0		3.0	
[PRR-VK]	Van Jct.-Kraft	0-1.4	1.4		
[PRR-VF]	Waveland-Colfax	37.0-71.2		34.2	

TOTALS		Conrail	PennC	Amtrak	PC System
	CCC	577.7	182.8		760.5
	LS	381.2	21.3		402.5
	MC	26.9	12.8	18.0	57.7
	PRR	933.9	374.2		1308.1
	P&E	76.1			76.1
	TOTAL	1995.8	591.1	18.0	2604.9

ACQUISITION/DISPOSITION RECORD (continued)

The lines retained by Penn Central:

Date	Act	PC--	End points	Change	Main	Note
1976	X	[CCC-GM]	Fairland-Franklin	-11.2		
	X	[CCC-GC]	In Columbus	(-2.5)		
	X	[CCC-LE]	IL state line-Evansville	-22.3		
	S1	[CCC-LE]	In Evansville	[5.9]		
	X	[CCC-H]	Zionsville-Lebanon	-11.6		
	X	[CCC-S]	OH state line-Lynn	-7.8		
	X	[LS-W]	MS-IL state line	-2.5		
	L1	[LS-TF]	MI state line-Pleasant Lake	<15.8>		
	X	[MC-WJ]	East Gary-Hartsdale	-12.8		
	S3	[PRR-LF]	Kenneth-Effner	[55.6]		
	S4	[PRR-CR]	Newman-New Castle	[23.9]		
	X	[PRR-CM]	Muncie-Mathews	-15.1		
	X	[PRR-CM]	In Muncie	(-0.7		
	X	[PRR-GR]	Richmond-Ridgeville	-30.7		
	X	[PRR-GR]	Ridgeville-Portland	-7.8		
	X	[PRR-GS]	Kendallville-MI state line	-25.4		
	X	[PRR-IA]	Clarksville-New Albany	-3.0		
	X	[PRR-IC]	Fenns-Shelbyville	-5.0		
	X	[PRR-IC]	Shelbyville-Rushville	-17.0		
	X	[PRR-IM]	Columbus-North Vernon	-16.6		
	X	[PRR-IV]	Bicknell-Vincennes	-14.9		
	X	[PRR-LE]	In Columbia City	-0.6		
	X	[PRR-LS]	Nutwood-S of South Bend	-3.0		
	X	[PRR-VF]	Waveland-Colfax	-34.2		
	X	[PRR-VM]	MP 0-MP 3	-3.0		
YEAR TOTALS			CCC=124.0 LS=3.0 MC=0 P&E=0 PRR=118.4 PC SYSTEM=245.4			
1977	X	[CCC-S]	Lynn-New Castle	-25.9		
	X	[CCC-S]	New Castle-Hunter	-10.4		
	X	[CCC-S]	Wilkinson-Hunter	-19.8		
	X	[PRR-LE]	Mexico-North Manchester	-22.7		
	L2	[PRR-GR]	Portland-Decatur	<28.4>		
	X	[PRR-IC]	Columbus-Flat Rock	-8.8		
	S5	[PRR-IM]	North Vernon-Madison	[25.8]		
YEAR TOTALS			CCC=67.9 LS=3.0 MC=0 P&E=0 PRR=32.7 PC SYSTEM=103.6			

(continued)

PENN CENTRAL

ACQUISITION/DISPOSITION RECORD (continued)
The lines retained by Penn Central:

Date	Act	PC--	End points	Change	Main	Note
1979/6	L3	[CCC-M]	Emporia-Carthage	<20.0>		
	L3	[CCC-S]	Shirley-Wilkinson	<1.7>		
	S6	[CCC-GW]	OH state line-Brookville	[19.2]		
	SL	[PRR-GR]	Portland-Decatur	<+28.4>		
	X	[PRR-GR]	Portland-Decatur	-26.9		
	T	[PRR-GR]	In Decatur	[1.5]		
	X	[PRR-LS]	N of Logansport-Culver	-32.7		
YEAR TOTALS			CCC=27.0 LS=3.0 MC=0 P&E=0 PRR=0 PC SYSTEM=30.0			
1981	X	[CCC-T]	Cory-Worthington Jct.	-27.0		
YEAR TOTALS			CCC=0 LS=3.0 MC=0 P&E=0 PRR=0 PC SYSTEM=3.0			
1986	S	[LS-TF]	Pleasant Lake-Steubenville	[3.0]		
YEAR TOTALS			CCC=0 LS=0 MC=0 P&E=0 PRR=0 PC SYSTEM=0			

ACT COLUMN KEY
B   Built by Conrail
L1   Leased to Hillsdale County
L2   Leased to Chicago & Indiana
L3   Leased to Indiana Eastern
L4   Leased to Indiana Interstate
S1   Sold to Louisville & Nashville
S2   Sold to Amtrak
S3   Sold to Toledo, Peoria & Western
S4   Sold to Norfolk & Western
S5   Sold to Madison RR
S6   Sold to Indiana & Ohio
S7   Sold to Whitewater Valley
X   Abandoned
XL   Lease terminated
Y   Converted to yard/industrial track

SOURCES
1. Indiana, *1995 Indiana State Rail Plan.*
2. Simons and Parker, *Railroads of Indiana.*

PENNSYLVANIA

PENNSYLVANIA

(continued)

L	Logansport Div., Columbus OH-Chicago	260-262
LE	" Logansport-Butler	265-266
LF	" Logansport-Effner	263-264
LO	" Van-Boone old line	263
LS	" Logansport-South Bend	264-265
LV	" LaCrosse-Valparaiso	263
SK	Shelbyville-Knightstown	268
SL	Shelbyville-Edinburg	271
V	St. Louis Div., Indianapolis-St. Louis	278-279
VB	" Brazil-Saline City	280
VF	" Terre Haute-Frankfort	283-284
VK	" Van Jct.-Kraft	277
VO	" Brazil-Seelyville old main line	279-280
VP	" Center Point Branch	281

FORT WAYNE DIVISION (PRR-F)

	Mileage	County	Crossings, junctions, etc.
Pittsburgh PA	0		
Crestline OH	188.7		
Dixon OH	300.4		
(OH/IN state line)	300.4		
Monroeville	304.2	Allen	
West Monroeville	305.5	"	
Maples	309.9	"	
Adams	314.4	"	J/PRR-GR 86.6
Linker	316.3	"	
Piqua Road	317.5	"	
Winter Street	318.6	"	
Wabash	319.2	"	X/WAB-M 146.0
Fort Wayne	319.8	"	
Broadway	320.2	"	
Junction	321.1	"	J/PRR-GS 93.3
(Crossing)	321.2	"	X/LS-TF 97.9
(Bridge)	324.6	"	B/NKP-C 375.2
Arcola	328.2	"	
Coesse	333.9	Whitley	
Columbia City	338.7	"	
Vandale	339.2	"	X/PRR-LE 55.3
West Vandale	341.1	"	
Larwill	346.2	"	
Pierceton	350.5	Kosciusko	
Winona Lake	357.1	"	X/WIN-B 1.8
Warsaw	358.7	"	X/CCC-M 79.7
West Warsaw	359.7	"	
(Bridge)	360.4	"	B/WIN-A 26.4
Atwood	365.5	"	
Etna Green	369.3	"	
Bourbon	373.0	Marshall	
Inwood	377.7	"	
Plymouth	383.9	"	X/PRR-LS 159.0, X/NKP-LM 118.3
West Plymouth	386.3	"	
Donaldson	391.7	"	
Groverton	394.3	Starke	
Hamlet	397.9	"	X/LS-WK 27.5
Davis	404	LaPorte	
Hanna	408.6	"	X/PM-W 8.94
East Wanatah	413.2	"	
Wanatah	414.9	"	X/MON-M 39.4

(continued)

PENNSYLVANIA

FORT WAYNE DIVISION (PRR-F) (continued)

	Mileage [Pittsburgh]	County	Crossings, junctions, etc.
Wanatah	414.9	LaPorte	
Valparaiso	424.1	Porter	
Grand Trunk	426.9	"	X/GTW-C 52.7
Wheeler	430.7	"	
East Bart	433.0	Lake	
(Junctiion)	433.8	"	J/NKP-C 487.5
Bart	434.4	"	X/EJE-A 45.7
Hobart	434.5	"	
Liverpool	437.4	"	X/MC-WJ 2.9
Virginia Street	439.9	"	
Broadway	440.4	"	
Tolleston	441.8	"	X/MC-W 256.3, X/IHB-G 5.1
Gary	442.9	"	
Clarke	443.8	"	
(Bridge)	445.3	"	B/EJE-G 7.8
Clarke Jct.	445.7	"	X/BOCT-A 449.3
Buffington	446.3	"	
Cline Avenue	447.4	"	
Indiana Harbor	448.1	"	X/IHB-A 0.2
Indiana Harbor Canal	448.5	"	
Mahoning	448.9	"	
Standard	450.6	"	
Whiting	450.8	"	X/BOCT-W 3.7
Lake Jct.	451.4	"	J/LS-WJ 0.4
Roby	452.1	"	
(Bridge)	452.6	"	B/IHB-WR 3.9
Colehour Yard Office	453.1	"	
(IN/IL state line)	453.3		
Colehour Jct. IL	453.7		
Chicago IL	467.8		

CONSTRUCTION/ABANDONMENT

Date	Act	End points	MP	Change	Main	Source	Note
1854/9	B9	OH state line-Ft. Wayne	300.4-319.8	+19.4	19.4	7	
1856/1/23	B10	Ft. Wayne-Columbia City	319.8-338.7	+18.9	38.3	7	
1858/12	B13	Columbia-IL state line	338.7-453.3	+114.6	152.9	7	2
1996	S1	Wabash-IL state line	319.2-453.3	-134.1	18.8	5	

OWNERSHIP

1854	Ohio & Indiana RR (B9), of part
1856/5/6	Fort Wayne & Chicago RR (B10), of part
1856/7/29	Pittsburgh, Fort Wayne & Chicago RR (B13), of part, merge O&I and FW&C
1862/3/2	Pittsburgh, Fort Wayne & Chicago Ry, reorganize PFW&C RR
1869/7/1	Pennsylvania RR, lease of PFW&C (Note ??e)
1871/4/1	Lease assigned to Pennsylvania Co. (PRR holding co.)
1918/1/1	Lease assigned to Pennsylvania RR
1968/2/1	Penn Central Co., merge PRR and New York Central
1969/10/1	Penn Central Transp. Co., acquire Penn Central Co.
1976/4/1	Conrail, acquire Penn Central Transp. and PFW&C
1996	Norfolk Southern, buy Ft. Wayne-Chicago line from Conrail

PENNSYLVANIA

CALUMET RIVER BRANCH (PRR-FR)

	Mileage	County	Crossings, junctions, etc.
River Branch Jct.	0		
Hegewisch IL	4.7		
(IL/IN state line)	5.8		
(Crossing)	5.9	Lake	X/IHB-W 1.2
Hammond	7.5	"	
(Crossing)	7.6	"	X/CSS-A 68.5, X/BOCT-A 5.2
East Chicago	9.2	"	

CONSTRUCTION/ABANDONMENT

Date	Act	End points	MP	Change	Main	Source	Note
							8

GRAND RAPIDS & INDIANA, SOUTHERN DIV. (PRR-GS)

	Mileage [Richmond]	County	Crossings, junctions, etc.
(Fort Wayne	91.9)	Allen	
--via PRR-F			
Junction	93.3	"	J/PRR-F 321.1
(Crossing)	93.6	"	X/LS-TF 97.7
(Crossing)	94.1	"	X/NKP-C 373.0
Spy Run	94.6	"	
Wallen	99.6	"	
Huntertown	104.1	"	
LaOtto	108.7	Noble	X/PRR-LE 73.7
Swans	110.4	"	
Avilla	113.6	"	X/B&O-C 133.1
Conlog	117.3	"	
Kendallville	120.2	"	X/NYC-T 379.74
Hoffman	121.5	"	
Rome City	127.3	"	
Kneipp Sanitarium	127.9	"	
Wolcottville	129.4	LaGrange	X/WAB-MC 136.8
Valentine	134.4	"	
LaGrange	138.4	"	
(Bridge)	139.9	"	B/SJV-A 34.3
Howe	143.7	"	
Crooked Creek	145.5	"	
(IN/MI state line)	146.4		
Sturgis MI	149.1		
Grand Rapids MI	234.0		

CONSTRUCTION/ABANDONMENT

Date	Act	End points	MP	Change	Main	Source	Note
1870/6/22	B30	Fort Wayne-Sturgis	93.3-146.4	+53.1	53.1	3	2

1976	Y	In Kendallville	120.1-121.0	(0.9)	52.2		
1979	X	Kendallville-MI state line	121.0-146.4	-25.4	26.8	2,5	
1982	X	MP 97.8-Kendallville	97.8-119.0	-21.2		2	
1982	Y	Junction-MP 97.8	93.3-97.8	(4.5)			
1982	Y	In Kendallville	119.0-120.1	(1.1)	0		
1984	x	In Kendallville	120.1-121.0	(-0.9)	0	2	
1996	L5	In Kendallville	119.0-120.1	<(1.1)>	0	2	

PENNSYLVANIA

GRAND RAPIDS & INDIANA, SOUTHERN DIV. (PRR-GS) (continued)
OWNERSHIP

1870	Grand Rapids & Indiana RR (B30)
1874	Pennsylvania RR, control of Grand Rapids & Indiana
1896/7/7	Grand Rapids & Indiana Ry, reorganized GR&I RR (controlled by Pennsylvania)
1953/12/1	Penndel Co. (Pennsylvania RR holding co.), merged GR&I
1968/2/1	Penn Central Co., control of Penndel
1969/10/1	Penn Central Transp. Co., acquired Penn Central Co.
1976/4/1	Conrail, buy of Penn Central Transp. and Penndel
1999/6/1	Norfolk Southern, buy Conrail line

GRAND RAPIDS & INDIANA, RICHMOND BRANCH (PRR-GR)

	Mileage	County	Crossings, junctions, etc.
(Richmond	0.0)	Wayne	
--via PRR-I			
(Newman	0.3)	"	
--via PRR-CR			
(Junction)	0.7	"	J/PRR-CR 75.3
(Bridge)	2.2	"	B/C&O-C 67.0
Parry		"	
Chester	4.3	"	
Woodford		"	
Fountain City	8.9	"	
Lynn	15.3	Randolph	X/CCC-S 69.3
Snow Hill	18.6	"	
Woods	19.6	"	
Winchester	24.5	"	X/CCc-I 207.9
Stone	28.9	"	
Ridgeville	33.0	"	X/PRR-L 117.3
Collett	38.9	Jay	
(Crossing)	42.9	"	X/NKP-LS 145.8, J/CBC-A 52
Portland	43.2	"	
Briant	50.3	"	
Geneva	54.2	Adams	
Berne	58.8	"	
Monroe	64.8	"	
DA	70.4	"	X/ERIE-C 96.1, X/NKP-TB 108.2
Decatur	70.7	"	
Williams	77.2	"	
Hoagland	79.6	Allen	
Adams	86.6	"	J/PRR-F 314.4
--via PRR-F			
(Fort Wayne	91.9)	"	J/(PRR-GS 91.9)

CONSTRUCTION/ABANDONMENT

Date	Act	End points	MP	Change	Main	Source	Note
1870/7	B31	Richmond Jct.-Winchester	0.7-24.5	+23.8	23.8	5	2
1871/12/25	B31	Winchester-Adams	24.5-86.6	+62.1	85.9	5	1

1976	Y	In Richmond	0.7-2.3	(1.6)			
1976	X	Richmond-Ridgeville	2.3-33.0	-30.7		2,5	
1976	Y	In Ridgeville	33.0-34.2	(1.2)			
1976	X	Ridgeville-Portland	34.2-42.0	-7.8	44.6	2,5	
1977	L4	Portland-DA	42.0-70.4	<28.4>	16.2	5	
1979	XL	Portland-DA	42.0-70.4	<+28.4>			
1979	X	Portland-Decatur	42.0-68.9	-26.9		2,5	
1979	Y	In Decatur	68.9-70.4	(1.5)	16.2	2	
1984	X	In Ridgeville	33.0-34.2	(-1.2)	16.2	2	
1984	X	In Decatur	68.9-70.4	(-1.5)	16.2	2	

PENNSYLVANIA

GRAND RAPIDS & INDIANA, RICHMOND BRANCH (PRR-GR) (continued)
OWNERSHIP

1870	Cincinnati, Richmond & Fort Wayne (B31)
1871/6/1	Grand Rapids & Indiana RR, leased Cincinnati, Richmond & Fort Wayne
1874	Pennsylvania RR, control of Grand Rapids & Indiana
1896/7/7	Grand Rapids & Indiana Ry, reorganized GR&I RR (controlled by PRR)
1927/6/9	Pittsburgh, Cincinnati, Chicago & St. Louis RR, (leased to PRR) buy CR&FW
1957 ca.	Ownership of PCC&SL transferred to Philadelphia, Baltimore & Washington
1968/2/1	Penn Central Co., merge PRR (with control of PB&W)
1969/10/1	Penn Central Transp. Co., acquire Penn Central Co.
1976/4/1	Conrail, buy Penn Central Transp.
1999/6/1	CSX Transportation, buy Conrail line

RICHMOND BRANCH (PRR-CR)

	Mileage	County	Crossings, junctions, etc.
Cincinnati OH (Union Term)	0.7		
Hamilton	30.7		
Camden	49.5		
Campbellstown OH	65.3		
(OH/IN state line)	68.5		
Glen	72.4	Wayne	J/PRR-I 117.4
--via PRR-I			
Newman	74.9	"	J/PRR-I 119.8
(Junction)	75.3	"	J/PRR-GR 0.7
Olive Hill	80	"	
Greens Fork	83.6	"	
NS	85.1	"	
Nolands	87	"	
Hagerstown	90.3	"	X/CCC-GW 87.7
Millville	95.6	Henry	
Ashland	98.3	"	
New Castle	101.5	"	
Broad	101.9	"	J/NKP-LF 83.6
(Bridge)	102.9	"	B/CCC-S 95.1
Foley	104.1	"	J/NKP-LF 80.8
Fayne	105.0	"	
Sulphur Springs	108.5	"	
Honey Creek	111.5	"	
Middletown	115.3	"	
Gridley	121.4	Madison	X/CCC-IA 245.7
Delco	122.2	"	X/CCC-I 246.7, X/CI-A 18.1, J/PRR-YA 0
Anderson	123.0	"	
Dow	124.8	"	X/CCC-M 162.6
Florida	127.3	"	
Frankton	132.8	"	
(Crossing)	137.5	"	X/NKP-LS 199.7
Elwood	137.8	"	
Curtisville	142.1	Tipton	
Windfall	146.4	"	
Nevada	149.9	"	
Hemlock	152.4	Howard	
Center	153.9	"	
(Crossing)	159.3	"	X/NKP-TB 180.9
Kokomo	159.5	"	
(Crossing)	159.6	"	X/NKP-LM 54.8
Galveston	165.9	Cass	
Lincoln	168.8	"	
Walton	172.2	"	
Anoka	177.4	"	J/PRR-L 192.6
(continued)			

PENNSYLVANIA

RICHMOND BRANCH (PRR-CR) (continued)
CONSTRUCTION/ABANDONMENT

Date	Act	End points	MP	Change	Main	Source	Note
1853	B8	OH state line-Richmond	68.5-72.4	+3.9		5	
1853	B8	Richmond-New Castle	74.9-101.5	+26.6	30.5	2,5	
1857	B11	New Castle-Anoka	101.5-177.4	+75.9	106.4	2	

1976	S1	Newman-New Castle	76.6-100.5	[23.9]	82.5		
1982	X	Anderson-Kokomo	127.0-155.7	-28.7			
1982	Y	In Anderson	119.3-127.0	(7.7)			
1982	S1	OH state line-Glen	68.5-72.4	[3.9]			
1982	S1	In Richmond	74.9-76.6	[1.7]	40.5		
1984	X	Delco-Dow	122.1-124.8	(-2.7)	40.5	2	
1986	X	In Kokomo	155.7-156.5	-0.8	39.7		
1993	X	Sulphur Springs-Anderson	110.7-119.3	-8.6		2,5	
1993	S1	New Castle-Foley	100.5-104.1	[3.6]			
1993/3/20	S5	Kokomo-Anoka	159.6-177.4	[17.8]		5	
1993	S1	In Kokomo	156.5-159.6	[3.1]			10
1993/10/1	S7	Foley-Sulphur Springs	104.1-110.7	[6.6]	0	2,5	

OWNERSHIP

1853	Cincinnati, Logansport & Chicago Ry (B8), of part
1854	Cincinnati & Chicago RR (B11), merge CL&C and other road
1860/7	Cincinnati & Chicago Air-Line RR, reorganize Cincinnati & Chicago
1865/5/15	Chicago & Great Eastern Ry, merge C&CAL and other road
1868/2/12	Columbus, Chicago & Indiana Central Ry, acquire C&GE
1869/2/1	Pennsylvania RR, lease Columbus, Chicago & Indiana Central
1884//4/3	Chicago, St. Louis & Pittsburgh RR, reorganize CC&IC
1884	Pittsburgh, Cincinnati & St. Louis Ry, manage CSL&P, controlled by Penna RR
1890/8/29	Pittsburgh, Cincinnati, Chicago & St. Louis Ry, merge CSL&P and others, controlled by Penna. RR
1917/1/1	Pittsburgh, Cincinnati, Chicago & St. Louis RR, merge PC&SL and others
1921/1/1	Pennsylvania RR, lease PCC&SL
1957 ca.	PCC&SL, ownership transfer to Philadelphia, Baltimore & Washington
1968/2/1	Penn Central Co., merge PRR and New York Central
1969/10/1	Penn Central Transp. Co., acquire Penn Central Co.
1976/4/1	Conrail, buy Penn Central Transp.

MUNCIE BRANCH (PRR-CM)

	Mileage	County	Crossings, junctions, etc.
Converse	0	Miami	J/PRR-L 168.6
Rich	2.5	Grant	
Swayzee	5.9	"	X/NKP-TB 164.2
Cole	8.7	"	
Radley	12.8	"	
Wright	15.7	"	
Fairmount	17.9	"	X/CCC-M 142.8
Fowlerton	22.1	"	X/C&O-C 121.0
Mathews	26.4	"	
Wheeling	28.6	Delaware	
Stockport	31.6	"	
Anthony	34.9	"	
Drew	38.1	"	X/C&O-C 103.5
(Crossing)	40.9	"	X/NKP-LF 65.7
Muncie	41.1	"	
Vance	41.8	"	X/CCC-I 228.5
(End)	42.9	"	

PENNSYLVANIA

MUNCIE BRANCH (PRR-CM) (continued)
CONSTRUCTION/ABANDONMENT

Date	Act	End points	MP	Change	Main	Source	Note
1895	B24	Fairmount-Mathews	17.9-26.4	+8.5	8.5	I	
1898	B24	Swayzee-Fairmount	6.0-17.9	+11.9	20.4	I	
1899	B24	Converse-Swayzee	0-6.0	+6.0	26.4	I	
1900	B24	Mathews-Vance	26.4-41.1	+14.7		I	
1900	B24	Muncie-MP 42.9	41.1-42.9	(+1.8)	41.1		
1933	X	Converse-Mathews	0-26.0	-26.0	15.1	R	

1976	X	Mathews-Muncie	26.0-41.1	-15.1			
1976	X	In Muncie	41.1-41.8	(-0.7)	0		
1984	X	In Muncie	41.8-42.9	(-1.1)	0		

OWNERSHIP

1895	Chicago, Indiana & Eastern Ry (B24)
1895	Pennsylvania RR, controlled CI&E, operated by Pittsb., Cinci., Chi. & St. L.
1917/1/1	Pittsburgh, Cincinnati, Chicago & St. Louis RR, merge CI&E and others
1968/2/1	Penn Central Co., merge PRR and New York Central
1969/10/1	Penn Central Transp. Co., acquire Penn Central Co.
1976/4/1	Conrail, buy Penn Central Transp. and Chicago, Indiana & Eastern

ANDERSON BELT (PRR-YA)

	Mileage	County	Crossings, junctions, etc.
Delco	0	Madison	J/PRR-CR 122.2
(Crossing)	0.9	"	X/CCC-M 166.3
(Crossing)	2.4	"	X/CCC-I 248.3
(Junction)	3.1	"	J/CI-A 20.5

CONSTRUCTION/ABANDONMENT

Date	Act	End points	MP	Change	Main	Source	Note
							8

OWNERSHIP

18--	Pittsburgh, Cincinnati & St. Louis Ry, controlled by Pennsylvania RR
1921/1/1	Pennsylvania RR, lease PCC&SL
1957 ca.	PCC&SL, ownership transfer to Philadelphia, Baltimore & Washington
1968/2/1	Penn Central Co., merge PRR and New York Central
1969/10/1	Penn Central Transp. Co., acquire Penn Central Co.
1976/4/1	Conrail, buy Penn Central Transp.

LOGANSPORT DIVISION (PRR-L)

	Mileage	County	Crossings, junctions, etc.
Columbus OH	0		
Woodington OH	96.6		
(OH/IN state line)	103.6		
(Crossing)	103.7	Randolph	X/CCC-I 198.7
Union City	103.8	"	
West Union City	105.2	"	
Saratoga	110.2	"	
Deerfield	113.9	"	
Ridgeville	117.3	"	X/PRR-GR 33.0
West Ridgeville	118.1	"	
Powers	121.2	Jay	
Red Key	124.9	"	X/NKP-LS 156.7
East Kirk	126.8	"	
Dunkirk	128.4	"	
West Kirk	130.5	"	
Mill Grove	132.5	Blackford	
(continued)			

PENNSYLVANIA

LOGANSPORT DIVISION (PRR-L) (continued)

	Mileage	County	Crossings, junctions, etc.
	[Columbus OH]		
Mill Grove	132.5	Blackford	
Hartford City	138.1	"	X/NKP-LF 47.4
Renner	141.9	"	
East Upland	144.1	Grant	
Upland	145.1	"	
Packy	150.5	"	
Gas City	152.2	"	
Bethevan	154.7	"	
Kent	156.9	"	X/CCC-M 133.4, X/NKP-TB 154.2
Marion	157.3	"	
Becker	160.0	"	
Goodman	161.0	"	
West Good	162.9	"	
Sweetser	163.2	"	
(Bridge)	168.0	"	B/C&O-C 142.9
Converse	168.6	Miami	J/PRR-CM 0
Amboy	171.4	"	
North Grove	174.0	"	
East Graw	174.8	"	
McGrawsville	176.8	"	
West Graw	178.9	"	
Loree	179.4	"	
Bunker Hill	181.8	"	X/NKP-LM 66.2
Onward	187.0	Cass	
Anoka	192.6	"	J/PRR-CR 177.4
Eighteenth Street	195.9	"	
Race	196.0	"	
Fourteenth Street	196.6	"	
Elm	197.1	"	X/WAB-P 218.7
Logansport	197.3	"	
Fort	197.6	"	
Van	198.3	"	J/PRR-LO 198.3, X/PRR-LS and PRR-IF 114.5
	[Logansport]		
Van	1.2	"	
Kenneth	5.7	"	J/PRR-LF 5.7
Deasy	8.9	"	
Boone	11.9	"	
	[Columbus OH via PRR-LO]		
Boone	206.8	"	J/PRR-LO 206.8
Royal Center	208.3	"	
Thornhope	212.8	Pulaski	
Star City	216.5	"	
West Star City	217.4	"	
Winimac	222.4	"	
Ripley	226.9	"	
Denham	231.4	"	
East North Judson	235.8	Starke	
North Judson	237.3	"	X/ERIE-C 199.7, X/LS-WK 43.33
English Lake	241.5	"	
La Crosse	246.3	LaPorte	X/PM-W 0
(Crossing)	246.6	"	X/MON-M 31.6, J/CAS-A 0
Kouts	253.1	Porter	X/ERIE-C 213.7
Sandy Hook	255.5	"	
Aynes	257.0	"	
Aylesworth	257.7	"	
(continued)			

PENNSYLVANIA

LOGANSPORT DIVISION (PRR-L) (continued)

	Mileage	County	Crossings, junctions, etc.
	[Columbus OH via PRR-LO]		
Aylsworth	257.7	Porter	
Hebron	262.5	"	
Leroy	267.1	Lake	
Crown Point	273.4	"	
Schererville	280.1	"	
(Bridge)	281.5	"	B/LS-WD 10.9
Hartsdale	281.7	"	X/EJE-A 33.8, X/MC-WJ 12.75
Maynard	284.8	"	X/GTW-C 31.56
(Crossing)	288.4	"	X/MON-A 25.4
(IN/IL state line)	286.1		
Lansing IL	286.6		
Chicago IL	314.1		

CONSTRUCTION/ABANDONMENT

Date	Act	End points	MP	Change	Main	Source	Note
1857	B11	Anoka-Logansport	192.8-197.7	+4.9	4.9	2	
1859	B12	Logansport-Van	197.7-198.3	+0.6			
1859	B12	Logansport-Kenneth	1.2-5.7	+4.5	10.0	2	
1861	B15	Boone-LaCrosse	206.8-249.2	+42.4	52.4		
1865	B14	LaCrosse-Chicago	249.2-286.1	+36.9	89.3	2	
1867	B16	Union City-Marion	103.6-157.6	+54.0	143.3	2	
1868	B17	Marion-Anoka	157.6-192.8	+35.2	178.5	2	
1893	B25	Kenneth-Boone	203.4-209.6	+6.2	184.7	2	

1980/7	S7	Marion-Sweetser	158.6-163.2	[4.6]	180.1	5	
1982	X	Winimac-Crown Point	225.4-274.2	-48.8	131.3	2,5	
1984	X	Crown Point-IL state line	274.2-286.1	-11.9		5	
1984	X	In Winimac	224.2-225.4	-1.2			
1984	X	Sweetser-Anoka	163.2-192.6	-29.4	88.8		
1985	X	In Winimac	223.9-224.2	-0.3	88.5		
1993	X	Union city-Red Key	105.4-124.9	-19.5		2	
1993	Y	In Union City	103.6-105.4	(1.8)			
1993/3/20	S5	Anoka-Van	192.6-198.3	[5.7]		5	
1993/3/20	S5	Van-Boone	1.2-11.9	[10.7]		5	
1993/3/20	S5	Boone-Winimac	206.8-223.9	[17.1]	33.7	5	

OWNERSHIP

1857	Cincinnati & Chicago RR (B11), of part
1859	Toledo, Logansport & Burlington RR (B12)
1860/7/11	Cincinnati & Chicago Air-Line RR, reorganize Cincinnati & Chicago
1861	Chicago & Cincinnati RR (B15), of part
1865/3/15	Chicago & Great Eastern Ry (B14), merge C&CAL and Chi. & Cinc.
1867	Columbus & Indiana Central (B16), merge Toledo, Logansport & Burlington
1868/2/12	Columbus, Chicago & Indiana Central Ry (B17), merge C&GE and C&IC and TL&B
1869/2/1	Pennsylvania RR, lease Columbus, Chicago & Indiana Central
1884/4/3	Chicago, St. Louis & Pittsburgh RR, reorganize CC&IC, controlled by Penna RR
1884	Pittsburgh, Cincinnati & St. Louis Ry, manage CSL&P
1890/8/29	Pittsburgh, Cincinnati, Chicago & St. Louis Ry (B25), merge CSL&P and others, controlled by Penna. RR
1917/1/1	Pittsburgh, Cincinnati, Chicago & St. Louis RR, merge Vandalia and others
1921/1/1	Pennsylvania RR, lease PCC&SL
1957 ca.	PCC&SL, ownership transfer to Philadelphia, Baltimore & Washington
1968/2/1	Penn Central Co., merge PRR and New York Central
1969/10/1	Penn Central Transp. Co., acquired Penn Central Co.
1976/4/1	Conrail, buy Penn Central Transp.

PENNSYLVANIA

VALPARAISO BRANCH (PRR-LV)

	Mileage	County	Crossings, junctions, etc.
LaCrosse	0	LaPorte	J/PRR-L 246.3
--route not determined between terminii			
Valparaiso	10.4	Porter	

CONSTRUCTION/ABANDONMENT

Date	Act	End points	MP	Change	Main	Source	Note
1861	B15	LaCrosse-Valparaiso	0-10.4	+10.4	10.4	S	
1865/3	X	LaCrosse-Valparaiso	0-10.4	-10.4	0	S	

OWNERSHIP

1861	Chicago & Cincinnati RR (B15)
1865/3/15	Chicago & Great Eastern Ry (B14), merge C&CAL and Chi. & Cinc

LOGANSPORT-ROYAL CENTER (PRR-LO)

	Mileage	County	Crossings, junctions, etc.
Van	198.3	Cass	J/PRR-L 198.3,J/PRR-LS 114.5,J/PRR-IF 114.4
Boone	206.8	"	J/PRR-L 11.9

CONSTRUCTION/ABANDONMENT

Date	Act	End points	MP	Change	Main	Source	Note
1861	B15	Van-Boone	198.3-206.8	+8.5	8.5	1	
1893	X	Van-Boone	198.3-206.8	-8.5	0	1	

OWNERSHIP

1861	Chicago & Cincinnati RR (B15)

EFFNER BRANCH (PRR-LF)

	Mileage [Logansport]	County	Crossings, junctions, etc.
Kenneth	5.7	Cass	J/PRR-L 5.7
Trimmer	6.8	"	f. Curveton
Lake Ciecott	8.7	"	
Burnettsville	12.1	White	
Idaville	15.1	"	
(Crossing)	21.5	"	X/MON-I 98.6
Monticello	21.6	"	
Reynolds	26.9	"	X/MON-N 95.8
Seafield	32.8	"	
Wolcott	35.8	"	
Remington	41.5	Jasper	
Goodland	48.9	Newton	X/CAS-A 48.5
Perkins	52.7	"	
Newton	53.1	"	
Kentland	57.2	"	X/LS-WD 61.87
SA	60.2	"	
Effner	61.2	"	
(IN/IL state line)	61.3		J/TPW

CONSTRUCTION/ABANDONMENT

Date	Act	End points	MP	Change	Main	Source	Note
1859	B12	Kenneth-Effner	5.7-61.3	+55.6	55.6	2	

1976	S4	Kenneth-Effner	5.7-61.3	[55.6]	0		

(continued)

PENNSYLVANIA

EFFNER BRANCH (PRR-LF) (continued)

OWNERSHIP

1859	Toledo, Logansport & Burlington RR (B12)
1862/7/31	Toledo, Logansport & Burlington Ry, reorganize TL&B RR
1867/9/1	Columbus & Indiana Central Ry, merge TL&B
1868/2/11	Columbus, Chicago & Indiana Central Ry, merge C&IC and other road
1869/2/1	Pennsylvania RR, lease Columbus, Chicago & Indiana Central which assigned to PCC&SL
1884/4/3	Chicago, St. Louis & Pittsburgh RR, reorganize CC&IC
1884	Pittsburgh, Cincinnati & St. Louis Ry, manage CSL&P, controlled by Penna RR
1890/8/29	Pittsburgh, Cincinnati, Chicago & St. Louis Ry, merge CSL&P and others, controlled by Penna. RR
1917/1/1	Pittsburgh, Cincinnati, Chicago & St. Louis RR, merge PC&SL and others
1921/1/1	Pennsylvania RR, lease PCC&SL
1957 ca.	PCC&SL, ownership transfer to Philadelphia, Baltimore & Washington
1968/2/1	Penn Central Co., merge PRR and New York Central
1969/10/1	Penn Central Transp. Co., acquired Penn Central Co.
1976/4/1	Toledo, Peoria & Western, bought line

SOUTH BEND BRANCH (PRR-LS)

	Mileage [Terre Haute]	County	Crossings, junctions, etc.
(Van	114.5)	Cass	J/PRR-L 198.9
(Junction)	115.9	"	J/PRR-LE 2.7
Bend	116.1	"	
Verona	120.5	"	
Lucerne	124.3	"	
Grass Creek	129.8	Fulton	
Kewanna	134.8	"	
(Crossing)	135.0	"	X/C&O-C 189.8
Bruce Lake	138.4	"	
DeLong	143.1	"	X/ERIE-C 179.7
Culver	148.8	Marshall	
Hibbard	151.7	"	X/NKP-C 438.9
Twin Lakes	154.8	"	
Plymouth	159.0	"	X/PRR-C 383.9, X/NKP-LM 118.3
Marshall	160.2	"	
Harris	163.7	"	
LaPaz Jct.	167.4	"	X/B&O-C 189.2
Lakeville	172.2	St.Joseph	X/WAB-MC 184.8
Nutwood	175.7	"	
DE	182.2	"	
South Bend	182.3	"	J/MC-J -2.6

CONSTRUCTION/ABANDONMENT

Date	Act	End points	MP	Change	Main	Source	Note
1884	B23	Van-South Bend	115.9-182.3	+66.4	66.4	2	

1973	X	N of Plymouth-Nutwood	160.9-176.0	-15.1		2,5	
1973	X	Culver-Plymouth	148.6-159.1	-10.5	40.8	2,5	
1976	Y	In Plymouth	159.1-160.9	(1.8)			
1976	X	Nutwood-S of South Bend	176.0-179.0	-3.0		2,5	
1976	Y	In South Bend	179.0-182.3	(3.3)	32.7		
1979	X	MP 115.9-Culver	115.9-148.6	-32.7	0	5	
1984	X	In South Bend	181.3-182.3	(-1.0)	0	2	
1985/5	L2	In Plymouth	159.1-160.9	<(1.8)>		5	
1990	X	In Plymouth	159.1-160.9	<(-1.8)>	0	5	

PENNSYLVANIA

SOUTH BEND BRANCH (PRR-LS) (continued)
OWNERSHIP

1884	Terre Haute & Logansport RR (B23)
1898/12/1	Terre Haute & Logansport Ry, reorganize TH&L RR
1905/1/1	Vandalia RR, merge Terre Haute & Logansport and other roads
1917/1/1	Pittsburgh, Cincinnati, Chicago & St. Louis RR, merge Vandalia and others, controlled by Penna. RR
1921/1/1	Pennsylvania RR, lease PCC&SL
1957 ca.	PCC&SL, ownership transfer to Philadelphia, Baltimore & Washington
1968/2/1	Penn Central Co., merge PRR and New York Central
1969/10/1	Penn Central Transp. Co., acquired Penn Central Co.
1976/4/1	Conrail, purchase of Penn Central Transp.

**NOTE. See also Michigan Central line MC-J which was controlled by this company between 1890 and 1900.

LOGANSPORT-BUTLER (PRR-LE)

	Mileage [Logansport]	County	Crossings, junctions, etc.
Van	1.2	Cass	J/PRR-L 198.3, J/PRR-IF 114.5
Fern	2.5	"	
(Junction)	2.6	"	J/PRR-NS 115.9
Log	3.1	"	
Adamsboro	5.7	"	
Hoover	10.1	"	X/C&O-C 170.0
Mexico	14.3	Miami	
(Crossing)	18.2	"	X/NKP-LM 81.9
Denver	18.8	"	
Chili	21.1	"	X/WIN-A 57.83
Pettysville	23.6	"	
Roann	27.2	Wabash	
Laketon	33.2	"	
Newton	33.9	"	X/ERIE-C 146.1
(Crossing)	36.9	"	X/CCC-M 99.0
North Manchester	37.1	"	
Liberty Mills	40.5	"	
South Whitley	47.1	Whitley	X/NKP-C 397.2
Wynkoop	51.5	"	
Vandale	55.3	"	X/PRR-F 339.2
Columbia City	56.0	"	
Collins	62.1	"	
Churubusco	66.1	"	
Ari	70.4	Allen	
LaOtto	73.7	Noble	X/PRR-GS 108.7
LaOtto Siding	74.3	"	
Cedar	76.3	DeKalb	
(Crossing)	81.3	"	X/LS-TF 76.58
Auburn Jct.	81.4	"	X/B&O-C 124.7
Auburn	82.4	"	
Moore	88.5	"	
Butler	93.1	"	
(Junction)	93.7	"	J/LS-T 358.46, J/WAB-M 114.3

CONSTRUCTION/ABANDONMENT

Date	Act	End points	MP	Change	Main	Source	Note
1874	B21	Van-Butler	1.2-93.7	+92.5	92.5	2	
1877/10	L1	Van-Butler	1.2-93.7	<92.5>	0	2	
1901	XL	Van-Butler	1.2-93.7	<+92.5>	92.5	2	
1954	X	Auburn-Butler	82.4-93.7	-11.3	81.2	2,5	
(continued)							

PENNSYLVANIA

LOGANSPORT-BUTLER (PRR-LE) (continued)

CONSTRUCTION/ABANDONMENT (continued)

1961	X	Columbia City-Churubusco	57.2-65.0	-7.8	73.4	2,5

1968	X	MP 3.4-Mexico	3.4-14.2	-10.8	62.6	2,5
1973	X	Churubusco-Auburn	65.0-82.4	-17.4	45.2	2,5
1975	X	N. Manchester-Columbia Cy.	38.0-55.3	-17.3	27.9	2,5
1976	Y	In North Manchester	36.9-38.0	(1.1)		
1976	Y	In Columbia City	55.3-56.6	(1.3)		
1976	X	In Columbia City	56.6-57.2	-0.6	24.9	2,5
1977	X	Mexico-North Manchester	14.2-36.9	-22.7	2.2	2,5
1982	X	In Columbia City	55.3-56.6	(-1.3)	2.2	2
1984	X	In North Manchester	36.9-38.0	(-1.1)	2.2	2
1989	S6	Van-MP 3.4	1.2-3.4	[2.2]	0	5

OWNERSHIP

1874	Detroit, Eel River & Illinois RR (B21)
1877/12/10	Eel River RR, reorganize Detroit, Eel River & Illinois
1877/10	Wabash Ry, lease Eel River
1901	Wabash RR, surrender lease of Eel River
1901/9/12	Logansport & Toledo Ry, bought Eel River
1905/1/1	Vandalia RR, merge Logansport & Toledo and other roads
1917/1/1	Pittsburgh, Cincinnati, Chicago & St. Louis, merge Vandalia and others, controlled by Penna. RR
1921/1/1	Pennsylvania RR, lease PCC&SL
1957 ca.	PCC&SL, ownership transfer to Philadelphia, Baltimore & Washington
1968/2/1	Penn Central Co., merge PRR and New York Central
1969/10/1	Penn Central Transp. Co., acquired Penn Central Co.
1976/4/1	Conrail, purchase of Penn Central Transp.

INDIANAPOLIS DIVISION (PRR-I)

	Mileage	County	Crossings, junctions, etc.
Columbus OH	0		
New Paris OH	113.8		
(OH/IN state line)	115.4		
Glen	117.4	Wayne	J/PRR-CR 72.4
Richmond	119.6	"	
(Bridge)	119.7	"	B/C&O-C 63.5
Newman	119.8	"	J/PRR-CR 74.9, J/PRR-GR 0.3
East Haven	121.7	"	
Hills	122.1	"	
Centerville	125.6	"	
Jax	126.9	"	
Germantown	133.1	"	
Cambridge City	134.9	"	J/PRR-ICA 63.4
(Crossing)	135.0	"	X/CCC-GW 81.0
(Crossing)	135.1	"	X/NKP-LF 97.2
East Dublin	137.0	"	
Dublin	137.3	"	
Dublin Jct.	138.4	"	J/PRR-IC 62.0
West Dublin	138.7	Henry	
Straughn	141.3	"	
Lewisville	144.6	"	
Dunreith	148.9	"	X/NKP-LR 94.1
Knightstown	153.9	"	X/CCC-M 188.2, J/PRR-SK 0
Chalottesville	158.7	Hancock	
Riley	164.8	"	
West Riley	166.3	"	
Greenfield	167.2	"	
(continued)			

PENNSYLVANIA

INDIANAPOLIS DIVISION (PRR-I) (continued)

	Mileage [Columbus OH]	County	Crossings, junctions, etc.
Greenfield	167.2	Hancock	
Philadelphia	170.9	"	
Gem	174.1	"	
Cumberland	176.8	Marion	
Thorne	180.8	"	J/PRR-IK 0
Irvington	183.0	"	
(Crossing)	184.8	"	X/IU-B 2.6
Pine	185.3	"	
ID	186.8	"	J/IU-E 0.9
--via IU			
(Indianapolis)	187.7)	"	

CONSTRUCTION/ABANDONMENT

Date	Act	End points	MP	Change	Main	Source	Note
1853/10	B7	Indianapolis-New Paris OH	186.8-115.4	+71.4	71.4	7	

1981	X	Cambridge City-Charlottesv.	136.6-157.9	-21.3	50.1	2	
1982	X	Charlottesville-Thorne	157.9-180.8	-22.9		2	
1982	X	Centerville-Cambridge City	126.5-136.6	-10.1		2	
1982	X	OH state line-Glen	115.4-117.4	-2.0		2	
1982	S1	Glen-Newman	117.4-119.8	[2.4]			
1982	Y	Thorne-ID	180.8-186.8	(6.0)	6.7		
1992	X	East Haven-Centerville	121.3-126.5	-5.2		2	
1992	S11	Newman-East Haven	119.8-121.3	[1.5]	0		

OWNERSHIP

1853	Indiana Central Ry (B7)
1864	Columbus & Indianapolis Central Ry, merge Indiana Central and other road
1868/2/12	Columbus, Chicago & Indiana Central Ry, merge Columbus & Indpls. Central
1869/2/1	Pennsylvania RR, lease Columbus, Chicago & Indiana Central
1884//4/3	Chicago, St. Louis & Pittsburgh RR, reorganize CC&IC
1884	Pittsburgh, Cincinnati & St. Louis Ry, manage CSL&P, controlled by Penna RR
1890/8/29	Pittsburgh, Cincinnati, Chicago & St. Louis Ry, merge CSL&P and others, controlled by Penna. RR
1917/1/1	Pittsburgh, Cincinnati, Chicago & St. Louis RR, merge PC&SL and others
1921/1/1	Pennsylvania RR, lease PCC&SL
1957 ca.	PCC&SL, ownership transfer to Philadelphia, Baltimore & Washington
1968/2/1	Penn Central Co., merge PRR and New York Central
1969/10/1	Penn Central Transp. Co., acquire Penn Central Co.
1976/4/1	Conrail, buy Penn Central Transp.

HAWTHORNE YARD BRANCH (PRR-IK)

	Mileage	County	Crossings, junctions, etc.
Thorne	0	Marion	J/PRR-I 180.8
(Bridge)	1.4	"	B/B&O-IH 118.2
Kitley Avenue	1.9	"	
Hawthorne Yards	2.0	"	
(West end yards)	4.5	"	
(Junction)	5.0	"	J/IU-B 3.0

CONSTRUCTION/ABANDONMENT

Date	Act	End points	MP	Change	Main	Source	Note
1922	B25	Line	0-2.0	+2.0		5	
1922	B25	Line in yard	2.0-5.0	(+3.0)	2.0		

1982	Y	Line	0-2.0	(2.0)	0		

PENNSYLVANIA

HAWTHORNE YARD BRANCH (PRR-IK) (continued)
OWNERSHIP

1922	Pittsburgh, Cincinnati, Chicago & St. Louis RR (B25), lease by Penna RR
1957 ca.	PCC&SL, ownership transfer to Philadelphia, Baltimore & Washington
1968/2/1	Penn Central Co., merge PRR and New York Central
1969/10/1	Penn Central Transp. Co., acquire Penn Central Co.
1976/4/1	Conrail, buy Penn Central Transp.
1999/6/1	CSX Transportation, buy Conrail line

KNIGHTSTOWN-SHELBYVILLE (PRR-SK)

	Mileage	County	Crossings, junctions, etc.
Knightstown	0	Henry	J/PRR-I 153.9
Carthage	4.5	Rush	
Morristown	12.5	Shelby	
Hanover		"	
Marion	19.5	"	
Shelbyville	26	"	J/PRR-SL 16

CONSTRUCTION/ABANDONMENT

Date	Act	End points	MP	Change	Main	Source	Note
1850	B27	Knightstown-Shelbyville	0-26	+26.0	26.0	5,6	
1854	X	Knightstown-Shelbyville	0-26	-26.0	0	5,6	

OWNERSHIP

1854	Knightstown & Shelbyville (B27)

COLUMBUS BRANCH (PRR-IC)

	Mileage	County	Crossings, junctions, etc.
Columbus	0	Bartholomew	J/PRR-IL 41.0, J/PRR-IM 0
Clifford	6.4	"	
St. Louis Crossing	9.2	"	
Flat Rock	12.4	Shelby	
Lewis Creek	15.1	"	
Fenns	19.2	"	
Vine (CP 82)	23.8	"	X/CCC-G 82.6
Shelbyville	24.0	"	
Rays Crossing	29.0	"	
Manilla	33.0	Rush	
Homer	35.2	"	
(Crossing)	41.8	"	X/CCC-M 204.7
(Crossing)	42.1	"	X/B&O-IH 85.2
Rushville	42.2	"	
North Rushville	44.1	"	
Gings	48.4	"	
Falmouth	52.7	Fayette	
Bentonville	57.3	"	J/PRR-ICA 0
Dublin Jct.	62.0	Wayne	J/PRR-I 138.4

CONSTRUCTION/ABANDONMENT

Date	Act	End points	MP	Change	Main	Source	Note
1850	B3	Rushville-Shelbyville	42.2-24.0	+18.2	18.2	2	
1853	B6	Shelbyville-Columbus	24.0-0	+24.0	42.2	2	
1867	B18	Rushville-Bentonville	42.2-57.3	+15.1	57.3	2	
1910	B25	Bentonville-Dublin Jct.	57.3-62.0	+4.7	62.0	2	
1955	X	Bentonville-Dublin Jct.	57.3-62.0	-4.7	57.3	2,5	
1962	X	North Rushville-Rushville	44.3-57.3	-13.0	44.3	2,5	

1972	X	Flat Rock-Fenns	12.6-18.8	-6.2	38.1	2,5	

(continued)

PENNSYLVANIA

COLUMBUS BRANCH (PRR-IC)
CONSTRUCTION/ABANDONMENT (continued)

1976	X	Fenns-Shelbyville	18.8-23.8	-5.0		2
1976	X	Shelbyville-Rushville	27.3-44.3	-17.0		2
1976	Y	In Shelbyville	23.8-27.3	(3.5)	12.6	
1977	X	Columbus-Flat Rock	3.8-12.6	-8.8		2,5
1977	Y	In Columbus	0-3.8	(3.8)	0	
1984	X	In Columbus	1.1-3.8	(-2.7)		2
1984	X	In Shelbyville	25.5-27.3	(-1.8)	0	2
1986	X	In Shelbyville	23.8-25.5	(-1.7)	0	2
1987	X	In Columbus	0-1.1	(-1.1)	0	2

OWNERSHIP

1850	Rushville & Shelbyville RR (B3), of part
1853	Columbus & Shelby RR (B6), of part
1853 ca.	Jeffersonville RR, lease Rushville & Shelbyville and Columbus & Shelby
1859/7/7	Shelby & Rush RR, reorganize Rushville & Shelbyville (leased to Jeffersonv.)
1866/5/1	Jeffersonville, Madison & Indianapolis RR, merge Jeffersonville and other
1867	Lake Erie & Louisville RR (B18), of part
1871	Pittsburgh, Cincinnati & St. Louis Ry, lease JM&I, controlled by Penna RR
1881/11/18	Jeffersonville, Madison & Indianapolis RR, bought Columbus & Shelby
1882/4/10	Jeffersonville, Madison & Indianapolis RR, bought Shelby & Rush
1890	Jeffersonville, Madison & Indianapolis RR, bought Lake Erie & Louisville
1890	Pittsburgh, Cincinnati & St. Louis, merge JM&I and other road
1890	Pittsburgh, Cincinnati, Chicago & St. Louis Ry (B25), merge PC&SL and others, controlled by Penna. RR
1921/1/1	Pennsylvania RR, lease PCC&SL
1957 ca.	PCC&SL, ownership transfer to Philadelphia, Baltimore & Washington
1968/2/1	Penn Central Co., merge PRR and New York Central
1969/10/1	Penn Central Transp. Co., acquire Penn Central Co.
1976/4/1	Conrail, buy Penn Central Transp.

ORIGINAL BENTONVILLE-CAMBRIDGE CITY LINE (PRR-ICA)

	Mileage [Columbus]	County	Crossings, junctions, etc.
Bentonville	57.3	Fayette	J/PRR-IC 57.3
(Crossing)	63.3	Wayne	X/CCC-GW 80.9, X/NKP-LF 97.3
Cambridge City	63.4	"	J/PRR-I 134.9

CONSTRUCTION/ABANDONMENT

Date	Act	End points	MP	Change	Main	Source	Note
1867	B18	Bentonville-Cambridge City	57.3-63.4	+6.1	6.1	2	
1910	X	Bentonville-Cambridge City	57.3-63.4	-6.1	0	2	

OWNERSHIP

1867	Lake Erie & Louisville RR (B18)
1890	Jeffersonville, Madison & Indianapolis RR, buy Lake Erie & Louisville
1890	Pittsburgh, Cincinnati & St. Louis, merge JM&I and other road
1890	Pittsburgh, Cincinnati, Chicago

INDIANAPOLIS-LOUISVILLE (PRR-IL)

	Mileage	County	Crossings, junctions, etc.
(Indianapolis --via IU-S	0)	Marion	
(Junction)	0.5	"	J/IU-S 0.5
Dale	1.7	"	X/IU-B 6.1
Southport (continued)	7.1	"	

PENNSYLVANIA

INDIANAPOLIS-LOUISVILLE (PRR-IL) (continued)

	Mileage	County	Crossings, junctions, etc.
Southport	7.1	Marion	
Greenwood	10.7	Johnson	
Whiteland	15.3	"	
Land	15.5	"	
Franklin	20.3	"	X/CCC-GM 101.8
Elvin	21.4	"	
Amity	25.1	"	
Atterbury	28.5	"	J/spur to Camp Atterbury
Edinburg	30.6	"	J/PRR-IEC 10, J/PRR-SL 0
Taylorsville	34.5	Bartholomew	
Brook	37.9	"	
Columbus	41.0	"	J/PRR-IC 0, J/PRR-IM 0, J/PRR-IEC 0, J/CCC-GC 88.6
Garden	42.5	"	
Walesboro	45.7	"	
Jonesville	51.8	"	
Reed	53.9	Jackson	
Peters	54.5	"	
Rockford	56.9	"	
(Crossing)	58.4	"	X/MILW-T 299.8
JD	58.9	"	X/B&O-SW 87.3
Seymour	59.0	"	
Crothersville	70.5	"	
Austin	74.5	Scott	
Scottsburg	79.3	"	
Vienna	81.7	"	
Underwood	84.8	Clark	
Henryville	89.3	"	
Caney	91.7	"	
Memphis	93.4	"	
Speed	98.3	"	
Sellersburg	99.6	"	
Cementville	102.7	"	
Boyd	104.9	"	X/B&O-SV 50.3, J/PRR-IW 0
Jeffersonville	107.2	"	J/PRR-IA 0
(Junction)	108.0	"	J/B&O-SJ 53.5
(IN/KY state line)	108.8		
Clagg KY	109.1		
Broadway Street	110.1		
Eleventh Street	110.5		
IC Jct.	110.6		
--via IC			
(Louisville KY	111.2)		

CONSTRUCTION/ABANDONMENT

Date	Act	End points	MP	Change	Main	Source	Note
1846/9/1	B2	Franklin-Edinburg	20.3-30.6	+10.3	10.3	6	
1847/10/1	B2	Indianapolis-Franklin	0.5-20.3	+19.8	30.1	2	6
1852	B4	Jeffersonville-Columbus	108.8-41.0	+67.8	97.9	2	
1853	B4	Columbus-Edinburg	41.0-30.6	+10.4	108.3	2	

1994/3/12	S10	Southport-KY state line	6.3-108.8	[102.5]	5.8	5	9
(continued)							

PENNSYLVANIA

INDIANAPOLIS-LOUISVILLE (PRR-IL) (continued)
OWNERSHIP

1846	Madison & Indianapolis RR (B2), of part
1852	Jeffersonville RR (B4), of part
1862/3/28	Indianapolis & Madison RR, reorganize Madison & Indianapolis
1866/5/1	Jeffersonville, Madison & Indianapolis RR, merge I&M and Jeffersonville
1871	Pittsburgh, Cincinnati & St. Louis Ry, lease JM&I, controlled by Penna RR
1890	Pittsburgh, Cincinnati & St. Louis, merge JM&I and other road
1890	Pittsburgh, Cincinnati, Chicago & St. Louis Ry, merge PC&SL and others, controlled by Penna. RR
1921/1/1	Pennsylvania RR, lease PCC&SL
1957 ca.	PCC&SL, ownership transfer to Philadelphia, Baltimore & Washington
1968/2/1	Penn Central Co., merge PRR and New York Central
1969/10/1	Penn Central Transp. Co., acquire Penn Central Co.
1976/4/1	Conrail, buy Penn Central Transp.

SHELBYVILLE LATERAL BRANCH (PRR-SL)

	Mileage	County	Crossings, junctions, etc.
Edinburg	0	Johnson	J/PRR-IL 30.6, J/PRR-IEC 10
Conovers		Shelby	
Marietta	8	"	
Clarks Depot		"	
Shelbyville	16	"	J/PRR-SK 26

CONSTRUCTION/ABANDONMENT

Date	Act	End points	MP	Change	Main	Source	Note
1849	B28	Edinburg-Shelbyville	0-16	+16.0	16.0	5,6	
1855	X	Edinburg-Shelbyville	0-16	-16.0	0	5,6	

OWNERSHIP

1849	Shelbyville Lateral Branch RR (B28)

MADISON BRANCH (PRR-IM)

	Mileage	County	Crossings, junctions, etc.
Columbus	0	Bartholomew	J/PRR-IL 41.0, J/PRR-IC 0, PRR-IEC 0
Haw	2.0	"	
Clifty Switch	3.5	"	
Wiggs	5	"	
Elizabethtown	8.0	"	X/MILW-T 312.7
Rock Creek	10.5	Jennings	
Hege	11.8	"	
Scipio	14.5	"	
Queensville	17.4	"	
North Vernon	21.5	"	X/B&O-SC/SW 72.2, J/B&O-SV 0, J/CCC-M 248.9
Wren	21.6	"	
Vernon	23.1	"	
Grayford	26.3	"	f. Graham
Dupont	32.0	Jefferson	
Middlefork	35.3	"	
Jeff	36.9	"	
Wirt	38.9	"	
North Madison	43.0	"	
Madison	45.2	"	
(continued)			

PENNSYLVANIA

MADISON BRANCH (PRR-IM) (continued)
CONSTRUCTION/ABANDONMENT

Date	Act	End points	MP	Change	Main	Source	Note
1838/11/29	B1	North Madison-Grayford	43.0-26.3	+16.7	16.7	4	
1839/6/6	B1	Grayford-Vernon	26.3-23.1	+3.2	19.9	4	
1841/6/1	B1	Madison-North Madison	45.2-43.0	+2.2		1,4	1
1841/6/1	B1	Vernon-Queensville	23.1-17.4	+5.7	27.8	4	
1843/6/1	B2	Queensville-Scipio	17.4-14.5	+2.9		4	
1843/9	B2	Scipio-Elizabethtown	14.5-8.0	+6.5	37.2	4	
1844/7	B2	Elizabethtown-Columbus	8.0-0	+8.0	45.2	4	

1976	X	Columbus-North Vernon	2.8-19.4	-16.6		2,5	
1976	Y	In Columbus	0-2.8	(2.8)	25.8		
1977	S2	North Vernon-Madison	19.4-45.2	[25.8]	0	5	
1984/3/12	S10	In Columbus	0-2.8	[(2.8)]	0		

OWNERSHIP

1838	State of Indiana (B1)
1843/2/20	Madison & Indianapolis RR (B2), lease line from State of Indiana
1856/2/26	Madison & Indianapolis RR, buy line from State of Indiana
1862/3/28	Indianapolis & Madison RR, reorganize Madison & Indianapolis
1866/5/1	Jeffersonville, Madison & Indianapolis RR, merge I&M and other road
1871	Pittsburgh, Cincinnati & St. Louis Ry, lease JM&I, controlled by Penna RR
1890	Pittsburgh, Cincinnati & St. Louis, merge JM&I and other road
1890	Pittsburgh, Cincinnati, Chicago & St. Louis Ry, merge PC&SL and other roads
1921/1/1	Pennsylvania RR, lease PC&SL
1957 ca.	PC&SL, ownership transfer to Philadelphia, Baltimore & Washington
1968/2/1	Penn Central Co., merge PRR and New York Central
1969/10/1	Penn Central Transp. Co., acquired Penn Central Co.
1976/4/1	Conrail, purchase of Penn Central Transp.

ORIGINAL EDINBURG-COLUMBUS LINE (PRR-IEC)

	Mileage	County	Crossings, junctions, etc.
Columbus	0	Bartholomew	J/PRR-IL 41.0, J/PRR-IM 0
Edinburg	10.5	Johnson	J/PRR-IL 30.6, J/PRR-SL 0

CONSTRUCTION/ABANDONMENT

Date	Act	End points	MP	Change	Main	Source	Note
1845/9/8	B2	Columbus-Edinburg	0-10.5	+10.5	10.5	6	
1864	X	Columbus-Edinburg	0-10.5	-10.5	0	2	

OWNERSHIP

1845	Madison & Indianapolis RR (B2)
1862/3/28	Indianapolis & Madison RR, reorganize Madison & Indianapolis

PENNSYLVANIA

NEW ALBANY BRANCH (PRR-IA)

	Mileage	County	Crossings, junctions, etc.
Jeffersonville	0	Clark	J/PRR-L 107.2
Clarksville	1.6	"	
New Albany	4.0	Floyd	B/KIT-A 0
New Albany, State Street	4.6	"	

CONSTRUCTION/ABANDONMENT

Date	Act	End points	MP	Change	Main	Source	Note
1865	B4	Jeffersonville-New Albany	0-4.6	+4.6	4.6	2	

1976	X	Clarksville-New Albany	1.6-4.6	-3.0	1.6	2	
1984	X	Jeffersonville-Clarksville	0-1.6	-1.6	0		

(continued)

PENNSYLVANIA

NEW ALBANY BRANCH (PRR-IA) (continued)

OWNERSHIP

1865	Jeffersonville RR (B4), of part
1866/5/1	Jeffersonville, Madison & Indianapolis RR, merge Jeffersonville
1871	Pittsburgh, Cincinnati & St. Louis Ry, lease JM&I, controlled by Penna RR
1890	Pittsburgh, Cincinnati & St. Louis, merge JM&I and other road
1890	Pittsburgh, Cincinnati, Chicago & St. Louis Ry, merge PC&SL and others, controlled by Penna. RR
1917/1/1	Pittsburgh, Cincinnati, Chicago & St. Louis RR, merge Vandalia and others
1921/1/1	Pennsylvania RR, lease PCC&SL
1957 ca.	PCC&SL, ownership transfer to Philadelphia, Baltimore & Washington
1968/2/1	Penn Central Co., merge PRR and New York Central
1969/10/1	Penn Central Transp. Co., acquire Penn Central Co.
1976/4/1	Conrail, buy Penn Central Transp.

WATSON BRANCH (PRR-IW)

	Mileage	County	Crossings, junctions, etc.
Boyd	0	Clark	J/PRR-IL 104.9
(Crossing)	3.2	"	X/SOIN-A 0.2
Watson	4.0	"	J/B&O-SV

CONSTRUCTION/ABANDONMENT

Date	Act	End points	MP	Change	Main	Source	Note
1941 ca.	B25	Line	0-4.0	+4.0	4.0		

1994/3/12	S10	Line	0-4.0	[4.0]	0		

OWNERSHIP

1941	Pittsburgh, Cincinnati, Chicago & St. Louis RR (B25), leased to Penns. RR
1957 ca.	PCC&SL, ownership transfer to Philadelphia, Baltimore & Washington
1968/2/1	Penn Central Co., merge Pennsylvania RR and New York Central
1969/10/1	Penn Central Transp. Co., acquire Penn Central Co.
1976/4/1	Conrail, buy Penn Central Transp.

ORIGINAL VINCENNES BRANCH (PRR-IVO)

	Mileage	County	Crossings, junctions, etc.
Kentucky Avenue	0	Marion	J/IU-W 0.3
(Crossing)	1.3	"	X/IU-B 7.9
Mars Hill	4.3	"	J/IV 6.2

CONSTRUCTION/ABANDONMENT

Date	Act	End points	MP	Change	Main	Source	Note
1868	B19	Kentucky Ave.-Mars Hill	0-4.3	+4.3	4.3	7	
1918 ca.	Y	Kentucky Ave.-Mars Hill	0-4.3	(4.3)	0		
1960 ca.	X	In Indianapolis	0-0.9	(-0.9)	0		

OWNERSHIP

1869	Indianapolis & Vincennes RR (B19))
1905/1/1	Vandalia RR, merge Indianapolis & Vincennes and other roads
1917/1/1	Pittsburgh, Cincinnati, Chicago & St. Louis RR, merge Vandalia and others, controlled by Penna. RR
1921/1/1	Pennsylvania RR, lease PCC&SL
1957 ca.	PCC&SL, ownership transfer to Philadelphia, Baltimore & Washington
1968/2/1	Penn Central Co., merge PRR and New York Central
1969/10/1	Penn Central Transp. Co., acquire Penn Central Co.

PENNSYLVANIA

VINCENNES BRANCH (PRR-IV)

	Mileage	County	Crossings, junctions, etc.
(Indianapolis	0)	Marion	
--via IU-W and PRR-V			
Kraft	3.0	"	J/PRR-V 3.0
Maywood	5.7	"	
(Junction)	6.2	"	J/PRR-IVO 4.3
Valley Mill(s)	8.5	"	
Camby	11.3	Hendricks	
Friendswood	12.8	"	
Mooresville	18.7	Morgan	
Brooklyn	21.5	"	
Bethany Park	22.1	"	
Centerton	23.8	"	
Campbells	27.3	"	
Elk	29.5	"	
Martinsville	30.6	"	J/CCC-GM 127.3
Hynds	34.2	"	
Browns crossing	35.5	"	
Paragon	38.4	"	
Whitaker	41.0	"	
Silex	43.1	Owen	
Gosport Jct.	44.1	"	X/MON-SA 203.1
Gosport	45.0	"	
Corinne	46.4	"	J/PRR-IVG 0
Romona	49.7	"	
Spencer	53.8	"	
Rudd	57.5	"	
Freedom	62.8	"	
Farmers	65.8	"	
Minich	72.2	Greene	
Worthington	72.3	"	
Worthington Jct.	72.5	"	(J/CCC-T 40.0)
Nelson	72.9	"	
Rincon Jct.	73.8	"	X/CCC-T 41.2
Switz City	79.8	"	X/IC-NI/NE 89.44, J/MON-SS 40.5
Lyons	83.2	"	
Bushrod	84.9	"	J/PRR-IG 0
Bee Hunter	86.2	"	X/MILW-T 218.3
Marco	88.0	"	
Sandborn	91.7	Knox	
Westphalia	94.9	"	
Edwardsport	98.5	"	
Howard	100.0	"	
Bicknell	102.9	"	J/PRR-IVC 0
(Junction)	104.3	"	J/PRR-IVK 0
Kirk	105.5	"	
Bruceville	109.3	"	
(Junction)	116.0	"	
(Crossing)	116.9	"	
Vincennes, Union Depot	117.3	"	X/B&O-SI 188.6
(Crossing)	117.4	"	X/CEI-E 234.7
Vincennes	117.8	"	
(Junction)	118.1	"	J/CCC-
(Junction)	118.3	"	J/CEI-E 235.7
(continued)			

PENNSYLVANIA

VINCENNES BRANCH (PRR-IV) (continued)
CONSTRUCTION/ABANDONMENT

Date	Act	End points	MP	Change	Main	Source	Note
1868	B19	MP 6.2-Gosport	6.2-45.0	+38.8	38.8	7	
1869	B19	Gosport-Vincennes	45.0-117.8	+72.8	111.6	1,2,7	
1918 ca.	B25	Kraft-MP 6.2	3.0-6.2	+3.2	114.8		

1976	X	Bicknell-Vincennes	102.9-117.8	-14.9	99.9	2	
1984	X	Sandborn-Bicknell	92.4-102.9	-10.5	89.4	2	
1992/4/11	S9	Kraft-Bicknell	3.0-92.4	[89.4]	0	5	

OWNERSHIP

1868	Indianapolis & Vincennes RR (B19)
1905/1/1	Vandalia RR, merge Indianapolis & Vincennes and other roads
1917/1/1	Pittsburgh, Cincinnati, Chicago & St. Louis RR (B25), merge Vandalia and others, controlled by PRR
1921/1/1	Pennsylvania RR, lease PCC&SL
1957 ca.	PCC&SL, ownership transfer to Philadelphia, Baltimore & Washington
1968/2/1	Penn Central Co., merge PRR and New York Central
1969/10/1	Penn Central Transp. Co., acquire Penn Central Co.
1976/4/1	Conrail, buy Penn Central Transp.

GREENE COUNTY COAL BRANCH (PRR-IG)

	Mileage	County	Crossings, junctions, etc.
Bushrod	0	Greene	J/PRR-IV 84.9
Sponsler	3.6	"	X/MILW-Y 214.7
Linton	5.3	"	
(Junction)	5.5	"	J/spur to Buckeye Mine, .7 mi., and J/spur to Island No. 2 Mine, .8 mi.
(Junction)	7.0	"	J/branch to Summit, 1.4 mi.
(Crossing)	8.0	"	X/MON-SL 48.0
(Junction)	8.6	"	J/spur to Vandalia No. 20 Mine, .7 mi.
Maumee No. 26	8.8	"	
Linton Summit	13.4	"	
(End)	15.4	"	

CONSTRUCTION/ABANDONMENT

Date	Act	End points	MP	Change	Main	Source	Note
1885	B18	Bushrod-Linton Summit	0-15.4	+15.4	15.4	2	
1956	X	MP 15.4-MP 14.3	15.4-14.3	-1.1	14.3	2	
1957	X	MP 14.3-MP 13.4	14.3-13.4	-0.9	13.4	2	

1973	X	Bushrod-Linton Summit	0-13.4	-13.4	0	2,5	

OWNERSHIP

1885	Indianapolis & Vincennes RR (B18)
1905/1/1	Vandalia RR, merge Indianapolis & Vincennes and other roads
1917/1/1	Pittsburgh, Cincinnati, Chicago & St. Louis RR, merge Vandalia and others, controlled by Penna. RR
1921/1/1	Pennsylvania RR, lease PCC&SL
1957 ca.	PCC&SL, ownership transfer to Philadelphia, Baltimore & Washington
1968/2/1	Penn Central Co., merge PRR and New York Central
1969/10/1	Penn Central Transp.

COLUMBIA BRANCH (PRR-IVC)

	Mileage	County	Crossings, junctions, etc.
Bicknell	0	Knox	J/PRR-IV 102.9
Knox Consolidated Mine	1.6	"	

PENNSYLVANIA

COLUMBIA BRANCH (PRR-IVC) (continued)
CONSTRUCTION/ABANDONMENT

Date	Act	End points	MP	Change	Main	Source	Note
1923	B25	Line	0-1.6	+1.6	1.6	6	
1956	X	Line	0-1.6	-1.6	0	2,6	

OWNERSHIP

1923	Pittsburgh, Cincinnati, Chicago & St. Louis RR (B25), leased to Penn. RR

GOSPORT BRANCH (PRR-IVG)

	Mileage	County	Crossings, junctions, etc.
Corinne	0	Owen	J/PRR-IV 46.4
North Bedford	4.3	"	

CONSTRUCTION/ABANDONMENT

Date	Act	End points	MP	Change	Main	Source	Note
1889	B19	Line	0-4.3	+4.3	4.3	6	
1906	X	Line	0-4.3	-4.3	0	6	

OWNERSHIP

1889	Indianapolis & Vincennes RR (B19)
1905	Vandalia RR, merged Indianapolis & Vincennes and other roads

KNOX COUNTY COAL BRANCH (PRR-IVK)

	Mileage	County	Crossings, junctions, etc.
(Junction)	0	Knox	J/PRR-IV 104.3
(Mine)	3.8	"	

CONSTRUCTION/ABANDONMENT

Date	Act	End points	MP	Change	Main	Source	Note
1911	B32	Line	0-3.8	+3.8	3.8	6	
1956	X	Line	0-3.8	-3.8	0	2,6	

OWNERSHIP

1911	Vandalia RR (B32)
1917/1/1	Pittsburgh, Cincinnati, Chicago & St. Louis RR (B25), merge Vandalia and others, controlled by Pennsylvania RR
1921/1/1	Pennsylvania RR, lease PCC&SL

I & F BRANCH (PRR-IF)

	Mileage	County	Crossings, junctions, etc.
(Indianapolis	0)	Marion	
--via IU-W and PRR-V			
Davis	6.9	"	J/PRR-V 6.9
South Hunt	8.6	"	X/CCC-L 9.4
Hunt	9.5	"	
(Bridge)	11.3	"	B/B&O-ID 132.6
Clermont	12.6	"	X/P&E-A 9.6
South Burr	17.9	Hendricks	
North Burr	19.6	"	
Herr	24.6	Boone	
South Lebanon	30.6	"	
(Bridge)	31.5	"	B/CI-A 6138
Lebanon	31.6	"	
(Bridge)	31.8	"	B/CCC-H 138.7
Pike	37.2	"	
Reagan	41.8	Clinton	
(continued)			

PENNSYLVANIA

I & F BRANCH (PRR-IF) (continued)

	Mileage	County	Crossings, junctions, etc.
Reagan	41.8	Clinton	
Frank	48.1	"	X/MON-I 136.0, J/PRR-VF 78.3
	[Terre Haute]		
Frank	78.3	"	
Frankfort	78.6	"	X/NKP-LF 234.2, X/NKP-TC 206.6
Moran	85.8	"	
Sedalia	87.9	"	
Cutler	92.2	Carroll	
Bringhurst	95.6	"	
Flora	97.0	"	
Camden	101.3	"	
Clymers	109.2	Cass	X/WAB-P 224.3
Long Cliff	113.3	"	
Van	114.5	"	J/PRR-L 198.3, J/PRR-LF 1.2

CONSTRUCTION/ABANDONMENT

Date	Act	End points	MP	Change	Main	Source	Note
1871	B22	Frank-Clymers	78.3-109.2	+30.9	30.9	5	3
1875	B22	Clymers-Van	109.2-114.4	+5.3	36.2	5	
1918	B29	Davis-Frank	6.9-48.1	+41.2	77.4	1	

1993/3/20	S5	Bringhurst-Van	94.0-114.5	[20.5]		5	
1993	X	Frankfort-Bringhurst	80.2-94.0	-13.8			
1993	Y	In Frankfort	78.6-80.2	(1.6)	41.5		

OWNERSHIP

1871	Logansport, Crawfordsville & South Western Ry (B22)
1879/11/1	Terre Haute & Logansport RR, reorganize LC&SW
1898/12/1	Terre Haute & Logansport Ry, reorganize TH&L
1905/1/1	Vandalia RR, merge Terre Haute & Logansport and other roads
1917/1/1	Pittsburgh, Cincinnati, Chicago & St. Louis RR, merge Vandalia and others, controlled by Penna. RR
1918	Indianapolis & Frankfort RR (B29), controlled by Pennsylvania RR
1921/1/1	Pennsylvania RR, lease PCC&SL
1953 ca.	Penndel Co. (Pennsylvania RR holding co.), merge Indianapolis & Frankfort
1957 ca.	PCC&SL, ownership transfer to Philadelphia, Baltimore & Washington
1968/2/1	Penn Central Co., merge PRR and New York Central
1969/10/1	Penn Central Transp. Co., acquire Penn Central Co.
1976/4/1	Conrail, buy Penn Central Transp. and Penndel

VAN JCT.-KRAFT (PRR-VK)

	Mileage	County	Crossings, junctions, etc.
Van Jct.	0	Marion	J/IU-B
Kraft	1.4	"	J/PRR-V 3.0

CONSTRUCTION/ABANDONMENT

Date	Act	End points	MP	Change	Main	Source	Note
1918 ca.	B25	Van Jct.-Kraft	0-1.4	+1.4	1.4		

OWNERSHIP

1918	Pittsburgh, Cincinnati, Chicago & St. Louis RR (B25), control by PRR
1921/1/1	Pennsylvania RR, lease PCC&SL
1957 ca.	PCC&SL, ownership transfer to Philadelphia, Baltimore & Washington
1968	Penn Central Co., buy Pennsylvania RR
1969/10/1	Penn Central Transp. Co., acquire Penn Central Co.
1976/4/1	Conrail, buy Penn Central Transp. and PB&W

PENNSYLVANIA

ST. LOUIS DIVISION (PRR-V)

	Mileage	County	Crossings, junctions, etc.
(Indianapolis)	0)	Marion	
--via IU-W			
West Street	0.4	"	J/IU-W 0.4
Woods	1.6	"	X/IU-B 8.9
Kraft	3.0	"	J/PRR-IV 3.0, J/PRR-VK 1.4
Davis	6.9	"	J/PRR-IF 6.9
West Davis	8.0	"	
Bridgeport	8.8	"	
Plainfield	13.5	Hendricks	
East Gibson	14.9	"	
West Gibson	16.0	"	
Cartersburg	16.8	"	
Clayton	20.1	"	
East Summit	20.3	"	
Summit	21.2	"	
West Summit	22.0	"	
Pecksburg	22.7	"	
Amo	24.9	"	
Coatesville	27.9	"	
East Marion	28.0	"	
Marion	29.0	"	
West Marion	30.0	Putnam	
Fillmore	32.5	"	
East Almeda	35.9	"	
Almeda	37.2	"	
Greencastle	38.9	"	
Limedale	40.3	"	X/MON-SA 180.0
West Limedale	41.4	"	
Hamrick	43.5	"	
Reelsville	47.7	"	
Eagles	49.8	"	
Harmony	53.2	Clay	
(Junction)	53.7	"	J/PRR-VHN 0
Knightsville	55.0	"	J/PRR-VP 0, J/PRR-VKN 0
(Junction)	55.2	"	J/spur to Rob Roy Mine, 1.6 mi. and J/spur to south, 1.5 mi.
Brazil	57.0	"	J/B&O-IB 25.1, J/CI-A 127.0, J/PRR-VB 0
(Junction)	57.1	"	J/CEI-EZ 184.6
(Junction)	57.3	"	J/PRR-VO 57.3
Seelyville	64.5	Vigo	J/PRR-VO 65.3
[Indianapolis, via PRR-VO]			
Seelyville	65.3	"	
(Junction)	66.7	"	J/spur to Glen Ayr Mine, 1.9 mi.
Prairie	68.6	"	
(Junction)	69.9	"	J/PRR-VT3 69.9
(Bridge)	70.3	"	B/MILW-T 177.3
Fruitridge Avenue	70.4	"	
East Yard	70.9	"	B/PRR-VT1 0
(Junction)	72.4	"	J/conn to CEI-E 177.8, 0.4 mi.
Union	72.6	"	X/CEI-E 177.5
Terre Haute	72.7	"	
Seventh Street	72.9	"	
Vigo	73.5	"	X/CCC-T 0.2
(Junction)	73.5	"	J/PRR-VT2 73.5
West Terre Haute	75.1	"	
(continued)			

PENNSYLVANIA

ST. LOUIS DIVISION (PRR-V) (continued)

	Mileage [Indianapolis]	County	Crossings, junctions, etc.
West Terre Haute	75.1	Vigo	
Macksville	75.3	"	J/PRR-VM 0
Liggett	77.4	"	
(IN/IL state line)	79.9		
Farrington IL	80.6		
Effingham	140.6		
Vandalia IL	172.0		
St. Louis MO	244.6		

CONSTRUCTION/ABANDONMENT

Date	Act	End points	MP	Change	Main	Source	Note
1852/2/16	B5	Indianapolis-Brazil	0.4-57.3	+56.9		7	
1852/2/16	B5	Seelyville-Terre Haute	65.3-72.7	+7.4	64.3	7	
1870/4/26	B20	Terre Haute-IL state line	72.7-79.9	+7.2	71.5	2	
1901 ca.	B20	Brazil-Seelyville	57.3-64.5	+7.2	78.7	5	4

1969 ca.	X	In Terre Haute	72.4-73.5	-1.1			
1969 ca.	Y	East Yard-Union	70.9-72.4	(1.5)	76.1		
1973	Y	MP 69.9-East Yard	69.9-70.9	(1.0)	75.1		
1982	X	Davis-Greencastle	6.9-35.0	-28.1	47.0	2	
1984	X	Greencastle-Limedale	35.0-40.3	-5.3			
1987	X	MP 69.9-Union	69.9-72.4	(-2.5)	41.7	2	
1987/5/1	S8	Limedale-Seelyville	40.3-64.5	[24.2]			
1987/5/1	S8	Seelyville-MP 69.9	65.3-69.9	[4.6]	12.9		

OWNERSHIP

1852	Terre Haute & Richmond RR (B5), of part
1865/3/6	Terre Haute & Indianapolis RR (B20), rename Terre Haute & Richmond
1905/1/1	Vandalia RR, merge Terre Haute & Indianapolis
1917/1/1	Pittsburgh, Cincinnati, Chicago & St. Louis RR, merge Vandalia and others, controlled by Penna. RR
1921/1/1	Pennsylvania RR, lease PCC&SL
1957 ca.	PCC&SL, ownership transfer to Philadelphia, Baltimore & Washington
1968/2/1	Penn Central Co., merge PRR and New York Central
1969/10/1	Penn Central Transp. Co., acquire Penn Central Co.
1976/4/1	Conrail, buy Penn Central Transp.
1987/5/1	Terre Haute, Brazil & Eastern, buy part of line

BRAZIL-SEELYVILLE OLD LINE (PRR-VO)

	Mileage [Indianapolis]	County	Crossings, junctions, etc.
(Junction)	57.3	Clay	J/PRR-V 57.3
Turner	58.4	"	
(Junction)	59.5	"	J/spur to Fortner Mine, .7 mi
(Junction)	60.0	"	J/spur to San Pedro Mine, 1.5 mi.
(Junction)	60.5	"	J/spur to Klondike Mine, 1 mi
Staunton	60.8	"	
Cloverland	63.1	"	
Seelyville	65.3	"	J/PRR-V 64.5/65.3

CONSTRUCTION/ABANDONMENT

Date	Act	End points	MP	Change	Main	Source	Note
1852/2/16	B5	Line	57.3-65.3	+8.0	8.0	7	
1901 ca.	X	Staunton-Seelyville	60.8-65.3	-4.5	3.5		

1984	X	Brazil-Staunton	57.3-60.8	-3.5	0		
(continued)							

PENNSYLVANIA

BRAZIL-SEELYVILLE OLD LINE (PRR-VO) (continued)

OWNERSHIP

1852	Terre Haute & Richmond RR (B5), of part
1865/3/6	Terre Haute & Indianapolis RR (B20), rename Terre Haute & Richmond
1905/1/1	Vandalia RR, merge Terre Haute & Indianapolis
1917/1/1	Pittsburgh, Cincinnati, Chicago & St. Louis RR, merge Vandalia and others, controlled by Penna. RR
1921/1/1	Pennsylvania RR, lease PCC&SL
1957 ca.	PCC&SL, ownership transfer to Philadelphia, Baltimore & Washington
1968	Penn Central Co., buy Pennsylvania RR
1969/10/1	Penn Central Transp. Co., acquire Penn Central Co.
1976/4/1	Conrail, buy Penn Central Transp.

BRAZIL-SALINE CITY (PRR-VB)

	Mileage	County	Crossings, junctions, etc.
Brazil	0	Clay	J/PRR-V 57.0
(Junction)	1.8	"	J/spur to Zeller Mine, 1.7 mi.
Stave Track	2	"	
Watson	3	"	
Ehrlich	4	"	
Prairie City	5.5	"	
(Junction)	5.8	"	J/spur to Crawford No. 8 Mine, 0.8 mi.
Vandalia	8	"	
Ashboro	8.8	"	
Saline City	11.5	"	J/CCC-T 20.0

CONSTRUCTION/ABANDONMENT

Date	Act	End points	MP	Change	Main	Source	Note
1887	B20	Brazil-Saline City	0-11.5	+11.5	11.5	2,6	
1887/6/3	L3	Brazil-Saline City	0-11.5	-11.5	0	6	h
1916 ca.	XL	Brazil-Saline City	0-11.5	+11.5	11.5		
1916	X	Saline City-north	4.0-11.5	-7.5	4.0	5,6	
1945	X	South of Brazil	2.0-4.0	-2.0	2.0	5	
1957	X	South of Brazil	1.0-2.0	-1.0		5	
1957	Y	In Brazil	0-1.0	(1.0)	0		

OWNERSHIP

1887	Terre Haute & Indianapolis RR (B20)
1888 ca.	Evansville & Indianapolis (L3), lease line
1905/1/1	Vandalia RR, merge Terre Haute & Indianapolis
1916 ca.	Lease to Evansville & Indianapolis terminated
1917/1/1	Pittsburgh, Cincinnati, Chicago & St. Louis RR, merge Vandalia and others, controlled by Penna. RR
1921/1/1	Pennsylvania RR, lease PCC&SL
1957 ca.	PCC&SL, ownership transfer to Philadelphia, Baltimore & Washington
1968/2/1	Penn Central Co., buy Pennsylvania RR
1969/10/1	Penn Central Transp. Co., acquire Penn Central Co.
1976/4/1	Conrail, buy Penn Central Transp. and PB&W

CHINOOK MINE BRANCH (PRR-VB2)

	Mileage	County	Crossings, junctions, etc.
Brazil	0	Clay	J/PRR-V 57.0
Chinook Mine	6.0	"	

CONSTRUCTION/ABANDONMENT

Date	Act	End points	MP	Change	Main	Source	Note
1984	X	Line	0-6.0	-6.0	0		8

(continued)

PENNSYLVANIA

CHINOOK MINE BRANCH (PRR-VB2) (continued)
OWNERSHIP

??	Pennsylvania RR, with lease of Pittsburgh, Cinci, Chi & St L
1957 ca.	PCC&SL, ownership transfer to Philadelphia, Baltimore & Washington
1968/2/1	Penn Central Co., buy Pennsylvania RR
1969/10/1	Penn Central Transp. Co., acquire Penn Central Co.
1976/4/1	Conrail, buy Penn Central Transp. and PB&W

CENTER POINT BRANCH (PRR-VP)

	Mileage	County	Crossings, junctions, etc.
Knightsville	0	Clay	J/PRR-V 55.0
(Junction)	4.0	"	J/spur to Crawford Mine, 2.0 mi.
Asherville	4.5	"	
Stearleys	6.5	"	
(Junction)	8.0	"	J/spur to Columbia No. 5 Mine, 1.0 mi.
Centerpoint	8.3	"	

CONSTRUCTION/ABANDONMENT

Date	Act	End points	MP	Change	Main	Source	Note
1870	B20	Knightsville-Centerpoint	0-8.3	+8.3	8.3	2	
1967	X	Knightsville-Centerpoint	0-8.3	-8.3	0	5	

OWNERSHIP

1865/3/6	Terre Haute & Indianapolis RR (B20), rename Terre Haute & Richmond
1905/1/1	Vandalia RR, merge Terre Haute & Indianapolis
1917/1/1	Pittsburgh, Cincinnati, Chicago & St. Louis RR, merge Vandalia and others, controlled by Penna. RR
1921/1/1	Pennsylvania RR, lease PCC&SL
1957 ca.	PCC&SL, ownership transfer to Philadelphia, Baltimore & Washington

HARMONY NORTH BRANCH (PRR-VHN)

	Mileage	County	Crossings, junctions, etc.
(Junction)	0	Clay	J/PRR-V 53.7
Gart Mine	1.5	"	

CONSTRUCTION/ABANDONMENT

Date	Act	End points	MP	Change	Main	Source	Note
							8

OWNERSHIP

KNIGHTSVILLE NORTH BRANCH (PRR-VKN)

	Mileage	County	Crossings, junctions, etc.
Knightsville	0	Clay	J/PRR-V 55.0
Benwood	2	"	
Otter Creek (Mine)	5	"	

CONSTRUCTION/ABANDONMENT

Date	Act	End points	MP	Change	Main	Source	Note
							8

OWNERSHIP

EAST YARD-PRESTON-DEWEY (PRR-VT1)

	Mileage	County	Crossings, junctions, etc.
East Yard	0	Vigo	J/PRR-V 70.9
Preston	2.1	"	X/CCC-L 68.6, MILW-T 175.2
Dewey Jct.	2.9	"	J/CEI-E 173.8 (J/PRR-VF 3.7)

PENNSYLVANIA

EAST YARD-PRESTON-DEWEY (PRR-VT1) (continued)
CONSTRUCTION/ABANDONMENT

Date	Act	End points	MP	Change	Main	Source	Note
1911	B32	East Yard-Dewey Jct.	0-2.9	+2.9	2.9		
1973 ca.	X	MP 1.7-Dewey Jct.	1.7-2.9	-1.2			
1973 ca.	Y	East Yard-MP 1.7	0-1.7	(1.7)	0		
1984 ca.	X	East Yard-MP 1.7	0-1.7	(-1.7)	0		

OWNERSHIP

1911	Vandalia RR (B32)
1917/1/1	Pittsburgh, Cincinnati, Chicago & St. Louis RR, merge Vandalia and others, controlled by Penna. RR
1921/1/1	Pennsylvania RR, lease PCC&SL
1957 ca.	PCC&SL, ownership transfer to Philadelphia, Baltimore & Washington
1968/2/1	Penn Central Co., merge PRR and New York Central
1969/10/1	Penn Central Transp. Co., acquire Penn Central Co.
1976/4/1	Conrail, buy Penn Central Transp.

IN TERRE HAUTE (PRR-VT2)

	Mileage	County	Crossings, junctions, etc.
CP Ringo	73.3	Vigo	J/CCC-L 72.0
(Junction)	73.5	"	J/PRR-V 73.5

CONSTRUCTION/ABANDONMENT

Date	Act	End points	MP	Change	Main	Source	Note
1969 ca.	B26	Line	73.3-73.5	+0.2	0.2		

OWNERSHIP

1968	Penn Central Co. (B26)
1969/10/1	Penn Central Transp. Co., acquire Penn Central Co.
1976/4/1	Conrail, buy Penn Central Transp.

PRARIE-PRESTON CONNECTION (PRR-VT3)

	Mileage	County	Crossings, junctions, etc.
(Junction)	69.9	Vigo	J/PRR-V 69.9
Preston	72.4	"	J/CCC-L 68.6, J/MILW-T 175.2
--via MILW-T			
(Dewey)	72.9	"	J/CEI-E 174.7--(PRR-VF 2.8)

CONSTRUCTION/ABANDONMENT

Date	Act	End points	MP	Change	Main	Source	Note
1973 ca.	B26	Line	69.9-72.4	+2.5	2.5		
1987/5/1	S8	Line	69.9-72.4	[2.5]	0		
1992/12/31	X	Line	69.9-72.4	[-2.5]	0		

OWNERSHIP

1973	Penn Central Transp. Co. (B26)
1976/4/1	Conrail, buy Penn Central Transp.
1987/12/31	Terre Haute, Brazil & Eastern, buy line

SOUTH BRANCH (PRR-VM)

	Mileage	County	Crossings, junctions, etc.
Macksville	0	Vigo	J/PRR-V 75.3
(End)	5.6	"	
(continued)			

PENNSYLVANIA

SOUTH BRANCH (PRR-VM) (continued)

CONSTRUCTION/ABANDONMENT

Date	Act	End points	MP	Change	Main	Source	Note
1910 ca.	B32	Line	0-5.6	+5.6	5.6		

1972	X	MP 3.0-MP 5.6	3.0-5.6	-2.6	3.0	2	
1976	X	MP 0-MP 3.0	0-3.0	-3.0	0	2	

OWNERSHIP

1910	Vandalia RR (B32)
1917/1/1	Pittsburgh, Cincinnati, Chicago & St. Louis RR, merge Vandalia and others, controlled by Penna.
RR1921/1/1	Pennsylvania RR, lease PCC&SL
1957 ca.	PCC&SL, ownership transfer to Philadelphia, Baltimore & Washington
1968/2/1	Penn Central Co., merge PRR and New York Central
1969/10/1	Penn Central Transp. Co., acquire Penn Central Co

TERRE HAUTE-FRANKFORT (PRR-VF)

	Mileage	County	Crossings, junctions, etc.
(Terre Haute)	0)	Vigo	
--via CEI-E			
(Dewey)	2.8)	"	J/PRR-VT3 72.9
--via CEI-E			
(Dewey)	3.7)	"	J/PRR-VT1 3.4
--via CEI-E			
Otter Creek Jct.	5.8	"	J/CEI-E 171.9
Rosedale	12.2	Parke	X/B&O-IB 12.1, J/spur to Parke No. 8 Mine, 1 mi.
Jessups	14.9	"	
(Junction)	15.1	"	J/spur to Minshall Mine, 3 mi.
Catlin	17.8	"	
KD	22.7	"	
Rockville	22.9	"	
Sand Creek	26.6	"	J/CI-A 105.3
(Junction)	28.5	"	J/spur to Nyesville, 2.0 mi.
Judson	29.9	"	
Guion	32.3	"	
GU	32.7	"	X/B&O-ID 176.4
Waveland Jct.	36.0	Montgomery	J/CI-A 95.9
Waveland	37.2	"	
Browns Valley	40.4	"	
New Market	45.6	"	
Ames	52.0	"	X/MON-SA 148.4, X/P&E-A 43.0
Crawfordsville	52.5	"	
GR	56.5	"	
Garfield	56.8	"	
Darlington	60.1	"	
Bowers	64.6	"	
Colfax	68.6	Clinton	X/CCC-H 154.0
Manson	73.7	"	
Fort	78.0	"	
Frank	78.3	"	J/PRR-IF 78.3

CONSTRUCTION/ABANDONMENT

Date	Act	End points	MP	Change	Main	Source	Note
1871	B22	Rockville-Frank	22.9-78.3	+55.4	55.4	5	
1872	L1	Otter Creek Jct.-Rockville	5.8-22.9	+17.1	72.5	2	5

1969	X	GU-Waveland	32.7-37.0	-4.3	68.2	2	
1972	X	Rockville-GU	23.3-32.7	-9.4	58.8	2	
1973	X	Otter Creek Jct.-Rockville	5.8-23.3	-17.5		2	
1973	X	Colfax-Frank	71.2-78.3	-7.1	34.2	2	
1976	X	Waveland-Colfax	37.0-71.2	-34.2	0	2	

PENNSYLVANIA

TERRE HAUTE-FRANKFORT (PRR-VF) (continued)
OWNERSHIP

1871	Logansport, Crawfordsville & South Western Ry (B22)
1872	Lease part of Evansville & Crawfordsville (L1)
1877	Evansville & Terre Haute, rename Evansville & Crawfordsville
1879/11/1	Terre Haute & Logansport RR, reorganize LC&SW
1898/12/1	Terre Haute & Logansport Ry, reorganize TH&L RR
1905/1/1	Vandalia RR, merge Terre Haute & Logansport and other roads
1911/7/20	Chicago & Eastern Illinois, merge Evansville & Terre Haute
1917/1/1	Pittsburgh, Cincinnati, Chicago & St. Louis RR, merge Vandalia and others, controlled by Penna. RR
1921/1/1	Pennsylvania RR, lease PCC&SL
1924	PCC&SL, buy leased line from Chicago & Eastern Illinois
1957 ca.	PCC&SL, ownership transfer to Philadelphia, Baltimore & Washington
1968/2/1	Penn Central Co., merge PRR and New York Central
1969/10/1	Penn Central Transp. Co., acquire Penn Central Co.

ACQUISITION/DISPOSITION RECORD

Date	Act	PRR-	End points	Change	Main	Note
1838/11/29	B1	IM	North Madison-Grayford	+16.7	16.7	
1839/6/6	B1	IM	Grayford-Vernon	+3.2	19.9	
1841/6/1	B1	IM	Madison-North Madison	+2.2		1
/6/1	B1	IM	Vernon-Queensville	+5.7	27.8	
1843/6/1	B2	IM	Queensville-Scipio	+2.9		
/9	B2	IM	Scipio-Elizabethtown	+6.5	37.2	
1844/7	B2	IM	Elizabethtown-Columbus	+8.0	45.2	
1845/9/8	B2	IEC	Columbus-Edinburg	+10.5	55.7	
1846/9/1	B2	IL	Franklin-Edinburg	+10.3	66.0	
1847/10/1	B2	IL	Indianapolis-Franklin	+19.8	85.8	
1849	B26	IJ	Edinburg-Shelbyville	+16.0	101.8	
1850	B3	IC	Rushville-Shelbyville	+18.2		
	B27	IK	Shelbyville-Knightstown	+26.0	146.0	
1852	B4	IL	Jeffersonville-Columbus	+67.8		
/2/16	B5	V,VO	Indianapolis-Terre Haute	+72.3	286.1	
1853	B4	IL	Columbus-Edinburg	+10.4		
/10	B7	I	Indianapolis-New Paris OH	+71.4		
	B6	IC	Shelbyville-Columbus	+24.0		
	B8	CR	OH state line-Richmond	+3.9		
	B8	CR	Richmond-New Castle	+26.6	422.4	
1854/9	B9	F	OH state line-Ft. Wayne	+19.4		
	X	IK	Shelbyville-Knightstown	-26.0	415.8	
1855	X	IJ	Edinburg-Shelbyville	-16.0	399.8	
1856/1/23	B10	F	Ft. Wayne-Columbia City	+18.9	418.7	
1857	B11	CR	New Castle-Anoka	+75.9		
	B11	L	Anoka-Logansport	+4.9	499.5	
1858/12	B13	F	Columbia City-IL state line	+114.6	614.1	2
1859	B12	L	Logansport-Kenneth	+5.1		
	B12	LE	Kenneth-Effner	+55.6	674.8	
1861	B15	L	Boone-LaCrosse	+42.4		
	B15	LO	Van-Boone	+8.5		
	B15	LV	LaCrosse-Valparaiso	+10.4	736.1	
1864	X	IEC	Columbus-Edinburg	-10.5	725.6	
1865	B4	IA	Jeffersonville-New Albany	+4.6		
	B14	L	LaCrosse-Chicago	+36.9		
	X	LV	LaCrosse-Valparaiso	-10.4	756.7	
1867	B18	IC	Rushville-Bentonville	+15.1		
	B16	L	Union City-Marion	+54.0		
	B18	ICA	Bentonville-Cambridge City	+6.1	831.9	

(continued)

PENNSYLVANIA

ACQUISITION/DISPOSITION RECORD (continued)

Date	Act	PRR-	End points	Change	Main	Note
1868	B17	L	Marion-Anoka	+35.2		
	B19	IV,IVO	Indianapolis-Gosport	+43.1	910.2	
1869	B19	IV	Gosport-Vincennes	+72.8	983.0	
1870	B20	VP	Knightsville-Centerpoint	+8.3		
/4/26	B20	V	Terre Haute-IL state line	+7.2		
/6/22	B1	GS	Junction-Sturgis MI	+53.1		
/7	B2	GR	Richmond-Winchester	+23.8	1075.4	
1871	B22	IF	Frank-Clymers	+30.9		3
	B22	VF	Rockville-Frank	+55.4		
/12/25	B2	GR	Winchester-Adams	+62.1	1223.8	
1872	L1	VF	Otter Creek Jct.-Rockville	+17.1	1240.9	
1875	B22	IF	Clymers-Van	+5.3	1246.2	
1884	B23	LS	Van-South Bend	+66.4	1312.6	
1885	B18	IG	Bushrod-Linton Summit	+15.4	1328.0	
1887	B20	VB	Brazil-Saline City	+11.5		
/6/3	L3	VB	Brazil-Saline City	<11.5>	1328.0	
1889	B19	IVI	Corinne-North Bedford	+4.8	1332.8	
1893	X	LO	Van-Boone	-8.5		
	B25	L	Kenneth-Boone	+6.2	1330.5	
1895	B24	CM	Mathews-Fairmount	+8.5	1339.0	
1898	B24	CM	Fairmount-Swayzee	+11.9	1350.9	
1899	B24	CM	Swayzee-Converse	+6.0	1356.9	
1900	B24	CM	Vance-Mathews	+14.7	1371.6	
1901 ca.	B20	V	Brazil-Seelyville	+7.2		4
	X	VO	Staunton-Seelyville	-4.5		
	XL	IE	Van-Butler	+92.5	1466.8	
1906	X	IVI	Corinne-North Bedford	-4.8	1462.0	
1910	B25	IC	Bentonville-Dublin Jct.	+4.7		
	X	ICA	Bentonville-Cambridge City	-6.1		
ca.	B32	VM	Line	+5.6	1466.2	
1911	B32	IVK	Knox County Coal Branch	+3.8		
	B32	vtl	East Yard-Dewey	+2.9	1472.9	
1916	XL	VB	Brazil-Saline City	<+11.5>		
	X	VB	Saline City-north	-7.5	1476.9	
1918	B29	IF	Davis-Frank	+41.2		
ca.	B25	IV	Kraft-MP 6.2	+3.2		
ca.	B25	VK	Van Jct.-Kraft	+1.4		
ca.	Y	IVO	Near Indianapolis	(4.3)	1518.4	
1922	B25	IK	Thorne-Hawthorne Yards	+2.0		
	B25	IK	In Hawthorne Yards	(+3.0)	1520.4	
1923	B25	IVC	Columbia Branch	+1.6	1522.0	
1933	X	CM	Mathews-Converse	-26.0	1496.0	
1941 ca.	B25	IW	Boyd-Watson	+4.0	1500.0	
1945	X	VB	South of Brazil	-2.0	1498.0	
1954	X	IE	Auburn-Butler	-11.3	1486.7	
1955	X	IC	Bentonville-Dublin Jct.	-4.7	1482.0	
1956	X	IG	MP 15.4-MP 14.3	-1.1		
	X	IVC	Columbia Branch	-1.6		
	X	IVK	Knox County Coal Branch	-3.8	1475.5	
1957	X	IG	MP 14.3-MP 13.4	-0.9		
	X	VB	Brazil-south	-1.0		
	Y	VB	In Brazil	(1.0)	1472.6	
1960 ca.	X	IVO	In Indianapolis	(-0.9)	1472.6	
1961	X	IE	Columbia City-Churubusco	-7.8	1464.8	
1962	X	IC	North Rushville-Rushville	-13.0	1451.8	
1967	X	VP	Knightsville-Centerpoint	-8.3	1443.5	7

(continued)

PENNSYLVANIA

ACQUISITION/DISPOSITION RECORD (continued)

On February 1, 1968, this company was conveyed to Penn Central. The Acquisition/-Disposition Record is continued to two places: under this company and under the name of the subsequent new owner.

Date	Act	PRR--	End points	Change	Main	Note
1968	X	LE	Logansport-Mexico	-10.8	1432.7	
1969	X	V	In Terre Haute	-1.1		
ca.	Y	v	East Yard-Union	(1.5)		
	B26	VT2	In Terre Haute	+0.2		
	X	VF	Guion-Waveland	-4.3	1426.0	
1972	X	IC	Flat Rock-Fenns	-6.2		
	X	VF	Rockville-Guion	-9.4		
1972	X	VM	MP 3.0-MP 5.6	-2.6	1407.8	
1973	X	IG	Bushrod-Linton	-13.4		
	X	LE	Churubusco-Auburn	-17.4		
	X	LS	Plymouth-Nutwood	-15.1		
	X	LS	Culver-Plymouth	-10.5		
	Y	V	Prairie-East Yard	(1.0)		
	X	VT1	East Yard-Dewey	-1.2		
	Y	VT1	At East Yard	(1.7)		
	B26	VT3	Prairie-Preston	+2.5		
	X	VF	Otter Creek Jct.-Rockville	-17.5		
	X	VF	Colfax-Frank	-7.1	1325.4	
1975	X	LE	North Manchester-Columbia City	-17.3	1308.1	

On April 1, 1976, part of this company was conveyed to Conrail and part retained by the Penn Central trustees. The Acquisition/Disposition Record is continued to two places: under Pennsylvania and under the subsequent new owner. The property conveyed was:

Date	End points	MP	Conrail Change	PennC Change	PRR Total
[PRR-F]	OH line-IL line	300.4-453.3	152.9		
[PRR-GR]	In Richmond	0.7-2.3	1.6		
[PRR-GR]	Richmond-Ridgeville	2.3-33.0		30.7	
[PRR-GR]	In Ridgeville	33.0-34.2	1.2		
[PRR-GR]	Ridgeville-Decatur	34.2-70.4		36.2	
[PRR-GR]	Decatur-Adams	70.4-86.6	16.2		
[PRR-GS]	Junction-Kendallville	93.3-121.0	27.7		
[PRR-GS]	Kendallville-MI line	121.0-146.4		25.4	
[PRR-L]	OH line-Van	103.6-198.3	94.7		
[PRR-L]	Van-Boone	1.2-11.9	10.7		
[PRR-L]	Boone-IL line	206.8-286.1	79.3		
[PRR-LF]	Kenneth-Effner	5.7-61.3		55.6	
[PRR-LS]	MP 115.9-Culver	115.9-148.6		32.7	
[PRR-LS]	In Plymouth	159.1-160.9	1.8		
[PRR-LS]	Nutwood-South Bend	176.0-179.0		3.0	
[PRR-LS]	In South Bend	179.0-182.3	3.3		
[PRR-LE]	Van-MP 3.4	1.2-3.4	2.2		
[PRR-LE]	Mexico-N. Manchester	14.2-36.9		22.7	
[PRR-LE]	In North Manchester	36.9-38.0	1.1		
[PRR-LE]	In Columbia City	55.3-56.6	1.3		
[PRR-LE]	In Columbia City	56.6-57.2		0.6	
[PRR-CR]	OH line-Glen	68.5-72.4	3.9		
[PRR-CR]	In Richmond	74.9-76.6	1.7		
[PRR-CR]	Newman-New Castle	76.6-100.5		23.9	
[PRR-CR]	New Castle-Anderson	100.5-127.0	26.5		
[PRR-CR]	Anderson-Kokomo	127.0-155.7	28.7		
[PRR-CR]	Kokomo-Anoka	155.7-177.4	21.7		
[PRR-YA]	Anderson Belt	0-3.1	(3.1)		

(continued)

PENNSYLVANIA

ACQUISITION/DISPOSITION RECORD (continued)
The property conveyed was:

Date	End points	MP	Conrail Change	PennC Change	PRR Total
[PRR-CM]	Muncie-Mathews	26.0-41.1		15.1	
[PRR-CM]	In Muncie	41.1-41.8		(0.7)	
[PRR-CM]	In Muncie	41.8-42.9	(1.1)		
[PRR-I]	OH line-Indianapolis	115.4-186.8	71.4		
[PRR-IK]	Thorne-Hawthorne Yard	0-2.0	2.0		
[PRR-IK]	In Hawthorne Yard	2.0-5.0	(3.0)		
[PRR-IL]	Indianapolis-KY line	0.5-108.8	108.3		
[PRR-IA]	Jeffersonville-Clarksv.	0-1.6	1.6		
[PRR-IA]	Clarksville-New Albany	1.6-4.6		3.0	
[PRR-IW]	Boyd-Watson	0-4.0	4.0		
[PRR-IM]	In Columbus	0-2.8	2.8		
[PRR-IM]	Columbus-Madison	2.8-45.2		42.4	
[PRR-IC]	In Columbus	0-3.8	3.8		
[PRR-IC]	Columbus-Flat Rock	3.8-12.6		8.8	
[PRR-IC]	Fenns-Shelbyville	18.8-23.8		5.0	
[PRR-IC]	In Shelbyville	23.8-27.3	3.5		
[PRR-IC]	Shelbyville-N. Rushville	27.3-44.3		17.0	
[PRR-IV]	Kraft-Vincennes	3.0-102.9	99.9		
[PRR-IV]	Bicknell-Vincennes	102.9-117.8		14.9	
[PRR-IVO]	In Indianapolis	0.9-4.3	(3.4)		
[PRR-IF]	Davis-Frank	6.9-48.1	41.2		
[PRR-IF]	Frank-Van	78.3-114.5	36.2		
[PRR-V]	Indianapolis-Seelyville	0.4-64.5	64.1		
[PRR-V]	Seelyville-Prairie	65.3-69.9	4.6		
[PRR-V]	Prairie-Union	69.9-72.4	(2.5)		
[PRR-V]	Terre Haute-IL line	73.5-79.9	6.4		
[PRR-VO]	Brazil-Staunton	57.3-60.8	3.5		
[PRR-VB2]	Brazil-Chinook Mine	0-6.0	(6.0)		
[PRR-VT1]	At East Yard	0-1.7	(1.7)		
[PRR-VT2]	In Terre Haute	73.3-73.5	0.2		
[PRR-VT3]	Prairie-Preston	69.9-72.4	2.5		
[PRR-VM]	Macksville-south	0-3.0		3.0	
[PRR-VK]	Van Jct.-Kraft	0-1.4	1.4		
[PRR-VF]	Waveland-Colfax	37.0-71.2		34.2	
		TOTALS	933.9	374.2	1308.1

ACQUISITION/DISPOSITION RECORD (continued)

Date	Act	PRR	End points	Conrail Change	PennC Change	PRR Total
1976	S1	CR	Newman-New Castle		[23.9]	
	X	CM	Muncie-Mathews		-15.1	
	X	CM	In Muncie		(-0.7)	
	Y	GR	In Richmond	(1.6)		
	X	GR	Richmond-Ridgeville		-30.7	
	Y	GR	In Ridgeville	(1.2)		
	X	GR	Ridgeville-Portland		-7.8	
	Y	GS	In Kendallville	(0.9)		
	X	GS	Kendallville-MI state line		-25.4	
	X	IA	Clarksville-New Albany		-3.0	
	X	IC	Fenns-Shelbyville		-5.0	
	X	IC	Shelbyville-Rushville		-17.0	
	Y	IC	In Shelbyville	(3.5))		

PENNSYLVANIA

ACQUISITION/DISPOSITION RECORD (continued)

Date	Act	PRR	End points	Conrail Change	PennC Change	PRR Total
1976	Y	IM	In Columbus	(2.8)		
	X	IM	Columbus-North Vernon		-16.6	
	X	IV	Bicknell-Vincennes		-14.9	
	X	LE	In Columbia City		-0.6	
	Y	LE	In Columbia City	(1.3)		
	Y	LE	In North Manchester	(1.1)		
	S4	LF	Kenneth-Effner		[55.6]	
	X	LS	Nutwood-S of South Bend		-3.0	
	Y	LS	In Plymouth	(1.8)		
	Y	LS	In South Bend	(3.3)		
	X	VM	MP 0-MP 3.0		-3.0	
	X	VF	Waveland-Colfax		-34.2	
YEAR TOTAL				916.4	118.4	1034.8
1977	L4	GR	Portland-DA		<28.4>	
	S2	IM	North Vernon-Madison		[25.8]	
	X	IC	Columbus-Flat Rock		-8.8	
	Y	IC	In Columbus	(3.8)		
	X	LE	Mexico-North Manchester		-22.7	
YEAR TOTAL				912.6	32.7	945.3
1979	XL	GR	Portland-DA		<+28.4>	
	X	GR	Portland-Decatur		-26.9	
	T	GR	In Decatur	+1.5	-1.5	11
	Y	GR	In Decatur	(1.5)		
	X	LS	MP 115.9-Culver		-32.7	
YEAR TOTAL				912.6	0	912.6
1980/7	S7	L	Marion-Sweetser	[4.6]		
YEAR TOTAL				908.0	0	908.0
1981	X	I	Cambridge City-Charlottesv.	-21.3		
YEAR TOTAL				886.7	0	886.7
1982	X	CR	Anderson-Kokomo	-28.7		
	Y	CR	In Anderson	(7.7)		
	S1	CR	OH state line-Glen	[3.9]		
	S1	CR	In Richmond	[1.7]		
	S1	GR	In Richmond	[(1.6)]		
	Y	GS	Junction-MP 97.8	(4.5)		
	X	GS	MP 97.8-Kendallville	-21.2		
	Y	GS	In Kendallville	(1.1)		
	X	I	OH state line-Glen	-2.0		
	S1	I	Glen-Newman	[2.4]		
	X	I	Centerville-Cambridge City	-10.1		
	X	I	Charlottesville-Thorne	-22.9		
	X	L	Winimac-Crown Point	-48.8		
	X	LE	In Columbia City	(-1.3)		
	X	V	Davis-Greencastle	-28.1		
	Y	I	Thorne-MP 186.8	(6.0)		
	Y	IK	Line	(2.0)		
YEAR TOTAL				695.6	0	695.6
1984	X	CM	In Muncie	(-1.1)		
	X	CR	Delco-Dow	(-2.7)		
	X	GR	In Ridgeville	(-1.2)		
	X	GR	In Decatur	(-1.5)		
	X	GS	In Kendallville	(-0.9)		
	X	IA	Jeffersonville-Clarksville	-1.6		
	X	IC	In Columbus	(-2.7)		
	X	IC	In Shelbyville	(-1.8)		

(continued)

PENNSYLVANIA

ACQUISITION/DISPOSITION RECORD (continued)

Date	Act	PRR	End points	Conrail Change	PennC Change	PRR Total
1984	X	IV	Sandborn-Bicknell	-10.5		
	X	L	Crown Point-IL state line	-11.9		
	X	L	In Winimac	-1.2		
	X	L	Sweetser-Anoka	-29.4		
	X	LE	In North Manchester	(-1.1)		
	X	LS	In South Bend	(-1.0)		
	X	V	Greencastle-Limedale	-5.3		
	X	VB2	Brazil-Chinook Mine	(-6.0)		
	X	VO	Brazil-Staunton	-3.5		
	X	VT1	East Yard-MP 1.7	(-1.7)		
YEAR TOTAL				632.2	0	632.2
1985	X	L	In Winimac	-0.3		
	/5	L2	LS	In Plymouth	<(1.8)>	
YEAR TOTAL				631.9	0	631.9
1986	X	CR	In Kokomo	-0.8		
	X	IC	In Shelbyville	(-1.7)		
YEAR TOTAL				631.1	0	631.1
1987/5/1	S8	V	Limedale-Seelyville	[24.2]		
/5/1	S8	V	Seelyville-Prairie	[4.6]		
/5/1	S8	VT3	Prairie-Preston	[2.5]		
	X	V	MP 69.9-Union	(-2.5)		
	X	IC	In Columbus	(-1.1)		
YEAR TOTAL				599.8	0	599.8
1989	S6	LE	Van-MP 3.4	[2.2]		
YEAR TOTAL				597.6	0	597.6
1990	X	LS	In Plymouth	<(-1.8)>		
YEAR TOTAL				597.6	0	597.6
1992	L5	GS	In Kendallville	<(1.1)>		
	X	I	East Haven-Centerville	-5.2		
	S11	I	Newman-East Haven	[1.5]		
/4/11	S9	IV	Kraft-Bicknell	[89.4]		
	X	IVO	In Indianapolis	(-3.4)		7
/12/31	X	V	Limedale-Seelyville	[-24.2]		
/12/31	X	V	Seelyville-Prairie	[-4.6]		
/12/31	X	VT3	Prairie-Preston	[-2.5]		
YEAR TOTAL				501.5	0	501.5
1993	S1	CR	In Kokomo	[3.1]		
	S1	CR	New Castle-Foley	[3.6]		
	X	CR	Sulphur Springs-Anderson	-8.6		
	X	L	Union city-Red Key	-19.5		
	Y	L	In Union City	(1.8)		
/10/1	S7	CR	Foley-Sulphur Springs	[6.6]		
1993/3/20	S5	CR	Kokomo-Anoka	[17.8]		
/3/20	S5	L	Anoka-Van	[5.7]		
/3/20	S5	L	Boone-Winimac	[17.1]		
/3/20	S5	L	Van-Boone	[10.7]		
/3/20	S5	IF	Bringhurst-Van	[20.5]		
	X	IF	Frankfort-Bringhurst	-13.8		
	Y	IF	In Frankfort	(1.6)		
YEAR TOTAL				371.1	0	371.1
1994/3/12	S10	IL	Southport-KY state line	[102.5]		
/3/12	S10	IW	Boyd-Watson	[4.0]		
/3/12	S10	IM	In Columbus	[(2.8)]		
YEAR TOTAL				264.6	0	264.6
1996	S1	F	Wabash-Clarke Jct.	[126.5]		
	L5	GS	In Kendallville	<(1.1)>		
YEAR TOTAL				138.1	0	138.1

(continued)

PENNSYLVANIA

ACQUISITION/DISPOSITION RECORD (continued)

On 1999/6/1 Conrail was conveyed to CSX Transportation and Norfolk Southern. The lines conveyed were:

Line desig. CSC/NS-	End points	MP	to CSX	to NS
[PRR-F]	OH state line-Wabash	300.4-319.2	18.8	
[PRR-F]	Clarke Jct.-IL state line	445.7-453.3	7.6	
[PRR-GR]	Decatur-Adams	70.4-86.6	16.2	
[PRR-GS]	In Fort Wayne	93.3-97.8		(4.5)
[PRR-CR]	In Anderson	119.3-122.1	(2.8)	
[PRR-CR]	In Anderson	124.8-127.0	(2.2)	
[PRR-YA]	Anderson Belt	0-3.1	(3.1)	
[PRR-I]	Thorne-ID	180.8-186.8	(6.0)	
[PRR-IL]	Indianapolis-Southport	0.2-6.3	5.8	
[PRR-IK]	Thorne-Hawthorne Yard	0-2.0	(2.0)	
[PRR-IK]	In Hawthorne Yard	2.0-5.0	(3.0)	
[PRR-IF]	Davis-Frank	6.9-48.1	41.2	
[PRR-IF]	Frank-Frankfort	78.3-78.6	0.3	
[PRR-IF]	In Frankfort	78.6-80.2	(1.6)	
[PRR-L]	Red Key-Marion	124.9-158.6	33.7	
[PRR-LS]	In South Bend	179.0-181.3		(2.3)
[PRR-V]	Indianapolis-Davis	0.4-6.9	6.5	
[PRR-V]	Terre Haute-IL line	73.5-79.9	6.4	
[PRR-VT2]	In Terre Haute	73.3-73.5	0.2	
[PRR-VK]	Van Jct.-Kraft	0-1.4	1.4	
		TOTAL	138.1	0

ACT COLUMN KEY
B1   Built by State of Indiana
B2   Built by Madison & Indianapolis RR
B3   Built by Rushville & Shelbyville RR
B4   Built by Jeffersonville RR
B5   Built by Terre Haute & Richmond RR
B6   Built by Columbus & Shelby RR
B7   Built by Indiana Central Ry
B8   Built by Cincinnati, Logansport & Chicago Ry
B9   Built by Ohio & Indiana RR
B10 Built by Fort Wayne & Chicago RR
B11 Built by Cincinnati & Chicago RR
B12 Built by Toledo, Logansport & Burlington RR
B13 Built by Pittsburgh, Fort Wayne & Chicago RR
B14 Built by Chicago & Great Eastern Ry
B15 Built by Chicago & Cincinnati RR
B16 Built by Columbus & Indiana Central RR
B17 Built by Columbus, Chicago & Indiana Central Ry
B18 Built by Lake Erie & Louisville RR
B19 Built by Indianapolis & Vincennes RR
B20 Built by Terre Haute & Indianapolis RR
B21 Built by Detroit, Eel River & Illinois RR
B22 Built by Logansport, Crawfordsville & South Western Ry
B23 Built by Terre Haute & Logansport RR
B24 Built by Chicago, Indiana & Eastern Ry
B25 Built by Pittsburgh, Cincinnati, Chicago & St. Louis Ry
B26 Built by Shelbyville Lateral Branch RR
B27 Built by Knightstown & Shelbyville RR
B29 Built by Indianapolis & Frankfort RR
B30 Built by Grand Rapids & Indiana
  (continued)

PENNSYLVANIA

ACT COLUMN KEY (continued)
B31 Built by Cincinnati, Richmond & Fort Wayne
B32 Built by Vandalia RR
L1   Leased to Wabash Ry
L2   Leased to Plymouth Short Line
L3   Leased to Evansville & Indianapolis
L4   Leased to Chicago & Indiana
L5   Leased to Michigan Southern RR
M1   Leased from Evansville & Crawfordsville
Q   Segment transferred between lines
S1   Sold to Norfolk Southern
S2   Sold to Madison RR
S3   Sold to Indian Creek RR
S4   Sold to Toledo, Peoria & Western
S5   Sold to Winimac Southern
S6   Sold to Logansport & Eel River
S7   Sold to Honey Creek
S8   Sold Terre Haute, Brazil & Eastern
S9   Sold to Indiana Southern
S10   Sold to Louisville & Indiana
T   Apparently transferred from Penn Central to Conrail
X   Abandoned
Y   Converted to yard use

SOURCES
1. Burgess and Kennedy, *Centennial History of the Pennsylvania Railroad Company.*
2. Indiana, *1995 Indiana State Rail Plan.*
3. Michigan, *Aids, Gifts, Grants.*
4. Sappington, "The Madison and Indianapolis Railroad."
5. Simons and Parker, *Railroads of Indiana.*
6. Sulzer, *Ghost Railroads of Indiana.*
7. Watt, *The Pennsylvania Railroad in Indiana.*

NOTES
   General. The Pennsylvania RR lease of the Pittsburgh, Fort Wayne & Chicago was assigned on April 1, 1871, to the Pennsylvania Co., a wholly-owned holding company. The lease was assigned back to the Pennsylvania RR effective Jan. 1, 1918.
   1. The Madison & Indianapolis line from Madison to Queensville was built and owned by the State of Indiana. Source 1 states that private parties operated the line from 1839 until 1843 and by the Madison & Indianapolis from 1843 to 1856 at which time the line was purchased by the Madison & Indianapolis RR.
   2. Source 1 states the line was completed to Englewood about Dec. 1, 1858, and on Jan. 1, 1859, was opened to the Van Buren Street station.
   3. Trackage rights between Clymers and Logansport on Wabash line WAB-P were used from 1871 until 1875.
   4. This construction was a relocation to line PRR-V replacing PRR-VO as the main line.
   5. This lease also apparently provided for trackage rights over the Evansville & Terre Haute between Union and Otter Creek Jct. Source 1 states that in Nov. 1879 the Terre Haute & Logansport leased the entire Terre Haute-Rockville line (apparently allowing the E&TH trackage rights between Terre Haute and Otter Creek Jct.), and that Chicago & Eastern Illinois purchased the Terre Haute-Otter Creek Jct. segment in 1911, and that after 1911 the TH&L successor Vandalia RR apparently retained trackage rights over the C&EI between Terre Haute and Otter Creek Jct. Source 5 states that the TH&L leased the Terre Haute-Rockville segment in 1872 and purchased it outright in 1924.
   6. The Indianapolis station of the Madison & Indianapolis was located near South St.
   7. This abandonment is assumed to coincide with the sale of PRR-IV to Indiana Southern.
   8. The date of construction or abandonment could not be determined and this is not included in the Acquisition/Disposition Record.
   9. This sale also included trackage rights on PRR-IL between MP 6.3 and Indianapolis.
   10. This sale is assumed from the abandonment of all other Conrail trackage into Kokomo.
   11. This segment apparently was transferred to conrail.

PEORIA & EASTERN

MAIN LINE (P&E-A)

	Mileage	County	Crossings, junctions, etc.
(Indianapolis	0)	Marion	
--via IU-W			
IJ	1.0	"	J/IU-W 1.0
KD	1.8	"	X/IU-B 9.4
Moorefield	2.1	"	
Brant	3.6	"	J/CCC-H 113.1
Speedway	4.6	"	
Indiana Girls School	7.4	"	
Clermont	9.6	"	X/PRR-IF 12.6
Brownsburg	14.0	Hendricks	
Pittsboro	17.9	"	
Raintown	20.6	"	
Lizton	22.3	"	
Jamestown	27.7	Boone	
New Ross	32.8	Montgomery	X/CI-A 75.6
Linnsburg	37.8	"	
Crawfordsville Jct.	43.0	"	
Ames	43.0	"	X/MON-SA 148.4, X/PRR-VF 52.0
Crawfordsville	43.8	"	
Tile Siding	49.8		
Wesley	50.7	"	
Waynetown	54.0	"	
Range Road	58.1	Fountain	
Hillsborough	59.3	"	
Raynear	62	"	
Veedersburg	64.7	"	X/CAS-A 95.7, X/NKP-TC 249.1
Layton	68.7	"	
Palmerton	70.2	"	
Covington	72.1	"	X/CEI-EC 15.6, J/WAB-PC 14.8
Kern Pit	73.9	Warren	
Olin	74.0	"	
Kern	74.4	"	
Foster	76.5	"	
(IN/IL state line)	79.9		
Walz IL	81.9		
Danville Jct.	84.3		
Danville IL	85.0		
Peoria IL	211.5		

CONSTRUCTION/ABANDONMENT

Date	Act	End points	MP	Change	Main	Source	Note
1869	B1	Indianapolis-Danville IL	1.0-79.9	+78.9	78.9	1	

1973	X	Speedway-Clermont	6.2-9.0	-2.8	76.1	1	
1982	X	Crawfordsville-Olin	46.0-74.0	-28.0	48.1	1	
1984	X	At Speedway	4.0-6.2	-2.2	45.9	1	

OWNERSHIP

1869	Indianapolis, Crawfordsville & Danville RR (B1)
1869	Indianapolis, Bloomington & Western Ry, merge Indpls., Crawf., & Danv.
1879/4	Indiana, Bloomington & Western RR, reorganize IB&W
1881/3	Indianapolis, Bloomington & Western Ry, merge Ind., Bloom'ton & W'n and Ohio, Indiana & Pacific
1887/11	Ohio, Indiana & Western Ry, reorganize Indpls., Bloom. & Western
1890/2/20	Peoria & Eastern RR, reorganize part of Ohio, Indiana & Western
1890	Cleveland, Cincinnati, Chicago & St. Louis Ry, lease Peoria & Eastern
1930/2/1	New York Central, leased Cleveland, Cincinnati, Chicago & St. Louis (with lease of Peoria & Eastern)
1968/2/1	Penn Central, assign lease of Cleveland, Cincinnati, Chicago & St. Louis (with lease of Peoria & Eastern)
1976/4/1	Conrail, purchase Penn Central
1999/6/1	CSX Transportation, purchase Conrail

PEORIA & EASTERN
ACQUISITION/DISPOSITION RECORD
See ownership record above for line P&E-A

On April 1, 1976, part of this company was conveyed to Conrail. The Acquisition/-Disposition Record is continued to two places: under this company and under the name of the subsequent new owner. The property conveyed was:

				to	to	
Line desig.	End points		MP	Conrail	PennC	Note
[P&E-A]	IJ-Speedway		1.0-6.2	5.2		
[P&E-A]	Clermont-IL state line		9.0-79.9	70.9		
			TOTAL	76.1	0	

Date	Act	P&E-	End points	Change	Main	Note
1982	X	A	Crawfordsville-Olin	-28.0	48.1	
1984	X	A	At Speedway	-2.2	45.9	

On 1999/6/1 Conrail was conveyed to CSX Transportation and Norfolk Southern. Its Acquisition/Disposition Record is continued in two places: under the name of the original company and under the name of the new company. The lines conveyed were:

				to	to
Line desig.	End points		MP	CSX	NS
CSC/NS-					
[P&E-A]	IJ-Speedway		1.0-4.0	3.0	
[P&E-A]	Clermont-Crawfordsville		9.0-46.0	37.0	
[P&E-A]	Olin-IL state line		74.0-79.9	5.9	
TOTAL				45.9	0

ACT COLUMN KEY
B1 Built by Indianapolis, Crawfordsville & Danville RR (B1)
X Abandoned

SOURCES
1. Indiana, *1995 Indiana State Rail Plan.*

PERE MARQUETTE
CHICAGO DIVISION (PM-C)

	Mileage	County	Crossings, junctions, etc.
Grand Rapids MI (old)	0		
New Buffalo (new)	115.1		old 114.86
Alfred MI	116.2		J/PM-W 34.2
(MI-IN state line)	117.9		
Merrick	119.9	LaPorte	
(Bridge)	122.5	"	B/CSS-A 31.3
(Bridge)	122.9	"	B/NKP-LM 156.6
Michigan City	125.3	"	
(Crossing)	126.7	"	X/MON-N 58.1
Doran	131.5	Porter	
Porter	136.6	"	J/LS-W 482.18

CONSTRUCTION/ABANDONMENT

Date	Act	End points	MP	Change	Main	Source	Note
1903/12/15	B2	Union Pier MI-Porter	117.9-136.6	+18.7	18.7	1	

OWNERSHIP
1903	Pere Marquette RR of Indiana (B2)
1907/8/12	Pere Marquette RR, merger of Pere Marquette of Indiana
1917/3/12	Pere Marquette Ry, reorganize Pere Marquette RR
1929/5	Chesapeake & Ohio, control of Pere Marquette Ry
1947/4/1	Chesapeake & Ohio, merger of Pere Marquette Ry
1973/6/15	Chessie System, control of Chesapeake & Ohio
1980/11/1	CSX Corp., merge Chessie System (with control of Chesapeake & Ohio)
1986/7/1	CSX Transportation, control of C&O from CSX Corp.
1987/9/2	CSX Transportation, merger of Chesapeake & Ohio

PERE MARQUETTE

LA CROSSE BRANCH (PM-W)

	Mileage	County	Crossings, junctions, etc.
(End)	(0.3)	LaPorte	J/MON-N 31.6, J/CAS-A 0
LaCrosse	0	"	X/PRR-L 246.3
Meadow	0.3	"	X/C&O-C 222.0
Machler	2.0	"	
Thomaston	6.1	"	X/NKP-C 463.0
Hanna	8.9	"	X/PRR-F 408.6
Chambers	11.9	"	
Wellsboro	15.1	"	X/B&O-C 213.8, X/GTW-C 71.1
Magee	17.5	"	X/WAB-MC 209.6
LaPorte	23.1	"	X/LS-W 463.8
Hilt	24.6	"	
Belfast IN	26.5	"	X/NKP-LM 149.5
Youngs	29.9	"	
(Bridge)	30.0	"	B/CSS-A 25.4
Ackerman	31.9	"	
(IN/MI state line)	33.0		
Alfred	34.2		J/PM-C 116.2

CONSTRUCTION/ABANDONMENT

Date	Act	End points	MP	Change	Main	Source	Note
1882/5/24	B1	LaPorte-New Buffalo MI	23.1-36.2	+9.9		1	
1882/11/12	B1	LaCrosse-LaPorte	0-23.1	+23.1	33.0	1	

1988	X	Wellsboro-Alfred MI	15.6-33.0	-17.4	15.6	2	

OWNERSHIP

1882	Chicago & West Michigan Ry, built by Indiana & Michigan (B1)
1899/12/7	Pere Marquette RR, merge Chicago & West Michigan Ry
1917/3/12	Pere Marquette Ry, reorganize Pere Marquette RR
1929/5	Chesapeake & Ohio, control of Pere Marquette Ry
1947/4/1	Chesapeake & Ohio, merge Pere Marquette Ry
1973/6/15	Chessie System, control of Chesapeake & Ohio
1980/11/1	CSX Corp. merge Chessie System (with control of Chesapeake & Ohio)
1986/7/1	CSX Transportation, control of C&O from CSX Corp.
1987/9/2	CSX Transportation, merger of Chesapeake & Ohio

ACQUISITION/DISPOSITION RECORD

Date	Act	PM-	End points	Change	Main	Note
1882/5/24	B1	W	LaPorte-New Buffalo MI	+9.9		
/11/12	B1	W	LaCrosse-LaPorte	+23.1	33.0	
1903/12/15	B2	C	Union Pier MI-Porter	+18.7	51.7	

On 1947/4/1 this company was acquired by Chesapeake & Ohio. The Acquisition/Disposition Record is continued in two places: under Pere Marquette and under Chesapeake & Ohio.

On 1973/6/15 Chessie System obtained control of Chesapeake & Ohio. The Acquisition/-Disposition Record is continued in two places: under Pere Marquette and under Chessie System.

On 1980/11/1 CSX Corporation merged Chessie System (with control of Chesapeake & Ohio). The Acquisition/Disposition Record is continued in two places: under Pere Marquette and under CSX Corporation.

On 1986/7/1 CSX Transportation obtained control and on 1987/9/2 merged Chesapeake & Ohio. The Acquisition/Disposition Record is continued in two places: under Pere Marquette and under CSX Transportation.

Date	Act	PM-	End points	Change	Main	Note
1988	X	W	Wellsboro-Alfred MI	-17.4	34.3	

PERE MARQUETTE

ACT COLUMN KEY
B1 Built by Indiana & Michigan
B2 Built by Pere Marquette RR of Indiana
X   Abandoned

SOURCES
1. Michigan, *Aid, Gifts, Grants, Donations..*
2. Simons and Parker, *Railroads of Indiana.*

PIGEON RIVER

ASHLEY-HUDSON - WOLCOTTVILLE (PGRV-[WAB-MC])
See Wabash line WAB-MC for arrangement of stations, prior construction/abandonment record, and prior ownership

CONSTRUCTION/ABANDONMENT

Date	Act	End points	MP	Change	Main	Source	Note
1985	L	Ashley-Hudson -Wolcottville	121.4-136.8	+15.4	15.4	1,2	
1985	XL	Ashley-Hudson -Wolcottville	121.4-136.8	-15.4	0	2	

OWNERSHIP
1985   Pigeon River RR, owned by South Milford Grain Co.

ACQUISITION/DISPOSITION RECORD
See ownership record above for line PGRV-[WAB-MC]

ACT COLUMN KEY
 L Leased from Norfolk Southern
 XL Lease terminated; part of property was transferred to Indiana Northeastern

SOURCES
1. Indiana, *1995 Indiana State Rail Plan.*
2. Simons and Parker, *Railroads of Indiana.*

PLYMOUTH SHORT LINE

IN PLYMOUTH (PLSL-[PRR-LS])
See Pennsylvania line PRR-LS for arrangement of stations, prior construction/abandonment record, and prior ownership

CONSTRUCTION/ABANDONMENT

Date	Act	End points	MP	Change	Main	Source	Note
1985/5	L	In Plymouth	159.1-160.9	+1.8	1.8	R	
1990/5	X	In Plymouth	159.1-160.9	-1.8	0	R	

OWNERSHIP
1985   Plymouth Short Line

ACQUISITION/DISPOSITION RECORD
See ownership record above for line PLSL-[PRR-LS]

ACT COLUMN KEY
L Leased from Conrail
X Abandoned

SOURCES
1. Simons and Parker, *Railroads of Indiana.*

POSEYVILLE & OWENSVILLE

MAIN LINE (PORR-[CEI-EM])
See Chicago & Eastern Illinois line CEI-EM for arrangement of stations, prior construction/abandonment record, and prior ownership

CONSTRUCTION/ABANDONMENT

Date	Act	End points	MP	Change	Main	Source	Note
1987/5	P	Owensville-Poseyville	270.8-281.8	+11.0	11.0	1	1
1996/7/22	S	Owensville-Poseyville	270.8.281.8	-11.0	0	1	

OWNERSHIP
Poseyville & Owensville RR, owned by Merchants Management Corp.

ACQUISITION/DISPOSITION RECORD
See ownership record above for line PORR-[CEI-EM]

ACT COLUMN KEY
P Purchased from CSX Transportation
S Sold to Owensville Terminal

SOURCES
1. Simons and Parker, *Railroads of Indiana.*

NOTES
1. This line was operated by Indiana Hi-Rail under contract with its owners.

SEABOARD SYSTEM

On 1983/1/1 this company acquired Louisville & Nashville. The L&N Acquisition/Disposition Record is continued in two places: under the name of the original constituent companies and under Seaboard System. The property acquired was:

Line desig. SBD-	End points	MP	Main	Note
CEI-E	Danville IL-Evansville	128.6-279.5	150.9	
CEI-E	In Evansville	279.5-287.2	(7.7)	
CEI-EB	In Evansville	279.5-287.4	7.9	
CEI-EJ	Evansville Belt	0-4.0	(4.0)	
CEI-EO	In Evansville	285.8-286.5	(0.7)	
CEI-EM	Mt. Vernon Jct.-Poseyville	265.3-281.8	16.5	
CEI-EM	In Mt. Vernon	300.5-301.1	(1.6)	
CEI-EU	Clinton-Universal	0-8.5	8.5	
L&N-S	Henderson KY-St. Louis MO	313.5-350.4	36.9	
L&N-SE	North Howell-Evansville	323.4-325.0	1.6	
MON-A	Chicago-Lafayette	19.2-117.9	98.7	
MON-I	Monon-Indianapolis	88.4-180.4	92.0	
MON-N	Monon-Medaryville	0-15.2	15.2	
MON-SA	Lafayette-Bloomington	117.9-221.5	103.6	
MON-SB	Bloomington-New Albany	221.5-317.5	96.0	
MON-SV	In New Albany	316.6-317.7	1.1	
MON-SBO	Clear Creek-Sanders	224.2-226.9	2.7	
MON-SL	Wallace Jct.-Midland	0-42.0	42.0	
MON-F	In Orleans	0-0.6	0.6	
1983	TOTAL CEI=183.8 L&N=38.5 MON=451.9 SOU SYSTEM=674.2			

SEABOARD SYSTEM

ACQUISITION/DISPOSITION RECORD

Date	Act	SBD-	End points	Change	Main	Note
1984	X	[MON-SL]	Wallace Jct.-Midland	-42.0		
YEAR TOTALS				CEI=183.8 L&N=38.5 MON=409.9 SYSTEM=632.2		
1985	X	[MON-I]	Frankfort-Sheridan	-17.9		
	L1	[MON-I]	Sheridan-Belt Jct.	<25.0>		
YEAR TOTALS				CEI=183.8 L&N=38.5 MON=367.0 SYSTEM=589.3		
1986 ca.	XL	[MON-I]	Sheridan-Belt Jct.	<+25.0>		
ca.	X	[MON-I]	Sheridan-Belt Jct.	-25.0		
YEAR TOTALS				CEI=183.8 L&N=38.5 MON=367.0 SYSTEM=589.3		

On 1986/7/1 this company was conveyed to CSX Transportation. Its Acquisition/Disposition Record is continued in two places: under the name of the original constituent companies and under CSX Transportation.

ACT COLUMN KEY
L1   Leased to Indiana Hi-Rail
X   Abandoned
XL   Lease terminated

SOURCES
1. Indiana, *1995 Indiana State Rail Plan.*
2. Simons and Parker, *Railroads of Indiana.*

SOO LINE

Effective 1986/1/1 (sale date 1985/2/19) this company acquired Chicago, Milwaukee, St. Paul & Pacific. The CMP&SP Acquisition/Disposition Record is continued in two places: under the Chicago, Milwaukee, St. Paul & Pacific and under Soo Line. The lines acquired were:

Line desig. SOO-	End points	MP	Main	Note
[MILW-T]	Fayette-Bedford	170.5-262.4	91.9	
[MILW-TL]	Latta Coal Branch	0-8.1	8.1	
1986		TOTAL	100.0	

ACQUISITION/DISPOSITION RECORD

Date	Act	SOO-	End points	Change	Main	Note
1990 ca.	X	[MILW-T]	Fayette-Dewey	-4.2	95.8	

ACT COLUMN KEY
X   Abandoned

SOURCES
1. Simons and Parker, *Railroads of Indiana.*

SOUTHERN

ST. LOUIS DIVISION (SOU-U)

	Mileage	County	Crossings, junctions, etc.
St. Louis MO	0		
East St. Louis IL	3.2		
Centralia	65.1		
Mt. Vernon	87.3		
Fairfield	117.7		
Mt. Carmel IL	151.1		
(IL/IN state line)	151.8		
Beck	152	Gibson	
(continued)			

SOUTHERN

ST. LOUIS DIVISION (SOU-U) (continued)

	Mileage [St. Louis MO]	County	Crossings, junctions, etc.
Beck	152	Gibson	
Lyle(s)	157.1	"	
Princeton Jct.	161.4	"	X/CEI-E 258.2
Princeton	162.5	"	
(Junction)	165.3	"	J/SOU-UA 2.4
Douglas	167.2	"	
(Junction)	168.5	"	J/CCC-TS 6.7
Francisco	170.0	"	
Oakland City	175.6	"	X/CCC-T 106.2
Ingleton	179	Pike	
(Bridge)	181.2	"	B/AWW-A 4.0
Ayrshire	182.1	"	
Winslow	183.8	"	
Hartwell Jct,	188.1	"	J/SOU-UH 0
Velpen	190.1	"	
Duff	194.9	Dubois	
Woods	196	"	
Huntingburg	199.6	"	J/SOU-UE 47.7, J/SOU-UF 47.7
Bretzville	203.9	"	
St. Anthony	206.9	"	
Kyana	209.0	"	
Mentor	213.3	"	
Birdseye	214.5	"	
Riceville	216.5	Crawford	
Eckerty	219.4	"	
Taswell	222.8	"	
English	228.9	"	
Temple	231.8	"	
Marengo	236.3	"	
Milltown	240.6	"	
De Pauw	244.4	Harrison	
Ramsey	248.0	"	
Corydon Jct.	251.2	"	J/LNAC-A 7.7
Mott	251.9	"	
Crandall	253.5	"	
Georgetown	259.4	Floyd	
Duncan	262.4	"	
Parkwood	266	"	
New Albany	268.3	"	J/KIT-A 0
--via KIT-A			
(Louisville KY	273.7)		

CONSTRUCTION/ABANDONMENT

Date	Act	End points	MP	Change	Main	Source	Note
1872	B1	Princeton-IL state line	151.8-162.5	+10.7	10.7	2	1
1880	B4	Princeton-Ingleton	162.5-179.0	+16.5	27.2	1,2	
1882	B4	Ingleton-New Albany	179.0-268.3	+89.3	116.5	1	
1957 ca.	X	Princeton Jct.-Princeton	161.4-163.0	-1.6			
1957 ca.	Y	In Princeton	163.0-165.3	(2.3)	112.6		

OWNERSHIP

1872	Louisville, New Albany & St. Louis Air Line Ry (B1)
1877/2/18	Louisville, New Albany & St. Louis Ry, reorganize LNA&SLAL
1878	Louisville, New Albany & St. Louis Air Line RR (B4), reorganize LNA&SL
1881	Louisville, Evansville & St. Louis RR, reorganize LNA&SLAL
1889	Louisville, Evansville & St. Louis Consolidated RR, reorganize LE&SL
1900	Southern Ry of Indiana, bought LE&SLC
1944	Southern Ry, merge Southern of Indiana
1990	Norfolk Southern, rename Southern Ry

SOUTHERN

PRINCETON BYPASS (SOU-UA)

	Mileage	County	Crossings, junctions, etc.
(Junction)	0	Gibson	J/CEI-A 259.9
(Junction)	2.4	"	J/SOU-U 165.3

CONSTRUCTION/ABANDONMENT

Date	Act	End points	MP	Change	Main	Source	Note
1893 ca.	B8	Line	0-2.4	+2.4	2.4	2	2

OWNERSHIP

1893	Louisville, Evansville & St. Louis Consolidated RR (B8)
1900	Southern Ry of Indiana, bought LE&SLC
1944	Southern Ry, merge Southern of Indiana
1990	Norfolk Southern, rename Southern Ry

EVANSVILLE BRANCH (SOU-UE)

	Mileage [Evansville]	County	Crossings, junctions, etc.
(Junction)	0.7	Vanderburgh	J/CEI-E 285.8, J/CEI-EO 285.8
Smythe	4.1	"	
Stevenson	7.4	Warrick	
Chandler	11.6	"	
DeForest	13	"	
(Crossing)	16.1	"	X/YANK-A 12
Boonville	16.9	"	
De Gonia	21.8	"	
Tennyson	26.8	"	
Pigeon	29.1	Spencer	
Gentryville	31.0	"	
Rockport Jct.	32.5	"	J/SOU-UR 1.0
Lincoln City	33.5	"	J/SOU-UC 0
Dale	36.8	"	
Hilltop	39	"	
Johnsburg	41.0	Dubois	f. Ferdinand
(Junction)	46.7	"	J/FERD-A 1.0
Huntingburg	47.7	"	J/SOU-UE 199.6

CONSTRUCTION/ABANDONMENT

Date	Act	End points	MP	Change	Main	Source	Note
1873	B2	Evansville-Boonville 0.7-16.9	+16.2	16.2	I		
1874	B3	Johnsburg-Rockport Jct.	41.0-32.5	+8.5	24.7	1	
1878	B3	Huntingburg-Johnsburg	47.7-41.0	+6.7	31.4	1	
1880	B5	Boonville-Rockport Jct.	16.9-32.5	+15.6	47.0	1	

OWNERSHIP

1873	Lake Erie, Evansville & Southwestern RR (B2), of part
1874	Cincinnati, Rockport & Southwestern RR (B3), of part
1879	Evansville Local Trade RR (B5), acquired LEE&SW
1880	Evansville, Rockport & Eastern Ry, merge CR&SW and ELT
1881	Louisville, Evansville & St. Louis RR, bought ER&E
1889	Louisville, Evansville & St. Louis Consolidated RR, reorganize LE&SL
1900	Southern Ry of Indiana, bought LE&SLC
1944	Southern Ry, merge Southern of Indiana
1990	Norfolk Southern, rename Southern Ry

SOUTHERN

CANNELTON BRANCH (SOU-UC)

	Mileage	County	Crossings, junctions, etc.
Lincoln City	0	Spencer	J/SOU-UE 33.5
Buffaloville	2.9	"	
Kennedy	6.8	"	
Evanston	11.9	"	
Troy	17.6	Perry	
Tell City	20.0	"	
Cannelton	22.7	"	

CONSTRUCTION/ABANDONMENT

Date	Act	End points	MP	Change	Main	Source	Note
1887	B6	Lincoln City-Cannelton	0-22.7	+22.7	22.7	1	
1989	L1	Lincoln City-Cannelton	0-22.7	<22.7>	0	2	

1994	XL	Lincoln City-Cannelton	0-22.7	<+22.7>			
1994	S2	Lincoln City-Tell City	0-19.8	<19.8>		2	
1994	X	Tell City-Cannelton	19.8-22.7	<-2.9>	0		

OWNERSHIP

1887	Huntington, Tell City & Cannelton RR (B6), controlled by next below
1887	Louisville, Evansville & St. Louis RR, ?merge ER&E
1889	Louisville, Evansville & St. Louis Consolidated RR, reorganize LE&SL
1900	Southern Ry of Indiana, bought LE&SLC
1944	Southern Ry, merge Southern of Indiana
1990	Norfolk Southern, rename Southern Ry

FRENCH LICK BRANCH (SOU-UF)

	Mileage	County	Crossings, junctions, etc.
Huntingburg	47.7	Dubois	J/SOU-U 199.6
Jasper	54.2	"	
Dubois	62.8	"	
Crystal	66.2	"	
Cuzco	69.5	"	
Norton	72.2	"	
French Lick	79.0	Orange	J/MON-F 17.7
--via MON-F			
(West Baden	80.0)	"	

CONSTRUCTION/ABANDONMENT

Date	Act	End points	MP	Change	Main	Source	Note
1878	B3	Huntingburg-Jasper	47.7-54.2	+6.5	6.5	1	
1907	B7	Jasper-French Lick	54.2-79.0	+24.8	31.3	1	
1978	S1	Dubois-French Lick	63.7-79.0	[15.3]	16.0	2	
1989	L1	Huntingburg-Dubois	47.7-63.7	<16.0>	0	2	

1993	LA1	Huntingburg-Dubois	47.7-63.7	<16.0>	0	2	

OWNERSHIP

1878	Cincinnati, Rockport & Southwestern RR (B3), of part
1880	Evansville, Rockport & Eastern Ry, merge CR&SW and ELT
1881	Louisville, Evansville & St. Louis RR, bought ER&E
1889	Louisville, Evansville & St. Louis Consolidated RR, reorganize LE&SL
1900	Southern Ry of Indiana (B7), bought LE&SLC
1944	Southern Ry, merge Southern of Indiana
1990	Norfolk Southern, rename Southern Ry

SOUTHERN

ROCKPORT BRANCH (SOU-UR)

	Mileage	County	Crossings, junctions, etc.
(Lincoln City	0)		
Rockport Jct.	1.0	Spencer	J/SOU-UE 32.5
Bradley	4.4	"	
Chrisney	7.9	"	
Ritchies	11.3	"	
Rock Hill	12.8	"	
Rockport	16.8	"	

CONSTRUCTION/ABANDONMENT

Date	Act	End points	MP	Change	Main	Source	Note
1874	B3	Rockport Jct.-Rockport	1.0-16.8	+15.8	15.8	1	
1989	L1	Rockport Jct.-Rockport	1.0-16.8	<15.8>	0	2	

1994	XL	Rockport Jct.-Rockport	1.0-16.8	<+15.8>	15.8	2	
1996	L2	Rockport Jct.-Rockport	1.0-16.8	<15.8>	0	2	

OWNERSHIP

1874	Cincinnati, Rockport & Southwestern RR (B3), of part
1880	Evansville, Rockport & Eastern Ry, merge CR&SW
1881	Louisville, Evansville & St. Louis RR, bought ER&E
1889	Louisville, Evansville & St. Louis Consolidated RR, reorganize LE&SL
1900	Southern Ry of Indiana, bought LE&SLC
1944	Southern Ry, merge Southern of Indiana
1990	Norfolk Southern, rename Southern Ry

HARTWELL BRANCH (SOU-UH)

	Mileage	County	Crossings, junctions, etc.
Hartwell Jct.	0	Pike	J/SOU-U 188.1
Hartwell	3.7	"	

CONSTRUCTION/ABANDONMENT

Date	Act	End points	MP	Change	Main	Source	Note
1899 ca.	B8	Hartwell Jct.-Hartwell	0-3.7	+3.7	3.7		
1934	X	Hartwell Jct.-Hartwell	0-3.7	-3.7	0		

OWNERSHIP

1899	Louisville, Evansville & St. Louis Consolidated RR (B8)
1900	Southern Ry of Indiana (B7), bought LE&SLC

ACQUISITION/DISPOSITION RECORD

Date	Act	SOU-	End points	Change	Main	Note
1872	B1	U	Princeton-IL state line	+10.7	10.7	1
1873	B2	UE	Evansville-Boonville	+16.2	26.9	
1874	B3	UE	Johnsburg-Rockport Jct.	+8.5		
	B3	UR	Rockport Jct.-Rockport	+15.8	51.2	
1878	B3	UE	Huntingburg-Johnsburg	+6.7		
	B3	UF	Huntingburg-Jasper	+6.5	64.4	
1880	B5	UE	Boonville-Rockport Jct.	+15.6		
	B4	U	Princeton-Ingleton	+16.5	96.5	
1882	B4	U	Ingleton-New Albany	+89.3	185.8	
1887	B6	UC	Lincoln City-Cannelton	+22.7	208.5	
1893 ca.	B8	UA	Princeton Bypass	+2.4	210.9	2
1899 ca.	B8	UH	Hartwell Jct.-Hartwell	+3.7	214.6	
1907	B7	UF	Jasper-French Lick	+24.8	239.4	
1934	X	UH	Hartwell Jct.-Hartwell	-3.7	235.7	
1957 ca.	X	U	Princeton Jct.-Princeton	-1.6		
	Y	U	In Princeton	(2.3)	231.8	
1978	S1	UF	French Lick-Dubois	[15.3]	216.5	

SOUTHERN

ACQUISITION/DISPOSITION RECORD
In 1982/6/1 this company was renamed Norfolk Southern. Its Acquisition/Disposition Record is continued in two places: under Southern and under Norfollk Southern.

Date	Act	SOU-	End points	Change	Main	Note
1989	L1	UF	Huntingburg-Dubois	<16.0>		
	L1	UC	Lincoln City-Cannelton	<22.7>		
	L1	UR	Rockport Jct.-Rockport	<15.8>	162.0	
1991	XL	UC	Lincoln City-Cannelton	<+22.7>	184.7	
1993	LA1	UF	Huntingburg-Dubois	<+-16.0>	184.7	
1994	S2	UC	Lincoln City-Tell City	[19.8]		
	X	UC	Tell City-Cannelton	-2.9		
	XL	UR	Rockport Jct.-Rockport	<+15.8>	177.8	
1996	L2	UR	Rockport Jct.-Rockport	<15.8>	162.0	

ACT COLUMN KEY
B1	Built by Louisville, New Albany & St. Louis Air Line Ry
B2	Built by Lake Erie, Evansville & Southwestern RR
B3	Built by Cincinnati, Rockport & Southwestern RR
B4	Built by Louisville, New Albany & St. Louis Air Line RR
B5	Built by Evansville Local Trade RR
B6	Built by Huntington, Tell City & Cannelton RR
B7	Built by Southern Ry of Indiana
B8	Built by Louisville, Evansville & St. Louis Consolidated RR
L1	Leased to Indiana Hi-Rail
L2	Leased to Hoosier Southern RR
LA1	Lease to Indiana Hi-Rail assigned to Dubois County Co
S1	Sold to French Lick, West Baden & Southern Ry
S2	Sold to Perry County Port Authority and leased to Hoosier Southern
X	Abandoned
XL	Lease terminated

SOURCES
1. Indiana, *1995 Indiana State Rail Plan*.
2. Simons and Parker, *Railroads of Indiana*..

NOTES
1. Source I states completion date of this segment to be 1871.
2. With this construction the company also obtained trackage rights on Chicago & Eastern Illinois line CEI-A between Princeton Jct. and CEI MP 259.9.

SOUTHERN INDIANA

MAIN LINE (SOIN-A)

	Mileage	County	Crossings, junctions, etc.
Watson Jct.	0	Clark	J/B&O-SJ 47.2
(Crossing)	0.2	"	X/PRR-IW 3.2, X/B&O-SV 47.1
(Junction)	0.3	"	J/spur to Watson, 0.9 mi.
Pass	3.5	"	
Sellersburg	4.2	"	
Speed	5.5	"	

CONSTRUCTION/ABANDONMENT
Date	Act	End points	MP	Change	Main	Source	Note
1939/10	P	Line	0-5.5	+5.5	5.5	1	

OWNERSHIP
1939		Southern Indiana Ry

SOUTHERN INDIANA

ACQUISITION/DISPOSITION RECORD
See ownership record above for line

ACT COLUMN KEY
P Purchased from Public Service Co. of Indiana, operated by Indiana Railroad, as shown under Indiana Railway line INDR-L, MP 104.1-107.4.

SOURCES
1. Simons and Parker, *Railroads of Indiana.*

SOUTHWIND SHORTLINE

MAIN LINE (SWND-A)

	Mileage	County	Crossings, junctions, etc.
(Junction)	0	Posey	J/L&N-S 340.2
(Southwind Maritime Center)	1.3	"	

CONSTRUCTION/ABANDONMENT

Date	Act	End points	MP	Change	Main	Source	Note
1992	B	Line	0-1.3	+1.3	1.3	1,2	

OWNERSHIP

1992	Southwind Shortline RR

ACQUISITION/DISPOSITION RECORD
See ownership record above for line SWND-A

ACT COLUMN KEY
B Built by Southwind Shortline

SOURCES
1. Indiana, *1995 Indiana State Rail Plan.*
2. Simons and Parker, *Railroads of Indiana.*

SYRACUSE & MILFORD

MAIN LINE (SYM-A)

	Mileage	County	Crossings, junctions, etc.
Syracuse	0	Kosciusko	J/B&O-C 160.6
Lake Wabee	5	"	
Milford	6.8	"	J/CCC-M 68.2

CONSTRUCTION/ABANDONMENT

Date	Act	End points	MP	Change	Main	Source	Note
1907	B	Syracuse-Wabee Lake	0-5.9	+5.9	5.9	1,2	
1910 ca.	B	Wabee Lake-Milford	5.9-6.8	+0.9	6.8	1,2	
1923	X	Syracuse-Milford	0-6.8	-6.8	0	1,2	

OWNERSHIP

1907	Syracuse & Milford RR (B)

ACQUISITION/DISPOSITION RECORD
See ownership record above for line SYM-A

ACT COLUMN KEY
B Built by Syracuse & Milford RR
X Abandoned

SOURCES
1. Simons and Parker, *Railroads of Indiana.*
2. Sulzer, *Ghost Railroads of Indiana.*

304   INDIANA RAILROAD LINES

TERRE HAUTE, BRAZIL & EASTERN

MAIN LINE (THBE-[PRR-V])
See Pennsylvania line PRR-V for arrangement of stations, prior construction/abandonment record, and prior ownership

CONSTRUCTION/ABANDONMENT

Date	Act	End points	MP	Change	Main	Source	Note
1987/5/1	P	Limedale-Seelyville	40.3-64.5	+24.2			
/5/1	P	Seelyville-Prairie	65.3-69.9	+4.6	28.8	2	
1992/12/31	X	Limedale-Prairie	40.3-69.9	-28.8	0	1,2	

OWNERSHIP
1987   Terre Haute, Brazil & Eastern RR

BRANCH (THBE-[PRR-VT3])
See Pennsylvania line PRR-VT1 for arrangement of stations, prior construction/abandonment record, and prior ownership

CONSTRUCTION/ABANDONMENT

Date	Act	End points	MP	Change	Main	Source	Note
1987/5/1	P	Prairie-Preston	69.9-72.4	+2.5	2.5		
1992/12/31	X	Prairie-Preston	69.9-72.4	-2.5	0		

OWNERSHIP
1987   Terre Haute, Brazil & Eastern RR

BRANCH (THBE-[PRR-VB2])
See Pennsylvania line PRR-VB2 for arrangement of stations, prior construction/abandonment record, and prior ownership

CONSTRUCTION/ABANDONMENT

Date	Act	End points	MP	Change	Main	Source	Note
1987/5/1	P	Brazil-Chinook Mine	0-6.0	(+6.0)	0		
1992/12/31	X	Brazil-Chinook Mine	0-6.0	(-6.0)	0		

OWNERSHIP
1987   Terre Haute, Brazil & Eastern RR

ACQUISITION/DISPOSITION RECORD

Date	Act	THBE-	End points	Change	Main	Note
1987/5/1	P	[PRR-V]	Limedale-Prairie	+28.8		
5/1	P	[PRR-VT1]	Prairie-Preston	+2.5		
5/1	P	[PRR-VB2]	Brazil-Chinook Mine	(+6.0)	31.3	
1992/12/31	X	[PRR-V]	Limedale-Prairie	-28.8		
12/31	X	[PRR-VT1]	Prairie-Preston	-2.5		
12/31	X	[PRR-VB2]	Brazil-Chinook Mine	(-6.0)	0	

ACT COLUMN KEY
P Purchased from Conrail
X Abandoned

SOURCES
1. Indiana, *1995 Indiana State Rail Plan*.
2. Simons and Parker, *Railroads of Indiana*.

TIPPECANOE
MAIN LINE (TIP-A)
See Erie line ERIE-C for arrangement of stations, prior construction/abandonment record, and prior ownership
(continued)

TIPPECANOE

MAIN LINE (TIP-A) (continued)
CONSTRUCTION/ABANDONMENT

Date	Act	End points	MP	Change	Main	Source	Note
1980/1	P	Monterey-North Judson	183.7-199.7	+16.0	16.0	1	
1990/4	S	Monterey-North Judson	183.7-199.7	-16.0	0	1	

OWNERSHIP
1980		Tippecanoe RR

ACQUISITION/DISPOSITION RECORD
See ownership record above for line TIP-A

ACT COLUMN KEY
P   Purchased by Tippecanoe RR from Erie
S   Sold to J.K.Line

SOURCES
1. Simons and Parker, *Railroads of Indiana*

TOLEDO, PEORIA & WESTERN

MAIN LINE (TPW-[PRR-L])
See Pennsylvania line PRR-L for arrangement of stations, prior construction/abandonment record, and prior ownership

CONSTRUCTION/ABANDONMENT

Date	Act	End points	MP	Change	Main	Source	Note
1976	P	Logansport-Van	195.1-198.3	+3.2		1	1
1976	P	Van-Kenneth	1.2-5.7	+4.5	7.7	1	1

OWNERSHIP
1976	Toledo, Peoria & Western RR (controlled by Santa Fe RR)
1983/12/31	Santa Fe RR, merge Toledo, Peoria & Western
1989/2/1	Toledo, Peoria & Western Ry, separated from Santa Fe RR to independent corp.

MAIN LINE (TPW-[PRR-LF])
See Pennsylvania line PRR-LF for arrangement of stations, prior construction/abandonment record, and prior ownership

CONSTRUCTION/ABANDONMENT

Date	Act	End points	MP	Change	Main	Source	Note
1976	P	Kenneth-Effner	5.7-61.3	+55.6	55.6	1	

OWNERSHIP
1976	Toledo, Peoria & Western RR (controlled by Santa Fe RR)
1983/12/31	Santa Fe RR, merge Toledo, Peoria & Western
1989/2/1	Toledo, Peoria & Western Ry, separated from Santa Fe RR to independent corp.

ACQUISITION/DISPOSITION RECORD

Date	Act	TPW-	End points	Change	Main	Note
1976	P	[PRR-L]	Logansport-Kenneth	+7.7		1
	P	[PRR-LF]	Kenneth-Effner	+55.6	63.3	

ACT COLUMN KEY
P   Purchased from Penn Central

SOURCES
1. Simons and Parker, *Railroads of Indiana*.

NOTES
1. The company provides running rights between Kenneth and Logansport to Winimac Southern.

TWIN BRANCH

MAIN LINE (TWBR-A)

	Mileage	County	Crossings, junctions, etc.
(Junction)	0	St.Joseph	J/LS-WE 12.1
(End, in Mishawaka)	1.7	"	

CONSTRUCTION/ABANDONMENT

Date	Act	End points	MP	Change	Main	Source	Note
1927/9	B	Line	0-1.7	+1.7	1.7	1	
1978/6	X	Line	0-1.7	-1.7	0	1	

OWNERSHIP

1927		Twin Branch RR (B)

ACQUISITION/DISPOSITION RECORD
See ownership record above for line TWBR-A

ACT COLUMN KEY
B Built by Twin Branch RR
X Abandoned

SOURCES.
1. Simons and Parker, *Railroads of Indiana..*

WABASH

MAUMEE BRANCH (WAB-MM)

	Mileage	County	Crossings, junctions, etc.
Toledo OH	0		
Antwerp OH	71.6		
(OH/IN state line)	75.7		
Woodburn	78.7	Allen	
Gar Creek	83.3	"	
New Haven	88.5	"	J/WAB-M 140.5

CONSTRUCTION/ABANDONMENT

Date	Act	End points	MP	Change	Main	Source	Note
1855	B1	Toledo OH-New Haven	75.7-88.5	+12.8	12.8		

1989	L8	Liberty Center OH-Woodburn	75.7-78.7	<3.0>	9.8	2	
1998	XL	Liberty Center OH-Woodburn	75.7-78.7	<+3.0>			
1998	S2	Liberty Center OH-Woodburn	75.7-78.7	[3.0]	9.8		
(continued)							

WABASH

MAUMEE BRANCH (WAB-MM) (continued)
OWNERSHIP

1855	Toledo & Illinois RR (B1)
1856/6	Toledo, Wabash & Western RR, merged Toledo & Illinois
1858/10/7	Toledo & Wabash Ry, reorganized Toledo, Wabash & Western
1865/6/30	Toledo, Wabash & Western Ry, merged Toledo & Wabash and other roads
1877/1/3	Wabash Ry, reorganized Toledo, Wabash & Western Ry
1879/11/10	Wabash, St. Louis & Pacific RR, merger of Wabash Ry and other road
1889/5/27	Wabash RR (B5), reorganize Wabash, St. Louis & Pacific
1915/10/22	Wabash Ry, reorganize Wabash RR
1928	Control of Wabash Ry acquired by Pennsylvania RR
1942/1/1	Wabash RR, reorganize Wabash Ry, controlled by Pennsylvania RR
1964/10/16	Norfolk & Western Ry, leased Wabash RR
1970/3/1	Norfolk & Western Ry, bought Wabash RR
1982/6/1	Norfolk Southern Corp., acquired Norfolk & Western

MONTPELIER DIVISION (WAB-M)

	Mileage	County	Crossings, junctions, etc.
Detroit MI	0		
Montpelier IN	96.9		
Blakesley OH	104.4		
(OH/IN state line)	109.3		
Artic	109.3	Dekalb	
(Crossing)	114.3	"	X/LS-T 358.46, J/PRR-LE 93.7
Butler	114.9	"	
St. Joe	122.7	"	X/B&O-C 116.5
Spencerville	125.3	"	
Grabill	130.6	Allen	
Thurman	137.0	"	
New Haven	140.5	"	J/WAB-MM 88.5
NE	140.5	"	X/NKP-F 365.4
(Junction)	145.8	"	J/B&O-F 80.0
Mike	146.0	"	X/PRR-F 319.2f. Wabash
Fort Wayne	146.5	"	
(Junction)	146.9	"	J/PRR-F 320.1
Hugo	149.2	"	X/NKP-LF 3.5, J/WAB-YF 0
Prairie Switch	154.8	"	f. Aboite
Roanoke Siding	157.3	Huntington	
Roanoke	161.7	"	
Mardenis	165.8	"	f. Union
(Crossing)	169.7	"	X/ERIE-C 126.3
Huntington	170.4	"	J/CBC-A 0
Andrews	176.2	"	
Andrews Yard	177.0	"	
Lagro	183.2	Wabash	
(Bridge)	187.6	"	B/CCC-M 112.7
Wabash	188.8	"	
Hartman	190.3	"	
Rich Valley	194.2	"	
Junction	200.2	Miami	J/WAB-MX 2.3, X/WIN-A 64.1
(Crossing)	202.2	"	X/NKP-LM 74.2
Peru	202.5	"	J/WAB-P 202.5

CONSTRUCTION/ABANDONMENT

Date	Act	End points	MP	Change	Main	Source	Note
1856	B2	New Haven-Peru	140.5-202.5	+62.0	62.0	1	
1881/8/15	B3	Delray MI-Butler	4.4-114.9	+5.6	67.6	1	
1902	B5	Butler-New Haven	114.9-140.5	+25.6	93.2	1	
(continued)							

WABASH

MONTPELIER DIVISION (WAB-M) (continued)

OWNERSHIP

1856	Lake Erie, Wabash & St. Louis RR (B2), of part
1856/6	Toledo, Wabash & Western RR, merged Lake Erie, Wabash & St. Louis
1858/10/7	Toledo & Wabash Ry, reorganized Toledo, Wabash & Western
1865/6/30	Toledo, Wabash & Western Ry, merged Toledo & Wabash and other roads
1877/1/3	Wabash Ry, reorganized Toledo, Wabash & Western Ry
1879/11/10	Wabash, St. Louis & Pacific RR, merger of Wabash Ry and other road
1881	Detroit, Butler & St. Louis (B3), of part
1881/9	Wabash, St. Louis & Pacific RR, merged Detroit, Butler & St. Louis
1889/5/27	Wabash RR (B5), reorganize Wabash, St. Louis & Pacific
1915/10/22	Wabash Ry, reorganize Wabash RR
1928	Control of Wabash Ry acquired by Pennsylvania RR
1942/1/1	Wabash RR, reorganize Wabash Ry, controlled by Pennsylvania RR
1964/10/16	Norfolk & Western Ry, leased Wabash RR
1970/3/1	Norfolk & Western Ry, bought Wabash RR
1982/6/1	Norfolk Southern Corp., acquired Norfolk & Western

LAKE ERIE & FORT WAYNE (WAB-YF)

	Mileage	County	Crossings, junctions, etc.
Hugo	0	Allen	J/WAB-M 146.9
(End)	2.0	"	

CONSTRUCTION/ABANDONMENT

Date	Act	End points	MP	Change	Main	Source	Note
1907	B7	Line	0-2.0	(+2.0)	(2.0)	2	
1982	X	Line	0-2.0	(-2.0)	0	2	

OWNERSHIP

1907	Lake Erie & Fort Wayne RR (B8)
1929	Wabash Ry, reorganize Wabash RR
1928	Control of Wabash Ry acquired by Pennsylvania RR
1942/1/1	Wabash RR, reorganize Wabash Ry, controlled by Pennsylvania RR
1964/10/16	Norfolk & Western Ry, leased Wabash RR
1970/3/1	Norfolk & Western Ry, bought Wabash RR
1982/6/1	Norfolk Southern Corp., acquired Norfolk & Western

STROH BRANCH (WAB-MS)

	Mileage	County	Crossings, junctions, etc.
Helmer	0	Steuben	J/WAB-MC 126.5
Stroh	4.6	LaGrange	

CONSTRUCTION/ABANDONMENT

Date	Act	End points	MP	Change	Main	Source	Note
1899	B5	Helmer-Stroh	0-4.6	+4.6	4.6	3	
1945	X	Helmer-Stroh	0-4.6	-4.6	0	2,3	

OWNERSHIP

1899	Wabash RR (B5)
1915/10/22	Wabash Ry, reorganize Wabash RR
1928	Control of Wabash Ry acquired by Pennsylvania RR
1942/1/1	Wabash RR, reorganize Wabash Ry, controlled by Pennsylvania RR

WABASH

CHICAGO DIVISION (WAB-MC)

	Mileage [Detroit]	County	Crossings, junctions, etc.
Montpelier OH	96.9		
Pergo	98.4		J/WAB-M 98.4
Edon OH	105.3		
(OH/IN state line)	107.2		
Hamilton	113.2	Steuben	
Steubenville	117.8	"	X/LS-TF 63.5
Ashley-Hudson	121.4	"	
Helmer	126.5	"	J/WAB-MS 0
South Milford	131.8	LaGrange	
Wolcottville	136.8	"	X/PRR-GS 129.4
Eddy	140.9	"	
Topeka	146.0	"	
Stony Creek	151.4	"	
Millersburg	154.0	Elkhart	
(Bridge)	154.1	"	B/LS-T 403.0
Benton	158.0	"	
New Paris	161.4	"	X/CCC-M 61.3, X/WIN-A 6.1
Foraker	166.5	"	
Wakarusa	171.3	"	
Wyatt	179.2	St.Joseph	
Lakeville	184.8	"	X/PRR-LS 172.2
Pine	187.4	"	J/NJI-A 11.6
North Liberty	192.9	"	X/LS-WK 13.7
Dillon	200.5	LaPorte	X/NKP-LM 137.3
Kingsbury Wye	203.0	"	
(Bridge)	205.6	"	B/GTW-C 74.82
Magee	209.6	"	X/PM-W 17.5
Westville	217.2	"	B/MON-M 47.1
(Crossing)	226.7	"	X/V&N-A 9.1
Crocker	230.5	"	
Willow Creek	233.7	"	X/B&O-C 236.9, X/MC-W 246.6
Aetna	239.2	Lake	B/IHB-G 7.2
Gary	241.1	"	
Tolleston	241.4	"	
(Bridge)	246.4	"	B/EJE-G 8.0
Clarke Jct.	246.7	"	J/BOCT-A 0.3

CONSTRUCTION/ABANDONMENT

Date	Act	End points	MP	Change	Main	Source	Note
1892	B5	Montpelier OH-Clarke Jct.	107.2-246.7	+139.5	139.5	1	

1982	X	Kingsbury-Clarke Jct.	205.6-246.7	-41.1	98.4	1	
1984	L6	Ashley-Hudson - Wolcottv.	121.4-136.8	<15.4>		2	
1984	X	Wakarusa IN-Wolcottville	171.0-136.8	-34.2	48.8		
1988	X	Pine-Wakarusa	187.4-171.0	-16.4	32.4	1,2	
1992/12	LA1	Ashley-Hudson - S. Milford	121.4-131.8	<<10.4>>		2	
1992	XL,X	S. Milford-Wolcottville	131.8-136.8	<+-5.0>	32.4	2	
1993	L7	Montpelier OH - Ashley-Hud.	107.2-121.4	<-14.2>	18.2	2	
1998	X	Pine-Dillon	187.4-200.5	-13.1	5.1		

OWNERSHIP

1892	Wabash RR (B5)
1915/10/22	Wabash Ry, reorganize Wabash RR
1928	Control of Wabash Ry acquired by Pennsylvania RR
1942/1/1	Wabash RR, reorganize Wabash Ry, controlled by Pennsylvania RR
1964/10/16	Norfolk & Western Ry, leased Wabash RR
1970/3/1	Norfolk & Western Ry, bought Wabash RR
1982/6/1	Norfolk Southern Corp., acquired Norfolk & Western

WABASH

EEL RIVER LINE (WAB-ME)
See Pennsylvania line PRR-LE for arrangement of stations, prior and subsequent construction/abandonment record, and prior and subsequent ownership

CONSTRUCTION/ABANDONMENT

Date	Act	End points	MP	Change	Main	Source	Note
1877/10	L1	Logansport-Butler	0-93.6	+93.6	93.6	4	6
1901	XL	Logansport-Butler	0-93.6	-93.6	0	2	5

OWNERSHIP

1877	Wabash Ry, leased Eel River RR
1879/11/10	Wabash, St. Louis & Pacific RR, merger of Wabash Ry (and lease assigned)
1889/5/27	Wabash RR, reorganize Wabash, St. Louis & Pacific (and lease of Eel River)
1901	Wabash RR, surrendered lease of Eel River RR

PERU-CHILI LINE (WAB-MX)

	Mileage	County	Crossings, junctions, etc.
(Peru)	0)	Miami	
--via WAB-M			
Junction	2.3	"	J/WAB-M 200.2
Brownell	7.1	"	
Chili	10.5	"	J/WAB-E 20.0

CONSTRUCTION/ABANDONMENT

Date	Act	End points	MP	Change	Main	Source	Note
1899	B6	Peru-Chili	0-10.5	+8.2	8.2	2,4	
1902	S1	Peru-Chili	0-10.5	-8.2	0	4	

OWNERSHIP

1899	Peru & Detroit Ry (B6)
1899	Wabash RR, acquired(?) Peru & Detroit

INDIANAPOLIS-MICHIGAN CITY LINE (WAB-IM)
For arrangement of stations and construction record, see Nickel Plate line NKP-LM

CONSTRUCTION/ABANDONMENT

Date	Act	End points	MP	Change	Main	Source	Note
1881/9	L2	Indianapolis-Michigan City	0-158.2	+158.2	158.2	2	4
1886/11	XL	Indianapolis-Michigan City	0-158.2	-158.2	0	2	4

OWNERSHIP

1881	Wabash, St. Louis & Pacific RR, leased Indianapolis, Peru & Chicago Ry
1886	Wabash, St. Louis & Pacific, surrendered lease

RANTOUL BRANCH (WAB-PR)
For arrangement of stations and construction record, see Illinois Central line IC-SR

CONSTRUCTION/ABANDONMENT

Date	Act	End points	MP	Change	Main	Source	Note
1881	L3	West Lebanon-Leroy IL	0-75.4	+8.4	8.4	4	
1884	XL	West Lebanon-Leroy IL	0-75.4	-8.4	0	4	2

OWNERSHIP

1881	Wabash, St. Louis & Pacific RR, leased Havana, Rantoul & Eastern RR
1884	Wabash, St. Louis & Pacific, surrendered lease

WABASH

PERU DIVISION (WAB-P)

	Mileage [Detroit]	County	Crossings, junctions, etc.
Peru	202.5	Miami	J/WAB-M 202.5
CW	204.4	"	X/C&O-C 164.2
New Waverly	209.2	Cass	
Danes	213.0	"	f. Cass
Logansport	218.5	"	
(Crossing)	218.7	"	X/PRR-L 197.5
Clymers	224.3	"	X/PRR-IF 109.2
Burrows	227.8	Carroll	
Rockfield	232.1	"	
Delphi	238.6	"	X/MON-I 111.0
Colburn	243.8	Tippecanoe	
Buck Creek	247.4	"	
East Yard	253.5	"	J/WAB-YL 0
Lafayette	255.4	"	
Lafayette Jct.	257.2	"	X/NKP-LP 257.7
(Bridge)	258.4	"	B/MON-SA 122.9
Shadeland	260.2	"	
Wea	263.5	"	
West Point	265.3	"	
Flint	268.8	"	
Riverside	272.2	Fountain	
Attica	276.8	"	J/WAB-PC 0, X/CAS-A 82.9
Williamsport	283.5	Warren	
West Lebanon	284.9	"	J/WAB-PR 0, J/IC-SR 0
Marshfield	288.7	"	
Johnsonville	291.2	"	
State Line	294.2	"	
(IN/IL state line)	294.3		
Eldan IL	296.2		
Danville	301.6		
Tilton IL	303.8		

CONSTRUCTION/ABANDONMENT

Date	Act	End points	MP	Change	Main	Source	Note
1856	B2	Peru-IL state line	202.5-294.3	+91.8	91.8	1	

OWNERSHIP

1856	Lake Erie, Wabash & St. Louis RR (B2), of part
1856/6	Toledo, Wabash & Western RR, merged Toledo & Illinois and Lake Erie, Wabash & St. Louis
1858/10/7	Toledo & Wabash Ry, reorganized Toledo, Wabash & Western
1865/6/30	Toledo, Wabash & Western Ry, merged Toledo & Wabash and other roads
1877/1/3	Wabash Ry, reorganized Toledo, Wabash & Western Ry
1879/11/10	Wabash, St. Louis & Pacific RR, merger of Wabash Ry and other road
1889/5/27	Wabash RR (B5), reorganize Wabash, St. Louis & Pacific
1915/10/22	Wabash Ry, reorganize Wabash RR
1928	Control of Wabash Ry acquired by Pennsylvania RR
1942/1/1	Wabash RR, reorganize Wabash Ry, controlled by Pennsylvania RR
1964/10/16	Norfolk & Western Ry, leased Wabash RR
1970/3/1	Norfolk & Western Ry, bought Wabash RR
1982/6/1	Norfolk Southern Corp., acquired Norfolk & Western

LAFAYETTE UNION (WAB-YL)

	Mileage	County	Crossings, junctions, etc.
East Yard	0	Tippecanoe	J/WAB-P 253.5
(End)	2.2	"	
(continued)			

WABASH

LAFAYETTE UNION (WAB-YL) (continued)
CONSTRUCTION/ABANDONMENT

Date	Act	End points	MP	Change	Main	Source	Note
1911/12/1	B8	Line	0-2.2	(+2.2)	0	1	

OWNERSHIP

1911	Lafayette Union RR (B8)
1915/10/22	Wabash Ry, lease Lafayette Union
1928	Control of Wabash Ry acquired by Pennsylvania RR
1942/1/1	Wabash RR, reorganize Wabash Ry, controlled by Pennsylvania RR
1964/10/16	Norfolk & Western Ry, leased Wabash RR
1970/3/1	Norfolk & Western Ry, bought Wabash RR
1982/6/1	Norfolk Southern Corp., acquired Norfolk & Western

LAFAYETTE-BLOOMINGTON LINE (WAB-PB)
For arrangement of stations and construction record, see Illinois Central line IC-SR

CONSTRUCTION/ABANDONMENT

Date	Act	End points	MP	Change	Main	Source	Note
1871	L4	Lafayette-Bloomington IL	0-116.3	+33.7	33.7	2	
1876	XL	Lafayette-Bloomington IL	0-116.3	-33.7	0	2	1

OWNERSHIP

1871	Lafayette, Muncie & Bloomington RR, leased by Toledo, Wabash & Western
1876	Toledo, Wabash & Western, surrendered lease of Lafayette, Muncie & Bloom.

COVINGTON BRANCH (WAB-PC)

	Mileage	County	Crossings, junctions, etc.
Attica	0	Fountain	J/WAB-P 276.8
Peacock	0.4	"	
Fountain	7.2	"	
Nebeker	11.1	"	
Shelby	12.3	"	
Covington	14.8	"	J/P&E-A 72.1

CONSTRUCTION/ABANDONMENT

Date	Act	End points	MP	Change	Main	Source	Note
1881/9/1	B4	Attica-Covington	0-14.8	+14.8	14.8	3	
1932/11/11 X		Attica-Covington	0-14.8	-14.8	0	3	7

OWNERSHIP

1881	Attica, Covington & Southern Ry (B4)
1881	Wabash, St. Louis & Pacific Ry, leased Attica, Covington & Southern
1889/5/27	Wabash RR, reorganize Wabash, St. Louis & Pacific
1904/1/15	Wabash RR, merged Attica, Covington & Southern
1915/10/22	Wabash Ry, reorganize Wabash RR
1928	Control of Wabash Ry acquired by Pennsylvania RR

VINCENNES BRANCH (WAB-CV)
For arrangement of stations and construction record, see Cleveland, Cincinnati, Chicago & St. Louis line CCC-LV.

CONSTRUCTION/ABANDONMENT

Date	Act	End points	MP	Change	Main	Source	Note
1881	L5	St. Francisville IL-Vincennes	0-8.7	+7.4	7.4	4	
1885	XL	St. Francisville IL-Vincennes	0-8.7	-7.4	0	4	3

OWNERSHIP

1881	Wabash, St. Louis & Pacific RR, leased Cairo & Vincennes RR
1885	Wabash, St. Louis & Pacific, surrendered lease

WABASH

ACQUISITION/DISPOSITION RECORD

Date	Act	WAB-	End points	Change	Main	Note
1855	B1	WT	Toledo OH-New Haven	+12.8	12.8	
1856	B2	M	New Haven-Peru	+62.0		
	B2	P	Peru-IL state line	+91.8	166.6	
1871	L4	LB	Lafayette-Bloomington IL	+33.7	200.3	
1876	XL	LB	Lafayette-Bloomington IL	-33.7	166.6	1
1877/10	L1	E	Logansport-Butler	+93.6	260.2	
1881/4	L5	CV	St. Francisville IL-Vincennes	+7.4		
/8/15	B3	M	Delray MI-Butler	+5.6		
	B4	PC	Attica-Covington	+14.8		
/9	L2	IM	Indianapolis-Michigan City	+158.2		
	L3	PR	West Lebanon-Leroy IL	+8.4	454.6	
1884	XL	PR	West Lebanon-Leroy IL	-8.4	446.2	2
1885	XL	CV	St. Francisville IL-Vincennes	-7.4	438.8	3
1886/11	XL	IM	Indianapolis-Michigan City	-158.2	280.6	4
1892	B5	MC	Montpelier OH-Clarke Jct.	+139.5	420.1	
1899	B5	CS	Helmer-Stroh	+4.6		
	B6	PX	Peru-Chili	+8.2	432.9	
1901	XL	E	Logansport-Butler	-93.6	339.3	5
1902	S1	PX	Peru-Chili	-8.2		
	B5	M	Butler-New Haven	+25.6	356.7	
1907	B7	YF	Lake Erie & Fort Wayne line	(+2.0)	356.7	
1911	B8	YL	Lafayette Union line	(+2.2)	356.7	
1932/11/11	X	PC	Attica-Covington	-14.8	341.9	7
1945	X	CS	Helmer-Stroh	-4.6	337.3	

On 1964/10/16 this company was leased to Norfolk & Western and on 1970/3/1 was merged by Norfolk & Western. The Acquisition/Disposition Record is continued under the Wabash and under Norfolk & Western.

On 1982/6/1 Norfolk & Western was merged to become Norfolk Southern. The Acqusition/-Disposition Record is continued under Wabash and under Norfolk Southern.

Date	Act	WAB-	End points	Change	Main	Note
1982	X	YF	Lake Erie & Fort Wayne line	(-2.0)		
	X	MC	Kingsbury-Clarke Jct.	-41.1	296.2	
1984	L6	MC	Ashley-Hudson - Wolcottville	<15.4>		
	X	MC	Wakarusa IN-Wolcottville	-34.2	246.6	
1988	X	MC	Pine-Wakarusa	-16.4	230.2	
1989	L8	MM	OH state line-Woodburn	<3.0>	227.2	
1992/12	LA1	MC	Ashley-Hudson - S. Milford	<+-10.4>		
	XL	MC	S. Milford-Wolcottville	<+5.0>		
	X	MC	S. Milford-Wolcottville	-5.0	227.2	
1993	L7	MC	Montpelier OH - Ashley-Hudson	<14.2>	213.0	
1998	X	MC	Pine-Dillon	-13.1		
	XL	MM	OH state line-Woodburn	<+3.0>		
	S2	MM	OH state line-Woodburn	[3.0]	199.9	

ACT COLUMN KEY
B1   Built by Toledo & Illinois RR
B2   Built by Lake Erie, Wabash & St. Louis RR
B3   Built by Detroit, Butler & St. Louis RR
B4   Built by Attica, Covington & Southern Ry
B5   Built by Wabash RR
B6   Built by Peru & Detroit Ry
B7   Built by Lake Erie & Fort Wayne RR
B8   Built by Lafayette Union RR
L1   Leased Eel River RR
L2   Leased Indianapolis, Peru & Chicago
(continued)

WABASH

ACT COLUMN KEY (continued)
L3   Leased Havana, Rantoul & Eastern RR
L4   Leased Lafayette, Bloomington & Mississippi Ry
L5   Leased Cairo & Vincennes RR
L6   Leased to Pigeon River, which see for subsequent record
L7   Leased to Indiana Northeastern
L8   Leased to Indiana Hi-Rail
LA1   Lease assigned from Pigeon River to Indiana Northeastern
S1   Sold to Winona Interurban Ry
S2   Sold to Maumee & Western
X   Abandoned
XL   Lease cancelled

SOURCES
1. Indiana, *1995 Indiana State Rail Plan.*
2. Simons and Parker, *Railroads of Indiana.*
3. Sulzer, *Ghost Railroads of Indiana.*
4. Swartz, "The Wabash Railroad."

NOTES
1. The lease of this line was terminated and the line eventually transferred to the Nickel Plate Road, see line NKP-LP.
2. The lease of this line was assigned to the Illinois Central, see line IC-SR.
3. This line was transferred to a predecessor of the Cleveland, Cincinnati & Chicago, see line CCC-LV.
4. This line was transferred to the Nickel Plate Road, see line NKP-LM.
5. This line was transferred to the Pennsylvania RR, see line PRR-LE.
6. The connecting route in Logansport between lines WAB-P and WAB-E could not be determined.
7. This is date the ICC authorized abandonment.

WABASH CENTRAL

CRAIGVILLE-VAN BUREN (WABC-[NKP-TB])
See New York, Chicago & St. Louis line NKP-TB for arrangement of stations, prior constructionabandonment record, and prior ownership

CONSTRUCTION/ABANDONMENT

Date	Act	End points	MP	Change	Main	Source	Note
1998	P	Craigville-Van Buren	117.8-144.2	+26.4	26.4		

OWNERSHIP

| 1998 | | Wabash Central | | | | | |

ACQUISITION/DISPOSITION RECORD
See ownership record above for line WABC-[NKP-TB]

ACT COLUMN KEY
P   Purchased from Norfolk Southern

WHITEWATER VALLEY

MAIN LINE (WWV-[CCC-GW])
See Cleveland, Cincinnati, Chicago & St. Louis line CCC-GW for arrangement of stations, prior construction/abandonment record, and prior ownership
(continued)

WHITEWATER VALLEY

MAIN LINE (WWV-[CCC-GW]) (continued)
CONSTRUCTION/ABANDONMENT

Date	Act	End points	MP	Change	Main	Source	Note
1974	L	Brookville-Connersville	43.9-68.0	+24.1	24.1	1	
1975	XL	Brookville-Metamora	43.9-50.1	-6.2	17.9	1	
1984/4	P1	Metamora-Connersville	50.1-68.0	[17.9]	17.9	1	
1990/2	P2	In Connersville	68.0-69.1	+1.1	19.0	1	

OWNERSHIP
1974   Whitewater Valley RR

ACQUISITION/DISPOSITION RECORD
See ownership record above for line WWV-[CCC-GW]

ACT COLUMN KEY
L   Leased from Penn Central
P1   Purchased from Penn Central
P2   Purchased from Indiana Hi-Rail
XL   Lease terminated

SOURCES
1. Simons and Parker, *Railroads of Indiana.*

WINIMAC SOUTHERN

MAIN LINE (WSRY-[PRR-L])
See Pennsylvania line PRR-L for arrangement of stations, prior construction/abandonment record, and prior ownership

CONSTRUCTION/ABANDONMENT

Date	Act	End points	MP	Change	Main	Source	Note
1993/3/20	P	Anoka-Van	192.6-198.3	+5.7		1	
1993/3/20	P	Kenneth-Boone	5.7-11.9	+6.2		1	1
1993/3/20	P	Boone-Winimac	206.8-223.9	+17.1	29.0	1	
1995	S	Kenneth-Boone	5.7-11.9	-6.2		1	
1995	S	Boone-Winimac	206.8-223.9	-17.1	5.7	1	

OWNERSHIP
1993/3/20   Winimac Southern RR

BRINGHURST-LOGANSPORT (WSRY-[PRR-IF])
See Pennsylvania line PRR-IF for arrangement of stations, prior construction/abandonment record, and prior ownership

CONSTRUCTION/ABANDONMENT

Date	Act	End points	MP	Change	Main	Source	Note
1993/3/20	P	Bringhurst-Van	94.0-114.5	+20.5	20.5	1	

OWNERSHIP
1993/3/20   Winimac Southern RR

KOKOMO-ANOKA (WSRY-[PRR-CR])
See Pennsylvania line PRR-CR for arrangement of stations, prior construction/abandonment record, and prior ownership

CONSTRUCTION/ABANDONMENT

Date	Act	End points	MP	Change	Main	Source	Note
1993/3/20	P	Kokomo-Anoka	159.5-192.8	+33.3	33.3	1	

OWNERSHIP
1993/3/20   Winimac Southern RR

WINIMAC SOUTHERN RR

ACQUISITION/DISPOSITION RECORD

Date	Act	WSRY-	End points	Change	Main	Note
1993/3/20	P	[PRR-L]	Anoka-Winimac	+29.0		1
/3/20	P	[PRR-CR]	Bringhurst-Van	+20.5		
/3/20	P	[PRR-L]	Kokomo-Anoka	+33.3	82.8	
1995	S	[PRR-L]	Kenneth-Winimac	-23.3	59.5	

ACT COLUMN KEY
P Purchased from Conrail
S Sold to A & R RR

SOURCES
1. Simons and Parker, *Railroads of Indiana*.

NOTES
1. This purchase also included trackage rights over Toledo, Peoria & Western between Kenneth and Van.

YANKEETOWN DOCK CORP.

MAIN LINE (YANK-A)

	Mileage	County	Crossings, junctions, etc.
Lynnville Mine	0	Warrick	J/CCC-TK 5.5
Boonville	12	"	X/SOU-UE 16.1
Yankeetown Dock	22	"	

CONSTRUCTION/ABANDONMENT

Date	Act	End points	MP	Change	Main	Source	Note
1954	B	Lynnville Mine-Yankeetown	0-22	+22.0	22.0	1	1

OWNERSHIP
1954   Yankeetown Dock Corp (B)

ACQUISITION/DISPOSITION RECORD
See ownership record above for line YANK-A

Act column KEY
B Built by Yankeetown Dock Corp (B1)

SOURCES
1. Simons and Parker, *Railroads of Indiana*.

NOTES
1. This railroad is not a common carrier.

5 COMPANY LISTING OF INTERURBAN LINES OF TRACK

BEECH GROVE TRACTION

MAIN LINE (BGT-A)

	Mileage	County	Crossings, junctions, etc.
Indianapolis	0	Marion	
Beech Grove	6	"	

CONSTRUCTION/ABANDONMENT

Date	Act	End points	MP	Change	Main	Source	Note
1911/4	B	Indianapolis-Beech Grove	0-6	+6.0	6.0	1,2	
1937	X	Indianapolis-Beech Grove	0-6	-6.0	0	1,2	

OWNERSHIP

1911	Beech Grove Traction Co. (B1)

ACQUISITION/DISPOSITION RECORD
See ownership record above for line BGT-A

ACT COLUMN KEY
B   Built by Beech Grove Traction Co.
X   Abandoned

SOURCES
1. Central, *Electric Railways of Indiana, Part I.*
2. Hilton and Due, *The Electric Interurban Railways.*

BLUFFTON, GENEVA & CELINA

MAIN LINE (BGCT-A)

	Mileage	County	Crossings, junctions, etc.
Bluffton	0	Wells	
Vera Cruz	6	"	
Linn Grove	11	Adams	
Geneva	19	"	

CONSTRUCTION/ABANDONMENT

Date	Act	End points	MP	Change	Main	Source	Note
1909/12	B1	Bluffton-Vera Cruz	0-6	+6.0	6.0	1	
1910/2	B1	Vera Cruz-Geneva	6-19	+13.0	19.0	1	
1918	X	Bluffton-Geneva	0-19	-19.0	0	1	

OWNERSHIP

1909	Bluffton, Geneva & Celina Traction Co.

ACQUISITION/DISPOSITION RECORD
See ownership record above for line BGCT-A

ACT COLUMN KEY
B1 Built by Bluffton, Geneva & Celina Traction Co.
X   Abandoned

SOURCES
1. Blackburn, "Interurban Railroads."
2. Central, *Electric Railways of Indiana, Part II.*

CHICAGO-NEW YORK ELECTRIC AIR LINE

MAIN LINE (CNAL-A)

	Mileage	County	Crossings, junctions, etc.
South LaPorte	0	LaPorte	
Goodrum	15	Porter	J/V&N-A 8.0

CONSTRUCTION/ABANDONMENT

Date	Act	End points	MP	Change	Main	Source	Note
1911/11	B	South LaPorte-Goodrum	0-15	+15.0	15.0	1	
1917/11/1	X	South LaPorte-Goodrum	0-15	-15.0	0	1	

OWNERSHIP

1911	Goshen, South Bend & Chicago RR (B1)
1913/1/28	Gary & Interurban RR, merged GSB&C
1917/9/18	Goshen, South Bend & Chicago RR, split from G&I

ACQUISITION/DISPOSITION RECORD
See ownership record above for line CNAL-A

ACT COLUMN KEY
B   Built by Goshen, South Bend & Chicago RR, owned by Chicago-New York Electric Air Line RR
X   Abandoned

SOURCES
1. Buckley, *Gary Railways.*

CHICAGO SOUTH SHORE & SOUTH BEND

MAIN LINE (CSS-A)

	Mileage	County	Crossings, junctions, etc.
South Bend	0	St.Joseph	
Cummins	0.9	"	
(Crossing)	1.3	"	X/LS-N2 2.3
Meade	1.9	"	
Bendix	2.2	"	f. Kaley
(Junction)	3.2	"	J/CSS-B 0
Ardmore	3.4	"	
Portage	3.8	"	
Fisher	5.4	"	
Chain Lakes	5.9	"	
Lydick	6.8	"	
(Crossing)	7.4	"	X/MC-J 5.9
Warren	8.7	"	f. Hubbard
Zigler	9.5	"	
Olive	10.4	"	
Risden	10.8	"	
Terre Coupee	11.8	"	
Plainview	12.9	"	
New Carlisle	13.6	"	
(Crossing)	13.7	"	X/NOIN-A 14.2
Hudson Lake	15.2	LaPorte	
Lake Park	15.8	"	
Hicks	16.8	"	
Sagunay	17.5	"	
Birchim	18.6	"	
Hillside	19.4	"	
Galena	20.5	"	
Smith	22.0	"	
(continued)			

CHICAGO SOUTH SHORE & SOUTH BEND

MAIN LINE (CSS-A) (continued)

	Mileage [South Bend]	County	Crossings, junctions, etc.
Smith	22.0	LaPorte	
Tee Lake	23.1	"	
LaLumiere	23.8	"	
Wilhelm	25.1	"	
(Bridge)	25.4	"	B/PM-W 30.0
Andry	26.6	"	
Springville	27.6	"	
Ambler	28.7	"	
Meer	29.8	"	
Davis	30.3	"	
Cook	31.0	"	
(Bridge)	31.3	"	B/PM-C 122.5
Trail Creek	32.0	"	
Shops	32.4	"	
(Crossing)	32.5	"	X/NKP-LM 157.3
Michigan City	34.0	"	
(Crossing)	34.5	"	X/MC-W 229.67, X/MON-M 59.0
Willard Avenue	34.7	"	
Sheridan	35.7	"	
Johnsfield	36.2	"	
Lake Shore	36.7	"	
Tamarack	38.5	Porter	
Beverly Shores	39.4	"	
Keiser	40.4	"	
Furnessville	42.0	"	
Tremont	43.1	"	
State Park Siding	43.4	"	f. Forsythe
Dune Park	43.6	"	
Port Chester	44.2	"	
Dune Acres	45.2	"	f. Mineral Springs
Oak Hill	46.1	"	
Bailey	46.8	"	
(Bridge)	47.2	"	B/LS-W 484.9
Meadowbrook	47.5	"	
Shadyside	48.0	"	
Wilson	49.3	"	
Midwest	49.8	"	
Ogden Dunes	50.9	"	f. Wickliffe
Paul	51.5	"	
Long Lake	52.3	"	
Fulton Road	52.7	Lake	
Wagner	53.3	"	
(Bridge)	54.9	"	B/B&O-C 241.1
Miller	55.0	"	
Aetna	56.9	"	
(Bridge)	57.6	"	B/IHB-G 7.4
(End two tracks)	57.7	"	
Virginia Street	58.5	"	
Gary	58.9	"	
Buchanan Street	59.7	"	
Tolleston Jct.	59.9	"	
Oak Ridge	60.3	"	
Ambridge	60.7	"	
Clark Road	61.8	"	
(Bridge)	63.2	"	B/EJE-G 6.3
Cavanaugh (continued)	63.4	"	J/CSS-AO 63.4

CHICAGO SOUTH SHORE & SOUTH BEND

MAIN LINE (CSS-A) (continued)

	Mileage [South Bend]	County	Crossings, junctions, etc.
Cavanaugh	63.4	Lake	J/CSS-AO 63.4
(Bridge)	65.2	"	B/LS-WD 3.9, B/IHB-A 3.3
East Chicago	66.2	"	
(Bridge)	67.2	"	B/EJE-GS 3.7, B/IHB-AW 1.6
(Bridge, Junction)	68.1	"	B/BOCT-A 4.6, B/PRR-spur, J/CSS-AO 68.1
Calumet Avenue	68.5	"	
Hammond	68.9	"	
(IN/IL state line)	69.3		
State Line IL	69.3		
Hegewisch	70.9		
Ford City	71.9		
Calumet Harbor	72.9		
Altgeld	73.4		
124th Street	74.5		
Kensington	75.7		
--via IC			
Chicago (Randolph St.)	89.9		

CONSTRUCTION/ABANDONMENT

Date	Act	End points	MP	Change	Main	Source	Note
1908/9/6	B2	South Bend-Gary	0-58.9	+58.9	58.9	1	
1909/7/1	B2	Gary-Cavanaugh	58.9-63.4	+4.5		1	
1909/7/1	B2	Calumet Ave.-Kensington IL	68.5-75.7	+7.6	71.0	1	
1956/9/1	B3	Cavanaugh-Calumet Ave.	63.4-68.5	+4.7	75.7	1	
1971	X	South Bend-Bendix Drive	0-2.2	-2.2	73.5		

OWNERSHIP

1903	Chicago & Indiana Air Line Ry (B1), of part
1904	Chicago, Lake Shore & South Bend Ry (B2), of part
1925	Chicago South Shore & South Bend RR (B3), of part

ORIGINAL LINE AT EAST CHICAGO (CSS-AO)

	Mileage [South Bend]	County	Crossings, junctions, etc.
Cavanaugh	63.4	Lake	J/CSS-A 63.4
Cudahy	64.1	"	
(Crossing)	64.4	"	X/IHB-AC 1.4
Shearson	64.8	"	X/EJE-GS 1.3
Empire	65.2	"	
Calumet	65.7	"	
(Crossing)	66.1	"	X/BOCT-spur
(Crossing)	66.4	"	X/IHB-A 2.1, X/LS-WD 2.7, X/EJE-GW 0.7
Railroad Avenue	66.7	"	X/BOCT-spur
East Chicago	67.0	"	
White Oak	67.5	"	
Standard	68.0	"	
(Junction)	68.1	"	J/CSS-A 68.1

CONSTRUCTION/ABANDONMENT

Date	Act	End points	MP	Change	Main	Source	Note
1909/7/1	B2	Line	63.4-68.1	+4.7	4.7	1	
1956/9/15	X	Line	63.4-68.1	-4.7	0	1	

OWNERSHIP

1909	Chicago, Lake Shore & South Bend RR (B2)
1925	Chicago South Shore & South Bend RR

CHICAGO SOUTH SHORE & CHICAGO

AIRPORT EXTENSION (CSS-B)

	Mileage	County	Crossings, junctions, etc.
(Junction)	0	St. Joseph	J/CSS-A 3.2
South Bend Airport	2.8	"	

CONSTRUCTION/ABANDONMENT

Date	Act	End points	MP	Change	Main	Source	Note
1992	B3	Line	0-2.8	+2.8	2.8		

OWNERSHIP

1992		Chicago South Shore & South Bend RR (B3)

MICHIGAN CITY-KINGSBURY (CSS-[NKP-LM])

See New York, Chicago & St. Louis line NKP-LM for arrangement of stations, prior construction/abandonment record, and prior ownership.

CONSTRUCTION/ABANDONMENT

Date	Act	End points	MP	Change	Main	Source	Note
1997	L	Kingsbury-Michigan City	135.5-159.0	+23.5	23.5		

OWNERSHIP

1997 ca.		Chicago South Shore & South Bend RR

ACQUISITION/DISPOSITION RECORD

Date	Act	CSS-	End points	Change	Main	Note
1908/9/6	B2	A	South Bend-Gary	+58.9	58.9	
/7/1	B2	A	Gary-Cavanaugh	+4.5		
/7/1	B2	AO	Cavanaugh-Calumet Ave.	+4.7		
/7/1	B2	A	Calumet Ave.-Kensington IL	+7.6	75.7	
1956/9/15	B3	A	Cavanaugh-Calumet Ave.	+4.7		
/9/15	X	AO	Cavanaugh-Calumet Ave.	-4.7	75.7	
1971	X	A	South Bend-Bendix Drive	-2.2	73.5	
1992	B3	B	South Bend Airport Extension	+2.8	76.3	
1997 ca.	L	[NKP-LM]	Kingsbury-Michigan City	+23.5	99.8	

ACT COLUMN KEY

B1   Built by Chicago & Indiana Air Line Ry
B2   Built by Chicago, Lake Shore & South Bend Ry
B3   Built by Chicago South Shore & South Bend RR
L   Leased from Norfolk Southern
X   Abandoned

SOURCES

1. Central, *Electric Railways of Indiana.*
2. Indiana, *1995 Indiana State Rail Plan.*

CINCINNATI, LAWRENCEBURG & AURORA

MAIN LINE (CLA-A)

	Mileage	County	Crossings, junctions, etc.
Cincinnati OH	0		
Delhi	4.2		
Sayler Park	4.6		
Fern Bank	6.0		
Addyston	7.0		
North Bend	8.7		
Cleves	10.0		
(continued)			

CINCINNATI, LAWRENCEBURG & AURORA

MAIN LINE (CLA-A) (continued)

	Mileage	County	Crossings, junctions, etc.
Cleves OH	10.0		
Valley Jct.	11.9		
Elizabethtown	13.7		
(OH/IN state line)	14.7		
Lawrenceburg Jct.	16.7	Dearborn	
Lawrenceburg	20.4	"	
Aurora	24.9	"	

CONSTRUCTION/ABANDONMENT

Date	Act	End points	MP	Change	Main	Source	Note
1900/5	B1	Cincinnati OH-Aurora	14.7-24.9	+10.2	10.2	1,2	
1930	X	Fern Bank OH-Aurora	14.7-24.9	-10.2	0	2	

OWNERSHIP

1900	Cincinnati, Lawrenceburg & Aurora Electric Street RR (B1)

ACQUISITION/DISPOSITION RECORD
See ownership record above for line CLA-A

ACT COLUMN KEY
B1 Built by Cincinnati, Lawrenceburg & Aurora Electric Street RR
X   Abandoned

SOURCES
1. Blackburn, "Interurban Railroads."
2. Central, *Electric Railways of Indiana, Part I.*

DAYTON & WESTERN

MAIN LINE (DAWE-A)

	Mileage	County	Crossings, junctions, etc.
Dayton OH	0		
(OH/IN state line)	35.4	Wayne	
West Driving Park	37.1	"	
Austin	37.6	"	
--via city line			
(Richmond)	39.5)	"	J/THIE-R 68.7

CONSTRUCTION/ABANDONMENT

Date	Act	End points	MP	Change	Main	Source	Note
1903	B1	Dayton OH-Richmond	35.4-37.6	+2.2	2.2	1,3	
1936/8/9	S	Dayton OH-Richmond	35.4-37.6	-2.2	0	2	

1937/5/9	X	Dayton OH-Richmond				2	

OWNERSHIP

1903	Dayton & Western Traction Co. of Indiana (B1)
1903	Dayton & Western Traction Co., lease D&WT of Indiana
1906/6/15	Indiana, Columbus & Eastern Traction Co., assigned lease of D&WT
1907/8/13	Ohio Electric Ry, assigned leases of IC&ET (and D&WT)
1920	Dayton & Western Traction, lease to IC&ET and OE terminated
1936/8	Indiana Ry, lease Dayton & Western Traction

ACQUISITION/DISPOSITION RECORD
See ownership record above for line DAWE-A
(continued)

DAYTON & WESTERN

ACT COLUMN KEY
B1 Built by Dayton & Western Traction Co. of Indiana
L   Leased to Indiana Ry
X   Abandoned

SOURCES
1. Bradley, *Indiana Railroad.*
2. Central, *Electric Railways of Indiana, Part I.*
3. Hilton and Due, *The Electric Interurban Railways.*

EVANSVILLE & OHIO VALLEY

ROCKPORT DIVISION (EOV-A)

	Mileage	County	Crossings, junctions, etc.
(Evansville)	0)	Vanderburgh	
--via city line			
Kentucky Avenue	1.95	"	
(Junction)	2.3	"	J/EOV-D 0
Wood	2.60	"	
Gun Club	3.65	"	
Green River	5.04	"	
Stacer	7.62	"	
Worsham	9.26	Warrick	
Darby	9.69	"	
Newburgh	9.93	"	
Hilltop	10.81	"	
Vanada	13.19	"	
Briscoe	14.94	"	
Yankeetown	16.11	"	
Posey	17.64	"	
County Line	18.52	"	
Car Shops	20.64	Spencer	
Hatfield	20.73	"	
Kensington	22.74	"	
Richland Jct.	23.40	"	J/EOV-B 0
Sandale	23.80	"	
Hardy	24.20	"	
Kincaid	25.83	"	
Fairview	28.04	"	
Figel	30.14	"	
Rockport	30.82	"	
Underhill	31.86	"	
Ray	35.13	"	
Grandview	36.53	"	

CONSTRUCTION/ABANDONMENT

Date	Act	End points	MP	Change	Main	Source	Note
1907/6/10	B2	Newburgh-Rockport	9.9-30.8	+20.9	20.9	2	1
1908/12	B2	Kentucky Ave.-Newburgh	1.9-9.9	+8.0	28.9	2	
1910/1	B2	Rockport-Grandview	30.8-36.5	+5.7	34.6	1	
1941	X	Kentucky Ave.-Posey	1.9-17.6	-15.7		3	
1941	X	Rockport-Grandview	30.8-36.5	-5.7	13.2	3	
1946	X	Posey-Rockport	17.6-30.8	-13.2	0	3	

OWNERSHIP

1907	Evansville & Eastern Electric Ry (B2), of part
1907/6/22	Evansville Railways, merge E&EE and Evansville & Mt. Vernon
1908/3/7	Evansville Railways, merge Evansville Terminal
1918/12/18	Evansville & Ohio Valley Rd, reorganize Evansville Rys

EVANSVILLE & OHIO VALLEY
RICHLAND BRANCH (EOV-B)

	Mileage	County	Crossings, junctions, etc.
Richland Jct.	0	Spencer	J/EOV-A 23.40
Richland	3.35	"	

CONSTRUCTION/ABANDONMENT

Date	Act	End points	MP	Change	Main	Source	Note
1907/10	B2	Richland Jct.-Richland	0-3.4	+3.4	3.4	2	
1946	X	Richland Jct.-Richland	0-3.4	-3.4	0	3	

OWNERSHIP

1907	Evansville & Eastern Electric Ry (B2)
1907/6/22	Evansville Railways, merge E&EE and Evansville & Mt. Vernon
1918/12/18	Evansville & Ohio Valley Rd, reorganize Evansville Rys

EVANSVILLE-MT. VERNON (EOV-C)

	Mileage	County	Crossings, junctions, etc.
(Evansville)	0	Vanderburgh	
--via city line			
New Harmony Road	3.0	"	
Mt. Vernon	12.9	"	

CONSTRUCTION/ABANDONMENT

Date	Act	End points	MP	Change	Main	Source	Note
1906/6/19	B1	Evansville-Mt. Vernon	3.0-12.9	+9.9	9.9	C1,B	
1941	X	Evansville-Mt. Vernon	3.0-12.9	-9.9	0	C1	

OWNERSHIP

1906	Evansville & Mt. Vernon Electric Ry (B1)
1907/6/22	Evansville Railways, merge E&MV and Evansville & Eastern Electric
1918/12/18	Evansville & Ohio Valley Rd, reorganize Evansville Rys

EVANSVILLE-HENDERSON (EOV-D)

	Mileage	County	Crossings, junctions, etc.
(Junction)	0	Vanderburgh	J/EOV-A 2.3
(IN/OH state line)	3		
Henderson KY			

CONSTRUCTION/ABANDONMENT

Date	Act	End points	MP	Change	Main	Source	Note
1912/8	L1	(Junction)-Henderson KY	0-3	+3.0	3.0	1	
1941	XL	(Junction)-Henderson KY	0-3	-3.0	0		

OWNERSHIP

1911	Evansville, Henderson & Owensboro Ry (L1), lease of Illinois Central line
ca.	Evansville Rys, control of EH&O
1918/12/18	Evansville & Ohio Valley Rd, reorganize Evansville Rys (with control of EH&O)

ACQUISITION/DISPOSITION RECORD

Date	Act	EOV-	End points	Change	Main	Note
1906/6/19	B1	C	Evansville-Mt. Vernon	+9.9	9.9	
1907/6/10	B2	A	Newburgh-Rockport	+20.9		1
/10	B2	B	Richland Jct.-Richland	+3.4	34.2	
1908/12	B2	A	Kentucky Ave.-Newburgh	+8.0	42.2	
1911/1	B2	A	Rockport-Grandview	+5.7	47.9	
1912/8	L1	D	Evansville-Henderson KY	+3.0	50.9	
(continued)						

EVANSVILLE & OHIO VALLEY

ACQUISITION/DISPOSITION RECORD (continued)

Date	Act	EOV-	End points	Change	Main	Note
1941	X	A	Kentucky Ave.-Posey	-15.7		
	X	A	Rockport-Grandview	-5.7		
	X	C	Evansville-Mt. Vernon	-9.9		
	XL	D	Evansville-Henderson KY	-3.0	16.6	
1946	X	A	Posey-Rockport	-13.2		
1946	X	B	Richland Jct.-Richland	-3.4	0	

ACT COLUMN KEY
B1   Built by Evansville & Mt. Vernon Electric Ry
B2   Built by Evansville & Eastern Electric Ry
L1   Leased from Illinois Central
X   Abandoned
XL   Lease terminated

SOURCES
1. Blackburn, "Interurban Railroads."
2. Central, *Electric Railways of Indiana, Part I.*
3. Hilton and Due, *The Electric Interurban Railways.*

NOTES
1. The company also held trackage rights on the Evansville Suburban & Newburgh between Evansville and Newburgh. These ended when the segment between Kentucky Avenue and Newburgh was completed in 1908.

EVANSVILLE SUBURBAN & NEWBURGH

EVANSVILLE-NEWBURGH (ESN-A)

	Mileage	County	Crossings, junctions, etc.
(Evansville)	0)	Vanderburgh	
--via city line			
(Junction)	0.4	"	
(Junction)	2.6	"	J/ESN-B 2.6
Woodmere	4.5	"	
Gilberts	5.1	"	
Barnetts	6.2	"	
Fuquay	7.2	"	
Stacers	8.0	"	
Coal Mine	9.3	Warrick	
Kueblers	10.0	"	
Newburgh	10.3	"	

CONSTRUCTION/ABANDONMENT

Date	Act	End points	MP	Change	Main	Source	Note
1889/8/1	B1	Evansville-Newburgh	0.4-10.3	+9.9	9.9	2	1
1941	X	MP 2.6-Newburgh	2.6-10.3	-7.7	2.2	2	
1948	X	MP 0.4-MP 2.6	0.4-2.6	-2.2	0	2	

OWNERSHIP

1889	Evansville Suburban & Newburgh Ry (B1)

EVANSVILLE SUBURBAN & NEWBURGH

BOONVILLE DIVISION (ESN-B)

	Mileage [Evansville]	County	Crossings, junctions, etc.
(Junction)	2.6	Vanderburgh	J/ESN-A 2.6
Stockwell	4.1	"	
Smyths	4.6	"	
Garvins	5.1	"	
Sub Station	7.5	Warrick	
Stephenston	8.3	"	
Lant Switch	9.1	"	
Castle Garden	10.8	"	
Stinson	11.5	"	
Chandler	12.7	"	
Harts	13.2	"	
St. Rowan	14.8	"	
Korffs	15.1	"	
Mitchems	15.5	"	
Newburgh Road	16.3	"	
Boonville	18.3	"	

CONSTRUCTION/ABANDONMENT

Date	Act	End points	MP	Change	Main	Source	Note
1906/7/3	B1	Junction-Boonville	2.6-18.3	+15.7	15.7	2	
1948	X	Junction-Boonville	2.6-18.3	-15.7	0	2	

OWNERSHIP

1906	Evansville Suburban & Newburgh Ry (B1)

ACQUISITION/DISPOSITION RECORD

Date	Act	ESN-	End points	Change	Main	Note
1889/8/1	B1	A	Evansville-Newburgh	+9.9	9.9	1
1906/7/3	B1	B	Junction-Boonville	+15.7	25.6	
1941	X	A	MP 2.6-Newburgh	-7.7	17.9	
1948	X	A	MP 0.4-MP 2.6	-2.2		
1948	X	B	Junction-Boonville	-15.7	0	

ACT COLUMN KEY
B1 Built by Evansville Suburban & Newburgh Ry
X   Abandoned

SOURCES
1. Blackburn, "Interurban Railroads."
2. Central, *Electric Railways of Indiana, Part I.*

NOTES
1. This line was operated by steam power until 1905. Electric operation began in May 1905, and continued until 1941, at which time steam power replaced it.

FORT WAYNE & DECATUR TRACTION

MAIN LINE (FWDT-A)

	Mileage	County	Crossings, junctions, etc.
(Fort Wayne)	0)	Allen	
--via city line			
Sherwood Terrace	2.7	"	
Philleys			
Thompsons			
Nine Mile			
(continued)			

FORT WAYNE & DECATUR TRACTION

MAIN LINE (FWDT-A) (continued)

	Mileage [Fort Wayne]	County	Crossings, junctions, etc.
Nine Mile			
Sub Station			
St. Johns			
Reiters Lane			
Monmouth			
Car Barns			
Decatur	22	Adams	

CONSTRUCTION/ABANDONMENT

Date	Act	End points	MP	Change	Main	Source	Note
1907/2/2	B1	Fort Wayne-Decatur	2.7-22	+19.3	19.3	1,2	
1927	X	Fort Wayne-Decatur	2.7-22	-19.3	0	2	

OWNERSHIP

1907	Fort Wayne & Springfield Ry (B1)
1916/7/1	Fort Wayne & Decatur Traction Co., reorganize Fort Wayne & Springfield

ACQUISITION/DISPOSITION RECORD
See ownership record above for line FWDT-A

ACT COLUMN KEY
B1 Built by Fort Wayne & Springfield Ry (B1)
X   Abandoned

SOURCES
1. Blackburn, "Interurban Railroads."
2. Central, *Electric Railways of Indiana, Part II.*

FORT WAYNE, VAN WERT & LIMA

MAIN LINE (FWVL-A)

	Mileage	County	Crossings, junctions, etc.
(Fort Wayne)	0)	Allen	
--via city line			
Walton Avenue	2.0	"	
Siding No. 20	2.3	"	
Roy	3.3	"	
Inca	3.8	"	
Grove	5.2	"	
New Haven	7.7	"	
Perry	8.1	"	
Siding No. 16	11.3	"	
Bly	12.1	"	
Tillman	15.6	"	
Giant	16.2	"	
Pit			
Monroeville	19.5	"	
Monroe	19.7	"	
(IN/OH state line)	23.4		
Dixon OH	23.5		
Ohio Siding	26.0		
Convoy	29.1		
Richey	32.5		
Stevens	35.1		
Van Wert	36.5		
(continued)			

FORT WAYNE, VAN WERT & LIMA

MAIN LINE (FWVL-A) (continued)

	Mileage	County	Crossings, junctions, etc.
Van Wert OH	36.5		
Morgan	37.1		
Cave Siding	37.5		
Gamble	41.6		
Frances Quarry	43.3		
Middlepoint	44.3		
Baxter Siding	44.9		
Siding No. 5	46.8		
Way	48.4		
Delphos	49.9		
Wright Siding	52.3		
Scott Siding	55.8		
Elida	58.1		
Tower Siding	61.2		
Grand Avenue Jct.	64.0		
--via city line			
(Lima OH)	64.7)		

CONSTRUCTION/ABANDONMENT

Date	Act	End points	MP	Change	Main	Source	Note
1905	B1	Fort Wayne-Monroeville	2.0-19.5	+19.5		2	
1905/Spr.	B2	Lima-IN state line	23.4-64.0			2	
1905/9/22	B1	Monroeville-OH state line	19.5-23.4	+3.9	23.4	2	
1932/6/30	XO	Fort Wayne-Lima	2.0-64.0	-23.4	0	2	

OWNERSHIP

1905	Fort Wayne, Van Wert & Lima Traction Co. (B1), of part
1905	Lima, Delphos, Van Wert & Fort Wayne Traction Co. (B2), of part
1905/4/1	Fort Wayne, Van Wert & Lima Traction Co, merge LDVW&FW
1916	Ohio Electric Ry, lease of FWVW&LT
1921	Lease terminated
1930	Indiana Ry, operated FWVW&LT

ACQUISITION/DISPOSITION RECORD
See ownership record above for line FWVL-A

ACT COLUMN KEY
B1   Built by Fort Wayne, Van Wert & Lima Traction Co.
B2   Built by Lima, Delphos, Van Wert & Fort Wayne Traction Co.
XO   Operations ended

SOURCES
1. Blackburn, "Interurban Railroads."
2. Central, *Electric Railways of Indiana, Part II.*

FRENCH LICK & WEST BADEN

MAIN LINE (FLWB-A)

	Mileage	County	Crossings, junctions, etc.
French Lick	0	Orange	
West Baden	1.1	"	

CONSTRUCTION/ABANDONMENT

Date	Act	End points	MP	Change	Main	Source	Note
1910 ca.	B	French Lick-West Baden	0-1.1	+1.1	1.1	1	
1924 ca.	X	French Lick-West Baden	0-1.1	-1.1	0	1	

OWNERSHIP

1910	French Lick & West Baden (B1)

FRENCH LICK & WEST BADEN

ACQUISITION/DISPOSITION RECORD
See ownership record above for line FLWB-A

ACT COLUMN KEY
B   Built by French Lick & West Baden
X   Abandoned

SOURCES
1. Central, *Electric Railways of Indiana, Part I.*

NOTES
General. Source 1 states that the company may also have a branch line extended to Abby Dell; no documentation is found for this.

GARY & INTERURBAN

GARY-CROWN POINT (GARY-A)

	Mileage	County	Crossings, junctions, etc.
(Gary)			
--via city line			
45th Ave./Oak Hill Cemetery	0	Lake	
45th Ave./Cleveland	0.3	"	
Lottavilla	1.3	"	
Crown Point (Main/Joliet)	5.5	"	

CONSTRUCTION/ABANDONMENT

Date	Act	End points	MP	Change	Main	Source	Note
1911/1	B1	Gary-Lottaville	0-1.3	+1.3		2	
1911/7/1	B1	Lottaville-Crown Point	1.3-5.5	+4.2	5.5	2	
1933/6/17	X	Gary-Crown Point	0-5.5	-5.5	0	2	

OWNERSHIP

1911	Gary & Southern Traction Co. (B1)
1928/10/1	Gary Railways Co., leased Gary & Southern Traction

GARY-GARYTON-WOODVILLE JCT. (GARY-B)

	Mileage	County	Crossings, junctions, etc.
(Gary)	0)		
--via city line			
East Gary	6.7	Porter	
Garyton	8.5	"	
Crisman	9.7	"	
McCool	11.5	"	
Babcock	13.4	"	
Esserman	15.1	"	
Woodville Jct.	16.9	"	J/VANE-A 7.5

CONSTRUCTION/ABANDONMENT

Date	Act	End points	MP	Change	Main	Source	Note
1912/8/14	B2	East Gary-Woodville Jct.	6.7-16.9	+10.2	10.2	2	
1938/10/23	XS	Garyton-Woodville Jct.	8.5-16.9	-8.4		2	
1938/10/23	XC	East Gary-Garyton	6.7-8.5	-1.8	0		

OWNERSHIP

1912	Gary Connecting Railways Co. (B2), owned by & leased to Goshen, South Bend & Chicago RR
1913/1/28	Gary & Interurban RR, merge Gary Connecting Rys and GSB&C
1917/9/18	Gary Connecting Railways Co., split from Gary & Interurban RR
/11/19	Gary & Valparaiso Ry, lease Gary Connecting Rys
1920/7/20	Gary & Connecting RR, buy Gary Connecting Rys, with lease to Gary & Valp.
1925/8/15	Gary Railways Co., buy Gary & Connecting and lease to G&V terminated

GARY & INTERURBAN

GARY-HOBART (GARY-C)

	Mileage	County	Crossings, junctions, etc.
(Gary)			
--via city line			
Broadway/37th Ave.	0	Lake	
37th/Froebel	2.1	"	
New Chicago	2.7	"	
Hobart	4.9	"	

CONSTRUCTION/ABANDONMENT

Date	Act	End points	MP	Change	Main	Source	Note
1912/9/21	B3	Gary-Hobart	0-4.9	+4.9	4.9	2	
1939/3/19	XS	Gary Hobart	0-4.9	-4.9	0	2	

OWNERSHIP

1912	Gary, Hobart & Eastern Traction Co. (B3)
1917/3/26	Gary & Hobart Traction Co., buy Gary, Hobart & Eastern Traction
1925/8/15	Gary Railways Co., merge Gary & Hobart Traction and other roads

ACQUISITION/DISPOSITION RECORD

Date	Act	GARY-	End points	Change	Main	Note
1911/1	B1	A	Gary-Lottaville	+1.3		
/7/1	B1	A	Lottaville-Crown Point	+4.2	5.5	
1912/8/14	B2	B	East Gary-Woodville Jct.	+10.2		
/9/21	B3	C	Gary-Hobart	+4.9	20.6	
1933/6/17	X	A	Gary-Crown Point	-5.5	15.1	
1938/10/23	XS	B	Garyton-Woodville Jct.	-8.4		
/10/23	XC	B	East Gary-Garyton	-1.8	4.9	
1939/3/19	XS	C	Gary Hobart	-4.9	0	

ACT COLUMN KEY

B1   Built by Gary & Southern Traction Co.
B2   Built by Gary Connecting Railways Co.
B3   Built by Gary, Hobart & Eastern Traction Co.
XC   Converted to city line
XS   Service ended

SOURCES

1. Blackburn, "Interurban Railroads."
2. Buckley, *Gary Railways.*
3. Hilton and Due, *The Electric Interurban Railways.*

NOTES

General. Much of Gary Railways property was city lines in Gary, Hammond, and Indiana Harbor, and these lines are not included in this outline of interurban services.

INDIANA RAILROAD

MAIN LINE (INDR-A)

	Mileage	County	Crossings, junctions, etc.
(Fort Wayne)	0)	Allen	
--via city line			
Broad	2.40	"	
Farm	2.80	"	
Point	3.90	"	
Mason	5.70	"	
Ferguson	8.00	"	
Land	9.50	"	
Yoder	11.40	"	
Sprang	11.90	"	
Ossian	14.90	Wells	
Erie	16.50	"	
Kingsland	16.60	"	
Mack	19.60	"	
Paxon	22.00	"	
Villa	23.60	"	
Bluffton	24.80	"	J/INDR-AB 31.80
Rotary	25.53	"	f. Barnett
Not	29.13	"	f. Nottingham
Bell	31.99	"	f. Bellevue
Key	35.78	"	f. Keystone
Oil	38.28	Blackford	
Pelier	38.79	"	f. Montpelier
Race	39.66	"	f. Race Track
Man	42.48	"	f. Manhattan
Burns	44.12	"	
Cleve	46.43	"	f. Cleveland
Blake	47.26	"	f. Blakes
Ford	48.11	"	f. Hartford City
Hurst	50.23	"	f. Winterhurst
Ervin	53.12	Delaware	f. County Line
Eaton	55.96	"	
Power	56.48	"	
(continued)			

INDIANA RAILROAD

MAIN LINE (INDR-A)

	Mileage [Fort Wayne]	County	Crossings, junctions, etc.
Power	56.48	Delaware	
Learnd	57.76	"	
Roy	61.36	"	f. Roysterton
Trent	64.38	"	
Granville	64.50	"	
Kuhner	65.27	"	
High	65.80	"	f. Highland
--via city line			
(Muncie)	66.72)	"	

CONSTRUCTION/ABANDONMENT

Date	Act	End points	MP	Change	Main	Source	Note
1903/1/24	B10	Muncie-Hartford City	65.8-48.1	+17.7		1	
1903/5/1	B10	Hartford City-Bluffton	48.1-24.8	+23.3	41.0	1	
1907/7/1	B15	Ft. Wayne-Bluffton	2.4-24.8	+22.4	63.4	1	
1941/1/18	XS	Ft. Wayne-Muncie	2.4-65.8	-63.4	0	2	

OWNERSHIP

1903	Muncie, Hartford & Fort Wayne Ry (B10), of part
1906	Indiana Union Traction Co., lease Muncie, Hartford & Ft. Wayne
1907	Ft. Wayne, Bluffton & Marion Traction Co. (B15), of part, controlled by Ft. Wayne & Wabash Valley Traction
1907 ca.	Ft. Wayne & Wabash Valley Traction, buy Ft. Wayne, Bluffton & Marion Tr.
1911	Ft. Wayne & Northern Indiana Traction Co., reorganize FW&WBT
1912/5/13	Union Traction Co. of Indiana, merge Indiana Union Traction
1920	Indiana Service Corp., merge Ft. Wayne & Northern Indiana and other roads
1930/7/2	Indiana Ry, buy Union Traction Co.

BLUFFTON-MARION (INDR-AB)

	Mileage	County	Crossings, junctions, etc.
Marion	0	Grant	
Marion Spur	0.30	"	
McClures Siding	0.70	"	
Feighner Siding	2.94	"	
Hicks Siding	5.10	"	
Oil Siding	6.94	"	
Race Siding	9.33	"	
Van Buren	10.20	"	
Studebaker Siding	12.55	"	
Barnes Siding	13.55	Huntington	
Warren	16.57	"	
Fair Siding	17.44	"	
Buckeye Siding	21.12	"	
Liberty Center	24.96	Wells	
Fisher Siding	27.34	"	
N. K. P. Transfer	29.90	"	
Car House	30.57	"	
Bluffton	31.80	"	J/INDR-A 24.80

CONSTRUCTION/ABANDONMENT

Date	Act	End points	MP	Change	Main	Source	Note
1905/12/1	B25	Marion-Bluffton	0-31.8	+31.8	31.8	1	
1931/8/16	XS	Marion-Bluffton	0-31.8	-31.8	0	2	

OWNERSHIP

1905	Marion, Bluffton & Eastern Traction Co. (B25)
1914	Marion & Bluffton Traction Co., merge Marion, Bluffton & Eastern
1920	Indiana Service Corp., merge Marion Bluffton & Traction and other roads

INDIANA RAILROAD

MUNCIE-PORTLAND (INDR-AP)

	Mileage	County	Crossings, junctions, etc.
(Muncie)	0)	Delaware	
--via city line			
??	1	"	
DeSoto	7	"	
Albany	12	"	
Dunkirk	17	Jay	
Redkey	21	"	
Como	25	"	
Blaine	27	"	
Delamore	30	"	
Portland	32	"	

CONSTRUCTION/ABANDONMENT

Date	Act	End points	MP	Change	Main	Source	Note
1906	B14	Muncie-Portland	1-32	+31.0	31.0	5	
1930/9/15	XS	Muncie-Portland	1-32	-31.0	0	2	

OWNERSHIP

1906	Muncie & Portland Traction Co. (B14)
1916/6/15	Indianapolis, New Castle & Eastern Traction Co., buy Muncie & Portland
1916/7/1	Union Traction Co. of Indiana, lease Indianapolis, New Castle & Eastern
1930/7/2	Indiana Ry, buy Union Traction Co.

MUNCIE-INDIANAPOLIS (INDR-B)

	Mileage	County	Crossings, junctions, etc.
(Muncie)	0)	Delaware	
--via city line			
Shops	1.56	"	
Hart	2.95	"	f. Siding No. 1
Russ	5.09	"	f. Siding No. 2
Yorktown	6.32	"	
Dolby	6.97	"	f. Siding No. 3
Make	9.27	"	f. Siding No. 4
Glass	11.09	"	f. Siding No. 5
Daleville	11.36	"	
Siding No. 6	12.40	"	
Camp	13.33	Madison	f. Siding No. 8
Chesterfield	13.34	"	
House	14.42	"	f. Siding No. 10
Pit	16.55	"	f. Siding No. 11
Cemetery	17.52	"	
--via city line			
(Siding No. A-11)	17.87	"	
(Anderson Jct.)	18.00	"	
(Anderson)	18.39	"	
(Madison Avenue)	19.07	"	
(Belt)	19.82	"	f. Siding No. B-11
--via city line			
Taft	22.60	"	f. Siding No. 12
Goul	25.38	"	f. Siding No. 13
Pendleton	26.96	"	
Tile	27.22	"	f. Siding No. 14
Rolla	29.00	"	f. Siding No. 15
Ingalls	31.72	"	
Bent	33.11	"	f. Siding No. 17
Hur	34.19	Hancock	f. Siding No. 18
Fortville	34.58	"	
(continued)			

INDIANA RAILROAD

MUNCIE-INDIANAPOLIS (INDR-B) (continued)

	Mileage	County	Crossings, junctions, etc.
Bucy	36.60	Hancock	f. Siding No. 19
McCordsville	39.44	"	aka Siding No. 20
Siding No. 21	41.31	Marion	
Oaklandon	41.66	"	
Siding No. 22	43.26	"	
Army Post	44.05	"	
Fort Harrison	44.47	"	
Valley	44.98	"	
Substation No. 23	45.96	"	
Lawrence	46.02	"	
Siding No. 23A	47.11	"	
Negley	48.31	"	f. Siding No. 24
Siding No. 24A	49.47	"	
Long	50.46	"	f. Siding No. 25
Siding No. 26	51.63	"	
Siding No. 26A	52.54	"	
Siding No. 27	53.45	"	
--via city line			
(Indianapolis)	56.52)	"	
(continued)			

CONSTRUCTION/ABANDONMENT

Date	Act	End points	MP	Change	Main	Source	Note
1900/Sum.	B4	Muncie-Anderson	1.6-17.5	+15.9		1	
1900/Sum.	B4	Anderson-Indianapolis	22.6-53.5	+30.9	46.8	1	1
1941/1/18	XS	Muncie-Anderson	1.6-17.5	-15.9		2	
1941/1/18	XS	Anderson-Indianapolis	22.6-53.5	-30.9	0	2	

OWNERSHIP

1900	Union Traction Co. of Indiana (B4)
1930/7/2	Indiana Ry, buy Union Traction Co.

MUNCIE-UNION CITY (INDR-BU)

	Mileage	County	Crossings, junctions, etc.
(Muncie	0)	Delaware	
--via city line			
??	2	"	
Selma	6	"	
Parker City	9	Randolph	
Farmland	14	"	
Winchester	22	"	
Union City	32	"	

CONSTRUCTION/ABANDONMENT

Date	Act	End points	MP	Change	Main	Source	Note
1904	B12	Union City-Farmland	32-14	+18.0	18.0	1	
1905/Fall	B12	Farmland-Muncie	14-2	+12.0	30.0	1	
1930/2/28	XS	Muncie-Union City	2-32	-30.0	0	2	

OWNERSHIP

1904	Dayton & Muncie Traction Co. (B12)
1906	Muncie & Union City Traction Co., buy Dayton & Muncie Traction
1906/7/1	Indiana Union Traction Co., buy Muncie & Union City Traction
1912/5/13	Union Traction Co. of Indiana, merge Indiana Union Traction Co.
1930/7/2	Indiana Ry, buy Union Traction Co.

INDIANA RAILROAD

ANDERSON-MIDDLETOWN (INDR-BM)

	Mileage	County	Crossings, junctions, etc.
(Anderson)	0)	Madison	
--via city line			
Siding No. 78	1.21	"	
Siding No. 79	2.27	"	
Mounds	3.63	"	
Siding No. 81	5.56	"	
Siding No. 82	7.55	Henry	
Middletown	9.61	"	

CONSTRUCTION/ABANDONMENT

Date	Act	End points	MP	Change	Main	Source	Note
1905/8/1	B4	Anderson-Middletown	1.2-9.6	+8.4	8.4	1	
1930/2/28	XS	Anderson-Middletown	1.2-9.6	-8.4	0	2	

OWNERSHIP

1905	Union Traction Co. of Indiana (B4)
1930/7/2	Indiana Ry, buy Union Traction Co.

WABASH-ANDERSON (INDR-C)

	Mileage	County	Crossings, junctions, etc.
(Anderson	0)	Madison	
(Shops	1.14)	"	
--via city line			
Yard	2.73	"	aka Siding No. 30
Hunt	4.04	"	aka Siding No. 31
Siding No. 32	6.16	"	
Linwood	6.22	"	
Strong	8.13	"	aka Siding No. 33
Castle	9.36	"	aka Siding No. 34
Block	10.44	"	aka Siding No. 35
Alexandria	11.38	"	
Monroe	11.68	"	aka Siding No. 36
Star	13.35	"	aka Siding No. 37
Allen	15.67	"	aka Siding No. 38
Summitville	17.08	"	aka Siding No. 39
Fairmount	22.49	"	
Clark	18.35	"	aka Siding No. 40
Dean	20.86	Grant	aka Siding No. 41
Sub Station 43	22.50	"	
Brick	25.69	"	aka Siding No. 44
School	26.63	"	aka Siding No. 45
Jonesboro	27.44	"	J/INDR-CG 0
City	27.87	"	aka Siding No. 46
Siding No. 47	28.64	"	
Siding No. 48	29.56	"	
Home	30.50	"	aka Siding No. 49
Marion	33.29	"	
Siding No. 50	36.47	"	
Fox	39.35	"	aka Siding No. 51
Siding No. 52	42.06	Wabash	
Siding No. 53	42.29	"	
La Fontaine	42.29	"	
Siding No. 54	44.03	"	
Siding No. 55	46.26	"	
Siding No. 56	48.40	"	
Siding No. 57	50.34	"	
Wabash	52.94	"	

INDIANA RAILROAD

WABASH-ANDERSON (INDR-C) (continued)
CONSTRUCTION/ABANDONMENT

Date	Act	End points	MP	Change	Main	Source	Note
1893/8/1	B1	Marion-Jonesboro	33.3-27.4	+5.9	5.9	1	
1894/Sum.	B1	Jonesboro-Summitville	27.4-17.1	+10.3	16.2	1	
1897/12/23	B2	Anderson-Alexandria	2.7-11.4	+8.7	24.9	1	
1898/Spr	B2	Alexandria-Summitville	11.4-17.1	+5.7	30.6	1	
1904/8	B11	Marion-Wabash	33.3-52.9	+19.6	50.2	1	
1930/9/15	XS	Marion-Wabash	33.3-52.9	-19.6	30.6	2	
1932/6/30	XS	Anderson-Marion	2.7-33.3	-30.6	0	2	

OWNERSHIP
1893	Marion Electric Street Ry (B1), of part
1897	Union Traction Co. (B2), of part
1899	Union Traction Co., buy Marion Electric Street Ry
1899/6/28	Union Traction Co. of Indiana, merge Union Traction Co.
1904	Indiana Northern Traction Co. (B11), of part
1905/12/2	Union Traction Co. of Indiana, buy Indiana Northern Traction
1930/7/2	Indiana Ry, buy Union Traction Co.

JONESBORO-GAS CITY (INDR-CG)

	Mileage	County	Crossings, junctions, etc.
Jonesboro	0	Grant	J/INDR-C 27.4
Gas City	2.26	"	
(continued)			

CONSTRUCTION/ABANDONMENT

Date	Act	End points	MP	Change	Main	Source	Note
1893/8/1	B1	Jonesboro-Gas City	0-2.3	+2.3	2.3	1	
1932/6/30	XS	Jonesboro-Gas City	0-2.3	-2.3	0	2	

OWNERSHIP
1893	Marion Electric Street Ry (B1)
1899	Union Traction Co., buy Marion Electric Street Ry
1899/6/28	Union Traction Co. of Indiana, merge Union Traction Co.
1930/7/2	Indiana Ry, buy Union Traction Co.

PERU-INDIANAPOLIS (INDR-D)

	Mileage	County	Crossings, junctions, etc.
(Peru)	0)	Miami	
--via city line			
River	0.48	"	
Creek	2.93	"	
Bets	5.62	"	
Bunker Hill	7.30	"	
Bunker	7.55	"	
Hagg	8.99	"	
Miami	10.40	"	
Shoe	11.61	"	
Bennetts	12.57	"	
Castor	13.21	"	
Cassville	14.31	Howard	
Len	15.29	"	
Pot	17.56	"	
--via city line			
Kokomo	19.51	"	
Markland Avenue	20.39	"	
Limit	21.25	"	
Dyer	23.82	"	
(continued)			

INDIANA RAILROAD

PERU-INDIANAPOLIS (INDR-D) (continued)

	Mileage [Peru]	County	Crossings, junctions, etc.
Dyer	23.82	"	
Fairfield	24.56	"	
Wilson	26.14	Tipton	
Sharp Spur	27.28	"	
Sharpsville	27.54	"	
Harp	29.11	"	
Jackson	31.27	"	
Jack	31.57	"	
Crail	33.71	"	
Tipton	34.92	"	
Innis	35.78	"	
Cox	37.73	"	
Atlanta	39.57	Hamilton	
Star	41.39	"	
Arcadia	42.61	"	
Midway	43.97	"	
Cicero	45.65	"	
Neal	46.48	"	
Bray	48.58	"	
Subville	51.31	"	
Noblesville	51.58	"	
Brick	52.82	"	
Moore	53.81	"	
Hazel	56.42	"	
Carmel	60.21	"	
Hawk	60.40	"	
Grove	62.80	"	
Akers	65.18	Marion	
Ripple	67.78	"	
--via city line			
(Indianapolis)	75.48)		

CONSTRUCTION/ABANDONMENT

Date	Act	End points	MP	Change	Main	Source	Note
1903	B4	Indianapolis-Kokomo	67.8-17.6	+50.2	50.2	4	
1904/8	B4	Kokomo-Peru	17.6-0.5	+17.1	67.3	1	
1938/9/5	XS	Peru-Indianapolis	0.5-67.8	-67.3	0	2	

OWNERSHIP

1905	Union Traction Co. of Indiana (B4), of part	
1930/7/2	Indiana Ry, buy Union Traction Co.	

LOGANSPORT-KOKOMO (INDR-DA)

	Mileage	County	Crossings, junctions, etc.
Logansport	0	Cass	
Siding No. 139	2.25	"	
Siding No. 137	4.75	"	
Siding No. 136	6.55	"	
Siding No. 135	8.45	"	
Walton	9.49	"	
Siding No. 134	10.82	"	
Lincoln	13.47	"	
Siding No. 132	13.47	"	
Siding No. 131	15.30	"	
Galveston	17.68	"	
(continued)			

INDIANA RAILROAD

LOGANSPORT-KOKOMO (INDR-DA) (continued)

	Mileage [Logansport]	County	Crossings, junctions, etc.
Galveston	17.68	Cass	
Siding No. 130	18.08	"	
Siding No. 129	19.98	Howard	
Siding No. 128	21.97	"	
--via city line			
(Kokomo)	23.77)	"	

CONSTRUCTION/ABANDONMENT

Date	Act	End points	MP	Change	Main	Source	Note
1904	B4	Logansport-Kokomo	0-22.0	+22.0	22.0	5	
1930/9/15	XS	Logansport-Kokomo	0-22.0	-22.0	0	2	

OWNERSHIP

1904	Union Traction Co. of Indiana (B4)
1930/7/2	Indiana Ry, buy Union Traction Co.

TIPTON-ALEXANDRIA (INDR-DC)

	Mileage	County	Crossings, junctions, etc.
Alexandria	0	Madison	
Sub Station	0.15	"	
Siding No. 60	1.98	"	
Orestes	3.22	"	
Siding No. 61	4.68	"	
Siding No. 62	7.78	"	
Sub Station 63	8.42	"	
Siding No. 64	9.49	"	
Elwood	9.5	"	
Siding No. 64A	9.98	"	
Siding No. 65	11.76	Tipton	
Siding No. 66	13.92	"	
Hobbs	15.07	"	
Siding No. 67	16.02	"	
Siding No. 68	18.14	"	
Tipton	20.00	"	

CONSTRUCTION/ABANDONMENT

Date	Act	End points	MP	Change	Main	Source	Note
1899/6/26	B3	Alexandria-Elwood	0-9.5	+9.5	9.5	1	
1902/12/31	B4	Elwood-Tipton	9.5-20.0	+10.5	20.0	1	2
1931/6/30	XS	Alexandria-Tipton	0-20.0	-20.0	0	2	

OWNERSHIP

1899	Elwood & Alexandria Ry (B3), of part
1900 ca.	Union Traction Co. of Indiana (B4), of part, buy Elwood & Alexandria
1930/7/2	Indiana Ry, buy Union Traction Co.

MARION-FRANKFORT (INDR-E)

	Mileage	County	Crossings, junctions, etc.
Marion	0	Grant	
Iron	1.10	"	
Belt	2.58	"	
Roseburg	4.82	"	
Babb	7.45	"	
Herbst	7.95	"	
Wye	9.88	"	
Swayzee	10.03	"	
(continued)			

INDIANA RAILROAD

MARION-FRANKFORT (INDR-E) (continued)

	Mileage [Marion]	County	Crossings, junctions, etc.
Swayzee	10.03	Grant	
Sims	11.81	"	
Marsh	13.62	Howard	
Sycamore	15.03	"	
Jinkens	17.59	"	
Greentown	17.84	"	
Pit	18.33	"	
Blakely	23.55	"	
Junction	25.50	"	
Kokomo	27.23	"	
Shops	28.79	"	
Busby	29.46	"	
Smith	31.55	"	
Middleton	33.63	"	
Russiaville	36.63	"	
Neff	39.20	"	
Forest	41.48	Clinton	
Nutter	41.72	"	
Hayes	45.54	"	
Michigantown	45.64	"	
Avery	48.52	"	
Frankfort	52.80	"	

CONSTRUCTION/ABANDONMENT

Date	Act	End points	MP	Change	Main	Source	Note
1903/fall	B9	Kokomo-Greentown	27.2-17.8	+9.4	9.4	4	
1905	B9	Greentown-Marion	17.8-0	+17.8	27.2	4	
1912/9/18	B22	Kokomo-Frankfort	27.2-52.8	+25.6	52.8	4	
1932/6/30	XS	Marion-Frankfort	0-52.8	-52.8	0	2	

OWNERSHIP

1903	Kokomo, Marion & Western Traction Co. (B9), of part
1912	Kokomo, Frankfort & Western Traction Co. (B22), of part
1912/12/7	Indiana Railways & Light Co., merge KM&WT and KF&WT
1922/11/7	Northern Indiana Power Co., merge IR&L and other roads

FORT WAYNE-LAFAYETTE (INDR-F)

	Mileage	County	Crossings, junctions, etc.
(Fort Wayne)	0)	Allen	
--via city line			
Taylor	1.6	"	
Freeman	2.6	"	
Ardmore	3.1	"	
Pauls	5.2	"	
Ellisons	7.5	"	
Ambers	10.3	"	
Weber	12.7	Huntington	
Roanoke	15.9	"	
Mahon	17.7	"	
Zint	20.2	"	
Rock	22.7	"	
McKees	23.5	"	
Wheel	24.8	"	
Huntington	25.3	"	
Diamond	25.8	"	
Park	27.6	"	
(continued)			

INDIANA RAILROAD

FORT WAYNE-LAFAYETTE (INDR-F) (continued)

	Mileage [Fort Wayne]	County	Crossings, junctions, etc.
Poplar	30.0	Huntington	
Andrews	31.6	"	
Coss	34.1	Wabash	
Fox	36.2	"	
Lagro	38.9	"	
Stoup	41.0	"	
Rankin	42.9	"	aka Dill
Wabash	45.1	"	
Wolf	46.6	"	
Kings	48.9	"	
Boyd	50.5	"	
Butts	53.1	Miami	
Hoover	55.4	"	
Smith	57.8	"	
--via city line			
(Peru)	58.7)	"	
--via city line			
Grant	59.4	"	
Gas	60.7	"	
Ogle	61.6	"	
Shurk	64.2	Cass	
Lewisburg	66.7	"	
Jones	70.1	"	
Keefer	70.7	"	
Baker	72.0	"	
I. R. R. Jct.	73.3	"	
Dorner	74.3	"	
Logansport	75.7	"	
Link	76.5	"	
Porter	79.3	"	
Clymers	81.4	"	
Grays	83.3	"	
Burrows	85.1	Carroll	
Martins	87.9	"	
Rockfield	89.5	"	
Loys	91.6	"	
Mears	93.5	"	
Camden	95.2	"	
Delphi	96.2	"	
Spring	98.0	"	
Vonn	100.1	Tippecanoe	
Colburn	101.1	"	
Elm	102.1	"	
Buck Creek	104.7	"	
Pence	106.4	"	
Hileman	108.7	"	
Vale	110.5	"	
Monon	111.3	"	
--via city line			
(Lafayette)	113.3)	"	

INDIANA RAILROAD

FORT WAYNE-LAFAYETTE (INDR-F) (continued)
CONSTRUCTION/ABANDONMENT

Date	Act	End points	MP	Change	Main	Source	Note
1901/8/3	B6	Peru-Wabash	57.8-45.1	+12.7	12.7	1	
1902	B7	Peru-Logansport	59.4-75.7	+16.3		1	
1902/3/30	B8	Ft. Wayne-Huntington	1.6-25.3	+23.7		1	
1902	B8	Huntington-Wabash	25.3-45.1	+19.8	72.5	1	
1907/7/1	B21	Logansport-Lafayette	75.7-111.3	+35.6	108.1	1	
1932/5/21	XS	Peru-Lafayette	59.4-111.3	-51.9	56.2	2	
1938/9/5	XS	Ft. Wayne-Peru	1.6-57.8	-56.2	0	2	

OWNERSHIP

1901	Wabash River Traction Co. (B6), of part
1902	Logansport, Rochester & Northern Traction Co. (B7), of part
1902	Ft. Wayne & Southwestern Traction Co. (B8), of part
1904/7	Ft. Wayne & Wabash Valley Traction Co., merge WRT, LR&NT, and FW&SWT
1911	Ft. Wayne & Northern Indiana Traction Co., reorganize FW&WVT
1920	Indiana Service Corp., merge Ft. Wayne & Northern Indiana Traction

FORT WAYNE-KENDALLVILLE (INDR-KA)

	Mileage	County	Crossings, junctions, etc.
(Fort Wayne)	0)	Allen	
--via city line			
Wells Street	1.0	"	
Home	1.2	"	
McAfee	1.6	"	
Adam	4.2	"	
Wallen	6.5	"	
Root	7.8	"	
Irene Byron Hospital	9.0	"	
Green	9.7	"	
Huntertown	11.3	"	
Shoaf	12.9	"	
Stoners	13.3	"	
Pit	16.0	DeKalb	
Ensley	16.7	"	
Hess	18.0	"	
Cedar	18.3	"	
Wagoner	19.7	"	
Garrett	20.4	"	J/INDR-KB 20.4
Altona	20.9	"	
Avilla	26.0	Noble	
Conlog	29.2	"	
Power House	31.5	"	
Kendallville	31.6	"	

CONSTRUCTION/ABANDONMENT

Date	Act	End points	MP	Change	Main	Source	Note
1907	B20	Ft. Wayne-Kendallville	1.0-31.6	+30.6	30.6	1	
1937/3/15	XS	Ft. Wayne-Kendallville	1.0-31.6	-30.6	0	2	

OWNERSHIP

1907	Toledo & Chicago Interurban Ry (B20)
1913	Ft. Wayne & Northwestern Ry, reorganize Toledo & Chicago Interurban
1924	Indiana Service Corp., buy Ft. Wayne & Northwestern

INDIANA RAILROAD

GARRETT-WATERLOO (INDR-KB)

	Mileage [Fort Wayne]	County	Crossings, junctions, etc.
Garrett	20.4	DeKalb	J/INDR-KA 20.4
Holman	23.8	"	
Auburn Jct.	24.1	"	
Auburn	25.2	"	
Waterloo	30.2	"	

CONSTRUCTION/ABANDONMENT

Date	Act	End points	MP	Change	Main	Source	Note
1907	B20	Garrett-Waterloo	20.4-30.2	+9.8	9.8	1	
1937/3/15	XS	Garrett-Waterloo	20.4-30.2	-9.8	0	2	

OWNERSHIP

1907	Toledo & Chicago Interurban Ry (B20)
1913	Ft. Wayne & Northwestern Ry, reorganize Toledo & Chicago Interurban
1924	Indiana Service Corp., buy Ft. Wayne & Northwestern

INDIANAPOLIS-LOUISVILLE (INDR-L)

	Mileage	County	Crossings, junctions, etc.
(Indianapolis)	0)	Marion	
--via city line			
The Loop	4.32	"	
Madison	5.80	"	
Edge	6.73	"	
Fort	7.89	"	
Oak	9.79	"	
Johnson	12.10	Johnson	
Green	12.60	"	
Miller	14.47	"	
Smith	17.19	"	
Story	20.83	"	
Franklin	21.62	"	
Stock	22.28	"	
Ham	23.55	"	
Barrow	26.01	"	
Ross	27.30	"	
Adams	28.70	"	
Durham	30.28	"	
Irwin	31.78	"	
Edinburg	31.97	"	
Elk	32.78	Bartholomew	
King	34.18	"	
Taylor	36.47	"	
Brook	40.63	"	
Long	42.80	"	
Columbus	43.31	"	
Brown	44.68	"	
Troy	47.28	"	
Newsom	49.33	"	
Azalia	52.37	"	
Crump	53.78	"	
Gibboons	55.73	Jackson	
Red	57.02	"	
Walsh	61.37	"	
Seymour	62.46	"	
(continued)			

INDIANA RAILROAD

INDIANAPOLIS-LOUISVILLE (INDR-L) (continued)

	Mileage [Indianapolis]	County	Crossings, junctions, etc.
Seymour	62.46	Jackson	
B. & O.	62.69	"	
Ward	63.20	"	
Farm	65.43	"	
Chest	67.85	"	
Langdon	71.71	"	
Rude	74.18	"	
Crothersville	74.62	"	
Austin	78.29	Scott	
Lake	82.19	"	
Scottsburg	82.92	"	
Vienna	85.41	"	
Hougland	87.26	"	
Wood	89.08	Clark	
Henry	93.08	"	
Memp	97.36	"	
Hill	99.96	"	
Speeds	101.85	"	
Sellersburg	103.34	"	
Pass	104.1	"	J/spur to cement plant, 2 mi.
Belknap	104.40	"	
Bridge	105.23	"	
Watson	107.43	"	J/INDR-LC 0
Pines	110.45	"	
River	111.71	"	
Jeff	113.84	"	J/INDR-LN 4
--via city line			
(Louisville KY)	117.16)		

CONSTRUCTION/ABANDONMENT

Date	Act	End points	MP	Change	Main	Source	Note
1901/5/31	B5	Indianapolis-Franklin	4.3-21.6	+17.3	17.3	1	
1902/9/4	B5	Franklin-Columbus	21.6-43.3	+21.7	39.0	1	
1906	B13	Louisville KY-Watson	113.8-107.4	+6.4	45.4	1	
1907/7	B18	Watson-Sellersburg	107.4-103.3	+4.1		1	
1907/9/28	B16	Columbus-Seymour	43.3-62.5	+19.2	68.7	1	
1908/2/10	B19	Sellersburg-Seymour	103.3-62.5	+40.8	109.5	1	
1939/10/31	XS	Seymour-Pass	62.5-104.1	-41.6		2	
1939/10	S1	Pass-Watson	104.1-107.4	[3.3]	58.2	2	3
1939/10/31	XS	Watson-Louisville KY	107.4-113.8	-6.4	58.2	2	
1941/9/8	XS	Indianapolis-Seymour	4.3-62.5	-58.2	0	2	

OWNERSHIP

1901	Indianapolis, Greenwood & Suburban Ry (B5), of part
1902/11/20	Indianapolis, Columbus & Southern Traction Co. (B16), of part, rename IC&S
1906	Louisville & Southern Indiana Traction Co. (B13), of part
1907	Louisville & Northern Ry & Lighting Co. (B18), of part
1907/9/7	Interstate Public Service Co., lease Indianapolis, Columbus & Southern
1908	Indianapolis & Louisville Traction Co. (B19), of part
1912/3/21	Indianapolis & Louisville Electric Ry, reorganize Indianapolis & Louisville Traction
1912/3/21	Interstate Public Service Co, reorganize Indianapolis & Louisville Electric
1921	Public Service Co. of Indiana, buy Interstate Public Service Co.

INDIANA RAILROAD

WATSON-CHARLESTOWN (INDR-LC)

	Mileage	County	Crossings, junctions, etc.
Watson Jct.	0	Clark	J/INDR-L 107.43
Crum	3.40	"	
Charlestown	6.86	"	

CONSTRUCTION/ABANDONMENT

Date	Act	End points	MP	Change	Main	Source	Note
1906	B13	Watson-Charlestown	0-6.9	+6.9	6.9	1	
1932/5/10	XS	Watson-Charlestown	0-6.9	-6.9	0	2	

OWNERSHIP

1906	Louisville & Southern Indiana Traction Co. (B13)
1907 ca.	Louisville & Northern Ry & Lighting Co., acquire Louisville & Southern Indiana Traction
1912/3/21	Interstate Public Service Co, apparently acquire Louisville & Northern Ry & Lighting
1921	Public Service Co. of Indiana, buy Interstate Public Service Co.

NEW ALBANY-JEFFERSONVILLE (INDR-LN)

	Mileage	County	Crossings, junctions, etc.
New Albany	0	Floyd	
Jeffersonville	4	Clark	J/INDR-L 113.8

CONSTRUCTION/ABANDONMENT

Date	Act	End points	MP	Change	Main	Source	Note
1907/4	B17	New Albany-Jeffersonville	0-4	+4.0	4.0	1	
1946	XS	New Albany-Jeffersonville	0-4	-4.0	0	3	

OWNERSHIP

1907	Jeffersonville City & Suburban Ry (B17)
1907 ca.	Louisville & Northern Ry & Lighting Co., acquire Jeffersonville City & Suburban
1912/3/21	Interstate Public Service Co, apparently acquire Louisville & Northern Ry & Lighting
1921	Public Service Co. of Indiana, buy Interstate Public Service Co.

INDIANAPOLIS-NEW CASTLE (INDR-N)

	Mileage	County	Crossings, junctions, etc.
(Indianapolis)	0)	Marion	
--via city line			
Brook	2.9	"	
Wood	4.1	"	
Shank	7.0	"	
Hall	10.1	"	
Comfort	14.5	Hancock	
Dunn	18.5	"	
Max	22.4	"	
Polk	27.0	"	
Wilk	29.7	"	
Shirley	33.3	"	
Ken	36.0	Henry	
Pitts	39.1	"	
Lowe	41.1	"	
Blue	44.0	"	
New Castle	44.9	"	J/INDR-NM 18.73, J/THIE-RN 0

CONSTRUCTION/ABANDONMENT

Date	Act	End points	MP	Change	Main	Source	Note
1910/1	B23	New Castle-Shirley	44.9-33.3	+11.6		1	
1910/7/1	B23	Shirley-Indianapolis	33.3-2.9	+30.4	42.0	1	
1938/5/8	XS	Indianapolis-New Castle	2.9-44.9	-42.0	0	2	

INDIANA RAILROAD

INDIANAPOLIS-NEW CASTLE (INDR-N) (continued)

OWNERSHIP

1910	Indianapolis, New Castle & Toledo Electric Ry (B23)
1912	Indianapolis, New Castle & Northeastern Traction Co., buy Indianapolis, New Castle & Toledo Electric
1912	Indianapolis, New Castle & Eastern Traction Co., buy Indianapolis, New Castle & Northeastern Tr.
1912/10/25	Union Traction Co. of Indiana, lease Indianapolis, New Castle & Eastern Traction
1930/7/2	Indiana RR, buy Union Traction Co. of Indiana

MUNCIE-NEW CASTLE (INDR-NM)

	Mileage	County	Crossings, junctions, etc.
(Muncie)	0)	Delaware	
--via city line			
5th Street	1.00	"	
Drag	4.11	"	
Cowan	6.19	"	
Oakville	7.99	"	
Springport	10.22	Henry	
Mt. Summit	13.29	"	
Bundy	15.56	"	
Burcutt	17.22	"	
New Castle	18.73	"	J/INDR-N 44.9, J/THIE-RN 0

CONSTRUCTION/ABANDONMENT

Date	Act	End points	MP	Change	Main	Source	Note
1913/8	B24	Muncie-New Castle	1.0-18.7	+17.7	17.7	1	
1941/1/18	XS	Muncie-New Castle	1.0-18.7	-17.7	0	2	

OWNERSHIP

1912	Indianapolis, New Castle & Eastern Traction Co. (B24)
1912/10/25	Union Traction Co. of Indiana, lease INC&ET
1930/7/2	Indiana RR, buy Union Traction Co. of Indiana

TERRE HAUTE, INDIANAPOLIS & EASTERN LINES (INDR-[THIE-x])

For arrangement of stations, construction record and prior ownership, see Terre Haute, Indianapolis & Eastern company individual line listings.

ACQUISITION/DISPOSITION RECORD

Date	Act	INDR-	End points	Change	Main	Note
1893/8/1	B1	C	Marion-Jonesboro	+5.9		
/8/1	B1	CG	Jonesboro-Gas City	+2.3	8.2	
1894/Sum.	B1	C	Jonesboro-Summitville	+10.3	18.5	
1897/12/23	B2	C	Anderson-Alexandria	+8.7	27.2	
1898/Spr	B2	C	Alexandria-Summitville	+5.7	32.9	
1899/6/26	B3	DC	Alexandria-Elwood	+9.5	42.4	
1900/Sum.	B4	B	Muncie-Anderson	+15.9		
/Sum.	B4	B	Anderson-Indianapolis	+30.9	89.2	
1901/5/31	B5	L	Indianapolis-Franklin	+17.3	106.5	
/8/3	B6	F	Peru-Wabash	+12.7	119.2	
1902	B7	F	Peru-Logansport	+16.3		
/3/30	B8	F	Ft. Wayne-Huntington	+23.7		
	B8	F	Huntington-Wabash	+19.8		
/9/4	B5	L	Franklin-Columbus	+21.7		
/12/31	B4	DC	Elwood-Tipton	+10.5	211.2	
1903/1/24	B10	A	Muncie-Hartford City	+17.7		
/5/10	B10	A	Hartford City-Bluffton	+23.3		
	B4	D	Indianapolis-Kokomo	+50.2		
/fall	B9	E	Kokomo-Greentown	+9.4	311.8	
(continued)						

INDIANA RAILROAD

ACQUISITION/DISPOSITION RECORD (continued)

Date	Act	INDR-	End points	Change	Main	Note
1904	B12	BU	Union City-Farmland	+18.0		
	B4	DA	Logansport-Kokomo	+22.0		
/8	B4	D	Kokomo-Peru	+17.1		
/8	B11	C	Marion-Wabash	+19.6	388.5	
1905/8/1	B4	BM	Anderson-Middletown	+8.4		
/Fall	B12	BU	Farmland-Muncie	+12.0		
/12/1	B25	AB	Marion-Bluffton	+31.8		
	B9	E	Greentown-Marion	+17.8	458.5	
1906	B14	AP	Muncie-Portland	+31.0		
	B13	L	Louisville KY-Watson	+6.4		
	B13	LC	Watson-Charlestown	+6.9	502.8	
1907/4	B17	LN	New Albany-Jeffersonville	+4.0		
/7/1	B15	A	Ft. Wayne-Bluffton	+12.4		
/7/1	B21	F	Logansport-Lafayette	+35.6		
/7	B18	L	Watson-Sellersburg	+4.1		
/9/28	B16	L	Columbus-Seymour	+19.2		
	B20	KA	Ft. Wayne-Kendallville	+30.6		
	B20	KB	Garrett-Waterloo	+9.8	628.5	
1908/2/10	B19	L	Sellersburg-Seymour	+40.8	669.3	
1910/1	B23	N	New Castle-Shirley	+11.6		
/7/1	B23	N	Shirley-Indianapolis	+30.4	711.3	
1912/9/18	B22	E	Kokomo-Frankfort	+25.6	736.9	
1913/8	B24	NC	Muncie-New Castle	+17.7	754.6	
1930/2/28	XS	BU	Muncie-Union City	-30.0		
/2/28	XS	BM	Anderson-Middletown	-8.4		
/9/15	XS	AP	Muncie-Portland	-31.0		
/9/15	XS	C	Marion-Wabash	-19.6		
/9/15	XS	DA	Logansport-Kokomo	-22.0	643.6	
1931/6/30	P1	[THIE-A]	Indianapolis-Terre Haute	+67.3		
/6/30	P1	[THIE-P]	Terre Haute-Paris IL	+9.5		
/6/30	P1	[THIE-R]	Indianapolis-Richmond	+61.4		
/6/30	P1	[THIE-RN]	Dunreith-New Castle	+10.9		
/6/30	XS	DC	Alexandria-Tipton	-20.0		
/8/16	XS	AB	Marion-Bluffton	-31.8	740.9	
1932/1/25	X	[THIE-P]	Terre Haute-Paris IL	-9.5		
/1/25	X	[THIE-R]	Indianapolis-Dunreith	-33.6		
/5/21	XS	F	Peru-Lafayette	-51.9		
/6/30	XS	C	Anderson-Marion	-30.6		
/6/30	XS	CG	Jonesboro-Gas City	-2.3		
/6/30	XS	E	Marion-Frankfort	-52.8		
/5/10	XS	LC	Watson-Charlestown	-6.9	553.3	
1936/8/9	L1	[D&W-A]	Dayton OH-Richmond	+2.2	555.5	
1937/3/15	XS	KA	Ft. Wayne-Kendallville	-30.6		
/3/15	XS	KB	Garrett-Waterloo	-9.8		
/5/8	XS	[THIE-R]	Dunreith-Richmond	-27.8		
/5/8	XS	[THIE-RN]	Dunreith-New Castle	-10.9		
/5/9	X	[D&W-A]	Dayton OH-Richmond	-2.2	474.2	
1938/5/8	XS	N	Indianapolis-New Castle	-42.0		
/9/5	XS	D	Peru-Indianapolis	-67.3		
/9/5	XS	F	Ft. Wayne-Peru	-56.2	308.7	
1939/10/31	XS	L	Seymour-Pass	-41.6		
/10	S1	L	Pass-Watson	[3.3]		3
/10/31	XS	L	Watson-Louisville KY	-6.4	257.4	
1940/1/10	X	[THIE-A]	Indianapolis-Terre Haute	-67.3	190.1	
(continued)						

INDIANA RAILROAD

ACQUISITION/DISPOSITION RECORD (continued)

Date	Act	INDR-	End points	Change	Main	Note
1941/1/18	XS	A	Ft. Wayne-Muncie	-63.4		
/1/18	XS	B	Muncie-Anderson	-15.9		
/1/18	XS	B	Anderson-Indianapolis	-30.9		
/1/18	XS	NM	Muncie-New Castle	-17.7		
/9/8	XS	L	Indianapolis-Seymour	-58.2	4.0	
1946	XS	LN	New Albany-Jeffersonville	-4.0	0	

ACT COLUMN KEY
B1   Built by Marion Electric Street Ry
B2   Built by Union Traction Co.
B3   Built by Elwood & Alexandria Ry
B4   Built by Union Traction Co. of Indiana
B5   Built by Indianapolis, Greenwood & Suburban Ry
B6   Built by Wabash River Traction Co.
B7   Built by Logansport, Rochester & Northern Traction Co.
B8   Built by Ft. Wayne & Southwestern Traction Co.
B9   Built by Kokomo, Marion & Western Traction Co.
B10 Built by Muncie, Hartford & Ft. Wayne Ry
B11 Built by Indiana Northern Traction Co.
B12 Built by Dayton & Muncie Traction Co.
B13 Built by Louisville & Southern Indiana Traction Co.
B14 Built by Muncie & Portland Traction Co.
B15 Built by Ft. Wayne, Bluffton & Marion Traction Co.
B16 Built by Indianapolis, Columbus & Southern Traction Co.
B17 Built by Jeffersonville City & Suburban Ry
B18 Built by Louisville & Northern Ry & Lighting Co.
B19 Built by Indianapolis & Louisville Traction Co.
B20 Built by Toledo & Chicago Interurban Ry
B21 Built by Lafayette & Logansport Traction Co.
B22 Built by Kokomo, Frankfort & Western Traction Co.
B23 Built by Indianapolis, New Castle & Toledo Electric Ry
B24 Built by Indianapolis, New Castle & Eastern Traction Co.
B25 Built by Marion, Bluffton & Eastern Traction Co.
L1   Leased Dayton & Western Traction
P1   Purchased from Terre Haute, Indianapolis & Eastern Traction Co.
S1   Sold to Southern Indiana
X   Abandoned
XS   Service ended

SOURCES
1. Blackburn, "Interurban Railroads."
2. Bradley, *Indiana Railroad.*
3. Central, *Electric Railways of Indiana, Part I.*
4. Central, *Electric Railways of Indiana, Part II.*
5. Hilton and Due, *The Electric Interurban Railways.*

NOTES
1. Source 1 states through Muncie-Indianapolis service began Jan. 3, 1901.
2. Source 1 states through Alexandria-Tipton service began Feb. 1903.
3. This sale included the spur from Pass to Speed (cement plant) and yard trackage at Watson.

INDIANAPOLIS & SOUTHEASTERN

INDIANAPOLIS-CONNERSVILLE (ISER-A)

	Mileage	County	Crossings, junctions, etc.
(Indianapolis)	0	Marion	
--via city line			
Harlan Loop	3.2	"	
Junction	4.32	"	J/ISER-B 4.32
Fenton	8.18	"	
Juliette	12.14	"	
New Palestine	15.94	Hancock	
Reedville	19.51	"	
Fountaintown	21.98	Shelby	
Morristown	26.46	"	
Gwynnsville	29.34	"	
Arlington	33.39	Rush	
Midway	37.03	"	
Dagler	39.91	"	
Rushville	40.52	"	
Rushville East Yard Limits	41.49	"	
Helm	44.42	"	
Mauzy	46.76	"	aka Griffin
Glenwood	48.81	"	
Bilby	52.05	Fayette	
Howard	54.68	"	
Wright	56.85	"	
Connersville	58.10	"	

CONSTRUCTION/ABANDONMENT

Date	Act	End points	MP	Change	Main	Source	Note
1902/9	B1	Indianapolis-Junction	3.2-4.3	+1.1	1.1	1,2	
1905/2/20	B2	Junction-Rushville	4.3-40.5	+36.2	37.3	2	
1906/10/28	B2	Rushville-Connersville	40.5-58.1	+17.6	54.9	2	
1932		XIndianapolis-Connersville	3.2-58.1	-54.9	0	2	

OWNERSHIP

1902	Indianapolis, Shelbyville & Southeastern Traction Co. (B1), of part
1903	Indianapolis & Cincinnati Traction Co. (B2), of part, acquired IS&SET
1929	Indianapolis & Cincinnati Ry, reorganize I&CT

INDIANAPOLIS-GREENSBURG (ISER-B)

	Mileage [Indianapolis]	County	Crossings, junctions, etc.
Junction	4.32	Marion	J/ISER-A 4.32
Heads	5.48	"	
Five Points	7.77	"	
New Bethel	10.41	"	
Acton	13.79	"	
Buck	15.54	Shelby	
London	17.93	"	
Moore	19.93	"	
Porter	21.37	"	
Totten	22.68	"	
Walser	25.32	"	
Barns	27.03	"	
Shelbyville	28.20	"	
Lewis	30.85	"	
Prescott	33.44	"	
Waldron	36.59	"	
St. Paul	38.38	Decatur	
Pleak	41.01	"	
(continued)			

INDIANAPOLIS & SOUTHEASTERN

INDIANAPOLIS-GREENSBURG (ISER-B) (continued)

	Mileage [Indianapolis]	County	Crossings, junctions, etc.
Pleak	41.01	Decatur	
Adams	43.89	"	
Zoller	48.08	"	
Greensburg	49.27	"	

CONSTRUCTION/ABANDONMENT

Date	Act	End points	MP	Change	Main	Source	Note
1902/9	B1	Junction-Shelbyville	4.3-28.2	+23.9	23.9	2	
1907/1/30	B2	Shelbyville-Greensburg	28.2-49.3	+21.1	45.0	1	
1932	X	Junction-Greensburg	4.3-49.3	-45.0	0	2	

OWNERSHIP

1902	Indianapolis, Shelbyville & Southeastern Traction Co. (B1)
1903	Indianapolis & Cincinnati Traction Co. (B2), of part, acquired IS&SET
1929	Indianapolis & Cincinnati Ry, reorganize I&CT

ACQUISITION/DISPOSITION RECORD

Date	Act	ISER-	End points	Change	Main	Note
1902/9	B1	A	Indianapolis-Junction	+1.1		
/9	B1	B	Junction-Shelbyville	+23.9	25.0	
1905/2/20	B2	A	Junction-Rushville	+36.2	51.2	
1906/10/28	B2	A	Rushville-Connersville	+17.6	78.8	
1907/1/30	B2	B	Shelbyville-Greensburg	+21.1	99.9	
1932	X	A	Indianapolis-Connersville	-54.9		
1932	X	B	Junction-Greensburg	-45.0	0	

ACT COLUMN KEY
B1 Built by Indianapolis, Shelbyville & Southeastern Traction Co.
B2 Built by Indianapolis & Cincinnati Traction Co.
X   Abandoned

SOURCES
1. Blackburn, "Interurban Railroads."
2. Central, *Electric Railways of Indiana, Part I.*

LEBANON & THORNTOWN

MAIN LINE (LETH-A)

	Mileage	County	Crossings, junctions, etc.
Lebanon	0	Boone	J/THIE-L 27.65, J/THIE-LC 27.65
Hazelrigg	5.2	"	
Thorntown	9.3	"	

CONSTRUCTION/ABANDONMENT

Date	Act	End points	MP	Change	Main	Source	Note
1905/7/12	B1	Lebanon-Thorntown	0-9.3	+9.3	9.3	1,2	
1926/7/6	X	Lebanon-Thorntown	0-9.3	-9.3	0	2	

OWNERSHIP
1905   Lebanon & Thorntown Traction Co. (B1)
ACQUISITION/DISPOSITION RECORD
See ownership record above for line LETH-A

ACT COLUMN KEY
B1 Built by Lebanon & Thorntown Traction Co.
X   Abandoned

SOURCES
1. Blackburn, "Interurban Railroads."
2. Central, *Electric Railways of Indiana, Part I.*

NORTHERN INDIANA

MICHIGAN CITY-SOUTH BEND (NOIN-A)

	Mileage	County	Crossings, junctions, etc.
(South Bend)	0)	St.Joseph	
--via city line			
Bendix	3.6	"	
Chain	6.9	"	
Log Cabin	10.3	"	
New Carlisle	13.9	"	
South Shore	14.2	"	
Hudson	15.6	LaPorte	
Wood	17.2	"	
Rolling Prairie	20.7	"	
Chicago Road	24.0	"	
Lake Erie	26.5	"	
LaPorte	27.6	"	
Weller Avenue	28.8	"	
Car Barn	30.1	"	
Pierce	31.6	"	
Waterford	35.3	"	
Timms	37.5	"	
Superior	39.7	"	
--via city line			
(Michigan City)	41.3)	"	

CONSTRUCTION/ABANDONMENT

Date	Act	End points	MP	Change	Main	Source	Note
1903/2/2	B3	Michigan City-LaPorte	39.7-27.6	+12.1	12.1	2	1
1908/8/26	B6	South Bend-LaPorte	3.6-27.6	+24.0	36.1	1	
1934/6/1	X	South Bend-Michigan City	3.6-39.7	-36.1	0		

OWNERSHIP

1903	Chicago & South Shore Ry (B3), of part
1905/5	LaPorte & Michigan City Traction Co., merge Chicago & South Shore
1905/7/1	South Bend, LaPorte & Michigan City Traction Co., merge L&MCT and South Bend Western Ry
1905/12/14	Northern Indiana Ry (B6), merge South Bend, LaPorte & Michigan City Traction and Indiana Ry
1907/1/25	Chicago, South Bend & Northern Indiana Ry, buy Northern Indiana
1930/2/1	Northern Indiana Ry, merge CSB&NI

ST. JOSEPH-SOUTH BEND LINE (NOIN-C)

	Mileage	County	Crossings, junctions, etc.
(South Bend)	0)	St.Joseph	
(Leepers)	1.2)	"	
--via city line			
St. Marys	2.0	"	
St. Marys Siding	2.8	"	
State Line	5.8		(IN/MI state line)
Bertrand	6.8		
Brandywine	8.4		
Brandy (Siding)	8.6		
(Bridge)	9.2		B/MC-N 2.2, B/CC-M 26.1
Wolf	9.9		
(enter 5th St at Superior)	10.1		
(5th & Main)	10.7		
(Main & Sycamore)	10.9		
Niles MI	11.0		
(continued)			

NORTHERN INDIANA

ST. JOSEPH-SOUTH BEND LINE (NOIN-C) (continued)

	Mileage [South Bend]	County	Crossings, junctions, etc.
Niles MI	11.0		
(Bridge)	11.3		B/MC-W 192.2
(enter 2nd St at Pokagon)	11.4		
(Bridge)	12.3		B/CC-M 22.6
River (Siding)	12.8		
River Bluff	12.8		
Thompsons	15.1		
Starkey	15.9		
Summit	17.7		
Berrien Springs	20.3		
College	22.1		
Twin (Siding)	24.0		
Twin Springs	24.0		
Rockeys	25.5		
Munich	26.5		
Smith	28.2		
Scotdale	28.7		
(Bridge)	28.9		B/PM-U 5.9
Royalton Heights	31.1		
M. C. (Siding)	31.7		
(Bridge)	31.9		B/MC-J 33.9
(State & Botham)	33.1		J/BHCL-1 3.68
--via city line--			
(Archer)	33.8		
(St. Joseph)	35.0		

CONSTRUCTION/ABANDONMENT

Date	Act	End points	MP	Change	Main	Source	Note
1903/8/17	B4	South Bend-Niles	2.0-5.8	+3.8	3.8	2	
1906/5/21	B5	Niles-St. Joseph					
1934/6/1	X	South Bend-St. Joseph	2.0-5.8	-3.8	0	2	

OWNERSHIP

1903	South Bend & Southern Michigan (B4)
1906/2/7	Southern Michigan Ry (B5), merge South Bend & Southern Michigan
1910	Chicago, South Bend & Northern Indiana, control of Southern Michigan
1930/2/3	Northern Indiana Ry, merge CSB&NI

SOUTH BEND-GOSHEN (NOIN-B)

	Mileage	County	Crossings, junctions, etc.
(South Bend)	0)	St.Joseph	
(Junction)			
(Mishawaka	4.4)	"	
--via city line			
Byrkett	5.7	"	
Lamport	9.6		
Osceola	10.1	"	
County Line	10.7	"	
Boss	13.3	Elkhart	
--via city line			
(Elkhart)	15.4)	"	
--via city line			
Hively	17.5	"	
Dunlap	20.4	"	
Keely	22.5	"	
Miller	24.2	"	
--via city line			
(Goshen)	25.9)	"	

NORTHERN INDIANA

SOUTH BEND-GOSHEN (NOIN-B) (continued)
CONSTRUCTION/ABANDONMENT

Date	Act	End points	MP	Change	Main	Source	Note
1898/12/22	B1	Elkhart-Goshen	17.5-24.2	+6.7	6.7	2	
1899/7/30	B2	South Bend-Elkhart	5.7-13.3	+7.6	14.3	2	2
1934/6/1	X	South Bend-Elkhart	5.7-13.3	-7.6		2	
1934/6/1	X	Elkhart-Goshen	17.5-24.2	-6.7	0	2	

OWNERSHIP

1898	Indiana Electric Ry (B1), of part
1898	South Bend & Elkhart Ry (B2), of part
1899/3/15	Indiana Ry, merge Indiana Electric Ry, South Bend & Elkhart and other roads
1905/12/14	Northern Indiana Ry, merge Indiana Ry and other roads
1907/1/25	Chicago, South Bend & Northern Indiana Ry, buy Northern Indiana
1930/2/1	Northern Indiana Ry, merge CSB&NI

ACQUISITION/DISPOSITION RECORD

Date	Act	NOIN-	End points	Change	Main	Note
1898/12/22	B1	B	Elkhart-Goshen	+6.7	6.7	
1899/7/30	B2	B	South Bend-Elkhart	+7.6	14.3	2
1903/2/2	B3	A	Michigan City-LaPorte	+12.1		1
/8/17	B4	C	South Bend-Niles	+3.8	30.2	
1908/9/6	B6	A	South Bend-LaPorte	+24.0	54.2	
1934/6/1	X	A	South Bend-Michigan City	-36.1		
/6/1	X	B	South Bend-Elkhart	-7.6		
/6/1	X	B	Elkhart-Goshen	-6.7		
/6/1	X	C	South Bend-St. Joseph	-3.8	0	

ACT COLUMN KEY
B1   Built by Indiana Electric Ry
B2   Built by Indiana Ry
B3   Built by Chicago & South Shore Ry
B4   Built by South Bend & Southern Michigan
B5   Built by Southern Michigan Ry
B6   Built by Northern Indiana Ry

SOURCES
1. Blackburn, "Interurban Railroads."
2. Bradley, *Northern Indiana Railway.*

NOTES
1. A portion of this line from LaPorte north to Pine Lake was in operation by September 1902.
2. Source 1 gives the South Bend-Elkhart segment opening as 1898/12.

ST. JOSEPH VALLEY

MAIN LINE (SJV-A)

	Mileage	County	Crossings, junctions, etc.
Elkhart	0	Elkhart	
City Limits	1.5	"	
Bickels	3.0	"	
Sparr	3.5	"	
Mitchell	4.3	"	
Carmein	4.6	"	
Keller	5.6	"	
Gregory	6.8	"	
Bristol	9.0	"	
(Crossing)	9.3	"	X/LS-A 430.1
Bonneyville	12.0	"	
(continued)			

ST. JOSEPH VALLEY

MAIN LINE (SJV-A) (continued)

	Mileage	County	Crossings, junctions, etc.
Bonneyville	12.0	Elkhart	
Pleasant Valley	14.0	"	
Middlebury	16.4	"	X/LS-TS 9.9
Shipshewana Lake	21.8	LaGrange	
Shipshewana	23.1	"	
Yoder	27.6	"	
LaGrange	32.7	"	
(Bridge)	34.3	"	B/PRR-GS 139.9
Pleasant Hill	35.3	"	
McCally	38.4	"	
Mongo	41.1	"	
Custer	44.7	"	
Orland	47.7	Steuben	
Lake Gage	51.5	"	
Inverness	52.6	"	
Crooked Lake	55.6	"	
Angola Jct.	58.7	"	J/SJV-B 0, B/LS-TF 55.5
Angola	59.7	"	

CONSTRUCTION/ABANDONMENT

Date	Act	End points	MP	Change	Main	Source	Note
1905/3/31	B1	Shipshewana-LaGrange	23.1-32.7	+9.6	9.6	2	
1907/5/4	B2	LaGrange-Orland	32.7-47.7	+15.0		2	
1907/8	B2	Orland-Angola	47.7-59.7	+12.0	36.6	2	
1910/7/16	B1	Elkhart-Bristol	0-9.0	+9.0	45.6	2	
1911/8/1	B1	Bristol-Shipshewana	9.0-23.1	+14.1	59.7	2	
1918/4/11	X	Bristol-LaGrange	9.0-32.7	-23.7		2	
1918/4/17	X	City Limits-Bristol	1.5-9.0	-7.5		2	
1918/4/18	X	Orland-Angola	47.7-59.7	-12.0		2	
1918/6/15	S1	Elkhart-City Limits	0-1.5	-1.5	15.0	2	1
1919/1	L1	Orland-LaGrange	47.7-32.7	(15.0)	15.0	2	2
1920/fall	XL	Orland-LaGrange	47.7-32.7	(15.0)		2	
1920/fall	X	Orland-LaGrange	47.7-32.7	-15.0	0		

OWNERSHIP

1905	St. Joseph Valley Traction Co. (B1), of part
1907	St. Joseph Valley Ry (B2), of part
1909/3/1	St. Joseph Valley Ry, lease of St. Joseph Valley Traction Co.
1919/1	LaGrange, Toledo & Eastern Ry (L1), lease of part of St. Joseph Valley

ANGOLA-COLUMBIA (SJV-B)

	Mileage	County	Crossings, junctions, etc.
Angola Jct.	0	Steuben	J/SJV-A 58.7
Berlein	6.8	"	
North Metz	9.8	"	
(IN/OH state line)	10.4		
Columbia OH	13.3		

CONSTRUCTION/ABANDONMENT

Date	Act	End points	MP	Change	Main	Source	Note
1911	B2	Angola-Berlien	0-6.8	+6.8	6.8	G	
1915/7	B2	Berlein-Columbia	6.8-10.4	+3.6	10.4	G	
1918/4/18	X	Angola Jct.-Columbia	0-10.4	-10.4	0	G	

OWNERSHIP

1911	St. Joseph Valley Ry (B2)

ST. JOSEPH VALLEY

ACQUISITION/DISPOSITION RECORD

Date	Act	SJV-	End points	Change	Main	Note
1905/3/31	B1	A	Shipshewana-LaGrange	+9.6	9.6	
1907/5/4	B2	A	LaGrange-Orland	+15.0		
/8	B2	A	Orland-Angola	+12.0	36.6	
1910/7/16	B1	A	Elkhart-Bristol	+9.0	45.6	
1911/8/1	B1	A	Bristol-Shipshewana	+14.1		
	B2	B	Angola-Berlien	+6.8	66.5	
1915/7	B2		Berlein-Columbia	+3.6	70.1	
1918/4/11	X	A	Bristol-LaGrange	-23.7		
/4/17	X	A	City Limits-Bristol	-7.5		
/4/18	X	A	Orland-Angola	-12.0		
/4/18	X	B	Angola Jct.-Columbia	-10.4		
/6/15	S1	A	Elkhart-City Limits	-1.5	15.0	1
1919/1	L1	A	Orland-LaGrange	(15.0)	0	2
1920/fall	X	A	Orland-LaGrange	-15.0	0	

ACT COLUMN KEY
B1   Built by St. Joseph Valley Traction Co.
B2   Built by St. Joseph Valley Ry
L1   Lease to LaGrange, Toledo & Eastern Ry
S1   Sold to Foster Traction Co.
X   Abandoned
XL   Lease cancelled

SOURCES
1. Blackburn, "Interurban Railroads."
2. Galloway and Buckley, *The St. Joseph Valley Railway.*

NOTES
1. The segment sold was operated by Northern Indiana Ry by agreement with SJV. Operations ended on June 2, 1934.
2. The lease was obtained from the road's purchaser at receivership, Benjamin Harris & Co.

SOUTHERN INDIANA GAS & ELECTRIC CO.

EVANSVILLE-PRINCETON (SIGE-A)

	Mileage	County	Crossings, junctions, etc.
(Evansville)	0)	Vanderburgh	
--via city line			
Weber	4.31	"	
Erskine	5.90	"	
Builtman	8.24	"	
Bauer	10.60	"	
Base Line	12.50	"	
Lamey Grove	16.50	Gibson	
Ft. Branch	20.88	"	
Robinson	22.84	"	
Kings	24.88	"	
Baldwin Heights	27.60	"	
Princeton	28.70	"	
Fair Grounds	29.62	"	
Patoka	33.00	"	
(continued)			

SOUTHERN INDIANA GAS & ELECTRIC CO.

EVANSVILLE-PRINCETON (SIGE-A) (continued)

CONSTRUCTION/ABANDONMENT

Date	Act	End points	MP	Change	Main	Source	Note
1903/12/8	B1	Evansville-Princeton	4.3-28.7	+24.4	24.4	1,2,3	1
1908	B2	Princeton-Patoka	28.7-33.0	+4.3	28.7	1,3	
1933	X	Evansville-Patoka	4.3-33.0	-28.7	0	3	

OWNERSHIP

1903	Evansville & Princeton Traction Co. (B1), of part
1906/6/30	Evansville, Princeton & Vincennes Interurban Ry, acquired Evansville & Princeton Traction
1908/12/24	Evansville & Southern Indiana Traction Co. (B2), of part, acquired Evansville, Princeton & Vincennes
1912/3	Public Service Co. of Evansville, merge Evansville & Southern Indiana Traction and a power co.
1921/3/7	Southern Indiana Gas & Electric Co., rename Public Service Co. of Evansville

ACQUISITION/DISPOSITION RECORD
See ownership record above for line SIGE-A

ACT COLUMN KEY
B1 Built by Evansville & Princeton Traction Co.
B2 Built by Evansville & Southern Indiana Traction Co.
X   Abandoned

SOURCES
1. Blackburn, "Interurban Railroads."
2. Central, *Electric Railways of Indiana, Part I.*
3. Hilton and Due, *The Electric Interurban Railways.*

NOTES
1. During 1907 the line between Evansville and Haubstadt was straightened. The change in mileage has not beeen determined. The mileage shown here is that after the relocation.

TERRE HAUTE, INDIANAPOLIS & EASTERN

INDIANAPOLIS-TERRE HAUTE (THIE-A)

	Mileage	County	Crossings, junctions, etc.
(Indianapolis)	0)	Marion	
--via city line			
Belt Railway	2.00	"	
Darnells	4.00	"	
Morris Road	4.7	"	
Indianapolis Heights	5.3	"	
Gun Club	5.47	"	
(continued)			

TERRE HAUTE, INDIANAPOLIS & EASTERN
INDIANAPOLIS-TERRE HAUTE (THIE-A)

	Mileage [Indianapolis]	County	Crossings, junctions, etc.
Gun Club	5.47	Marion	
Mickley	5.9	"	
Ben Davis	6.52	"	
Sterling Heights	7.2	"	
Wishmeyer	7.5	"	
Huffman	8.0	"	
Reagan	8.6	"	
Bridgeport	9.31	"	
Hobbs	9.6	"	
Six Points	10.1	"	
Smiths	10.9	"	
Vestals	12.18	Hendricks	
Raper	13.2	"	
Plainfield	14.01	"	
Boys School	14.41	"	
National Road	15.2	"	
Miles	16.4	"	
Cartersburg	17.5	"	
Dilley	17.86	"	
Van Jct.	18.38	"	
Gilliland	18.7	"	
Belville Road	19.2	"	
Kynerson	20.47	"	
Clayton	20.67	"	
Summit	21.8	"	
Pecksburg	23.21	"	
Harlan	24.6	"	
Amo	25.50	"	
Quinland	27.4	"	
Coatesville	28.66	"	
Ellis	29.2	"	
Hessler	29.9	"	
Gibson	31.2	Putnam	
Bryan	31.93	"	
Delmar Road	32.5	"	
Fillmore	33.23	"	
Browning	34.0	"	
Bunton	34.95	"	
McNarys	35.7	"	
Almeda	37.5	"	
Tucker	37.70	"	
Commercial Place	38.4	"	
Hays	38.7	"	
Greencastle	39.63	"	
Duffs	39.92	"	
Shops	40.58	"	
Limedale	41.80	"	
Stoner	42.3	"	
Mt. Olive	42.6	"	
Torrs	44.14	"	
Hutchinson	44.7	"	
Big Walnut	45.3	"	
Wilton Mill Road	45.9	"	
Johns	46.39	"	
Fox	47.5	"	
Girton	48.3	"	

(continued)

TERRE HAUTE, INDIANAPOLIS & EASTERN

INDIANAPOLIS-TERRE HAUTE (THIE-A) (continued)

	Mileage [Indianapolis]	County	Crossings, junctions, etc.
Girton	48.3	Putnam	
Mullinix	48.7	"	
Canaan Chapel	49.9	Clay	
Eagles	50.4	"	
Reberger	50.9	"	
Croy Creek	51.5	"	
Rock Cut	52.1	"	
Appel	52.68	"	
Harmony	53.2	"	
Tripletts	53.7	"	
Knightsville	54.2	"	
Junction	54.37	"	
Morgans	55.71	"	
Brazil	56.55	"	
Cottage Hill	57.7	"	
Millers	59.30	"	
Billtown	59.5	"	
Staunton	59.6	"	
Yocums	59.7	"	
Gravel Pit	60.1	"	
Purdys	60.3	"	
Bowles Crossing	60.7	"	
Jones	61.2	"	
Cloverland	62.1	"	
Carpenter	62.2	"	
West Cleveland	62.3	"	
Miami	62.61	Vigo	
Pines	63.3	"	
Blue Goose	63.6	"	
Seelyville	63.9	"	
West Seelyville	64.41	"	
Lost Creek	64.7	"	
Farrell	65.1	"	
Chamberlains	65.5	"	
East Glenn	65.6	"	
Glenn Home	65.9	"	
Stock Farm	66.75	"	
Hullmans	67.2	"	
Cedar Grove	67.7	"	
Country Club	68.1	"	
Highland Lawn	68.6	"	
Fruitridge Avenue	69.33	"	
--via city line			
(Terre Haute)	71.88)	"	J/THIE-P 0, J/THIE-S 0, J/THIE-T 0

CONSTRUCTION/ABANDONMENT

Date	Act	End points	MP	Change	Main	Source	Note
1893/7/16	B1	Brazil-Harmony	56.6-53.2	+3.4	3.4	1.2	
1900/9	B6	Terre Haute-Brazil	69.3-56.6	+12.7	16.1	2	
1902/Fall	B4	Indianapolis-Plainfield	2.0-14.0	+12.0	28.1	2	
1907		B10 Plainfield-Greencastle	14.0-39.6	+25.6	53.7	1	
1908/1	B11	Greencastle-Harmony	39.6-53.2	+13.6	67.3	1,2	
1931/6/30	S1	Indianapolis-Terre Haute	2.0-69.3	-67.3	0	3	

(1940/1/10	X	Indianapolis-Terre Haute	2.0-69.3	-67.3	0	3	

TERRE HAUTE, INDIANAPOLIS & EASTERN

INDIANAPOLIS-TERRE HAUTE (THIE-A) (continued)
OWNERSHIP

1893	Brazil Rapid Transit Street Ry (B1), of part
1902	Indianapolis & Plainfield Electric RR (B4), of part
1903	Terre Haute Electric Co. (B6), of part
1903/6/1	Terre Haute Traction & Light Co., buy Terre Haute Electric and Brazil R. T.
1903/8/29	Indianapolis Coal Traction Co. (B10), merge Indianapolis & Plainfield Electric (Note 2)
1907/3/1	Terre Haute, Indianapolis & Eastern Traction Co. (B11), merge Indianapolis Coal Traction T
1907/3/25	Terre Haute, Indianapolis & Eastern Traction, lease Terre Haute Traction & Ligh
1931/6/30	Indiana RR, buy Terre Haute, Indianapolis & Eastern Traction

LEBANON-CRAWFORDSVILLE (THIE-C)

	Mileage	County	Crossings, junctions, etc.
(Indianapolis)	0)	Marion	
--via city line			
Speedway	5.0	"	
Rancks	7.2	"	
Girls School	8.1	"	
Clermont	9.9	"	
Turpin	12.2	Hendricks	
Brownsville	14.5	"	
Holloways	16.1	"	
Pittsboro	18.5	"	
West Pittsboro	19.4	"	
Hale	20.7	"	
Lizton	22.9	"	
Youngs	25.4	"	
Jamestown	28.0	Boone	
Gardners	30.3	"	
Walls	32.5	Montgomery	
New Ross	33.4	"	
Vannce	35.4	"	
Brattons	37.3	"	
Linnsburg	38.5	"	
Gregg	39.7	"	
Smiths	42.9	"	
Crawfordsville Jct.	43.9	"	J/THIE-TG 49.67
--via INDR-T			
(Crawfordsville)	45.0)	"	

CONSTRUCTION/ABANDONMENT

Date	Act	End points	MP	Change	Main	Source	Note
1907/7/7	B12	Indianapolis-Crawfordsv.	5.0-43.9	+38.9	38.9	1	
1930/10/30	XS	Indianapolis-Crawfordsv.	5.0-43.9	-38.9	0	2	

OWNERSHIP

1907	Indianapolis, Crawfordsville & Western Traction Co. (B11)
1912/4	Indianapolis, Crawfordsville & Danville Electric Ry, reorganize IC&WT
1912/5/1	Terre Haute, Indianapolis & Eastern Traction Co., lease of IC&DE

INDIANAPOLIS-DANVILLE (THIE-D)

	Mileage	County	Crossings, junctions, etc.
(Indianapolis)	0)	Marion	
--via city line			
Mt. Jackson	3.0	"	
Salem Park	3.3	"	
Lynnhurst	5.0	"	
Whitcomb Street	5.4	"	
State Farm	5.5	"	
(continued)			

TERRE HAUTE, INDIANAPOLIS & EASTERN

INDIANAPOLIS-DANVILLE (THIE-D) (continued)

	Mileage [Indianapolis]	County	Crossings, junctions, etc.
State Farm	5.5	Marion	
Holt	6.0	"	
White Lick	8.2	"	
Tremont Gardens	8.5	"	
Taylors	10.3	Hendricks	
Griswold	10.9	"	
Huron	12.4	"	
Avon	12.9	"	
Gravel Pit	13.7	"	
Gale	16.5	"	
Underwood	16.8	"	
Danville	19.8	"	

CONSTRUCTION/ABANDONMENT

Date	Act	End points	MP	Change	Main	Source	Note
1905/9/1	B8	Indianapolis-Danville	3.0-19.8	+16.8	16.8	2	1
1930/10/30	XS	Indianapolis-Danville	3.0-19.8	-16.8	0	2	

OWNERSHIP

1905	Indianapolis & Western Ry (B8)
1907/3/1	Terre Haute, Indianapolis & Eastern Traction Co., merge I&W

INDIANAPOLIS-LAFAYETTE (THIE-L)

	Mileage	County	Crossings, junctions, etc.
(Indianapolis)	0)	Marion	
--via city line			
3rd Street	3.67	"	
Townsend	5.96	"	
Augusta	9.22	"	
County Line	12.39	"	
Zionsville	14.44	"	
Gravel Pit	14.79	"	
Eldridge	18.58	Boone	
Whitestown	20.56	"	
Perrine	24.60	"	
Power House	27.20	"	
Lebanon	27.65	"	J/THIE-LC 27.65, J/LETH-A 0
Park Siding	28.51	"	
Whites	31.78	"	
Mechanicsburg	35.40	"	
School House	38.54	Clinton	
Sub Station	42.57	"	
Clinton	43.25	"	
Frankfort	44.27	"	
Bunn	46.26	"	
Martz	50.37	"	
East Mulberry	53.65	"	
Mulberry	54.00	"	
Wikle	57.32	Tippecanoe	
Dayton	59.90	"	
West Dayton	60.41	"	
Matke	64.02	"	
City Limits	65.44	"	
Top Oakland Hill	66.77	"	
--via city line			
(Lafayette)	67.72)	"	
(continued)			

TERRE HAUTE, INDIANAPOLIS & EASTERN

INDIANAPOLIS-LAFAYETTE (THIE-L) (continued)
CONSTRUCTION/ABANDONMENT

Date	Act	End points	MP	Change	Main	Source	Note
1903/Fall	B7	Indianapolis-Lafayette	3.7-66.8	+63.1	63.1	1,2	
1930/10/30	XS	Indianapolis-Lafayette	3.7-66.8	-63.1	0	2	

OWNERSHIP
1903	Indianapolis & Northwestern Traction Co. (B7)
1907/4/1	Terre Haute, Indianapolis & Eastern Traction Co., lease I&NWT

LEBANON-CRAWFORDSVILLE (THIE-LC)

	Mileage [Indianapolis]	County	Crossings, junctions, etc.
Lebanon	27.65	Boone	J/THIE-L 27.65, J/LETH-A 0
Midland	28.45	"	
Youngs	32.45	"	
Caldwell	36.74	"	
Becks	41.16	Montgomery	
Pettigrew	45.40	"	
East Englewood	46.31	"	
Crawfordsville Jct.	49.67	"	J/THIE-C 48.9
Crawfordsville	50.86	"	

CONSTRUCTION/ABANDONMENT

Date	Act	End points	MP	Change	Main	Source	Note
1903/9	B7	Lebanon-Crawfordsville	27.7-50.9	+23.2	23.2	1	
1930/10/30	XS	Lebanon-Crawfordsville	27.7-50.9	-23.2	0	2	

OWNERSHIP
1904	Indianapolis & Northwestern Traction Co. (B7)
1907/4/1	Terre Haute, Indianapolis & Eastern Traction Co., lease I&NWT

INDIANAPOLIS-MARTINSVILLE (THIE-M)

	Mileage	County	Crossings, junctions, etc.
(Indianapolis)	0)	Marion	
--via city line			
Stock Street	1.93	"	
Maywood	4.63	"	
Harmons	6.24	"	
Valley Mills	8.24	"	
Camby	10.97	"	
Friendswood	12.50	Morgan	
Jessups	13.79	"	
Mooresville	16.50	"	
Car Barns	16.83	"	
Newbys	20.02	"	
Brooklyn	22.16	"	
Bethany	22.35	"	
Centerton	23.00	"	
Riverside	26.30	"	
Hendricks	28.66	"	
Martinsville	30.64	"	

CONSTRUCTION/ABANDONMENT

Date	Act	End points	MP	Change	Main	Source	Note
1902/8/11	B5	Indianapolis-Mooresville	1.9-16.5	+14.6	14.6	1	
1903/4	B5	Mooresville-Martinsville	16.5-30.6	+14.1	28.7	1,2	
1930/10/30	XS	Indianapois-Martinsville	1.9-30.6	-28.7	0	2	

TERRE HAUTE, INDIANAPOLIS & EASTERN

INDIANAPOLIS-MARTINSVILLE (THIE-M) (continued)
OWNERSHIP

1902	Indianapolis & Martinsville Rapid Transit Co. (B5) (Note 3)
1907/4/1	Terre Haute, Indianapolis & Eastern Traction Co., lease I&MRT

INDIANAPOLIS-RICHMOND (THIE-R)

	Mileage	County	Crossings, junctions, etc.
(Indianapolis)	0)	Marion	
--via city line			
Sheridan Avenue	5.7	"	
Morris	8.4	"	
Memorial Park	8.8	"	
Bertermanns	9.1	"	
German Church	10.5	"	
Cumberland	11.3	"	
Gem	14.5	Hancock	
Park Jct.	16.7	"	
Philadelphia	17.1	"	
Coopers	18.6	"	
Fruit Farm	19.5	"	
Lillys	19.7	"	
Glass Works	20.3	"	
Greenfield	21.3	"	
Tyners	23.2	"	
Criders	23.8	"	
Tree's Shop	24.5	"	
Range Line	25.5	"	
Davis	26.5	"	
Cleveland	27.8	"	
Charlottsville	29.6	"	
Herford Place	32.3	Henry	
Knightstown	34.3	"	
Raysville	35.1	"	
Ogden	37.6	"	
Dunreith	39.3	"	J/THIE-RN 10.9
Lewisville	43.8	"	
Straughns	47.2	"	
Dublin	51.6	Wayne	
Mt. Auburn	52.5	"	
Cambridge City	53.6	"	J/THIE-RM 0
East Germantown	55.4	"	
Pennville	56.8	"	
Hisers	58.5	"	
Washington Road	58.9	"	
Jackson Park	60.7	"	
Centerville	62.9	"	
Reidston	64.0	"	
Graves	66.3	"	
East Haven Jct.	66.6	"	
City Limits	67.1	"	
--via city line			
(Richmond)	68.7)	"	

CONSTRUCTION/ABANDONMENT

Date	Act	End points	MP	Change	Main	Source	Note
1900/6	B2	Indianapolis-Greenfield	5.7-21.3	+15.6	15.6	1	
1902/5	B2	Greenfield-Charlottesville	21.3-29.6	+8.3		1	
1902/1	B3	Richmond-Centerville	67.1-62.9	+4.2	28.1	1	
(continued)							

TERRE HAUTE, INDIANAPOLIS & EASTERN

INDIANAPOLIS-RICHMOND (THIE-R)
CONSTRUCTION/ABANDONMENT (continued)

Date	Act	End points	MP	Change	Main	Source	Note
1903/9	B2	Charlottesville-Dublin	29.6-51.6	+22.0		1	
1903/9	B3	Dublin-Centerville	51.6-62.9	+11.3	61.4	1	
1931/6/30	S1	Indianapols-Richmond	5.7-67.1	-61.4	0	3	
(1932/1	X	Indianapolis-Dunreith	5.7-39.3				

OWNERSHIP

1900	Indianapolis & Eastern Ry (B2), of part
1902	Richmond Street & Interurban Ry (B3), of part
1907/3/1	Terre Haute, Indianapolis & Eastern Traction Co., merge I&E and RS&I

CAMBRIDGE CITY-MILTON (THIE-RM)

	Mileage	County	Crossings, junctions, etc.
Cambridge City	0	Wayne	J/THIE-R 53.6
Milton	2	"	

CONSTRUCTION/ABANDONMENT

Date	Act	End points	MP	Change	Main	Source	Note
1902 ca.	B3	Cambridge City-Milton		0-2	+2.0	2.0	3
1925	XS	Cambridge City-Milton		0-2	-2.0	0	2,3

OWNERSHIP

1902	Richmond Street & Interurban Ry (B3), of part
1907/3/1	Terre Haute, Indianapolis & Eastern Traction Co., merge I&E and RS&I

DUNREITH-NEW CASTLE (THIE-RN)

	Mileage	County	Crossings, junctions, etc.
New Castle	0	Henry	J/INDR-
Chambers	1.3	"	
Carpenter	4.8	"	
Cates	7.1	"	
Spiceland	9.3	"	
Draper	9.8	"	
Dunreith	10.9	"	J/THIE-R 39.3

CONSTRUCTION/ABANDONMENT

Date	Act	End points	MP	Change	Main	Source	Note
1903/9	B3	Dunreith-New Castle	0-10.9	+10.9	10.9	2	
1931/6/30	S1	Dunreith-New Castle	0-10.9	-10.9	0	4	

OWNERSHIP

1903	Richmond Street & Interurban Ry (B3)
1907/3/1	Terre Haute, Indianapolis & Eastern Traction Co, merged RS&I
1931/6/30	Indiana RR, buy THI&E

TERRE HAUTE-PARIS (THIE-P)

	Mileage	County	Crossings, junctions, etc.
(Terre Haute)	0)	Vigo	
--via city line			
City Limits	0.8	"	
Grade	1.6	"	
West Terre Haute	2.3	"	
Tile Works	2.8	"	
St. Marys	5.6	"	
(continued)			

TERRE HAUTE, INDIANAPOLIS & EASTERN

TERRE HAUTE-PARIS (THIE-P) (continued)

	Mileage [Terre Haute]	County	Crossings, junctions, etc.
St. Marys	5.6	Vigo	
Mickelberrys	6.5	"	
Mars	10.0	"	
Sandford	10.2	"	
(IN/IL state line)	10.3		
Thompsons IL	11.2		
McFarlands	11.8		
Trogden	12.8		
Vermillion	14.0		
Kentuck	15.5		
Stepps	17.9		
Sugar Creek	18.9		
Paris IL	20.8		

CONSTRUCTION/ABANDONMENT

Date	Act	End points	MP	Change	Main	Source	Note
1902/12/1	B9	Terre Haute-West T. H.	0.8-2.3	+1.5	1.5	1	
1907/10	B12	West Terre Haute-Paris IL	2.3-10.3	+8.0	9.5	1	
1931/6/30	S1	Terre Haute-Paris IL	0.8-10.3	-9.5	0	3	
(1932/1/25	XS	Terre Haute-Paris IL	0.8-10.3	-9.5	0)	2	

OWNERSHIP

1902	Terre Haute Traction & Light Co. (B9), of part
1907/3/25	Terre Haute, Indianapolis & Eastern Traction Co. (B12), lease THT&L
1931/6/30	Indiana RR, buy THI&E (with lease of THT&L)

TERRE HAUTE-SULLIVAN (THIE-S)

	Mileage	County	Crossings, junctions, etc.
(Terre Haute)	0)	Vigo	
--via city line			
City Limits	1.8	"	
Halsteads	4.1	"	
Allendale	5.2	"	
Forks	5.7	"	
Youngstown	7.5	"	
Pimento	11.2	"	
Turman	13.0	"	
Siefert	14.2	"	
Farmersburg	15.0	Sullivan	
Odell	18.1	"	
Curryville	19.7	"	
Shelburn	20.3	"	
Morrison Creek	22.9	"	
Scotts	23.3	"	
City Limits	25.4	"	
Sullivan	26.3	"	

CONSTRUCTION/ABANDONMENT

Date	Act	End points	MP	Change	Main	Source	Note
1906/6	B9	Terre Haute-Sullivan	1.8-26.3	+24.5	24.5	1	
1931/Spr	XS	Terre Haute-Sullivan	1.8-26.3	-24.5	0	2	

OWNERSHIP

1906	Terre Haute Traction & Light Co. (B9)
1907/3/25	Terre Haute, Indianapolis & Eastern Traction, leased Terre Haute Traction & Light

TERRE HAUTE, INDIANAPOLIS & EASTERN

TERRE HAUTE-CLINTON (THIE-T)

	Mileage	County	Crossings, junctions, etc.
(Terre Haute)	0)	Vigo	
--via city line			
Maple Avenue	2.30	"	
Carl Avenue	3.05	"	
Phillips	4.52	"	
North Terre Haute	5.17	"	
Crabbs	6.78	"	
Atherton	10.72	"	
Walkers	11.58	Parke	
Numa	12.26	"	
Lyford	13.44	"	
Clinton	15.29	Vermillion	
Italy	16.25	"	

CONSTRUCTION/ABANDONMENT

Date	Act	End points	MP	Change	Main	Source	Note
1903/11	B10	Terre Haute-Italy	2.3-16.3	+14.0	14.0	1	
1931/Spr	XS	Terre Haute-Italy	2.3-16.3	-14.0	0	2	

OWNERSHIP

1903	Terre Haute Traction & Light Co. (B10)
1907/3/25	Terre Haute, Indianapolis & Eastern Traction, lease THL&T

ACQUISITION/DISPOSITION RECORD

Date	Act	THIE-	End points	Change	Main	Note
1893/7/16	B1	A	Brazil-Harmony	+3.4	3.4	
1900/9	B6	A	Terre Haute-Brazil	+12.7		
	B2	R	Indianapolis-Greenfield	+15.6	31.7	
1902	B2	R	Greenfield-Charlottesville	+8.3		
/1	B3	R	Richmond-Centerville	+4.2		
/8	B5	M	Indianapolis-Mooresville	+14.6		
/Fall	B4	A	Indianapolis-Plainfield	+12.0		
/12/1	B9	P	Terre Haute-West Terre Haute	+1.5		
ca.	B3	RM	Cambridge City-Milton	+2.0	74.3	
1903/4	B5	M	Mooresville-Martinsville	+14.1		
/Fall	B7	L	Indianapolis-Lafayette	+63.1		
/9	B3	RN	Dunreith-New Castle	+10.9		
/9	B7	LC	Lebanon-Crawfordsville	+23.2		
/11	B6	T	Terre Haute-Italy	+14.0		
	B3	R	Charlottesville-Centerv.	+33.3	232.9	
1905/9/1	B8	D	Indianapolis-Danville	+16.8	249.7	
1906	B9	S	Terre Haute-Sullivan	+24.5	274.2	
1907	B11	A	Plainfield-Greencastle	+25.6		
/10	B12	P	West Terre Haute-Paris IL	+8.0		
/7	B12	C	Indianapolis-Crawfordsv.	+38.9	346.7	
1908/1	B11	A	Greencastle-Brazil	+13.6	360.3	
1925	XS	RM	Cambridge City-Milton	-2.0	358.3	
1930/10/30	XS	L	Indianapolis-Lafayette	-63.1		
/10/30	XS	C	Indianapolis-Crawfordsv.	-38.9		
/10/30	XS	D	Indianapolis-Danville	-16.8		
/10/30	XS	LC	Lebanon-Crawfordsville	-23.2		
/10/30	XS	M	Indianapois-Martinsville	-28.7	187.6	
1931/Spr	XS	S	Terre Haute-Sullivan	-24.5		
/Spr	XS	T	Terre Haute-Italy	-14.0		
/6/30	S1	A	Indianapolis-Terre Haute	-67.3		
/6/30	S1	P	Terre Haute-Paris IL	-9.5		
/6/30	S1	R	Indianapols-Richmond	-61.4		
/6/30	S1	RN	Dunreith-New Castle	-10.9	0	

TERRE HAUTE, INDIANAPOLIS & EASTERN

ACT COLUMN KEY
B1   Built by Brazil Rapid Transit Street Ry
B2   Built by Indianapolis & Eastern Ry
B3   Built by Richmond Street & Interurban Ry
B4   Built by Indianapolis & Plainfield Electric RR
B5   Built by Indianapolis & Martinsville Rapid Transit Co.
B6   Built by Terre Haute Electric Co.
B7   Built by Indianapolis & Northwestern Traction Co.
B8   Built by Indianapolis & Western Ry
B9   Built by Terre Haute Traction & Light Co.
B10 Built by Indianapolis Coal Traction Co.
B11 Built by Terre Haute, Indianapolis & Eastern Traction Co.
B12 Built by Indianapolis, Crawfordsville & Western Traction Co.
S1   Sold to Indiana RR
X   Abandoned
XS   Service ended

SOURCES
1. Blackburn, "Interurban Railroads."
2. Central, *Electric Railways of Indiana, Part I.*
3. Hilton and Due, *The Electric Interurban Railways.*

NOTES
 1. Source 3 states service began 1906.
 2. The McGowen-Schoepf-Dolan-Morgan syndicate bought control this company in 1905.
 3. The Stone & Webster syndicate bought control of this company in June 1905 and "soon after" control was transferred to the McGowen-Schoepf-Dolan-Morgan syndicate.

VALPARAISO & NORTHERN

MAIN LINE (VANE-A)

	Mileage	County	Crossings, junctions, etc.
Valparaiso	0	Porter	
Grand Trunk	0.6	"	X/GTW-C 55.80
Vale Park	1.9	"	
Burlington Beach	3.1	"	
Flint Lake	3.6	"	
Long Lake			
Wahob	5.4	"	
Woodville Jct.	7.5	"	J/GARY
(Bridge)	7.6	"	B/B&O-C 229.6
Goodrum Jct.	8.0	"	J/CNAL-A 15
(Crossing)	9.1	"	X/WAB-MC 226.7
Chesterton	10.9	"	

CONSTRUCTION/ABANDONMENT

Date	Act	End points	MP	Change	Main	Source	Note
1910/7/4	B	Valparaiso-Flint Lake	0-3.6	+3.6	3.6	1	
1911/2/18	B	Goodrum-Chesterton	8.0-10.9	+2.9		1	
1911/10/7	B	Flint Lake-Woodville	3.6-7.5	+3.9	10.4	1	
1912/2/17	B	Woodville-Goodrum	7.5-8.0	+0.5	10.9	1	
1922	X	Woodville-Chesterton	7.5-10.9	-3.4	7.5	1	
1938/10/23	X	Valparaiso-Woodville	0-7.5	-7.5	0	1	

OWNERSHIP

1910	Valparaiso & Northern Ry (B1)
1913/1/28	Gary & Interurban RR, merged V&N
1917/9/18	Valparaiso & Northern Ry, split from G&I
1917/11/19	Gary & Valparaiso Ry, acquired V&N

VALPARAISO & NORTHERN

ACQUISITION/DISPOSITION RECORD
See ownership record above for line VANE-A

ACT COLUMN KEY
B   Built by Valparaiso & Northern Ry
X   Abandoned

SOURCES
1. Buckley, *Gary Railways.*

WINONA

MAIN LINE (WIN-A)

	Mileage	County	Crossings, junctions, etc.
(Goshen)	0)	Elkhart	
--via city line			
College	1.45	"	
Fairlawn	2.81	"	
New Paris	6.07	"	X/WAB-MC 161.4
Arnolds	9.63	"	
Milford Jct.	11.01	Kosciusko	X/B&O-C 165.7
Wright	12.00	"	
Milford	12.31	"	
Felkner	13.96	"	
Leesburg	18.06	"	
Wren	18.37	"	
Hancock	20.60	"	
Shop	23.79	"	
Big Four	23.99	"	
Center Street	24.56	"	J/WIN-B 0.15
Warsaw	24.71	"	
Lake Street	24.81	"	
Fair Ground	25.94	"	
Cook	29.67	"	
Latta	31.81	"	
Mentone	35.71	"	X/NKP-C 419.8
Jeffries	37.73	"	
Doran	39.70	"	
Beaver Dam	41.70	"	
Bear	42.71	"	
Polo	44.68	Fulton	
Akron	46.05	"	
Erie	46.56	"	X/ERIE-C 158.6
Craig	48.29	Miami	
Gilead	50.55	"	
Dix	50.89	"	
Whistler	52.28	"	
King	53.97	"	
Love	55.93	"	
Ray	57.83	"	X/PRR-IE 21.1
Chili	58.12	"	
Brownell	60.77	"	
Wabash Jct.	64.14	"	X/WAB-M 200.2
Belt	65.47	"	
Oakdale	66.09	"	
Columbia	66.74	"	
Elmwood	66.84	"	
Peru	67.83	"	
(continued)			

WINONA

MAIN LINE (WIN-A) (continued)
CONSTRUCTION/ABANDONMENT

Date	Act	End points	MP	Change	Main	Source	Note
1906/6	B2	Goshen-Warsaw	1.5-24.7	+23.2		1	
1906/8/6	P1	Ray-Wabash Jct.	57.8-64.1	+6.3	29.5	4	
1907/5	B2	Wabash Jct.-Peru	64.1-67.8	+3.7	33.2	4	
1908/1	B2	Akron-Ray	46.1-57.8	+11.7	44.9	2	
1909/3	B2	Warsaw-Mentone	24.7-35.7	+11.0	55.9	2	
1910/2/4	B2	Mentone-Akron	35.7-46.1	+10.4	66.3	2	
1934	X	Goshen-New Paris	1.5-6.1	-4.6		3	
1934	X	Wabash Jct.-Peru	64.1-67.8	-3.7	58.0	3	
1947	X	Warsaw-Wabash Jct.	24.7-64.1	-39.4	18.6	3	
1952	X	New Paris-Warsaw	6.1-24.7	-18.6	0	3	

OWNERSHIP

1906	Winona Interurban Ry (B2), of part
1924	Winona Service Co., reorganize Winona Interurban Ry
1935 ca.	Winona RR, rename Winona Service Co.

WINONA LAKE LINE (WIN-B)

	Mileage	County	Crossings, junctions, etc.
(Warsaw	0)	Kosciusko	
(Junction)	0.15	"	J/WIN-A 24.56
(Crossing)	0.20	"	X/CCC-M 79.6
(Crossing)	1.80	"	X/PRR-F 357.1
Winona Lake	2.00	"	

CONSTRUCTION/ABANDONMENT

Date	Act	End points	MP	Change	Main	Source	Note
1903/5/1	B1	Line	0.2-2.0	+1.8	1.8	3	
1947	X	Line	0.2-2.0	-1.8	0	3	

OWNERSHIP

1903	Winona & Warsaw Ry (B1)
1910/1/1	Winona Interurban Ry, lease of Winona & Warsaw
1924	Winona Service Co., reorganize Winona Interurban Ry
1935 ca.	Winona RR, rename Winona Service Co.

ACQUISITION/DISPOSITION RECORD

Date	Act	WIN-	End points	Change	Main	Note
1903/5/1	B1	B	Warsaw-Winona Lake	+1.8	1.8	
1904/6	B2	A	Warsaw-Goshen	+23.2	25.0	
1906/8/6	P1	A	Ray-Wabash Jct.	+6.3	31.3	
1907/5	B2	A	Wabash Jct.-Peru	+3.7	35.0	
1908/1	B2	A	Akron-Ray	+11.7	46.7	
1909/3	B2	A	Warsaw-Mentone	+11.0	57.7	
1910/2/4	B2	A	Mentone-Akron	+10.4	68.1	
1934	X	A	Goshen-New Paris	-4.6		
	X	A	Wabash Jct.-Peru	-3.7	59.8	
1947	X	A	Warsaw-Wabash Jct.	-39.4		
	X	B	Warsaw-Winona Lake	-1.8	18.6	
1952	X	A	New Paris-Warsaw	-18.6	0	

ACT COLUMN KEY
B1 Built by Winona & Warsaw Ry
B2 Built by Winona Interurban Ry
P1 Purchased from Wabash RR
X   Abandoned

SOURCES
1. Blackburn, "Interurban Railroads."
2. Central, *Electric Railways of Indiana, Part II.*

RAILROADS	1838	1839
State of Indiana	16.7	19.9
RAILROAD YEAR TOTAL	16.7	19.9
RAILROAD YEAR CHANGE	16.7	3.2

RAILROADS	1840	1841	1842	1843	1844	1845	1846	1847	1848	1849
Madison & Indianapolis						10.5	20.8	40.6	40.6	40.6
State of Indiana				37.2	45.2	45.2	45.2	45.2	45.2	45.2
Shelbyville Lateral Branch										16.0
State of Indiana	19.9	27.8	27.8							
RAILROAD YEAR TOTAL	19.9	27.8	27.8	37.2	45.2	55.7	66.0	85.8	85.8	101.8
RAILROAD YEAR CHANGE	0.0	7.9	0.0	9.4	8.0	10.5	10.3	19.8	0.0	16.0

RAILROADS	1850	1851	1852	1853	1854	1855	1856	1857	1858	1859
Cincinnati & Chicago					30.5	30.5	30.5	111.3	111.3	111.3
Cincinnati & Indianapolis Jct.			40.1	40.1	40.1	40.1	40.1	40.1	40.1	40.1
Cincinnati, Logansport & Chicago				30.5						
Cincinnati, Peru & Chicago						29.2	29.2	29.2	29.2	29.2
Evansville & Crawfordsville				109.0	109.0	109.0	109.0	109.0	109.0	109.0
Greenville & Union			0.2	0.2	0.2	0.2	0.2	0.2	0.2	0.2
Indiana Central				71.4	71.4	71.4	71.4	71.4	71.4	71.4
Indianapolis & Bellefontaine		84.9	84.9	84.2	84.2					
Indianapolis & Cincinnati				91.7	91.7	91.7	91.7	91.7	91.7	91.7
Indianapolis, Pittsburgh & Clev.						84.2	84.2	84.2	84.2	84.2
Indianapolis Union			1.8	1.8	1.8	1.8	1.8	1.8	1.8	1.8
Jeffersonville			67.8	78.2	78.2	78.2	78.2	78.2	78.2	78.2
Columbus & Shelby				24.0	24.0	24.0	24.0	24.0	24.0	24.0
Rushville & Shelbyville				18.2	18.2	18.2				
Shelby & Rush							18.2	18.2	18.2	18.2
Knightstown & Shelbyville	26.0	26.0	26.0	26.0						
Lafayette & Indianapolis		59.7		59.5	59.5	59.5	59.5	59.5	59.5	59.5
Louisville, NewAlbany & Chi.										287.2
Madison & Indianapolis	40.6	40.6	40.6	40.6	40.6	40.6	85.8	85.8	85.8	85.8
Martinsville & Franklin				25.5	25.5	25.5	25.5	25.5		
Peru & Indianapolis					72.0	72.0	72.0	72.0	72.0	72.0
State of Indiana	45.2	45.2	45.2	45.2	45.2	45.2				
Martinsville & Franklin									25.5	25.5
Michigan Central	6.2	6.2	42.5	42.5	42.5	42.5	42.5	42.5	42.5	42.5
Joliet & Northern Indiana					15.7	15.7	15.7	15.7	15.7	15.7
Mich. South. & No. Indiana						111.3	111.3	111.3	167.4	167.4
Buffalo & Mississippi						14.0				
New Albany & Salem		56.0	83.3	230.6	287.2	287.2	287.2	287.2	287.2	
Northern Indiana		29.8	111.3	111.3	111.3					
Buffalo & Mississippi		14.0	14.0	14.0	14.0					
Ohiio & Indiana					19.4	19.4				
Ohio & Mississippi								172.6	172.6	172.6
Peru & Indianapolis		20.3	20.3	72.0						

RAILROADS continued	1850	1851	1852	1853	1854	1855	1856	1857	1858	1859
Pittsburgh, Ft. Wayne & Chgo						38.3	38.3	152.9	152.9	
Rushville & Shelbyville	18.2	18.2	18.2							
St. Louis, Alton & Terre Haute							8.4	8.4	8.4	8.4
Shelbyville Lateral Branch	16.0	16.0	16.0	16.0	16.0					
Toledo & Illinois						12.8				
Toledo & Wabash									166.6	166.6
Toledo, Logansport & Burl.										60.7
Toledo, Wabash & Western							166.6	166.6		
Terre Haute & Richmond			72.7	72.3	72.3	72.3	72.3	72.3	72.3	72.3
RAILROAD YEAR TOTAL	152.2	357.2	702.7	1234.2	1299.9	1296.7	1493.0	1665.6	1836.3	1897.0
RAILROAD YEAR CHANGE	107.0	205.0	345.5	531.5	65.7	-3.2	196.3	172.6	170.7	60.7

RAILROADS	1860	1861	1862	1863	1864	1865	1866	1867	1868	1869
Bellefontaine					84.2	84.2	84.2	84.2		
Chicago & Cincinnati		61.3	61.3	61.3	61.3					
Chicago & Great Eastern						257.8	257.8	311.5		
Chicago, Cincinnati & Louisville								29.2	29.2	73.6
Cincinnati & Chicago Air-Line	111.3	111.3	111.3	111.3	111.3					
Cincinnati & Indianapolis Jct.	40.1	40.1	40.1	40.1	40.1	40.1	40.1	78.6	78.6	78.6
Cincinnati & Martinsville						25.5	38.0	38.0	38.0	38.0
Cinci., Connersville & Muncie									43.3	
Cincinnati, Peru & Chicago	29.2	29.2	29.2	29.2	29.2	29.2	29.2			
Cleve., Col., Cinci. & Indpls.									84.2	84.2
Columbus & Indiana Central					71.4	71.4	71.4	132.7		
Columbus, Chgo & Ind. Cent.									421.3	
Connersville & New Castle Jct.						25.0	25.0	25.0		
Dayton & Union				0.2	0.2	0.2	0.2	0.2	0.2	0.2
Evansville & Crawfordsville	131.9	131.9	131.9	131.9	131.9	131.9	131.9	131.9	131.9	131.9
Fort Wayne, Muncie & Cinci.										43.3
Greenville & Miami	0.2	0.2	0.2							
Indiana Central	71.4	71.4	71.4	71.4						
Indianapolis & Cincinnati	91.7	91.7	91.7	91.7	91.7	91.7	91.7			
Indianapolis & Lafayette	70.2	70.2	70.2	70.2	70.2	70.2	70.2			
Indianapolis & Madison			85.8	85.8	85.8	45.2				
Indianapolis, Peru & Chicago					72.0	72.0				
Peru & Indianapolis			72.0	72.0						
Indianapolis & St. Louis										
St. Louis, Alton & Terre Haute								8.4	8.4	8.4
Indianapolis, Bloomingt'n & W.										78.9
Indianapolis, Cinci. & Lafayette								152.7	152.7	152.7
White Water Valley									63.0	63.0
Indianapolis, Peru & Chicago							72.0	72.0	72.0	72.0
Indianapolis, Pittsburgh & Clev.	84.2	84.2	84.2	84.2						
Indianapolis Union	1.8	1.8	1.8	1.8	1.8	2.2	2.2	2.2	2.2	2.8
Indianapolis & Vincennes									43.1	115.9
Jeffersonville	78.2	78.2	78.2	78.2	78.2	112.9				
Columbus & Shelby	24.0	24.0	24.0	24.0	24.0	24.0				
Shelby & Rush	18.2	18.2	18.2	18.2	18.2	18.2				

RAILROADS continued	1860	1861	1862	1863	1864	1865	1866	1867	1868	1869
Jeffersonv., Madison & Indpls.						158.1	158.1	158.1	158.1	
Columbus & Shelby							24.0	24.0	24.0	24.0
Shelby & Rush							18.2	18.2	18.2	18.2
Lafayette & Indianapolis	59.5	59.5	59.5	59.5	59.5	59.5	59.5			
Lake Erie & Louisville								21.2	21.2	21.2
Lake Shore & Mich. Southern										167.4
Louisville, NewAlbany & Chi.	287.2	287.2	287.2	287.2	287.2	287.2	287.2	287.2	287.2	287.2
Martinsville & Franklin	25.5	25.5	25.5	25.5	25.5					
Madison & Indianapolis	85.8	85.8								
Peru & Indianapolis	72.0	72.0								
Michigan Central	42.5	42.5	42.5	42.5	42.5	42.5	42.5	42.5	42.5	42.5
Joliet & Northern Indiana	15.7	15.7	15.7	15.7	15.7	15.7	15.7	15.7	15.7	15.7
Northern Indiana	167.4	167.4	167.4	167.4	167.4	167.4	167.4	167.4	167.4	
Ohio & Mississippi	172.6	172.6	172.6	172.6	172.6	172.6	172.6	172.6	172.6	225.6
Pennsylvania										
Columbus, Chicago & Ind. Cent.										420.4
Pittsburgh, Ft. Wayne & Chi.										152.9
Pittsburgh, Ft. Wayne & Chi.	152.9	152.9	152.9	152.9	152.9	152.9	152.9	152.9	152.9	
St. Louis, Alton & Terre Haute	8.4	8.4	8.4	8.4	8.4	8.4	8.4			
Toledo & Wabash	166.6	166.6	166.6	166.6						
Toledo, Logansport & Burl.	60.7	60.7	60.7	60.7	60.7	60.7	60.7			
Toledo, Wabash & Western					166.6	166.6	166.6	166.6	166.6	166.6
Terre Haute & Indianapolis							72.3	72.3	72.3	72.3	72.3
Terre Haute & Richmond	72.3	72.3	72.3	72.3	72.3					
RAILROAD YEAR TOTAL	2141.5	2202.8	2202.8	2202.8	2202.8	2307.5	2320.0	2365.3	2466.8	2715.6
RAILROAD YEAR CHANGE	841.6	61.3	0.0	0.0	0.0	104.7	12.5	45.3	101.5	248.8

RAILROADS	1870	1871	1872	1873	1874	1875	1876	1877	1878	1879
Baltimore & Ohio							146.3	146.3	146.3	146.3
Baltimore, Pittsburg & Ohio					146.3	146.3				
Bedf., Spr., Owensb. & Bloomf'd								33.6	33.6	33.6
Bloomfield									6.2	6.2
Cairo & Vincennes			8.6	8.6	8.6	8.6	8.6	8.6	8.6	8.6
Chicago & Block Coal										12.8
Chicago & Eastern Illinois								19.0	19.0	8.4
Chicago & Lake Huron									56.4	55.3
Chicago, Cincinnati & Louisville	73.6									
Chicago, Danville & Vincennes			8.4	19.0	19.0	19.0	19.0			
Cincinnati & Indianapolis Jct.	78.6	78.6								
Cincinnati & Martinsville	38.0	38.0	38.0	38.0	38.0	38.0				
Cincinnati & Terre Haute							25.5	25.5		
Cincinnati, Hamilton & Indpls.			78.6	78.6	78.6	78.6	78.6	78.6	78.6	78.6
Cinci., Richmond & Ft. Wayne	23.8									
Cinci., Rockport & SW					24.3	24.3	24.3	24.3	37.5	37.5
Cinci, Wabash & Michigan		43.7	58.1	77.4	77.4	87.5	110.2	110.2	110.2	110.2
Cleve., Col., Cinci. & Indpls.	84.2	84.2	84.2	84.2	84.2	84.2	84.2	84.2	84.2	84.2
Cleve., Indiana & St. Louis							18.4	18.4	18.4	18.4
Dayton & Union	0.2	0.2	0.2	0.2	0.2	0.2	0.2	0.2	0.2	0.2

RAILROADS continued	1870	1871	1872	1873	1874	1875	1876	1877	1878	1879
Delphos, Bluffton & Frankfort									13.8	
Detroit, Eel River & Illinois					92.5	92.5	92.5			
Evansville & Crawfordsville	131.9	131.9	116.0	116.0	116.0	116.0	116.0			
Evansville & Terre Haute								116.0	116.0	116.0
Evansville Local Trade RR										16.2
Evansv., Terre Haute & Chicago		43.3	43.3	43.3	43.3	43.3	43.3	43.3	43.3	43.3
Fort Wayne & Jackson										55.3
Ft. Wayne, Jackson & Saginaw	55.3	55.3	55.3	55.3	55.3	55.3	55.3	55.3	55.3	
Ft. Wayne, Muncie & Cinci.	107.4	107.4	107.4	107.4	107.4	107.4	107.4	107.4	107.4	107.4
Frankfort & Kokomo					25.1	25.1	25.1	25.1	25.1	25.1
Frankfort & State Line										11.6
Indiana & Block Coal									12.7	12.7
Indiana & Illinois Central				8.3	8.3					
Indiana, Bloomington & West'n										78.9
Indiana North & South					12.8	12.8	12.8	12.8	12.8	
Indianapolis & Cincinnati										
Cincinnati & Martinsville										
Indianapolis & St. Louis	71.8	71.8	71.8	71.8	71.8	71.8	71.8	71.8	71.8	71.8
St. Louis, Alton & Terre Haute	8.4	8.4	8.4	8.4	8.4	8.4	8.4	8.4	8.4	8.4
Indianapolis & Vincennes	115.9	115.9	115.9	115.9	115.9	115.9	115.9	115.9	115.9	115.9
Indianapolis, Bloomington & W	78.9	78.9	78.9	78.9	78.9	78.9	78.9	78.9	78.9	
Indpls., Cinci. & Lafayette	152.7	152.7	176.3	176.3	176.3	174.2	174.2	174.2	174.2	174.2
Cincinnati & Martinsville							38.0			
Fairland, Franklin & Martinsv.								38.0	38.0	38.0
White Water Valley	63.0									
Indpls., Decatur & Springfield						8.3	8.3	8.3	8.3	8.3
Indpls., Delphi & Chicago									38.0	38.0
Indianapolis, Peru & Chicago	72.0	145.6	145.6	145.6	145.6	145.6	145.6	145.6	145.6	145.6
Michigan City & Indianapolis		11.5	11.5	11.5	11.5	11.5	11.5	11.5	11.5	11.5
Indianapolis Union	2.8	2.8	2.8	2.8	2.8	2.8	14.6	14.6	14.6	14.6
Jeffersonv., Madison & Indpls.	158.1									
Columbus & Shelby	24.0									
Shelby & Rush	18.2									
Lake Erie & Louisville	21.2	21.2	21.2	21.2	21.2	21.2	21.2	21.2	21.2	21.2
Lafayette, Muncie & Bloomington			18.6	35.7			120.7	120.7	120.7	
Lake Erie & Western										158.1
Lake Erie, Evansville & SW				16.2	16.2	16.2	16.2	16.2	16.2	
Lake Shore & Mich. Southern	167.4	167.4	167.4	167.4	167.4	167.4	167.4	167.4	167.4	167.4
Logansport, Crawfordsv. & SW		86.3	86.3	86.3	86.3	91.6	91.6	91.6	91.6	
Evansville & Crawfordsville			17.1	17.1	17.1	17.1	17.1			
Evansville & Terre Haute								17.1	17.1	
Louisville, NewAlbany & Chi.	287.2	287.2	287.2	287.2	287.2	287.2	287.2	287.2	287.2	287.2
Louisv., N. A. & St. L. Air Line RR									10.7	10.7
Louisv., N. A. & St. L. Air Line Ry			10.7	10.7	10.7	10.7	10.7			
Louisv., N. A. & St. Louis Ry								10.7		
Martinsville & Franklin										
Michigan Central	42.5	42.5	42.5	42.5	42.5	42.5	42.5	42.5	42.5	42.5
Joliet & Northern Indiana	15.7	15.7	15.7	15.7	15.7	15.7	15.7	15.7	15.7	15.7
Michigan Air Line			5.9	5.9	5.9	5.9	5.9	5.9	5.9	5.9

RAILROADS continued	1870	1871	1872	1873	1874	1875	1876	1877	1878	1879
North Western Grand Trunk										25.2
Ohio & Mississippi	225.6	225.6	226.1	226.1	226.1	226.1	226.1	226.1	226.1	226.1
Peninsular			10.6	56.4	56.4	56.4	56.4	56.4		
Pennsylvania										
Columbus, Chgo. & Ind. Cent.	420.4	420.4	420.4	420.4	420.4	420.4	420.4	420.4	420.4	420.4
Grand Rapids & Indiana	53.1	53.1	53.1	53.1	53.1	53.1	53.1	53.1	53.1	53.1
Cinci., Richm. & Ft. Wayne		85.9	85.9	85.9	85.9	85.9	85.9	85.9	85.9	85.9
Pittsburgh, Cinci. & St. L.										
Jeffersonv., Madison & Indpls.		158.1	158.1	158.1	158.1	158.1	158.1	158.1	158.1	158.1
Columbus & Shelby		24.0	24.0	24.0	24.0	24.0	24.0	24.0	24.0	24.0
Shelby & Rush		18.2	18.2	18.2	18.2	18.2	18.2	18.2	18.2	18.2
Pittsburgh, Ft. Wayne & Chi.	152.9	152.9	152.9	152.9	152.9	152.9	152.9	152.9	152.9	152.9
St. Louis & South Eastern				28.6	28.6	28.6	28.6	28.6	28.6	28.6
Terre Haute & Indianapolis	87.8	87.8	87.8	87.8	87.8	87.8	87.8	87.8	87.8	87.8
Terre Haute & Logansport										91.6
Evansville & Terre Haute										17.1
Terre Haute & Southeastern									25.5	25.5
Toledo, Delphos & Burlington										37.3
Toledo, Wabash & Western	166.6	166.6	166.6	166.6	166.6	166.6	166.6			
Lafayette, Bloom'ton & Miss.			35.7	35.7	35.7	35.7				
Wabash Ry								166.6	166.6	
Eel River								92.5	92.5	
Wabash, St. Louis & Pacific										166.6
Eel River										92.5
Warsaw, Goshen & Wh. Pigeon	24.4									
White Water Valley		63.0	63.0	63.0	63.0	63.0	63.0	63.0	63.0	63.0
RAILROAD YEAR TOTAL	3023.6	3246.1	3412.9	3530.2	3795.5	3808.8	3972.2	4005.8	4089.7	4175.7
RAILROAD YEAR CHANGE	820.8	222.5	166.8	117.3	265.3	13.3	163.4	33.6	83.9	86.0

RAILROADS	1880	1881	1882	1883	1884	1885	1886	1887	1888	1889
Baltimore & Ohio	146.3	146.3	146.3	146.3	146.3	146.3	146.3	146.3	146.3	146.3
Bedfod & Bloomfield				33.6	39.8	39.8	0.0			
Bedf., Spr., Owensb. & Bloomf.	33.6	33.6	33.6	0.0						
Bloomfield	37.2	37.2	37.2	6.2	0.0					
Cairo & Vincennes	8.6					8.6	8.6	8.6	8.6	
Cairo, Vincennes & Chicago										8.6
Canada & St. Louis									25.6	
Chicago & Atlantic			159.2	159.2	159.2	159.2	159.2	159.2	159.2	159.2
Chicago & Block Coal	12.8	12.8	19.9	0.0						
Chicago & Eastern Illinois RR										
Evansville, Terre Haute & Chi.	43.3	43.3	43.3	43.3	43.3	43.3	43.3	43.3	43.3	43.3
Indiana Block Coal	12.7	12.7	12.7	12.7	12.7	12.7	12.7	12.7	12.7	12.7
Chicago & Grand Trunk	80.5	80.5	80.5	80.5	80.5	80.5	80.5	80.5	80.5	80.5
Chicago & Great Southern				76.2	76.2	118.1				
Chicago & Indiana Coal							118.1	144.7	165.7	165.7
Chicago & West Michigan			33.0	33.0	33.0	33.0	33.0	33.0	33.0	33.0
Cincinnati, Hamilton & Dayton										
Cincinnati, Hamilton & Indpls.							78.6	78.6	78.6	78.6

RAILROADS continued	1880	1881	1882	1883	1884	1885	1886	1887	1888	1889
CH&D-CCC&SL										
Dayton & Union	0.2	0.2	0.2	0.2	0.2	0.2	0.2	0.2	0.2	0.2
Cincinnati, Hamilton & Indpls.	78.6	78.6	78.6	78.6	78.6	78.6				
Cinci., Indpls., St. Louis & Chi.	212.2	212.2	212.2	212.2	212.2	212.2	212.2	212.2	212.2	
Cinci. & So. Ohio River								3.7	3.7	
Columbus, Hope & Greensburg					24.4	24.4	24.4	24.4	24.4	
Vernon, Greensburg & Rushv.		44.4	44.4	44.4	44.4	44.4	44.4	44.4	44.4	
Cinci., Wabash & Michigan	110.2	110.2	130.3	130.3	130.3	130.3	130.3	130.3	130.3	130.3
Cleve., Cinci., Chi. & St. Louis										421.0
Cinci. & So. Ohio River										3.7
Columbus, Hope & Greensburg										24.4
Cleve., Col., Cinci. & Indpls.	84.2	84.2	84.2	84.2	84.2	84.2	84.2	84.2	84.2	
Cleve., Indiana & St. Louis	18.4	18.4	18.4	18.4	18.4					
Delphos, Bluffton & Frankfort	13.8	13.8								
Elgin, Joliet & Eastern									21.3	21.3
Evansville & Indianapolis							137.5	137.5	137.5	137.5
Terre Haute & Indianapolis									11.5	11.5
Evansville & Terre Haute	116.0	116.0	116.0	152.8	152.8	152.8	152.8	160.9	160.9	160.9
Evansville Belt		4.0	4.0	4.0	4.0	4.0	4.0	4.0	4.0	4.0
Evansville, Rockport & Eastern	69.3									
Evansv., Washington & Brazil						43.0	0.0			
Fort Wayne & Jackson	55.3	55.3								
Fort Wayne, Cinci. & Louisville		107.4	107.4	107.4	107.4	107.4	130.6	130.6	130.6	130.6
New Castle & Rushville		23.2	23.2	23.2	23.2	23.2				
Ft. Wayne, Muncie & Cincinnati	107.4									
Frankfort & Kokomo	25.1									
Frankfort & State Line	11.6									
Havana, Rantoul & Eastern					8.4	8.4	8.4			
Henderson Bridge Co.						9.9	9.9	9.9	9.9	9.9
Illinois Central										
Rantoul								8.4	8.4	8.4
Indiana & Illinois Southern RR							31.0	31.0	31.0	31.0
Indiana & Illinois Southern Ry				31.0	31.0	31.0				
Indiana, Bloomington & West'n	78.9	78.9	153.7	153.7	153.7	153.7	153.7			
Indiana, Illinois & Iowa RR				38.9	38.9	38.9	48.3	48.3	48.3	48.3
Indianapolis & Evansville					51.2	51.2	0.0			
Indianapolis & St. Louis	71.8	71.8	71.8	71.8	71.8	71.8	71.8	71.8	71.8	
St. Louis, Alton & Terre Haute	8.4	8.4	8.4	8.4	8.4	8.4	8.4	8.4	8.4	
Indianapolis & Vincennes	115.9	115.9	115.9	115.9	115.9	131.3	136.1	136.1	136.1	136.1
Indpls., Decatur & Springifled	76.3	76.3	76.3	76.3	76.3	76.3	76.3			
Indpls., Decatur & Western								76.3	76.3	76.3
Indpls., Delphi & Chicago	38.0	0.0								
Indianapolis, Peru & Chicago	145.6						145.6			
Michigan City & Indianapolis	11.5									
Indianapolis Union	14.6	14.6	16.1	16.1	16.1	16.1	16.1	16.1	16.1	16.1
Kentucky & Indiana Terminal							0.4	0.4	0.4	0.4
Lake Erie & Louisville	21.2	21.2	21.2	21.2	21.2	21.2	21.2	21.2	21.2	21.2
Lake Erie & Western	158.1	158.1	158.1	158.1	158.1	158.1	169.6	316.3	316.3	316.3
Michigan City & Indianapolis							11.5			

RAILROADS continued	1880	1881	1882	1883	1884	1885	1886	1887	1888	1889
Lake Shore & Mich. Southern	167.4	167.4	167.4	167.4	167.4	167.4	167.4	167.4	167.4	167.4
Fort Wayne & Jackson			55.3	55.3	55.3	55.3	55.3	55.3	55.3	55.3
Louisville & Nashville										
South East & St. Louis		28.6	28.6	28.6	28.6	28.6	28.6	28.6	28.6	28.6
Louisville, Evansville & St. Louis		96.5	185.8	185.8	185.8	185.8	185.8	208.5	208.5	
Louisv., Evansv. & St. L. Consol.										208.5
Louisville, New Albany & Chi.	287.2	369.2	450.8	450.8	450.8	450.8	490.6	490.6	490.6	490.6
Orleans,W.Baden&Fr.Lick Sprs								17.7	17.7	17.7
Louisv., New Albany & Corydon				7.7	7.7	7.7	7.7	7.7	7.7	7.7
Louisv., N. A. & S. L. Air Line	27.2									
Michigan Central	42.5	42.5	42.5	42.5	42.5	42.5	42.5	42.5	42.5	42.5
Joliet & Northern Indiana	15.7	15.7	15.7	15.7	15.7	15.7	15.7	15.7	15.7	15.7
Michigan Air Line	5.9	5.9	5.9	5.9	5.9	5.9	5.9	5.9	5.9	5.9
Midland Ry						18.4	18.4	18.4	18.4	18.4
New Albany & Eastern								7.4		
New York, Chicago & St. Louis		17.6	150.7	150.7	150.7	150.7	150.7	150.7	150.7	150.7
Ohio & Mississippi	226.1	226.1	226.1	226.1	226.1	226.1	226.1	226.1	233.5	233.5
Ohio, Indiana & Western								153.7	153.7	153.7
Pennsylvania										
Columbus, Chgo. & Ind. Cent.	420.4	420.4	420.4	420.4						
Grand Rapids & Indiana	53.1	53.1	53.1	53.1	53.1	53.1	53.1	53.1	53.1	53.1
Cinci., Richm. & Ft. Wayne	85.9	85.9	85.9	85.9	85.9	85.9	85.9	85.9	85.9	85.9
Pittsburgh, Cincinnati & St. L.										
Chicago, St. Louis & Pacific					420.4	420.4	420.4	420.4	420.4	420.4
Jeffersonv., Mad. & Indpls.	158.1	182.1	200.3	200.3	200.3	200.3	200.3	200.3	200.3	200.3
Columbus & Shelby	24.0									
Shelby & Rush	18.2	18.2								
Pittsburgh, Ft. Wayne & Chi.	152.9	152.9	152.9	152.9	152.9	152.9	152.9	152.9	152.9	152.9
Peoria, Decatur& Evansville		37.4	37.4	37.4	37.4	37.4	37.4	37.4	37.4	37.4
South East & St. Louis	28.6									
Sturgis, Goshen & St. Louis										25.6
Terre Haute & Indianapolis	87.8	87.8	87.8	87.8	87.8	87.8	87.8	87.8	87.8	87.8
Terre Haute & Logansport	91.6	91.6	91.6	91.6	158.0	158.0	158.0	158.0	158.0	158.0
Evansville & Terre Haute	17.1	17.1	17.1	17.1	17.1	17.1	17.1	17.1	17.1	17.1
Terre Haute & Southeastern	25.5	25.5	39.3	39.3	39.3	39.3				
Toledo, Cincinnati & St. Louis		89.8	171.0	171.0	171.0	171.0				
Toledo, Delphos & Burlington	53.6	81.2								
Toledo, St. Louis & Kansas City							171.0	171.0	171.0	171.0
Wabash RR										172.2
Attica, Covington & Southern										14.8
Eel River										92.5
Wabash, St. Louis & Pacific	166.6	172.2	172.2	172.2	172.2	172.2	172.2	172.2	172.2	
Attica, Covington & Southern		14.8	14.8	14.8	14.8	14.8	14.8	14.8	14.8	
Cairo & Vincennes		8.6	8.6	8.6	8.6					
Eel River	92.5	92.5	92.5	92.5	92.5	92.5	92.5	92.5	92.5	
Havana, Rantoul & Eastern		8.4	8.4	8.4						
Indianapolis, Peru & Chicago		145.6	145.6	145.6	145.6	145.6				
Michigan City & Indianapolis		11.5	11.5	11.5	11.5	11.5				
White Water Valley	63.0	63.0	63.0	63.0	63.0	63.0	63.0	63.0	63.0	63.0

RAILROADS continued	1880	1881	1882	1883	1884	1885	1886	1887	1888	1889
RAILROAD YEAR TOTAL	4182.2	4458.3	5062.0	5168.1	5303.9	5414.1	5484.0	5559.8	5639.2	5639.2
RAILROAD YEAR CHANGE	386.7	276.1	603.7	106.1	135.8	110.2	69.9	75.8	79.4	0.0

RAILROADS	1890	1891	1892	1893	1894	1895	1896	1897	1898	1899
Baltimore & Ohio	146.3	146.3	146.3	146.3	146.3	146.3	146.3	146.3	146.3	146.3
Baltimore & Ohio Southwestern				244.3	244.3	244.3	244.3	244.3	244.3	244.3
Bedford Belt				4.8	4.8	4.8	4.8	4.8	4.8	4.8
Cairo, Vincennes & Chicago	8.6	8.6	8.6	8.6	8.6	8.6	8.6	8.6	8.6	8.6
Chicago & Calumet Terminal	3.7	3.7	3.7	3.7	3.7	3.7	3.7	3.7		
Chicago & Eastern Illinois RR										359.2
Chicago & Indiana Coal			165.7	165.7	165.7	165.7	165.7	165.7	165.7	
Evansville, Terre Haute & Chi.	43.3	43.3	43.3	43.3	43.3	43.3	43.3	43.3	43.3	
Indiana & Block Coal	12.7	12.7	12.7	12.7	12.7	12.7	12.7	12.7	12.7	
Terre Haute & Indianapolis										11.5
Chicago & Grand Trunk	80.5	80.5	80.5	80.5	80.5	80.5	80.5	80.5	80.5	80.5
Chicago & Indiana Coal	165.7	165.7								
Chicago & South Eastern		77.1	93.6	93.6	93.6	93.6	93.6	93.6	93.6	112.4
Ft. Wayne, Terre Haute & St. L.			9.7	9.7	9.7	9.7	9.7	9.7	9.7	5.2
Chicago & West Michigan	33.0	33.0	33.0	33.0	33.0	33.0	33.0	33.0	33.0	
Chicago, Hammond & Western								3.1		
Chicago, Indianapolis & Lousv.								508.3	508.3	508.3
Indiana Stone										8.6
Chicago Junction										
Chicago, Hammond & West'n									3.1	3.1
East Chicago Belt									3.5	3.5
Chicago, Lake Shore & Eastern							7.9	7.9	7.9	7.9
Chicago Terminal Transfer						6.0	6.0	6.0	9.7	9.7
Cincinnati, Hamilton & Dayton										
Cincinnati, Hamilton & Indpls.	78.6	78.6	78.6	78.6	78.6	78.6	78.6	78.6	78.6	78.6
CH&D-CCC&SL										
Dayton & Union	0.2	0.2	0.2	0.2	0.2	0.2	0.2	0.2	0.2	0.2
Cinci., Wabash & Michigan	130.3	169.3								
Cleve., Cinci., Chgo. & St. Lou.	495.8	495.8	500.2	500.2	500.2	500.2	500.2	500.2	500.2	500.2
Cinci. & So. Ohio River	3.7	3.7	3.7	3.7	3.7	3.7	3.7	3.7	3.7	3.7
Cinci., Wabash & Michigan			169.3	169.3	169.3	169.3	169.3	169.3	169.3	169.3
Columbus, Hope & Greensbg.	24.4	24.4	24.4	24.4	24.4	24.4	24.4	24.4	24.4	24.4
Louisv. & Jeffersonville Bridge				0.7	0.7	0.7	0.7	0.7	0.7	0.7
Peoria & Eastern	78.9	78.9	78.9	78.9	78.9	78.9	78.9	78.9	78.9	78.9
White Water Valley	63.0	63.0	63.0	63.0	63.0	63.0	63.0	63.0	63.0	63.0
East Chicago Belt							3.5	3.5		
Elgin, Joliet & Eastern	21.3	213.0	21.3	25.9	25.9	25.9	25.9	26.9	43.7	43.7
Elkhart & Western				12.9	12.9	12.9	12.9	12.9		
Erie										
Chicago & Erie	159.2	159.2	159.2	159.2	159.2	159.2	159.2	159.2	161.0	161.0
Evansville & Indianapolis	137.5	137.5	137.5	137.5	137.5	137.5	137.5	137.5	137.5	
Terre Haute & Indianapolis	11.5	11.5	11.5	11.5	11.5	11.5	11.5	11.5	11.5	
Evansville & Richmond	101.8	101.8	101.8	101.8	101.8	101.8	101.8			
Evansville & Terre Haute	160.9	160.9	160.9	169.9	169.9	169.9	169.9	169.9	169.9	169.9
Evansville Belt	4.0	4.0	4.0	4.0	4.0	4.0	4.0	4.0	4.0	4.0

RAILROADS continued	1890	1891	1892	1893	1894	1895	1896	1897	1898	1899
Findlay, Ft. Wayne & Western						18.0	18.0	18.0	18.0	18.0
Ft. Wayne, Terre Haute & St. L.		9.7								
Hammond & Blue Island							3.1			
Henderson Bridge Co.	9.9	9.9	9.9	9.9	9.9	9.9	9.9	9.9	9.9	9.9
Indpls., Decatur & Western	76.3	76.3	76.3	76.3	76.3	76.3	76.3	76.3	76.3	76.3
Illinois & Indiana										31.0
Illinois Central										
Rantoul	8.4	8.4	8.4	8.4	8.4	8.4	8.4	8.4	8.4	8.4
Indiana, Illinois & Iowa RR	48.3	48.3	48.3							
Indiana, Illinois & Iowa Ry				48.3	82.0	82.0	82.0	82.0		
Indianapolis & Vincennes	136.1	136.1	136.1	136.1	136.1	136.1	136.1	136.1	136.1	136.1
Indianapolis Union	16.1	16.1	16.1	16.1	16.1	16.1	16.1	16.1	16.1	16.1
Kentucky & Indiana Terminal	0.4	0.4	0.4	0.4	0.4	0.4	0.4	0.4	0.4	0.4
Lake Erie & Western	443.6	443.6	443.6	443.6	443.6	443.6	443.6	443.6	443.6	443.6
Lake Shore & Mich. Southern	167.4	167.4	167.4	167.4	167.4	167.4	167.4	167.4	167.4	167.4
Elkhart & Western									12.9	12.9
Fort Wayne & Jackson	55.3	55.3	55.3	55.3	55.3	55.3	55.3	55.3	55.3	55.3
Indiana, Illinois & Iowa RR									82.0	82.0
Sturgis, Goshen & St. Louis	25.6	25.6	25.6	25.6	25.6	25.6	25.6	25.6	25.6	25.6
Louisville & Nashville										
South East & St. Louis	28.6	28.6	28.6	28.6	28.6	28.6	28.6	28.6	28.6	28.6
Louisv., Evansv. & St. L. Consol.	208.5	208.5	208.5	210.9	210.9	210.9	210.9	210.9	210.9	214.6
Louisville, New Albany & Chi.	490.6	490.6	490.6	490.6	490.6	490.6	490.6			
Orleans,W.Baden&Fr.Lick Sprs	17.7	17.7	17.7	17.7	17.7	17.7	17.7			
Louisv., New Alb. & Corydon	7.7	7.7	7.7	7.7	7.7	7.7	7.7	7.7	7.7	7.7
Michigan Central	42.5	42.5	42.5	42.5	42.5	42.5	42.5	42.5	42.5	42.5
Joliet & Northern Indiana	15.7	15.7	15.7	15.7	15.7	15.7	15.7	15.7	15.7	15.7
Michigan Air Line	5.9	5.9	5.9	5.9	5.9	5.9	5.9	5.9	5.9	5.9
Midland Ry	77.1									
New York, Chicago & St. Louis	150.7	150.7	150.7	150.7	150.7	150.7	150.7	150.7	150.7	150.7
Ohio & Mississippi	233.5	233.5	233.5							
Pennsylvania										
Chicago, Indiana & Eastern						8.5	8.5	8.5	20.4	26.4
Grand Rapids & Indiana	53.1	53.1	53.1	53.1	53.1	53.1	53.1	53.1	53.1	53.1
Cinci., Rich. & Ft. Wayne	85.9	85.9	85.9	85.9	85.9	85.9	85.9	85.9	85.9	85.9
Pittsburgh, Cinci., Chi. & St. L.	641.9	641.9	641.9	641.9	639.6	639.6	639.6	639.6	639.6	639.6
Pittsburgh, Ft. Wayne & Chi.	152.9	152.9	152.9	152.9	152.9	152.9	152.9	152.9	152.9	152.9
Peoria, Decatur & Evansville	37.4	37.4	37.4	37.4	37.4	37.4	37.4	37.4	37.4	37.4
Pere Marquette RR										33.0
St. Joseph, S. Bend & Southern										14.3
St. Louis, Indpls. & Eastern	31.0	31.0	31.0	31.0	31.0	31.0	31.0	31.0	31.0	
Southern Indiana								101.8	101.8	101.8
Terre Haute & Indianapolis	87.8	87.8	87.8	87.8	87.8	87.8	87.8	87.8	87.8	87.8
Indiana & Lake Michigan	14.3	14.3	14.3	14.3	14.3	14.3	14.3	14.3	14.3	
Terre Haute & Logansport	158.0	158.0	158.0	158.0	158.0	158.0	158.0	158.0	158.0	158.0
Evansville & Terre Haute	17.1	17.1	17.1	17.1	17.1	17.1	17.1	17.1	17.1	17.1
Toledo, St. Louis & Kansas City	171.0	171.0	171.0	171.0	171.0	171.0	171.0	171.0	171.0	171.0

RAILROADS continued	1890	1891	1892	1893	1894	1895	1896	1897	1898	1899
Wabash RR	172.2	172.2	316.3	316.3	316.3	316.3	316.3	316.3	316.3	324.5
Attica, Covington & Southern	14.8	14.8	14.8	14.8	14.8	14.8	14.8	14.8	14.8	14.8
Eel River	92.5	92.5	92.5	92.5	92.5	92.5	92.5	92.5	92.5	92.5
RAILROAD YEAR TOTAL	5960.7	6201.1	6174.4	6219.6	6251.0	6283.5	6298.0	6299.0	6329.5	6370.3
RAILROAD YEAR CHANGE	321.5	240.4	-26.7	45.2	31.4	32.5	14.5	1.0	30.5	40.8

RAILROADS	1900	1901	1902	1903	1904	1905	1906	1907	1908	1909
Baltimore & Ohio	390.6	387.6	387.6	387.6	387.6	387.6	387.6	387.6	387.6	387.6
Bedford & Wallner								2.8	2.8	2.8
Bedford Belt	4.8	4.8	4.8	4.8	4.8	4.8	4.8	4.8	4.8	4.8
Bedford Stone		3.0	3.0	3.0	3.0	3.0	3.0	3.0	3.0	3.0
Cairo, Vincennes & Chicago	8.6	8.6	8.6	8.6	8.6	8.6				
Central Indiana				117.6	117.6	117.6	117.6	117.6	117.6	117.6
Chicago & Eastern Illinois RR	375.0	376.8	376.8	383.7	383.7	383.7	383.7	383.7	383.7	383.7
Terre Haute & Indianapolis	11.5	11.5	11.5	11.5	11.5					
Vandalia							11.5	11.5	11.5	11.5	11.5
Chicago & South Eastern	112.4	117.6	117.6							
Ft. Wayne, Terre Haute & S.L.	5.2									
Chicago & Wabash Valley	20.4	22.0	26.0	30.4	30.4	30.4	35.2	35.2	35.2	35.2
Chicago, Cincinnati & Louisville					195.0					
Chicago, Indianapolis & Louisv.	508.3	508.3	508.3	508.3	515.8	515.8	515.8	515.8	515.8	515.8
Indiana Stone	8.6	8.6	8.6	8.6	8.6	8.6	8.6	8.6	8.6	8.6
Indianapolis & Louisville								59.5	59.5	59.5
Chicago Junction										
Chicago, Hammond & West'n	3.1	3.1	3.1	3.1	3.1	3.1	3.1			
East Chicago Belt	3.5	3.5	3.5	3.5	3.5	3.5	3.5			
Chicago, Lake Shore & Eastern	7.9									
Chicago Terminal Transfer	9.7	9.7	9.7	9.7	9.7	9.7	9.7	9.7	9.7	9.7
Cincinnati, Bluffton & Chicago				19.0	29.0	29.0	29.0	29.0	52.0	52.0
Cincinnati, Hamilton & Dayton										
Cincinnati, Findl. & Ft. Wayne				18.0	18.0	18.0	18.0	18.0	18.0	18.0
Cincinnati, Hamilton & Indpls.	78.6	78.6								
Cincinnati, Indpls. & Western			154.9	154.9	154.9	154.9	154.9	154.9	154.9	154.9
Findlay, Ft. Wayne & Western		18.0	18.0							
Pere Marquette						33.0	33.0	51.7	51.7	51.7
Chicago, Cincinnati & Louisv.						221.0	221.0	227.6	227.6	227.6
Pere Marquette of Indiana						18.7	18.7			
CH&D-CCC&SL										
Dayton & Union	0.2	0.2	0.2	0.2	0.2	0.2	0.2	0.2	0.2	0.2
Cincinnati, Richmond & Muncie		58.1	195.0	195.0						
Cleve., Cinci., Chgo. & St. Lou,	500.2	500.2	500.2	500.2	497.8	496.3	496.3	496.3	496.3	496.3
Cairo, Vincennes & Chicago								8.6	8.6	8.6
Cinci. & So. Ohio River	3.7	3.7	3.7	3.7	3.7	3.7	3.7	3.7	3.7	3.7
Cinci., Wabash & Michigan	169.3	169.3	169.3	169.3	169.3	169.3	169.3	169.3	169.3	169.3
Columbus, Hope & Greensb'g	24.4	24.4	24.4	24.4	24.4	24.4	24.4	24.4	24.4	24.4
Louisv. & Jeffersonville Bridge	0.7	0.7	0.7	0.7	0.7	0.7	0.7	0.7	0.7	0.7
Peoria & Eastern	78.9	78.9	78.9	78.9	78.9	78.9	78.9	78.9	78.9	78.9
White Walter Valley	63.0	63.0	63.0	63.0	63.0	63.0	63.0	63.0	63.0	63.0

RAILROADS continued	1900	1901	1902	1903	1904	1905	1906	1907	1908	1909
Elgin, Joliet & Eastern	43.7	43.7	43.7	43.7	43.7	43.7	44.5	44.5	44.5	44.5
Chicago, Lake Shore & Eastern		7.9	7.9	7.9	7.9	7.9	11.3	11.3	11.3	11.3
Erie										
Chicago & Erie	161.0	161.0	161.0	161.0	161.0	161.0	161.0	161.0	161.0	161.0
Evansville & Terre Haute	152.8	152.8	152.8	152.8	152.8	152.8	152.8	152.8	152.8	152.8
Evansville Belt	4.0	4.0	4.0	4.0	4.0	4.0	4.0	4.0	4.0	4.0
Ferdinand										6.4
Findlay, Ft. Wayne & Western	18.0									
Grand Trunk Western Ry	80.5	80.5	80.5	80.5	80.5	80.5	80.5	80.5	80.5	80.5
Henderson Bridge Co.	9.9	9.9	9.9	9.9	9.9	9.9				
Illinois & Indiana	31.0	31.0	31.0	31.0	31.0					
Illinois Central	37.4	37.4	37.4	37.4	37.4	68.4	68.4	68.4	68.4	68.4
Indianapolis Southern						89.2	89.2	89.2	89.2	89.2
Rantoul	8.4	8.4	8.4	8.4	8.4	8.4	8.4	8.4	8.4	8.4
Indiana Harbor					4.9	4.9				
Indiana Harbor Belt								13.2	13.2	13.2
indianapolis & Vincennes	136.1	136.1	136.1	136.1	136.1					
Indpls., Decatur & Westerm	76.3	76.3								
Indianapolis Union	16.1	16.1	16.1	16.1	16.1	16.1	16.1	16.1	16.1	16.1
Kentucky & Indiana Bridge	0.4	0.4	0.4	0.4	0.4	0.4	0.4	0.4	0.4	0.4
Lake Shore & Mich. Southern	167.4	167.4	167.4	167.4	167.4	167.4	167.4	167.4	167.4	167.4
Chicago, Indiana & Southern				4.9	4.9	4.9	184.7	184.7	184.7	184.7
Elkhart & Western	12.9	12.9	12.9	12.9	12.9	12.9	12.9	12.9	12.9	12.9
Fort Wayne & Jackson	55.3	55.3	55.3	55.3	55.3	55.3	55.3	55.3	55.3	55.3
Indiana, Illinois & Iowa	82.0	82.0	82.0	82.0	82.0	83.9				
St.Joseph, S.Bend & Southern	14.3	14.3	14.3	14.3	14.3					
Lake Erie & Western	443.6	443.6	443.6	443.6	443.6	443.6	443.6	443.6	443.6	443.6
Sturgis, Goshen & St. Louis	25.6	25.6	25.6	25.6	25.6	25.6	25.6	25.6	25.6	25.6
Logansport & Toledo		92.5	92.5	92.5	92.5					
Louisville & Nashville							9.9	9.9	9.9	9.9
South East & St. Louis	28.6	28.6	28.6	28.6	28.6	28.6	28.6	28.6	28.6	28.6
Louisv., New Albany & Corydon	7.7	7.7	7.7	7.7	7.7	7.7	7.7	7.7	7.7	7.7
Michigan Central	42.5	42.5	42.5	42.5	42.5	43.8	43.8	43.8	43.8	43.8
Joliet & Northern Indiana	15.7	15.7	15.7	15.7	15.7	15.7	15.7	15.7	15.7	15.7
Michigan Air Line	5.9	5.9	5.9	5.9	5.9	5.9	5.9	5.9	5.9	5.9
St.Joseph, S.Bend & Southern						14.3	14.3	14.3	14.3	14.3
New Jersey, Indiana & Illinois						11.6	11.6	11.6	11.6	11.6
New York, Chicago & St. Louis	150.7	150.7	150.7	150.7	150.7	150.7	150.7	150.7	150.7	150.7
Pennsylvania										
Grand Rapids & Indiana	53.1	53.1	53.1	53.1	53.1	53.1	53.1	53.1	53.1	53.1
Cinci., Rich. & Ft. Wayne	85.9	85.9	85.9	85.9	85.9	85.9	85.9	85.9	85.9	85.9
Pittsburgh, Cinci, Chi., & St. L.	639.6	639.6	639.6	639.6	639.6	639.6	639.6	639.6	639.6	639.6
Pittsburgh, Ft. Wayne & Chi.	152.9	152.9	152.9	152.9	152.9	152.9	152.9	152.9	152.9	152.9
Chicago, Indiana & Eastern	41.1	41.1	41.1	41.1	41.1	41.1	41.1	41.1	41.1	41.1
Vandalia						477.1	472.3	472.3	472.3	472.3
Evansville & Terre Haute						17.1	17.1	17.1	17.1	17.1
Pere Marquette RR	33.0	33.0	33.0	33.0	33.0					
Chicago, Cincinnati & Louisv.					221.0					
Pere Marquette of Indiana				18.7	18.7					

RAILROADS continued	1900	1901	1902	1903	1904	1905	1906	1907	1908	1909
Southern Indiana	136.2	136.2	136.2	170.3	170.3	226.5	226.5	226.5	226.5	226.5
Southern Ry of Indiana	214.6	214.6	214.6	214.6	214.6	214.6	214.6	239.4	239.4	239.4
Syracuse & Milford								5.0	5.0	5.0
Terre Haute & Indianapois	87.8	90.5	90.5	90.5	90.5					
Terre Haute & Logansport	158.0	158.0	158.0	158.0	158.0					
Evansville & Terre Haute	17.1	17.1	17.1	17.1	17.1					
Toledo, Cincinnati & St. Louis	171.0	171.0	171.0	171.0	171.0	171.0	171.0	171.0	171.0	171.0
Wabash RR	324.5	324.5	341.9	341.9	341.9	356.7	356.7	356.7	356.7	356.7
Attica, Covington & Southern	14.8	14.8	14.8	14.8	14.8					
Eel River	92.5									
RAILROAD YEAR TOTAL	6438.5	6502.7	6661.0	6753.9	6990.0	6948.8	7048.9	7154.2	7177.2	7183.6
RAILROAD YEAR CHANGE	68.2	64.2	158.3	92.9	236.1	-41.2	100.1	105.3	23.0	6.4

RAILROADS	1910	1911	1912	1913	1914	1915	1916	1917	1918	1919
Baltimore & Ohio	387.6	387.6	387.6	387.6	387.6	387.6	387.6	387.6	387.6	387.6
Baltimore & Ohio Chgo. Tm.	9.7	9.7	9.7	9.7	9.7	9.7	9.7	9.7	9.7	9.7
Bedford & Wallner	2.8	2.8	2.8	2.8	2.8	2.8	2.8	2.8	2.8	2.8
Bedford Stone	3.0	3.0	3.0	3.0	3.0	3.0	3.0	3.0		
Central Indiana	117.6	117.6	117.6	117.6	117.6	117.6	117.6	117.6	117.6	117.6
Chesapeake & Ohio Chesapeake & Ohio of Indiana	227.6	227.6	227.6	227.6	227.6	227.6	227.6	227.6	227.6	227.6
Chicago & Eastern Illinois RR	373.0	538.5	538.5	538.5	538.5	538.5	538.5	536.9	536.9	536.5
Vandalia	11.5	11.5	11.5	11.5	11.5	11.5				
Chicago & Wabash Valley	31.2	31.2	36.0	36.0						
Chicago, Indianapolis & Louisv.	515.8	515.8	519.8	560.8	519.8	519.8	623.9	623.9	623.9	623.9
Chicago & Wabash Valley					36.0	36.0				
Indiana Stone	8.6	8.6	8.6	8.6	8.6	8.6				
Indianapolis & Louisville	59.5	59.5	59.5	59.5	59.5	59.5				
Chicago, Terre Haute & SE	229.4	229.4	229.4	242.7	242.7	238.7	239.7	239.7	239.7	239.7
Cincinnati, Bluffton & Chicago	52.0	52.0	52.0	52.0	52.0	52.0	52.0			
Cincinnati, Hamilton & Dayton										
Cincinnati, Find. & Ft. Wayne	18.0	18.0	18.0	18.0	18.0	18.0	18.0	18.0	18.0	
Cincinnati, Indpls. & Western	154.9	154.9	154.9	154.9	154.9	154.9	154.9	154.9	154.9	154.9
CH&D-CCC&SL										
Dayton & Union	0.2	0.2	0.2	0.2	0.2	0.2	0.2	0.2	0.2	0.2
Cleve., Cinci., Chgo. & St. Lou,	496.3	496.3	496.3	533.1	533.1	769.1	769.1	769.1	769.1	769.1
Cairo, Vincennes & Chicago	8.6	8.6	8.6							
Cinci. & So. Ohio River	3.7	3.7	3.7	3.7	3.7					
Cinci., Wabash & Michigan	169.3	169.3	169.3	169.3	169.3					
Columbus, Hope & Greensb.	24.4	24.4	24.4	24.4	24.4	24.4	24.4	24.4	24.4	24.4
Evansville, Mt. Carmel & No.		28.2	28.2							
Louisv. & Jeffersonville Bridge	0.7	0.7	0.7	0.7	0.7	0.7	0.7	0.7	0.7	0.7
Peoria & Eastern	78.9	78.9	78.9	78.9	78.9	78.9	78.9	78.9	78.9	78.9
White Water Valley	63.0	63.0	63.0	63.0	63.0					
Elgin, Joliet & Eastern	44.5	44.5	44.5	44.5	44.5	44.5	44.5	44.5	44.5	44.5
Chicago, Lake Shore & Eastern	11.3	11.3	11.3	11.3	11.3	11.3	11.3	11.3	11.3	11.3
Erie										
Chicago & Erie	161.0	161.0	161.0	161.0	161.0	161.0	161.0	161.0	161.0	161.0

RAILROADS continued	1910	1911	1912	1913	1914	1915	1916	1917	1918	1919
Evansville & Terre Haute	152.8									
Evansville Belt	4.0									
Ferdinand	6.4	6.4	6.4	6.4	6.4	6.4	6.4	6.4	6.4	6.4
Grand Trunk Western Ry	80.5	80.5	80.5	80.5	80.5	80.5	80.5	80.5	80.5	80.5
Illinois Central	68.4	157.6	157.6	157.6	157.6	157.6	157.6	157.6	157.6	157.6
Bloomington Southern					8.2	8.2	8.2	8.2	8.2	8.2
Indianapolis Southern	89.2									
Rantoul	8.4	8.4	8.4	8.4	8.4	8.4	8.4	8.4	8.4	8.4
Indiana Harbor Belt	29.4	29.4	29.4	29.4	29.4	29.4	29.4	29.4	29.4	29.4
Indianapolis Union	16.1	16.1	16.1	16.1	16.1	16.1	16.1	16.1	16.1	16.1
Kentucky & Indiana Terminal	0.4	0.4	0.4	0.4	0.4	0.4	0.4	0.4	0.4	0.4
Lake Shore & Mich. Southern	167.4	167.4	167.4	167.4	167.4					
Chicago, Indiana & Southern	184.7	184.7	184.7	184.7	184.7					
Elkhart & Western	12.9	12.9	12.9	12.9	12.9					
Fort Wayne & Jackson	55.3	55.3	55.3	55.3	55.3					
Lake Erie & Western	443.6	443.6	443.6	443.6	443.6					
Sturgis, Goshen & St. Louis	25.6	25.6	25.6	25.6	25.6					
Louisville & Nashville	9.9	9.9	9.9	9.9	9.9	9.9	9.9	9.9	9.9	9.9
South East & St. Louis	28.6	28.6	28.6	28.6	28.6	28.6	28.6	28.6	28.6	28.6
Louisv., New Alb. & Corydon	7.7	7.7	7.7	7.7	7.7	7.7	7.7	7.7	7.7	7.7
Michigan Central	42.5	42.5	42.5	42.5	42.5	42.5	49.7	49.7	49.7	49.7
Joliet & Northern Indiana	15.7	15.7	15.7	15.7	15.7	15.7	15.7	15.7	15.7	15.7
Michigan Air Line	7.2	7.2	7.2	7.2	7.2	7.2				
St.Joseph, S.Bend & Southern	14.3	14.3	14.3	14.3	14.3	14.3	14.3	14.3	14.3	14.3
New Jersey, Indiana & Illinois	11.6	11.6	11.6	11.6	11.6	11.6	11.6	11.6	11.6	11.6
New York Central						390.6	390.6	390.6	390.6	390.6
Fort Wayne & Jackson						55.3	55.3	55.3	55.3	55.3
Lake Erie & Western						443.6	443.6	443.6	443.6	443.6
New York, Chicago & St. Louis	150.7	150.7	150.7	150.7	150.7	150.7	150.7	150.7	150.7	150.7
Pennsylvania										
Grand Rapids & Indiana	53.1	53.1	53.1	53.1	53.1	53.1	53.1	53.1	53.1	53.1
Cinci., Rich. & Ft. Wayne	85.9	85.9	85.9	85.9	85.9	85.9	85.9	85.9	85.9	85.9
Indianapolis & Frankfort									41.2	41.2
Pittsburgh, Cinci, Chi., & St. L.	638.2	638.2	638.2	638.2	638.2	638.2	638.2	1159.3	1168.2	1168.2
Chicago & Eastern Illinois								17.1	17.1	17.1
Pittsburgh, Ft. Wayne & Chi.	152.9	152.9	152.9	152.9	152.9	152.9	152.9	152.9	152.9	152.9
Chicago, Indiana & Eastern	41.1	41.1	41.1	41.1	41.1	41.1	41.1			
Vandalia	477.9	484.6	484.6	484.6	484.6	484.6	488.6			
Chicago & Eastern Illinois		17.1	17.1	17.1	17.1	17.1	17.1			
Evansville & Terre Haute	17.1									
Pere Marquette RR	51.7	51.7	51.7	51.7	51.7	51.7	51.7			
Pere Marquette Ry								51.7	51.7	51.7
Southern Ry of Indiana	239.4	239.4	239.4	239.4	239.4	239.4	239.4	239.4	239.4	239.4
Syracuse & Milford	6.8	6.8	6.8	6.8	6.8	6.8	6.8	6.8	6.8	6.8
Toledo, St. Louis & Western	171.0	171.0	171.0	171.0	171.0	171.0	171.0	171.0	171.0	171.0
Wabash RR	356.7	356.7	356.7	356.7	356.7					
Wabash Ry						356.7	356.7	356.7	356.7	356.7

RAILROADS continued	1910	1911	1912	1913	1914	1915	1916	1917	1918	1919
RAILROAD YEAR TOTAL	7189.2	7232.8	7241.6	7295.9	7263.1	7259.1	7252.6	7190.4	7237.5	7219.1
RAILROAD YEAR CHANGE	5.6	43.6	8.8	54.3	-32.8	-4.0	-6.5	-62.2	47.1	-18.4

RAILROADS	1920	1921	1922	1923	1924	1925	1926	1927	1928	1929
Algers, Winslow & Western								10.1	10.1	10.1
Baltimore & Ohio	387.6	387.6	412.7	412.7	401.9	401.9	401.9	556.8	556.8	556.8
Baltimore & Ohio Chgo. Tm.	9.7	9.7	9.7	9.7	9.7	9.7	9.7	9.7	9.7	9.7
B&O-CCC&SL										
Dayton & Union								0.2	0.2	0.2
Bedford & Wallner	2.8	2.8	2.8	2.8	2.8	2.8	2.8			
Central Indiana	117.6	117.6	117.6	117.6	117.6	117.6	117.6	117.6	64.0	52.3
Chesapeake & Ohio										
Chesapeake & Ohio of Ind.	227.6	227.6	227.6	227.6	227.6	227.6	227.6	227.6	227.6	227.6
Chicago & Eastern Illinois Ry	411.5	409.7	244.0	244.0	244.0	244.0	244.0	244.0	244.0	244.0
Chicago, Attica & Southern			140.6	140.6	140.6	140.6	140.6	140.6	140.6	140.6
Chicago, Indianapolis & Louisv.	623.9	623.9	623.9	623.9	623.9	623.9	623.9	623.9	623.9	623.9
Chicago, Milwaukee & St. Paul										
Chicago, Terre Haute & SE		239.7	239.7	239.7	239.7	239.7	239.7	239.7		
Chicago, Milw. St. Paul & Pac.										
Chicago, Terre Haute & SE									239.7	239.7
Chicago, Terre Haute & SE	239.7									
Cincinnati, Hamilton & Dayton										
Cincinnati, Indpls. & Western	154.9	154.9	154.9	154.9	154.9	154.9	154.9			
CH&D-CCC&SL										
Dayton & Union	0.2	0.2	0.2	0.2	0.2	0.2	0.2			
Cleve., Cinci., Chgo. & St. Lou,	769.1	769.1	769.1	769.1	769.1	769.1	769.1	769.1	769.1	769.1
Columbus, Hope & Greensbg.	24.4	24.4	24.4	24.4	24.4	24.4	24.4	24.4	24.4	24.4
Evansv. Indpls. & Terre Haute	134.0	134.0	134.0	134.0	140.7	140.7	140.7	146.5	158.6	157.8
Louisv. & Jeffersonville Bridge	0.7	0.7	0.7	0.7	0.7	0.7	0.7	0.7	0.7	0.7
Peoria & Eastern	78.9	78.9	78.9	78.9	78.9	78.9	78.9	78.9	78.9	78.9
Elgin, Joliet & Eastern	44.5	44.5	44.5	44.5	44.5	44.5	44.5	44.5	44.5	44.5
Chicago, Lake Shore & Eastern	11.3	11.3	11.3	11.3	11.3	11.3	11.3	11.3	11.3	11.3
Erie										
Chicago & Erie	161.0	161.0	161.0	161.0	161.0	161.0	161.0	161.0	159.2	159.2
Ferdinand	6.4	6.4	6.4	6.4	6.4	6.4	6.4	6.4	6.4	6.4
Grand Trunk Western RR									80.5	79.2
Grand Trunk Western Ry	80.5	80.5	80.5	80.5	80.5	80.5	80.5	80.5		
Illinois Central	157.6	157.6	157.6	157.6	157.6	157.6	157.6	157.6	157.6	157.6
Bloomington Southern	8.2	8.2	8.2	8.2	8.2	8.2	8.2	8.2	8.2	8.2
Rantoul	8.4	8.4	8.4	8.4	8.4	8.4	8.4	8.4	8.4	8.4
Indiana Harbor Belt	29.4	29.4	29.4	29.4	29.4	29.4	29.4	29.4	29.4	29.4
Indianapolis Union	16.1	16.1	16.1	16.1	16.1	16.1	16.1	16.1	16.1	16.1
Kentucky & Indiana Terminal	0.4	0.4	0.4	0.4	0.4	0.4	0.4	0.4	0.4	0.4
Louisville & Nashville	9.9	9.9	9.9	9.9	9.9	9.9	9.9	9.9	9.9	9.9
South East & St. Louis	28.6	28.6	28.6	28.6	28.6	28.6	28.6	28.6	28.6	28.6
Louisv., New Alb. & Corydon	7.7	7.7	7.7	7.7	7.7	7.7	7.7	7.7	7.7	7.7
Michigan Central	49.7	49.7	49.7	49.7	49.7	49.7	49.7	49.7	49.7	49.7
Joliet & Northern Indiana	15.7	15.7	15.7	15.7	15.7	15.7	15.7	15.7	15.7	15.7
St.Joseph, S.Bend & Southern	14.3	14.3	14.3	14.3	14.3	14.3	14.3	14.3	14.3	14.3

RAILROADS continued	1920	1921	1922	1923	1924	1925	1926	1927	1928	1929
New Jersey, Indiana & Illinois	11.6	11.6	11.6	11.6	11.6	11.6				
New York Central	390.6	390.6	390.6	390.6	390.6	390.6	390.6	390.6	390.6	390.6
Fort Wayne & Jackson	55.3	55.3	55.3	55.3	55.3	55.3	55.3	55.3	55.3	55.3
Lake Erie & Western	445.8	445.8								
New York, Chicago & St. Louis	150.7	150.7	765.3	765.3	765.3	765.3	765.3	765.3	765.3	765.3
Pennsylvania										
Grand Rapids & Indiana	53.1	53.1	53.1	53.1	53.1	53.1	53.1	53.1	53.1	53.1
Cinci., Rich. & Ft. Wayne	85.9									
Indianapolis & Frankfort	41.2	41.2	41.2	41.2	41.2	41.2	41.2	41.2	41.2	41.2
Pittsburgh, Cinci., Chi. & St. L.	1168.2	1254.1	1256.1	1257.7	1274.8	1274.8	1274.8	1274.8	1274.8	1274.8
Chicago & Eastern Illinois	17.1	17.1	17.1	17.1						
Pittsburgh, Ft. Wayne & Chi.	152.9	152.9	152.9	152.9	152.9	152.9	152.9	152.9	152.9	152.9
Pere Marquette Ry	51.7	51.7	51.7	51.7	51.7	51.7	51.7	51.7	51.7	51.7
Southern Ry of Indiana	239.4	239.4	239.4	239.4	239.4	239.4	239.4	239.4	239.4	239.4
Syracuse & Milford	6.8	6.8	6.8							
Toledo, Cincinnati & St. Louis	171.0	171.0								
Twin Branch								1.7	1.7	1.7
Wabash Ry	356.7	356.7	356.7	356.7	356.7	356.7	356.7	356.7	356.7	356.7
New Jersey, Indiana & Illinois							11.6	11.6	11.6	11.6
RAILROAD YEAR TOTAL	7230.3	7228.5	7228.3	7223.1	7219.0	7219.0	7219.0	7233.8	7190.5	7176.7
RAILROAD YEAR CHANGE	11.2	-1.8	-0.2	-5.2	-4.1	0.0	0.0	14.8	-43.3	-13.8

RAILROADS	1930	1931	1932	1933	1934	1935	1936	1937	1938	1939
Algers, Winslow & Western	10.1	10.1	10.1	10.1	10.1	10.1	10.1	10.1	10.1	10.1
Baltimore & Ohio	556.8	556.8	556.8	556.8	556.8	556.8	556.8	557.0	557.0	557.0
Baltimore & Ohio Chgo. T'm.	9.7	9.7	9.7	9.7	9.7	9.7	9.7	9.7	9.7	9.7
Central Indiana	52.3	52.3	52.3	52.3	52.3	52.3	52.3	52.3	52.3	52.3
Chesapeake & Ohio					227.6	227.6	227.6	227.6	227.6	227.6
Chesapeake & Ohio of Ind.	227.6	227.6	227.6	227.6						
Pere Marquette Ry	51.7	51.7	51.7	51.7	51.7	51.7	51.7	51.7	51.7	51.7
Chicago & Eastern Illinois Ry	243.0	241.0	241.0	241.0	241.0	241.0	241.0	237.7	237.7	237.7
Chicago, Attica & Southern	140.6	140.6	140.6	140.6	140.6	140.6	140.6	140.6	140.6	140.6
Chicago, Indianapolis & Louisv.	623.9	623.9	623.9	623.9	623.9	554.1	554.1	554.1	554.1	554.1
Chicago, Milw. St. Paul & Pac.										
Chicago, Terre Haute & SE	239.7	239.7	239.7	239.7	239.7	236.5	236.5	236.5	236.5	236.5
Elgin, Joliet & Eastern	44.5	44.5	44.5	40.3	40.3	40.3	40.3	40.3	51.6	51.6
Chicago, Lake Shore & Eastern	11.3	11.3	11.3	11.3	11.3	11.3	11.3	11.3		
Erie										
Chicago & Erie	159.2	159.2	159.2	159.2	159.2	159.2	159.2	159.2	159.2	159.2
Ferdinand	6.4	6.4	6.4	6.4	6.4	6.4	6.4	6.4	6.4	6.4
Grand Trunk Western RR	79.2	79.2	79.2	79.2	79.2	79.2	79.2	79.2	79.2	79.2
Illinois Central	157.6	157.6	157.6	157.6	157.6	157.6	157.6	157.6	157.6	157.6
Bloomington Southern	8.2	8.2	8.2	8.2	8.2	8.2	8.2	8.2	8.2	8.2
Rantoul	8.4	8.4	8.4	8.4	8.4	8.4				
Indiana Harbor Belt	29.4	29.4	29.4	29.4	29.4	29.4	29.4	29.4	29.4	29.4
Indianapolis Union	16.1	16.1	16.1	16.1	16.1	16.1	16.1	16.1	16.1	16.1
Kentucky & Indiana Terminal	0.4	0.4	0.4	0.4	0.4	0.4	0.4	0.4	0.4	0.4
Louisville & Nashville	9.9	9.9	9.9	9.9	9.9	9.9	38.5	38.5	38.5	38.5

RAILROADS continued	1930	1931	1932	1933	1934	1935	1936	1937	1938	1939
South East & St. Louis	28.6	28.6	28.6	28.6	28.6	28.6				
Louisv., New Alb. & Corydon	7.7	7.7	7.7	7.7	7.7	7.7	7.7	7.7	7.7	7.7
New York Central	390.6	390.6	390.6	390.6	390.6	390.6	390.6	390.6	390.6	390.6
Cleve., Cinci., Chi. & St. Louis	769.1	755.8	755.8	755.8	755.8	755.8	755.8	755.8	755.8	755.8
Columbus, Hope & Greensb.	24.4	24.4	24.4	24.4	24.4	24.4	24.4	24.4	24.4	24.4
Evansville, Indpls. & Terre H.	157.8	157.8	157.8	157.8	157.8	157.8	151.1	151.1	151.1	151.1
Louisv. & Jeffersonville Br.	0.7	0.7	0.7	0.7	0.7	0.7	0.7	0.7	0.7	0.7
Peoria & Eastern	78.9	78.9	78.9	78.9	78.9	78.9	78.9	78.9	78.9	78.9
Fort Wayne & Jackson	55.3	55.3	55.3	55.3	55.3	55.3	55.3	55.3	55.3	55.3
Michigan Central	49.7	49.7	49.7	49.7	49.7	49.7	49.7	49.7	49.7	49.7
Joliet & Northern Indiana	15.7	15.7	15.7	15.7	15.7	15.7	15.7	15.7	15.7	15.7
St.Joseph, S.Bend & Southern	14.3	14.3	14.3	14.3	14.3	14.3	14.3	14.3	14.3	14.3
New York, Chicago & St. Louis	765.3	765.3	765.3	765.3	765.3	765.3	765.3	765.3	765.3	765.3
Pennsylvania										
Grand Rapids & Indiana	53.1	53.1	53.1	53.1	53.1	53.1	53.1	53.1	53.1	53.1
Indianapolis & Frankfort	41.2	41.2	41.2	41.2	41.2	41.2	41.2	41.2	41.2	41.2
Pittsburgh, Cinci., Chi. & St. L.	1274.8	1274.8	1274.8	1274.8	1248.8	1248.8	1248.8	1248.8	1248.8	1248.8
Pittsburgh, Ft. Wayne & Chi.	152.9	152.9	152.9	152.9	152.9	152.9	152.9	152.9	152.9	152.9
Southern Ry of Indiana	239.4	239.4	239.4	239.4	235.7	235.7	235.7	235.7	235.7	235.7
Southern Indiana										5.5
Twin Branch	1.7	1.7	1.7	1.7	1.7	1.7	1.7	1.7	1.7	1.7
Wabash Ry	356.7	356.7	341.9	341.9	341.9	341.9	341.9	341.9	341.9	341.9
New Jersey, Indiana & Illinois	11.6	11.6	11.6	11.6	11.6	11.6	11.6	11.6	11.6	11.6
RAILROAD YEAR TOTAL	7175.5	7160.2	7145.4	7141.2	7111.5	7038.5	7023.4	7020.3	7020.3	7025.8
RAILROAD YEAR CHANGE	-1.2	-15.3	-14.8	-4.2	-29.7	-73.0	-15.1	-3.1	0.0	5.5

RAILROADS	1940	1941	1942	1943	1944	1945	1946	1947	1948	1949
Algers, Winslow & Western	10.1	10.1	10.1	10.1	10.1	10.1	10.1	10.1	10.1	10.1
Baltimore & Ohio	557.0	557.0	557.0	557.0	557.0	557.0	557.0	557.0	557.0	557.0
Baltimore & Ohio Chgo. Tm.	9.7	9.7	9.7	9.7	9.7	9.7	9.7	9.7	9.7	9.7
Central Indiana	52.3	52.3	52.3	44.0	44.0	44.0	44.0	44.0	44.0	44.0
Chesapeake & Ohio	227.6	227.6	227.6	227.6	227.6	227.6	227.6	279.3	279.3	279.3
Pere Marquette Ry	51.7	51.7	51.7	51.7	51.7	51.7	51.7			
Chicago & Eastern Illinois RR	237.7	237.7	236.2	236.2	236.2	236.2	236.2	236.2	236.2	236.2
Chicago, Attica & Southern	140.6	140.6	140.6	65.7	65.7	65.7	0.0			
Chicago, Indianapolis & Louisv.	554.1	554.1	551.5	547.3	547.3	541.3	541.3	540.7	540.7	540.7
Chicago, Milw. St. Paul & Pac.									212.2	212.2
Chicago, Terre Haute & SE	231.3	231.3	221.5	212.2	212.2	212.2	212.2	212.2		
Elgin, Joliet & Eastern	51.6	51.6	51.6	51.6	51.6	51.6	51.6	51.6	51.6	51.6
Erie		159.2	159.2	159.2	159.2	159.2	159.2	159.2	159.2	159.2
Chicago & Erie	159.2									
Ferdinand	6.4	6.4	6.4	6.4	6.4	6.4	6.4	6.4	6.4	6.4
Grand Trunk Western RR	79.2	79.2	79.2	79.2	79.2	79.2	79.2	79.2	79.2	79.2
Illinois Central	157.6	157.6	157.6	157.6	157.6	157.6	157.6	157.6	157.6	157.6
Bloomington Southern	8.2	8.2	8.2	8.2	8.2	8.2	8.2	8.2	8.2	8.2
Indiana Harbor Belt	29.4	29.4	29.4	29.4	29.4	29.4	29.4	29.4	29.4	29.4
Indianapolis Union	16.1	16.1	16.1	16.1	16.1	16.1	16.1	16.1	16.1	16.1
Kentucky & Indiana Terminal	0.4	0.4	0.4	0.4	0.4	0.4	0.4	0.4	0.4	0.4

RAILROADS continued	1940	1941	1942	1943	1944	1945	1946	1947	1948	1949
Louisville & Nashville	38.5	38.5	38.5	38.5	38.5	38.5	38.5	38.5	38.5	38.5
Louisv., New Alb. & Corydon	7.7	7.7	7.7	7.7	7.7	7.7	7.7	7.7	7.7	7.7
New York Central	390.6	390.6	390.6	390.6	390.6	390.6	390.6	390.6	390.6	390.6
Cleve., Cinci., Chi. & St. Louis	755.8	755.8	717.7	717.7	717.7	717.7	717.7	717.7	717.7	717.7
Columbus, Hope & Greensb.	24.4	24.4	24.4	24.4	24.4	24.4	24.4	24.4	24.4	24.4
Evansville, Indpls. & Terre H.	151.1	151.1	151.1	151.1	151.1	151.1	151.1	151.1	151.1	151.1
Louisv. & Jeffersonville Br.	0.7	0.7	0.7	0.7	0.7	0.7	0.7	0.7	0.7	0.7
Peoria & Eastern	78.9	78.9	78.9	78.9	78.9	78.9	78.9	78.9	78.9	78.9
Fort Wayne & Jackson	55.3	55.3	55.3	55.3	55.3	55.3	55.3	55.3	55.3	55.3
Michigan Central	64.0	64.0	49.7	49.7	49.7	49.7	49.7	49.7	49.7	49.7
Joliet & Northern Indiana	15.7	15.7	15.7	15.7	15.7	15.7	15.7	15.7	15.7	15.7
St.Joseph, S.Bend & Southern	14.3	14.3								
New York, Chicago & St. Louis	765.3	765.3	765.3	765.3	765.3	765.3	765.3	765.3	765.3	765.3
Pennsylvania										
Grand Rapids & Indiana	53.1	53.1	53.1	53.1	53.1	53.1	53.1	53.1	53.1	53.1
Indianapolis & Frankfort	41.2	41.2	41.2	41.2	41.2	41.2	41.2	41.2	41.2	41.2
Pittsburgh, Cinci., Chi. & St. L.	1248.8	1252.8	1252.8	1252.8	1252.8	1252.8	1250.8	1250.8	1250.8	1250.8
Pittsburgh, Ft. Wayne & Chi.	152.9	152.9	152.9	152.9	152.9	152.9	152.9	152.9	152.9	152.9
Southern Ry					235.7	235.7	235.7	235.7	235.7	235.7
Southern Ry of Indiana	235.7	235.7	235.7	235.7						
Southern Indiana	5.5	5.5	5.5	5.5	5.5	5.5	5.5	5.5	5.5	5.5
Twin Branch	1.7	1.7	1.7	1.7	1.7	1.7	1.7	1.7	1.7	1.7
Wabash RR			341.9	341.9	341.9	337.3	337.3	337.3	337.3	337.3
New Jersey, Indiana & Illinois			11.6	11.6	11.6	11.6	11.6	11.6	11.6	11.6
Wabash Ry	341.9	341.9								
New Jersey, Indiana & Illinois	11.6	11.6								
RAILROAD YEAR TOTAL	7034.9	7038.9	6958.3	6861.6	6861.6	6851.0	6783.3	6782.7	6782.7	6782.7
RAILROAD YEAR CHANGE	9.1	4.0	-80.6	-96.7	0.0	-10.6	-67.7	-0.6	0.0	0.0

RAILROADS	1950	1951	1952	1953	1954	1955	1956	1957	1958	1959
Algers, Winslow & Western	20.0	20.0	20.0	20.0	20.0	20.0	20.0	20.0	20.0	20.0
Baltimore & Ohio	557.0	557.0	557.0	557.0	557.0	557.0	557.0	557.0	557.0	557.0
Baltimore & Ohio Chgo. Tm.	9.7	9.7	9.7	9.7	9.7	9.7	9.7	9.7	9.7	9.7
Central Indiana	44.0	44.0	44.0	44.0	44.0	44.0	44.0	44.0	44.0	44.0
Chesapeake & Ohio	279.3	279.3	279.3	279.3	279.3	279.3	279.3	279.3	279.3	279.3
Chicago & Eastern Illinois RR	234.4	234.4	234.4	234.4	234.4	230.9	230.9	230.9	230.9	230.9
Chicago, Indianapolis & Louisv.	531.8	531.8	531.8	531.8	531.8	516.9				
Chicago, Milw. St. Paul & Pac.	212.2	212.2	209.3	208.2	208.2	208.2	197.7	197.7	197.7	197.7
Elgin, Joliet & Eastern	51.6	51.6	51.6	51.6	51.6	51.6	51.6	51.6	51.6	51.6
Erie	159.2	159.2	159.2	159.2	159.2	159.2	159.2	159.2	159.2	159.2
Ferdinand	6.4	6.4	6.4	6.4	6.4	6.4	6.4	6.4	6.4	6.4
Grand Trunk Western RR	79.2	79.2	79.2	79.2	79.2	79.2	79.2	79.2	79.2	79.2
Illinois Central	157.6	157.6	157.6	157.6	157.6	157.6	157.6	157.6	157.6	157.6
Bloomington Southern	8.2	8.2	8.2	8.2	8.2	8.2	8.2	8.2	8.2	8.2
Indiana Harbor Belt	29.4	29.4	29.4	29.4	29.4	29.4	29.4	29.4	34.0	34.0
Indianapolis Union	16.1	16.1	16.1	16.1	16.1	16.1	16.1	16.1	16.1	16.1
Kentucky & Indiana Terminal	0.4	0.4	0.4	0.4	0.4	0.4	0.4	0.4	0.4	0.4
Louisville & Nashville	38.5	38.5	38.5	38.5	38.5	38.5	38.5	38.5	38.5	38.5

RAILROADS continued	1950	1951	1952	1953	1954	1955	1956	1957	1958	1959
Louisv., New Alb. & Corydon	7.7	7.7	7.7	7.7	7.7	7.7	7.7	7.7	7.7	7.7
Monon RR							516.9	516.9	516.9	516.9
New York Central	390.6	390.6	390.6	390.6	390.6	390.6	390.6	390.6	385.7	385.7
Cleve., Cinci., Chi. & St. Louis	717.7	717.7	717.7	717.7	717.7	717.7	717.7	717.7	717.7	717.7
Columbus, Hope & Greensb.	24.4	24.4	24.4	24.4	24.4	24.4	24.4	24.4	24.4	24.4
Evansville, Indpls. & Terre H.	148.1	148.1	148.1	148.1	143.8	143.8	143.8	143.8	143.8	143.8
Louisv. & Jeffersonville Br.	0.7	0.7	0.7	0.7	0.7	0.7	0.7	0.7	0.7	0.7
Peoria & Eastern	78.9	78.9	78.9	78.9	78.9	78.9	78.9	78.9	78.9	78.9
Fort Wayne & Jackson	55.3	55.3	55.3	55.3	55.3	55.3	55.3	55.3	55.3	55.3
Michigan Central	49.7	49.7	49.7	49.7	49.7	49.7	49.7	49.7	44.1	44.1
Joliet & Northern Indiana	15.7	15.7	15.7	15.7	15.7	15.7	15.7	15.7	15.7	15.7
New York, Chicago & St. Louis	765.3	765.3	765.3	761.8	761.8	761.8	761.8	761.8	761.8	761.8
Pennsylvania				53.1	53.1	53.1	53.1	53.1	53.1	53.1
Grand Rapids & Indiana	53.1	53.1	53.1							
Indianapolis & Frankfort	41.2	41.2	41.2	41.2	41.2	41.2	41.2	41.2	41.2	41.2
Philadelphia, Baltimore & Wash.								1225.4	1225.4	1225.4
Pittsburgh, Cinci., Chi. & St. L.	1250.8	1250.8	1250.8	1250.8	1239.5	1234.8	1228.3			
Pittsburgh, Ft. Wayne & Chi.	152.9	152.9	152.9	152.9	152.9	152.9	152.9	152.9	152.9	152.9
Southern Ry	235.7	235.7	235.7	235.7	235.7	235.7	235.7	231.8	231.8	231.8
Southern Indiana	5.5	5.5	5.5	5.5	5.5	5.5	5.5	5.5	5.5	5.5
Twin Branch	1.7	1.7	1.7	1.7	1.7	1.7	1.7	1.7	1.7	1.7
Wabash RR	337.3	337.3	337.3	337.3	337.3	337.3	337.3	337.3	337.3	337.3
New Jersey, Indiana & Illinois	11.6	11.6	11.6	11.6	11.6	11.6	11.6	11.6	11.6	11.6
Yankeetown Dock					22.0	22.0	22.0	22.0	22.0	22.0
RAILROAD YEAR TOTAL	6778.9	6778.9	6776.0	6771.4	6777.8	6754.7	6737.7	6730.9	6725.0	6725.0
RAILROAD YEAR CHANGE	-3.8	0.0	-2.9	-4.6	6.4	-23.1	-17.0	-6.8	-5.9	0.0

RAILROADS	1960	1961	1962	1963	1964	1965	1966	1967	1968	1969
Algers, Winslow & Western	20.0	20.0	20.0	20.0	20.0	20.0	20.0	20.0	20.0	20.0
Baltimore & Ohio	557.0	557.0	557.0							
Baltimore & Ohio Chgo. Tm.	9.7	9.7	9.7							
Central Indiana	44.0	44.0	44.0	44.0	44.0	44.0	44.0	44.0	44.0	44.0
Chesapeake & Ohio	279.3	279.3	279.3	279.3	279.3	279.3	279.3	279.3	279.3	279.3
Baltimore & Ohio				557.0	557.0	531.9	531.9	531.9	531.9	531.9
Baltimore & Ohio Chgo. Term.				9.7	9.7	9.7	9.7	9.7	9.7	9.7
Chicago & Eastern Illinois RR	230.9	230.9	230.9	230.9	230.9	228.2	228.2			
Chicago, Milw. St. Paul & Pac.	197.7	171.6	168.8	168.8	168.8	168.8	168.8	168.8	168.8	168.8
Elgin, Joliet & Eastern	51.6	51.6	51.6	51.6	51.6	51.6	51.6	51.6	51.6	51.6
Erie-Lackawanna	159.2	159.2	159.2	159.2	159.2	159.2	159.2	159.2	159.2	159.2
Ferdinand	6.4	6.4	6.4	6.4	6.4	6.4	6.4	6.4	6.4	6.4
Grand Trunk Western RR	79.2	79.2	79.2	79.2	79.2	79.2	79.2	79.2	79.2	79.2
Illinois Central	157.6	157.6	157.6	157.6	157.6	157.6	157.6	157.6	157.6	157.6
Bloomington Southern	8.2	8.2	8.2	8.2	8.2	8.2	8.2	8.2	8.2	8.2
Indiana Harbor Belt	34.0	34.0	34.0	34.0	34.0	34.0	34.0	34.0	34.0	34.0
Indianapolis Union	16.1	16.1	16.1	16.1	16.1	16.1	16.1	16.1	16.1	16.1
Kentucky & Indiana Terminal	0.4	0.4	0.4	0.4	0.4	0.4	0.4	0.4	0.4	0.4
(Louisv. & Jeffersonville Br.)		0.7	0.7	0.7	0.7	0.7	0.7	0.7	0.7	0.7
Louisville & Nashville	38.5	38.5	38.5	38.5	38.5	38.5	38.5	259.8	259.8	259.8

RAILROADS continued	1960	1961	1962	1963	1964	1965	1966	1967	1968	1969
Louisv., New Alb. & Corydon	7.7	7.7	7.7	7.7	7.7	7.7	7.7	7.7	7.7	7.7
Missouri Pacific								6.9	6.9	6.9
Monon RR	516.9	516.9	516.9	516.9	516.9	516.9	516.9	516.9	516.9	516.9
New York Central	377.0	377.0	377.0	377.0	377.0	377.0	377.0	377.0		
Cleve., Cinci., Chi. & St. Louis	717.7	710.0	710.0	710.0	710.0	710.0	710.0	710.0		
Columbus, Hope & Greensb.	24.4	24.4	24.4	24.4	24.4	24.4	24.4	24.4		
Evansville, Indpls. & Terre H.	143.8	143.8	143.8	143.8	143.8	143.8	143.8	143.8		
Louisv. & Jeffersonville Br.	0.7									
Peoria & Eastern	78.9	78.9	78.9	78.9	78.9	78.9	78.9	78.9		
Fort Wayne & Jackson	55.3	55.3	55.3	55.3	55.3	55.3	55.3	55.3		
Michigan Central	44.1	44.1	44.1	44.1	44.1	44.1	44.1	44.1		
Joliet & Northern Indiana	15.7	15.7	15.7	15.7	15.7	15.7	15.7	15.7		
New York, Chicago & St. Louis	761.8	761.8	761.8	761.8						
Norfolk & Western					761.8	761.8	761.8	761.8	761.8	761.8
New Jersey, Indiana & Illinois					11.6	11.6	11.6	11.6	11.6	11.6
Wabash RR					337.3	337.3	337.3	337.3	337.3	337.3
Penn Central									1657.2	1651.1
Cleve., Cinci., Chi. & St. Louis									701.4	701.4
Columbus, Hope & Greensb.									24.4	24.4
Evansville, Indpls. & Terre H.									143.8	137.1
Fort Wayne & Jackson									55.3	55.3
Michigan Central									44.1	44.1
Joliet & Northern Indiana									15.7	15.7
Peoria & Eastern									78.9	78.9
Pittsburgh, Ft. Wayne & Chi.									152.9	152.9
Pennsylvania	53.1	53.1	53.1	53.1	53.1	53.1	53.1	53.1		
Indianapolis & Frankfort	41.2	41.2	41.2	41.2	41.2	41.2	41.2	41.2		
Philadelphia, Balti. & Wash.	1225.4	1217.6	1204.6	1204.6	1204.6	1204.6	1204.6	1196.3		
Pittsburgh, Ft. Wayne & Chi.	152.9	152.9	152.9	152.9	152.9	152.9	152.9	152.9		
Southern Ry	231.8	231.8	231.8	231.8	231.8	231.8	231.8	231.8	231.8	231.8
Southern Indiana	5.5	5.5	5.5	5.5	5.5	5.5	5.5	5.5	5.5	5.5
Twin Branch	1.7	1.7	1.7	1.7	1.7	1.7	1.7	1.7	1.7	1.7
Wabash RR	337.3	337.3	337.3	337.3						
New Jersey, Indiana & Illinois	11.6	11.6	11.6	11.6						
Yankeetown Dock	22.0	22.0	22.0	22.0	22.0	22.0	22.0	22.0	22.0	22.0
RAILROAD YEAR TOTAL	6716.3	6674.7	6658.9	6658.9	6658.9	6631.1	6631.1	6622.8	6603.8	6591.0
RAILROAD YEAR CHANGE	-8.7	-41.6	-15.8	0.0	0.0	-27.8	0.0	-8.3	-19.0	-12.8

RAILROADS	1970	1971	1972	1973	1974	1975	1976	1977	1978	1979
Algers, Winslow & Western	20.0	20.0	20.0	20.0	20.0	20.0	20.0	20.0	20.0	20.0
Amtrak								18.0	18.0	18.0	18.0
Central Indiana	44.0	44.0	44.0	44.0	44.0	44.0				
Chesapeake & Ohio	279.3	279.3	279.3							
Baltimore & Ohio	531.9	531.9	531.9							
Baltimore & Ohio Chgo. Term.	9.7	9.7	9.7							
Chessie System										
Chesapeake & Ohio					279.3	279.3	279.3	279.3	279.3	279.3
Baltimore & Ohio					531.9	531.9	531.9	533.6	533.6	533.6

RAILROADS continued	1970	1971	1972	1973	1974	1975	1976	1977	1978	1979
Baltimore & Ohio Chicago Term.				9.7	9.7	9.7	9.7	9.7	9.7	9.7
Cicago & Indiana										
Erie-Lackawanna										159.2
Chicago, Milw. St. Paul & Pac.	168.8	168.8	168.8	168.8	168.8	168.8	168.8	168.8	131.4	131.4
Chicago South Shore & S. Bend	75.7	73.5	73.5	73.5	73.5	73.5	73.5	73.5	73.5	73.5
Conrail							1977.6	1973.8	1973.8	1953.7
Elgin, Joliet & Eastern	51.6	51.6	51.6	51.6	51.6	51.6	51.6	51.6	51.6	51.6
Erie-Lackawanna	159.2	159.2	159.2	159.2	159.2	159.2	159.2			
Erie Western										
Erie-Lackawanna								159.2	159.2	
Penn Central								28.4	28.4	
Ferdinand	6.4	6.4	6.4	6.4	6.4	6.4	6.4	6.4	6.4	6.4
French Lick, W. Baden & South.									15.3	15.3
Grand Trunk Western RR	79.2	79.2	79.2	79.2	79.2	79.2	79.2	79.2	79.2	79.2
Hillsdale County										
Penn Central							15.8	15.8	15.8	15.8
Illinois Central	157.6	157.6								
Bloomington Southern	8.2	8.2								
Illinois Central Gulf			157.6	157.6	157.6	157.6	151.3	151.3	151.3	151.3
Bloomington Southern			8.2	8.2	8.2	8.2	8.2	8.2	8.2	8.2
Indiana & Ohio										20.7
Indiana Eastern										
Penn Central										23.0
Indiana Harbor Belt	34.0	34.0	34.0	34.0	34.0	34.0	34.0	34.0	34.0	34.0
Indiana Interstate										
Penn Central									1.0	17.2
Indianapolis Union	16.1	16.1	16.1	16.1	16.1	16.1				
Kentucky & Indiana Terminal	0.4	0.4	0.4	0.4	0.4	0.4	0.4	0.4	0.4	0.4
(Louisv. & Jeffersonville Br.)	0.7	0.7	0.7	0.7	0.7	0.7	0.7	0.7	0.7	0.7
Louisville & Nashville	259.8	776.7	776.7	776.7	776.7	776.7	760.9	748.2	748.2	748.2
Louisv., New Alb. & Corydon	7.7	7.7	7.7	7.7	7.7	7.7	7.7	7.7	7.7	7.7
Madison RR										
City of Madison Port Auth.								25.8	25.8	25.8
Missouri Pacific	6.9	6.9	6.9							
Monon RR	516.9									
Norfolk & Western	1099.1	1099.1	1099.1	1099.8	1099.6	1099.6	1099.6	1099.6	1099.6	1123.5
New Jersey, Indiana & Illinois	11.6	11.6	11.6	11.6	11.6	11.6	11.6	11.6	11.6	11.6
Penn Central	1651.1	1651.1	1632.3	1549.9	1549.9	1532.6	121.4	37.4	37.4	3.0
Cleve., Cinci., Chi. & St. Louis	701.4	701.4	701.4	623.1	599.0	599.0	124.0	67.9	67.9	27.0
Columbus, Hope & Greensb.	24.4	24.4	24.4	24.4	24.4	24.4				
Evansville, Indpls. & Terre H.	137.1	137.1	137.1	137.1	137.1	137.1				
Fort Wayne & Jackson	55.3	55.3	55.3	25.1	25.1	25.1				
Michigan Central	44.1	44.1	44.1	44.1	44.1	42.0				
Joliet & Northern Indiana	15.7	15.7	15.7	15.7	15.7	15.7				
Peoria & Eastern	78.9	78.9	78.9	76.1	76.1	76.1				
Pittsburgh, Ft. Wayne & Chi.	152.9	152.9	152.9	152.9	152.9	152.9				
Southern Ry	231.8	231.8	231.8	231.8	231.8	231.8	231.8	231.8	216.5	216.5
Southern Indiana	5.5	5.5	5.5	5.5	5.5	5.5	5.5	5.5	5.5	5.5
Toledo, Peoria & Western							63.3	63.3	63.3	63.3

RAILROADS continued	1970	1971	1972	1973	1974	1975	1976	1977	1978	1979
Twin Branch	1.7	1.7	1.7	1.7	1.7	1.7				
Whitewater Valley										
Penn Central					24.1	17.9	17.9	17.9	17.9	17.9
Yankeetown Dock	22.0	22.0	22.0	22.0	22.0	22.0	22.0	22.0	22.0	22.0
RAILROAD YEAR TOTAL	6666.7	6664.5	6645.7	6445.8	6445.6	6420.0	6053.0	5950.6	5914.2	5874.2
RAILROAD YEAR CHANGE	75.7	-2.2	-18.8	-199.9	-0.2	-25.6	-367.0	-102.4	-36.4	-40.0

RAILROADS	1980	1981	1982	1983'	1984	1985	1986	1987	1988	1989
Algers, Winslow & Western	20.0	20.0	20.0	20.0	20.0	20.0	20.0	20.0	20.0	20.0
Amtrak	18.0	18.0	18.0	18.0	18.0	18.0	18.0	18.0	18.0	18.0
Benton Central									6.0	
Carthage, Knightstown & Shirley								20.5	5.0	5.0
Central Indiana & Western							9.3	9.3	9.3	9.3
Central RR of Indiana		63.5	63.5	63.5	63.5	63.5	63.5	63.5	63.5	63.5
Central RR of Indianapolis										
Norfolk Southern										86.9
Chicago, Milw. St. Paul & Pac.	104.8	104.8	104.8	104.8	100.0	100.0				
Chicago South Shore & S. Bend	73.5	73.5	73.5	73.5	73.5	73.5	73.5	73.5	73.5	73.5
Conrail	1949.1	1920.8	1640.1	1640.1	1571.8	1538.3	1535.1	1503.8	1503.8	1495.6
CSX Corp.										
Chesapeake & Ohio	279.3	279.3	249.7	249.7	249.7	249.7				
Baltimore & Ohiio	505.1	503.4	503.4	503.4	503.4	491.6				
Baltimore & Oh. Chgo. Tm.	9.7	9.7	9.7	9.7	9.7	9.7				
Port Authority of Auburn IN		1.7	1.7	1.7	1.7	1.7				
CSX Transportation							589.3	1293.4	1238.0	1125.4
Chesapeake & Ohio							249.7			
Baltimore & Ohiio							491.6			
Baltimore & Ohio Chgo. Term.							9.7	9.7	9.7	9.7
Port Authority of Auburn IN							1.7	1.7	1.7	1.7
Elgin, Joliet & Eastern	51.6	51.6	51.6	51.6	31.3	31.3	31.3	31.3	31.3	31.3
Ferdinand	6.4	6.4	6.4	6.4	6.4	6.4	6.4	6.4	6.4	6.4
French Lick, W. Baden & South.	15.3	15.3	15.3	15.3	15.3	15.3	15.3	15.3	15.3	15.3
Fulton County										
Erie-Lackawanna	15.4	15.4	15.4							
Grand Trunk Western RR	79.2	79.2	79.2	79.2	79.2	79.2	79.2	79.2	79.2	79.2
Hillsdale County										
Penn Central	15.8	15.8	15.8	15.8	15.8	15.8	18.8	18.8	18.8	18.8
Illinois Central									10.4	
Illinois Central Gulf	151.3	151.3	151.3	151.3	150.1	150.1	10.4	10.4	10.4	
Bloomington Southern	8.2	8.2	8.2	8.2	8.2	8.2	8.2	8.2		
Indian Creek	4.6	4.6	4.6	4.6	4.6	4.6	4.6	4.6	4.6	4.6
Indiana & Ohio	20.7	20.7	20.7	20.7	20.7	20.7	20.7	20.7	20.7	20.7
Indiana Eastern										
Conrail	23.0	23.0	23.0	23.0	23.0					
Indiana Harbor Belt	34.0	34.0	34.0	34.0	34.0	34.0	34.0	34.0	34.0	34.0
Indiana Hi-Rail		6.1	6.1	6.1	30.0	30.0	59.5	59.5	59.5	67.0
Central RR of Indianapolis										34.4
Norfolk Southern						26.3				111.4

RAILROADS continued	1980	1981	1982	1983'	1984	1985	1986	1987	1988	1989
Indiana Midland										
Penn Central						23.0	23.0			
Indiana RR							109.6	109.6	109.6	120.0
Kankakee, Beaverville & South.										39.2
Kentucky & Indiana Terminal	0.4	0.4	0.4	0.4	0.4	0.4	0.4	0.4	0.4	0.4
Logansport & Eel River Shore L.										2.2
(Louisv. & Jeffersonville Br.)	0.7	0.7	0.7	0.7	0.7	0.7	0.7	0.7	0.7	0.7
Louisville & Nashville	703.4	694.5	674.2							
Louisv., New Alb. & Corydon	7.7	7.7	7.7	7.7	7.7	7.7	7.7	7.7	7.7	7.7
Madison RR										
City of Madison Port Auth.	25.8	25.8	25.8	25.8	25.8	25.8	25.8	25.8	25.8	25.8
Norfolk & Western	1123.5	1123.5								
New Jersey, Indiana & Illinois	11.6	9.5								
Norfolk Southern			1316.4	1316.4	1242.9	1242.9	1242.9	1203.2	1161.8	871.9
Penn Central	3.0	3.0	3.0	3.0	3.0	3.0	0.0	0.0		
Cleve., Cinci., Chi. & St. Louis	27.0									
Pigeon River										
Norfolk Southern						15.4	15.4	15.4	15.4	15.4
Plymouth Shore Line										
Conrail						1.8	1.8	1.8	1.8	1.8
Poseyville & Owensville								11.0	11.0	11.0
Seaboard System				674.2	632.2	589.3				
Soo Line							100.0	100.0	100.0	100.0
Southern Ry	216.5	216.5								
Southern Indiana	5.5	5.5	5.5	5.5	5.5	5.5	5.5	5.5	5.5	5.5
Terre Haute, Brazil & Eastern								31.3	31.3	31.3
Tippecanoe RR	16.0	16.0	16.0	16.0	16.0	16.0	16.0	16.0	16.0	16.0
Toledo, Peoria & Western	63.3	63.3	63.3	63.3	63.3	63.3	63.3	63.3	63.3	63.3
Whitewater Valley					17.9	17.9	17.9	17.9	17.9	17.9
Penn Central	17.9	17.9	17.9	17.9						
Yankeetown Dock	22.0	22.0	22.0	22.0	22.0	22.0	22.0	22.0	22.0	22.0
RAILROAD YEAR TOTAL	5609.3	5612.6	5248.9	5233.5	5047.3	5002.6	4981.8	4913.4	4809.3	4663.8
RAILROAD YEAR CHANGE	-264.9	3.3	-363.7	-15.4	-186.2	-44.7	-20.8	-68.4	-104.1	-145.5

RAILROADS	1990	1991	1992	1993	1994	1995	1996	1997	1998	1999
A & R Line						26.3	26.3	26.3	26.3	26.3
Algers, Winslow & Western	20.0	20.0	20.0	20.0	20.0	20.0	20.0	20.0	20.0	20.0
Amtrak	18.0	18.0	18.0	18.0	18.0	18.0	18.0	18.0	18.0	18.0
Auburn Ind. Port Authority										
Bee Line					10.8	10.8	10.8	10.8	10.8	10.8
C&NC RR									3.0	3.0
Carthage, Knightst'n & Shirley	5.0	5.0	5.0	5.0	5.0	5.0	5.0	5.0	5.0	5.0
Central Indiana & Western	9.3	9.3	9.3	9.3	9.3	9.3	9.3	9.3	9.3	9.3
Central RR of Indiana		63.5	63.5	63.5	62.0	62.0	62.0	62.0	62.0	62.0
Central RR of Indianapolis										
Norfolk Southern	86.9	86.9	86.9	86.9	86.9	86.9	70.2	70.2	47.5	47.5
Chicago South Shore & S. Bend	73.5	73.5	76.3	76.3	76.3	76.3	76.3	76.3	76.3	76.3
Norfolk Southern										

RAILROADS continued	1990	1991	1992	1993	1994	1995	1996	1997	1998	1999
Conrail	1495.6	1431.5	1235.1	1101.1	966.2	966.2	772.8	772.8	772.8	
Corman, R. J.										
Norfolk Southern				9.5	9.5	9.5	9.5	9.5	9.5	9.5
CSX Transportation	1110.2	1110.0	1068.8	1029.3	999.7	989.4	989.4	985.1	985.1	1501.0
Baltimore & Ohio Chgo. Tm.	9.7	9.7	9.7	9.7	9.7	9.7	9.7	9.7	9.7	9.7
Port Authority of Auburn IN	1.7	1.7	1.7	1.7	1.7	1.7	1.7	1.7	1.7	1.7
Dubois County										
Norfolk Southern				16.0	16.0	16.0	16.0	16.0	16.0	16.0
Elgin, Joliet & Eastern	31.3	31.3	31.3	31.3	31.3	31.3	31.3	31.3	31.3	31.3
Evansville Terminal Co.							29.5	18.7	18.7	18.7
Ferdinand	6.4									
French Lick, W. Baden & South.	15.3	15.3	15.3	15.3	15.3	15.3	15.3	15.3	15.3	15.3
Fulton County									13.0	13.0
Grand Trunk Western RR	79.2	79.2	79.2	79.2	79.2	79.2	79.2	79.2	79.2	79.2
Heritage		3.1	3.1	3.1	3.1	3.1	3.1	3.1	3.1	3.1
Hillsdale County										
Penn Central	18.8	18.8								
Honey Creek				13.5	13.5	13.5	13.5	13.5	13.5	13.5
Hoosier Southern										
Norfolk Southern							15.8	15.8	15.8	15.8
Perry Co. Port Authority					19.8	19.8	19.8	19.8	19.8	19.8
Indian Creek	4.6	4.6	4.6	4.6	4.6	4.6	4.6	4.6	4.6	4.6
Indiana & Ohio	20.7	20.7	20.7	20.7	20.7	20.7	20.7	20.7	20.7	20.7
Indiana Harbor Belt	34.0	34.0	34.0	34.0	34.0	34.0	34.0	34.0	34.0	34.0
Indiana Hi-Rail	61.1	61.1	61.1	54.2	54.2	54.2	24.7	24.7		
Central RR of Indianapolis	34.4	34.4	34.4	34.4	34.4	34.4				
Norfolk Southern	111.4	111.4	111.4	111.4	56.9	56.9	56.9	39.0		
Indiana Northeasern			18.8	18.8	18.8	18.8	18.8	18.8	18.8	18.8
Norfolk Southern			10.4	24.6	24.6	24.6	24.6	24.6	24.6	24.6
Indiana RR	120.0	120.0	120.0	120.0	120.0	120.0	120.0	120.0	120.0	120.0
Norfolk Southern	37.6	37.6	37.6	37.6	37.6	37.6				
Indiana Southern			189.7	189.7	171.5	171.5	171.5	171.5	171.5	171.5
Indianapolis Union										
J K Line	16.0	16.0	16.0	16.0	16.0	16.0	16.0	16.0	16.0	16.0
Kankakee, Beaverville & South.	39.2	39.2	39.2	39.2	56.8	56.8	62.7	62.7	62.7	62.7
Kentucky & Indiana Terminal	0.4	0.4	0.4	0.4	0.4	0.4	0.4	0.4	0.4	0.4
Kokomo Rail			12.6	12.6	12.6	12.6	12.6	12.6	12.6	12.6
Logansport & Eel River Short Li.	2.2	2.2	2.2	2.2	2.2	2.2	2.2	2.2	2.2	2.2
Louisville & Indiana					106.5	106.5	106.5	106.5	106.5	106.5
(Louisv. & Jeffersonville Br.)	0.7	0.7	0.7	0.7	0.7	0.7	0.7	0.7		
Louisv., New Alb. & Corydon	7.7	7.7	7.7	7.7	7.7	7.7	7.7	7.7	7.7	7.7
Madison RR										
City of Madison Port Auth.	25.8	25.8	25.8	25.8	25.8	25.8	25.8	25.8	25.8	25.8
Maumee & Western									3.0	3.0
MG Rail										
Michigan Southern										
Conrail							9.8	9.8	9.8	
Norfolk Southern										9.8
Muncie & Western										

RAILROADS continued	1990	1991	1992	1993	1994	1995	1996	1997	1998	1999
Norfolk Southern	834.3	857.0	857.0	832.1	825.2	825.2	948.9	925.4	912.5	1169.4
Owensville Terminal							11.0	11.0	4.6	4.6
Pigeon River										
Norfolk Southern	15.4	15.4								
Poseyville & Owensville	11.0	11.0	11.0	11.0	11.0	11.0				
Soo Line	95.8	95.8	95.8	95.8	95.8	95.8	95.8	95.8	95.8	95.8
Southern Indiana	5.5	5.5	5.5	5.5	5.5	5.5	5.5	5.5	5.5	5.5
Southwind Shortline				1.3	1.3	1.3	1.3	1.3	1.3	1.3
Terre Haute, Brazil & Eastern	31.3	31.3	0.0							
Toledo, Peoria & Western	63.3	63.3	63.3	63.3	63.3	63.3	63.3	63.3	63.3	63.3
Wabash Central									26.4	26.4
Whitewater Valley	19.0	19.0	19.0	19.0	19.0	19.0	19.0	19.0	19.0	19.0
Winimac Southern				82.8	82.8	59.5	59.5	59.5	59.5	59.5
Yankeetown Dock	22.0	22.0	22.0	22.0	22.0	22.0	22.0	22.0	22.0	22.0
RAILROAD YEAR TOTAL	4594.3	4612.9	4544.1	4476.1	4385.2	4377.9	4251.0	4194.5	4133.5	4133.5
RAILROAD YEAR CHANGE	-69.5	18.6	-68.8	-68.0	-90.9	-7.3	-126.9	-56.5	-61.0	0.0

TABLE OF INTERURBAN MILEAGE, 1890–1959

INTERURBANS	1880	1881	1882	1883	1884	1885	1886	1887	1888	1889
Evansville Suburban & Newburgh										9.9
INTERURBAN YEAR TOTAL	0.0	0.0	0.0	0.0	0.0	0.0	0.0	0.0	0.0	9.9
INTERURBAN YEAR CHANGE	0.0	0.0	0.0	0.0	0.0	0.0	0.0	0.0	0.0	9.9

INTERURBANS	1890	1891	1892	1893	1894	1895	1896	1897	1898	1899
Brazil Rapid Transit				3.4	3.4	3.4	3.4	3.4	3.4	3.4
Elwood & Alexandria Ry										9.5
Evansville Suburban & Newb.	9.9	9.9	9.9	9.9	9.9	9.9	9.9	9.9	9.9	9.9
Indiana Electric									6.7	
Indiana Ry										14.3
Marion Electric Street Ry				8.2	18.5	18.5	18.5	18.5	18.5	
Union Traction Co								8.7	14.4	
Union Traction Co. of Indiana										32.9
INTERURBAN YEAR TOTAL	9.9	9.9	9.9	21.5	31.8	31.8	31.8	40.5	52.9	70.0
INTERURBAN YEAR CHANGE	0.0	0.0	0.0	11.6	10.3	0.0	0.0	8.7	12.4	17.1

INTERURBANS	1900	1901	1902	1903	1904	1905	1906	1907	1908	1909
Bluffton, Geneva & Celina										6.0
Brazil Rapid Transit	3.4	3.4	3.4							
Chicago & South Shore				12.1	12.1					
Chicago, Lake Shore & S. Bend									58.9	75.7
Chicago, S. Bend & No. Ind.								26.4	50.4	50.4
Cinci., Lawrenceburg & Aurora	10.2	10.2	10.2	10.2	10.2	10.2	10.2	10.2	10.2	10.2
Dayton & Muncie Traction					18.0	30.0				
Dayton & Western										

INTERURBANS CONT'D	1900	1901	1902	1903	1904	1905	1906	1907	1908	1909
Dayton & Western of Indiana				2.2	2.2	2.2				
Evansville & Mt. Vernon							9.9			
Evansville & Princeton Traction				24.4	24.4	24.4				
Evansville & So. Indiana Tract.									28.7	28.7
Evansville, Princeton & Vincennes							24.4	24.4		
Evansville Rys										
Evansville & Eastern								24.3	24.3	24.3
Evansville & Mt. Vernon Elec.								9.9	9.9	9.9
Evansville Terminal									8.0	8.0
Evansville Suburban & Newb.	9.9	9.9	9.9	9.9	9.9	9.9	25.6	25.6	25.6	25.6
Fort Wayne & Southwestern Tr.			43.5	43.5						
Fort Wayne & Springfield								19.3	19.3	19.3
Fort Wayne & Wabash Valley Tr.				72.5	72.5	72.5		130.5	130.5	130.5
Ft. Wayne, Van Wert & Lima						23.4	23.4	23.4	23.4	23.4
Indiana, Columbus & Western										
Dayton & Western of Indiana							2.2			
Indiana Northern Traction				19.6						
Indianapolis & Cincinnati Tr.				25.0	25.0	51.2	78.8	99.9	99.9	99.9
Indianapolis & Eastern	15.6	15.6	23.9	23.9	23.9	23.9	23.9			
Indianapolis & Louisville Tract.									40.8	40.8
Indianapolis & Martinsville Rap.Tr.			14.6	28.7	28.7	28.7	28.7			
Indianapolis & Northwestern				86.3	86.3	86.3	86.3			
Indianapolis & Plainfield Electric			12.0							
Indianapolis & Western						16.8	16.8			
Indianapolis Coal Traction				12.0	12.0	12.0	12.0			
Indpls, Columbus & Southern			39.0	39.0	39.0	39.0	39.0			
Indpls., Crawfordsville & West.								38.9	38.9	38.9
Indpls., Greenwood & Suburban		17.3								
Indianapolis, Shelbyville & SE			25.0							
Indiana Ry	14.3	14.3	14.3	14.3	14.3					
Indiana Union Traction							30.0	30.0	30.0	30.0
Muncie, Hartf'd & Ft. Wayne							41.0	41.0	41.0	41.0
Interstate Public Service Co.										
Indpls., Columbus & South.								58.2	58.2	58.2
Kokomo, Marion & Western				9.4	9.4	27.2	27.2	27.2	27.2	27.2
Lebanon & Thorntown						9.3	9.3	9.3	9.3	9.3
Logansport, Rochester & North.			16.3	16.3						
Louisville & Northern Ry. & Light.								21.4	21.4	21.4
Louisville & So. Indiana Tr.							13.3			
Marion, Bluffton & Eastern Tr.						31.8	31.8	31.8	31.8	31.8
Muncie, Hartford & Ft. Wayne				41.0	41.0	41.0				
Muncie & Portland Traction							31.0	31.0	31.0	31.0
Northern Indiana Ry						26.4	26.4			
Oho Electric										
Dayton & Western of Indiana								2.2	2.2	2.2
Richmond Street & Interurban			6.2	50.4	50.4	50.4	50.4			
St. Joseph Valley						9.6	9.6	36.6	36.6	36.6
Terre Haute Electric	12.7	12.7	12.7							
Terre Haute, Indianapolis & E.								128.7	142.3	142.3

INTERURBANS CONT'D	1900	1901	1902	1903	1904	1905	1906	1907	1908	1909
Indianapolis & Martinsville								28.7	28.7	28.7
Indianapolis & Northwestern								86.3	86.3	86.3
Terre Haute Traction & Light								64.1	64.1	64.1
Terre Haute Traction & Light			1.5	31.6	31.6	31.6	56.1			
Toledo & Chicago Interurban								40.4	40.4	40.4
Union Traction Co. of Indiana	89.2	89.2	99.7	149.9	189.0	217.0	217.0	217.0	217.0	217.0
Wabash River Traction Co.		12.7	12.7	12.7						
Winona & Warsaw				1.8	1.8	1.8				
Winona Interurban							25.0	32.9	37.0	48.0
Wabash								9.7	9.7	9.7
INTERURBAN YEAR TOTAL	155.3	185.3	344.9	644.6	721.3	876.6	1021.8	1329.3	1483.0	1516.8
INTERURBAN YEAR CHANGE	85.3	30.0	159.6	299.7	76.7	155.3	145.2	307.5	153.7	33.8

INTERURBAN	1910	1911	1912	1913	1914	1915	1916	1917	1918	1919
Beech Grove Traction		6.0	6.0	6.0	6.0	6.0	6.0	6.0	6.0	6.0
Bluffton, Geneva & Celina	19.0	19.0	19.0	19.0	19.0	19.0	19.0	19.0	0.0	
Chicago, Lake Shore & S. Bend	75.7	75.7	75.7	75.7	75.7	75.7	75.7	75.7	75.7	75.7
Chicago-New York El. Air Line										
Goshen, South Bend & Chicago		15.0	15.0	15.0	15.0	15.0	15.0			
Chicago, S. Bend & No. Ind.										
Southern Michigan	3.8	3.8	3.8	3.8	3.8	3.8	3.8	3.8	3.8	3.8
Cinci,, Lawrenceburg & Aurora	10.2	10.2	10.2	10.2	10.2	10.2	10.2	10.2	10.2	10.2
Evansville & Ohio Valley									47.9	47.9
Illinois Central									3.0	3.0
Evansville & So. Indiana Tr.	28.7	28.7								
Evansville Rys										
Evansville & Eastern	38.0	38.0	38.0	38.0	38.0	38.0	38.0	38.0		
Evansville & Mt. Vernon Elec.	9.9	9.9	9.9	9.9	9.9	9.9	9.9	9.9		
Evansv., Henderson & Owens.										
Illinois Central			3.0	3.0	3.0	3.0	3.0	3.0		
Evansville Suburban & Newb.	25.6	25.6	25.6	25.6	25.6	25.6	25.6	25.6	25.6	25.6
Fort Wayne & Decatur								19.3	19.3	19.3
Ft. Wayne & Northern Indiana		130.5	130.5	130.5	130.5	130.5	130.5	130.5	130.5	130.5
Fort Wayne & Northwestern				40.4	40.4	40.4	40.4	40.4	40.4	40.4
Fort Wayne & Springfield	19.3	19.3	19.3	19.3	19.3	19.3				
Fort Wayne & Wabash Valley	130.5									
Ft. Wayne, Van Wert & Lima	23.4	23.4	23.4	23.4	23.4	23.4				
French Lick & West Baden	1.1	1.1	1.1	1.1	1.1	1.1	1.1	1.1	1.1	1.1
Gary & Hobart Traction								4.9	4.9	4.9
Gary & Interurban				25.2	36.1	36.1	36.1	0.0		
Gary & Southern Traction		5.5	5.5	5.5	5.5	5.5	5.5	5.5	5.5	5.5
Gary & Valparaiso								10.9	10.9	10.9
Gary Connecting Rys								10.2	10.2	10.2
Gary Connecting Rys			10.2							
Gary, Hobart & Eastern Tr.			4.9	4.9	4.9	4.9	4.9			
Goshen, South Bend & Chicago		15.0	15.0							
Indiana Rys & Light Co.			52.8	52.8	52.8	52.8	52.8	52.8	52.8	52.8
Indiana Union Traction	30.0	30.0								

INTERURBAN CONT'D	1910	1911	1912	1913	1914	1915	1916	1917	1918	1919
Muncie, Hartf'd & Ft. Wayne	41.0	41.0								
Indianapolis & Cincinnati	99.9	99.9	99.9	99.9	99.9	99.9	99.9	99.9	99.9	99.9
Indianapolis & Louisville Trac.	40.8	40.8								
Indpls., Crawfordsville & West.	38.9	38.9								
Indpls., New Castle & Toledo	42.0	42.0								
Interstate Public Service Co.			120.4	120.4	120.4	120.4	120.4	120.4	120.4	120.4
Indpls., Columbus & South.	58.2	58.2								
Kokomo, Marion & Western	27.2	27.2								
LaGrange, Toledo & Eastern										
St. Joseph Valley										15.0
Lebanon & Thorntown	9.3	9.3	9.3	9.3	9.3	9.3	9.3	9.3	9.3	9.3
Louisville & Northern Ry. & L.	21.4	21.4								
Marion & Bluffton Traction					31.8	31.8	31.8	31.8	31.8	31.8
Marion, Bluffton & Eastern Tr.	31.8	31.8	31.8	31.8						
Muncie & Portland Traction	31.0	31.0	31.0	31.0	31.0	31.0				
Northern Indiana Ry	50.4	50.4	50.4	50.4	50.4	50.4	50.4	50.4	50.4	50.4
Ohio Electric										
Dayton & Western of Indiana	2.2	2.2	2.2	2.2	2.2	2.2	2.2	2.2	2.2	2.2
Ft. Wayne, Van Wert & Lima							23.4	23.4	23.4	23.4
Public Service Co. of Evansville			28.7	28.7	28.7	28.7	28.7	28.7	28.7	28.7
St. Joseph Valley	45.6	59.7	59.7	59.7	59.7	59.7	59.7	59.7	15.0	
Terre Haute, Indianapolis & E.	142.3	142.3	142.3	142.3	142.3	142.3	142.3	142.3	142.3	142.3
Indianapolis & Martinsville	28.7	28.7	28.7	28.7	28.7	28.7	28.7	28.7	28.7	28.7
Indianapolis & Northwestern	86.3	86.3	86.3	86.3	86.3	86.3	86.3	86.3	86.3	86.3
Indpls., Crawfordsville & West.			38.9	38.9	38.9	38.9	38.9	38.9	38.9	38.9
Terre Haute Traction & Light	64.1	64.1	64.1	64.1	64.1	64.1	64.1	64.1	64.1	64.1
Toledo & Chicago Interurban	40.4	40.4	40.4							
Union Traction Co. of Indiana	217.0	217.0	330.0	347.7	347.7	347.7	378.7	378.7	378.7	378.7
Valparaiso & Northern	3.6	10.4	10.9	10.9	0.0					
Winona Interurban	58.4	58.4	58.4	58.4	58.4	58.4	58.4	58.4	58.4	58.4
Wabash	9.7	9.7	9.7	9.7	9.7	9.7	9.7	9.7	9.7	9.7
INTERURBAN YEAR TOTAL	1605.4	1667.8	1712.0	1729.7	1729.7	1729.7	1729.7	1699.7	1636.0	1636.0
INTERURBAN YEAR CHANGE	88.6	62.4	44.2	17.7	0.0	0.0	0.0	-30.0	-63.7	0.0

INTERURBAN	1920	1921	1922	1923	1924	1925	1926	1927	1928	1929
Beech Grove Traction	6.0	6.0	6.0	6.0	6.0	6.0	6.0	6.0	6.0	6.0
Chicago, Lake Shore & S. Bend	75.7	75.7	75.7	75.7	75.7					
Chicago, S. Bend & No. Ind.										
Southern Michigan	3.8	3.8	3.8	3.8	3.8	3.8	3.8	3.8	3.8	3.8
Chicago South Shore & S. Bend						75.7	75.7	75.7	75.7	75.7
Cinci,, Lawrenceburg & Aurora	10.2	10.2	10.2	10.2	10.2	10.2	10.2	10.2	10.2	10.2
Dayton & Western Traction	2.2	2.2	2.2	2.2	2.2	2.2	2.2	2.2	2.2	2.2
Evansville & Ohio Valley	47.9	47.9	47.9	47.9	47.9	47.9	47.9	47.9	47.9	47.9
Illinois Central	3.0	3.0	3.0	3.0	3.0	3.0	3.0	3.0	3.0	3.0
Evansville Suburban & Newb.	25.6	25.6	25.6	25.6	25.6	25.6	25.6	25.6	25.6	25.6
Fort Wayne & Decatur	19.3	19.3	19.3	19.3	19.3	19.3	19.3	0.0		
Fort Wayne & Northwestern	40.4	40.4	40.4	40.4						
Ft. Wayne, Van Wert & Lima		23.4	23.4	23.4	23.4	23.4	23.4	23.4	23.4	23.4

INTERURBAN CONT'D	1920	1921	1922	1923	1924	1925	1926	1927	1928	1929
French Lick & West Baden	1.1	1.1	1.1	1.1						
Gary & Hobart Traction	4.9	4.9	4.9	4.9	4.9	4.9				
Gary & Southern Traction	5.5	5.5	5.5	5.5	5.5	5.5	5.5	5.5		
Gary & Valparaiso	10.9	10.9	7.5	7.5	7.5	7.5	7.5	7.5	7.5	7.5
Gary & Connecting RR	10.2	10.2	10.2	10.2	10.2	10.2				
Gary Railways							15.1	15.1	15.1	15.1
Gary & Southern Traction									5.5	5.5
Indiana Public Service Co.					40.4					
Indiana Rys & Light Co.	52.8	52.8								
Indiana Service Corp.	162.3	162.3	162.3	162.3	202.7	202.7	202.7	202.7	202.7	202.7
Interstate Public Service Co.	120.4									
Lebanon & Thorntown	9.3	9.3	9.3	9.3	9.3	0.0				
Northern Indiana Power Co.			52.8	52.8	52.8	52.8	52.8	52.8	52.8	52.8
Northern Indiana Ry	50.4	50.4	50.4	50.4	50.4	50.4	50.4	50.4	50.4	50.4
Ohio Electric										
Ft. Wayne, Van Wert & Lima	23.4									
Public Service Co. of Evansville	28.7									
Public Service Co. of Indiana		120.4	120.4	120.4	120.4	120.4	120.4	120.4	120.4	120.4
Southern Indiana Gas & Electric		28.7	28.7	28.7	28.7	28.7	28.7	28.7	28.7	28.7
Terre Haute, Indianapolis & E.	142.3	142.3	142.3	142.3	142.3	140.3	140.3	140.3	140.3	140.3
Indianapolis & Martinsville	28.7	28.7	28.7	28.7	28.7	28.7	28.7	28.7	28.7	28.7
Indianapolis & Northwestern	86.3	86.3	86.3	86.3	86.3	86.3	86.3	86.3	86.3	86.3
Indpls., Crawfordsville & W.	38.9	38.9	38.9	38.9	38.9	38.9	38.9	38.9	38.9	38.9
Terre Haute Traction & Light	64.1	64.1	64.1	64.1	64.1	64.1	64.1	64.1	64.1	64.1
Union Traction Co. of Indiana	378.7	378.7	378.7	378.7	378.7	378.7	378.7	378.7	378.7	378.7
Winona Interurban	58.4	58.4	58.4	58.4	58.4					
Wabash	9.7	9.7	9.7	9.7	9.7					
Winona Service						58.4	58.4	58.4	58.4	58.4
Wabash						9.7	9.7	9.7	9.7	9.7
INTERURBAN YEAR TOTAL	1521.1	1521.1	1517.7	1517.7	1557.0	1505.3	1505.3	1486.0	1486.0	1486.0
INTERURBAN YEAR CHANGE	-114.9	0.0	-3.4	0.0	39.3	-51.7	0.0	-19.3	0.0	0.0

INTERURBAN	1930	1931	1932	1933	1934	1935	1936	1937	1938	1939
Beech Grove Traction	6.0	6.0	6.0	6.0	6.0	6.0	6.0			
Chicago South Shore & S. Bend	75.7	75.7	75.7	75.7	75.7	75.7	75.7	75.7	75.7	75.7
Dayton & Western Traction	2.2	2.2	2.2	2.2	2.2	2.2				
Evansville & Ohio Valley	47.9	47.9	47.9	47.9	47.9	47.9	47.9	47.9	47.9	47.9
Illinois Central	3.0	3.0	3.0	3.0	3.0	3.0	3.0	3.0	3.0	3.0
Evansville Suburban & Newb.	25.6	25.6	25.6	25.6	25.6	25.6	25.6	25.6	25.6	25.6
Ft. Wayne, Van Wert & Lima	23.4	23.4	0.0							
Gary & Valparaiso	7.5	7.5	7.5	7.5	7.5	7.5	7.5	7.5		
Gary Railways	15.1	15.1	15.1	15.1	15.1	15.1	15.1	15.1	4.9	0.0
Gary & Southern Traction	5.5	5.5	5.5	5.5						
Indiana Ry	267.7	396.8	320.8	320.8	320.8	320.8	320.8	282.1	172.8	172.8
Dayton & Western Traction							2.2	0.0		
Indiana Service Corp.	202.7	170.9	119.0	119.0	119.0	119.0	119.0	78.6	22.4	22.4
Northern Indiana Power Co.	52.8	52.8	0.0							
Public Service Co. of Indiana	120.4	120.4	113.5	113.5	113.5	113.5	113.5	113.5	113.5	62.2

INTERURBAN CONT'D	1930	1931	1932	1933	1934	1935	1936	1937	1938	1939
Indianapolis & Cincinnati	99.9	99.9	99.9	99.9	99.9	99.9	99.9	99.9	99.9	99.9
Northern Indiana Power Co.	52.8	52.8								
Northern Indiana Ry	54.2	54.2	54.2	54.2	0.0					
Southern Indiana Gas & Electric	28.7	28.7	28.7							
Terre Haute, Indianapolis & E.	123.5	0.0								
Terre Haute Traction & Light	64.1									
Winona RR					53.8	53.8	53.8	53.8	53.8	53.8
Wabash					6.0	6.0	6.0	6.0	6.0	6.0
Winona Service	58.4	58.4	58.4	58.4						
Wabash	9.7	9.7	9.7	9.7						
INTERURBAN YEAR TOTAL	1346.8	1256.5	992.7	964.0	896.0	896.0	896.0	808.7	625.5	569.3
INTERURBAN YEAR CHANGE	-139.2	-90.3	-263.8	-28.7	-68.0	0.0	0.0	-87.3	-183.2	-56.2

INTERURBAN	1940	1941	1942	1943	1944	1945	1946	1947	1948	1949
Chicago South Shore & S. Bend	75.7	75.7	75.7	75.7	75.7	75.7	75.7	75.7	75.7	75.7
Evansville & Ohio Valley	47.9	16.6	16.6	16.6	16.6	16.6	0.0			
Illinois Central	3.0									
Evansville Suburban & Newb.	25.6	17.9	17.9	17.9	17.9	17.9	17.9	17.9	0.0	
Indianapolis & Cincinnati	99.9	99.9	0.0							
Indiana Ry	105.5	0.0								
Indiana Service Corp.	22.4	0.0								
Public Service Co. of Indiana	62.2	4.0	4.0	4.0	4.0	4.0	0.0			
Winona RR	53.8	53.8	53.8	53.8	53.8	53.8	53.8	18.6	18.6	18.6
Wabash	6.0	6.0	6.0	6.0	6.0	6.0	6.0			
INTERURBAN YEAR TOTAL	0.0	273.9	174.0	174.0	174.0	174.0	153.4	112.2	94.3	94.3
INTERURBAN YEAR CHANGE	0.0	273.9	-99.9	0.0	0.0	0.0	-20.6	-41.2	-17.9	0.0

INTERURBAN	1950	1951	1952	1953	1954	1955	1956	1957	1958	1959
Chicago South Shore & S. Bend	75.7	75.7	75.7	75.7	75.7	75.7	75.7	75.7	75.7	75.7
Winona RR	18.6	18.6	0.0							
INTERURBAN YEAR TOTAL	94.3	94.3	75.7	75.7	75.7	75.7	75.7	75.7	75.7	75.7
INTERURBAN YEAR CHANGE	0.0	0.0	-18.6	0.0	0.0	0.0	0.0	0.0	0.0	0.0

----Beginning in 1960 Interurban mileage is included with Railroad mileage.

APPENDIX 1. KEY TO DATA IN CHAPTERS 4 AND 5

Each individual main line or branch line of each individual railroad or interurban company is detailed separately, and each line has the information shown in the example below:

(A)

(1)
PENNSYLVANIA

(2)   **(3)**
RICHMOND BRANCH (PRR-CR)

(4)

	(5) Mileage [Cincinnati]	(6) County	(7) Crossings, junctions, etc.
Campbellstown OH	65.3		
(OH/IN state line)	68.5		
Glen	72.4	Wayne	J/PRR-Z 3.6
--via PRR-I			
(Junction)	75.3	"	J/PRR-Z 0.7
Olive Hill	80	"	
Millville	95.6	Henry	
Ashland	98.3	"	
New Castle	101.5	"	
Broad	101.9	"	J/NKP-LF 83.6
(Bridge)	102.9	"	B/CCC-S 95.1
Foley	104.1	"	J/NKP-LF 80.8
(Crossing)	159.6	"	X/NKP-LM 54.8
Galveston	165.9	Cass	
Anoka	177.4	"	J/PRR-L 192.6

(B)

(8) Date	(9) Act	(10) End points	(11) MP	(12) Change	(13) Main	(14) Source	(15) Note
CONSTRUCTION/ABANDONMENT							
1853	B8	OH state line-Richmond	68.5-72.4	+3.9		2	
1853	B8	Richmond-New Castle	74.9-101.5	+26.6	31.4	1,2	
1857	B11	New Castle-Anoka	101.5-177.4	+75.9	106.4	2	
---------- (16)							
1976	S1	OH state line-Glen	68.5-72.4	[3.9]			
1976	Y	In Richmond	74.9-76.6	(1.7)			
1976	S1	Newman-New Castle	76.6-100.5	[23.9]	76.9		
1982	X	Anderson-Kokomo	127.0-155.7	-28.7			
1982	Y	In Anderson	119.3-127.0	(7.7)	40.5		
1986	X	In Kokomo	155.7-156.5	-0.8	39.7		
1993	X	Sulphur Springs-Anderson	108.7-119.3	-10.6		1,2	4
1993	S1	New Castle-Foley	100.5-104.1	[3.6]			
1993	S1	In Kokomo	156.5-159.6	[3.1]			
1993/10/1	S7	Foley-Sulphur Springs	104.1-108.7	[4.6]	0	1	

(C) (17)
OWNERSHIP   **(18)**

1853	Cincinnati, Logansport & Chicago Ry (B8), of part
1854	Cincinnati & Chicago RR (B11), merge CL&C and other road
1860/7	Cincinnati & Chicago Air-Line RR, reorganize Cincinnati & Chicago
1865/5/15	Chicago & Great Eastern Ry, merge C&CAL and other road
1868/2/12	Columbus, Chicago & Indiana Central Ry, acquired C&GE
1869/2/1	Pennsylvania RR, lease Columbus, Chicago & Indiana Central
1968/2/1	Penn Central Co., merge PRR and New York Central
1969/10/1	Penn Central Transp. Co., acquire Penn Central Co.
1976/4/1	Conrail, buy Penn Central Transp.

Each individual line's listing has three sets of data:

A. Arrangement of stations showing:
1. Company name. A complete list of companies is in Chapter 1.
2. Line name.
3. Line designation. The construction of these is discussed in detail in Appendix 2.
4. List of stations and, in parentheses, other unnamed places. A cross-index of place names for railroads is in Chapter 2. Stations on railroad lines located outside of Indiana and all of those on interurban lines are not included in Chapter 2.
5. Mileage of each place or location from the beginning of the line, using when possible actual Mile Post numbers placed on the line. If Mile Posts are numbered from a point off the line, the name of that place is given.
6. County in which each place or location is situated. A cross-index of each county and the companies operating in each county is in Chapter 3.
7. Additional information about the place:
       Intersections with other railroads with "X/" indicating a crossing, "J/" a junction, "C/" a track connection, and "B/" a bridge) followed by the intersecting line designation and mileage on that line.
       Former names shown by "f."
       Subsequent former names shown by "th."
       Non-railroad name shown by "aka."
       Alternate post office names shown by "P.O."

B. Below the arrangement of stations, under the head *CONSTRUCTION/ABANDONMENT*, is a chronological record of construction, abandonment, and disposition events of the line's trackage:
8. Date of the Act event given in the next right column.
9. "Act" column gives the corporate action. These are given in full detail at the end of the listing for each company under the heading **ACT COLUMN KEY**. Generally B (with or without a number following) indicates construction, P is purchase, L is lease, LA is assignment of lease to another road, S is sale, X is abandonment, XL is termination of lease, and Y is a conversion of main line track to yard track use.
10. Named end points of the project segment.
11. "MP" column gives the beginning and ending mileage locations.
12. Change in the line's main track mileage caused by the Act event. This relates the event in number 9 data and also indicates effect on number 13 mileage as shown below:
       + with B, P in "Act" column, L; construction or acquisition; adds to mileage
       - with X in "Act" column; abandonment; reduces mileage
       ( ) with Y in "Act" column; converted from main to yard track; reduces mileage
       [ ] with S in "Act" column; sold to another company; reduces mileage
       < > with L in "Act" column; leased to another company; reduces mileage
       (-), [-], <- > with X in "Act" column; track abandoned; no change in mileage
13. Cumulative main track mileage in Indiana at year end. The definition of main track mileage is discussed in more detail in Appendix 2.
14. Source of data. The source(s) of the data are given at the end of the listing for each company under the heading **SOURCES**, and a full bibliographic listing is in the Bibliography.
15. Notes. Clarifying detail for the Act on this line is given at the end of the listing for each company under the heading **NOTES**.
16. A dashed line (--------) indicates the line was sold to another company and that the Construction/-Abandonment record is continued, but that the acts and changes of mileage are for information purposes. The record also is continued under the new owner of the line.

C. Below the *CONSTRUCTION/ABANDONMENT* heading is *OWNERSHIP*, which gives a a chronological record of the ownership of the line:
16. Date of a change of ownership or control of the line.
17. Name of the acquiring/succeeding company and the type of change.
       NOTE about *OWNERSHIP*. If the line was sold to another company, the chronological ownership record is not continued here but is continued under the subsequent owner.

At the end of listing for each individual company listing is:

D. A chronological **ACQUISITION/DISPOSITION RECORD** listing the folloiwng events for all lines of the company, if it had more than one line:

21. Date of act, number, shown in number 8 above.
22. "Act" showing type of work on segment, shown in number 9.
23. Line designation, shown in number 3.
24. End points of segment reported, shown in number 10.
25. Change in mileage of the segment, shown in number 12.
26. Year end total of main track mileage in Indiana. For several major railroads that resulted from mergers after 1950, the company record includes a detail of lines conveyed, followed by a continuation of the **ACQUISITION/DISPOSITION RECORD** for information purposes. For the acquiring lines the company record includes a detail of lines acquired, followed by an **ACQUISITION/DISPOSITION RECORD** for the merged company. A year end total of mileage is given from the record of each of acquired road and summed for the owning road.

E. ACT COLUMN KEY A list of all corporate actions shown in B 9 and in C 22.

F. SOURCES. Short names of bibliographic sources in C 14. The full Bibliography is at the end of the book.

G. NOTES. The text of clarifying notes shown in C 15 above.

APPENDIX 2. DEFINITION OF "MAIN TRACK" MILEAGE

The table of mileage that comprises chapter 6 invites comparison with the mileage reported by other sources, particularly by the Indiana regulatory authorities and by the Interstate Commerce Commission. Their definitions of trackage to be included are to meet specific legal and regulatory purposes, and are critical to the performance of their responsibilities, particularly taxation and rate-making. The intent of this tabulation herein is to indicate the economic impact of Indiana's railroads, using route mileage as a measurement. The table groups together all of the lines owned or controlled by each company at the end of each year. This allows easy comparison between companies as they grew and waned in importance from year to year. In recent years it shows the concentration of strength in fewer and fewer companies as well as the decline in the size of the state's rail network.

A "route mile," as used herein, is the length of an intercity railroad line between two given points without regard to the number of tracks or whether it is a main line or a branch line. The problem is what trackage to include and what to exclude in determining the route mileage of the individual railroad companies. A "main track" is, by railroad definition, a "track extending through yards and between stations, upon which trains are operated by time-table or train order, or both, or the use of which is governed by block signals." A given route may have more than one track main track (called "double track" or "triple track") and using route miles derives a measurement that ignores the effect of two- and three-track main tracks on a route. A "main line" usually is the principal or most heavily trafficked main track route of a company. The intercity main line of each company certainly must be included in the table. A main line or main track of a company such as the Fort Wayne Union or the Kokomo Belt does not, properly speaking, extend between stations but rather is within the area of one municipality. For this reason the main lines of such intra-city and intra-terminal companies are not included in the state's railroad mileage shown in Chapter 6. A few roads like the Indianapolis Union and the Indiana Harbor Belt, however, are included because they have, to my mind, some intercity characteristics.

Branch lines pose a different sort of problem. For many companies many branch line main tracks do appear in public and employee timetables and such these included herein. But there is no long-standing clear definition of what is and is not a branch line that can be brought to this work. The Interstate Commerce Commission's definition, as it was generally understood and generally used, turns on whether the branch line has a common carrier function, which is determined by whether it serves more than one shipper. By serving more than one customer the I. C. C. concludes it is a line that is to be included in mileage. This approach has merit on a current basis, but it proves difficult to implement for lines that were abandoned a hundred years ago. In their annual reports some railroad companies include every scrap of branch as it built and abandoned them, down to 0.2 and 0.3 miles in length, while other companies considered many short branches as spurs and sidings and not to have main track characteristics. With no a uniform approach at the corporate level, and with the difficulties inherent in using the I. C. C. standard, the writer has elected to use an inclusive approach for branch lines. A branch line main track, when it extends away from the station or location where it connects with another main track and when it can be considered an intercity line, is included in mileage whenever possible. The result is that the tabulation includes a great many branches of the common carrier companies when both the construction and abandonment dates could be determined or reasonably estimated. If either or both dates could not be determined it is so noted and the line is not included in the **ACQUISITION/DISPOSITION RECORD.**

Each main line and branch line of each company has its own designation, comprised of a company identifier and a unique line identifier. A company's initials often are a quite recognizable abbreviation of its name and are used herein as the company identifier. After the company identifier and a hyphen is the line identifier. The line identifier often is the first letter of the division or branch name. However, the larger the system the more difficult it is to hold to this practice. Subsidiary and branch lines usually have two- or three-letter line identifiers, and these may include numbers.

Lines constructed as intra-city, terminal, or yard lines by intercity carriers, are given a line identifier that begins with the letter Y, which generally is followed by the first letter of the city in which it is located, and then another number or letter if more than one such line exists in that city. Mileage of these lines is not shown in the Acquisition/Disposition Record for the company.

When a main track is abandoned in part and two separate parts are retained for intercity service, or if any parts of it are retained for intra-city terminal service, no attempt has been made to provide a distinct line identifier for each segment. Such a conversion to yard track is shown by a "Y" entry in the "Act" column for the line and the mileage change shown in the "Change" column is enclosed in parentheses. Subsequent changes in yard track mileage are shown in parentheses with a plus or minus sign.

In the sale of a line to another company, the event is identified by an "S" in the "Act" (B 9)column. On the purchasing company record the line identifier used is: the purchasing company's road identifier, a hyphen, followed by the selling company's road identifier and line identifier that are enclosed in brackets. Example, the Pennsylvania main line between Richmond and Indianapolis is designated as line PRR-I; Penn Central's purchase of this line changes the designation to PC-[PRR-I]. Lines leased by one company from another generally are treated in the same way, using an "L" in the "Act" (B 9) column.

BIBLIOGRAPHY AND ESSAY

BIBLIOGRAPHIC ESSAY

A work of this sort relies heavily on the efforts of others. It would have been impossible to assemble the data compiled in this book without their contributions. For their efforts I offer my great appreciation and thanks. I have found three studies to be particularly useful: Simons and Parker's *Railroads of Indiana*, Sulzer's *Ghost Railroads of Indiana*, and the *1995 Indiana State Rail Plan*. Simons and Parker have used a considerable number of sources in compiling their very creditable history of the state's railroad business; their bibliography is very useful for anyone looking for further reading. The body of work by the Central Electric Railfans' Association has been invaluable in determining data for the state's electric lines, although the depth of its research varies widely. The on-line records of the Surface Transportation Board (found at: www.stb.gov)have been useful for the years after 1995, but have not been cited a source herein.

Blackburn, Glen A. "Interurban Railroads of Indiana." *Indiana Magazine of History* XX (1924).

Bradley, George K. *Indiana Railroad: the Magic Interurban.* (Bulletin no. 128) Chicago: Central Electric Railfans' Association, 1991.

Bradley, George K. *Northern Indiana Railway.* (Bulletin no. 132) Chicago: Central Electric Railfans' Association, 1998.

Buckley, James J. *Gary Railways.* (Bulletin no. 84) Chicago: Central Electric Railfans' Association, reissue 1975.

Burgess, George H. and Kennedy, Miles C. *Centennial History of the Pennsylvania Railroad Company.* Philadelphia: Pennsylvania Railroad, 1949.

Central Electric Railfans' Association. *Electric Railways of Indiana, Part I.* (Bulletin no. 101) Chicago: Central Electric Railfans' Association, 1958.

Central Electric Railfans' Association. *Electric Railways of Indiana, Part II.* (Bulletin no. 102) Chicago: Central Electric Railfans' Association, 1958.

Central Electric Railfans' Association. *Electric Railways of Indiana,* (Bulletin no. 104) Chicago: CERA, 1960.

Galloway, Joseph A. and Buckley, James J. *The St. Joseph Valley Railway.* Chicago: Electric Railway Historical Society, 1955.

Hilton, George W. and Due, John F. *The Electric Interurban Railways in America.* Stanford, Calif.: Stanford University Press, 1960.

Hilton, George W. *Monon Route.* Berkeley Calif.: Howell-North, 1978.

Hopper, A. B. and Kearney, T. *Canadian National Railways: Synoptical History...as of December 31, 1960.* Montreal: Canadian National Railways, 1962.

Indiana, Department of Transportation, Rail Section, 1995 *Indiana State Rail Plan.* Indianapolis, 1996.

Meints, Graydon M. *Michigan Railroads and Railroad Companies.* East Lansing, Mich.: Michigan State University Press, 1992.

Michigan, Railroad Commission. *Aids, Gifts, Grants and Donations to Railroads including Outline of Development and Successions in Titles to Railroads in Michigan.* Lansing Mich.: Wynkoop Hallenbeck Crawford, 1919.

Simons, Richard S. and Parker, Francis H. *Railroads of Indiana.* Bloomington Ind.: Indiana University Press, 1997.

Sulzer, Elmer G. *Ghost Railroads of Indiana.* Bloomington Ind.: Indiana University Press, 1998, reprint of 1970.

Swartz, William. "The Wabash Railroad." *Railroad History.* No. 133 (Fall 1975).

Sappington, C. G. "The Madison and Indianapolis Railroad." *Indiana Magazine of History.* XXI (1925).

Watt, William J. *The Pennsylvania Railroad in Indiana.* Bloomington Ind.: Indiana University Press, 1999.

After working for 10 years on the New York Central Railroad as a small town station agent, towerman, and telegraph operator, GRAYDON MEINTS joined Fidelity Savings Bank and retired as vice president after 32 years of service. He has served as president of the Kalamazoo County Historical Society and as trustee and treasurer of the Historical Society of Michigan. He has written three books about Michigan Railroads. This is his first about Indiana Railroads.